Barts and The London

Queen Mary's School of Medicine and Dentistry

Handbo WHITECHAPEL LIBRARY, TURNER STREET, LONDON E1 2AD
020 7882 7110

4 WEEK LOAN
Books are to be returned on or before the last date below,
otherwise fines may be charged.

Blackwell Handbooks of Research Methods in Psychology

Created for advanced students and researchers looking for an authoritative definition of the research methods used in their chosen field, the *Blackwell Handbooks of Research Methods in Psychology* provide an invaluable and cutting-edge overview of classic, current, and future trends in the research methods of psychology.

- Each handbook draws together 20–25 newly commissioned chapters to provide comprehensive coverage of the research methodology used in a specific psychological discipline.
- Each handbook is introduced and contextualized by leading figures in the field, lending coherence and authority to each volume.
- The international team of contributors to each handbook has been specially chosen for its expertise and knowledge of each field.
- Each volume provides the perfect complement to non-research based handbooks in psychology.

Handbook of Research Methods in Industrial and Organizational Psychology
Edited by Steven G. Rogelberg

Handbook of Research Methods in Clinical Psychology
Edited by Michael C. Roberts and Stephen S. Ilardi

Handbook of Research Methods in Experimental Psychology
Edited by Stephen F. Davis

Handbook of Research Methods in Developmental Psychology
Edited by Douglas M. Teti

Handbook of Research Methods in Clinical Psychology

Edited by

Michael C. Roberts and Stephen S. Ilardi

© 2003, 2005 by Blackwell Publishing Ltd
except for editorial material and organization © 2003, 2005 by Michael C. Roberts and
Stephen S. Ilardi

BLACKWELL PUBLISHING
350 Main Street, Malden, MA 02148-5020, USA
9600 Garsington Road, Oxford OX4 2DQ, UK
550 Swanston Street, Carlton, Victoria 3053, Australia

First published 2003
First published in paperback 2005 by Blackwell Publishing Ltd

1   2005

Library of Congress Cataloging-in-Publication Data

Handbook of research methods in clinical psychology / edited by Michael
C. Roberts and Stephen S. Ilardi.
        p. cm. – (Blackwell handbooks of research methods in psychology; 2)
Includes bibliographical references and index.
    ISBN 0-631-22673-7 (hardback) – ISBN 1-4051-3279-5 (paperback)
    1. Clinical psychology–Research–Methodology–Handbooks, manuals,
etc. I. Roberts, Michael C. II. Ilardi, Stephen S., 1963– III. Series.

RC467.8 .H36 2003
616.89'0072–dc21

                                                              2002151836

ISBN-13: 978-0-631-22673-4 (hardback) – ISBN-13: 978-1-4051-3279-4 (paperback)

A catalogue record for this title is available from the British Library.

Set in 10.5/12.5 pt Adobe Garamond
by Graphicraft Ltd, Hong Kong
Printed and bound in the United Kingdom
by TJ International, Padstow, Cornwall

For further information on
Blackwell Publishing, visit our website:
www.blackwellpublishing.com

To Our Wives:

Karen, whose bemused tolerance of the mess in the basement office and of my general distraction when a book is in progress permitted its development.

Michael

Maria, whose love, friendship, and encouragement made this project possible.

Steve

Contents

List of Contributors   x

Part I Clinical Psychology Research   1

1   Research Methodology and Clinical Psychology: An Overview   3
Michael C. Roberts and Stephen S. Ilardi

2   Addressing Validity Concerns in Clinical Psychology Research   13
Michael S. Finger and Kevin L. Rand

3   The Scientific Process and Publishing Research   31
Michael C. Roberts, Keri J. Brown, and Julianne M. Smith-Boydston

4   Ethical Considerations in Clinical Psychology Research   52
William A. Rae and Jeremy R. Sullivan

Part II Research Designs   71

5   Evaluating Treatment Efficacy With Single-Case Designs   73
Cynthia M. Anderson and Christine Kim

6   Design and Analysis of Experimental and Quasi-Experimental Investigations   92
Andrea Follmer Greenhoot

7   The Analysis of Correlational Data   115
Charles M. Judd and Melody S. Sadler

8   Structural Equation Modeling in Clinical Psychology Research   138
Samuel B. Green and Marilyn S. Thompson

9   Qualitative Methods in Psychological Research   176
Gloria L. Krahn and Michelle Putnam

10   Basic Principles of Meta-Analysis   196
Joseph A. Durlak

Part III Topics of Research   211

11   Research Methods for Developmental Psychopathology   213
Eric M. Vernberg and Edward J. Dill

    Vignette: Research Methods for Developmental Psychopathology   232
Anne K. Jacobs

12   Adult Experimental Psychopathology   234
John P. Kline, Steven D. LaRowe, Keith F. Donohue,
Jennifer Minnix, and Ginette C. Blackhart

    Vignette: Adult Experimental Psychopathology   260
Anne K. Jacobs

13   Child and Adolescent Assessment and Diagnosis Research   262
Paul J. Frick and Amy H. Cornell

    Vignette: Child and Adolescent Assessment and Diagnostic Research   282
Anne K. Jacobs

14   Adult Clinical Assessment and Diagnosis Research: Current Status and
Future Directions   284
Thomas E. Joiner, Jr., and Jeremy W. Pettit

    Vignette: Adult Clinical Assessment and Diagnosis   305
Anne K. Jacobs

15   Therapy and Interventions Research with Children and Adolescents   307
Ric G. Steele and Michael C. Roberts

    Vignette: Therapy and Interventions Research with Children, Youth,
and Families   327
Anne K. Jacobs

16   Therapy and Interventions Research with Adults   329
Anne D. Simons and Jennifer E. Wildes

    Vignette: Therapy and Interventions Research with Adults   352
Anne K. Jacobs

17   Research in Prevention and Promotion   354
George C. Tremblay and Barbara Landon

    Vignette: Research in Prevention and Promotion   374
Anne K. Jacobs

18 Research in Ethnic Minority Communities: Cultural Diversity
Issues in Clinical Psychology 376
Yo Jackson

Vignette: Research in Ethnic Minority Communities 394
Anne K. Jacobs

19 Investigating Professional Issues in Clinical Psychology 396
Michael C. Roberts, Jodi L. Kamps, and Ephi J. Betan

Vignette: Investigating Professional Issues in Clinical Psychology 418
Anne K. Jacobs

20 Reflections on the Future of Clinical Psychological Research 420
Stephen S. Ilardi and Michael C. Roberts

Index 433

Contributors

Cynthia M. Anderson, Department of Psychology, West Virginia University, Morgantown, West Virginia

Ephi J. Betan, Georgia School of Professional Psychology, Atlanta, Georgia

Ginette C. Blackhart, Department of Psychology, Florida State University, Tallahassee, Florida

Keri J. Brown, Clinical Child Psychology Program, University of Kansas, Lawrence, Kansas

Amy H. Cornell, Department of Psychology, University of New Orleans, New Orleans, Louisiana

Edward J. Dill, Clinical Child Psychology Program, University of Kansas, Lawrence, Kansas

Keith F. Donohue, Department of Psychology, Florida State University, Tallahassee, Florida

Joseph A. Durlak, Department of Psychology, Loyola University, Chicago, Illinois

Michael S. Finger, Department of Psychology, University of Kansas, Lawrence, Kansas

Paul J. Frick, Department of Psychology, University of New Orleans, New Orleans, Louisiana

Samuel B. Green, Division of Psychology in Education, Arizona State University, Tempe, Arizona

Andrea Follmer Greenhoot, Department of Psychology, University of Kansas, Lawrence, Kansas

Stephen S. Ilardi, Department of Psychology, University of Kansas, Lawrence, Kansas

Yo Jackson, Clinical Child Psychology Program, University of Kansas, Lawrence, Kansas

Anne K. Jacobs, Clinical Child Psychology Program, University of Kansas, Lawrence, Kansas

Thomas E. Joiner, Jr., Department of Psychology, Florida State University, Tallahassee, Florida

Charles M. Judd, Department of Psychology, University of Colorado, Boulder, Colorado

Jodi L. Kamps, Clinical Child Psychology Program, University of Kansas, Lawrence, Kansas

Christine Kim, Department of Psychology, West Virginia University, Morgantown, West Virginia

John P. Kline, Department of Psychology, Florida State University, Tallahassee, Florida

Gloria L. Krahn, Child Development and Rehabilitation Center, Oregon Health and Science University, Portland, Oregon

Barbara Landon, Department of Clinical Psychology, Antioch New England Graduate School, Keene, New Hampshire

Steven D. LaRowe, Department of Psychology, Florida State University, Tallahassee, Florida

Jennifer Minnix, Department of Psychology, Florida State University, Tallahassee, Florida

Jeremy W. Pettit, Department of Psychology, Florida State University, Tallahassee, Florida

Michelle Putnam, George Warren Brown School of Social Work, Washington University, St. Louis, Missouri

William A. Rae, Department of Educational Psychology, Texas A & M University, College Station, Texas

Kevin L. Rand, Department of Psychology, University of Kansas, Lawrence, Kansas

Michael C. Roberts, Clinical Child Psychology Program, University of Kansas, Lawrence, Kansas

Melody S. Sadler, Department of Psychology, University of Colorado, Boulder, Colorado

Anne D. Simons, Department of Psychology, University of Oregon, Eugene, Oregon

Julianne M. Smith-Boydston, Bert Nash Mental Health Center, Lawrence, Kansas

Ric G. Steele, Clinical Child Psychology Program, University of Kansas, Lawrence, Kansas

Jeremy R. Sullivan, Department of Educational Psychology, Texas A & M University, College Station, Texas

Marilyn S. Thompson, Division of Psychology in Education, Arizona State University, Tempe, Arizona

George C. Tremblay, Department of Clinical Psychology, Antioch New England Graduate School, Keene, New Hampshire

Eric M. Vernberg, Clinical Child Psychology Program, University of Kansas, Lawrence, Kansas

Jennifer E. Wildes, Department of Psychology, University of Oregon, Eugene, Oregon

PART I

Clinical Psychology Research

CHAPTER ONE

Research Methodology and Clinical Psychology: An Overview

Michael C. Roberts and Stephen S. Ilardi

Scientific and Professional Foundations of Clinical Psychology

The field of clinical psychology has a rich history of empirical research across a number of domains: assessment, diagnosis, psychotherapy, experimental psychopathology, and many others (Reisman, 1981; Routh, 1994; Routh and DeRubeis, 1998; Walker, 1991). In fact, an emphasis on the generation of clinically relevant knowledge through rigorous research has been a hallmark of clinical psychology from its inception as a distinct field. Many of the earliest clinical psychologists came to the field with a background in the natural sciences, integrating their scientific proclivities with an interest in generating practical knowledge as a means of addressing an array of clinical problems. Such a foundational merging of science and clinical practice was fortuitous, and it has resulted in a robust empirical foundation for the field. In fact, we would argue that the continued existence of clinical psychology as a vital discipline is contingent upon both the enduring soundness of the field's scientific framework and the demonstrable application of its scientific knowledge as a means of improving human lives.

The founder of clinical psychology, Lightner Witmer, established the first psychology clinic and training program in 1896. Later, Witmer founded and edited the first scientific and professional journal for the developing field, *Psychological Clinic*. Thus, even at the outset, there was an implicit recognition of the value of integrated science and practice. Nevertheless, the research methodologies which characterized most early clinical psychology investigations (and many of the conclusions derived therefrom) are generally regarded as flawed, even primitive, by today's standards. Clinical psychology has benefited from an ongoing process of scientific development and advancement, a process which has tended over time to correct for many methodological and conceptual foibles (even those vigorously embraced, at one time or another, by most of the field). In fact, the sensibility of employing scientific scrutiny to critically evaluate and refine existing concepts and practices has permeated the history of clinical psychology.

There are three principal professional roles which have emerged in clinical psychology – that of *clinical scientist* (with a primary emphasis on conducting clinical research), that of *scientist–practitioner* (reflecting an equal emphasis on science and clinical practice), and that of *applied clinical scientist* (with a preeminent focus on the application of existing scientific knowledge) – and despite their differing emphases, each role reflects the field's intrinsic balance between the scientific generation of knowledge and the applied aspects of clinical assessment and intervention. Clinical science and practice are inextricably interwoven and reciprocally inform one another, and (fortunately) many areas of clinical psychology emphasize their integration rather than bifurcation.

The need for extensive research training of aspiring clinical psychologists is a point repeatedly stressed in the field's historic training conferences (e.g., the famous Boulder Conference of 1949: Raimy, 1950) and the ensuing reports which have come to define clinical psychology as a discipline (American Psychological Association Committee on Accreditation, 2002; Belar and Perry, 1992; Korman, 1976; Roberts et al., 1998; Trierweiler and Stricker, 1998). This sensibility is also reflected in the stated program philosophies, goals, and educational curricula of master's-level and doctoral programs in clinical psychology and allied fields. For example, the Clinical Child Psychology Program at the University of Kansas (which one of us, MCR, directs) affirms in its philosophy statement that graduates should be "ready for future changes and needs, to produce original contributions to clinical child psychology, and to evaluate their own work and others . . . Equally important in the program is the preparation of students to contribute to and evaluate the scientific knowledge base guiding psychological practice" (www.ku.edu/~clchild). Variations on this and related themes are endorsed by clinical psychology programs of many different orientations and foci. The consensus view is that all clinical psychology graduates should be the beneficiaries of research training sufficient to enable them – at a minimum – to critically evaluate the existing research literature and to engage in informed applications thereof in an array of practice activities.

Today's clinical psychologist likely will have more formal training than his or her predecessors, inasmuch as the amount of material to be mastered has grown commensurate with growth in the field's scientific underpinnings. Due in large part to the increasingly rigorous research methodology which has come to characterize clinical psychology, the field has witnessed many important advances in recent decades, including the introduction of novel interventions of high demonstrated efficacy, concurrent with the occasional identification of less effective or even detrimental clinical procedures. Consequently, professionals in the field – regardless of their level of experience – are wise to remain abreast of all new developments in the discipline's science and practice, and continually to evaluate their own work and that of others in light of relevant scientific advances.

Professional and Research Challenges for Clinical Psychology

Numerous challenges confront today's clinical psychologist, regardless of his or her theoretical orientation or area of activity, and it is our view that such challenges can be met successfully only in tandem with a clear research emphasis. Because the full delineation of all such challenges would be formidable, we will briefly highlight several which appear especially noteworthy. First, research is needed to facilitate a deeper understanding of the fundamental processes of psychological development (normal and abnormal; prenatal to senescence), as an essential precursor to the field's development of more comprehensive models of human behavior. Such enhanced understanding, we believe, will lead to improved preventive and therapeutic interventions on the part of psychologists and other healthcare professionals. While developmental considerations might naturally seem most applicable to clinical child practice, adult clinical psychologists are increasingly recognizing that the process of psychological development continues throughout adulthood. Thus, improved models of psychological change for adult clinical psychology are also needed. Moreover, just as child-oriented researchers and practitioners have long recognized the complexity of families and peers in influencing the process of change over time – as observed, for example, in psychotherapy outcomes – so too will adult-oriented clinical psychologists need to develop such comprehensive multi-person systemic conceptualizations. Second (but relatedly), there remains a need for greater emphasis upon examination of the mediators and moderators of psychological change (including, of course, therapeutic change) as a means of advancing the field beyond overly simplistic understandings (e.g., this therapy *somehow* seems to lead to some improvement for some individuals) toward increasingly sophisticated models which reflect more adequately the full complexity of human functioning.

A third contemporary challenge to clinical psychology to be met by research is to develop clinical assessment devices and methods of greater reliability and validity. Correspondingly, existing diagnostic schemes and taxonomies of psychological disorder are in considerable need of refinement on the basis of applied scientific investigation. Fourth, research can help identify valid and invalid psychotherapies, psychological interventions, and prevention efforts. Improvements in therapy techniques, and in the more precise identification of the processes by which psychotherapies exert their effects, can be accomplished through targeted research informed by the methodologies outlined in this handbook. Measurement of treatment procedures, treatment integrity, behavioral changes, functional performance, objective measurements, perceptions of change, and satisfaction from a variety of sources, follow-up assessment, etc., are needed to establish the "scientific credentials" of each therapeutic approach. Fifth, measurement of the range of outcomes following psychotherapies and preventive interventions can help establish the associated costs and benefits associated with each. Relevant outcomes can include all aspects of a patient's life, such as personal perceptions and functioning, work, and significant relationships (parents, spouses, friends, siblings, offspring). Additionally, research is required to determine the costs, benefits, and harm of clinical psychology activities (e.g., assessment, prevention, therapy) – both with respect to direct as well as indirect effects of such activities (e.g., practice patterns and charges for psychologist's time; medical cost offsets, insurance reimbursement patterns). The effects of psychological practice (and research) on society in general stand in great need of more rigorous investigation.

A sixth domain of professional challenge and research effort concerns evaluation of the organization and delivery of a variety of clinical services through *program evaluation*. There is an ongoing need within the field for evaluative frameworks, methodologies, and instruments that may be applied across the wide variety of settings (e.g., inpatient/ outpatient units; clinics and hospitals; private practice) and problems faced by clinical psychology (e.g., different sets of psychologically related symptoms and diagnoses). At this time, clinical psychology is no longer a single specialty, but is now an amalgam of more specialized substantive foci: clinical child, pediatric, adult clinical, clinical neuropsychology, geropsychology, health, and others. The varieties of these foci require development and acceptance of a multitude of approaches within the scientific traditions of the overarching field of clinical psychology.

A seventh challenging issue, as noted by the Clinical Treatment and Services Research Workgroup (1998) of the National Institute of Mental Health, is reflected in the fact that improvement in research and clinical practice requires an iterative investigational process across a continuum of treatment research emphases: *efficacy* (i.e., demonstrated treatment-related improvements as observed in controlled research studies), *effectiveness* (i.e., the degree to which the treatment is efficacious across the wide array of individuals and therapists found in real-world settings), *practice* (i.e., how services are delivered), and *service systems* (i.e., how mental health services are structured). The translation of re-search to applied clinical settings with the aim of improving practice is clearly important; equally important, however, is the principle that the research itself be informed by psychology practice. Finding the appropriate mechanisms by which to accomplish such translating/informing actions poses an ongoing challenge for clinical researchers. Finally, informing each of the aforementioned current and future challenges is the fact that clinical psychologists conduct research and practice in an increasingly diverse society, especially in the United States. Populations underserved by mental health service provid-ers are typically those which have been under-researched as well. Finding ways to in-crease the representativeness of participants in clinical research will enhance the field's ability to respond effectively to each of its principal challenges.

Numerous commentators have highlighted these and other complex challenges facing clinical psychology at present (e.g., Compas and Gotlib, 2002). For example, similar issues have been articulated specifically for the area of pediatric psychology (e.g., Brown and Roberts, 2000; Roberts, Brown, and Puddy, 2002) and clinical neuroscience (Ilardi, 2002), areas in which we have personal interests. We encourage readers of this handbook to remain alert both to the delineation of such challenges as they are outlined in detail in the chapters to follow, and to the many exciting future research opportunities discussed in the book's final chapter. It is our hope that the highlighting of such challenges and opportunities will serve to help catalyze research in such areas for decades to come. We recognize, however, that some of the field's current assumptions and enthusiasms – even some of those emphasized in this text! – will likely be replaced over time as the evidence mounts (as it inevitably does). Indeed, new and completely unanticipated questions will doubtless arrive at the offices, clinics, and laboratories of clinical researchers and practitioners. Nevertheless, the research methods and principles outlined in this handbook, we believe, will remain important to the field's advancement in the years ahead.

Purpose and Overview of this Handbook

Some students (and even some graduated professionals) approach the general topic of "research" with a groan, a dread of boredom, or even with unmitigated fear and loathing – this despite perhaps a grudging recognition of the necessity of research training as a means of fulfilling requirements of courses and/or theses and dissertation projects. Still others view research and the scientific process as interesting detective work, a means of solving important problems and resolving questions tinged with the thrill of discovery. It is this latter sense of excitement at the prospects of discovery which we seek to emphasize in this handbook, though with a clear recognition that individual results may vary. The organization of this handbook reflects the editors' attempt to be comprehensive in coverage, i.e., not providing merely a collection of essays related to research, but an integrated framework allowing the reader to see a broad range of methodologies and their respective applications in advancing the science and practice of clinical psychology. In developing this book we wanted the contributors to convey the excitement of conducting empirical research, utilizing a variety of methodologies, to answer a broad range of enormously important questions facing clinical psychology at present. As noted, such questions may be regarded as challenges to be met through the use of evidence-based approaches outlined herein.

We hope that this book meets the needs for a concise textbook for students, instructors, professionals, and scientists interested in expanding their base of knowledge regarding research methods in clinical psychology. The chapters cover the major approaches to research and design for clinical psychology, with attention to both child and adult populations. In addition, brief research vignettes describe examples of projects with exemplary designs and methodologies as a means of illustrating the essential elements of many of the research topics covered herein. This handbook consists of twenty chapters, each covering a different facet of clinical research. The first two parts of the text examine important issues which affect all clinical researchers – areas such as ethics, research validity, research designs, methodology, and data analysis; the third part focuses on specific topical areas of application in clinical psychology. For many of the latter topics, separate discussions are provided for research with adult and child populations, inasmuch as the research with these populations has become increasingly specialized and independent (although common questions and methods are highlighted as well).

Part one on *Clinical Psychology Research* covers topics of important relevance to all aspects of scientific work in the field. In fact, these are areas which require the researcher's continual attention when applying the content of later chapters on methodology and focal research topics. In a foundational chapter, Michael S. Finger and Kevin L. Rand describe the manner in which confidence in the professional psychologist's findings (and clinical activities) is contingent upon careful attention to numerous validity issues. The authors define and illustrate four principal types of research validity concerns (internal, external, construct, and statistical conclusion) and illustrate ways of addressing them. They also elucidate many common potential threats to validity in clinical psychology research, and discuss strategies for addressing in simultaneous fashion internal and external validity concerns in research projects. In chapter 3, Michael C. Roberts, Keri J. Brown, and Julianne M. Smith-Boydston outline issues germane to moving research through the review process to the publication end stage. They discuss how to determine what is publishable, how to select a publication outlet, how to prepare a manuscript, and many possible outcomes of the editorial review process. In chapter 4, William A. Rae and Jeremy R. Sullivan elucidate ethical considerations in clinical psychology research. These authors articulate important ethical concerns that may arise in each of four phases of the research process: research planning, institutional review boards, informed consent, and analysis and write-up for publication. They focus special attention on issues of confidentiality, research with vulnerable populations (including children), and use of deception and recording (e.g., audio/video).

In part two of this handbook the focus shifts to the foundational research designs and statistical approaches requisite to conducting appropriate research on the central questions posed in clinical psychology. In chapter 5, Cynthia M. Anderson and Christine Kim describe specific strategies for examining data obtained from the individual psychotherapy client, as opposed to larger groups of participants. Derived from applied behavior analysis, these single-case techniques are particularly applicable to heuristic, exploratory investigations in the early stages of intervention research, as well as for practicing clinicians attempting to evaluate the effects of their therapeutic activities. Anderson and Kim note that single-case approaches are widely applicable to clinical psychology practice, regardless of the theoretical orientation of the practitioner. Next, in chapter 6, Andrea Follmer Greenhoot discusses the design and analysis of experimental and quasi-experimental investigations. She presents the principal types of experimental designs and the set of related statistical techniques commonly used to investigate between-group differences on key variables (e.g., to evaluate the effects of a psychotherapy intervention versus a control condition). In chapter 7, Charles M. Judd and Melody S. Sadler focus attention on the analysis of datasets in which the variables of interest are measured as they are found (*observational data*); i.e., the key variables are not manipulated in an experiment. These authors address the conceptualization of correlational research, the pragmatic concerns of correlational data analysis, and strategies for the resolution of interpretational difficulties. In chapter 8, Samuel B. Green and Marilyn S. Thompson describe a specific form of statistical analysis which has become widely used by psychological scientists over the past two decades: structural equation modeling. Clinical psychology research involves the examination of human behavior and change via increasingly complex theoretical models capable of representing causal interrelationships among a large number of variables over time; structural equation modeling provides one such useful modeling approach. In chapter 9, Gloria L. Krahn and Michelle Putnam describe the applicability of qualitative research in clinical psychology. They demonstrate how qualitative research, if undertaken systematically and with proper training, may constitute a useful scientific approach. They outline principles involved in selecting qualitative techniques, the practical applications of the various qualitative methods, and optimal ways to resolve challenges of sampling, data collection techniques, and analyses. Part two concludes with chapter 10, Joseph A. Durlak's treatment of the basic principles of meta-analysis as applied to clinical psychology topics. He notes that meta-analytic techniques are useful statistical methods of reviewing and summarizing clinical psychology research that may be dispersed across many studies. Durlak describes the basic methodology of meta-analysis and provides examples to illustrate his points. He also notes that meta-analytic studies help elucidate problems with extant research studies and indicate where further work is needed.

In the third and final part of this handbook, a wide range of more focal *topics of research* is considered. Many of these topics are covered across two separate chapters, with emphases on child and adolescent versus adult populations, respectively. In chapter 11, Eric M. Vernberg and Edward J. Dill outline developmentally oriented research frameworks for examining the manner in which psychological problems emerge, intensify, and remit. Although the term *developmental psychopathology* is often thought to refer exclusively to child/adolescent disorders, developmental approaches are those based on consideration of change over time (and thus applicable to adults as well). Vernberg and Dill present the core research issues in this area by means of a series of "research tasks" for research in developmental psychopathology. Chapter 12 has a parallel focus on psychopathology research among adult populations. Written by John P. Kline, Steven D. LaRowe, Keith F. Donohue, Jennifer Minnix, and Ginette C. Blackhart, this chapter describes the manner in which experimental psychopathology encompasses the investigation of causal mechanisms associated with psychological disorders across multiple intersecting levels of analysis (e.g., neurophysiological, cognitive, affective, interpersonal, etc.). As the term implies, experimental psychopathology derives from the tradition of lab-based experimental psychology, and involves the application of experimental principles and methods to the study of psychological disorders. Both psychopathology chapters demonstrate the importance to clinical psychology of the ongoing development of a scientific knowledge-base regarding the processes through which psychological problems develop and progress.

In the book's next two chapters, the emphasis shifts to the assessment and diagnosis of children and adults, respectively, with extensive coverage given to research methodologies used to develop assessment instruments and to conduct empirical evaluations thereof. Diagnostic assessment has always been an important aspect of clinical psychology, and the field continues to witness important new conceptualizations and evaluative approaches in this area. In chapter 13 on child and adolescent assessment and diagnosis research, Paul J. Frick and Amy H. Cornell demonstrate the techniques of psychological assessment with children and the applicability of scientific research techniques in evaluating the instruments used in assessment. Throughout their chapter, Frick and Cornell indicate that, all too often, instruments used in psychopathology research are different from those which are useful in applied clinical assessment settings with children and adolescents. In chapter 14, Thomas E. Joiner, Jr., and Jeremy W. Pettit describe the primary conceptual issues germane to research in the area of clinical assessment and diagnosis, and they suggest several strategies for implementing research with the existing array of clinical assessment techniques. In particular, they highlight three common approaches used in this work – structured clinical interviews, symptom scales, and projective tests – and discuss the degree to which the extant empirical literature which supports (or fails to support) major assessment instruments within each of these domains. The authors also highlight limitations associated with the field's DSM-based diagnostic classification system, and suggest ways of facilitating research progress in assessing and diagnosing psychopathology.

Another significant area of activity for clinical psychologists has been the development, evaluation, and application of psychotherapeutic interventions for the various clinical concerns. In chapter 15, Ric G. Steele and Michael C. Roberts detail therapy and interventions research with children, youths, and families. These authors emphasize empirically supported treatment approaches and discuss such issues as efficacy, effectiveness, treatment selection, study participant selection, internal and external validity, and treatment integrity. In chapter 16 on therapy and interventions research with adults, Anne D. Simons and Jennifer E. Wildes provide an overview of issues central to conducting psychotherapy research with adults. They explain that such research examines whether an intervention works, how and why it might work, factors which might affect its efficacy, and how long the effects might last. The authors also provide an overview of the methods and current trends in research regarding the effects of adult psychotherapy.

An important aspect of clinical psychology, sometimes neglected, is the fact that often the most efficient means of alleviating distress is to intervene *before* any problems are evident – for example, by creating healthier psychological environments for at-risk individuals, especially during temporal windows of vulnerability at key stages of development. Consequently, in chapter 17 on research in prevention and promotion, George C. Tremblay and Barbara Landon emphasize that a developmental perspective underlies most effective prevention approaches. They detail the salient issues facing prevention research in clinical psychology, and describe the prevailing methodologies for conducting scientifically sound research on prevention programs. In an overview of material germane to each of the aforementioned topics in part three, in chapter 18 Yo Jackson explicates research in ethnic minority communities. She calls for greater multicultural competence among clinical psychology researchers, and describes the research challenges raised by an ethnically diverse population in the need for more research with different groups. She attends to the conceptual and pragmatic issues of conducting such research in order to generate useful findings, while remaining attentive to the importance of accounting for cultural differences.

As clinical psychology has developed as a profession, it has increasingly examined a range of professional issues, such as training and education, ethics, licensing and credentialing, practice, and service activities. The methodologies requisite for the empirical investigation of such issues are described in chapter 19 by Michael C. Roberts, Jodi L. Kamps, and Ephi J. Betan. The authors report on existing research covering a range of topics and methodologies, such as surveys regarding outcomes of training (e.g., student placement) and attitudes about various issues affecting the field (e.g., managed care, ethics), clinical case analysis and practice pattern studies, and even research on the research activities of clinical psychologists.

Finally, in chapter 20, Stephen S. Ilardi and Michael C. Roberts focus attention on a number of important windows of opportunity for scientific discovery in the discipline of clinical psychology in the years immediately ahead. They give primary coverage to areas of exploration which represent the extension of existing productive research programs that aim to address myriad important unresolved questions regarding psychotherapy, assessment, and experimental psychopathology. In addition, the editors discuss research which is likely to emerge in the context of clinical psychology's ongoing "prescription privileges movement." Finally, they provide a brief overview of groundbreaking statistical techniques which are likely to be of importance to the field for years ahead.

Throughout the chapters that constitute part three there are interwoven nine illustrative research vignettes by Anne K. Jacobs. These vignettes were chosen to highlight, by means of critical attention to actual published research articles, the principles discussed by each set of chapter authors. In addition to selecting and succinctly describing exemplary research articles, Dr. Jacobs explains the limitations and strengths of each in contributing to the science and practice of clinical psychology.

Conclusions

Clinical psychology has distinguished itself from other helping professions by an enduring and unabashed reliance on its foundation of scientific research. Accordingly, the chapters to follow in this handbook provide an in-depth overview of both the basic methods of research in clinical psychology and the principal research domains that continue to engage the field – with treatment, assessment, and psychopathology preeminent among them. Considerable attention is accorded throughout the text to a description of new developments and cutting-edge advances in knowledge and research methodology, with an eye toward both equipping and inspiring the next generation of clinical researchers. To this end, we are pleased and honored to have obtained for this handbook the contributions of an eminent and talented set of scholars, who have provided herein insightful coverage of leading-edge methodologies and an overview of the areas of inquiry which continue to command the attention of clinical psychological researchers throughout the world. As scientist–practitioners ourselves, we anticipate a bright future for the discipline of clinical psychology, but only to the extent that clinical psychologists remain committed to the century-old process of strengthening and building upon the field's scientific foundation.

References

American Psychological Association Committee on Accreditation (2002). *Guidelines and principles for accreditation of programs in professional psychology.* Washington, DC: American Psychological Association.

Belar, C. D., and Perry, N. W. (1992). The national conference on scientist–practitioner education and training for the professional practice of psychology. *American Psychologist, 47,* 71–5.

Brown, K. J., and Roberts, M. C. (2000). Future issues in pediatric psychology: Delphic survey. *Journal of Clinical Psychology in Medical Settings, 7,* 5–15.

Clinical Treatment and Services Research Workgroup, National Institute of Mental Health (1998). *Bridging science and service.* Bethesda, MD: National Institutes of Health. Retrieved December 22, 2000, from http://nimh.nih.gov/research/bridge.htm

Compas, B. E., and Gotlib, I. H. (2002). *Introduction to clinical psychology: Science and practice.* Boston, MA: McGraw-Hill.

Ilardi, S. S. (2002). The cognitive neuroscience perspective: A brief primer for clinical psychologists. *The Behavior Therapist, 25,* 49–52.

Korman, M. (1976). National conference on levels and patterns of professional training in psychology: The major themes. *American Psychologist, 29,* 441–9.

Raimy, V. C. (ed.) (1950). *Training in clinical psychology.* New York: Prentice-Hall.

Reisman, J. M. (1981). History and current trends in clinical psychology. In C. E. Walker (ed.), *Clinical practice of psychology: A guide for mental health professionals* (pp. 1–32). New York: Pergamon.

Roberts, M. C., Brown, K. J., and Puddy, R. W. (2002). Service delivery issues and program evaluation in pediatric psychology. *Journal of Clinical Psychology in Medical Settings, 9,* 3–13.

Roberts, M. C., Carlson, C. I., Erickson, M. T., Friedman, R. M., La Greca, A. M., Lemanek, K. L., Russ, S. W., Schroeder, C. S., Vargas, L. A., and Wohlford, P. F. (1998). A model for training psychologists to provide services for children and adolescents. *Professional Psychology: Research and Practice, 29,* 293–9.

Routh, D. K. (1994). *Clinical psychology since 1917: Science, practice, and organization.* New York: Plenum.

Routh, D. K., and DeRubeis, R. J. (eds.) (1998). *The science of clinical psychology: Accomplishments and future directions.* Washington, DC: American Psychological Association.

Trierweiler, S. J., and Stricker, G. (1998). *The scientific practice of professional psychology.* New York: Plenum.

Walker, C. E. (ed.) (1991). *Clinical psychology: Historical and research foundations.* New York: Plenum.

CHAPTER TWO

Addressing Validity Concerns in Clinical Psychology Research

Michael S. Finger and Kevin L. Rand

Validity concerns are pervasive in psychological research, from simple correlational investigations to the most complex experimental studies. Research in clinical psychology is no exception, as clinical researchers must address validity issues ranging from the demonstrated construct validity of clinical treatment manipulations to the generalizability of findings from the laboratory to applied settings. Generally speaking, the researcher's confidence in his or her findings will be commensurate with the degree to which he or she has adequately addressed validity concerns. Moreover, the process of addressing validity issues during the design phase of a study will help the investigator identify potential flaws in study design (e.g., treatment manipulation, variable measurement, etc.) that could confound the interpretation of any observed causal relationships.

Arguably, the four most common types of research validity addressed in the literature are *internal, external, construct,* and *statistical conclusion.* This chapter will describe and explicate each of these types of validity. In addition, it will identify potential confounds that threaten each type of validity in any given study. It is often the case that internal validity is maximized at the sacrifice of external validity, or vice versa. Accordingly, a discussion on the optimal balancing of internal and external validity concerns is included in the final section of this chapter.

Four Types of Research Validity

Defining the validity of research

Within the domain of psychological measurement, the concept of validity generally refers to the theorized relationship between a psychological inventory and its associated hypothetical construct(s). An instrument is said to be *valid* to the extent that it actually reflects the construct that it purports to measure. Valid conclusions regarding the theoretical constructs are possible if empirical observations are obtained from construct-valid measures of the variables.

While *measurement validity* is a central concern in the development of psychological tests, the need to demonstrate *research validity* arises in the context of empirical investigations. For example, to what extent does an employed treatment manipulation accurately reflect the theoretical treatments or therapies under investigation? To what extent are the conclusions drawn from statistical analysis of empirical data appropriate? To what extent do the results of the study at hand generalize to a different setting or population? Each of these questions pertains to research validity, and by asking and addressing such questions, the researcher strengthens the justification of results and conclusions from psychological investigations.

A research study on optimism training

To help elucidate the present discussion of research validity, we will reference the following hypothetical research scenario throughout the chapter; it will be referred to as the *Optimism Study*.

> A team of academic researchers, affiliated with a mental health center in a large, midwestern city, investigated the effects of a novel psychotherapy technique – *optimism training* – for the treatment of unipolar major depression. *Optimism training* was provided concurrently with a standard cognitive–behavioral therapy protocol (CBT; Beck, Shaw, Rush, and Emery, 1979). Initial assessment at the center entailed administration of the SCID-I (Spitzer, Williams, Gibbon, and First, 1993), a structured diagnostic interview. Clients, who were self- or physician-referred to the center after the initial start date of the investigation, and who met the criteria for unipolar depression based on the SCID-I, were recruited to participate in the study. Study participants were randomly assigned either to the combined treatment condition (CBT and optimism training) or to the standard condition (CBT only). Over a 12-week period, one clinic psychotherapist treated all clients from the treatment condition, while a different clinic psychotherapist treated the clients from the control condition. All study participants were administered the Beck Depression Inventory-II (BDI-II; Beck, Steer, Ball, and Ranieri, 1996) prior to treatment, again at the completion of treatment, and once more during a 6-month follow-up visit.

Internal validity

Accounting for changes in a dependent measure by group membership or treatment manipulation is common in psychological research. Thus, it is important that certainty can be placed on any research conclusions that draw causal inferences from one or more independent variables (IVs) to a dependent variable (DV). *Internal validity addresses whether changes on a DV are attributable to the IVs*, or due to alternative, extraneous variables, called confound variables. Confounds of the IVs present competing explanations for a study's findings and they diminish confidence in the observed effects of the given IVs. By addressing such threats to internal validity before commencing data collection, the researcher may take into account possible confound variables and exclude alternative explanations for results (i.e., other than the effect of IVs).

For present purposes, an IV is any variable that is manipulated or that could potentially be manipulated. IVs may also include preexisting groups from which participants can be sampled. A true experimental IV, such as drug dosage, is actively varied or manipulated across participants in a study. On the other hand, persons from preexisting populations are sampled to form a quasi-experimental IV, sometimes because active manipulation on such a variable is undesirable and/or harmful to participants. Examples of quasi-experimental IVs based upon group membership include smoking, marital status, and reported history of sexual abuse.

Threats to internal validity will be grouped based on the categorization of research designs of Campbell (1957). A unique set of internal validity threats is associated with each design. Such organization will demonstrate how potential threats to internal validity can be identified through attention to experimental design.

Correlation and quasi-experimental designs

One-group pretest–posttest

In the one-group pretest–posttest design, a single group of individuals receives a single form of experimental manipulation. An initial measurement or observation of the dependent variable(s) is taken prior to the manipulation, and a second measurement is taken after its completion. Often helpful in behavioral research and applications, the one-group pretest–posttest design can be used to demonstrate the efficacy of a specific treatment intervention, although without regard to the effects of alternative treatments (including the option of *no treatment*). The *Optimism Study* would have been a one-group pretest–posttest design if a single group of clients received CBT and optimism training (and the 6-month follow-up assessment was not conducted). The following five confounds can threaten the internal validity of a study using the one-group pretest–posttest design: history, maturation, testing, instrumentation, and regression to the mean.

History. Specific events can occur in the lives of participants during an investigation, aside from treatment or experimental manipulation that participants receive. Such events present possible explanations for changes in the DV. These events can occur within or outside of the research setting. In the one-group version of the *Optimism Study*, suppose that the mean depression level among participants was significantly lower after treatment than at the beginning of treatment. However, suppose further that over the course of the study, a long-standing economic recession in the area lifted, dramatically easing a local unemployment crisis. Such economic events would compete with the treatment as an explanation for the observed reduction in mean depression levels. However, history effects can be accounted for in an experimental design by the inclusion of a control group, i.e., a group receiving no treatment at all. If the average change in DV scores in a control group was statistically similar to the change observed in the treatment group, then some variable, aside from the treatment manipulation, would be influencing levels on the DV.

Maturation. Developmental changes that occur over time within the participants can compete with treatments in explaining changes in the DV. These developmental changes include not only factors associated with growth, as maturation implies (e.g., growing older, getting stronger, etc.), but also with degeneration (e.g., growing tired or getting annoyed from extended participation, unexpected brain damage, etc.). In the example of the optimism training study, although the improvement in clients' mood appears likely due to the treatment intervention, it is also the case that most clients experience spontaneous remission of depressive symptoms in the absence of any intervention (American Psychiatric Association, 1994). As was the case for the threat of history, maturation effects can be controlled for with the use of a control comparison group.

Testing. The method of observation, or testing, can itself lead to changes in the dependent variable. Taking a test once can influence a participant's performance on subsequent administrations of that test. For example, a participant who completes the BDI-II may report fewer depressive symptoms merely on the basis of having been previously exposed to the BDI-II. In fact, the repetition of assessments can directly lead to an improved score on any measure of personality pathology or maladjustment (Kazdin, 1998).

Thus, it becomes important to distinguish between reactive and nonreactive measures (e.g., Campbell, 1957, 1977). The reactivity of a psychological measure can be considered to lie on a continuum, ranging from a relatively nonreactive measure (e.g., measuring someone's height) to a considerably reactive measure (e.g., observing someone's eating habits). Often, the optimal method for controlling the effect of testing is to select the most nonreactive measure possible. Note that assessing the degree of reactivity for a measure is a subjective decision, which can depend on the setting and use of a particular instrument.

Instrumentation. Instrumentation, or *instrumental decay*, refers to any changes in the measurement instruments, procedures, or observers used during a study that might lead to changes in the dependent variable(s). Changes in observers, such as fatigue, may threaten the internal validity of a study through instrumentation. (In contrast, the threat of maturation is specific to changes only within the participants.) Longitudinal studies are especially susceptible to this threat, as changes in technology and knowledge may lead to changes in measurement devices. The threat of instrumentation also occurs when the instructions for a questionnaire change over time.

In the *Optimism Study*, giving different instructions for completing the BDI-II – such as changing the rating scales of the items – between the first and second administration could affect the obtained BDI-II scores. Alternatively, if the BDI-I (Beck, Shaw, Rush, and Emery, 1979) had been used for the first administration and the BDI-II for the second administration, the differences in scale construction between forms could have caused unintentional (artifactual) differences in the obtained scores.

Statistical regression. Regression toward the mean occurs whenever the extreme scores on some measure from an initial administration become less extreme at subsequent repeated administrations. For example, when participants are selected for the study because they score very high on a measure of depressive symptomatology, there is the danger that their subsequent scores will tend to be closer to the population average. In the case of repeated administrations, a person who initially obtains an extreme score on a measure will typically see his or her long-run average of scores on the measure converge (*regress*) toward the population average.

Note that this phenomenon applies only to measurements containing some degree of measurement error (e.g., scores from paper-and-pencil tests). Assessment techniques that are virtually error free (e.g., measuring a person's height) will not be threatened by statistical regression effects.

Correlational group comparison design

A popular design in clinical research is the correlational group comparison, in which two or more groups that have not been selected through strict randomization are compared. Generally, one group has a certain preexisting characteristic (e.g., clinical depression) that the other group lacks. Several types of confounds can compromise the internal validity of such research studies: selection bias, attrition, causal ambiguity, and selection bias interactions.

Selection bias. Selection bias is a systematic difference between groups due to participant self-selection. In the optimism training study example, clients were assigned randomly to the two treatment conditions, and selection bias is not a threat. However, if clients had themselves chosen in which of the two groups to participate, there may have been systematic reasons why particular clients would have elected to be in particular groups. Such reasons could themselves have accounted for any observed changes in depressive symptoms over the course of the study. For example, participants that are highly motivated to change might tend to select the treatment condition that involves the most work.

Attrition. Attrition (sometimes called *mortality*) becomes an internal validity threat when the potential for loss in participants differs across groups. For example, if optimism training involves a great deal of extra work on the part of the client, then one might expect more clients to drop out from this condition. Further, the more severely depressed individuals in the optimism group might be especially likely to drop out by virtue of having to do such work. The result could be an illusory decline in mean depressive symptoms, simply because all of the severely depressed clients left the study.

Causal ambiguity. Ambiguity about the causal direction is a concern if it cannot be ascertained whether the independent or predictor variable is the causal agent of the DV, or vice versa. Confusion about whether Variable *A* causes *B*, Variable *B* causes *A*, or another variable, *C*, causes both Variables *A* and *B*, often plagues correlation research. When the independent variable does not reflect an active manipulation, the chronological and causal relationships of two or more variables cannot be determined. As such, in a comparison of samples from two preexisting groups, the direction of causation between group membership and the dependent variable cannot be ascertained. For an excellent discussion of the difficulties inherent in inferring causation on the basis of correlation data, see Bollen (1989: ch. 3).

Selection bias interaction. It is possible for selection bias to interact with any other threat to internal validity. In cases of such interaction, one or more of the aforementioned threats to internal validity may affect one self-selected group more than they may affect another. For example, an interaction of selection bias and maturation could result in a motivated group of clients volunteering for the optimism training condition over the other condition. These clients may then mature differently than the other clients because they work more diligently. When any threat to internal validity affects only one group in an experiment, there is always the potential for a selection bias interaction (Shadish, Cook, and Campbell, 2002).

Non-randomized pretest–posttest control-group design

A more experimental version of the correlational group comparison design is the non-randomized pretest–posttest control-group design, in which two or more groups are measured on a dependent variable before and after active manipulation of the independent variable. However, because the group members are not sampled at random, such quasi-experimental studies suffer from most of the threats to internal validity characteristic of correlational group comparisons: selection bias, attrition, and interactions with selection bias. The main advantage of this quasi-experimental design over simple correlational group comparisons is that there is no causal ambiguity. The independent variable is actively manipulated, allowing for a degree of certainty in attributions of causality.

Fully experimental designs

Pretest–posttest control-group design

The optimism training study is an example of a pretest–posttest control-group design. History, maturation, testing, instrumentation, regression, and selection bias in pretest–posttest control-group studies are controlled for through random assignment. Still, other threats to internal validity can occur with this type of study design.

Attrition. As with the other group comparison designs, attrition may differentially eliminate participants of one treatment group in a study.

Treatment diffusion. In clinical settings it is possible for the treatment condition of one group to "bleed" into another group, especially when there is considerable cross-group contact among treatment group members. For example, suppose that the clients from the control group (CBT) of the *Optimism Study* begin to notice that their counterparts are engaging in new positive attitudes toward events (i.e., optimism). The clients from the control group might then engage in this new positive outlook on the world, thereby giving themselves a form of optimism training. This could conceivably make the control group appear more similar to the experimental group on outcome BDI-II scores, thereby masking any superiority of the optimism treatment condition over the control condition.

Reaction of controls. In some situations participants from the control group may be treated differently than participants from the treatment group (i.e., in ways other than that of the treatment manipulation). The manner in which participants react to such differential treatment can impact the outcome of a study. For example, threats to validity from the reactions of controls can occur when blinded studies unintentionally become "unblinded." For example, participants in a control group for a psychotropic medication may figure out that they are receiving a placebo due to the absence of expected side effects. This discovery could disappoint or anger members of the control group who had hoped to receive a new medication to treat their condition. Such a response could in turn exacerbate existing symptoms in a manner that would obscure the effect of the medication being tested.

Solomon four-group design

The mere exposure of a participant to a pretest may increase a participant's sensitivity to the variable(s) being studied. Therefore, the observed results from studies with a pretesting condition may not generalize to populations not exposed to such a pretest condition. To control for this, the Solomon design was developed as a modification of the pretest–posttest control-group design, with two addition groups utilized. The other two groups represent a posttest-only treatment group and a posttest-only control group. Accordingly, the reaction to the pretest can be independently evaluated. Although the Solomon four-group design suffers from the same threats to internal validity as the pretest–posttest control-group design, the Solomon design is more externally valid, or generalizable (see section on external validity), to populations that will not experience any pretest. See Braver and Braver (1988) for an overview on analyzing data from a Solomon design.

External validity

External validity refers to the generalizability of the research findings (Campbell and Stanley, 1963). To what degree do the conclusions from one study – based on specific populations, settings, and treatment variables – extend to additional populations, settings, and treatment variables? External validity refers to the extent to which a study's results can be expanded beyond the study's boundaries (Campbell, 1957). Although different sets of threats to internal validity apply to different research designs, every research design is susceptible to all external validity threats. The differences in generalizability among the various designs are only a matter of degree.

Threats to external validity

Testing interaction and sensitivity

Being aware that you are in a research study may alter your behavior. Hence, research findings obtained with participants who know they are being examined may not generalize to people in their everyday lives. Obtrusive measures or treatments may also cause reactivity in participants though a process called *sensitization*. Through completing an assessment measure or receiving a treatment, participants may gain new awareness of specific thoughts or behaviors pertaining to the variables under investigation. When sensitization of participants to variables occurs, the effect of the given independent variable(s) may not generalize to a broader, untested population.

Although sensitization can hinder the interpretation of study results, sensitization can also help optimize a treatment strategy. In the *Optimism Study*, through answering the items from the BDI-II, the participants might become more aware of depressive symptoms during the study period. If so, the self-report would be said to sensitize the participants to the construct under study, perhaps resulting in some of the participants becoming more motivated to work in treatment to ameliorate symptoms of depression. Thus, even if the intended treatment effect were found, it would not be clear whether the treatment would be effective without a pretreatment administration of the self-report measure. Note that this form of threat to validity inherent in the assessment process is present in all research that employs reactive assessment techniques. In other words, in science it is often impossible to study a phenomenon without fundamentally altering it.

The characteristics of research settings and stimuli can also threaten external validity. A laboratory environment is often dramatically different from the real world. Hence, the results of treatment manipulations performed in lab settings may not translate to other settings.

Selection bias interactions

Selection biases have the potential to interact with treatment variable(s), resulting in a threat to external validity. Because most research in psychology is conducted on samples of homogeneous populations, any special characteristics of such populations can interact with the variables being investigated. This interaction limits the extent to which the findings of a study may be generalized to other populations.

For example, much of the research in the social sciences is conducted on convenience samples of college students. This population of people has many distinguishing characteristics (e.g., youth, education level) that set it apart from the broader population. Suppose the participants from the *Optimism Study* had been recruited from a student mental health center at a local university. Optimism training for depression may have been shown to be effective in college populations because it interacted favorably with students' characteristically high eagerness to learn. As such, it would not be certain whether optimism training would work as well in broader populations of individuals less motivated to learn.

It is worth pointing out that this phenomenon poses less of a threat to the validity of research conducted with nonrandomized samples than with full-randomized samples. In the general population, groups of people tend to self-select based on a variety of factors. Hence, studies examining such self-selected groups in their real-world state (as opposed to the artificial homogeneity created by randomization) are more externally valid. For example, in the *Optimism Study*, participants are made up of individuals who present themselves to a clinic for help. They are not randomly sampled from the overall population. Hence, the study's results will generalize well to the population of interest, namely, people who intentionally seek out help for depression in similar outpatient treatment settings.

Multiple-treatment interference

Generalization of clinical research results can be threatened when a series of several treatments is being investigated. When each participant receives multiple levels of the treatment variable, such as in the case of a within-subjects experimental factor, exposure to the treatment from one condition may affect the efficacy of the treatment from another condition.

For example, suppose the *Optimism Study* was conducted on patients that had previously participated in a study that investigated the efficacy of a medication for the treatment of depression. Because the effects of medication treatment cannot be completely reversed, the results of the *Optimism Study* might not generalize to populations of clients who had not received depression medication prior to optimism training and CBT.

Novelty

The effects of a novel treatment might depend on the method's novelty or uniqueness. A client's initial exposure to a newly developed treatment may produce significant progress in recovery, but in the long term, the progress of the client may be more limited. This phenomenon can be generated by a therapist's initial enthusiasm for a new type or method of treatment. Note that this is a variation on the theme of an investigator "allegiance effect."

In the case of the *Optimism Study* the therapist from the experimental group might be quite excited about the potential of combination of optimism training with CBT for depression treatment. Because of her initial enthusiasm she devotes more energy and effort into the therapy sessions than she would have devoted to a more common treatment regimen. Amelioration of clients' depression from the treatment condition might then be due in part to the improved efficacy of the treatment generated from the therapist's enthusiasm, not the efficacy of the treatment itself. If so, the apparent efficacy of optimism training might disappear upon the more widespread use by less enthusiastic clinicians.

Multiple-testing

The timing of measurement is also a crucial factor in evaluating a study's external validity. For example, the *Optimism Study* might demonstrate that optimism training plus CBT is superior to CBT alone in reducing depressive symptoms immediately upon completion of the treatment. However, it is uncertain if this difference will remain after 6 months or a year. It is for this reason that standard treatment outcome research requires assessment to be made at the conclusion of the study and at certain follow-up times (e.g., 6 months, 12 months, and 18 months). Follow-up assessments are crucial so that the longer-term (as well as acute) effects of a treatment can be ascertained.

Construct validity

The ability to attribute group-level changes in measured outcomes to the treatment manipulations of an experimental study is paramount in experimental research. The validity of inferred causal relations from a study is threatened when extraneous variables confound the treatment variables. For the purposes of a discussion regarding the construct validity of a study, it will be assumed that any important confound variables have been controlled for, e.g., by random assignment and/or equivalent group assessment.

If a treatment or intervention is found to affect an outcome variable, two questions follow: "What exactly is the treatment?" and "Why did the treatment have an effect on the behavior under examination?" Construct validity is concerned with the extent to which extraneous variables interfere with the interpretation of the treatment itself. Whereas in psychological measurement the demonstration of construct validity involves an exploration of the traits or attitudes underlying a psychological inventory (e.g., Cronbach, 1990), construct validity in the present context involves an exploration of the variable(s) underlying a treatment manipulation or intervention.

Threats to construct validity

Experimenter contact with clients
In the *Optimism Research Scenario* the clients in the treatment condition interact with therapists during both CBT and optimism training sessions. Alternatively, the clients in the control condition interact with therapists only during CBT sessions. Because clients from the treatment condition spent additional time in treatment with a therapist, relative to the control condition clients, there might have been greater opportunity to address personal concerns. If so, the greater attention paid toward the treatment condition clients is confounded with the treatment variable. As such, the effects of the novel treatment and the additional time in treatment afforded to treatment condition clients cannot be fully separated.

Treatment implementation

In the transition from the conceptual to the operational definition of a treatment or intervention, researchers must make decisions regarding how the treatment is to be executed for the purposes of a study. In the *Optimism Training Scenario* each therapist in the study conducts therapy with either the treatment or control condition clients. As such, the therapist is confounded with the treatment condition to which he or she is assigned. If a treatment effect were found, it would then be unclear if the combination of CBT and optimism training were truly superior to CBT alone, or if the therapist from the combination treatment condition was simply better than the therapist from the CBT control condition. This confound would be remedied, of course, by having each therapist see clients from both the treatment and control conditions.

Experimenter expectations

A researcher's theoretical orientation can affect the outcome of an experimental study. Whether intentionally or unintentionally, experimenters can communicate specific, or even vague, expectations to participants – through side comments about study treatments, nonverbally communicated expectations, and so forth – regarding which among a set of competing treatments will show greatest efficacy. When the experimenters who execute the various treatment conditions are not blind to which condition a given participant belongs, the potential for communication of experimenter expectations is increased. In cases with significant potential for the influence of experimenter expectations, single- or double-blind procedures should be implemented to help control for this confound.

In some cases, such as the *Optimism Study*, a single- or double-blind process is not feasible. The therapist conducting the optimism training knows that the clients she sees belong to the treatment condition. As such, if sessions are videotaped, independent raters can review the tapes to look for any biased comments or statements made by the therapist regarding the particular treatment. This information can help identify if either therapist from the study exhibited significant biased behavior, in turn helping the interpretation of study results.

Statistical conclusion validity

Whereas internal validity focuses on systematic biases that confound substantive conclusions, statistical conclusion validity focuses on whether random variation and sampling and measurement error have invalidated statistical conclusions (Cook, Campbell, and Peracchio, 1990). As such, the validity of statistical conclusions is controlled through the appropriate use of statistical and measurement techniques.

Threats to statistical conclusion validity

Statistical power
In a review of the 1960 volume of the *Journal of Abnormal and Social Psychology*, Cohen (1962) found the average level of statistical power sufficient to detect medium-sized effects was equal to 0.48. As such, averaged across studies reviewed, there was only about a 50 percent chance of rejecting a null hypothesis. Two decades later, Sedlmeier and Gigerenzer (1989) found similar results in a review of the 1984 volume of the same journal (renamed the *Journal of Abnormal Psychology*).

The problems that result from inadequate statistical power can be eliminated by evaluating statistical power, both before and after data collection. Before data collection, power analysis can be used to determine the optimal and/or practical number of participants needed to achieve a given level of power. After data collection, power analysis may be employed to indicate the probability of rejecting the null hypothesis from the particular sample of persons collected. Fortunately, easy-to-use power analysis software is now readily available through such commercially available programs as *Power and Precision 2.0* (Borenstein et al., 2001).

Significance testing

Null hypothesis significance testing is prevalent throughout behavioral science research. For some, $p < .05$ is *sine qua non* of hypothesis testing. However, significance test results convey only one kind of information, Type I error values. Recently, researchers in psychology have paid increased attention to the use of effect sizes in tandem with *p*-values (e.g., Cohen, 1994; Wilkinson, 1999). In fact, the reporting of effect sizes in tandem with *p*-values is now a standard requirement for some academic journals (e.g., the *Journal of Community Psychology*, the *Journal of Consulting and Clinical Psychology*, the *Journal of Counseling and Development*, and the *Journal of Learning Disabilities*).

Effect sizes convey information not supplied by *p*-values, such as the magnitude and direction of an effect. Whereas a *p*-value indicates whether an effect is statistically significant, an effect size indicates the extent of the effect. Furthermore, because formulae for test statistics involve the value of sample size and formulae for effect sizes do not, the finding of a significant *p*-value does not necessarily equate to a nontrivial effect size (e.g., the use of extremely large samples will render even minuscule effects statistically significant at the $p = .05$ level). Conversely, the finding of a nonsignificant *p*-value is not necessarily tantamount to a trivial effect size. As such, sole reliance on *p*-values can result in negligible effects treated as important and sizable effects treated as nonexistent. For primers on computing effect sizes, see Friedman (1968), Kirk (1996), and Snyder and Lawson (1993).

Measurement reliability

Often, psychological inventories are employed as dependent measures in clinical research (e.g., BDI-II, SCID-I, and NEO-PI-R) (Costa and McCrae, 1992). Excessive levels of measurement error can interfere with detecting effects. First, the implicit unreliability of a psychological instrument with substantial measurement error will attenuate the magnitude of estimated Pearson correlations – or any other measure of effect (e.g., Cohen's *d*) – between that instrument and other study variables of interest (e.g., Crocker and Algina, 1986; Hunter and Schmidt, 1990; McNemar, 1962). Thus, in those situations in which an estimate of the degree of correlation between two theoretical constructs is desired, it may be useful to correct correlations for attenuation (Hunter and Schmidt, 1990).

At times, deciding when to correct for attenuation can be complex, and even within a study, some analyses might use disattenutated correlations while other analyses use the uncorrected values. For example, in a recent meta-analysis (Finger and Ones, 1999) the computerized and booklet forms of the MMPI (Butcher et al., 1989; Hathaway and McKinley, 1942) were compared for psychometric equivalence (the three criteria for measurement equivalence are equal means and variances, and a high positive correlation between forms). Finger and Ones corrected cross-form correlations for attenuation, because an estimate of the correlation between the *theoretical* or *construct-level* scores on the two forms was desired. However, the Cohen's *d* values between the two forms were not disattenuated because an estimate of mean difference between the *actual* or *observed*

MMPI scale scores was desired. Whereas the mean differences were indicative of observed scores with measurement error, the cross-form correlations were indicative of true scores without measurement error (Crocker and Algina, 1986; Cronbach, 1990).

Type I error and multiple comparisons

Multiple dependent significance tests are all too prevalent in published research, the end result of which is inflated familywise Type I error rates. For example, conducting all possible pairwise *t*-tests from a one-way within-subjects design (i.e., testing for differences in means between all pairwise treatment levels) will appreciably increase the familywise *p*-value past the nominal .05 level. Similarly, testing each element of a correlation matrix for statistical significance (i.e., $r \neq 0$) inflates the familywise Type I error in an equivalent sense.

Consider the case of 5×5 correlation matrix, in which there are ten distinct correlations.[1] By testing each of the ten correlations for significance at the .05 level, the familywise Type I error rate[2] is actually .226. Accordingly, there is a 22.6 percent chance that at least one of the ten observed correlations would be found significant under the Null Hypothesis scenario in which all ten correlations in the population were truly equal to 0. For a 10×10 correlation matrix with 45 distinct elements, the familywise Type I error rate is .901. As such, there is a 90.1 percent chance that at least one of the 45 observed correlations would be found significant even if all such correlations in the population were equal to 0.

An appropriate alternative is testing whether the joint set of correlations differs significantly from zero (e.g., Cohen and Cohen, 1983; Steiger, 1980). This is equivalent to testing whether the correlation matrix differs significantly from an identity matrix. An identity matrix has 1's on the diagonals and 0's on the off-diagonals. In situations in which only a specific subset of elements from the correlation matrix is hypothesized to differ from zero, it is possible to test whether this subset of correlations jointly statistically differs from zero, with the remaining correlations not differing from zero (Steiger, 1980). By using alternative techniques that provide better control over Type I error, more precise and accurate conclusions can be drawn regarding systematic patterns found in empirical datasets.

Choosing an appropriate data analytic model

Model selection is often associated with structural equation modeling (e.g., Bollen, 1989) or multiple linear regression analysis (Cohen and Cohen, 1983; Keppel and Zedeck, 1989). However, statistical models underlie most parametric statistical methods, from the analysis of variance (ANOVA; Keppel, 1991; Keppel and Zedeck, 1989) to log-linear analysis (e.g., Agresti, 1990). The degree to which the model assumptions of a given analysis are appropriate can vary across datasets. While overly restrictive assumptions can mask an observed effect, overly relaxed assumptions can create the false appearance of an observed effect. In either case, the statistical conclusion validity of a research study can be compromised when unrealistic statistical assumptions are placed on a given dataset.

As an example, a mixed-factorial ANOVA might be used to study the pattern of mean differences from the *Optimism Study*. However, if the sphericity assumption[3] (e.g., Kirk,

1996) placed on the patterns of covariation among the three levels of the within-factor variable (pretreatment, post-treatment, and 6-month follow-up BDI scores) were not met, a time-series analysis (e.g., Tabachnick and Fidell, 2001), with more flexible underlying assumptions regarding study variable distributions, might be considered. Through an appropriate pairing of the statistical analysis with an empirical dataset, the validity of the statistical conclusions is strengthened.

Relating Internal and External Validity

The goals of maximizing internal and external validity are often in conflict with each other. In order to increase the internal validity of a study, a researcher may tightly control all variables to the extent that the study does not resemble any real-world scenario. This concept is particularly important in clinical research. Researchers often select participants that neatly fit into one diagnostic category (e.g., major depressive disorder). This is done to ensure that the efficacy of a treatment can be demonstrated for one disorder, and that other disorders do not confound the results.

However, in applied, real-world settings, it is rare for clients to meet the diagnostic criteria for only one mental disorder. Rather, cases with diagnostic comorbidity are the norm (e.g., Kessler et al., 1997; Krueger et al., 1998; Krueger and Finger, 2001). Moreover, boundaries among mental disorders can blur, and labeling discrete disorders can often be difficult. Hence, the external validity of such tightly controlled studies is questionable, to some degree. More importantly, because of the prevailing attention to the internal validity of clinical studies, one might question the degree to which real-world practical information is being discovered.

The most salient example of the distinction between internal and external validity in clinical settings stems from psychotherapy outcome research studies. In the middle of the 1990s the Society of Clinical Psychology (Division 12) of the American Psychological Association initiated the Task Force on Promotion and Dissemination of Psychological Procedures (1995). The purpose of forming this task force was to establish which psychotherapy treatments are supported by empirical evidence. Unfortunately, the task force initially decided to use the phrase "empirically validated treatments."[4] This was unfortunate because it implies that the evidence is complete and final, when in fact the research is still ongoing (Ingram, Hayes, and Scott, 2000).

The task force has emphasized that their validation criteria apply more to internal validity than to external validity concerns, and that the internally valid research findings demonstrate "treatment efficacy." Based on the task force criteria, a psychotherapy process that has demonstrated treatment efficacy has been shown to produce treatment outcomes superior to that of a no-treatment (e.g., wait list) control group or equivalent to that of an already established treatment in a randomized clinical trial with homogeneous samples. The participants in these trials are usually carefully chosen so that they are diagnosed with a single and distinct mental disorder from the Diagnostic and Statistical Manual of Mental Disorders (*DSM-IV*; American Psychiatric Association, 1994). However, psychotherapists in real-world clinical settings rarely treat clients from populations of a single, clearly diagnosed disorder. The people seeking treatment often operate under some self-selection bias, and rarely present for treatment with a single diagnosable problem. Highly controlled outcome studies, such as those required by the Division 12 Task Force, do little to elucidate the external validity of psychotherapy, given numerous real-world concerns (e.g., heterogeneous patient populations, therapists with various backgrounds and levels of training, different clinical settings, etc.; Ingram, Hayes, and Scott, 2000). Please note that more recently the task force has significantly increased its focus on generalizability concerns (see Chambless and Hollon, 1998).

A theory driven approach to research validity

Traditionally, concerns with internal validity have been paramount in the stated priorities of clinical researchers. Campbell and Stanley (1963) went so far as to call internal validity the *sine qua non* of research. This emphasis on internal validity led to widespread application of the experimental paradigm in clinical research. More recently, some have begun to question the "real-world" value of such tightly controlled research methodologies. In particular, Cronbach (1982) argued that external validity, or generalizability, was of greatest importance to researchers (see also Cronbach and Snow, 1977). Cronbach questioned the use of knowing something if it could not be applied in a practical manner. From this perspective, Cronbach placed primary emphasis on the external, rather than internal, validity of scientific research.

From this historic and long-standing debate over internal versus external validity, the notion has arisen that internal and external validity are inversely related. In order to have high internal validity, a researcher must sacrifice external validity (the generalizability of research findings), and vice versa. While some researchers attended mostly to the demonstration of one type of validity at the expense of the other, some researchers have sought to balance both internal and external validity concerns (Chen and Rossi, 1987; Shadish, Cook, and Campbell, 2002).

For example, Chen and Rossi (1987) described a number of instances that allow for the simultaneous consideration of internal and external validity. They suggested that *theory* should form the basis for identifying the potential threats to validity. If it is unlikely, based on theoretical considerations, for a certain threat to be present in a given study, then research methodologies need not be tailored to control for that threat (e.g., via randomization). In other words, methodological actions are meant to strengthen, rather than replace, relevant psychological models or theories.

Conclusions

Four types of research validity must be addressed in research studies to ensure that the conclusions drawn and the causal inferences made therefrom are valid and appropriate. While internal and external validity concerns are often addressed by clinical researchers, in practice it is all too often one concern at the expense of the other. However, theorists are beginning to elaborate methods through which internal and external validity may be addressed simultaneously, rather than as competing concerns. Perhaps through such complementary methods of examining validity concerns, clinical researchers will be able to draw sounder and stronger causal inferences from their observed results.

Notes

1   The number of distinct correlations from an $n \times n$ correlation matrix is the number of lower or upper off-diagonal elements, or $n(n - 1)/2$. Therefore, a 5×5 correlation matrix has $5(4)/2 = 10$ distinct elements, and a 10×10 correlation matrix has $10(9)/2 = 45$ distinct elements.
2   The familywise Type I error rate for a set of p comparisons is equal to $1 - (1 - \alpha)^p$, where α is the per comparison Type I error rate. The familywise Type I error rate for five comparisons, each of which is tested at the $p = .05$ level, is $1 - (1 - .05)^5 = 1 - .95^5 = 1 - .774 = .226$.
3   In a repeated-measures ANOVA, the sphericity assumption refers to the assumption of equal variances among all possible difference scores – differences in DV scores based on all possible pairs of levels from the within-subjects IV.
4   The task force has since changed the designation to "empirically supported" treatments.

References

Agresti, A. (1990). *Categorical data analysis*. New York: Wiley.

American Psychiatric Association (1994). *Diagnostic and statistical manual of mental disorders* (4th edn.). Washington, DC: American Psychiatric Association.

Beck, A. T., Shaw, B. F., Rush, A. J., and Emery, G. (1979). *Cognitive therapy of depression*. New York: Guilford Press.

Beck, A. T., Steer, R. A., Ball, R., and Ranieri, W. F. (1996). Comparison of Beck Depression Inventories-IA and -II in psychiatric outpatients. *Journal of Personality Assessment, 67*, 588–97.

Bollen, K. A. (1989). *Structural equations with latent variables*. New York: Wiley.

Borenstein, M. T., Rothstein, H., Cohen, J., Schoenfeld, D., Berlin, J., and Lakatos, E. (2001). Power and Precision (Version 2): A computer program for statistical power analysis and confidence intervals [Computer software]. Mahway, NJ: Lawrence Erlbaum.

Braver, M. C. W., and Braver, L. S. (1988). Statistical treatment of the Solomon four-group design: A meta-analytic approach. *Psychological Bulletin, 104*, 150–4.

Butcher, J. N., Dahlstrom, W. G., Graham, J. R., Tellegen, A., and Kaemmer, B. (1989). *MMPI-2 (Minnesota Multiphasic Personality Inventory-2): Manual for administration and scoring*. Minneapolis: University of Minnesota Press.

Campbell, D. T. (1957). Factors relevant to the validity of experiments in social settings. *Psychological Bulletin, 54*, 297–312.

Campbell, D. T. (1977). Reforms as experiments. In F. G. Caro (ed.), *Readings in evaluation research* (2nd edn.). New York: Russell Sage Foundation.

Campbell, D. T., and Stanley, J. C. (1963). *Experimental and quasi-experimental designs for research*. Chicago, IL: Rand McNally.

Chambless, D. L., and Hollon, S. D. (1998). Defining empirically supported therapies. *Journal of Consulting and Clinical Psychology, 66*, 7–18.

Chen, H. T., and Rossi, P. T. (1987). The theory-driven approach to validity. *Evaluation and Program Planning, 10,* 95–103.

Cohen, J. (1962). The statistical power of abnormal-social psychological research: A review. *Journal of Abnormal and Social Psychology, 65,* 145–53.

Cohen, J. (1994). The earth is round (p < .05). *American Psychologist, 49,* 997–1003.

Cohen, J., and Cohen, P. (1983). *Applied multiple regression correlation analysis for the behavioral sciences* (2nd edn.). Hillsdale, NJ: Lawrence Erlbaum.

Cook, T. D., and Campbell, D. T. (1979). *Quasi-experimentation: Design and analysis issues for field settings.* Skokie, IL: Rand McNally.

Cook, T. D., Campbell, D. T., and Peracchio, L. (1990). Quasi experimentation. In M. D. Dunnette and L. M. Hough (eds.), *Handbook of industrial and organizational psychology* (2nd edn., vol. 1, pp. 491–576). Palo Alto, CA: Consulting Psychologists Press.

Costa, P. T., and McCrae, R. R. (1992). *Professional manual for the NEO-PI-R.* Odessa, FL: Psychological Assessment Resources.

Crocker, L., and Algina, J. (1986). *Introduction to classical and modern test theory.* Fort Worth, TX: Harcourt Brace.

Cronbach, L. J. (1982). *Designing evaluations of educational and social programs.* San Francisco, CA: Jossey-Bass.

Cronbach, L. J. (1990). *Essentials of psychological testing* (5th edn.). New York: Harper Collins.

Cronbach, L. J., and Snow, R. E. (1977). *Aptitudes and instructional methods: A handbook for research on interactions.* New York: Halsted Press/Wiley.

Finger, M. S., and Ones, D. S. (1999). Psychometric equivalence of the computer and booklet forms of the MMPI: A meta-analysis. *Psychological Assessment, 11,* 58–66.

Friedman, H. (1968). Magnitude of experimental effect and a table for its rapid estimation. *Psychological Bulletin, 70,* 245–51.

Hathaway, S. R., and McKinley, J. C. (1942). *The Minnesota Multiphasic Personality Schedule.* Minneapolis: University of Minnesota Press.

Hunter, J. E., and Schmidt, F. L. (1990). *Methods of meta-analysis: Correcting error and bias in research findings.* Newbury Park, CA: Sage.

Ingram, R. E., Hayes, A., and Scott, W. (2000). Empirically supported treatments: A critical analysis. In C. R. Snyder and R. E. Ingram (eds.), *Handbook of psychological change: Psychotherapy processes and practices for the 21st Century* (pp. 40–60). New York: John Wiley and Sons.

Kazdin, A. E. (1998). *Research design in clinical psychology.* Needham Heights, MA: Allyn and Bacon.

Keppel, G. (1991). *Design and analysis: A researcher's handbook* (3rd edn.). Upper Saddle River, NJ: Prentice-Hall.

Keppel, G., and Zedeck, S. (1989). *Data analysis for research designs: Analysis of variance and multiple regression/correlation approaches.* New York: Freeman.

Kessler, R. C., Crum, R. M., Warner, L. A., Nelson, C. B., Schulenberg, J., and Anthony, J. C. (1997). Lifetime co-occurrence of *DSM-III-R* alcohol abuse and dependence with other psychiatric disorders in the National Comorbidity Survey. *Archives of General Psychiatry, 54,* 313–21.

Kirk, R. (1996). Practical significance: A concept whose time has come. *Educational and Psychological Measurement, 56,* 746–59.

Krueger, R. F., Caspi, A., Moffitt, T. E., and Silva, P. A. (1998). The structure and stability of common mental disorders (*DSM-III-R*): A longitudinal–epidemiological study. *Journal of Abnormal Psychology, 107,* 216–27.

Krueger, R. F., and Finger, M. S. (2001). Using item response theory to understand comorbidity among anxiety and unipolar mood disorders. *Psychological Assessment, 13,* 140–51.

McNemar, Q. (1962). *Psychological statistics* (3rd edn.). New York: Wiley.

Parker, R. M. (1993). Threats to the validity of research. *Rehabilitation Counseling Bulletin, 36,* 130–8.

Sedlmeier, P., and Gigerenzer, G. (1989). Do studies of statistical power have an effect on the power of studies? *Psychological Bulletin, 105,* 309–16.

Shadish, W. R., Cook, T. D., and Campbell, D. T. (2002). *Experimental and quasi-experimental designs for generalized causal inference.* Boston, MA: Houghton Mifflin.

Snyder, P., and Lawson, S. (1993). Evaluating results using corrected and uncorrected effect size estimates. *Journal of Experimental Education, 61,* 334–49.

Spitzer, R. L., Williams, J. B., Gibbon, M., and First, M. B. (1993). The Structured Clinical Interview for DSM-III-R (SCID): I. History, rationale, and description. *Archives of General Psychiatry, 49,* 624–9.

Steiger, J. M. (1980). Tests for comparing elements of a correlation matrix. *Psychological Bulletin, 87,* 245–51.

Tabachnick, B. G., and Fidell, L. S. (2001). *Using multivariate statistics* (4th edn.). Needham Heights, MA: Allyn and Bacon.

Task Force on Promotion and Dissemination of Psychological Procedures (1995). Training in and dissemination of empirically validated psychological treatments. *The Clinical Psychologist, 48,* 3–23.

Wilkinson, L. (1999). Statistical methods in psychology journals: Guidelines and explanations. *American Psychologist, 54,* 594–604.

CHAPTER THREE

The Scientific Process and Publishing Research

Michael C. Roberts, Keri J. Brown, and Julianne M. Smith-Boydston

The publication of research and theory is a fundamental aspect of science. Psychology, as the science of behavior, shares this emphasis on disseminating information via the publication process. Similarly, the publishing of advances in technique, process, and outcome of therapeutic interventions contributes to the clinical, or applied, side of psychology. Thus, both the art and science of psychology progress through its publication record. There have been numerous expositions in the philosophy of science germane to the role of publishing in science (cf. Mahoney, 1976; Medawar, 1979), and it is clear that scientists engage in the publication process for reasons ranging from the noble to the prosaic. Some of the more notable reasons identified for publishing research include the following: (a) to test hypotheses derived from theory and answer significant theoretical questions, (b) to present experiments and theoretical thinking for public and peer scrutiny and replication, (c) to join the ranks of scientists in advancing the cause of science, (d) to receive recognition and validation for ideas, and (e) to enhance chances for jobs, promotion, tenure, salary increases, etc. Whatever the reason for wanting to publish, the formula for "getting published" is an admixture of competence-based abilities (e.g., knowledge and training), careful research and preparation of the manuscript, compulsivity, perseverance, and some luck.

Despite the importance of scientific and applied psychological publishing, journal editors, senior researchers, and professors often assume that the skills and information requisite to successful publishing are somehow acquired through observation and experience. Often this unstructured learning process leads to haphazard, trial-and-error attempts at publishing. As a result, the potential author may be left frustrated, rejected, and worst of all, unpublished. The present chapter outlines central issues regarding publishing in psychology. The discussion will examine how to: (a) determine what is publishable, (b) select a publication outlet, (c) prepare the manuscript, and (d) anticipate outcomes from the editorial review process.

What is Publishable?

The first step in publishing is obvious: have something to describe in the publication. If research or theory is the content, then an experiment should have been conducted or a theoretical analysis developed. If psychological application is the content, then a psychosocial intervention should have been undertaken. Thus, the first step assumes the author has something available to publish and, admittedly, that may be difficult to accomplish. Fortunately for aspiring authors, there is a large number of topics and content which may serve as material for published articles. The following sections discuss the various content domains for articles which may be produced by psychologists, physicians, social workers, and other professionals.

Literature review

Literature reviews constitute either selected or comprehensive reviews based on existing research articles. The format of a review paper should not just be an annotated listing of one study after another. A good author innovatively considers the literature and combines or synthesizes what has been done in a specific area. Relationships between ideas and results should be clearly communicated. A theoretical framework might be formulated which places into perspective previous research while suggesting how future research might test hypotheses drawn from this framework. In addition to theoretical reviews, there are methodological critiques which review a specific area of research, comment upon the scientific procedures which may have influenced the obtained results, and suggest improvements. There are relatively fewer journals devoted to literature and theoretical reviews in comparison with research studies (e.g., *Clinical Psychology: Science and Practice*; *Applied and Preventive Psychology*; *Clinical Psychology Review*; *Clinical Child and Family Psychology Review*; *American Psychologist*; *Psychological Science*; *Psychological Bulletin*). Editors of other journals sometimes resist overloading their pages with these usually lengthy articles when there are more empirical articles needing publication. A useful distinction might be made between review and overview. As stated before, a review is a more focused detailed analysis, while an overview paper takes a broader topic and, at best, samples the literature, e.g., "behavior therapy with children" or "analytic therapy with adults." Such topics as these are so broad that entire books are devoted to them, and one article would rarely do justice to the material. Nevertheless, overviews can be publishable as articles if they propose a unique approach or analysis of the topic.

Prospective authors should carefully consider the choice of topic and potential publication outlets before investing the immense amount of time necessary to produce a true contribution in the form of a literature review. Students also should be cautious about submitting a literature review based on a class term paper or introduction to a thesis or dissertation until they have carefully assessed the quality and size of its contribution (i.e., to ensure that it constitutes a novel analysis of an important content area). Invariably, the length will need to be shortened. Some of the journals publishing review or theoretical papers are typically among the most prestigious, and published articles become highly cited because of their unique contribution to the literature.

Research articles

The more common (and probably most respected) article published is one based on scientific investigation, because research is the crux of progress for the discipline of psychology and the specialty of clinical psychology. Such articles describe original experimental studies (either one experiment or several in one paper). These articles contain sufficient detail to convey the theoretical or logical origin of an idea, the hypotheses tested by the experiment, the procedures the experimenter employed (to allow replication by others and the readers' judgment of the experimenter's methodological soundness), the statistical analyses and findings, a discussion of results which relates them to the introduction/hypotheses, and ideas for future research. For most psychological journals, the *Publication Manual of the American Psychological Association* (fifth edition) details the standard format of research articles (American Psychological Association, 2001). The APA website also answers frequently asked questions (FAQs) about the publication style (www.apa.org). Individual journals should also be examined for the style required for submission of an article.

There are, of course, differing opinions in psychology as to what constitutes a researchable topic and appropriate methodology. Regarding methodology, some psychologists favor the use of several participants in groups with analysis and comparison of group (nomothetic) data, while others prefer to examine a single participant's behavior in greater individual (ideographic) detail. These differences often serve as benchmarks in different theoretical and methodological camps to define what research is and is not.

There is a fairly uniform bias against publishing research results which fail to reject the null hypothesis (i.e., "nonsignificant results"). Many alternative hypotheses may be offered for failure to find predicted differences (e.g., poor methodology). Unfortunately, the overemphasis on statistically significant results often leads to data "snooping," falsification of data, and other scientifically unsound practices. Many competently conducted studies with statistical nonsignificance may be filed away and never published, creating what is called the "file drawer" problem. Consequently, the field never reads of these challenges to theory and failures to replicate previous studies. Convincing arguments may be offered for the publication of nonsignificant results because even these findings may be very important for theory and practice and may better reflect the research that has been conducted in a given area. A similar bias of nonpublication extends to replication studies. All in all, authors are well advised to consider the values and opinions held by researchers in each subarea of psychology when looking at the results of their own study.

Case studies

Clinical case studies are a third type of material published in clinical psychology. Case studies generally take one or more participants and review the development or etiology of a psychological disorder, and present the therapeutic intervention initiated to alleviate the disorder. Several questions should be asked before submitting a case study: Does the case illustrate a particular problem in a unique or definitive way? Is the intervention adequately described? Is the problem and treatment related to a theoretical superstructure? Case studies are frequently valuable because they suggest areas in which further research with larger groups of subjects might be made. Additionally, some disorders are relatively infrequent and, therefore, not conducive to multiple subjects design or group intervention. Case studies can frequently demonstrate the potential of a therapy technique or support particular components of a theoretical model. Case reports vary in the kind of information provided, and the type of case and methodology presented will differ according to the type of journal publishing the article. The orientation of the journal determines its acceptance of case studies. For example, *Behavior Therapy* publishes case descriptions of behavior change interventions from a behavioral orientation. Similarly, the *Journal of Applied Behavior Analysis* publishes cases that rely on the objective measurement of actual behavior prior to intervention, during an intervention, and following the intervention. These detailed analyses of individuals' behaviors often utilize methodologies of multiple baseline or ABA design (see chapter 5, this volume). In addition, *Cognitive and Behavioral Practice* publishes a section of articles and commentary entitled "The Cognitive-Behavior Therapy Case Conference," with different cases discussed. In contrast, the *Psychoanalytic Study of the Child* publishes studies consisting of descriptions of the clinician's conceptualization of a particular client and problem, with considerable detail devoted to the process of therapeutic intervention.

Comments and topical discussions

A fourth type of publication comments upon events or other publications in a topical discussion. "Letters to the Editor" or "Comments" are usually relatively brief and attend to a very specific issue. For example, the *American Psychologist* and *Professional Psychology: Research and Practice* publish written commentaries, several paragraphs in length, which discuss professional issues or other articles published in that same journal. Recently, *Clinical Psychology: Science and Practice* (Barlow, 2000) and the *Journal of Consulting and Clinical Psychology* (Kendall, 2000) have become receptive to this form of published communication. Such letters and comments mostly deal with such matters as the methodological rigor (or lack thereof) or conclusions of recently published studies. Various professional organizations (e.g., the Society of Clinical Psychology, the Association for the Advancement of Behavior Therapy, the Division of Health Psychology) include materials of this type in their organizational newsletters (e.g., *The Clinical Psychologist, The Behavior Therapist, The Health Psychologist*).

Book reviews

Journals sometimes publish book reviews relevant to a particular topic or field of psychology. Evaluations of books help define the progress of psychological thinking, and help potential book buyers judge whether or not to acquire a book. Different journals publish different styles and contents of their book reviews. Not all journals publish reviews, nor do all those that publish them accept unsolicited reviews. One journal, *Contemporary Psychology*, is devoted entirely to invited book reviews, and a relatively high standard is imposed on those accepted.

Convention presentations

Oral presentation of research findings at psychology conventions is another form of scientific publication. The session at which research is presented on posters, with the researcher standing nearby for discussion, is another convention or conference format common for research dissemination. Conventions and conferences now rarely publish proceedings with presented papers included, but preparing a project for such presentation is an excellent first step in getting to the write-up for journal submission. An additional benefit is the opportunity to get feedback and discuss implications of the project from fellow conference participants to include in the manuscript.

Research topics

A great deal of fad research exists in clinical psychology, with "hot" topics waxing and then waning in popularity in a manner not dissimilar to the latest fashion trends. Most researchers and practitioners want to be on the cutting edge of the scientific discipline. However, the novice researcher is frequently misled by a perceived *zeitgeist* reflected in the published literature. There are several difficulties with attempting to determine "hot" topics. First, what may be popular this year may not be publishable next year. Second, by the time an article reaches publication and is read by other researchers, a great deal of time will have passed due to the usual publication lag of one to two years (i.e., between the time an article is submitted and when it subsequently appears in print). In all likelihood, the article's author has moved beyond his or her original idea and the "catchy" research topic is no longer so innovative that journal editors will be attracted to it. Beginning researchers need also to think long term in developing a research program and becoming experts in a topic area. Although some publications may result from serendipitous collaborations, a planned series of research projects eventuating in publications is important to establishing a programmatic research effort. This program can be organized around a theoretical question, a particular problem, or clinical population. A central theme should run through the various projects. Students often have the opportunity to work with different researchers, sometimes resulting in a potpourri of articles and interests. This is to be expected. However, a narrowing of activity to one or two lines of clinical research and theory is important to demonstrate expertise and a program of research.

Quality of the Article

Personal standards

Authors often find it difficult to judge the quality of their own work in deciding what is potentially publishable. Criticism of something in which authors have become invested may be difficult to accept. It should always be remembered that criticism will come, if not from oneself, then from the journal reviewers and/or other researchers in the field. However, standards of quality vary among individual researchers and among journals. No one standard can be applied to determine the quality of all articles published in psychology. Therefore, authors first apply their own standards to identify potential worth of the topic and results of their writing.

Colleagues' critique

In view of the difficulty in arriving at an objective assessment of the quality of one's own work, there are other ways to determine the publishability of a particular article. Researchers can discuss topics and perhaps prepare an article for critical review by trusted colleagues. However, some readers may hesitate to make many negative comments because of their personal relationship with the author. Potential readers need to be told that a "good" friend will make critical comments which are useful in improving the paper. Seeking a mentoring relationship with an established author for advice can have many benefits for the nascent researcher in mastering the process, receiving support, and enhancing chances of getting published. Feedback from a presubmission reviewer should be of detail and quality similar to that of the journal to which the manuscript will be submitted. It is frequently useful to send presubmission manuscripts to other researchers familiar with a topic to elicit ideas and criticisms which might improve a paper. Help received during manuscript preparation has been shown to be related to the quality of the published article (Bauer and Hammer, 1996).

Editorial standards

After having colleagues critique a manuscript, the author may take the final step toward establishing what is publishable, which is of course to let journal editors and reviewers decide. Some of the most useful feedback will come from the objective reviews by the journal referees, because this is truly evaluation by one's peers. Novice authors should actively seek out this evaluation, and experienced authors also should not neglect continual feedback on the quality of their work. However, not all journals in psychology and other scientific disciplines employ a peer review system. The researcher who only publishes in nonrefereed journals is not obtaining an objective measure of the quality of his or her work and standing in the field. On the other hand, potentially valuable articles are lost to science when authors are overly strict in their own standards and do not submit their work. An editor is charged with determining what should be published, and it makes sense to allow him or her to do that job with input from reviewers.

Selecting the Most Appropriate Publication Outlet

Two axioms for selecting an outlet

One axiom to follow as a strategy is that authors should never aim an article to only *one* journal. If an article is too narrowly focused and appropriate to only one journal, and if it is rejected by that outlet, it may end up never getting published. A good strategy is to make a list of four or five appropriate journals and to rank-order them from the "best" down to "acceptable." Submission can start at the top of the list and work down in the case of initial rejections. The flexibility of the article for several outlets is an advantage, and it may get in at the first submission in a top-notch journal. If rejected by the better journal, the reviewers' comments may contain useful feedback for the author to consider while revising and resubmitting to another journal. Some editors and reviewers complain about "journal shoppers" who persist in submitting the same poor manuscript to a succession of journals (Webb, 1979). There is enough evidence for inconsistency in the reviewing process to mitigate this complaint. For example, reviewers can often be unreliable, and may make individualized comments on aspects of a manuscript not shared by the other reviewers. Sometimes, the reviewing process may come down to the "luck of the draw" in getting favorable reviewers.

The catch phrase in academia is "publish or perish." Therefore, researchers should do what they ethically can to enhance the chances of publication of their work. Submission to a reasonable number of journals seems appropriate, particularly if reviewers' objections are accommodated in the revisions and improve the quality. Repeated rejections should tell an author something about the quality of the paper.

A second axiom follows from the one above: submit a manuscript to only one journal at a time. It is unethical to submit the same manuscript simultaneously to several journals and then to select which one of these in which to publish; in fact, many journals now require a statement in the cover letter which indicates that the manuscript is not under editorial review elsewhere. Granted, submitting to one journal at a time and going through the usual lengthy review process (often 3–9 months) may impede or delay publication, but the ethical researcher should not misrepresent an article. It is, however, entirely appropriate to submit the same manuscript to another journal once it has been officially rejected by one journal editor, or after the author has formally withdrawn it from editorial consideration by that journal.

The American Psychological Association (1997) publishes a compendium of information on over 350 journals regarding editorial policy, topic coverage, and instructions to contributors. There are several issues associated with various journals and editorial policies which should influence selection of a publication outlet. Therefore, in this section, these various considerations will be examined, including the prestige of the journal, publishing a line of research in the same or a different journal, types of readership to target, journal content, rejection rates, use of peer reviewers, paying for publication, submitting to new or established journals, electronic journals, and strategies for submitting. These issues need to be weighed together in determining where to submit; no one priority issue can solely determine publishing strategy.

Prestige of the journal

There are several axioms which hold true much of the time with regard to selecting a publication outlet. The first axiom is that the prestige of the journal will help to: (a) determine the impact of the article on the field, (b) influence the frequency of citations of the published article by other researchers, (c) influence the amount of respect colleagues will have for both the author and the published research, and (d) determine whether or not the article is accepted (i.e., generally, the better the journal's reputation, the higher the rejection rate). One objective evaluation technique to consider is citation impact. Citation impact refers to how many times articles from a particular journal are cited in other published works. This information is available from the Social Science Citation Index (Institute for Scientific Information, see www.isinet.com). One indicator, journal prestige, is often overemphasized and other characteristics should be considered as well when selecting a publication outlet. Citation index (or citation impact) refers to how many times other authors cite one author's papers (or a journal) in their reference lists. The Social Science Citation Index (SSCI), a database produced each year, lists articles according to senior (first) author that have been referenced by other publications during the year (www.isinet.com). Most research libraries at universities have this reference available. The greater the number of citations, the more impact an author is presumed to have on the field (unless everybody is repeatedly citing the work as an example of poor research!). The citation index may be used as a criterion for promotion or as a measure of an individual's eminence in a field. Productivity ratings for groups of researchers can be generated from the data on individual researchers to reflect on a department faculty, for example, with an implication for a department's reputation. Similarly, journals can be ranked according to the impact they are having on the field by checking the citation impact (the average rate of others' citations of articles published in a particular journal).

At the basic level, the number of publications is often used as a measure of productivity. This, however, interacts with the quality of the journal, rejection rates, etc. Citation rates are a little more sophisticated, but also have problems. For example, citation rates do not reflect the effect an article may have on clinical applications. Citation rates are also affected by the length of time an article has been in print and in what journal. Journals with larger audiences, but not necessarily better quality articles, seem to get cited most often. Some highly cited articles and books are basic references or standardized assessment devices. These reflect an impact, but may not be comparable to that of a theoretical review or important research study.

Same or different journals

A second axiom is that, in general, an author should not publish his or her work only in one journal, but not always in a different one either. Publishing in only one journal limits the impact of the research largely to the readership of that journal. Additionally, depending on the prestige of that journal, publishing in only one journal may indicate to other workers in the area that the author cannot get material published elsewhere. However, one reason for not publishing in many different journals is that a scientist's research work needs to show continuity and programmatic efforts. That is, scattering articles across a wide number of journals might give the appearance of a fragmented research program, or even scattered thinking. A second reason is that researchers in a specialized area may not read or subscribe to a wide variety of journals, and may not take the time to investigate an author's publications in several journals. Third, publishing in too many different journals may indicate that an author is unable to convince the journal editor to repeat the "mistake" of publishing his or her first article in that journal. A qualification on the "same or different" axiom above is that if the author is always publishing in the top journals within the field, then no negative inferences can be drawn. Thus, in the clinical psychology area, publishing in the *Journal of Consulting and Clinical Psychology* repeatedly or exclusively would be viewed as very respectable. The axiom holds truest for journals in the middle-to-lower range of reputation.

Journal readership

The decision to submit an article to a particular journal should also be based on the readership a researcher wants to target. Workers in a specialized area often do not subscribe to or read journals in another area, and may not subscribe to the more generic journals in their fields. Clinical child/pediatric psychologists may pay closest attention to articles published in the *Journal of Clinical Child and Adolescent Psychology, Children's Services: Social Policy, Research, and Practice*, the *Journal of Pediatric Psychology*, or the *Journal of Abnormal Child Psychology*. Similarly, adult clinical psychologists might attend more to the *Journal of Abnormal Psychology* or the *Journal of Clinical Geropsychology*. More generic clinical journals might be accessed by a variety of specialists within clinical psychology, such as the *Journal of Consulting and Clinical Psychology, Clinical Psychology: Science and Practice*, the *Journal of Clinical Psychology in Medical Settings*, and *Mental Health Services Research*. There is also some research which indicates that authors publishing in one particular journal tend to cite other articles also published in that same journal, rather than articles from other journals (e.g., Kazdin, 1975; Kazak, 2000). This finding suggests that authors likely read and use material from a limited number of publication sources, usually those most relevant to the topic.

The main point here is that authors should consider to which readership they want to target their articles, and who will respect the publication outlet. Hence, one might choose the *Journal of Clinical Child and Adolescent Psychology* to have an impact on specialists in this area. On the other hand, if exposure to pediatricians about clinical child psychology material is desired, then a medical journal may be more appropriate (e.g., *Pediatrics* or the *Journal of Developmental and Behavioral Pediatrics*). If one wants to build a "name" in behavioral psychology, then publishing in such journals as the *Journal of Behavior Research and Experimental Psychiatry, Behavior Therapy,* or *Child and Family Behavior Therapy* would be important. It is usually easy to tell if a journal has a particular orientation or bias which may attract a particular readership and, thus, might be amenable to one's work. An author can often determine a potential publication outlet by examining his or her own reference list for where cited articles are published.

Journal content

To determine whether an article is appropriate for a journal, the prospective author may examine back issues of that journal. Searching back too far, however, may lose track of what the current editorial policy and *zeitgeist* of the field is in that specific area (two to three years should be adequate). A check of journal content will reveal those journals which may be attracted to a research topic an author is studying. A journal editor sometimes likes to maintain continuity of the journal's articles and, thus, may be willing to publish studies related to material previously published in that journal. However, the editor may also negatively react to too much material on one topic in his or her journal and wish to limit it. Of course, the editor may also use a previous author on the topic to do the review, and this reviewer may help or hurt chances of acceptance, depending on his or her predilection to see the submitted manuscript as enhancing or competing with the published article. Despite exhortations to be objective, scientific, and scholarly, reviewers' biases sometimes do creep into the review process and may act against manuscripts, particularly ones that are seen as critical of the reviewer's own previously established article.

Other journal editors may be attracted to a topic if it has never been published in their particular journal. Editors like their journals to publish material which is perceived to be at the "cutting edge" of research in a field, and are often particularly receptive to submissions. In selecting a publication outlet based on journal content, one may also examine the paper's reference list to see where the articles cited therein were published. This is a good indication of the interest in a particular topic by the journal's reviewers and editors, particularly within the last few years. Often, as new editors assume the editorship of a journal, they write statements of interest and coverage for their terms. Of course, the mastheads of the journal provide a general statement of coverage. Content analyses of journal publications may also help in selecting journals (e.g., Roberts, 1992).

Rejection rates

Journals vary in their rates of accepting and rejecting submitted manuscripts. In general, psychology (like other social sciences) has a higher rate of rejection than do other scientific areas. Psychology journals average about 80 percent rejection (range 20–95 percent).

Generally, the more selective and prestigious journals have higher rates of rejection. (Interestingly, such "hard" science areas as chemistry and physics have rejection rates of only 20 to 30 percent.) The average length and number of submitted psychology papers relative to the number of available journal pages determine the rejection rate. The rate of acceptance of a journal obviously has direct implications for the probability of a sub-mitted paper being accepted. Prospective authors can find rates summarized in editorial statements or summary reports (e.g., APA journals, see Summary Report of Journal Operations for 2001, 2002).

Peer reviewed/refereed journals

One characteristic of a journal which affects its prestige and respectability is its use of referees or reviewers to aid in accepting or rejecting manuscripts for publication. While the editor and/or associate editor are the gatekeepers for science, reviewers play a major role by adding their particular expertise in evaluating articles. Reviewers are usually selected from the journal's board of editors or appointed "ad hoc" by the editor to read and review a submitted manuscript. This review aspect of the editorial process will be elaborated in a subsequent section. Refereed or peer-reviewed journals are almost invari-ably more prestigious than nonrefereed journals. The latter usually do not have outside or ad hoc reviewers; instead, an editor alone makes determination of the publishability of a particular article. Some nonrefereed journals may not have the same level of quality standards as refereed journals. Also, some journals claim to utilize an editorial board and reviewers, while in actual practice, they may not. Additionally, some nonrefereed journals charge authors for publishing their articles.

The importance of refereed journals is that one's work is reviewed by a panel of expert peers and, if accepted and published, implies some value to the work. Additionally, no critical feedback is received from a nonrefereed journal, and an author may erroneously infer that his or her work is of high quality when, in reality, no such inference should be made. It is to an author's advantage to publish in refereed journals whenever possible, both for the respect it may bring and the feedback the review process provides. A more pragmatic reason is that academic promotions and awarding of tenure are frequently based on a requirement to publish in refereed journals.

Pay for publication

Some journals require payment from the author or his or her institution for publication costs of the article. There are advantages and disadvantages to such "pay journals." As noted above, some pay journals are nonrefereed, but not all. Thus, one disadvantage is the lower respectability for these journals. In addition, some charges for publication include what are called "page costs" and special table and figure "set up" charges. An additional disadvantage or advantage, depending on one's perspective, is that pay journals have a reputation for taking almost any type of manuscript without regard to quality. Pay journals usually have short backlogs of articles waiting to be published.

Consequently, many pay journals guarantee publication within two months of final acceptance and receipt of payment. Sometimes an author may desire to have fast turn-around and publication of papers which may be related to other manuscripts of his or hers being published (e.g., have the two articles come out close in time). Thus, the quick publication offered by pay journals may have particular advantages. Other journals may not charge for the publication of a manuscript, but will charge an author for reprint copies (sometimes optional or mandatory). Some journals provide at least a few reprints free of charge (authors should check the journal's submission instructions).

New versus well-established journals

When considering outlets for publishing an article, the prospective author may wish to consider whether a journal is new or established. There are advantages to each situation. If the journal is fairly new (e.g., established in the last one to five years), then it may need to acquire publishable material rapidly with somewhat lower quality standards early in its development. A new journal usually has the advantage that there is no backlog of accepted articles waiting to be published and faster turnaround may be accomplished. A disadvantage of a new journal is that it has yet to obtain a universal scholarly reputation, although a well-known, reputable editor can contribute to its respectability. Unless the journal is backed by a professional organization or reputable publishing company, it may also go defunct. An article published in a defunct journal may also fade into oblivion. Publishing with an established journal generally has the advantage of a prestigious reputation. As a disadvantage, more established journals have higher rejection rates, higher quality standards, and a lengthy publication lag for backlogged articles. Sometimes when there is an editor change for a journal, the policy shift or pool of potential reviewers will change sufficiently to increase (or decrease) the possibility of placing a paper with the journal.

Electronic journals

Most journals are now available both in print and in digital versions accessible through the world wide web. A few journals are now published solely in electronic format. For example, *Prevention and Treatment* is "web published" by the American Psychological Association. The editorial process is conducted primarily through the Internet. Articles are peer reviewed and those selected are published on the APA website (see www.apa.org), often with invited commentary. One added feature of web publication is that readers can post their own comments and analyses in reaction to the article. Hard copy versions can be printed (e.g., through Adobe Acrobat). The Society for the Scientific Study of Social Issues began a web-based journal under the title of ASAP (*Analysis of Social Issues and Public Policy*; see www.asap-spssi.org). Print versions of ASAP's web-published articles will be published by Blackwell Publishing. Another electronic journal, *Behavioral Technology Today*, appears at www.behavior.org. Currently, there are some perceived drawbacks to digital journals, such as the need for more permanent archiving and preservation, and the ambiguous reception in the academic reward system for such publications (see www.createchange.org and www.arl.org/sparc/). In all likelihood, this modality will increase in prestige and popularity over time (Fowler, 1996). Electronic articles may also benefit from enhanced technical features not found in hard copy publications, such as video and audio clips, color pictures, and links to other information sites.

Strategies for submitting

In addition to the above factors, there are a few other important considerations in selecting a publication outlet: (a) What is the circulation of the journal? Generally, the larger the circulation, the better suited it is for wider dissemination and enhanced citation of its articles. To determine circulation rates, the "Statement of Ownership, Management, and Circulation" is a form required of all periodicals by the US Postal Service, and is usually printed in the last journal issue of each year. (b) Does the journal go to members of any scientific or professional organizations? If yes, then there usually is a guaranteed readership the author may want to target. Sponsored journals generally have better reputations. (c) Is the journal well advertised? The critical question is: Do other people know about it and recognize its quality? Familiarity with a journal generally enhances its rating of scientific reputation. (d) Where are the journal's articles indexed or abstracted? There are several important abstracting services (e.g., PsycInfo; PubMed) which generate wider impact and larger citation rates of journal publications. This result is because secondary sources that cite articles are often consulted more than original issues of the journals themselves.

Preparation of the Manuscript

Writing

It seems self-evident that an author should use the best grammar, spelling, and punctuation of which he or she is capable. Unfortunately, Medawar (1979) asserts that "most scientists do not know how to write" (p. 63). Authors should learn the conventional style for articles published in psychology journals. Authors may need to consult the APA *Publication Manual* (APA, 2001) and writing guides (Becker, 1986; Lester, 1999; O'Connor, 1992; Strunk and White, 1979). Although the use of jargon has been challenged by both lay readers and fellow scientists, the precision of certain words and shorthand communication has a high priority. Communication with fellow psychologists and professionals often requires an ability different from that of communicating with the lay public. Certainly, writing should be tailored to the audience targeted. Even more certainly, brevity in writing is better than verbosity. Careful attention should be given to the abstract because it is the first (or only) thing read and may color perceptions of the manuscript.

Submission guidelines

"Submission Guidelines," "Instructions to Authors," and "Notes to Contributors" present the style for each journal to standardize the preparation of manuscripts submitted. A complete set of instructions is usually given in at least one issue of the journal each year, and journal or publisher websites typically present this necessary information. Many journals request that authors use a standardized style manual in preparing manuscripts. The American Psychological Association *Publication Manual* (APA, 2001) has been adopted by most psychology journals and many related disciplines. Other scientific and professional fields (e.g., medicine, psychiatry) have developed their own styles. Additionally, some journals in psychology use a style different from the APA manual. Several websites provide links to numerous journals and their instructions for authors: www.mco.edu/lib/instr/libinsta.html and www.clas.ufl.edu/users/gthursby/psi/journal.htm. These are not comprehensive (and nothing helps as much as examining the journal directly). One important alternative format to the APA style is the Uniform Requirements for Manuscripts submitted to Biomedical Journals; information on these may be accessed at www.acponline.org/journals/resource/unifreqr.htm. Authors are advised to follow the submission requirements for each journal very closely, including page limits, reference style, etc. Otherwise, manuscripts may be returned unreviewed by the editor with a request that the paper be revised to conform with the journal's submission requirements. Or the journal may review the manuscript in its submitted style, but delay its publication in order to return it to the author for the required revisions or because of copy-editing problems. A journal may require authors to sign a document which states that the submitted manuscript is not under editorial review elsewhere and/or a form transferring copyright privileges to the journal publisher should the manuscript be accepted for publication. Increasingly, journals are requiring that *all* authors listed on the manuscript cover page sign permission forms. In the preparation of the manuscript, authors should be compulsive in checking all aspects of the write-up. For example, statistics and tables should be compared with hard copies of the original data analyses (e.g., computer printouts, etc.). Line-by-line proofreading of the manuscript should be sufficient to catch most typographical errors and to identify any left-out phrases or sentences. It is an axiom in academia that when preparing a manuscript or paper, "care may help acceptance, sloppiness is almost guaranteed to bring rejection." Word processing programs have spell-check features that can catch many typographical errors and misspellings. However, spell check cannot identify correctly spelled words used inappropriately, such as homonyms (e.g., there, their, they're).

Masked/blind review

Some journals utilize a review process known as "blind review" or more recently as "masked review." This simply means that those reviewers chosen by the editor to read and comment on the manuscript are not informed of the author's name or institutional affiliation. This procedure was developed to ensure equal opportunity for publishing regardless of one's stature in the field or an institution's prestige. Some studies have shown that without such masking of authors, reviewers rated manuscripts more favorably when they were informed they came from "big name" authors than when they were informed the papers were by unknown authors. Masked review is a goal which is not always realized, inasmuch as reviewers can frequently guess at the identity of an author (e.g., through frequent self-reference by the author or statements in the procedure section about where the research took place). The procedure for preparing a masked review paper should include removing all identifying names from the copies of the manuscript except for the cover sheet. In general, it is to the advantage of a novice author to utilize a "masked review" privilege when a journal offers that option.

Submission of the manuscript

Manuscripts should be sent to the editor with a typed cover letter explaining that the enclosed copies are for consideration in the journal. One paragraph in the cover letter should describe for the editor what is presented in the manuscript. This paragraph will assist the editor in determining whether the topic fits the journal's content. This is an opportunity for the author to emphasize the importance of the study, how it fits into the theoretical or applied field, and why it is relevant to the journal. Editors of journals receiving multitudes of manuscripts may not read the submitted papers until they have been recommended for acceptance by the reviewers. Thus, the cover letter may be the only way the author can affect the editorial judgment. In the cover letter, the author may also choose to suggest possible reviewers of the manuscript. Some, but not all, journals allow authors to nominate two or three reviewers in the topic area. Suggested reviewers should not be one's colleagues, students, professors, or collaborators on previous or current research. An author may also ask the editor to exclude some particular person in a field from serving as a reviewer of the submitted manuscript. Editors likely will not ask to know *why* a potential reviewer was excluded, because they will assume an author would have a valid reason (e.g., hostile competitor, negative history, ex-lover). The privilege of excluding reviewers should be used cautiously, lest the editor becomes irritated, but such exclusion may be necessary for a fair and objective review.

Editorial Review Process

Editor and reviewers

The process of reviewing a submitted manuscript is relatively straightforward; however, it also contains more than a modicum of chance. Some journals and editors make explicit their editorial policy and process (e.g., *Journal of Abnormal Psychology*, Strauss, 1995; *Journal of Consulting and Clinical Psychology*, Kendall, 1997; *Clinical Psychology: Science and Practice*, Barlow, 1999; *Professional Psychology: Research and Practice*, Kunkel,

2001; *Journal of Counseling Psychology*, Hansen, 2000; *American Psychologist*, Fowler, 1993, 1996; *Journal of Pediatric Psychology*, Kazak, 1998; *Health Psychology*, Stone, 2001; *Applied and Preventive Psychology*, Smith, 2000). Prospective authors may find it useful to sleuth out what a journal editor is thinking about, what topics he or she wants to encourage, and how the journal's procedures might be changed in the future. Depending on the journal, editors may have 5-year or 6-year terms, with new editors appointed by a sponsoring academic society. In other cases, the publishing company owns the journal and will select the editor, usually for longer terms. Researchers have investigated the editorial process ever since the beginning of scientific publication. Each discipline has studied editorial reviewing and decision-making, often finding flaws and recommending corrections (e.g., Bedeian, 1996; Brysbaert, 1996; Epstein, 1995; Fine, 1996; Levenson, 1996; Rabinovich, 1996). Despite occasional calls for reform, the general review process is accepted within the psychology discipline.

The editor, upon receipt of the manuscript, initially makes a global decision about the appropriateness of the paper for the journal's topic area. At this point, he or she may return the manuscript to the author with a notation that it does not fit the content area of the journal and suggestion for submission elsewhere. If retained, the editor will usually send the manuscript out for review by members of the editorial board or select reviewers on an ad hoc basis from the field at large. Usually two reviewers are utilized, although more may be solicited. Selection of reviewers is generally made on the basis of their expertise on the topic presented in the submitted paper. Often, editors will scan the reference list of the manuscript to gain an idea of possible reviewers. As noted above, the editor may also use reviewers recommended in the author's cover letter, but he or she is not under any obligation to do so.

Most journals list the names of the editorial board in the masthead (front pages or cover of a journal issue) and the names of reviewers used on an ad hoc basis during a year to acknowledge their contributions. Reviewers or referees are not paid for their efforts, and get only intrinsic reinforcement for their behavior at best. These acknowledgment lists do not associate the names with the reviewed papers, but they are useful for indicating some likely candidates for reviewers the editor will consider. Reviewers have the obligation of objectively reading the manuscript in a timely manner and providing written comments to the editor regarding the various aspects of the manuscript. These referees are ethically mandated to maintain confidentiality of the scientific communication in a manuscript under review and must not advance their own work through the review. Reviewers are asked to read the manuscript and to examine such scientific considerations as its conception, design, execution, data analysis, results, interpretation, and importance to the field. Clarity of writing is assessed and ratings are often made on forms regarding significance of the problem, rigor of the methodology, logic and reasoning, new information contributed, and appropriateness for the journal. Referees are allowed to return the manuscript to the editor, if necessary, without reviewing it for a number of reasons including other time commitments, personal affiliation with the author, self-perceived biases against topic or author, etc. Many journals attempt to maintain a 2–4 month turnaround on reviews. However, it is probably more common for editorial disposition letters to be returned between 6–9 months after submission. Some journals publish their editorial lag statistics (i.e., the length of time from date of submission to date of acceptance) as well as publication lag (i.e., the length of time from acceptance to publication; e.g., APA journals, see Summary Report of Journal Operations for 2001, 2002). Lengthy lags frequently occur in this field wherein after acceptance, it may be as long as two years before an article is published. Fortunately, some journals have much shorter lags.

Editorial decision-making

Upon receipt of the reviews, the editor will then determine whether to accept or reject the manuscript. A third alternative open to the editor is to solicit another set of reviews or make his or her own judgment when two conflicting reviews are obtained. Two negative recommendations will usually result in an outright rejection by the journal. Generally positive reviews with recommendations for acceptance with "low priority" or "if space allows" may result in editorial rejection because most journals have no extra space for such marginal articles. Two very positive reviews or two out of three positive recommendations will generally result in acceptance for publication in the journal. Journals with very high numbers of submissions may impose a requirement for unanimity for all reviewers in order to justify acceptance.

Sometimes an editor will stipulate that a manuscript must be revised prior to acceptance. O'Connor (1979) adapted another article (*Lancet*, 1970) to give general tips for shortening a manuscript:

1   Shorten the Introduction by cutting out all references to previous work that are not directly related to the work described; citing a review article will probably cover most of them.
2   Omit details of methods described in other publications. The principles on which the methods are based are often more significant; on the other hand, major modifications must be described exactly.
3   Do not repeat in the text information provided in tables or legends to illustrations.
4   Reduce speculation in the Discussion to reasonable, testable hypotheses.
5   Use the active voice and first person whenever appropriate; they are usually more succinct.
6   Cut out all flabby introductory phrases such as "It is interesting that . . ." – and all woolly words of uncertain meaning. (O'Connor, 1979: 44)

Editors' and reviewers' comments

Although psychology has a tradition of constructive criticism, some comments by reviewers are not necessarily useful. For example, they may make such statements as "the author has succeeded in reinventing the wheel" or "the best thing about this research is the researcher has debriefed the participants." Such comments are not only obnoxious, but also do not help the research process. Some reviews contain one line stating acceptance or rejection, while others are fairly lengthy in attending not only to the study but also to the writing style and use of grammar. The greater the detail, the more information the author has as insight into how the reviewers perceive the paper and how it (and later research) can be improved.

Because colleagues rarely share with each other the negative comments made by reviewers about their manuscripts, most authors are unaware of the range of things that can be said. Thus, the novice author has no baseline for comparison; he or she is unprepared for the seemingly overwhelming hostility and casual reading of one's cherished work. Although infrequent, some harsh and sarcastic things are written under the guise of constructive "feedback." As an example of the worst type of comment, the following is a slightly edited version of a reviewer's comments to one of us: "In general, the manuscript suffers from an amazing lack of any understanding about the phenomenon with which they are dealing and the various concepts and processes used to explain it. There are gargantuan conceptual and design flaws in their flimsy attempt to measure the behavior and relate it to an underlying mechanism. This manuscript should be rejected, since it would only add to the confusion already rampant in the area. Below are only a few of the more serious problems with this study; they are presented here in order to justify my strong recommendation to reject this paper and urge the author to seek other avenues of investigation." (We should note that this paper was eventually published in a more respected journal than the one for which this referee was reviewing.) A responsible editor will withhold those reviews that attack an author personally, but one may slip by him or her on occasion. Fortunately, the majority of comments will be unbiased, considerate, and constructive, even if not supporting acceptance for publication. Some journals and some disciplines (e.g., medicine) generally do not provide detailed feedback, opting for a form letter of rejection. If accepted for publication, then more detailed revisions are outlined.

Handling rejection: read, react, rewrite, resubmit

If a submitted manuscript gets rejected, the author should follow the following axiom: read, react, rewrite, and resubmit. First, the author should read the editorial letter and reviewers' comments closely while trying not to overreact, but considering carefully the suggestions and reasoning. Authors can learn from perceived mistakes in order to improve the submitted manuscript for later submission and to improve the overall research program. An author should look at the concerns of the reviewers and attempt to see the manuscript through their eyes.

For the second step, authors may *react* to a review by exclaiming "Why didn't the reviewer read paragraph 2 on page 10?" or some other squeal of anguish. We will consider how to approach erroneous reviews later, but for now authors are urged not to take rejection as personal insult. We suggest the author put the letter aside for a while (two weeks) before returning to it to move forward.

In terms of *rewriting* the manuscript, an author should make those changes recommended by the reviewers only if they appear valid. Indeed, over the span of time taken for the review, a researcher may have changed his or her own ideas in ways which can improve the paper. Obviously, some reviewers' comments may seem off-base, but they can certainly alert the author to how others may perceive the paper. Should the paper be submitted to another journal, the same reviewer may be selected to review it again. One strategy for revising to accommodate the reviewer's comments is to put counterarguments in the paper for the next submission. For example, an author could include a phrase "it can be argued that . . ." and then proceed to refute that argument.

The fourth step to the axiom above is to *resubmit* the manuscript to another journal. Following from the earlier recommendation of rank-ordering possible journals, the author can submit the article to the next highest one on the list. There is some chance that the paper will get more favorable reviews by a different set of referees. A decision to revise and resubmit can be made based on two considerations: (a) the number of times rejected (i.e., how far down on the list of possible journals is the author willing to go), and (b) the reviewers' and editor's reasons for rejection. In the latter case, if a manuscript is rejected because of concerns regarding the ethics of the research or due to poor methodology, further attempts to publish may lead to an exhausting and impossible search. Worse yet, if poor research is published, it may damage the reputation of the authors involved.

Appealing decisions

Should an author feel that the journal editor or reviewer did not give a fair and objective review of a submitted manuscript, the rejected author can appeal to the editor for additional consideration. Appealing a decision is usually only justified when there has been a marginal decision (split vote or assignment of low priority). The most important reason for objecting is when one can discern a bias in a review arising from professional or personal differences. In our experience, appeals succeed approximately one out of three times. In most cases, the editor will want to ensure fairness in the process. On the other hand, as a defensive reaction, the editor may choose a third reviewer who is tougher in order to generate a negative decision corresponding with the previous editorial decision. At the least, a protest of a biased review should be made to alert the editor that his or her reviewers may not be abiding by scientific ethics. An appeal should be relatively low-keyed with a simple statement of the facts. A particular bias in the theory, methodological procedure, or personal proclivities of the reviewer can be noted. Errors in the reviewer's analysis should be noted. Any new information which can be provided to the editor to answer reviewers' questions should be noted. An appeal should not be made *just* because the journal rejected a manuscript. There should be substantial grounds for the request. P. B. Medawar, in *Advice to a Young Scientist* (1979), advised: "rejection of a paper is always damaging to the pride, but it is usually better to try to find another home for it than to wrangle with referees" (p. 67).

A Final Axiom

New faculty (or aspiring professors) may find two handbooks on entering and surviving the academic profession helpful (Bianco-Mathis and Chalofsky, 1999; Boice, 2000). All clinical psychology researchers will find useful the handbook edited by Drotar (2000). Although written for clinical child and pediatric psychology, its insights are applicable to all clinical psychology. Whatever the reasons for wanting to publish, having a paper accepted for publication is an exciting experience. One's name always looks good in print at the top of a published article. One last axiom: prospective authors never become published authors unless they keep trying and submit manuscripts. An idea or project cannot become published unless it is written up and submitted.

References

American Psychological Association (1997). *Journals in psychology: A resource listing for authors* (5th edn.). Washington, DC: American Psychological Association.

American Psychological Association (2001). *Publication manual of the American Psychological Association* (5th edn.). Washington, DC: American Psychological Association.

Barlow, D. (1999). Mission and publication formats for *Clinical Psychology: Science and Practice*. *Clinical Psychology: Science and Practice, 6*, iii.

Barlow, D. (2000). Announcement. *Clinical Psychology: Science and Practice, 7*, 242.

Bauer, T. N., and Hammer, L. B. (1996). Help received during the journal article writing process: The outcomes of quality and quantity. *Journal of Social Behavior and Personality, 11*, 213–24.

Becker, H. S. (1986). *Writing for social scientists: How to start and finish your thesis, book, or article.* Chicago, IL: University of Chicago Press.

Bedeian, A. G. (1996). Improving the journal review process: The question of ghostwriting. *American Psychologist, 51*, 1189.

Bianco-Mathis, V., and Chalofsky, N. (eds.) (1999). *The full-time faculty handbook.* Thousand Oaks, CA: Sage.

Boice, R. (2000). *Handbook for new faculty members.* Needham Heights, MA: Allyn and Bacon.

Brysbaert, M. (1996). Improving the journal review process and the risk of making the poor poorer. *American Psychologist, 51*, 1193.

Drotar, D. (2000). *Handbook of research in pediatric and clinical child psychology: Practical strategies and methods.* New York: Kluwer/Plenum.

Epstein, S. (1995). What can be done to improve the journal review process. *American Psychologist, 50*, 883–5.

Fine, M. A. (1996). Reflections on enhancing accountability in the peer review process. *American Psychologist, 51*, 1190–1.

Fowler, R. D. (1993). Statement of editorial policy. *American Psychologist, 48*, 5–7.

Fowler, R. D. (1996). 1996 Editorial: 50th anniversary issue. *American Psychologist, 51*, 5–7.

Hansen, J. C. (2000). Editorial. *Journal of Counseling Psychology, 47*, 3–4.

Kazak, A. E. (1998). Editorial: Change and continuity in the *Journal of Pediatric Psychology*. *Journal of Pediatric Psychology, 23*, 1–3.

Kazak, A. E. (2000). *Journal of Pediatric Psychology*: A brief history (1969–1999). *Journal of Pediatric Psychology, 25*, 463–70.

Kazdin, A. E. (1975). The impact of applied behavior analysis of diverse areas of research. *Journal of Applied Behavior Analysis, 8*, 213–29.

Kendall, P. C. (1997). Editorial. *Journal of Consulting and Clinical Psychology, 65*, 3–5.

Kendall, P. C. (2000). I've got mail! *Journal of Consulting and Clinical Psychology, 68*, 747.

Kunkel, M. B. (2001). Editorial: Research informing practice in *Professional Psychology*. *Professional Psychology: Research and Practice, 32*, 3–4.

Lancet (1970) *2*, 1077–8.

Lester, J. D. (1999). *Writing research papers: A complete guide* (9th edn.). New York: Longman.

Levenson, R. L. (1996). Enhance the journals, not the review process. *American Psychologist, 51*, 1191–3.

Mahoney, M. J. (1976). *Scientist as subject: The psychological imperative*. Cambridge, MA: Ballinger.

Medawar, P. B. (1979). *Advice to a young scientist*. New York: Harper and Row.

O'Connor, M. (1979). *The scientist as editor: Guidelines for editors of books and journals*. New York: Wiley.

O'Connor, M. (1992). *Writing successfully in science*. New York: Routledge.

Rabinovich, B. A. (1996). A perspective on the journal review process. *American Psychologist, 51*, 1190.

Roberts, M. C. (1992). Vale dictum: An editor's view of the field of pediatric psychology and its journal. *Journal of Pediatric Psychology, 17*, 785–805.

Smith, D. A. (2000). Editorial: Applied is *not* atheoretical. *Applied and Preventive Psychology, 9*, 1–3.

Stone, A. A. (2001). *Health Psychology*: 2001–2006. *Health Psychology, 20*, 3.

Strauss, M. (1995). Editorial. *Journal of Abnormal Psychology, 104*, 555–7.

Strunk, W., and White, E. B. (1979). *The elements of style* (3rd edn.). New York: Macmillan.

Summary Report of Journal Operations for 2001 (2002). *American Psychologist, 57*, 659.

Webb, W. B. (1979). Continuing education: Refereeing journal articles. *Teaching of Psychology, 6*, 59–60.

CHAPTER FOUR

Ethical Considerations in Clinical Psychology Research

William A. Rae and Jeremy R. Sullivan

Conducting research in clinical psychology requires special attention to ethical issues. Empirical studies focusing on interventions, therapy, assessment, diagnosis, and psychopathology are common to clinical psychology; research in clinical psychology is therefore often concerned with intimate, personal psychological information about a patient's life and has the potential to disrupt the lives of vulnerable research participants. Although always present to some degree in the past, recent initiatives in the field of clinical psychology have strongly promoted intervention research in an attempt to identify empirically supported psychological treatments (Task Force on Promotion and Dissemination of Psychological Procedures, 1995). Unfortunately, with this enthusiasm there also lies potential to erode ethical standards in the desire to pursue a research agenda.

The issues discussed in the present chapter are based on the previous and recently revised editions of the *Ethical Principles of Psychologists and Code of Conduct* (APA, 1992, 2002), as this code is most applicable to clinical psychology research. It is worth noting that the APA ethics code has been recently revised, effective June 1, 2003, and is available in printed form (APA, 2002) and online at www.apa.org/ethics. Other professional groups (e.g., social workers, physicians, licensed professional counselors) also have their own ethics codes. The Belmont Report (OPRR, 1979) describes basic ethical principles in research, including respect for persons, beneficence, and justice, and preeminent federal guidelines outline ethical procedures in research (OPRR, 1991). These documents can give the clinical psychology investigator additional guidance while planning and conducting research.

The purpose of this chapter is to discuss the ethical practices that apply to the four phases of research in clinical psychology. First, research planning will be discussed. This phase includes designing quality research, protecting the welfare and rights of research participants, and conducting a cost-benefit analysis. Second, the issues concerning approval of a research plan and working with institutional review boards are described.

Third, the parameters of informed consent will be highlighted. Fourth, special ethical concerns with regard to analysis and dissemination of results (e.g., publication) will be described. Finally, ethical issues surrounding special topics in clinical psychology research will be discussed, including confidentiality, research with vulnerable populations, increased inclusion of children in clinical research, use of deception, recording, and international perspectives. A consideration of resolving ethical dilemmas also is included.

Planning Research

Many potential ethical and legal problems can be avoided with a sound research plan. From the initial conceptualization of a project, protecting the welfare and rights of human participants should be of highest importance to the researcher. Clinical psychology researchers should always consider the APA ethical code and if an ethical issue is unclear, the psychologist should seek to resolve the issue through consultation with peers, institutional review boards, or other appropriate authorities (APA, 1992). In the same way, psychologists should consult with other professionals with expertise concerning studies with special populations. This is particularly important if conducting research with participants who are children; the researcher should always consult with a child specialist in the area being studied.

Psychological research should yield some benefit to all stakeholders. These stakeholders include not only research participants, but also the community, researchers, funding agencies, and society at large (Sieber, 2000). The researcher also should be cognizant of the degree of risk inherent in the research being planned. The risk can range from a nearly no-risk situation (e.g., filling out an anonymous questionnaire) to a high-risk situation (e.g., engaging in a stressful experimental clinical treatment). The assessment of the degree of risk will affect how the research is planned and what research choices are ultimately made in terms of the experimental manipulation, research participants chosen, research setting, and hypotheses. Although the investigator should always minimize risk, the research participants must always be fully informed as to the nature and extent of any possible risk.

During these initial stages of research planning, the ethical issues involved may seem difficult to conceptualize and resolve (Sieber, 2000). An initial assessment should be made to weigh the risk and benefit of any research intervention to a participant. The assessment of risks and benefits presents an opportunity to think about and gather systematic information regarding the planned research project. Research should have a favorable risk–benefit ratio that is related to the general ethical principle of beneficence (i.e., doing good). Risk is often conceptualized in terms of degree (e.g., high or low risk), which pertains to both the probability of experiencing harm and the magnitude of the potential harm. In contrast, benefit is often conceptualized as a positive value related to health or welfare without any connotation of probabilities (OPRR, 1979). Therefore, risk and benefit are often analyzed using different schema and are not always comparable.

Clinical psychology research often entails minimal or no risk; it almost never involves any physical risk. Because of this comparatively lower risk, it is possible that researchers might minimize the psychological impact of an "unpleasant emotional experience" or "distress." At times, the researcher's need to complete a research project might lead to taking ethical shortcuts as regards participants' welfare. For example, a psychologist might feel work-related pressures (e.g., publish-or-perish, grant deadline) to complete a research project while sometimes not allowing for a meticulous evaluation of possible ethical conflicts. In this situation, carefully attending to ethical issues might jeopardize completing research that would be crucial to the psychologist's career. Thus, it would be less difficult for the researcher who is under professional duress to underestimate the distress or unpleasant emotions that the research participant might experience.

Similarly, the researcher's perceived higher power and status may inadvertently influence the research participant. Although attempts are usually made to eliminate the power differential between researcher and participant during the informed consent process, patients, for example, cannot help but be influenced by the authority of the "doctor" suggesting that they should participate in the research.

In the same way, researchers might be prone to overestimate the potential benefits of their research in order to justify a risky intervention or to "win over" potential participants. For example, in research involving the treatment of debilitating anxiety, a researcher might be tempted to try a distressing procedure (e.g., exposing the patient to intense doses of a feared situation). One could argue that the risk of performing a potentially unsafe procedure is counterbalanced by the benefit of discovering a new treatment for anxiety that could benefit many people. As long as the research participant's rights are protected (which in this example is questionable), the interest to society can be used to justify the risky intervention. A complete cost-benefit analysis also requires that the researcher be concerned about the loss of benefit to society if the research is *not* undertaken. If the risks are reasonable relative to anticipated benefits, it is generally justified to go ahead with the study. Risk in research must be evaluated carefully by external reviewers (e.g., Institutional Review Boards or IRBs) in order to ensure that an overzealous researcher has not biased the risk-benefit analysis.

Designing the highest quality research is important to meeting high ethical standards in planning clinical psychology research. Psychologists must always design and conduct research in accordance with recognized standards of scientific competence. The employment of inappropriate design, procedures, methods, and statistical analyses within a research study is unethical for two major reasons. First, poorly designed and conducted studies are likely to yield invalid results that can lead psychological science and practice in the wrong direction. Second, such studies waste participants' time and journals' space (assuming they get published), which could have been devoted to more methodologically sound research (Koocher and Keith-Spiegel, 1998). Rosenthal (1994) has argued that the general investment that society has made in supporting science and its practitioners is not well served by pursuing bad science.

It is clear that research ethics and methods are interrelated; one cannot be addressed without affecting the other (Adair, Dushenko, and Lindsay, 1985). Indeed, the inescapable interaction between methodology and ethics is an extremely important concept. This situation is complicated by the fact that clinical psychology has numerous research designs from which to choose (as detailed in this volume), such as the case study, single-case experimental design, clinical replication, between-group design, and analogue study

(Sanderson and Barlow, 1991). Each research design must be evaluated in terms of applicability to the experimental question and degree of adherence to ethical guidelines. Meta-analysis is thought to be an especially ethical method of data analysis, as this technique maximizes the utility and scope of the results of individual studies, including all of the time and effort invested in those individual studies (Rosenthal, 1994). When meta-analyses are conducted, the individual study becomes more useful and worthwhile. In contrast, experimental group designs can be much more intrusive into the lives of participants and thus potentially more risky.

Research should begin with a written plan that includes research questions that are grounded in the literature. Included in the research plan should be adequate documentation of the hypotheses being investigated, a rationale for the research, the number and type of research participants required, the research methods, and proposed data analysis (Pettifor, 1996). The research methods should be based on sound methodology with adequate experimental control. For example, if a researcher haphazardly implements an experimental clinical treatment lacking in proper experimental controls (i.e., no manualized procedures implemented by trained assistants), the results might be worthless since the intervention might have changed with each research participant. In this instance, not only would the results be spurious, but also the research participants possibly would have received no benefit and have been exposed to unnecessary risk. Another example of problematic research might be dependent variable "shotgunning." A researcher might require the study participants to complete multiple surveys (i.e., dependent variables) hoping that one might yield statistically significant results without reviewing the previous research literature examining variables that might be sensitive to the effect of the intervention, and thus would make more sense to investigate.

Institutional Approval

With regard to research conducted in the United States, after the research plan is developed, Institutional Review Board (IRB) approval of a project is the next crucial step in the research process. In fact, federal funds can be withheld from any institution not participating in an IRB process. Psychologists must provide accurate information about the proposed research and agree to conduct their research in accordance with the IRB-approved research protocol. In institutions where behavioral science research is less common (e.g., medical centers), the researcher must educate the IRB about the nature of the clinical psychology research and which, if any, special considerations must be taken into account. In the same way, if the IRB does not have expertise about a participant population being studied, the researcher should also provide additional information or help facilitate consultation by experts in that area. The IRB serves to reassure the community at large that the welfare of human participants is seriously considered by people who do not have a vested interest in the outcome of the research. The IRB also ensures the fair application of federal regulations and ethical principles in order to balance the need for scientific inquiry while at the same time protecting the welfare of research participants. When the IRB approves a project, it provides an affirmation of the ethical and scientific quality of the research (OPRR, 1979). Unfortunately, IRBs also have been shown to be inconsistent in their decision-making, mirroring the changing standards of fields that are in constant ebb and flow (Rosnow et al., 1998).

Recently, there has been some debate with regard to the role and function of IRBs. Some researchers (e.g., Rosenthal, 1995) believe that IRBs should expand their duties to include evaluating the scientific merit of proposed research projects (including issues such as the methodological soundness of studies discussed above). Other researchers (e.g., Colombo, 1995) feel that such an evaluative role should not be assumed by IRBs, as board members do not have the expertise required to consider all issues necessary to accurately evaluate the methodological quality and scientific merit of proposed studies across a wide range of scientific disciplines. For example, does an IRB member who has been trained in engineering or geological sciences have the background knowledge to make an informed evaluation of the scientific quality or utility of a research project proposed by researchers from the psychology department? Surely, such decisions would require a substantial amount of background knowledge of the specific field (in this case, psychology) in order to determine where the results of the proposed study would fit in with the established knowledge base and whether the proposed study is worthwhile. The proposed role expansion of IRBs to evaluate the scientific quality or utility of research proposals is in stark contrast to the current functions of IRBs (i.e., to determine whether proposed studies involving human participants are ethically sound and whether the research poses potential risk to participants). Such an expanded role may actually serve to inhibit scientific progress in various disciplines due to lack of expertise and lack of consistency in decision-making among board members (Colombo, 1995). Rosenthal (1995) suggested that when IRB members do not feel qualified to evaluate the scientific quality of a given proposal, the board could consult with experts in the specific area of inquiry. According to Mordock (1995), many IRBs in applied (as opposed to university) settings currently evaluate the scientific quality and costs of proposed research, though Mordock noted that "the IRB in an applied setting reviews a small number of proposals with an extremely narrow range of research and has a membership of individuals with experience in the field being researched. Moreover, the importance of the research for the clients of the agency is more easily judged" (p. 320). The role of university-based IRBs in the evaluation of scientific merit will likely be the subject of future debate.

After IRB approval, researchers are responsible for the ethical conduct of not only themselves, but their research team as well. Researchers and their assistants are permitted to perform only those tasks for which they are appropriately trained and prepared. It is clear that the responsibility of enforcing ethical standards and protecting participants lies not only with the primary investigator(s), but also with the entire research team.

Informed Consent

After a study has been carefully planned and has received IRB approval, participants must be recruited and data must begin to be collected. In most clinical psychology research, documented informed consent of each participant is required. On the consent form and through conversation, the researcher explains the nature of the study in language that participants can understand. Great care must be taken to be sure the participant can read the written material and that the researcher can explain the research in the participant's indigenous language. The researcher must ensure that participants have a reasonable understanding of what the research is about and what their participation will entail. Using understandable language means resisting the temptation to use professional jargon in an attempt to impress would-be participants. If participants consent to become involved, then this consent must be documented by having them sign an approved consent form.

The consent form should clarify the responsibilities of each party (i.e., researcher and participant), and should include the following: (1) an invitation to participate, (2) an explanation of the nature and purpose of the research, (3) an explanation of the basis for participant selection, (4) the study's expected duration and procedures, (5) a statement that participants are free to decline or withdraw at any time, (6) a description of how confidentiality will be maintained, (7) an explanation of consequences of declining or withdrawing, (8) a description of anticipated benefits that the study's results may produce, (9) a description of any inducements or compensation for participation, (10) important factors that may influence participants' decision to participate (e.g., risks, emotional or physical discomfort, limitations regarding confidentiality), and (11) contact information of the principal investigator (APA, 1992; Fischman, 2000; Kitchener, 2000). Further, researchers must be willing to respond to participants' questions and concerns.

Informed consent must be provided voluntarily and without coercion. Prospective participants must be given the option to decline participation or withdraw at any time, even after they have provided consent. In order for consent to be voluntary, prospective participants should understand the benefits and risks of participation, all relevant aspects of the research, and the consequences of declining participation, all of which should have been included on the consent form.

Investigators have a duty to protect prospective participants from adverse consequences of declining or withdrawing participation. In order for consent to be truly voluntary, participants must feel safe to refuse to become involved in a study, or to decline participation once the study has begun. Research in clinical psychology often involves faculty members recruiting their undergraduate students to participate in the professors' research studies. These students may be offered extra credit or some similar academic benefit as compensation for their participation. Of course, the mere participation in a research study is felt to have some educative benefit for the student. In order for consent to be given voluntarily, however, students who are potential recruits must be offered an *equitable alternative* to participation in the research study. For example, a 25-page research paper is not equitable to one hour of research participation; the alternative must be reasonable and of equal educative value to the student. Suggested alternatives include assisting in an ongoing research project, writing brief reviews of high-quality research articles, attending research presentations, observing studies or experiments as they are being conducted, and completing additional readings about research (Kimmel, 1996). If a student declines research participation and opts for the alternative activity, then this student must not be treated differently by the professor or suffer any adverse consequences for declining or withdrawing. Similarly, if research is to be conducted on the effectiveness of a particular form of treatment or intervention, patients must be assured that they will still receive appropriate treatment if they decline participation in a research protocol.

The issue of voluntary consent is sometimes difficult to accomplish in clinical or psychotherapeutic research due to the influence that therapists may have over their patients. Thus, therapists must be sure that their patients understand that consenting to or declining participation will have no bearing on the quality of treatment that they receive. Importantly, the researcher should discontinue any intervention if it is determined that the participant is receiving a negative or deteriorating effect from the intervention (Welfel, 1998).

When offering inducements or compensation for participation, researchers should not offer excessive financial rewards or other inappropriate inducements, as these may lead to coerced participation. Of course, what is considered excessive or inappropriate is relative and depends on the specific participants, as $10 may be coercive to a poor or homeless child but not to a business professional or wealthy family (Canter et al., 1994; Sales and Lavin, 2000). In clinical research, inducement or compensation may take the form of clinical services (e.g., therapy sessions, an assessment report) in return for participation. In these cases, the researcher must be forthcoming about the nature of these services, including risks, obligations, and limitations (e.g., maximum number of therapy sessions). Psychologists must honor all commitments that they have made to research participants, including providing any agreed-upon compensation for participation or sending a report of the research results.

The APA ethics code (APA, 1992) does provide some exceptions to the informed consent process. For example, naturalistic observations, anonymous questionnaires or surveys, and archival research may not require informed consent due to the nature of the research. Canter et al. (1994) described these as situations in which the research participants are either unaware of their own involvement in the study and, as a result, are unaffected by it, or in which they choose to be anonymous in their participation. Still, the APA ethics code encourages researchers to consider institutional regulations, IRB requirements, and the guidance of colleagues before dispensing with informed consent. At the same time, even archival reviews of clinic records may be ethically questionable since many patients in clinics are not fully informed that their unidentified diagnostic or treatment data might be used for future research purposes (Welfel, 1998).

Analyzing and Disseminating Research Results

After implementing the study, the researcher should provide an opportunity for research participants to obtain appropriate information about the nature, results, and conclusions of the study. However, researchers bear a broader social responsibility to *not* report research findings if they are considered to reflect deficiencies or negative characteristics regarding groups of individuals (e.g., as a function of age, gender, or ethnicity), as reporting such findings may lead to discrimination against these groups (Kazdin, 1998).

Once data are collected, they usually are analyzed statistically before being reported to the scientific community. The following sections will consider some of the ethical issues surrounding the statistical analysis and publication of research results.

Ethical issues in statistical analysis

In order for research results to be valid, it is an ethical imperative to use the most appropriate statistical analysis for the question being asked. As discussed above, good science generally leads to good ethics, and vice versa (Welfel, 1998). For example, researchers are expressly forbidden to fabricate or misrepresent data. This includes simply fabricating research results and publishing them, in addition to the subtler form of manipulating data until the results say what the investigator wants them to say. This outcome can be obtained by excluding data or cases that are counter to the researcher's expectations and desired results. Investigators often feel strongly about what they want their results to say and which hypotheses they are aiming to support. Obtaining grant money for further research in a given area is often dependent upon producing significant results (Kitchener, 2000; Koocher and Keith-Spiegel, 1998). For example, if a researcher is attempting to demonstrate the efficacy of a particular intervention for the treatment of post-traumatic stress disorder and the intervention is shown to be effective, then the researcher will likely receive continued financial support to study the area further. Thus, the researcher may be tempted to exclude cases for which the treatment was ineffective in order to obtain a large effect size for the entire sample of participants. However, this practice is dishonest and unethical, and seems especially pernicious when considering the potential impact on future patients.

If researchers decide to remove several participants from the statistical analysis because they happened to be outliers, a practice not uncommon in clinical psychology research, then this procedure should be explained and justified (McGue, 2000). It also would be desirable for the researcher to include, perhaps in a footnote, the results that would have been obtained had the outliers been included in the analysis (Rosenthal, 1994). Psychologists are also responsible for communicating and correcting any errors in their results that are discovered after the results have been published. Such communication and correction may take the form of an erratum, retraction, or other appropriate means.

Ethical issues in scholarly publication

Preparing the results of a completed study for publication in a scholarly journal or for presentation at a conference or convention may be seen as the final stage of a research project. Indeed, publication or presentation is often the ultimate goal of conducting a particular study in clinical psychology, as doing so adds to the knowledge base of the field, serves to further the careers of the investigators, and has the potential to shape the practice and future research of clinical psychology. There are several ethical issues that must be attended to when preparing and reporting results, including publication credit, duplicate publication of data, sharing original data, and plagiarism.

Publication credit

Researchers should only take authorship credit if they have made significant contributions to the project. Further, order of authorship should be determined by the relative intellectual contribution of each author. In clinical psychology graduate training programs it is common for one or more faculty members to head research teams composed of graduate students. In these situations it is often difficult to determine order of authorship given the large size of some teams and the huge amount of work that may go unnoticed by others. Authorship matters should be discussed at the outset of the project, in order to avoid tension and hurt feelings when the time comes to write up the results for publication. The APA guidelines also state that one's title or position (e.g., Department Chair, Director of Training, Clinic Director) do not automatically qualify an individual for authorship without significant contribution to the study. Authorship is often not justified for individuals whose contributions are limited to collecting or coding data, conducting routine statistical analyses under the supervision of others, typing the manuscript, or providing editorial comments or proofreading; minor or routine contributions such as these may be best acknowledged in a footnote within the manuscript (Koocher and Keith-Spiegel, 1998; McGue, 2000). These tasks may not warrant being included as an author since authorship should be reserved for major intellectual, statistical, methodological, conceptual, and written contributions. Graduate student publications bring up unique issues. If a student decides to publish his or her dissertation or thesis, the student usually is listed as principal author, followed by members of the committee (APA, 1992).

All of the potential conflicts that may arise with regard to order of authorship point to the importance of discussing authorship issues prior to beginning the study, or prior to preparing the results for publication. Will all team members contribute to each publication, or will the research produce a database large enough to answer multiple questions, thereby allowing different members to take their own "piece" of the results and prepare and publish their own pieces independently or in smaller groups? These questions are especially important for large research teams and should receive due consideration as early as possible in the life of the research team.

Duplicate publication of data

Duplicate publication of data refers to submitting for publication data that have already been published, and presenting the data as novel or original. Sometimes published data are used more than once, for example in meta-analysis or in a study demonstrating the use of a novel statistical technique with already-published data. This practice is acceptable as long as the author states that the data have already been published elsewhere, and does not attempt to present the data as new. It used to be common practice to publish the same data in different journals in order to reach different audiences who may benefit equally from reading about the study (e.g., school psychologists, counseling psychologists). In the current day of ubiquitous access to centralized, computerized databases, however, this practice no longer seems necessary (Canter et al., 1994). Moreover, given the huge number of useful manuscripts submitted and very limited journal space, republishing old data on its own is unethical because it impedes the publication of new, equally deserving data. A similar practice, called piecemeal publication, also is discouraged, as this involves submitting for publication numerous smaller manuscripts that report few results when a single large manuscript reporting many results would better represent and integrate the results of a research study.

Sharing original data

Psychologists must be willing to share the original data for a given study after the results have been published. For example, if another researcher reads a particular article and is astonished at the findings, and believes them to be in error, he or she may then ask the author to provide the original data so that the statistical analyses can be rechecked. Investigators are not required to share data if another researcher wants to investigate another hypothesis. Psychologists should provide this data *unless* legal rights concerning proprietary data or concerns regarding protection of confidentiality of the participants preclude doing so.

Plagiarism

Plagiarism involves presenting the work of others as one's own, including but not limited to data, ideas, text, measures, and instruments. Plagiarism is expressly forbidden by the APA (1992) ethical code. The protection of intellectual property rights has been described as a basic principle of scientific inquiry (Canter et al., 1994). The psychologist should acknowledge the source of any idea either by quoting the source directly or by annotating from whom the idea was obtained. In short, credit must be given where credit is due, and sources must always be cited for both quoted and paraphrased material.

Implications of issues surrounding publication ethics

The ethical issues involved in preparing and reporting data become very important when considering how research results are used. In a scientist-practitioner field such as clinical psychology, significant research results (ideally) shape clinical practice. Different treatments and interventions utilized every day by clinicians are based on research findings. Clinicians change or modify their treatments based on research that reports on effectiveness for different populations. Thus, publishing research that is anything less than accurate and honest is unfair to both the science and practice of clinical psychology, and may ultimately be harmful to patients.

Special Topics in Research Ethics

Confidentiality and privacy

The APA code clearly states that psychologists have a primary obligation to take precautions with respect to confidentiality (APA, 1992). Unless otherwise stipulated, the research participant should expect and receive privacy for any intervention, measure, procedure, or experimental manipulation involved in the research. In the same way, researchers discuss personal research data only for appropriate professional or scientific purposes and only reveal information germane to the purpose of a professional communication. If any information is discussed, it is only with persons who clearly need to be informed. Researchers inform participants of their anticipated further use or sharing of personally identifiable research data and of unanticipated future uses, if possible.

The limits to confidentiality need to be fully explained to the research participant before research begins. This disclosure can also include situations when the research participant might permit voluntary disclosure of information. Because clinical psychology research often requires the research participant to reveal private or personal information, the clinical psychology investigator has a special obligation. Like the practicing clinician with patients, the researcher is ethically required to break confidentiality in order to protect the research participant from harm to self or others. For example, while conducting a study on depression, the researcher might learn that a research participant is contemplating suicide. The researcher must then assess the potential for danger to self (or others) and then decide whether or not to disclose that information to appropriate authorities. The decision to break confidentiality is often influenced by the researcher's clinical experience and personal values. Even in practice situations, psychologists have a range of responses to breaking confidentiality with patients reporting a danger to self or others (Rae and Worchel, 1991). Legal mandates to break confidentiality for certain behaviors by licensed psychologists (e.g., child abuse) also can guide the researcher's ethical decision-making process.

Researchers must maintain appropriate confidentiality in creating, storing, accessing, transferring, and disposing of research records. This includes records in any medium (e.g., written, electronic). If personal identifiers are included in a research protocol, they are deleted before the information is made available to others not described in the original consent agreement. On the other hand, if personal identifiers cannot be deleted, the researcher takes steps to obtain appropriate consent of participants before the researcher transfers the data to others. Finally, the researcher should make sure that plans for disposal of research data are made in advance in case of incapacity or death of the researcher (APA, 1992).

Research with vulnerable populations

Special care should be taken when performing research with vulnerable populations. In fact, the researcher must demonstrate that studying any vulnerable population is integral to the research questions posed. Included in the judgment of appropriateness are the nature and degree of risk, the condition of the specific population involved, and the anticipated benefits. Vulnerable populations can include persons with disabilities (e.g., mental retardation, hearing impairment, vision impairment), persons with financial or educational disadvantages, institutionalized persons (e.g., prisoners, hospitalized patients), or persons with impaired capacity or limited autonomy (e.g., children) (Kimmel, 1996). These populations should be considered vulnerable for two reasons. First, participants in these populations may be more prone to be coerced into research participation. Because of their easy availability in certain research settings, groups such as the economically disadvantaged, the institutionalized, or the hospitalized are frequently sought as research participants. These groups are often dependent and thus have a compromised capacity for free consent. Especially in the case of institutionalized or economically disadvantaged persons, coercion can be subtle by promising an inappropriate inducement. For example, a prisoner could be offered a favorable parole recommendation. In the same way, an economically disadvantaged person might be offered a monetary inducement that would not appear excessive except for the fact that the participant has no monetary resources whatsoever.

Second, participants from these populations may not have appropriate judgment or mental capacity to make an informed decision about research participation. For example, children, individuals with mental retardation, and individuals with impaired capacity (e.g., persons with schizophrenia) would fit into this category. When using these individuals as participants, it is necessary to obtain consent from a legally authorized person, such as the participant's parent or legal guardian. Thus, the first step is to assess the individual's mental and legal capacity to provide informed consent, and then based on this assessment, consent should be obtained either from the individual or other appropriate source (Fischman, 2000). Most young children lack the cognitive ability and experience to understand the potential risks and benefits of a research project, which makes consent nearly impossible. Thus, it has been argued that children should not be participants in psychosocial research that has any potential for even minimal risk (Rae and Fournier, 1986). Researchers must attempt to explain the research to such potential participants in a language that they can understand, so that they can *assent* to participate after their legal authority has consented (Koocher and Keith-Spiegel, 1990). Obtaining assent from children with disabilities common to school settings (e.g., mental retardation, learning disabilities, emotional disturbance) may be problematic since these children may have difficulty understanding the concepts of risk and benefit.

Increasing the inclusion of children

Relevant to the above discussion on conducting research with vulnerable populations, the National Institutes of Health (NIH) recently issued an encouragement for investigators to include children in clinical research to a greater extent (NIH, 1997; Oesterheld, Fogas, and Rutten, 1998). This encouragement was in response to a paucity of research examining the treatment of certain childhood disorders. The result of this lack of research has been the application of treatment methods found to be effective with adult patients to children with similar disorders, in the absence of research data suggesting that these methods also are efficacious with child populations. More recently, the NIH (1998) presented specific guidelines for the inclusion of children in clinical research, and in so doing formally implemented the policy *requiring* investigators to include children in *all* human subjects research supported by the NIH, unless the investigators can provide adequate scientific or ethical justification for excluding children. (The policy also includes circumstances under which such exclusion would be acceptable.) The guidelines make clear that investigators applying for NIH funding must address issues related to the inclusion (or exclusion) of children in their proposals.

The implication of this requirement is that adult-oriented researchers will likely be encouraged to include children in their research projects in order to maximize the likelihood that their proposals will be approved, yet these researchers may be unfamiliar with the unique issues surrounding research with children. The NIH recognizes that the formal implementation of such a policy will require educative efforts targeted toward members of the scientific community and IRBs, but the exact logistical nature (i.e., who will do what, when and how will they do it) and content of these efforts are not included in the organization's policy statements or guidelines. The NIH (1999) recently issued notice of a website created to provide up-to-date information regarding the Inclusion of Children policy; the address is http://grants.nih.gov/grants/funding/children/children.htm.

Deception in research

The use of deception involves neglecting to inform participants of the true purpose of a study. Deception is used when knowledge of the study's purpose may influence participants' performance or behavior in a manner that would affect or invalidate the study's results. Thus, deception may be conceptualized as a protective methodological measure, used to maximize the validity and accuracy of a study's results. Historically, the practice of deception is most associated with social psychology research, but many clinical psychologists conduct similar research (Adair et al., 1985; Koocher and Keith-Spiegel, 1998).

According to the APA ethics code (APA, 1992), deception should be used only when it is justified by the potential scientific, educational, or applied value of the study's results. Further, researchers are obligated to consider alternative designs or procedures, and deception should be used only when these alternatives are not equally effective in meeting the purposes of the study. Most importantly, participants should never be deceived or misled about aspects of the study that would influence their decision to consent to participate (e.g., potential harm, physical discomfort, adverse emotional experiences).

If it is decided that the study's potential value warrants the use of deception, and alternative methods would be less effective at answering the research questions or testing the hypotheses, then the investigator is obligated to explain the true purpose of the experiment to participants as early as possible. This explanation should also include a rationale as to why deception was necessary. Researchers must be prepared to answer questions and address participants' feelings of embarrassment, confusion, or even anger as a result of being "duped" (Koocher and Keith-Spiegel, 1998). This process has been termed "debriefing," and it is generally accepted that deception without debriefing is less than ethical. Ideally, participants should be debriefed when their individual or collective participation is concluded. If this is not feasible, then participants must be debriefed at the conclusion of the research study. As with the process of obtaining informed consent, researchers must debrief in a language that participants can understand; this is especially true with children and other special populations (Canter et al., 1994).

The APA code reserves the use of deception only as a last resort, and deception has been harshly criticized in the literature (e.g., Baumrind, 1985). Yet it also has been argued that neglecting to conduct a study that may serve to significantly reduce pain and suffering or improve well-being simply because the design employs deception is also ethically questionable (Rosenthal and Rosnow, 1984; Rosnow, 1990). In this case, *failing* to conduct a particular study using deception may have ethical implications. For example, research conducted to determine the relative effectiveness of psychiatric medication often employs a treatment group, placebo group, and perhaps a wait-list control group that receives neither the medication nor the placebo, but receives treatment at the conclusion of the study. It could be reasonably argued that these studies are employing deception, as participants within the placebo group are under the impression that they may be receiving the actual medication under study (Imber et al., 1986). However, without the inclusion of placebo or control groups it would be difficult to determine the relative effectiveness (or lack thereof) and side effects of the medication under study. In this case, the debriefing process would include optional access to the medication for the placebo and control groups following data collection if it was determined anytime during the course of the research trial that the medication was effective. Imber et al. (1986) described these issues within the context of clinical trials psychotherapy research, and suggested the use of an alternative or already-established efficacious treatment (i.e., a "standard reference treatment") in place of the placebo or no treatment condition, so that participants not receiving the experimental psychotherapeutic treatment are not harmed or left untreated for the duration of the study.

Recording in research

Clinical psychology research designs may involve recording clinical therapy sessions using audiotape or videotape, and then examining these sessions at a later time for coding and analysis. Such a design may be employed when researchers attempt to study patients' reactions to the specific behaviors or verbalizations of the therapist, or wish to analyze the integrity with which a manualized treatment was implemented by the psychologist. In these instances, and any others in which participants may be personally identified, participants must consent specifically to having sessions recorded. Consent is not required for recording naturalistic observations in public places if the recording will not be used in a way that would identify participants or cause them harm.

International perspectives on research ethics

While the discussion within the present chapter is based on the ethical code of the American Psychological Association (APA, 1992), psychological organizations in other countries have developed their own ethical standards as applied to conducting research with human participants. For example, the *Canadian Code of Ethics for Psychologists* (Canadian Psychological Association, 2000) is based on four general principles: Respect for the Dignity of Persons, Responsible Caring, Integrity in Relationships, and Responsibility to Society. The code contains no specific section on research ethics; rather, research ethics (and ethics related to practice, education, training, etc.) are discussed throughout the code in terms of these overriding principles. The Canadian guidelines also provide a model for ethical decision-making, inclusion of a role for personal conscience, and inclusion of both minimum and idealized standards (Sinclair, 1998). The British Psychological Society (2000) relies on its *Code of Conduct, Ethical Principles and Guidelines* in the regulation of research. The British guidelines for ethical research are discussed separately within the code, and particular attention is paid to issues such as deception, debriefing, and protection from risk. Finally, the Australian *Code of Ethics* (Australian Psychological Society, 1999) has separate sections for research and for reporting and publishing research results. The Australian guidelines are very similar to those contained in the APA (1992) code. In sum, each of these organizations' guidelines pertaining to research ethics are organized and presented differently within their respective codes, but the content of the regulations is more similar than different across organizations.

Resolving Ethical Dilemmas

Researchers in the area of clinical psychology would probably be wise to recognize that at some point in their careers, ethical dilemmas or uncertainties will emerge. Answers to these situations will not always come easily, and will depend upon the unique circumstances of each research program or study. While the APA code (APA, 1992) provides some clear-cut guidance for many ethical issues, not all situations can be reduced to black and white concepts. Indeed, in contrast to abstract discussions of ethics, decisions are much more complex in the real world of psychological research. When answers are elusive, perhaps the most valuable resource is one's colleagues. Senior faculty members, experienced practitioners or researchers, and other trusted colleagues may be consulted for assistance. Sometimes these sources may provide discrepant advice. When this occurs, and the researcher is still struggling, members of his or her institution's IRB can be consulted. Because the IRB ultimately decides whether any empirical research study can be pursued, its members will be able to tell the researcher with certainty whether the research design meets ethical standards. If the IRB finds certain aspects of the proposed study unacceptable, the committee will provide recommendations that, if followed, may result in approval.

Sales and Lavin (2000) described a heuristic model for investigators to consider when faced with ethical dilemmas in research. This model involves examining existing professional ethics codes and using professional ethical standards, following more general ethical and moral principles, knowing legal responsibilities and standards, applying professional ethics codes and standards, and consulting with colleagues and experts. Similarly, Canter et al. (1994) stated the importance of knowing the APA ethics code, being aware of state laws and federal regulations, knowing the regulations of the researcher's institution, and consulting with colleagues. Bass et al. (1996) provide a useful checklist with which researchers can evaluate the ethicality of their research designs and procedures. Following detailed checklists such as this may be one way to keep researchers on the right track.

The critical rule to remember with regard to ethical decision-making and resolving ethical dilemmas is that one should always be able to reasonably defend one's ethical decisions, and should be able to show that all relevant factors were considered during the decision-making process. Finally, researchers should keep up to date on changes or revisions to ethical standards and guidelines by reading professional journals, going to workshops, and attending professional conferences.

Conclusions

Teachers of ethics may want to consider employing innovative techniques presented in the literature (e.g., Beins, 1993; Fisher and Kuther, 1997; Rosnow, 1990; Strohmetz and Skleder, 1992) in order to introduce students to the complexities of ethical decision-making in clinical psychology research. Further, readers are encouraged to consult seminal volumes and articles related to research ethics for comprehensive information and guidance (e.g., Bersoff, 1999; Canter et al., 1994; Kimmel, 1996; Kitchener, 2000; Nagy, 2000; Rosenthal, 1994; Sales and Folkman, 2000). Cooper and Gottlieb (2000) provided a thoughtful and detailed account of the ethical issues increasingly faced by both clinicians and researchers with the advent of managed care. Interestingly, the NIH (2000) recently implemented a policy requiring investigators applying for NIH funding to document that they have received education and training in the protection of human research participants. The NIH (2000) provides links to training modules that investigators or institutions may use in order to meet these education requirements. Requirements such as this point to the importance of not only receiving formal education and training in ethical issues, but also suggest the value of staying aware of current trends with regard to ethical issues and dilemmas.

Future areas of inquiry in clinical psychology research ethics include evaluating different methods of debriefing, exploring ways of enhancing participants' understanding of consent or assent information (especially as applied to special populations such as children), evaluating the effects of research involvement on participants, examining the ethical practices of investigators and review boards, and determining optimal methods of education and training in research ethics (Oesterheld, Fogas, and Rutten, 1998; Stanley, Sieber, and Melton, 1987). It has been found that the procedures used to conform to ethical guidelines are rarely reported in published research articles (Adair, Dushenko, and Lindsay, 1985; Sifers et al., 2002). This practice is unfortunate, as reporting ethical procedures would facilitate the development of systematic knowledge on which other researchers could base their own ethical decisions, and may allow other researchers to enhance their knowledge of the effects of deception, effective methods of debriefing, common practices with regard to informed consent, and trends in other ethical aspects of research (Adair, 1988; Adair, Dushenko, and Lindsay, 1985). In preparing empirical research for publication, therefore, researchers are encouraged to describe the means by which they maximized the ethicality of their studies, including the ethical procedures and processes used.

When researchers invite participants to become involved in research studies, and when participants provide informed consent, researchers have a responsibility to be as honest as possible with their participants, and are obligated to treat them ethically. The present chapter has discussed some of the ethical issues involved in clinical psychology research, as related to the APA's (1992) ethical code. It is critical that researchers maintain continued awareness and consideration of these issues in order to protect the well-being of their participants, and to preserve the reputation of the science of clinical psychology.

References

Adair, J. G. (1988). Research on research ethics. *American Psychologist, 43*, 825–6.

Adair, J. G., Dushenko, T. W., and Lindsay, R. C. L. (1985). Ethical regulations and their impact on research practice. *American Psychologist, 40*, 59–72.

American Psychological Association (1992). Ethical principles of psychologists and code of conduct. *American Psychologist, 47*, 1597–1611.

American Psychological Association (2001, February). Ethical principles of psychologists and code of conduct: Draft for comment. *APA Monitor, 32* (2), 77–89.

American Psychological Association (2002). Ethical principles of psychologists and code of conduct. *American Psychologist, 57*, 1060–73.

Australian Psychological Society (1999). *Code of ethics* (revd. edn.). Victoria, Australia: Australian Psychological Society.

Bass, L. J., DeMers, S. T., Ogloff, J. R. P., Peterson, C., Pettifor, J. L., Reaves, R. P., Rétfalvi, T., Simon, N. P., Sinclair, C., and Tipton, R. M. (eds.) (1996). *Professional conduct and discipline in psychology*. Washington, DC: American Psychological Association.

Baumrind, D. (1985). Research using intentional deception: Ethical issues revisited. *American Psychologist, 40*, 165–74.

Beins, B. C. (1993). Using the Barnum effect to teach about ethics and deception in research. *Teaching of Psychology, 20*, 33–5.

Bersoff, D. N. (ed.) (1999). *Ethical conflicts in psychology* (2nd edn.). Washington, DC: American Psychological Association.

British Psychological Society (2000). *Code of conduct, ethical principles and guidelines*. Leicester, England: British Psychological Society.

Canadian Psychological Association (2000). *Canadian code of ethics for psychologists* (3rd edn.). Ottawa, Ontario: Canadian Psychological Association.

Canter, M. B., Bennett, B. E., Jones, S. E., and Nagy, T. F. (1994). *Ethics for psychologists: A commentary on the APA ethics code*. Washington, DC: American Psychological Association.

Colombo, J. (1995). Cost, utility, and judgments of institutional review boards. *Psychological Science, 6*, 318–19.

Cooper, C. C., and Gottlieb, M. C. (2000). Ethical issues with managed care: Challenges facing counseling psychology. *The Counseling Psychologist, 28*, 179–236.

Fischman, M. W. (2000). Informed consent. In B. D. Sales and S. Folkman (eds.), *Ethics in research with human participants* (pp. 35–48). Washington, DC: American Psychological Association.

Fisher, C. B., and Kuther, T. L. (1997). Integrating research ethics into the introductory psychology course curriculum. *Teaching of Psychology, 24*, 172–5.

Imber, S. D., Glanz, L. M., Elkin, I., Sotsky, S. M., Boyer, J. L., and Leber, W. R. (1986). Ethical issues in psychotherapy research: Problems in a collaborative clinical trials study. *American Psychologist, 41*, 137–46.

Kazdin, A. E. (ed.) (1998). *Methodological issues and strategies in clinical research* (2nd edn.). Washington, DC: American Psychological Association.

Kimmel, A. J. (1996). *Ethical issues in behavioral research: A survey.* Cambridge, MA: Blackwell.

Kitchener, K. S. (2000). *Foundations of ethical practice, research, and teaching in psychology.* Mahwah, NJ: Erlbaum.

Koocher, G. P., and Keith-Spiegel, P. C. (1990). *Children, ethics, and the law: Professional issues and cases.* Lincoln: University of Nebraska Press.

Koocher, G. P., and Keith-Spiegel, P. C. (1998). *Ethics in psychology: Professional standards and cases* (2nd edn.). New York: Oxford University Press.

McGue, M. (2000). Authorship and intellectual property. In B. D. Sales and S. Folkman (eds.), *Ethics in research with human participants* (pp. 75–95). Washington, DC: American Psychological Association.

Mordock, J. B. (1995). Institutional review boards in applied settings: Their role in judgments of quality and consumer protection. *Psychological Science, 6,* 320–1.

Nagy, T. F. (2000). *Ethics in plain English: An illustrative casebook for psychologists.* Washington, DC: American Psychological Association.

National Institutes of Health. (1997, January 31). Policy on the inclusion of children as subjects in clinical research. *NIH Guide for Grants and Contracts, 26* (3), 2.

National Institutes of Health. (1998, March 6). NIH policy and guidelines on the inclusion of children as participants in research involving human subjects. *NIH Guide for Grants and Contracts.* Retrieved July 17, 2001, from http://grants.nih.gov/grants/guide/notice-files/not98-024.html

National Institutes of Health. (1999, May 14). New website for the NIH policy and guidelines on the inclusion of children as participants in research involving human subjects. *NIH Guide for Grants and Contracts.* Retrieved July 17, 2001, from http://grants.nih.gov/grants/guide/notice-files/not99-082.html

National Institutes of Health. (2000, June 9). Required education in the protection of human research participants. *NIH Guide for Grants and Contracts.* Retrieved July 17, 2001, from http://grants.nih.gov/grants/guide/notice-files/not-od-00-039.html

Oesterheld, J. R., Fogas, B., and Rutten, S. (1998). Ethical standards for research on children. *Journal of the American Academy of Child and Adolescent Psychiatry, 37,* 684–5.

Office for Protection From Research Risks, Protection of Human Subjects. National Commission for the Protection of Human Subjects of Biomedical and Behavioral Research (1979). *The Belmont Report: Ethical principles and guidelines for the protection of human subjects of research* (GPO 887-809). Washington, DC: US Government Printing Office.

Office for Protection From Research Risks, Protection of Human Subjects. (1991, June 18). Protection of human subjects: Title 45, Code of Federal Regulations, Part 46 (GPO 1992 O-307-551). *OPRR Reports,* pp. 4–17.

Pettifor, J. L. (1996). Maintaining professional conduct in daily practice. In L. J. Bass, S. T. DeMers, J. R. P. Ogloff, C. Peterson, J. L. Pettifor, R. P. Reaves, T. Rétfalvi, N. P. Simon, C. Sinclair, and R. M. Tipton (eds.), *Professional conduct and discipline in psychology* (pp. 91–116). Washington, DC: American Psychological Association.

Rae, W. A., and Fournier, C. J. (1986). Ethical issues in pediatric research: Preserving psychosocial care in scientific inquiry. *Children's Health Care, 14,* 242–8.

Rae, W. A., and Worchel, F. F. (1991). Ethical beliefs and behaviors of pediatric psychologists: A survey. *Journal of Pediatric Psychology, 16,* 727–45.

Rosenthal, R. (1994). Science and ethics in conducting, analyzing, and reporting psychological research. *Psychological Science, 5,* 127–34.

Rosenthal, R. (1995). Ethical issues in psychological science: Risk, consent, and scientific quality. *Psychological Science, 6,* 322–3.

Rosenthal, R., and Rosnow, R. L. (1984). Applying Hamlet's question to the ethical conduct of research: A conceptual addendum. *American Psychologist, 39*, 561–3.

Rosnow, R. L. (1990). Teaching research ethics through role-play and discussion. *Teaching of Psychology, 17*, 179–81.

Rosnow, R. L., Rotheram-Borus, M. J., Ceci, S. J., Blanck, P. D., and Koocher, G. P. (1998). The Institutional Review Board as a mirror of scientific and ethical standards. In A. E. Kazdin (ed.), *Methodological issues and strategies in clinical research* (2nd edn., pp. 673–85). Washington, DC: American Psychological Association.

Sales, B. D., and Folkman, S. (eds.) (2000). *Ethics in research with human participants.* Washington, DC: American Psychological Association.

Sales, B. D., and Lavin, M. (2000). Identifying conflicts of interest and resolving ethical dilemmas. In B. D. Sales and S. Folkman (eds.), *Ethics in research with human participants* (pp. 109–28). Washington, DC: American Psychological Association.

Sanderson, W. C., and Barlow, D. H. (1991). Research strategies in clinical psychology. In C. E. Walker (ed.), *Clinical psychology: Historical and research foundations* (pp. 37–49). New York: Plenum.

Sieber, J. E. (2000). Research planning: Basic ethical decision-making. In B. D. Sales and S. Folkman (eds.), *Ethics in research with human participants* (pp. 13–26). Washington, DC: American Psychological Association.

Sifers, S. K., Puddy, R. W., Warren, J. S., and Roberts, M. C. (2002). Reporting of demographics, methodology, and ethical procedures in journals in pediatric and child psychology. *Journal of Pediatric Psychology, 27*, 19–25.

Sinclair, C. (1998). Nine unique features of the Canadian Code of Ethics for Psychologists. *Canadian Psychology, 39*, 167–76.

Stanley, B., Sieber, J. E., and Melton, G. B. (1987). Empirical studies of ethical issues in research: A research agenda. *American Psychologist, 42*, 735–41.

Strohmetz, D. B., and Skleder, A. A. (1992). The use of role-play in teaching research ethics: A validation study. *Teaching of Psychology, 19*, 106–8.

Task Force on Promotion and Dissemination of Psychological Procedures (1995, winter). Training in and dissemination of empirically validated psychological treatments: Report and recommendations. *The Clinical Psychologist, 48*, 3–23.

Welfel, E. R. (1998). *Ethics in counseling and psychotherapy: Standards, research, and emerging issues.* Pacific Groves, CA: Brooks/Cole.

PART II

Research Designs

CHAPTER FIVE

Evaluating Treatment Efficacy With Single-Case Designs

Cynthia M. Anderson and Christine Kim

The vast majority of research evaluating the efficacy of therapeutic interventions in clinical psychology relies on group designs and statistical evaluation. Though such research may be useful for confirming hypotheses about the effectiveness of an intervention for a given population (e.g., the utility of exposure and response prevention for individuals diagnosed with obsessive-compulsive disorder), such designs are less useful for clinicians who wish to evaluate the effect of an intervention with a specific client. Thus, clinicians often rely on such indirect measures as client report of functioning, whether the client continues to attend therapy sessions, or inferences about whether the client appears to be following the intervention directives. Unfortunately, such measures do not provide objective information about the effects of an intervention; just because a client continues to come to therapy does not necessarily mean the intervention is resulting in behavior change – perhaps the client simply enjoys having someone to talk to. Also, if the intervention is not working, or is only marginally effective, the clinician does not have access to information which would assist him or her in determining which treatment variables could be altered to increase intervention efficacy.

An alternative to subjective measures of intervention success is the use of single-case methodology. Although single-case designs have most often been used in research studies in the field of applied behavior analysis, they also are very useful for evaluating the effect of an intervention with a specific client in applied settings regardless of theoretical orientation. This chapter reviews single-case design, focusing on the utility of this methodology for clinicians working in applied settings. Much has been written about unique characteristics of single-subject design that differentiate it from group designs and this issue will not be reviewed here. The interested reader is referred instead to Barlow, Hayes, and Nelson (1984) or Johnston and Pennypacker (1993). The chapter begins with a discussion of the critical components of single-case design – therapist behaviors necessary for successful implementation and analysis. Next, we review the purpose and rationale of single-case design. Finally, we provide an overview of single-case designs useful in clinical settings. The rationale of each design is presented, and examples are given. Also, the advantages and disadvantages of each design are discussed.

Critical Therapist Behaviors

Implementing a single-case design involves careful preparation. The clinician must conduct an assessment, collect data, develop a visual display of the data, and finally select a design. Each of these steps is discussed in the context of the following hypothetical case.

> Jack is a 24-year-old man presenting with significant social anxiety. He reports that he has been anxious in social situations for as long as he can remember. He states that he feels very uncomfortable in large groups, when he is around unfamiliar people, or in a one-to-one setting with a woman, and he is convinced that those around him view him as "stupid." Further evaluation reveals that Jack meets criteria for a diagnosis of social phobia.

The initial stage of therapy typically involves assessment. At the least, the clinician must determine what specific problem or problems the client presents with, the events that seem to trigger and maintain problems, and the severity of the client's difficulties. This information is critical when preparing to use single-case design to evaluate an intervention. A clinician must carefully define the problem (i.e., develop an operational definition) so that the client and the therapist recognize when the problem is and is not occurring. Importantly, an operational definition should be objective, consisting of the specific things that a person says or does. If necessary, target behaviors might be covert (e.g., thoughts, heart rate, upset stomach), but it is imperative that the client be able to recognize specific instances of them. Thus, clinicians should avoid using constructs such as "anxiety" and instead assist the client in identifying specific behaviors that are problematic. This is important because, as will be discussed next, the client (and possibly the clinician) must be able to record occurrences of the targeted behaviors.

In the case example, Jack and the therapist worked together to develop a definition of anxiety. Anxiety for Jack consisted of averting his eyes in the presence of others, "pounding" heart, mumbling or speaking in a whisper, negative self-statements in the presence of others, and walking away from individuals or avoiding situations involving social interactions.

After development of an operational definition it is important to collect information about the target behavior. As discussed by Kazdin (1982), initial data collection – collection of baseline data – provides the clinician with critical information. First, baseline data provide descriptive information about the target behavior, including its frequency, intensity, and the situations under which it occurs. Second, baseline data serve a predictive function – they are used to estimate the client's behavior in the future if no intervention were implemented. Third, baseline data are used to evaluate the effect of intervention. This is done by comparing some dimension of the behavior (e.g., frequency, intensity) in baseline to changes observed when intervention is implemented. Because intervention efficacy is evaluated by comparing data obtained in baseline to intervention data, it is crucial that the clinician obtains repeated measures of the behavior in baseline and once intervention has begun.

In the example, Jack's therapist collected baseline data in two ways. First, the therapist had Jack record incidences of target behaviors and the situations under which they occurred. Second, the therapist observed Jack in two analogue situations: in the first situation Jack interacted with a female clinic staff member, and in the second situation Jack gave a brief presentation to several other staff members. The therapist recorded instances of overt anxious behaviors, including averting eye contact, changes in speech tone or rate, and whether or not Jack ended the situation early (by stating that he wanted to stop). Strategies for developing operational definitions and methods of data collection are comprehensively reviewed by Hawkins, Matthews, and Hamdan (1999).

After data collection has begun, the therapist must graph the data to evaluate trends and determine when to begin intervention (for detailed instructions on graphing and visual inspection, see Cooper, Heron, and Heward, 1989: 142–62; or Hawkins, Matthews, and Hamdan, 1999). Figure 5.1 depicts three possible trends that might be observed after collection of five baseline data points.

The closed squares represent a stable baseline – the frequency of behavior is relatively consistent across all measured points. Such stability is ideal as it allows for accurate evaluation of intervention effects. If the intervention results in either increases or decreases in behavior, such change will be readily apparent when compared to a stable baseline. In contrast, the data represented by closed circles illustrate an increasing trend.

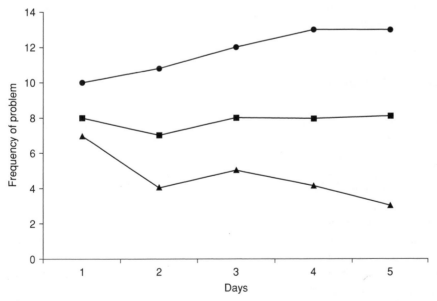

Figure 5.1 Hypothetical data exhibiting stable rates (closed squares), increasing trend (closed circles), and decreasing trend (closed triangles).

If the goal of intervention were to increase a behavior (e.g., to increase the duration of Jack's conversations), the therapist would be ill advised to begin intervention at this point. If the behavior continues to increase once intervention is begun, it would be difficult to argue that improvement would not simply have happened on its own – after all, the behavior was improving in baseline. The reverse situation is depicted by the closed triangles – in this case the frequency of behavior is decreasing. This is problematic if the goal of intervention is to decrease a behavior in terms of clearly demonstrating change (e.g., to decrease Jack's avoidance of social situations). When collecting baseline data the clinician should continue to collect data until stability is achieved. It is only with stable data that the clinician will be able to evaluate an intervention. If responding continues to be highly erratic over an extended period of time, the clinician should discuss the data with the client, and attempt to pinpoint the sources of variability. For example, the first author once had a female client presenting with periodic panic attacks. Initial data collection suggested that panic attacks were not cued or related to any other events and thus occurred sporadically. After further discussion, the woman stated that her husband worked in a coal mine several hours from their home, and was gone for 2–3 days at a time. The woman began to record the number of panic attacks occurring when her husband was home on a different sheet of paper, and it was revealed that attacks were far more likely to occur on the first day after her husband left.

Once a stable baseline is achieved, the clinician is ready to implement an intervention. At this time the therapist chooses a specific type of single-case design to use to evaluate the impact of the intervention. Single-case designs vary somewhat in how they are implemented, and certain designs are more applicable to certain situations; however, all single-case designs share the same goal – evaluating treatment efficacy – and accomplish this goal through similar means. The purpose and rationale of single-case designs are discussed next, and this discussion is followed by a thorough review of strategies of single-case design.

Purpose of Single-Case Design

The goal of single-case design in clinical practice is to assist the clinician in evaluating the effect of an intervention on a client's behavior. That is, it allows the clinician to determine whether an intervention is effective, and if so, to what extent. Through the use of single-case design a clinician can demonstrate that behavior change is the result of the therapeutic intervention and not some other extraneous variable. For example, suppose that a clinician is working with a couple experiencing marital discord. The therapist teaches the couple specific communication strategies, and the couple begins to use them. Now suppose that at approximately the same time as the couple begins using these skills their son – a notorious troublemaker and the topic of many of the couple's disputes – leaves for college. If the couple's relationship improves it would be difficult to assert that the change was due to the intervention (as opposed to their son no longer being in the home) without the use of a single-case design that would systematically control for the potential effects of the child leaving.

In addition to assisting clinicians in determining the cause of a client's improvement (or worsening), single-case designs also are useful in helping clinicians modify an intervention as treatment progresses, so as to improve treatment outcome. This is possible because evaluation of an intervention is not conducted at the end of treatment (as is the case in large group designs) but instead takes place throughout the assessment and treatment process. This allows clinicians to determine the extent to which an intervention is resulting in desired behavior change, and if the intervention is not proceeding as planned the therapist can make specific changes to improve outcome.

A variety of single-case designs exist, and though they appear quite distinct in the manner they are conducted, all demonstrate the effect of an intervention through prediction, verification, and replication (Cooper, Heron, and Heward, 1989; Sidman, 1960). *Prediction* involves analyzing baseline data and developing a hypothesis about the rate, intensity, or frequency with which a response will occur in the future. As previously discussed, stable baseline data allow a clinician to predict the occurrence of the target behavior in the future if no intervention (or other changes relevant to the behavior) occurred. As noted by Cooper, Heron, and Heward (1989), "Using the prediction of behavior measures in the absence of the [intervention] represents the behavior analyst's effort to approximate the ideal but impossible simultaneous measurement of the dependent variable [client's behavior] in both the presence and the absence of the independent variable [intervention]" (pp. 156–7). In other words, the effect of the intervention is determined, in part, by comparing the behavior once intervention has begun to rates of the behavior in baseline – which is used to predict what responding would have continued to look like had intervention not been implemented. Prediction has to do with inferring the future level of behavior based on baseline observations; however, *verification* is necessary to demonstrate that changes in behavior subsequent to intervention are due to the intervention – that the prediction was correct; had intervention not occurred, the level of responding observed in baseline would have continued.

Finally, *replication* involves repeating observed changes; that is, withdrawing the intervention, and reimplementing it, to determine whether behavior change occurs again. As Cooper, Heron, and Heward (1989) stated, demonstrating that the intervention reliably changes behavior reduces the likelihood that the observed change was due to some factor other than intervention (e.g., medication, fluctuation in stressors). Each of these factors – prediction, verification, and replication – will be discussed further within the context of specific single-case designs.

Types of Single-Case Designs

There exist a variety of single-case designs and the choice of a specific design depends on a number of factors, including characteristics of the behavior (e.g., severity) and the location in which the behavior occurs. Although the various designs appear quite distinct, they each assist the clinician in evaluating the impact of intervention on the client's presenting problems. Commonly used single-case designs that may be useful in clinical settings include AB, reversal, alternating treatments, multiple baseline, and changing criterion designs.

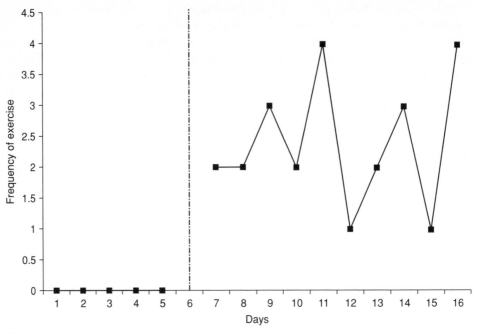

Figure 5.2   Frequency of exercising emitted by a man attempting to lose weight.

AB design

The AB design is perhaps the most commonly used design in clinical practice. In this design, baseline (phase A) is followed by intervention (phase B). The effects of an intervention are tentatively evaluated by comparing performance in baseline to performance in treatment. This evaluation is possible because obtaining a stable baseline (phase A) allows the clinician to *predict* the extent to which the behavior would continue to occur if intervention were not implemented. It is important to note that, because the baseline and intervention phase occur only once, the effect of intervention can be neither verified nor replicated. To illustrate, consider the graph in figure 5.2. These data depict the frequency of physical exercise (e.g., walking for 20 or more minutes, weight lifting) engaged in by a man attempting to lose weight. During baseline (no intervention), the man did not report any instances of physical exercise. After intervention (monitoring weight, differential reinforcement for exercise) began, the frequency of exercising increased. In this example, the improvements observed in the man's behavior following intervention could have been due to intervention. Alternatively, the improvement might be due to some other uncontrolled variable. Perhaps the man's physician told him to begin exercising to avoid a heart attack, or perhaps his partner threatened to leave him if he did not lose weight. Due to this limitation, AB designs should be used only when it is not possible to use a more rigorous design. Also, when using an AB design, clinicians must be careful not to draw unwarranted conclusions about the efficacy of their interventions.

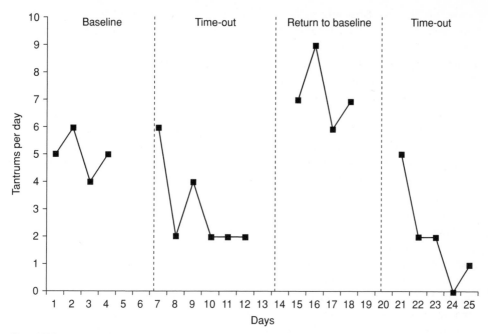

Figure 5.3 Frequency of tantrums emitted by a 4-year-old boy.

ABAB or reversal design

The ABAB design extends the AB design by including a return to a no-intervention phase following the first implementation of intervention. Thus, following baseline (phase A), intervention (phase B) is implemented. When rates of behavior are stable, the intervention is withdrawn (reversal; phase A), and then reimplemented (phase B). The effects of the intervention are demonstrated if, when the intervention is withdrawn, rates of behavior approximate those observed during the initial baseline. Thus, the ABAB design permits *prediction* by collecting baseline data prior to intervention. *Verification* is demonstrated if, when the intervention is temporarily removed, levels of responding are similar to those observed during the initial baseline. Finally, *replication* is demonstrated if, when intervention is reinstituted, the levels of responding approximate those obtained during the initial implementation of intervention.

To illustrate, examine the data depicted in figure 5.3. These data were collected by the parent of a 4-year-old boy who was exhibiting frequent, intense tantrums. Prior to intervention (baseline), this child was exhibiting frequent tantrums, averaging 5 per day. When the rates of tantrums in baseline were relatively stable, his mother was taught to implement a 2-minute chair time-out contingent on tantrums. Data from this phase are depicted in phase B (labeled time-out). When the rates of behavior in phase B are compared to baseline, the intervention appears to be successful. That is, the tantrums occur more often in baseline and the stable nature of the baseline data allow the clinician to *predict* that tantrums would have continued to occur at that frequency had intervention not occurred. The temporary withdrawal of the intervention allows for verification of that effect. This involved having the child's mother temporarily stop using time-out (data shown in the "return to baseline" phase), with the result being an increase in tantrums. To replicate the finding, time-out was reimplemented, with the result being a decrease in the frequency of tantrums.

The ABAB design clearly demonstrates causal relations through prediction, verification, and replication. Behavior change is repeatedly observed when intervention is withdrawn and reintroduced. Because this design relies on observed changes between baseline and intervention, stability of the data is critical. If rates of behavior are extremely variable during baseline, it may be very difficult to determine if observed patterns in intervention are due to the intervention or simply are a continuation of fluctuating patterns observed in baseline.

Reversal designs require temporary withdrawal of an intervention to evaluate the effects of the intervention. This methodology may be problematic in clinical settings for several reasons. First, if the intervention involves teaching a skill (e.g., teaching Jack conversation skills), it may be difficult to return to baseline because skills cannot be "untaught." Second, if the intervention focuses on a severe or dangerous behavior (e.g., suicidal behaviors, aggression) it may be unethical to remove intervention – even temporarily. A third difficulty is that, once the intervention is removed, the client's behavior may not worsen. Indeed, in a clinical situation – this often is the ultimate goal – after all, clinical psychologists do not want their clients to continue in therapy forever. Unfortunately, if the rates of behavior do not return to those observed in baseline, a causal relation between intervention and behavior change cannot be determined. Thus, such designs are seldom practical in applied settings.

Alternating treatments design

When considering intervention options for a client, clinicians often must choose between two or more potential treatments. The question to be answered is, which intervention will be most effective for this client? One way to answer this question would be to use a reversal design, implementing baseline then the first intervention, returning to baseline, then implementing the second intervention, returning to baseline, and then perhaps repeating the entire sequence. Unfortunately, such a design would require an extensive amount of time to conduct. Additionally, order effects may be observed; perhaps the effects of the second intervention were observed because that intervention followed the first intervention – if it had been implemented first, its effects might have differed.

Alternating treatments designs provide an efficient means of comparing two interventions. An alternating treatments design involves rapidly alternating conditions – either a baseline and intervention or sometimes two different interventions – and comparing behavior change associated with each condition. Alternating treatments designs depend on the client's ability to discriminate between conditions (i.e., stimulus control). Thus, a distinct stimulus must be associated with each condition. For example, the first author used an alternating treatments design to evaluate the impact of token economy on the off-task behavior of a second grader. On days that the intervention was in place, the teacher put a blue circle on the chalkboard. On days that the intervention was not used, the teacher put an orange circle on the chalkboard. If clear stimuli are not associated with the conditions being compared it is possible that the client will have difficulty making initial discriminations between conditions and thus it may take a significant amount of time for differentiation to occur. Continuing with the school example, if circles were not used to help the children discriminate which condition was in effect, the only way they would have known would be through the contingencies on their behavior. Thus, they would have had to emit target responses and experience the consequences, before their behavior was changed.

When using an alternating treatments design, conditions can be alternated daily, every couple of days, or within a single day. For example, in the classroom mentioned above, intervention might have been used in one half of the day, and the intervention could have been removed during the second half. Importantly, the order in which different conditions occur must be counterbalanced to control for the possibility that other variables are impacting behavior. Continuing with the classroom example, if the intervention was never implemented on Mondays and Fridays, it is possible that intervention might have appeared more effective not due to the specifics of the intervention but due instead to the days in which no intervention was implemented (just after and just before a weekend).

Alternating treatments designs allow for evaluation of the impact of an intervention through prediction, verification, and replication. Consider the data obtained from the above-mentioned classroom study, which are depicted in figure 5.4. First, prediction is based on evaluating previously plotted data points. Each point is used to *predict* the location of the next data point. Early in clinical interventions it is difficult to predict the occurrence of future behavior, but as it progresses, prediction becomes easier. In this dataset the percentage of intervals that off-task behavior occurred is depicted for both interventions. The data in both conditions are relatively stable and the clinician can predict with some confidence that those trends would continue into the future. *Verification* is accomplished through each additional data point. For example, consider only the first three data points for intervention and no intervention in figure 5.4. Based on these data points, one would predict that off-task behavior in the intervention condition would occur in between 40–45 percent of intervals, and that in the no-intervention condition, off-task behavior would be predicted to occur in about 70–75 percent of intervals. Now examine the fourth data point for each condition. The data collected on this day serve as *verification* of those predictions because the percentage of off-task behavior during intervention is within the predicted range. *Replication* also is accomplished if, each time the intervention is reinstituted, the percentage of off-task behavior differs from that observed when the intervention was not in place.

The unique features of alternating treatments designs render them particularly useful in many applied situations. First, alternating treatments designs are useful when it is not feasible to carry out extended baseline data collection, for example if the client's behavior is dangerous or is causing significant distress. Second, this design also is advantageous because the clinician does not have to withdraw an intervention that appears to be working to evaluate the impact of the treatment. A third advantage of alternating

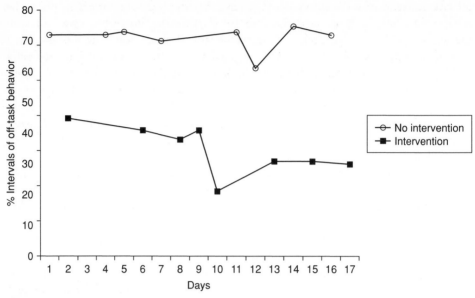

Figure 5.4   Percentage of intervals of off-task behavior exhibited by a first grader whose classroom teacher compared the effect of an intervention designed to address off-task and disruptive behaviors exhibited by students to no intervention. Percentage of off-task behavior exhibited when the intervention was used is represented by closed squares. Percentage of off-task behavior exhibited during days when intervention was not used are represented by open circles.

treatments designs is that carry-over effects are unlikely to occur. Carry-over effects threaten the validity of a study when the effects of an intervention are due, at least in part, to the sequencing of interventions. Because alternating treatments designs involve randomly ordered, rapid alternations between interventions, there is no set sequence of interventions. Fourth, alternating treatments designs often demonstrate the effect of an intervention relatively rapidly. The data in figure 5.4 illustrate this point. Although the study was carried out for only 17 days, effects were quite apparent and appeared stable by the third day. Although carrying out the intervention beyond this point allowed for more confidence in the observed effect of intervention, if data collection had to be foreshortened – for example, if the child's teacher wanted to stop alternating – the clinician would have had sufficient data to be reasonably confident in the recommendation to use the intervention.

Although the alternating treatments design is advantageous for many reasons, features of this design do yield three disadvantages. First, only a limited number of interventions can be assessed – typically no more than three and often just two (Cooper, Heron, and Heward, 1989; Miltenberger, 2001). This is the case for at least two reasons: (1) clients may have difficulty discriminating between different interventions if more than two to three are alternated; (2) because the clinician must counterbalance conditions to control for the possible effects of such factors as day of the week or number of people present, managing the design becomes increasingly cumbersome as more interventions are added.

Second, alternating treatments designs call for rapid alternation between treatment and no treatment or two or more treatments. Although this is necessary to evaluate the impact of the intervention, it creates a somewhat artificial situation – interventions typically are not introduced and withdrawn in a rapid fashion. A third potential difficulty has to do with what often is called multiple treatment interference (Cooper, Heron, and Heward, 1989). Multiple treatment interference occurs when the observed effects of an intervention are not due solely to the intervention, but rather are a factor of the intervention condition being alternated with another condition or conditions. Cooper, Heron, and Heward (1989) noted that, by following the alternating treatments design with implementation of one (usually the most effective) intervention, one could evaluate whether the effects were due to the intervention itself or to multiple treatment interference. One way to evaluate whether this has occurred is to implement the most effective treatment by itself, after the alternating treatments design has revealed which treatment seems most effective. If the target behavior changes in some way when conditions are no longer being alternated it is possible that multiple treatment interference was a factor. If, however, the target behavior continues to occur at approximately the same rate, frequency, etc. as it did when that intervention was alternated with another condition, the clinician can be confident that multiple treatment interference did not affect the results, and thus be more confident in the efficacy of the chosen intervention. Because most clinicians would use this design to determine an effective intervention, implementing that intervention alone would be the next logical step, and so this evaluation should be relatively easy to do.

Multiple baseline design

Multiple baseline designs are frequently used in the field of applied behavior analysis because they allow the practitioner to evaluate the impact of the intervention on behavior without withdrawing the treatment (as in an ABAB design) or comparing it to either another intervention or no intervention (as in the alternating treatments design). Using a multiple baseline design the practitioner can evaluate the impact of intervention by comparing its effect across behaviors, settings, or participants. The multiple baseline across behaviors design entails sequentially administering the intervention to two or more behaviors exhibited by the same client while holding other factors (e.g., setting) constant. When conducted across settings it involves sequentially administering the intervention across two or more settings with the same client (e.g., at home, then at work). Finally, the multiple baseline across participants involves targeting the same behavior (e.g., reports of anxious thoughts) emitted by two or more clients and administering the same intervention to each client sequentially.

An example of a multiple baseline across subjects design is depicted in figure 5.5. This study, conducted by Morin et al. (1995), examined the effects of cognitive behavior therapy combined with a supervised medication-tapering schedule on hypnotic-dependent patients with insomnia. A multiple baseline design across patients was used to evaluate the effects of the intervention on use of hypnotic medications and sleep efficiency (e.g., early awakenings, latency to sleep onset, awakening after onset of sleep). In baseline,

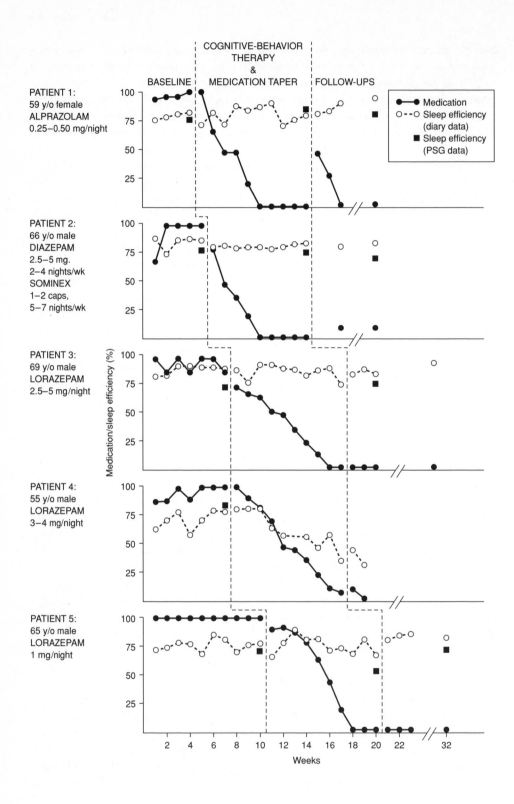

all patients reported using hypnotic medications on a nightly basis and relatively high sleep efficiency. Following treatment, all patients exhibited a gradual reduction in hypnotic usage and (with the exception of one patient) continued high sleep efficiency. Gains were maintained at 1- and 3-month follow-up appointments.

In all multiple baseline designs, intervention is introduced sequentially across behaviors, settings, or participants. As with all single-case designs, the multiple baseline design allows for prediction, verification, and replication. Prediction is achieved for each behavior, setting, or person by obtaining stable rates of the target response in baseline prior to implementing intervention. Stable responding prior to intervention allows the clinician to *predict* the pattern of responding if intervention were not administered. In the Morin et al. (1995) study, prediction is accomplished via the relatively stable baselines for all groups. *Verification* is achieved by comparing the level of responding on the behavior, setting, or clients where treatment has begun to those in which baseline data are still being collected. If responding in the remaining baselines remains relatively similar after treatment was introduced on another response (or setting, or client), the prediction of no change in responding had baseline continued for the first behavior, setting, or client is verified. Also, because change did not occur in situations where intervention was not introduced, there is some evidence that the change in the situation where intervention occurred is due to the intervention. Once responding has stabilized after intervention, the intervention is applied to the second behavior, setting, or client. This allows for further prediction and verification by comparing responding for the first two behaviors, settings, or clients (now under intervention) to the third (still in baseline). Finally, if the intervention similarly affects responding when it is implemented with the second response (or setting, or client), *replication* is achieved – the effect of the intervention observed with the first behavior, setting, or client is replicated with the second. The intervention is sequentially administered across the remaining responses, settings, or clients, and the resulting data are compared to data obtained with the other responses, settings, or clients.

Multiple baseline designs often are used in applied settings. This is the case for several reasons. First, and as is true with the alternating treatments design, the clinician does not have to remove an intervention that appears to be effective. Second, the multiple baseline design allows the clinician to target several behaviors or settings for intervention. It is rarely the case that a clinician plans on targeting only one behavior – typically a whole class of behaviors (e.g., assertiveness, which is made up of making eye contact, speaking in an appropriate tone of voice, and voicing concerns) is targeted. Multiple baseline designs allow the clinician to evaluate the effects of an intervention across all relevant behaviors.

Figure 5.5 (*opposite*) Percentage of medication and sleep efficiency among hypnotic-dependent patients with insomnia. Intervention for all participants consisted of a combination of a medication tapering schedule and cognitive behavior therapy. Percent medication used is indicated by the closed circles, percent sleep efficiency based on the patient's diary data is indicated by the open circles, and the percent sleep efficiency based on polysomnographic data is indicated by the closed squares. (From Morin, Colecchi, Ling, and Sood (1995). Copyright 1995 by the Association for the Advancement of Behavior Therapy. Reprinted by permission.)

Although multiple baseline designs have great utility in applied settings, their applicability may be limited in certain situations. This is because demonstration of the efficacy of the intervention requires that the intervention be systematically implemented across at least three behaviors, settings, or clients. The result of this is that intervention is necessarily delayed for some baselines; and if responding does not rapidly stabilize in the other behaviors, settings, or clients, the delay could be rather long. Thus, if clinicians are targeting behaviors that must be intervened upon immediately, the multiple baseline design might not be a good choice. In addition, each type of multiple baseline design has specific limiting conditions.

First, the *multiple baseline across behaviors* design is useful only if the behaviors typically do not occur together. For example, if a woman's "anxious behaviors" occurred in interactions with individuals in positions of authority and involved avoiding eye contact, talking in a quiet tone, and folding her arms in front of her, a multiple baseline design across these behaviors might not be an effective demonstration of treatment efficacy – as soon as one behavior was targeted, the others most likely would be impacted as well. However, the clinician must be careful to pick behaviors that will require the same intervention; thus, if the behaviors targeted for change were avoiding eye contact – which might be maintained by avoiding social interaction, and sleeping late – maintained by extra sleep, a multiple baseline design could not be used because the two responses necessitate different interventions.

The multiple baseline across settings design is useful when only one behavior (e.g., anxiety) is targeted for intervention; however, a potential problem is generalization. That is, when the intervention is applied to the behavior in the first setting, it may result in improvements in the behavior across all settings, thereby eliminating the possibility of demonstrating that changes in behavior were due to implementation of the intervention. Also, it may be difficult to obtain measures of the behavior in different settings, unless the client is using self-monitoring or there are trained observers in each setting.

The *multiple baseline across participants* design may be difficult to conduct in clinical settings because clinicians do not necessarily have several people presenting with the same problem at the same time. One alternative is to conduct a nonconcurrent multiple baseline across participants. In this design, participants do not enter the study at the same point in time. Because of the differences in time, it is difficult to draw strong conclusions about the efficacy of the intervention. Also, from an applied perspective, using a nonconcurrent multiple baseline design would not allow the clinician to draw immediate conclusions about the effects of an intervention for a given client – the clinician would have to withhold judgment until data from all three participants were available for comparison. Also, it may be unethical to have some participants remain without intervention for extended periods. Finally, if the participants talk to one another about the intervention, improvements might be seen before the intervention is actually administered.

Changing criterion design

Clinicians sometimes are interested in evaluating the impact of interventions that will be implemented in a stepwise fashion. For example, we recently worked with a child

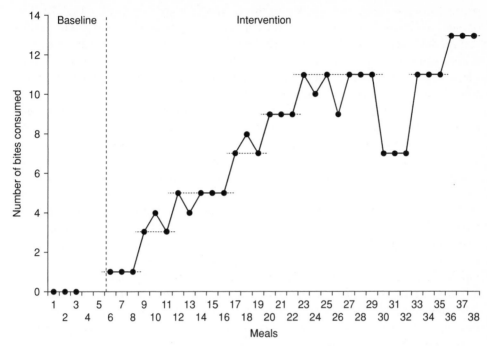

Figure 5.6 Number of bites of nonpreferred foods consumed during baseline and intervention. The criterion for reinforcement is indicated by the dashed line.

– Rudy – who exhibited significant food selectivity. Intervention consisted of ignoring interruptions, such as turning away his face or crying, and reinforcing acceptances with bites of preferred food. Rather than expect Rudy to eat typical portions of fruits, vegetables, and meats immediately after beginning intervention, we set a specific criterion to be met at each stage. For example, during the first treatment meal, he was required to eat one bite of fruit. When the criterion was met, Rudy earned a bite of preferred food and brief access to preferred toys. After the criterion was met for three consecutive meals, the number of bites required was increased by two. A graph of this treatment is shown in figure 5.6. The graph shows that, prior to intervention, Rudy did not consume any foods his parents had suggested were nonpreferred (fruits, vegetables, meat). Once intervention began, and Rudy was required to eat one bite of fruit to gain access to the reinforcer, he quickly did so. The amount of food that Rudy consumed systematically increased as the criterion for reinforcement was increased.

Changing criterion designs also demonstrate the utility of an intervention through prediction, replication, and verification. *Prediction* is possible when stable responding in baseline or at any given criterion is achieved. The clinician can predict that, if intervention was not implemented (or the criterion for reinforcement did not change), then responding would continue in a similar manner as has been observed. *Verification* can be obtained by returning briefly to a former criterion (Hall and Fox, 1977). If the rate of responding decreases to the previous criterion, verification has been obtained. For example, after Rudy met the criterion of consuming eleven bites of food, we returned to a previous criterion of seven bites. When this occurred, Rudy consumed only seven bites of food, and continued to do so until the criterion was once again increased. This verifies that the changes in responding most likely were due to the intervention. Finally, *replication* is demonstrated when, following a criterion change, responding changes systematically. For example, it was only when the criterion was increased from three to five bites that Rudy began consuming more bites of food.

Changing criterion designs can be useful to clinicians because they do not require removing the intervention to evaluate intervention efficacy. This design is especially useful when clinicians are evaluating behaviors that are expected to increase gradually, in a systematic fashion. Examples of behaviors that might be evaluated in this way include compliance, number of tasks completed correctly, calories consumed, or number of cigarettes smoked. One potential limiting factor for the use of changing criterion designs is that reinforcement (or punishment) must be delivered immediately contingent on responding at criterion. If an intervention involves some other behavior change technique, this design is not appropriate. A second limiting factor is the necessary imposition of a set criterion for responding. In many cases, client behavior may improve more rapidly than this design allows. For example, if a client is attempting to reduce the number of calories consumed, the criterion for reinforcement should be relatively easily achievable (e.g., 50 calories lower per criterion). It is possible that, if this criterion were not imposed, the client would begin to consume far fewer calories more rapidly, simply as a function of the intervention.

Thus far, several single-case designs have been reviewed. The logic of each design has been discussed, and the advantages and limitations of each design in clinical settings have been presented. Next, we briefly discuss strategies clinicians can use when attempting to evaluate the outcome of an intervention.

Evaluating Treatment Efficacy

When large group designs are used to evaluate the effect of an intervention, analysis typically takes place after completion of the study, and statistical analyses typically are performed to determine whether any differences between groups are statistically significant. In contrast, data analysis in single-case design is most often formative analysis. That is, data are analyzed as they are collected, and changes often are made in an intervention based on the data collected thus far. For example, if the collected data suggest that an intervention is not having the desired effect, or if a client reports difficulty in implementing an intervention, the intervention might be altered to make it more powerful.

Additionally, evaluation in single-case designs does not often involve statistical analysis. Instead, clinicians and researchers using single-case designs are interested in clinically significant changes – changes that are apparent to the clinician and the client. Thus, analysis of single-case designs most often involves visually inspecting data presented graphically. Visual inspection most often involves analyzing the magnitude and rate of changes following implementation of intervention.

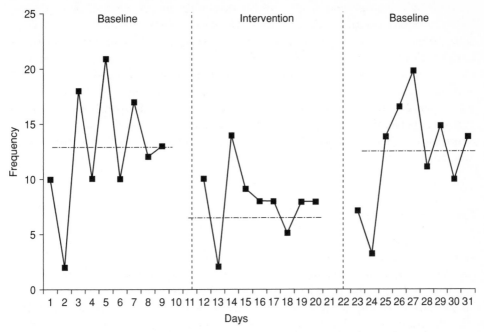

Figure 5.7 Hypothetical data illustrating behavior change between baseline and intervention. Mean response rates are indicated by the dashed lines.

When evaluating magnitude it is important to examine changes in mean rate of responding and changes in the level of responding. When evaluating changes in mean rate of responding, the average response rate in each condition is examined. For example, in figure 5.7 the mean response rate per condition is denoted by a dashed line. Examining the data and the mean lines, it is obvious that the intervention resulted in changes in mean rate of responding. Evaluation of level of responding involves comparing responding when one phase ends (e.g., baseline) and another phase begins (e.g., intervention). When evaluating whether a change in level occurred, the clinician might ask, "Could I tell where the intervention began if the phase line was not on the graph?" Examining the data in figure 5.7, we see that the change in level of responding between baseline and intervention is rather obvious, even if the phase line were not present.

Evaluation of the rate of changes entails examining both changes in the trend of behaviors and the latency until change occurs. When examining trend the goal is to look for systematic increases or decreases (or stable responding) over time. Ideally, intervention should reverse the trend evidenced in baseline. For example, if the target response is complaints, and the goal of the intervention is to decrease the frequency of complaining, one would hope that the frequency of verbal complaints would be either stable or slightly increasing in baseline. Once intervention commenced, a decreasing trend in verbal complaints should be observed. If responding in baseline is extremely unstable, it may be difficult to discern changes in trend unless the result of intervention is more stable responding.

Finally, visual inspection might involve examining latency until change occurred following implementation of intervention. The data in figure 5.7 illustrate a relatively rapid change in responding, once intervention was implemented. When behavior changes relatively close in time to manipulation of intervention (either introducing or removing the intervention), the effects of that intervention are more convincing. If changes in responding are delayed, it is more difficult to argue convincingly that the intervention was responsible for the change without the use of a reversal (ABAB) design. When changes are quite delayed, it is possible that they are due, not to the intervention, but rather to some extraneous variable that occurred around the time behavioral changes were observed.

Conclusions

Students in masters and doctoral programs in psychology often are taught that practicing psychologists function as scientist-practitioners. As such, psychologists attend to new empirical findings and apply relevant findings to their work, they evaluate the efficacy of interventions they implement, and they function as researchers, reporting data to the scientific community (Hayes, Barlow, and Nelson-Gray, 1999). Unfortunately, these goals often are not met. One reason is that practitioners may view the results of large, carefully controlled clinical trials as relatively irrelevant to their individual clients. Second, many practitioners do not systematically evaluate the utility of their interventions. A third reason why many clinicians do not consider themselves scientist-practitioners is that they are unable to conduct large group research designs – few practitioners have access to large numbers of clients presenting with sufficiently similar characteristics (e.g., diagnosis, age, gender) that they could use to conduct such research.

In this chapter we discussed the relevance of single-case design to practicing psychologists. It is our belief that, if single-case designs were more prevalent in psychology, more psychologists could function as scientist-practitioners. We believe this to be the case for several reasons. First, the use of single-case designs in research studies would allow practitioners to evaluate the results of an intervention for individual participants – not the average of many participants. Also, clinicians could visually inspect the data to determine whether the results were clinically – not just statistically – significant. Third, if single-case designs were more prevalent in clinical psychology journals, practitioners would have an avenue to publish their work with 2–3 clients, and thus might be encouraged to conduct research in their practice. Fourth, single-case designs provide clinicians with a means of evaluating the efficacy of interventions with a given client. The inherent flexibility of single-case designs allows clinicians to choose a design that will most benefit the client while simultaneously providing evidence of the utility of the intervention. Finally, because single-case designs involve analyzing the data as intervention progresses, the clinician is able to make informed judgments about the impact of intervention, and to make any needed changes along the way.

References

Barlow, D. H., Hayes, S. C., and Nelson, R. O. (1984). *The scientist practitioner: Research and accountability in clinical and educational settings.* New York: Pergamon.

Cooper, J. O., Heron, T. E., and Heward, W. L. (1989). Introduction to analysis. *Applied behavior analysis* (pp. 142–62). Upper Saddle River, NJ: Prentice-Hall.

Hall, R. V., and Fox, R. G. (1977). Changing-criterion designs: An alternative applied behavior analysis procedure. In B. C. Etzel, J. M. LeBlanc, and D. M. Baer (eds.), *New developments in behavioral research: Theory, method, and application* (pp. 151–66). Hillsdale, NJ: Lawrence Erlbaum Associates.

Hawkins, R. P., Matthews, J. R., and Hamdan, L. (1999). *Measuring behavioral health outcomes: A practical guide.* New York: Plenum.

Hayes, S. C., Barlow, D. H., and Nelson-Gray, R. O. (1999). *The scientist practitioner* (2nd edn.). Boston, MA: Allyn and Bacon.

Johnston, J. M., and Pennypacker, H. S. (1993). *Strategies and tactics of human behavioral research* (2nd edn.). Hillsdale, NJ: Lawrence Erlbaum Associates.

Kazdin, A. E. (1982). *Single-case research designs: Methods for clinical and applied settings.* New York: Oxford University Press.

Kazdin, A. E. (1998). *Research designs in clinical psychology* (3rd edn.). Boston, MA: Allyn and Bacon.

Miltenberger, R. G. (2001). *Behavior modification: Principles and procedures* (2nd edn.). Belmont, CA: Wadsworth.

Morin, C. M., Colecchi, C. A., Ling, W. D., and Sood, R. K. (1995). Cognitive behavior therapy to facilitate benzondiazepine discontinuation among hypnotic-dependent patients with insomnia. *Behavior Therapy, 26,* 733–45.

Sidman, M. (1960). *Tactics of scientific research.* Boston, MA: Authors Cooperative.

CHAPTER SIX

Design and Analysis of Experimental and Quasi-Experimental Investigations

Andrea Follmer Greenhoot

This chapter is concerned with experimental and quasi-experimental designs and the statistical approaches most commonly employed in conjunction with them. The section on design describes basic configurations of true experiments and quasi-experiments, explains the advantages and disadvantages of each of these two families of design, and discusses some general considerations for either type of design. The section on analysis focuses on the analysis of experimental and quasi-experimental data with continuous response variables (see chapter 9, this volume, for information about the analysis of qualitative dependent variables). This section begins with a brief discussion of preliminary, descriptive analyses, followed by a description of methods for inferential analyses. Because experimental and quasi-experimental studies are designed to address questions about group differences in average performance, data from these studies are typically analyzed using some form of an analysis of variance (ANOVA) or extensions of that technique. However, it is important to note that the statistical techniques discussed here may be appropriate for the analysis of nonexperimental data; indeed, these procedures are appropriate for the analysis of data from any investigation in which the primary research questions involve an assessment of differences in group performance.

Design

Experimental designs

True experiments involve the manipulation of one or more independent variables by the investigator and random assignment of subjects to experimental groups or treatments.

An experiment with two or more independent variables (i.e., factors) that are completely crossed has a *factorial design*. Combinations of levels of the independent variables form the groups or cells of the experimental design. For example, an experimenter might measure depressive symptoms of patients who took one of three drugs (drug *A*, drug *B*, or a placebo) and participated in one of two types of therapy. By combining the three levels of the drug factor with the two levels of therapy, six cells or groups are formed. With random assignment of subjects to groups, each individual has an equal chance of being assigned to any experimental group, reducing the likelihood of differences between treatment groups being due to initial differences in the group samples. As such, true experiments permit the investigator to make strong cause and effect conclusions about the relations between the independent and dependent variables.

Random assignment procedures

Two general procedures can be used to randomly assign subjects to experimental conditions. With the simpler procedure, free random assignment, subjects are randomly distributed among experimental groups; this procedure leads to a *completely randomized* experimental design. The alternative procedure, matched random assignment, is often used when an investigator suspects that certain subject characteristics (e.g., age, IQ, or prior hospitalization) are related to the dependent variable. This method is particularly desirable when the influence of a confounding variable is likely to be strong enough that it will mask experimental effects. Pretest scores or existing records are used to create blocks of subjects who are similar on the confounding variable(s), and treatment levels are assigned at random to subjects within each block. By controlling for initial differences among subjects on confounding factors, the blocking procedure facilitates detection of experimental effects. When this randomization procedure is used, the experiment has a *randomized block design*.

Posttest-only versus pretest–posttest designs

In the simplest experimental design one or more experimental groups are compared to a control group in a "posttest." In other words, subjects are randomly assigned to groups, and responses are measured once after the introduction of the experimental manipulation. Group differences in mean scores on the response variable are assumed to reflect the effect of the independent variable because the randomization process reduces the probability of initial group differences in the outcome variable. Posttest-only designs work particularly well with large samples, because larger samples increase the likelihood that random assignment will actually lead to equality between groups. To strengthen the claim that the randomization process resulted in initially equivalent groups, also it is common practice to measure other characteristics of the sample that might be related to the outcome of interest.

Whereas posttest-only designs only permit the evaluation of between-subject effects, pretest–posttest designs allow for the assessment of within-group changes in response to an experimental manipulation. In some pretest–posttest designs subjects are first randomly assigned to groups and then pretested before the experimental manipulation. Pretest scores allow the investigator to verify the success of random assignment in creating equivalent groups. Other pretest–posttest designs involve pretesting subjects first, matching them on the basis of pretest scores, and randomly assigning members of matched pairs to groups. This procedure helps to ensure that equivalent groups are created in the first place. A pretest–posttest design is especially preferable when the number of subjects is small or when the subjects are likely to differ substantially on a characteristic related to the outcome of interest. The design is also recommended if a researcher suspects that subjects' responses to a manipulation depend on their initial scores on the dependent measure; with the pretest–posttest design the investigator can statistically control for initial levels, making it easier to detect experimental effects. Further, when the examination of within-subject changes in the outcome is an explicit goal of the research, a pretest–posttest design is clearly the more appropriate one. One disadvantage of pretest–posttest designs is that repeated testing sometimes introduces the problem of differential carryover effects (see Maxwell and Delaney, 1990). When carryover effects are likely, a posttest-only design is preferred.

Quasi-experimental designs

Quasi-experiments have some of the characteristics of true experiments, including direct manipulation of one or more variables of interest. As in basic experiments, combinations of the different levels of the independent variables form the experimental groups. What distinguishes quasi-experiments from true experiments is that they do not involve random assignment of subjects to conditions. Quasi-experimental designs can be categorized into two subtypes: *nonequivalent control group designs* and *interrupted time series designs.*

Nonequivalent control group designs

In research with human subjects it is sometimes impossible for an investigator to randomly assign subjects to treatment groups. In many institutions individuals are assigned to groups for educational or social purposes. For example, children are aggregated into schools, grades, and classrooms, and patients are aggregated into hospitals and wards. In these situations researchers are rarely permitted to reassign individuals to test a hypothesis, and instead must compare preexisting groups that receive different treatments. Intact groups, however, might differ on characteristics related to the outcome variable. For example, patients assigned to different wards might vary in symptom level or demographic characteristics such as age. Similarly, children attending different schools might come from different socioeconomic and educational backgrounds. Within schools, children may be aggregated into classrooms by school staff on the basis of academic or behavioral characteristics, or by parents who request particular teachers for their children. Because of the potential for initial group differences, the ability to draw causal inferences from nonequivalent control group investigations depends on other features of the study design, such as whether the design includes a pretest.

Posttest-only versus pretest–posttest designs

Posttest-only designs for nonequivalent control group designs are not ordinarily recommended (e.g., see Morgan, Gliner, and Harmon, 2000). The researcher is unable to rule out the threat of selection bias because baseline information about the equivalence of groups is not collected. That is, group differences in the outcome could be attributable to either the experimental manipulation or initial group differences. Although measurements of sample characteristics that might be related to the variables of interest could be used to strengthen the claim of group equivalence, the results of a posttest-only quasi-experiment are generally more difficult to interpret than those of the pretest–posttest alternative. Quasi-experiments that employ some sort of pretest provide clearer information about the relationships between the independent and dependent variables, because the use of a pretest permits an assessment of the initial equivalence of the experimental groups. Pretest–posttest designs, however, do not eliminate the threat of "local history," or an experience occurring between pretest and posttest for one group that might influence the outcome of interest. Thus, the likelihood of such experiences for the different groups should be assessed.

Interrupted time series designs

In contrast to nonequivalent control group designs, which involve between-subjects comparisons to test treatment effects, interrupted time series designs assess treatment effects through within-subjects comparisons. These designs, including ABA, ABAB, and multiple baseline designs, can be applied to either groups of subjects or single subjects. The logic of the designs is generally the same regardless of whether one or several subjects are involved: subjects are exposed to a series of changes in the independent variable, and their responses are measured in each phase. To illustrate, in ABA designs, baseline measurements on the outcome variable are taken repeatedly for a given time period, followed by the introduction of an experimental manipulation and the measurement of responses to the manipulation. Finally, the manipulation is removed and baseline conditions are reinstated. Changes in subjects' responses during the experimental manipulation phase combined with reversal of the effects in the final phase provide strong evidence for a causal link between the independent and dependent variable (see Gelfand and Hartmann, 1984; and chapter 5, this volume, for a more detailed description of these procedures).

Inclusion of additional explanatory variables

Both true experiments and quasi-experiments frequently include measurements of non-manipulated classificatory or continuous variables. For instance, an investigator might be interested in whether subjects from two or more populations (e.g., males and females) respond similarly to an experimental manipulation (e.g., drug *A* and a placebo). Alternatively, a researcher might want to control for continuous extraneous variables, such as age or prior hospitalizations, when assessing experimental effects. The inclusion of such variables permits the investigator to demonstrate the generalizability of treatment effects, and increases the sensitivity of tests of treatment effects by accounting for some within-group variability. In data analysis, classificatory variables can simply be treated as additional factors. Methods for dealing with continuous covariates (i.e., analysis of covariance) will be discussed at some length in the analysis section of this chapter.

Advantages of factorial designs

How many independent variables should be examined in an experiment or quasi-experiment? Methodologists generally agree that factorial designs have several advantages over a series of single-factor studies (e.g., Maxwell and Delaney, 1990; Kirk, 1982). One major benefit of factorial experiments is their ability to detect the presence of interactions between factors. That is, factorial studies provide information about whether each variable operates in the same way across levels of the other variables. For example, a researcher interested in the effects of a new drug on depressive symptoms could use a factorial design to determine whether the drug affects subjects receiving therapy differently from those not receiving therapy. Even if no interactions are expected, a factorial design enhances generalizability of the findings because effects can be generalized across levels of the other factor. Finally, factorial experiments employ subjects more economically than a series of experiments focusing on one factor at a time. These advantages do not imply that investigators should try to design studies manipulating all factors that could possibly affect the outcome of interest. The high-order interactions created by four- or five-factor designs are usually too complex to be informative. Thus, designs with several manipulated factors (i.e., more than three) are uncommon in the behavioral sciences (Maxwell and Delaney, 1990).

Between-subjects versus within-subjects designs

Most of the discussion of design thus far has centered on between-subjects factors, but very often experiments and quasi-experiments include factors that vary within subjects. For example, rather than exposing different groups to different treatment conditions, a researcher could apply two or more treatment conditions to the same subjects, counter-balancing the order of treatments between subjects (note that this type of design is desirable only when treatment effects are expected to be temporary). Other within-subjects designs involve comparing subjects' scores on several different outcome variables, as in the case of profile analysis, or comparing subjects' scores on the same variables measured repeatedly, as in pretest–posttest designs or longitudinal studies. The within-subjects approach may be adopted for several reasons. First and foremost, within-subjects designs are often used to explore research questions that between-subjects designs cannot address (e.g., questions about changes in individuals over time). In addition, participants are used more efficiently in within-subjects designs than in between-subjects designs; more information is gathered from each subject and the number of subjects required for a particular level of power is lower (Maxwell and Delaney, 1990). Finally, within-subjects factors remove some variability due to individual differences among subjects from the error term, reducing the error variance and increasing power to detect experimental effects (Vonesh, 1983; Winer, 1971). The most serious disadvantage of within-subject designs is the potential for differential carryover from repeated measures, which may bias estimates of treatment effects (e.g., see Maxwell and Delaney, 1990). Thus, the effects of some factors are better assessed in between-subjects designs.

Analysis

Research questions about experimental and quasi-experimental data involve comparisons between experimental conditions on one or more outcome variables. Measures of individual performance are combined into measures of typical performance for each condition, and differences between conditions provide information about whether there is evidence for a cause and effect relationship between the independent and dependent variables. More generally, examination of the data involves measuring one or more dependent variables under conditions that are identified by one or more categorical variables. Thus, as mentioned earlier, the techniques for analyzing experimental and quasi-experimental data are also appropriate for examining nonexperimental data in which subjects are aggregated into groups according to one or more classification variables, such as age, gender, or disease diagnosis.

Data analysis can be partitioned into two phases, each of which is critical to the investigator's scientific conclusions. The first phase is a preliminary descriptive phase in which the investigator becomes familiar with the data. Once the preliminary phase has been applied, formal inferential analyses are used to determine the likelihood that patterns identified in the descriptive analyses could have occurred by chance (i.e., the statistical significance of patterns). Each of these two phases will be discussed in turn.

Descriptive analyses

Preliminary descriptive analyses are essential to understanding the meaning of data. In this phase of analysis, the investigator constructs graphs or plots and calculates descriptive statistics to become familiar with data, looking for important or unexpected patterns. All too often, after completing data collection, investigators are eager to look for statistically significant effects and conduct formal inferential tests prematurely, before taking the time to familiarize themselves with their data. Yet the descriptive phase of analysis is as critical for drawing scientific conclusions as the formal inferential phase; indeed, it is difficult to interpret the results of inferential analyses without actually understanding what the data look like.

To become familiar with experimental and quasi-experimental data, investigators often construct histograms or stem and leaf plots to illustrate the frequency distribution of scores (see figures 6.1 and 6.2). These graphic displays provide information about the shape of the distribution, so that the investigator can examine the symmetry, modality, and peakedness of the distribution for departures from normality. For example, the frequency distribution in figure 6.1 shows a positively skewed distribution, suggesting that there might be a floor effect on the assessment instrument. In contrast, figure 6.2 is an illustration of an approximately normal distribution. As we will see below, the assumption that scores are normally distributed is required for the most common statistical procedures used to analyze continuous response variables. Frequency distributions should also be examined for deviations or outliers that fall well outside the overall pattern, as illustrated in figure 6.1. In this case the researcher should search for explanations for the

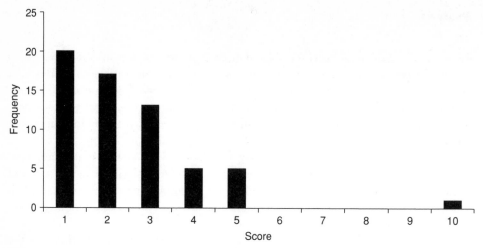

Figure 6.1 Illustration of a frequency distribution that is positively skewed and contains an outlier.

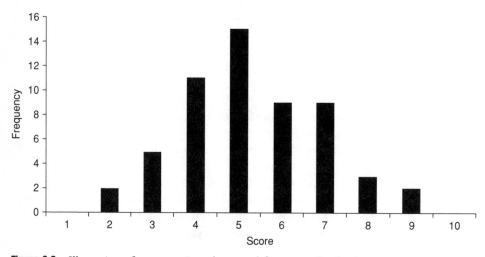

Figure 6.2 Illustration of an approximately normal frequency distribution.

atypical response, and decide how to handle it (see Stevens, 1984 or Tukey, 1977, for detailed discussions of the detection and treatment of outliers).

When research questions focus on differences between groups or experimental conditions the most commonly used descriptive statistics are the mean, which measures the central tendency of the scores, and the standard deviation, which measures the spread or variability of the scores. Means and standard deviations are ordinarily calculated and compared for each cell of the experimental design, as well as for the total sample. When more than one independent variable (or classification variable) is being investigated, *marginal means* may also be calculated. A marginal mean is the mean score for a particular level of one independent variable, averaged across levels of the other factor. Comparisons

Table 6.1 Sample cell means for a 2-factor study

| | *Program* | | |
Gender	Control	Intervention	Marginal mean (gender)
Females	$Y_{11} = 90.3$	$Y_{21} = 79.9$	$Y_{.1} = 85.1$
Males	$Y_{12} = 83.8$	$Y_{22} = 84.4$	$Y_{.2} = 84.1$
Marginal mean (program)	$Y_{1.} = 87.1$	$Y_{2.} = 82.2$	$Y_{..} = 84.6$

of marginal means for an independent variable provide information about the main effect of that variable. Comparisons of individual cell means provide information about interactions between independent variables. To illustrate, table 6.1 shows cell, marginal, and overall means for an artificial example of a study examining the effects of an exercise program on resting heart rate in male and female subjects, assuming equal cell sample sizes. Thus, two explanatory variables, gender and program, are considered here, each of which has two levels. Comparison of the marginal means for males and females suggests no differences according to gender. The marginal mean for the control program is somewhat higher than that for the intervention program. Comparison of the cell means suggests the presence of an interaction between gender and program; among females, average heart rate was lower in the intervention program than in the control program, whereas there appear to be no differences between programs among the males. Of course, it is not possible at this point to determine whether these differences are simply the result of chance variation. Inferential statistics must be used to determine whether the observed mean differences are statistically significant.

Inferential analyses

Once an investigator has explored patterns in the data, formal inferential tests are used to determine the extent to which these patterns could have arisen by chance. Experimental and quasi-experimental studies are designed to address questions about mean differences between treatment conditions in one or more response variables. Thus, the analysis of experimental or quasi-experimental data typically involves relating one or more categorical independent variables (e.g., an experimental treatment) to one or more continuous outcome variables. When all factors are manipulated between subjects, the most appropriate analysis strategy is an analysis of variance (ANOVA). The following sections begin with a discussion of the basic assumptions and principles of ANOVA, followed by an overview and illustration of the use of several types of ANOVA models and extensions of ANOVA, for dealing with continuous covariates or within-subjects factors.

Assumptions of ANOVA
ANOVA requires several assumptions that are associated with either the F statistic or linear models. First, it is assumed that all observations are random samples from the k populations or groups. Second, random errors of the observations are assumed to be

independent and normally distributed within each population, with a mean of 0. Thus, the observations are also independent and normally distributed within each population. Finally, the variance of the random errors (and therefore the variance of the observations) is assumed to be the same in all populations.

Computational details

ANOVA partitions the variation in a dependent variable into different parts that are attributed to one of the explanatory variables or to random error. The variation attributable to random error is represented by the within-group variation, calculated as the sum of the squared deviations of the individual scores from the group means, or the *sum of squares due to error* (SSE). The SSE, divided by its corresponding degrees of freedom (the *error mean square*, or MSE), is an estimate of the random error or common population variance, σ^2. The variation associated with each explanatory variable is measured as the variability between treatment groups, calculated as the sum of squared deviations of treatment group means from the overall sample mean, or the *sum of squares due to treatments* (SST). When SST is large compared to SSE, we know that most of the variability in the dependent variable is due to differences between groups rather than differences within groups. The SST divided by its degrees of freedom is called the treatment mean square (MST), and under the null hypothesis of no group differences MST is also an estimate of the common population variance σ^2. When MST is much larger than MSE, the null hypothesis can be rejected. Thus, tests of the null hypothesis are constructed as a ratio of these two mean squares, MST/MSE, which has an F distribution under the null hypothesis. The probability of an F value at least as large as the one observed (the *p* value) can be calculated, providing a test of significance of group differences.

Table 6.2 presents the formulas for the calculation of variance components for a simple one-way ANOVA, in which a single classification variable is related to one dependent variable. Two subscripts are used in these formulas. The first subscript indicates the treatment group ($i = 1^{st}$ to k^{th} group), whereas the second subscript indicates the individual observation within each group ($j = 1^{st}$ to n_i^{th} observation). The calculations are only slightly more complicated when more than one explanatory variable is involved, provided there are equal numbers of observations in each cell. For example, the SST for each independent variable is indicated by the deviations of the marginal means, rather

Table 6.2   General one-way ANOVA table

Source	Df	SS	MS	F
Between	k–1	$SST = \sum_{i=1}^{k} \bar{Y}_{i\cdot}^2/n_{i\cdot} - \bar{Y}^2/n$	MST = SST/(k–1)	MST/MSE
Within	n–k	$SSE = \sum_{i=1}^{k}\sum_{j=1}^{ni} \bar{Y}_{ij}^2 - \bar{Y}_{i\cdot}^2/n_{i\cdot}$	MSE = SSE/(n–k)	
Total	n–1	$Total\ SS = \sum_{i=1}^{k}\sum_{j=1}^{ni} \bar{Y}_{ij}^2 - \bar{Y}^2/n$		

than the cell means, from the overall mean, and the sums of squares for interaction effects are indicated by deviations of the cell means from the overall mean, less the sums of squares components for the main effects.

ANOVA as a general linear model

The computational details described above correspond to the traditional sum of squares approach to analysis of variance. This approach to ANOVA was developed in the day of desk calculators and uses a formula simple enough for hand calculation. This approach is limited, however, because it cannot be used in two or more factor studies with unbalanced data[1] (i.e., data with unequal cell sizes). A more general analytic approach called a general linear model (GLM) can be used with balanced or unbalanced data, but requires computer software packages that can manipulate matrices. Although ANOVA and regression are traditionally viewed as distinct approaches to data analysis, both can actually be written as specific cases of the GLM. In the GLM framework a subject's score on a dependent variable is defined as a linear combination of main effects, interaction effects, and an error. In the GLM approach to ANOVA, group means are estimated as linear combinations of regression parameters. Groups are defined by combinations of indicator variables that take the value of 0 or 1. For instance, a one-way ANOVA can be written by the use of a single indicator variable for each level of the categorical variable. To illustrate, if variable A has three levels, indicator variables are created as follows:

$X_1 = 1$ for A = 1
$\quad = 0$ for A = 2 or 3
$X_2 = 1$ for A = 2
$\quad = 0$ for A = 1 or 3
$X_3 = 1$ for A = 3
$\quad = 0$ for A = 1 or 2

The linear model for this example is:

$$y_i = \beta_0 + \beta_1 X_{1i} + \beta_2 X_{2i} + \beta_3 X_{3i}$$

Variation is partitioned into a portion attributable to the regression model (or explanatory variables) and a portion due to random error. These variance components are a function of predicted values, calculated using least squares estimates of the regression parameters, and observed values. For example, in a model with one explanatory variable, the regression sum of squares (SSR) is calculated as the sum of squared deviations of the predicted values from the overall observed mean. Variation due to random error (SSE) is calculated as the sum of squared deviations of individual observed values from the predicted values. As in ANOVA, the error mean square in GLM is an estimate of the population variance, σ^2. When the null hypothesis is true, the regression mean square is also an estimate of σ^2; thus F-tests for the effects of explanatory variables are constructed as ratios of the regression and error mean squares.

When the data are balanced (i.e., when cell sizes are equal) the GLM approach and the traditional approach give identical solutions. The GLM approach is more flexible than the traditional approach because it can handle both balanced and unbalanced data and it can also be more readily extended to incorporate continuous explanatory variables and repeated measures. These characteristics, as well as the prevalence of computers for data analysis, make GLM the current preferred approach (Kirk, 1982; Kleinbaum, Kupper, and Muller, 1988). It is often argued, however, that students should continue to learn about the traditional sum of squares approach to ANOVA because it elucidates many of the basic concepts of experimental design (e.g., Kirk, 1982; Collier and Hummel, 1977). Moreover, even when GLM machinery is used to predict a continuous outcome variable from one or more group variables, the term ANOVA continues to be used simply because it is a convenient way of conveying these characteristics of the analysis strategy. Indeed, in the remainder of this chapter, the analysis examples are conducted using GLM machinery, but the more traditional terms will be used to describe them.

One-way ANOVA

One-way ANOVA deals with the effect of a single between-subjects factor or variable on a single outcome variable. The independent variable can have two or more levels; thus a one-way ANOVA assesses differences in two or more population means. In the simplest case, a one-way ANOVA that compares two population means is equivalent to a two-sample *t*-test. If there are *k* population means, the null hypothesis is that all *k* means are equal, whereas the alternative hypothesis is that all means are not equal.

To illustrate a one-way ANOVA, consider a recent study by Donnelly et al. (1996), which examined the effectiveness of an intervention program in promoting physical fitness and preventing obesity among elementary school children. The investigation had a quasi-experimental design with a pretest, a posttest, and two intermediate observations. For two years, three cohorts of children (in the 3rd through 5th grades at the beginning of the study) at the intervention school participated in a program with enhanced physical activity, nutrition education, and a modified school lunch (low fat and sodium), whereas children in the control school continued with their regular school lunch and physical activity programs. Several measures of physical fitness, such as aerobic capacity, resting heart rate, lat pulls, bench presses, and knee extensions, were measured at the beginning and end of each school year.

Suppose Donnelly and his colleagues were interested in age differences in physical fitness as measured by lat pull scores at the initial assessment. To examine this issue, mean bench press scores would first be calculated for each grade. These data are shown in table 6.3, and as can be seen, lat pull scores seemed to increase with age. A one-way

Table 6.3   Mean scores and standard deviations for lat pull scores (lbs.), by age

Grade (at pretest)	Mean	SD
3rd graders (n = 29)	52.7	8.2
4th graders (n = 47)	55.7	11.2
5th graders (n = 26)	61.5	10.2

Table 6.4 Results of one-way ANOVA examining age differences in lat pull scores

Source	Df	SS	MS	F
Grade	2	1114.3	557.1	5.41
Error	99	10201.8	103.0	
Total	101	11316.0		

ANOVA could then be used to determine whether grade differences were statistically significant. Table 6.4 summarizes the results of a one-way ANOVA with grade as the classification variable and lat pulls as the dependent measure. As can be seen, the mean square for grade is larger than the error mean square. The resulting F ratio of 5.41 is significant at $p = .006$, indicating that lat pull scores do differ between the three age cohorts.

The F ratio associated with the grade effect does not provide information about which grades performed differently from each other. When a factor has more than two levels, the overall F test is only a first step in analyzing the data. If the omnibus F test is significant, more specific mean comparisons or contrasts are then considered to determine which means are significantly different from each other. A contrast is defined by a set of known, ordered coefficients applied to the means such that at least two coefficients are nonzero, and all coefficients sum to zero (Ramsey, 1993). Some contrasts involve pairwise comparisons between means. For example, in the Donnelly et al. (1996) example, one might wish to determine whether the 3rd graders' lat pull scores differ from those of the 4th graders. The null hypothesis for this contrast is H_o: $u_{3rd} = u_{4th}$, which can be rewritten as H_o: $u_{3rd} - u_{4th} = 0$. The contrast for testing this hypothesis is identified by the coefficients $(-1\ 1\ 0)$. Other contrasts involve more complex comparisons. For instance, the coefficients $(-1\ \frac{1}{2}\ \frac{1}{2})$ could be used to determine whether 3rd graders' lat pull scores differ from the average of 4th and 5th graders' scores. If multiple follow-up tests are conducted, the researcher runs the risk of inflating the Type I error rate. In addition, some contrasts may have been hypothesized before the data were collected (*a priori* or planned comparisons), whereas others might arise after the data are examined (*a posteriori* or post hoc comparisons). When decisions about mean comparisons are made after examining the data, the testing procedure is further biased in favor of rejecting the null hypothesis because only comparisons that appear to be significant would be tested. A variety of procedures have been developed for controlling the Type I error rate when carrying out multiple tests of planned and post hoc contrasts.

Multiple comparison procedures
Each of the multiple comparison methods discussed here involves calculating an F statistic for each contrast and comparing it to a critical value. When all comparisons are planned in advance, the Type I error rate can be adjusted by reducing the significance level (e.g., $\alpha = .05$) for each contrast by dividing it by the number of planned contrasts. This procedure is called the Bonferroni or Dunn procedure and can be used with simple pairwise comparisons or more complex contrasts. For example, if an investigator plans to

test two contrasts, each would be tested at a significance level of $\alpha = .025$. Tukey's HSD (honestly significant difference) is designed specifically to test all pairwise comparisons, either planned or unplanned. The logic of this method is that each observed F is compared to a critical value ($q^2/2$) selected such that the largest pairwise difference will exceed that value only 5 percent of the time when the null hypothesis is true. Although Tukey's HSD is limited to situations in which sample sizes are equal across treatment levels, Tukey (1953) and Kramer (1956) proposed a modification to Tukey's HSD for unequal cell sizes (the Tukey–Kramer method). This method has been shown to be more powerful than the Bonferroni method for testing pairwise comparisons. When more complex, post hoc comparisons are of interest, Scheffe's method is recommended. Following a similar logic to Tukey's HSD, Scheffe's approach involves comparing observed F values for each contrast to a critical value of $(k-1)F_{.05;k-1,n-k}$ (where k is the number of groups), which ensures that the largest F value for *any* possible contrast in the data (pairwise or complex) will exceed that value only 5 percent of the time when the null hypothesis is true. Scheffe's method should be used only when the investigator is interested in complex comparisons and when these contrasts are unplanned (e.g., Maxwell and Delaney, 1990). When only paired comparisons are of interest, Tukey's HSD or the Tukey–Kramer extension are more powerful than Scheffe's method. In the case of planned complex comparisons, Bonferroni's procedure is typically more powerful than Scheffe's method. Although the Bonferroni, Tukey, and Scheffe methods are the most commonly used multiple comparison procedures, several additional approaches have been suggested in the statistical literature. More comprehensive reviews of these procedures can be found elsewhere (e.g., Miller, 1981; Kirk, 1982).

To test all pairwise grade comparisons in lat pull scores for the Donnelly et al. (1996) example, the most appropriate procedure is the Tukey–Kramer adjustment. Table 6.5 shows the F values for each contrast and the associated *p* values according to the Tukey–Kramer criteria. As can be seen, 3rd graders differ from the 5th graders, whereas the 4th graders do not significantly differ from either the 3rd or 5th graders.

Two-way (and higher) ANOVA

Two-way ANOVAs are designed to assess the relations between two classification variables, each with two or more levels, and an outcome variable. Thus, factorial designs are typically analyzed with two-way or higher-way ANOVAs. This strategy can also be used with randomized block designs, with block considered an additional factor, although this method is less powerful than analysis of covariance (Maxwell and Delaney, 1990;

Table 6.5   F and *p* values for pairwise grade comparisons

Contrast	F(1,99)	Tukey–Kramer p value
3rd vs. 4th graders	1.60	.419
4th vs. 5th graders	5.55	.053
3rd vs. 5th graders	10.48	.005

Kirk, 1982). For the sake of simplicity, the discussion here will focus on two-factor studies, but these methods are easily generalized to multifactor studies.

Hypothesis testing in two-way ANOVAs involves an assessment of the main effects of each factor as well as the interaction between the factors. Most statisticians recommend that the interaction effects be considered before main effects (e.g., Applebaum and Cramer, 1974). If the interaction is significant, simple effect tests should be carried out to assess the effect of each independent variable at each level of the other independent variable (more on simple effects below). If the interaction is not significant, the investigator should then test main effects. There are several methods for calculating the sums of squares for main effects in two-way ANOVAs. These methods yield equivalent results when cell sizes are equal. When cell sizes are unequal, the different methods can lead to dramatically different conclusions about the presence of main effects. Type I sums of squares, or "added in order" tests, test the main effect of the first factor entered in the model ignoring the effects of the other factor and the interaction. The test of the second factor allows for main effects of the first factor, but ignores the interaction. Type II sums of squares test the main effects of each factor allowing for the effect of the other factor, but ignoring the interaction effect. Finally, Type III sums of squares test the main effects of each factor allowing for all other specified effects, including the interaction. The Type I approach is not usually recommended because ignoring the effects of one factor defeats the purpose of a factorial design (Maxwell and Delaney, 1990). The choice between Type II and Type III sums of squares is somewhat controversial (e.g., Cramer and Applebaum, 1980). The Type II method is more powerful than the Type III approach when the population interaction is zero. However, the statistical test of the interaction could fail to detect a true interaction in the population. As a result, many statisticians recommend using the Type III approach, unless there are strong theoretical arguments for a nonzero population interaction (e.g., Maxwell and Delaney, 1990; Kleinbaum, Kupper, and Muller, 1988). Most statistics programs (e.g., SAS and SPSS) automatically provide the results for Type III sums of squares.

In two-way and higher-way ANOVAs, main effects for multilevel factors may be investigated in the same manner as in one-way ANOVAs, using contrasts and the multiple comparison procedures described earlier. To further explore interactions, tests of simple effects are used to examine the effects of each factor at each level of the other factor. If a simple effect test is significant and the factor has more than two levels, one usually compares individual cell means. To control the Type I error rate, the Bonferroni adjustment is usually recommended (Maxwell and Delaney, 1990; Kirk, 1982). For example, tests of factor A at b different levels of factor B are conducted using $\alpha = .05/b$. Likewise, tests of factor B at a different levels of factor A are conducted using $\alpha = .05/a$.

In the physical fitness example, a two-way ANOVA could be used to examine the effects of both grade level and gender on children's physical fitness measured by their initial lat pull scores. The mean scores shown in table 6.6 suggest that lat pulls increase with age, and that gender differences might vary across grades. Specifically, females' scores were higher than those of males in the 3rd and 4th grades, but male scores were higher than those of females in the 5th grade, suggesting that there may be an interaction between gender and grade. Table 6.7 summarizes the results of the 2 × 3 ANOVA analyzing these data, using the Type III sums of squares. As can be seen, the F test for

Table 6.6   Mean scores (and standard deviations) for lat pull scores (lbs.), by age and gender

Grade (at pretest)	Females	Males
3rd graders	54.9 (8.3)	50.0 (7.4)
4th graders	57.2 (9.3)	53.3 (13.6)
5th graders	59.1 (8.5)	66.1 (11.9)

Table 6.7   Results of a two-way ANOVA examining grade and gender differences in lat pull scores

Source	df	Type III SS	MS	F	p
Grade	2	1421.05	710.53	7.12	.0013
Gender	1	7.46	7.46	0.07	.7851
Grade × gender	2	567.19	283.59	2.84	.0632
Error	96	9579.68	99.79		
Total	101	11316.05			

the interaction does not reach significance, making tests of simple effects unnecessary. As in the one-way ANOVA, a significant main effect of grade was observed. To further investigate this main effect, pairwise grade comparisons were conducted using the Tukey–Kramer method. These tests indicated that both 3rd and 4th graders scored significantly lower than 5th graders, $Fs(1, 96) > 8.35$, $ps < .013$.

Analysis of covariance (ANCOVA)

Sometimes an investigator wishes to control for extraneous variables when assessing the relation between an independent variable and a response. One way to control for such a variable is to include it in the analysis model, so that the effects of the independent variable are adjusted for the presence of the control variable, or *covariate*, in the model. The usual statistical technique for carrying out this adjustment process is called an analysis of covariance (ANCOVA). In the typical analysis of covariance, one of the predictors is continuous and the other is categorical. Separate parallel regression lines are estimated for each level of the classification variable. Thus, ANCOVA assumes equivalent slopes for all groups, or that there is no interaction between the classification variable and the continuous covariate. Main effects of the classification variable are represented as intercept differences, or differences in the relative levels of the regression lines. More complex ANCOVA models can include more than one factor and more than one covariate (see Maxwell, Delaney, and O'Callaghan, 1993, for a discussion of these more complex models).

ANCOVA is also the preferred method for analyzing data from randomized block designs (Feldt, 1958; Maxwell and Delaney, 1990). In contrast to the ANOVA approach in which block is treated as a factor, the ANCOVA approach uses all the quantitative information in the covariate or blocking variable, and consumes fewer degrees of freedom. ANCOVA can also be used to analyze pretest–posttest data, as long as the analysis of change from pretest to posttest is not of interest to the investigator. In the ANCOVA approach, group differences in posttest scores are assessed with the pretest score included as a covariate. This method is highly recommended for the analysis of pretest–posttest data because it is usually more powerful than the alternative method of analyzing change scores (Huck and McLean, 1975; Maxwell, Delaney, and Dill, 1984).

Most methodologists recommend that investigators test the assumption of parallelism of regression lines before proceeding with the standard ANCOVA strategy (e.g., Kleinbaum, Kupper, and Muller, 1988; Maxwell and Delaney, 1990). The test of parallelism, or homogeneity of slopes, is essentially a test of the interaction between the covariate and the classification variable to determine whether the relation between the covariate and the dependent variable differs at different levels of the classification variable. The model used to test the parallelism hypothesis is referred to by a variety of names, including ANCOVA with heterogeneous slopes or the heterogeneous regressions model. Maxwell and Delaney (1990) suggest that the heterogeneous regressions model be used if the test of the interaction term approaches significance ($p < .20$) or if there are theoretical reasons to suspect heterogeneity of regressions. If neither of these two conditions applies, the investigator should proceed with the standard ANCOVA assuming parallel slopes.

When the heterogeneous regressions model applies, the interpretation of the main effect of the classification variable is complicated, especially if the covariate is considered a nuisance variable by the investigator. In ANCOVA the main effect of the classification variable is represented by the distance between the regression lines; if the regression lines are not parallel, however, this distance varies continuously as a function of the covariate. How should this distance be estimated? There are two ways to address this problem. One approach, elaborated by Rogosa (1980), involves selecting a single point along the covariate dimension at which to test the main effect of the classification variable. The estimate will be most accurate when the selected point is at the center of the covariate's distribution. The alternative approach involves testing for main effects at multiple points along the covariate's distribution to identify regions in which treatment effects are significant (Potthoff, 1964, developed a method for simultaneously conducting these tests so as to control the Type I error rate). This procedure is recommended when a researcher is interested in the covariate itself, or when the regression lines intersect. The approach is especially useful when a researcher is using the covariate to identify ranges within which particular treatments will be effective. The reader is advised to consult Neter, Wasserman, and Kutner (1985), Maxwell, Delaney, and O'Callaghan (1993), or Maxwell and Delaney (1990) for further details about these procedures.

To demonstrate these procedures, ANCOVA was used with the Donnelly et al. (1996) physical fitness data to assess the effects of the intervention program controlling for pretest fitness levels. Specifically, group (intervention versus control) and pretest bench press scores were used to predict bench press scores at the final assessment. An initial test of the interaction between group and pretest bench press scores was not significant, $F(1, 98) = 0.05$, $p = .82$, thus a standard ANCOVA model was examined.

Table 6.8   Results of ANCOVA examining group differences in posttest bench press scores, controlling for pretest scores

Source	df	Type III SS	MS	F	p
Group	1	1315.98	1315.98	16.14	.0001
Pretest bench press	1	3748.60	3748.60	45.97	.0001
Error	99	8072.78	81.54		
Total	101	14044.10			

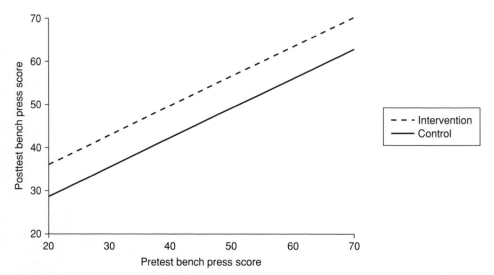

Figure 6.3   Estimated posttest bench press scores as a function of group, adjusting for pretest bench press scores (data from Donnelly et al., 1996).

The results of this model are shown in table 6.8. As can be seen, both group and pretest scores were related to posttest bench press scores. To further illustrate the nature of the effects, the slope and intercept estimates from this model were used to plot the regression lines for each group (see figure 6.3). The distance between the two lines indicates that children in the intervention group had higher bench press scores at the end of the program than children in the control group. The slope of the lines indicates that in both groups, individuals with higher baseline bench press scores had higher posttest scores as well.

Multivariate analysis of variance (MANOVA)

When more than one measurement is taken on the same subjects, the measurements are often correlated with each other. To account for these correlations it often makes sense to use a multivariate analysis strategy. MANOVA is used when the investigator measures more than one dependent variable, each representing qualitatively different constructs that share some conceptual meaning. For example, MANOVA is appropriate for analyzing several different measures of physical fitness, such as lat pull scores, aerobic capacity, and bench press scores. In the standard MANOVA the investigator is interested in jointly testing the effects of one or more between-subjects classification variables on the set of outcome measures. The procedure is a generalization of ANOVA in which linear combinations of the dependent variables are formed to maximize the differences between the levels of the independent variable. The resulting composite scores, rather than scores on the separate dependent measures, are tested for significance. There are several reasons for considering a MANOVA rather than a series of separate univariate ANOVAs (Stevens, 1992; Harris, 1993). When there is a weak treatment effect across several outcome variables, MANOVA has greater power for detecting the effect than single ANOVAs. In addition, the MANOVA approach reduces the probability of a Type I error when the dependent variables are correlated.

When the multivariate test of a between-subjects effect is significant, several follow-up tests may be of interest. For example, when the factor has more than two levels, contrasts can be used to determine which groups differ from one another at the multivariate level. In addition, an investigator will often want to determine which dependent variables contribute to multivariate significance, most often by examining univariate tests of each dependent variable. Some methodologists argue that multiple comparison procedures for controlling Type I error are not necessary in multivariate analyses because the overall multivariate test provides adequate protection (e.g., Hummel and Sligo, 1971). Others suggest the Bonferroni adjustment for multiple planned comparisons and pairwise post hoc comparisons (e.g., Stevens, 1992; Maxwell and Delaney, 1990; Timm, 1975). For complex post hoc comparisons a multivariate extension of Scheffe's method developed by Roy and Bose (1953) is sometimes recommended for the selection of the appropriate critical value (e.g., Morrison, 1976; Harris, 1993). This method controls Type I error rate for all possible pairwise and complex group comparisons for each dependent variable, as well as for different linear combinations of the variables. As such, this procedure allows for unrestricted analysis, but is highly conservative (Hummel and Sligo, 1971; Stevens, 1992). For additional detail about multiple comparison procedures in MANOVA, the reader should refer to Stevens (1992) or Harris (1993).

Suppose Donnelly et al. (1996) were interested in assessing grade and gender differences in baseline scores on several indicators of physical fitness. To address this question, a MANOVA was used to examine the joint effects of grade and gender on a set of four outcome measures: aerobic capacity, knee extensions, lat pulls, and bench presses. The multivariate test statistics for this analysis are summarized in table 6.9. As shown in the table, the MANOVA revealed significant multivariate main effects of both grade and gender. To further investigate the grade effect, pairwise multivariate tests were conducted. Even with the significance level adjusted according to the Bonferroni procedure ($\alpha = .05/3 = .017$), all three contrasts were significant, $Fs(4, 93) > 4.95$, $ps < .0012$. Univariate tests of these differences were then examined to determine which dependent measures contributed to the pairwise multivariate significance, adjusting the significance level for the number of dependent variables ($\alpha = .05/4 = .0125$). These tests indicated

Table 6.9 Results of MANOVA examining grade and gender differences in four physical fitness measures (aerobic capacity, knee extensions, lat pulls, and bench presses)

Source	Num df	Den df	F	p
Grade	8	186	6.95	.0001
Gender	4	93	8.99	.0001
Grade × gender	8	186	1.05	.40

that the difference between 3rd graders and 4th graders was limited to knee extensions, $F(1, 96) = 18.06$, $p = .0001$. Fifth graders outperformed 3rd graders on both knee extensions and lat pulls, $Fs(1, 96) > 13.49$, $ps < .0004$. Fifth graders also outperformed 4th graders on knee extensions and lat pulls, $Fs(1, 96) > 8.38$, $ps < .0047$. The contributions of the four dependent measures to the significant multivariate gender effect were also examined through univariate tests, which indicated that males outperformed females in aerobic capacity and bench press scores, $Fs(1, 96) > 14.53$, $ps < .0002$.

Repeated measures ANOVA

Like MANOVA, a repeated measures ANOVA is used to analyze multiple measurements on the same subjects. The repeated measures approach is typically used to examine multiple measurements on the same outcome variable. In the simplest repeated measures ANOVAs, the researcher is interested in within-subjects differences in the repeated measure. In more complex repeated measures ANOVAs, between-subjects effects of one or more classification variables, as well as interactions between the within-subjects and between-subjects variables, are also of interest. In contrast, in MANOVA the investigator is primarily interested in between-subjects effects, tested jointly across a set of dependent measures. Repeated measures ANOVAs are recommended for investigations in which change over time is of particular interest, such as longitudinal or developmental studies, studies of learning and memory, and some pretest–posttest studies.

There are two approaches to repeated measures ANOVAs. The univariate approach involves blocking the data by subject, and treating block as a factor in a univariate ANOVA to account for individual differences in subjects' responses to the repeated measure. Thus, the univariate repeated measures ANOVA will always have at least two factors, one representing subjects and the other representing the within-subjects or repeated measures variable (e.g., time). The univariate approach requires an assumption of sphericity, or homogeneity of the treatment difference variances. In other words, it is assumed that all pairs of levels of the within-subjects variable have equal correlations. This assumption, however, is frequently violated; measurements taken close in time are often more highly correlated than measurements taken farther apart in time. Several adjusted univariate tests have been developed to handle violations of the sphericity assumption, including the Geisser–Greenhouse lower bound correction, the Box adjustment, and the Huynh–Feldt adjustment (see Stevens, 1992, for greater detail). Alternatively, an investigator could choose to use the multivariate approach to repeated measures ANOVAs, which require no sphericity assumption. The multivariate strategy involves transforming the dependent variables into a set of difference scores and testing the hypothesis that these scores equal zero. Between-subjects effects are measured by averaging across levels of the within-subjects variable. When the within-subjects variable has only two levels, the univariate and multivariate approaches provide identical results. When sphericity holds, the univariate approach is the more powerful strategy; when sphericity is violated, the choice between the adjusted univariate procedures and the multivariate approach is complicated (see Davidson, 1972). Some methodologists (e.g., Cole and Grizzle, 1966; Maxwell and Delaney, 1990) recommend routine use of the multivariate approach for theoretical reasons (e.g., because repeated measures data are essentially multivariate in nature).

In repeated measures ANOVAs, significant overall tests for within-subjects effects, between-subjects effects, and their interactions can be followed up with a variety of more specific comparisons, depending on the hypotheses of interest. Comparisons involving between-subjects effects with more than two levels can be tested with contrasts that average over scores on the within-subject factor. The multiple comparison procedures recommended for univariate ANOVAs are also appropriate for between-subjects comparisons in the repeated measures case (Maxwell and Delaney, 1990). Contrasts may also be used to determine the nature of within-subject effects. For example, the investigator might want to test for linear, quadratic, and cubic trends in the repeated measure (see Morrison, 1976, for more details about trend analysis). One way to explore a significant interaction between within- and between-subjects variables is to test the simple effect of the between-subjects variable at each level of the within-subjects variable. For instance, the researcher could examine the univariate one-way ANOVAs of the between-subjects variable at each level of the within-subjects variable. The Bonferroni adjustment is recommended to control the Type I error rate when testing multiple planned contrasts or unplanned pairwise comparisons involving within-subjects effects. For post hoc complex comparisons, the Roy and Bose method is preferred (e.g., Morrison, 1976; Harris, 1993).

In the physical fitness example, a multivariate repeated measures ANOVA was used to assess change over time in physical fitness scores as a function of group (intervention versus control). The model included the four-level within-subjects variable of time, the between-subjects variable group, and the interaction between time and group. As shown in table 6.10, all three effects were significant, indicating that the effect of group varied across time. To explore the nature of this interaction, univariate tests of the group effect

Table 6.10 Results of a repeated measures ANOVA examining group differences in bench press scores over time

Source	Num df	Den df	F	p
Group	1	97	10.92	.0013
Time	3	95	18.83	.0001
Group × time	3	95	4.29	.007

were conducted at each level of time. These analyses revealed that the intervention group had higher bench press scores than the control group at the final assessment, $F(1, 97) = 20.78$, $p < .0001$, but not at the earlier three time points. Thus, these findings suggest that only after two academic years did the intervention program lead to significant strength gains relative to the control group.

Conclusions

The goal of this chapter is to provide an overview of common experimental and quasi-experimental designs and the statistical analysis strategies most often associated with them. The information presented here is by no means exhaustive; a multitude of more complex extensions of these methods are possible. Kirk (1982) provides in-depth coverage of a variety of experimental designs for the behavioral sciences. More complex designs than those described here can usually be analyzed using some form of the general linear model. These strategies are likely to be generalizations of those presented here, which are also based on the general linear model. The interested reader is referred to Graybill (1961) or Kirk (1982) for further information about the general linear model.

Note

1   The method of unweighted means is an adaptation of the traditional sum of squares approach for unbalanced data, but this technique provides test statistics that only approximate F statistics under the null hypothesis.

References

Applebaum, M. I., and Cramer, E. M. (1974). Some problems with nonorthogonal analysis of variance. *Psychological Bulletin, 81,* 335–43.

Cole, J. W. L., and Grizzle, J. E. (1966). Applications of multivariate analysis to repeated measures experiments. *Biometrics, 22,* 810–28.

Collier, R. O., and Hummel, T. J. (1977). *Experimental design and interpretation.* Berkeley, CA: McCutchan.

Cramer, E. M., and Applebaum, M. I. (1980). Nonorthogonal analysis of variance – once again. *Psychological Bulletin, 87,* 51–7.

Davidson, M. L. (1972). Univariate versus multivariate tests in repeated measures experiments. *Psychological Bulletin, 77,* 446–52.

Donnelly, J. E., Jacobsen, D. J., Whatley, J. E., Hill, J. O., Swift, L. L., Cherrington, A., Polk, B, Tran, Z. V., and Reed, G. (1996). Nutrition and physical activity program to attenuate obesity and promote physical and metabolic fitness in elementary school children. *Obesity Research, 4,* 229–43.

Feldt, L. S. (1958). A comparison of the precision of three experimental designs employing a concomitant variable. *Psychometrika, 23,* 335–54.

Gelfand, D. M., and Hartmann, D. P. (1984). *Child behavior analysis and therapy* (2nd edn.). New York: Pergamon.

Graybill, F. A. (1961). *An introduction to linear statistical models, volume 1*. New York: McGraw-Hill.

Harris, R. J. (1993). Multivariate analysis of variance. In L. K. Edwards (ed.), *Applied analysis of variance in behavioral science* (pp. 255–96). New York: Marcel Dekker.

Huck, S. W., and McLean, R. A. (1975). Using a repeated measures ANOVA to analyze the data from a pretest–posttest design: A potentially confusing task. *Psychological Bulletin, 82*, 511–18.

Hummel, T. J., and Sligo, J. (1971). Empirical comparison of univariate and multivariate analysis of variance procedures. *Psychological Bulletin, 76*, 49–57.

Keselman, H. J., and Keselman, J. C. (1993). Analysis of repeated measurements. In L. K. Edwards (ed.), *Applied analysis of variance in behavioral science* (pp. 105–46). New York: Marcel Dekker.

Kirk, R. E. (1982). *Experimental design: Procedures for the behavioral sciences* (2nd edn.). Pacific Grove, CA: Brooks/Cole.

Kleinbaum, D. G., Kupper, L. L., and Muller, K. E. (1988). *Applied regression analysis and other multivariable methods*. Boston, MA: PWS-Kent.

Kramer, C. Y. (1956). Extension of multiple range test to group means with unequal numbers of replications. *Biometrics, 12*, 307–10.

Maxwell, S. E. (1998). Longitudinal designs in randomized group comparisons: When will intermediate observations increase statistical power? *Psychological Methods, 3*, 275–90.

Maxwell, S. E., and Delaney, H. D. (1990). *Designing experiments and analyzing data: A model comparison perspective*. Belmont, CA: Brooks/Cole.

Maxwell, S. E., Delaney, H. D., and Dill, C. A. (1984). Another look at ANCOVA versus blocking. *Psychological Bulletin, 95*, 136–47.

Maxwell, S. E., Delaney, H. D., and O'Callaghan, M. F. (1993). Analysis of covariance. In L. K. Edwards (ed.), *Applied analysis of variance in behavioral science* (pp. 63–104). New York: Marcel Dekker.

Miller, R. G., Jr. (1981). *Simultaneous statistical inference* (2nd edn.). New York: Springer-Verlag.

Morgan, G. A., Gliner, J. A., and Harmon, R. J. (2000). Quasi-experimental designs. *Journal of the American Academy of Child and Adolescent Psychiatry, 39*, 794–6.

Morrison, D. F. (1976). *Multivariate statistical methods*. New York: McGraw-Hill.

Neter, J., Wasserman, W., and Kutner, M. H. (1985). *Applied linear statistical models*. Homewood, IL: Richard D. Irwin.

Potthoff, R. F. (1964). On the Johnson–Neyman technique and some extensions thereof. *Psychometrika, 29*, 241–56.

Ramsey, P. H. (1993). Multiple comparisons of independent means. In L. K. Edwards (ed.), *Applied analysis of variance in behavioral science* (pp. 25–62). New York: Marcel Dekker.

Rawlings, J. O. (1988). *Applied regression analysis: A research tool*. Pacific Grove, CA: Wadsworth.

Rogosa, D. (1980). Comparing non-parallel regression lines. *Psychological Bulletin, 88*, 307–21.

Roy, S. N., and Bose, R. C. (1953). Simultaneous confidence interval estimation. *Annals of Mathematical Statistics, 24*, 513–36.

Stevens, J. (1992). *Applied multivariate statistics for the social sciences*, 2nd edn. Hillsdale, NJ: Erlbaum.

Stevens, J. P. (1984). Outliers and influential data points in regression analysis. *Psychological Bulletin, 95*, 334–44.

Timm, N. H. (1975). *Multivariate analysis with applications in education and psychology*. Monterey, CA: Brooks-Cole.

Tukey, J. W. (1953). *The problem of multiple comparisons.* Mimeographed monograph.

Tukey, J. W. (1977). *Exploratory data analysis.* Reading, MA: Addison-Wesley Publishing.

Vonesh, E. F. (1983). Efficiency of repeated measures designs versus completely randomized designs based on multiple comparisons. *Communications in Statistics: Theory and Methods, 12,* 289–302.

Winer, B. J. (1971). *Statistical principles in experimental design* (2nd edn.). New York: McGraw-Hill.

CHAPTER SEVEN

The Analysis of Correlational Data

Charles M. Judd and Melody S. Sadler

Introduction

Defining correlational data

The initial question to be posed concerns the definition of the term "correlational" in our title. In what sense does this limit what we are about? In what sense is this chapter not just about the analysis of data in general? When do we have correlational data and when do we not?

From an analytic point of view, all datasets are correlational. The meaningful information in any dataset consists of the means, variances, and covariances among the measured variables. All data analyses, from simple *t*-tests through the most complicated structural equation analysis that one might conduct, rest on the information contained in the variance/covariance matrix.

Accordingly, "correlational" in our title does not limit what we are about if we are talking only about analytic issues. But that is not the focus of this chapter. Rather, our focus is on the analysis of data from "correlational" research designs: designs where the variables in the dataset are exclusively measured, rather than experimentally manipulated. From the legacy of Campbell and Stanley (1963) we have all learned about the distinction between correlational designs and experimental designs. The latter involve independent variables whose values are systematically and randomly varied across participants. Correlational designs are everything else. They are designs in which none of the variables in the dataset have values that have been randomly determined.

Preparation of this chapter was partially supported by NIMH grant R01 MH45049 to the first author.

Experimental designs necessarily involve longitudinal data. The independent variable(s) are manipulated and subsequently the dependent ones are measured. Correlational data may be longitudinal or not. In other words, measurements may be taken at multiple points in time. Accordingly, our definition of correlational datasets includes many sorts of designs that have been labeled elsewhere quasi-experimental research designs (e.g., Cook and Campbell, 1979; Judd and Kenny, 1981).

Although variables in a correlational design may be measured at different points in time, an important distinction between correlational datasets and experimental ones is that in the former the designation of variables as "independent" versus "dependent" is a theoretical decision that one makes. In other words, there is nothing inherent in the research design that specifies that one variable is an independent one and another a dependent one, even though they may be measured at different points in time. In experimental datasets this is not the case. Variables whose values have been manipulated and randomly determined are the independent variables of interest. Any variable subsequently measured may be considered a dependent variable.

A frequent confusion involves scales of measurement and research designs. Variables in a correlational dataset may be measured on nominal, ordinal, interval, or ratio scales of measurement. Research designs are not defined by the scale of measurement of the independent variables. Accordingly, as we will see, analytic procedures are not design specific. A common misconception is that analysis of variance is used with experimental designs (having nominally scaled independent variables) while multiple regression is used for correlational designs (having continuously varying independent variables).

Overview of analytic approach

At the most basic level, the analysis of data from correlational designs involves the estimation and testing of parameters of linear models, predicting one variable or set of variables from some other variable or sets of variables. Parameter estimation is most typically done by deriving coefficients that minimize the sum of squared errors (Ordinary Least Squares estimation), although other approaches, involving generalized least squares or maximum likelihood estimation, are increasingly used (see Judd, McClelland, and Culhane, 1995).

Although the models that are estimated are typically linear additive models, this is true in form only. As we review in later sections of this chapter, appropriate transformations of variables in these models permit the testing of many nonlinear and interactive hypotheses.

The specification of the models to be estimated requires strong theoretical assumptions on two fronts. First, because measured variables in the behavioral sciences are typically errorful, assumptions about what we will call the "measurement model" must be articulated and critically examined. The measurement model specifies the relationships between the measured variables and the constructs that are of theoretical interest. In the next section of this chapter we lay out procedures used to specify and critically examine the measurement model.

Once the measurement model has been specified, then theoretical assumptions must be clearly articulated to guide the analysis. In particular, decisions about which linear models to estimate, about the identification of dependent and independent variables in these models, and about implicit causal models must be made. Data analysis cannot be accomplished as a blind exploration of patterns of covariances among variables in a dataset. Rather, data analysis presumes a theoretical model that guides model estimation and testing. This theoretical model needs to be made explicit and critically examined.

In most analyses the specification of the measurement model precedes the actual conduct of the analysis, estimating linear models that relate dependent to independent variables. However, in the last 25 years, procedures have been developed for estimating the parameters of both the measurement model and the data analytic model (or structural model) simultaneously. These procedures, generally known as structural equation modeling procedures, have been implemented in a number of commonly available computer programs (e.g., Lisrel, EQS; Bentler, 1995; Joreskog and Sorbom, 1993). Chapter 8 in the present volume presents a comprehensive introduction to the specification and testing of structural equation models.

This chapter will treat data analysis in the way it is more traditionally and typically conducted. We will first lay out procedures for specifying and examining the measurement model. Once these have been developed, we will turn to data analytic procedures for estimating and testing the linear models that examine the relations among constructs specified in the measurement model. We will conclude by examining the assumptions which underlie hypothesis testing in these linear models and procedures that can be adopted to deal with assumption violations.

Specification of the Measurement Model

In far too many cases, measurement models remain implicit and unexamined. Researchers in essence presume that they know what each measured variable represents and they proceed with data analysis based on these unexamined measurement assumptions. Most typically, this involves using single indicators of constructs and analyzing these indicators as if they were the constructs themselves, thereby implicitly assuming the absence of measurement error.

Another frequently adopted but problematic approach is to assume that someone else's measurement model applies in the current situation. This occurs with great regularity whenever one uses a scale that someone else has developed and validated without examining whether that scale continues to be reliable and valid in the situation in which it is currently being used. It may well turn out that a set of items that someone has previously shown to scale nicely and capture some construct of theoretical interest continues to function quite well in the current situation. But this possibility should be critically examined, using the procedures we outline below for assessing the adequacy of a measurement model.

Although prior validation of a scale by others is clearly an asset, one should not presume that successful measurement requires that. All too frequently we have encountered situations where researchers presume that they must use measures that have been previously validated even when those measures do not seem to exactly capture the constructs of theoretical interest in the current situation. So long as the assumptions underlying a measurement model are critically examined, there is nothing wrong in developing measures of key constructs rather than relying exclusively on previously validated scales.

The key concept in validating a measurement model is that of multiple operationalizations (Campbell and Fiske, 1959). Only by having multiple variables that are expected to measure each of the key theoretical constructs can one approach the tasks of establishing convergent and discriminant validity. To review quickly, convergent validity concerns the extent to which multiple measures of the same construct all converge on the same answer (i.e., are highly intercorrelated), while discriminant validity concerns the extent to which measures of different constructs tend not to give the same answer (i.e., lower correlations between measures of different constructs than between measures of the same construct). These notions have been most elaborately addressed in analyses of Multitrait–Multimethod matrices (Campbell and Fiske, 1959; Kenny and Kashy, 1992).

The assessment of a measurement model begins with the analysis of the structure of the correlation matrix among measured variables. Probably the most important procedures used to evaluate this structure are common factor analysis and principal components analysis. Although often used interchangeably, common factor analysis and principal components analysis are in fact very different procedures. The former builds a model of the measured variables, attempting to identify a set of common factors that explains the covariation in the measured variables, while allowing unique variation in each measured variable. The latter procedure, principal components analysis, turns the situation around: it identifies linear composites of measured variables that account for as much variance in the measured variables as possible. (See Gorsuch, 1983; Harmon, 1976; and Wegener and Fabrigar, 2000, for a more detailed discussion of the difference.)

Although the common factor analysis model is the more appropriate model if the goal is to "uncover" the underlying structure of a covariance matrix among measured variables (i.e., to identify the dimensions or latent variables that are responsible for the observed covariation), principal components analysis is more appropriate if one wishes to construct composite variables that are linear combinations of the measured variables. It is our belief that the second goal should be the primary one in most correlational research. One is usually not so much interested in determining the underlying dimensional structure of an observed covariation matrix. Rather, one has certain constructs that one hopes to have measured, each with multiple indicators, and one wishes to construct linear composites of those measured variables that capture the theoretical constructs as closely as possible.

To clarify further, the common factor analysis model starts with the presumption that there is some meaningful universe of measured variables (e.g., all possible measures of different forms of intelligence). The goal is then to discover the underlying regularities in these variables. This is not the situation most researchers face. Rather, they have ideas about what the theoretical constructs are that they wish to measure. They then construct or borrow from others variables that they think will capture those constructs. They then want to form indices of their measured variables that capture as best as possible the hypothesized constructs. It is this last goal that is well served by principal components analysis.

To establish convergent validity for variables presumed to measure the same construct, the first unrotated component from a principal components analysis of just those variables ought to be examined. If there is convergent validity then that first principal component should have a large eigenvalue, relative to the eigenvalues of the residual components. This will be the case when most of the measured variables have substantial correlations with the first component (i.e., factor loadings; the eigenvalue equals the sum of all the squared loadings of the variables on the component). A quick measure of the degree to which the measured variables all converge in what they are measuring (i.e., load on a single component) is given by the eigenvalue for the first unrotated component divided by the number of variables included in the analysis. This number represents the proportion of the variance across the variables explained by the component, assuming standardization or equal variances of the items.

A conceptually similar measure is given by Cronbach's (1951) coefficient alpha measure of internal consistency of the set of variables. It too can be computed from the eigenvalue of the first unrotated component (λ) and the number of measures (k):

$$\alpha = \left(\frac{k}{k-1} \right)\left(1 - \frac{1}{\lambda} \right)$$

This is equivalently the reliability of the weighted sum of all the variables, standardizing and weighting each by the variable's loading on the first component. This has been shown to be the maximum possible reliability of any weighted linear combination of the set of items (Bentler, 1968).

Practically, assuming that the eigenvalue is large, relative to the number of variables, and assuming the computed value of alpha is relatively large (e.g., > .70), one has evidence that the set of variables presumed to measure a common construct are in fact converging in what they are measuring. One can then either compute a weighted sum or average of the standardized items, weighting by the factor loadings, or a simple sum or average of the standardized items, reversing those that have negative loadings.[1]

The above approach helps establish the convergent validity of a set of variables that are presumed to measure the same construct. Further work, however, is needed to establish discriminant validity, i.e., that one set of variables is measuring something different from another set. The goal here is to show that one set loads on a different component from the other set, when a rotated principal components solution is computed on the two sets of variables. Again, we do not recommend a strategy that conducts a factor analysis of a large number of variables to uncover the underlying constructs that they measure. Rather, we favor a theoretically driven analysis, one that explores whether or not measures of a few constructs, previously shown to have convergent validity, are discriminable.

Let us assume, for instance, that we have three sets of variables, with five variables in each set, and previous principal components analyses have established reasonable levels of internal consistency or convergent validity within each set (i.e., separate component analyses of each set revealing high alpha levels). Now, we want to verify that these three sets manifest discriminant validity, i.e., that they are in fact measuring different constructs. A single principal components analysis would be conducted on all fifteen variables, forcing a rotated solution with three factors (since that is the number of constructs that theory has dictated underlie the variables), and allowing an oblique rotation of those three components (since the expectation should be that the underlying constructs are correlated with each other). Discriminant validity would be shown if in fact the rotated solution showed that variables in each set loaded on the different factors and the patterns of loadings were similar to those obtained in the three separate component analyses conducted previously.

The strategy recommended here has considerable advantages over the typical use of factor analysis to "uncover" the latent constructs in a set of variables. It avoids arbitrary decisions about the number of factors that exist and ought to be rotated. Rather, one starts with theoretical ideas about the number of discriminable constructs and examines whether the data are consistent with those ideas. The approach here is very similar to that used in a confirmatory factor analysis (see chapter 8), although an overall test of the measurement model is not conducted.

Although this analysis could be extended to include all variables in a given dataset, attempting to show the discriminant validity of all of the underlying constructs of interest, we recommend examining issues of discriminant validity only in cases where one might reasonably suspect that two or more constructs may be similar to each other. Including all variables in a single component analysis is likely to be unwieldy and sample sizes insufficient.

Finally, although the assessment of a measurement model can only be conducted if each construct is measured with multiple variables, there are practical limits to the increase in internal consistency that can be achieved by adding additional measures. The well-known Spearman–Brown prophecy formula (see Judd and McClelland, 1998; Lord and Novik, 1968) defines those limits. Assuming that items that measure the same construct correlate at least .3 or more, increases in the internal consistency of a composite score constructed from those items become negligible beyond eight or nine items. We are not a fan of often-used scales that employ thirty or more items to measure a single construct. They try participants' patience and the benefits over shorter scales are negligible.

Analysis of Relations Among Constructs

Once a measurement model has been fleshed out, with composite scores for most of the constructs of interest,[2] then one is ready to examine the relationships among those constructs, specifying a series of linear additive models and estimating these, typically through ordinary least squares regression. The process of specifying and estimating these models must be a theoretically driven process, estimating and testing the coefficients of a system of linear models that derive from theoretical considerations. Although those theoretical considerations may be tentative and subject to considerable revision in light of the data, it is simply impossible to conduct a fully exploratory analysis at this point, "allowing the data to tell whatever story they have to tell."

This point is made most clearly by the simple deliberation about which variables are to be used as criterion or dependent variables in this system of equations and which variables will serve as predictors or independent variables. Of course, in a series of equations, it is exceedingly likely that a dependent variable in one estimated equation serves as a predictor variable in another. Nevertheless, for each equation estimated, the decisions about which variable should be the criterion (dependent variable) and which variables should be predictors (independent variables) must be theoretically driven. There are certainly likely to be indications from the employed research design about which variables are likely to fall into these two classes. For instance, with longitudinal data, it would be exceedingly unlikely that the criterion variable would be one measured earlier than the predictor(s). Similarly, stable individual differences variables (e.g. demographic variables) would be most likely included simply as predictor variables in the models. Nevertheless, the fundamental point is that with correlational data – even longitudinal correlational data – decisions about model specification necessarily are theoretical decisions.

Because of this, we strongly recommend that so-called automatic model building strategies, widely implemented in multiple regression software, not be utilized. For instance, stepwise regression and similar procedures that attempt to maximize the multiple R-squared of a model by selecting subsets of predictor variables, are to be avoided. Data analysis necessarily involves theory testing. Procedures such as stepwise regression simply attempt to minimize errors of prediction, regardless of whether the resulting model makes any theoretical sense at all. And, typically, such procedures are not even successful at accomplishing their stated aims.

Rather than using such automatic model building strategies, the data analyst needs to estimate a series of linear models that make theoretical sense. Of course, other analysts might look at the same set of data and estimate an entirely different set of models. Accordingly, one needs to be prepared to justify at a theoretical level the choices that one has made in specifying the models to be estimated. Once these models are estimated, then hypothesis testing proceeds via a model comparison process, the basics of which we outline in the following paragraphs. Additionally, we discuss the important issue of interpretation of parameter estimates in these models.

Model specification, comparison, and interpretation

As we have outlined elsewhere (Judd and McClelland, 1989; Judd, McClelland, and Culhane, 1995), hypothesis testing in the context of ordinary least squares regression models can be integrated under a "model comparison" approach. According to this approach, all inferential hypothesis testing involves the specification of an augmented model, in which some number of parameters are estimated from the data, and a compact model in which one or more of those parameters are constrained at *a priori* values. The number of parameters estimated in the augmented model is designated as PA. The number of parameters in the compact model is designated as PC (PC < PA, since the compact model constrains one or more parameters). The difference between the two models embodies the null hypothesis that is being tested by their comparison (i.e., that the parameter(s) equal the value(s) constrained in the compact model).

Each of these models, the augmented and compact, has an associated sum of squared errors, SSE(A) for the augmented model and SSE(C) for the compact one, which can be compared to determine whether the constraint(s) imposed under the compact model significantly reduce the quality of the fit of the model (or, equivalently, increase the sum of squared errors).

The comparison of augmented and compact models involves computing the proportional reduction in error (PRE) as one moves from the compact to the augmented model:

$$PRE = \frac{SSE(C) - SSE(A)}{SSE(C)}$$

Given degrees of freedom of PA − PC and N − PA (where N is the number of observations in the dataset), the computed value of PRE can be compared to critical values, tabled in Judd and McClelland (1989), to determine whether the reduction in error is significant (i.e., whether the constraint(s) embodied in Model C should be rejected). More conventionally, PRE can be converted to the usual F ratio, again with degrees of freedom equal to PA − PC and N − PA:

$$F_{PA-PC, N-PA} = \frac{PRE/(PA - PC)}{(1 - PRE)/(N - PA)}$$

and this statistic can be compared to commonly available tabled values of F.

This general outline of the process of hypothesis testing in ordinary least squares regression can be applied to many types of questions. The specifics of some of these are outlined in the following sections, in which we consider particular model comparisons likely to be of interest.

(A) Simple regression: Is X predictive of Y?

Model A: $\hat{Y}_i = b_0 + b_1 X_i$

Model C: $\hat{Y}_i = b_0$

The PRE associated with this model comparison is the squared Pearson product moment correlation. The null hypothesis is that the slope of the predictor equals zero, and equivalently that the correlation between Y and X equals zero. The square root of the resulting F statistics is the *t* statistic that is typically computed to determine whether a correlation differs from zero.

The parameter estimates in model A are the slope and intercept of simple regression. The slope represents the predicted difference in Y associated with a 1-unit difference in X. The intercept represents the predicted Y when X equals zero. When X is centered (i.e., computing $X'_i = (X_i - \bar{X})$ for each case and regressing Y on X′), the intercept equals the mean of Y.

(B) Multiple regression: Is a set of X's useful as predictors?

Model A: $\hat{Y}_i = b_0 + b_1 X_{1i} + b_2 X_{2i} + \ldots + b_p X_{pi}$

Model C: $\hat{Y}_i = b_0$

In this model comparison the null hypothesis is that all of the slopes are equal to zero. The resulting PRE for testing this null hypothesis is equivalent to the Multiple R-squared from model A. Equivalently, therefore, the null hypothesis is that the set of p predictor variables is unrelated to Y.

(C) Partial effects: Is a particular X useful as a predictor over and above the others?

Model A: $\hat{Y}_i = b_0 + b_1X_{1i} + b_2X_{2i} + \ldots + b_{p-1}X_{p-1i} + b_pX_{pi}$

Model C: $\hat{Y}_i = b_0 + b_1X_{1i} + b_2X_{2i} + \ldots + b_{p-1}X_{p-1i}$

This model comparison asks whether a particular predictor variable, designated as X_p, is useful over and above a set of other predictor variables. The null hypothesis is that its associated partial regression coefficient equals zero. PRE for this comparison equals the squared partial correlation between X_p and Y controlling for the set of other X's. An equivalent null hypothesis is that this partial correlation, as well as the partial regression coefficient, equals zero.

The F statistic that results from the above comparison is equivalent to the F that can be computed from the difference between the Multiple R-squares of the two models, commonly given in multiple regression texts (e.g., Cohen and Cohen, 1983). Note however, that the difference between two Multiple R-squares is itself not a PRE.

One could also compare a model A with the full set of predictors to a model C which leaves out two or more predictors. The resulting PRE and F from such a comparison can be estimated from the sums of squares of the two models. In general, we prefer model comparisons in which PA − PC equals 1 (i.e., the compact model only constrains a single parameter estimated in the augmented model), since rejection of a null hypothesis with multiple degrees of freedom in the numerator of F (i.e., PA − PC > 1) does not lead to unambiguous theoretical conclusions.

The parameter estimates associated with the predictors in model A are partial regression coefficients, or partial slopes. They are interpreted as the predicted difference in Y associated with a 1-unit difference in the particular X, holding constant all other predictors in the model. The power of multiple regression over simple regression models is this ability to "hold constant" other predictor variables, to examine a predicted difference "over and above" or "within-levels" of the other predictor variables. But this power is potentially misleading, as measurement error in the predictors can seriously bias the resulting coefficients. Additionally, of course, no degree of "partialling out other variables" can permit confident causal inference in the absence of a true randomized experimental design (Cook and Campbell, 1979; Judd and Kenny, 1981).

If all predictor variables are centered around their mean, then the intercept will continue to equal the mean value of Y, just as it does in the simple regression case.

(D) Tests of a priori values other than zero
All of the above model comparisons test null hypotheses that one or more regression coefficients equal zero. Although this is typically the question of interest, the model comparison approach permits one to formulate null hypotheses about any *a priori* value of a regression coefficient. For instance, suppose one measured the exact same variable at

two different points in time, Y_1 and Y_2. A test of perfect reliability, or equivalently the absence of regression to the mean (Campbell and Kenny, 1999), would be given by the following model comparison:

Model A: $\hat{Y}_{2i} = b_0 + b_1 Y_{1i}$

Model C: $\hat{Y}_{2i} = b_0 + Y_{1i}$

In model C the regression coefficient for Y_1 is set to the *a priori* value of 1, implying the absence of regression to the mean. To calculate PRE and F for this comparison, the least squares parameter estimates for both models need to be calculated, in order to compute the SSEs for both models. Although all regression procedures will estimate the model A parameters, only some statistical packages (e.g., SAS) permit one to estimate some parameters in a model while constraining others at nonzero values (for instance to estimate b_0 in model C).

If two predictors are measured in the same metric, then one can also compare models to ask whether they have equivalent effects. For instance, imagine that one wanted to know whether scores on the SAT math test and on the SAT verbal test were equally predictive of subsequent performance in college, as measured for instance by first year GPA. One would regress GPA on both SAT predictors and then ask whether they have equivalent slopes. The following models accomplish this:

Model A: $\hat{Y}_i = b_0 + b_1 X_{1i} + b_2 X_{2i}$

Model C: $\hat{Y}_i = b_0 + b_1 X_{1i} + b_1 X_{2i}$

Model C can be written equivalently as:

Model C: $\hat{Y}_i = b_0 + b_1 (X_{1i} + X_{2i})$

Thus, the appropriate PRE and F come from comparing an augmented model, in which both SAT variables are used as predictors, to a compact one in which their sum is used as a single predictor.

The question that this comparison asks (whether two predictors have the same partial regression coefficients) demands that the predictors be measured in the same metric, since partial regression coefficients are metric-specific (i.e., their magnitude depends on the units of measurement of the predictor and the criterion variable). To compare the effects of different predictors measured in different metrics, standardized slopes (commonly called beta weights) are often computed, redefining the metrics of all variables in standard deviation units. We do not encourage this practice, since the metric used in computing these standardized slopes is the sample variance. Sampling error will thus unduly impact standardized slopes even more than it does unstandardized ones.

(E) Categorical predictors and the analysis of variance and covariance

Our model comparison approach using multiple regression estimation can be easily extended to include categorical predictors as well as continuously varying ones. One

Table 7.1   Example illustrating the definition of contrast-coded predictors

	Category levels			
Predictors	A	B	C	D
X1	−1	−1	1	1
X2	−1	1	0	0
X3	0	0	−1	1

must code those categorical predictors using some numerical convention. We strongly endorse the use of contrast-coded predictors for this purpose (Abelson and Prentice, 1997; Judd and McClelland, 1989; Rosenthal and Rosnow, 1985). In general, if a categorical predictor has m discrete levels, then $m-1$ contrast-coded predictors must be used. Two conditions define contrast-coded predictors. First, the sum of the category values for any one predictor must add up to zero. Second, the sum of the product of category values for every pair of predictors, summed across categories, must equal zero.

To illustrate, consider the example in table 7.1. Here we have a categorical variable with four discrete levels: A, B, C, and D. Accordingly, three contrast-coded predictors must be defined, and every observation is given values on these three predictors according to the category in which it resides. The three contrast-coded predictors we have chosen to define this categorical variable are X1, X2, and X3, with values as indicated in the table. Thus, an observation in level B of the categorical variable would be assigned values of −1, +1, and 0 on the three predictors. For each of these three predictors, the sum of the values across category levels (summing within any row of the table) equals zero. Additionally, the sum of the product of values between any two predictors, across category levels, also equals zero.[3]

A model in which the dependent variable is regressed on a set of contrast-coded predictors is equivalent to a one-way analysis of variance (ANOVA). The overall test of the model, testing whether the set of contrast-coded predictors is useful, asks whether there are any significant mean differences in Y among the levels of the categorical predictor. The partial regression coefficient associated with any given contrast-coded predictor estimates the mean difference in Y across the levels of the categorical predictor coded by that particular contrast code. Thus, tests of individual parameters associated with individual predictors are tests of single degree of freedom contrasts among condition means coded by those predictors. For instance, given the codes defined in table 7.1, a test of the partial regression coefficient for X1 would test whether there is a significant difference between the means of categories C and D and the means of categories A and B. A test of the X2 coefficient would compare the means of categories B and A. And a test of the X3 coefficient would test the D − C mean difference.

When a model includes both categorical and continuous predictors, then it is equivalent to an analysis of covariance model (ANCOVA). Testing the set of contrast-coded predictors associated with a categorical predictor asks whether there are differences in Y across the levels of the categorical variable controlling for the continuous predictor (i.e., the coviariate). Equivalently, it asks whether the "adjusted" means, adjusted for the covariate, differ. Such adjusted means are computed as:

$$\bar{Y}'_k = \bar{Y}_k - b_c(\bar{C}_k - \bar{C}_{\bullet})$$

where $\bar{Y}_k$ is the mean of the kth level of the categorical variable, $\bar{Y}'_k$ is the adjusted mean for that level, b_c is the partial regression coefficient for the covariate, $\bar{C}_k$ is the mean of the covariate for the kth level of the categorical variable, and $\bar{C}_{\bullet}$ is the covariate grand mean (computed across all observations). Tests of individual partial regression coefficients for the contrast-coded predictor variables ask whether the adjusted cell means coded by that particular contrast-coded predictor differ. Again, one must be cautious in interpreting these differences. While cell differences on the covariate are "controlled" (or "held constant") in these comparisons, causal inference remains impossible in the absence of random assignment to levels of the categorical predictor.

(F) Moderation or interaction models

Theory often predicts interactions among variables: the effect of one predictor variable depends on the level of another one. Indeed, important theoretical traditions have interactions at their core, wherein behavior is a result of the interaction of the person with the situation.

Interactions are modeled by using partialled products as predictors (Cohen, 1978). That is, a predictor is included that is the product of two variables that are also used as predictors. Thus the following model comparison tests whether the effect of one predictor depends on the second:

Model A: $\hat{Y}_i = b_0 + b_1 X_{1i} + b_2 X_{2i} + b_3(X_{1i}X_{2i})$

Model C: $\hat{Y}_i = b_0 + b_1 X_{1i} + b_2 X_{2i}$

The coefficient for the product in model A captures the interaction between X_1 and X_2. It is the coefficient of a *partialled* product, since the two component variables that are used to compute the product are included simultaneously as predictors.

To understand why the partialled product estimates the interaction, it is helpful to rewrite the above model A, focusing on the "simple" relationship between Y and one of the two X predictors (Judd and McClelland, 1989). The following is an equivalent expression of models A and C, focusing on the "simple effect" of X_2:

Model A: $\hat{Y}_i = (b_0 + b_1 X_{1i}) + (b_2 + b_3 X_{1i})X_{2i}$

Model C: $\hat{Y}_i = (b_0 + b_1 X_{1i}) + (b_2)X_{2i}$

As these re-expressions make clear, model C assumes that as the value of X_1 changes, the "simple" intercept for X_2 changes, but its slope is invariant. Model A, on the other hand, allows both the "simple" intercept and the "simple" slope for X_2 to vary as X_1 changes in value.

The interpretation of parameter estimates in models with product predictor variables must be done carefully. The key to this interpretation lies in the simple effects re-expression of model A given immediately above. In this simple effects re-expression, the simple slope for X_2 equals $(b_2 + b_3X_1)$. This slope can be interpreted as any simple slope: it tells us the predicted difference in Y for each unit difference in X_2. Clearly that predicted difference varies in magnitude as X_1 varies in value. As X_1 increases in value by one unit, the simple slope for X_2 increases by X_3 units. Thus the regression coefficient for the product predictor tell us the change in the simple slope for one of the predictors as the other predictor increases by 1 unit. This is the meaning of an interaction: the slope for one predictor depends on the value of another.

The other partial regression coefficients in the model are also simple slopes, but they are simple slopes for one of the variables when (and only when) the other variable in the interaction equals zero. From the simple slope for X_2 given above $(b_2 + b_3X_1)$, it is clear that b_2, the regression coefficient for X_2 in the interactive model, equals the simple slope for X_2 when (and only when) X_1 equals zero. The same interpretation holds for b_1, given an equivalent re-expression of model A that enables us to focus on the simple slope for X_1:

Model A: $\hat{Y}_i = (b_0 + b_2X_{2i}) + (b_1 + b_3X_{2i})X_{1i}$

Because of the fact that the interactive model can be re-expressed in these two different ways, focusing on the simple slope for either X_1 or X_2, the regression coefficient for the product predictor has either of the following two equivalent interpretations: (1) the change in the simple slope for X_1 as X_2 increases in value 1 unit; (2) the change in the simple slope for X_2 as X_1 increases in value 1 unit. The regression coefficients associated with the two component variables, b_1 and b_2, tell us about the simple slope for each variable when and only when the other component variable equals zero. Importantly, these should *not* be interpreted as the overall partial regression coefficient or the "main effect" of the component variable. They estimate the effect of each component variable when and only when the other component variable equals zero. For many variables, of course, values of zero may not be meaningful.

Aiken and West (1991) recommend centering both component variables (i.e., recomputing the scores of every observation on each variable as deviations from the variable's mean), computing the product of the centered variables, and then estimating model A with the centered components and their product as predictors. Doing this changes the meaning of a zero value on the components: now zero equals the mean value of each variable. Accordingly, such centering will change the values of both b_1 and b_2, but will leave the coefficient for the interaction product unchanged. The values of b_1 and b_2 can, with centering, be interpreted as simple effects of each component variable at the mean level of the other component variable. This seems to us to be a very helpful recommendation.

The variables could be centered around other values than their mean, if one desired to estimate simple effects at values other than the mean. In general, if one of the component variables, say X_1, is centered around some value, C, then the coefficient for the other component variable, X_2, in the model that includes the product of the two as a predictor, estimates the simple effect of X_2 when X_1 equals C.

As Aiken and West (1991) have discussed, standardized regression coefficients in interactive models are particularly difficult to interpret because the product of two standardized variables is itself not standardized. This is one more reason why we prefer to avoid the interpretation of standardized regression coefficients.

Higher order interactions can be modeled by higher ordered products (e.g., the product of X_1, X_2, and X_3), with the restriction that all components of such products, including the component variables themselves as well as the lower order product components, are partialled. For instance, if the triple interaction among X_1, X_2, and X_3 is tested, both models A and C must include as predictors the three two-way products between all possible pairs of the predictors. Interpretation of partial regression coefficients for the components follows the general rule given above for two-way interactions: the regression coefficient for any component of a higher order product included in a model estimates the simple effect of that component when the other component(s) with which one must multiply it to get the highest order product in the model equals zero. For example, if the $X_1X_2X_3$ triple product is included as a predictor (along with all of its components), the partial regression coefficient for the X_1X_2 product estimates the effect of that two-way interaction when and only when X_3 equals zero. In general, given such complications, centering component variables in moderator models around their means is a highly recommended practice.

(G) Models of mediation

Judd and Kenny (1981) and Baron and Kenny (1986) have outlined analyses to be conducted in support of the theoretical argument that one variable mediates the effect of a treatment variable on an outcome. By mediation here, we mean that the mediating variable is responsible for the causal process that links the treatment variable with the outcome, i.e., it is because the treatment induces a change in the mediator that the ultimate outcome variable is affected.

Frequently the mediational analyses recommended in this literature have been used with correlational data, where causal treatment effects cannot be clearly demonstrated because observations have not been randomly assigned to treatment versus control conditions. We have substantial reservations about talking about mediation in this case, since mediation seems to us to imply the prior demonstration of a causal effect of the treatment on the outcome. Nevertheless, the analyses that have been recommended for assessing mediation can be conducted with purely correlational data.

Mediational analyses involve the estimation of a series of models. First, an overall treatment effect must be demonstrated, showing that the treatment variable of interest has an effect on the outcome variable. This analysis involves a model comparison which tests whether the slope of the treatment variable is different from zero. Of course, with correlational data, all that really can be concluded from this comparison is that the treatment variable is predictive of the outcome rather than that it exerts a causal effect on the outcome.

Second, one must demonstrate that the treatment variable is predictive of the mediator, estimating and testing an additional simple regression model with the mediator as the dependent variable.

Third, one estimates a model in which both the treatment variable and the mediator are used to predict the outcome variable. Two results are obtained if mediation is to be argued. First, the mediator must significantly predict the outcome once the treatment variable is controlled. Second, the slope associated with the treatment variable must be reduced (in absolute value) compared to its slope in the model where only the treatment is used to predict the outcome and the mediator is not controlled. While the first of these results can be tested with a simple model comparison between this model (using both treatment and mediator as predictors) and a model where only the treatment variable is a predictor, the second result cannot be easily accomplished in a model comparison framework. Rather, the magnitude of two dependent regression coefficients must be compared. The most frequently recommended procedure for doing this involves using the Sobel test, presented in detail in Kenny, Kashy, and Bolger (1998).

It is important to recognize that this mediational analysis is in fact no different from any other partialled analysis, in which one wishes to argue that a partialled slope is different in magnitude from an unpartialled one, i.e., in which some other variable is not statistically controlled. The only thing that distinguishes a mediational analysis from one in which partialled effects are estimated is the causal theoretical model that the data analyst has in mind. A clear causal chain is hypothesized in which the treatment variable affects the mediator, which in turn affects the outcome. This is a rather different model from one in which there are numerous simultaneous predictors of an outcome and one seeks simply to estimate the effects of each, partialling out the others. But the difference lies in the implicit (and hopefully explicit) causal model, not in the analyses that are actually conducted.

One partial approach to examining the adequacy of the theoretical model of mediation comes if one switches the role of the mediator and outcome variables. Consider the two causal models in figure 7.1. The top one is the mediational model, in which variable M is presumed to mediate the effect of X (the treatment) on O (the outcome). The analyses described in the preceding paragraphs provide estimates of the effects in this model. Instead of this model, one might estimate the second model, switching the roles of M and O. Hopefully, this would lead to the conclusion that O fails to mediate the

Mediation: M mediates the X – O effect

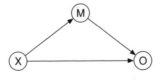

Reverse mediation: O does not mediate the X – M effect

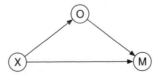

Figure 7.1 Mediational and reverse mediational models.

X – M relationship. To do this, one would estimate the regression models previously described, but the third one would involve regressing the mediator on the treatment variable and the outcome variable, rather than the outcome variable on the treatment variable and the mediator. One would like to argue that the slope of the treatment variable on the outcome is reduced in magnitude once the mediator is controlled. The argument for mediation is certainly strengthened if in the model where the mediator is treated as the dependent variable, the slope of the treatment variable is not reduced in magnitude once the outcome variable is controlled.

Assumptions, Their Violation, and Other Data Problems

Inferential tests of parameters in linear models estimated through ordinary least squares procedures (including analysis of variance and multiple regression) require three assumptions about the distribution of residuals or errors. First, it is assumed that those residuals are normally distributed around predicted values. Second, it is assumed that they come from a single normal distribution, with a constant variance. This second assumption is known as the homoscedasticity assumption. Third, it is assumed that residuals are sampled independently from their distribution. In other words, knowing the value of one residual tells you nothing about the value of any other.

Outliers in a dataset may lead to serious violations of the first two assumptions. We start this section of the chapter by considering procedures for detecting and dealing with outliers. Our discussion here relies largely on McClelland (2000). We then consider other remedies for violations of the first two assumptions. Finally, we discuss in some detail the third assumption, since dependence in data can result in serious bias in inferential tests of parameters.

Outliers

There are three types of outliers that can be identified. Each type of outlier has a different impact on the analysis, and identification of each requires computation of a different statistic. All three of these are readily obtainable with most general purpose multiple regression programs.

Outliers with extreme values on a predictor variable

Extreme values on a predictor affect the magnitude of the slope found between the predictor (X) and criterion (Y) because more weight is given to extreme predictor values in calculating the slope. Extreme values on the predictor also artificially increase the range of the predictor, thereby inflating the observed partial correlation between the predictor and criterion over and above the other predictors. As a result, one is more likely to make a Type I error and falsely conclude there is a relationship between X and Y if there are extreme values on X. To identify outliers on X, one should examine levers for each observation (also called hat statistics, commonly given as a regression diagnostic statistic in most regression software; in SPSS called LEVER; in SAS called H). Levers indicate the degree to which a parameter(s) is determined by each single data point. Any observation with a lever at or near 1.0 should be of concern, as that value indicates that the observation is essentially completely determining one of the model parameters. The maximum lever value is the number of parameters estimated in the model.

Outliers with extreme values on the criterion
Extreme values on the criterion have a different effect. Outliers on Y increase the overall error in the model. As a result, they increase the chances of making Type II errors. Identification of outliers on Y is accomplished by calculating the studentized deleted residual for each observation (again, this is a common regression diagnostic statistic, called SDRESID in SPSS and RSTUDENT in SAS). This statistic is distributed as a *t* statistic and tests whether errors of prediction are significantly reduced when a single additional parameter is dedicated to predicting a particular observation's Y value perfectly. Since one computes this statistic for every observation, one expects many of them, in large datasets, to exceed typical .05 cutoffs for the *t* distribution. Accordingly, values of 3 or 4 are typically indicative of serious outlier problems.

Outliers with extreme values on both the predictor and the criterion
Even though a particular outlier may not emerge as worrisome in either of the above cases, it may still problematically influence parameter estimates if it is relatively extreme simultaneously on both Y and X. The Cook's D statistic is conceptually similar to the product of the lever and studentized deleted residual for each observation (in SPSS called COOK; in SAS called COOKD). Hence, relatively large values of this statistic can be used to identify observations that are relatively extreme simultaneously on the predictor and criterion.

Once outliers have been identified, we suggest dropping them from the data. Although this recommendation may be considered controversial, it is consistent with the goal of constructing a story about the relationships present in a set of data. If a few observations have the potential to dramatically alter that story, we find it less averse to delete them from the analysis than to report a story that is really due to those observations.

We do not recommend going through the process of identifying and deleting outliers iteratively. Because outliers are determined by the relative position of observations in a sample, it is possible that after deleting the first set of outliers, one would find more unusual observations in successive examinations of the data, even though the observations appeared fine in the initial diagnosis. This iterative process could be practically unending. Accordingly, we recommend that for each model estimated, outlier statistics be computed once, and appropriate remedial actions taken. But an iterative process is generally not helpful.

Detecting violations of the normality assumption

The normality assumption concerns only the residuals in a regression model. There is no need to assume that predictor variables are normally distributed, nor is a nonnormally distributed criterion variable necessarily a problem. Rather, it is the errors of prediction from a model that are assumed to be normally distributed.

Violations of normality can result from a variety of factors. Tails of residual distributions that are thicker than those of a normal distribution, or tails skewed toward more extreme observations at one end of a distribution, produce nonnormal distributions. The primary concern in checking the normality assumption is to detect especially thick or skewed tails of a distribution of residuals. Although several approaches to diagnosing nonnormal distributions have been suggested (inspection of the partial regression plots, tests for nonnormality), they often focus on deviations from normality that do not endanger the validity of an analysis. McClelland (2000) suggested that the best tool for detecting departures from normality is the normal quantile–quantile plot. Basically, the normal quantile–quantile plot displays residuals in rank-order on the ordinate against the quantiles one would expect if the data were normally distributed on the abscissa. (See McClelland, 2000, for precise methods of computing the normal quantile–quantile plot.) If the data are normally distributed, then the points should all fall along a straight line on the diagonal of the plot. If the data are not normal, on the other hand, there will be systematic departures from this diagonal line. Of particular concern is the behavior of points at the bottom and top of the distribution. If the points toward either end produce a flatter slope than the diagonal, then the tails of the distribution are thinner than one would expect in a normal distribution. But if the points form a slope that is steeper than the diagonal line at either end, then fatter-than-expected tails are indicated. Skewness is present if one tail is relatively fat and one is relative thin. Fat tails at both ends (e.g., a Cauchy distribution; McClelland, 2000) are particularly problematic.

Detecting violations of the homogeneity of variance assumption

Violations of the homogeneity of variance assumption exist when the variability or spread of residuals is systematically related to the magnitude of predicted values. Most statistical packages will produce plots of errors of prediction as a function of predicted values. Departures from the homogeneity assumption are indicated if such plots reveal a funnel shape (i.e., if the variance of residuals either increases or decreases at higher predicted values) or other departures from a spherical shape, indicating nonlinear relations between the spread of residuals and predicted values. Even more useful than residual-by-prediction plots are spread-location plots (Cleveland, 1993) that display the absolute errors (or square roots of the absolute errors) as a function of the predicted values.

Methods to treat nonnormality and heterogeneity of variance

In general, we recommend data transformations to correct problems of nonnormality and heterogeneity of variance. It is rare in the behavioral sciences for our measured variables to be measured in psychologically meaningful metrics. Accordingly, we see little reason to avoid monotonic data transformation that effectively deal with assumption violations.

Power transformations (Tukey, 1977; Box and Cox, 1964) are most useful for dealing with skewed distributions. One simply computes a new criterion variable, W_i, as follows:

$$W_i = Y_i^p$$

where p can be any positive or negative value. Power transformations with values of p larger than 1 reduce negative skew in Y; power transformations with values of p smaller than 1 reduce positive skew in Y. The larger the departure of p from 1, the more potent the transformation. Of course when $p = 0$, the transformation is undefined. The log transformation is commonly used in its stead (i.e., to remove positive skew).

Other transformations can be effective as well depending on the ways in which the model assumptions are violated. One very useful transformation is the rank transformation, in which one analyzes simply the rank ordering of individual observations on Y. Such analyses can be shown to be equivalent to many nonparametric statistical procedures (McClelland, 2000). There exist other commonly used transformations which are particularly useful for measures whose departures from nonnormality take characteristic forms. For instance, a square root transformation is recommended for data that consist of frequency counts, log or inverse transformations are recommended for reaction time data, and logit or probit transformations are useful for proportions. (See Judd and McClelland, 1989, for other examples.)

If a measured variable is only dichotomous, then such transformations will have no effect. Accordingly, in such cases one must use procedures such as logistic regression, where the normality of residuals assumption is not made. However, the full range of models that we outlined earlier can be estimated with logistic regression.

Violations of the independence assumption

Although normality and homogeneity of variance assumptions are considered to be robust to violation (but see McClelland, 2000), the independence assumption is not. The assumption is violated whenever there exist links between individual observations in a dataset, and linked observations are more (or less) similar than unlinked ones. Links can arise from many different factors. For instance, if participants are measured more than once, observations within a participant are linked. If multiple individuals from different families are measured, observations within families are linked. In general, whenever there are nestings in the data, such that observations are nested within persons, couples, families, classrooms, etc., dependence is a potential problem. Positive dependence exists when linked observations are more similar than unlinked ones; negative dependence exists when linked observations are less similar than unlinked ones.

The bias introduced by dependence depends on three factors: the magnitude of dependence, whether that dependence is positive or negative, and the nature of the relationship between a predictor variable and the nestings responsible for the dependence. A thorough discussion of all three factors can be found in Kenny, Kashy, and Bolger (1998). Kenny and Judd (1986) consider dependence-induced bias in analysis of variance designs.

In general, to assess dependence one calculates an intraclass correlation, estimating the degree to which linked observations are more or less similar than unlinked ones. Although tests of the intraclass correlation can be conducted to determine whether dependence is significant, any degree of dependence must be treated carefully, since serious bias can result from only relatively modest intraclass correlations.

Procedures for dealing with dependent data have been well worked out in analysis of variance, where within-subject or repeated measures analysis of variance are routinely conducted. Procedures within a multiple regression framework are much less widely known, although models in which sums and differences among linked observations serve as the criterion variables avoid the assumption violations (see Judd, 2000; Judd and McClelland, 1989). Judd, Kenny, and McClelland (2001) have expanded this approach to incorporate models involving mediation and moderation.

More general and highly recommended approaches to the analysis of dependent data involve what are known as multilevel modeling procedures that have now been implemented in a number of different computer programs (Bryk and Raudenbush, 1992; Kenny, Kashy, and Bolger, 1998; Snijders and Bosker, 1999). Such approaches can also be incorporated within a latent variable structural equation approach to data analysis. (Again, see chapter 8, this volume.)

In this section we have emphasized the importance of examining assumptions and correcting their violations more than many other treatments. Additionally, we strongly encourage the search for obviously outlying data points and their elimination from datasets prior to analysis. It seems to us very unwise to let a few unruly data points and strange distributions seriously distort the theoretical story that a set of data has to tell.

Conclusions

Large correlational datasets present imposing analytic challenges. The most important of these is that analyses must be guided by theoretical models since there is no structure to the data, other perhaps than time lags, that can be used to determine the status of particular variables in analyses. Decisions about which variables are treated as dependent, which ones are predictors, and which are potential mediators and moderators, must be guided almost exclusively by theoretical considerations.

As a result, the conclusions that are reached from data analysis speak only to the particular theoretical model that has guided that analysis. Those conclusions can certainly refine and qualify the model that one started with, but there will always remain plausible alternative models to explain the covariances among the variables in the dataset. In other words, as in most science, what we hope to take away from the data is a reasonable and clear theoretical story. That story is not the exclusive one that could be told, but if the data permit a compelling story, then that story is given increased credence and may guide others in constructing their own theoretical stories.

We have highlighted a number of dangers or pitfalls that lie along the path of constructing a reasonable theoretical story through the analysis of a correlational dataset. One obvious one involves the use of single indicator measurement models, in essence assuming the absence of measurement error. Another danger arises from the likely existence of outlying observations in datasets that can considerably alter the story one tells. Similarly, violations of assumptions that underlie the least squares analytic model, particularly the independence assumption, can substantially bias the story one tells. Finally, and perhaps most importantly, ultimately the best we can do with correlational datasets is argue that the data are consistent with stories about causal mechanisms that link theoretical constructs. They lend support to these mechanisms, but other data structures (i.e., involving randomized experimental designs) are required if one really wants to elaborate a causal argument.

At the same time, and in conclusion, we do not want to be too pessimistic about what can be learned through the analysis of correlational datasets. There is nothing that feels better than having a theoretical story that one would like to tell and having a rich dataset, with constructs well measured, that permits one both to tell that story in a convincing manner and to refine it at the same time. That is ultimately the pleasure of data analysis.

Notes

1   Because the specific loadings have associated with them sampling error, unit weights generally perform as well as using the factor loadings as weights. It is obviously important, however, to reverse items that have negative loadings. Additionally, summing standardized scores is preferable to summing the raw values, unless all variables are measured in the same metric and have equivalent variances.
2   Some constructs are reasonably measured with single indicators, making the assumption of error-free measurement. Gender is one such.
3   These codes are one set among many sets that could have been used. A perfectly good alternative set, for instance, would have values for X1 of 3, −1, −1, −1, for X2 of 0, 2, −1, −1, and for X3 of 0, 0, 1, −1 across the A, B, C, and D levels. The choice of sets of codes depends on the specific comparisons among the various category means that one wishes to make, following the logic in the next paragraph.

References

Abelson, R. P., and Prentice, D. A. (1997). Contrast tests of interaction hypothesis. *Psychological Methods, 2*, 315–28.

Aiken, L. S., and West, S. G. (1991). *Multiple regression: Testing and interpreting interactions.* Newbury Park, CA: Sage.

Baron, R. M., and Kenny, D. A. (1986). The moderator–mediator variable distinction in social psychological research: Conceptual, strategic, and statistical considerations. *Journal of Personality and Social Psychology, 51*, 1173–82.

Bentler, P. M. (1968). Alpha-maximized factor analysis and its relation to alpha and canonical factor analysis. *Psychometrika, 33*, 335–46.

Bentler, P. M. (1995). *EQS structural equations program manual.* Encino, CA: Multivariate Software.

Box, G. E. P., and Cox, D. R. (1964). An analysis of transformations (with discussion). *Journal of the Royal Statistical Society B, 26*, 211–46.

Bryk, A. S., and Raudenbush, S. W. (1992). *Hierarchical linear models*. Newbury Park, CA: Sage.

Campbell, D. T., and Fiske, D. W. (1959). Convergent and discriminant validation by the multitrait–multimethod matrix. *Psychological Bulletin, 56*, 81–105.

Campbell, D. T., and Kenny, D. A. (1999). *A primer on regression artifacts*. New York: Guilford Press.

Campbell, D. T., and Stanley, J. C. (1963). *Experimental and quasi-experimental designs for research*. Chicago, IL: Rand McNally.

Campbell, D. T., and Stanley, J. C. (1966). *Experimental and quasi-experimental designs for research*. Boston, MA: Houghton Mifflin.

Cleveland, W. S. (1993). *Visualizing data*. Summit, NJ: Hobart Press.

Cohen, J. (1978). Partialed products are interactions; partialed powers are curve components. *Psychological Bulletin, 85*, 858–66.

Cohen, J., and Cohen, P. (1983). *Applied multiple regression/correlation for the behavioral sciences* (2nd edn.). Hillsdale, NJ: Erlbaum.

Cook, T. D., and Campbell, D. T. (1979). *Quasi-experimentation: Design and analysis issues for field settings*. Boston, MA: Houghton Mifflin.

Cronbach, L. J. (1951). Coefficient alpha and the internal structure of tests. *Psychometrika, 16*, 297–334.

Gorsuch, R. L. (1983). *Factor analysis* (2nd edn.). Hillsdale, NJ: Erlbaum.

Harmon, H. H. (1976). *Modern factor analysis* (3rd edn.). Chicago, IL: University of Chicago Press.

Joreskog, K. G., and Sorbom, D. (1993). *LISREL 8: Structural equation modeling with the SIMPLIS command language*. Chicago, IL: Scientific Software International.

Judd, C. M. (2000). Everyday data analysis in social psychology: Comparisons of linear models. In H. T. Reis and C. M. Judd (eds.), *Handbook of research methods in social and personality psychology* (pp. 370–92). Cambridge: Cambridge University Press.

Judd, C. M., and Kenny, D. A. (1981). *Estimating the effects of social interventions*. New York: Cambridge University Press.

Judd, C. M., and McClelland, G. H. (1989). *Data analysis: A model comparison approach*. San Diego, CA: Harcourt, Brace, Jovanovich.

Judd, C. M., and McClelland, G. H. (1998). Measurement. In D. Gilbert, S. T. Fiske, and G. Lindzey (eds.), *The handbook of social psychology* (4th edn., pp. 180–232). New York: McGraw-Hill.

Judd, C. M., Kenny, D. A., and McClelland, G. H. (2001). Estimating and testing mediation and moderation in within-participant designs. *Psychological Methods, 6*, 115–34.

Judd, C. M., McClelland, G. H. and Culhane, S. E. (1995). Data analysis: Continuing issues in the everyday analysis of psychological data. *Annual Review of Psychology, 46*, 433–65.

Kenny, D. A., and Judd, C. M. (1986). Consequences of violating the independence assumption in analysis of variance. *Psychological Bulletin, 99*, 422–31.

Kenny, D. A., and Kashy, D. A. (1992). Analysis of the multitrait–multimethod matrix by confirmatory factor analysis. *Psychological Bulletin, 112*, 165–72.

Kenny, D. A., Kashy, D. A., and Bolger, N. (1998). Data analysis in social psychology. In D. Gilbert, S. T. Fiske, and G. Lindzey (eds.), *The handbook of social psychology* (4th edn., vol. 1, pp. 233–65). New York: McGraw-Hill.

Lord, F., and Novick, M. R. (1968). *Statistical theories of mental tests*. New York: Addison Wesley.

McClelland, G. H. (2000). Nasty data: unruly, ill-mannered observations can ruin your analysis. In H. T. Reis and C. M. Judd (eds.), *Handbook of research methods in social and personality psychology* (pp. 393–411). Cambridge: Cambridge University Press.

Rosenthal, R., and Rosnow, R. L. (1985). *Contrast analysis: Focused comparisons in the analysis of variance*. Cambridge: Cambridge University Press.

Snijders, T. A. B., and Bosker, R. J. (1999). *Multilevel analysis: An introduction to basic and advanced multilevel modeling*. London: Sage.

Tukey, J. W. (1977). *Exploratory data analysis*. Reading, MA: Addison-Wesley.

Wegener, D. T., and Fabrigar, L. R. (2000). Analysis and design for nonexperimental data: Addressing causal and noncausal hypotheses. In H. T. Reis and C. M. Judd (eds.), *Handbook of research methods in social and personality psychology* (pp. 412–50). Cambridge: Cambridge University Press.

CHAPTER EIGHT

Structural Equation Modeling in Clinical Psychology Research

Samuel B. Green and Marilyn S. Thompson

Increasingly, clinical psychologists are discovering the utility of structural equation modeling (SEM) for testing a wide range of hypotheses. SEM is commonly applied to research problems that include validating the factor structure of psychological instruments and evaluating complex theories specifying the causal relationships among constructs. We focus the present chapter on SEM topics selected based on our review of current statistical practice in clinical research. We chose to discuss a limited number of specific topics rather than present a broad overview because of the extensive literature that already exists on SEM. This literature includes introductory-level (e.g., Kline, 1998) and more advanced textbooks (e.g., Bollen, 1989; Kaplan, 2000), chapters in the *Annual Review of Psychology* (Bentler and Dudgeon, 1996; MacCallum and Austin, 2000), annotated bibliographies of the SEM literature (Austin and Wolfle, 1991; Austin and Calerón, 1996), and the journal *Structural Equation Modeling*, as well as a special section on SEM in the *Journal of Consulting and Clinical Psychology* in 1994. The five SEM topics we discuss are coefficient alpha and SEM alternatives, multivariate analyses of means, nonnormal data, exploratory analyses, and model equivalency. Below, we briefly describe these five topics and our rationale for including them in this chapter.

Many researchers may not identify the first two topics – coefficient alpha and multivariate analyses of means – as associated with SEM. Coefficient alpha is commonly used to support the psychometric quality of measurement instruments, and multivariate analysis of variance (MANOVA) is routinely applied to assess group differences on multiple dependent variables. We argue coefficient alpha and MANOVA are not well understood and are frequently misapplied and misinterpreted. Methods using SEM offer alternatives to these approaches, although they must be judiciously applied.

The remaining topics discussed in this chapter – analysis of nonnormal data, exploratory analyses, and model equivalency – are methodological issues that apply to many clinical applications of SEM. Clinical psychologists frequently analyze dichotomous or polytomous items or scale scores with skewed distributions. Because of the pervasiveness of nonnormal data in clinical research, we summarize the consequences of ignoring nonnormality and provide a review of current techniques for analzying nonnormal data.

Clinical researchers construct complex theories to account for a variety of abnormal behaviors and model the treatment processes for individuals who display these behaviors. The initially specified models based on these theories may not fit well. However, a researcher may feel it would be wasteful and unproductive not to explore further these models and attempt to modify them to produce better fit, particularly since these studies often involve large samples of participants who are difficult to recruit. Additionally, the guidelines for conducting and reporting model modifications are not well documented, so we felt it important to discuss exploratory SEM methods.

Finally, we discuss equivalent models. If a hypothesized model is found to be consistent with the data, it is tempting to conclude that the model was affirmed and, therefore, that the hypothesized causal relationships were substantiated. However, these conclusions are unwarranted unless alternative explanations for the causal relationships can be ruled out. Researchers should routinely examine their models to determine whether equivalent models are viable alternative explanations for their results.

In the next two sections we first describe the results of a review that documents the growth of SEM applications in the clinical literature. We then give a brief overview of SEM to offer a foundation for our discussion of the five specific SEM topics presented in the remaining part of the chapter.

SEM Applications in the Clinical Psychology Literature

In order to better describe the increasing frequency and diversity of SEM applications in clinical psychology research, we surveyed empirical articles appearing in the *Journal of Consulting and Clinical Psychology* (*JCCP*) and *Psychological Assessment* (*PA*) for 1989 and 1999. In both publications the proportion of empirical articles employing SEM was substantially greater in 1999 than in 1989. Specifically, in *JCCP*, the percent of empirical articles utilizing SEM was 4.1 percent in 1989 and 7.0 percent in 1999. In *PA*'s first year of publication, 1989, 5.4 percent of empirical articles employed SEM, increasing to 27.5 percent in 1999.

Particularly in *JCCP*, the models evaluated using SEM have broadened from confirmatory factor analysis (CFA) and path analysis to more elaborate applications, including longitudinal models involving structural relationships among latent variables. In 1989 only 4 of 98 empirical articles published in *JCCP* utilized SEM approaches. Two of these applications were path analyses in which parameter estimates were obtained via multiple regression analysis rather than solving simultaneously for the multiple parameters using SEM software (Atwood, Gold, and Taylor, 1989; Draucker, 1989). LISREL was used in one case to estimate a path analytic model (Swaim et al., 1989), and only one study published in *JCCP* in 1989 specified and evaluated measurement and structural models containing latent variables (Fisher et al., 1989). In 1999, 7 of 100 empirical articles in

JCCP utilized SEM approaches, but more noteworthy is the observation that all except one of these SEM applications involved latent variables. The types and frequencies of models represented were path analysis (1), CFA (2), and models with structural relations among latent variables (4). Of the full latent variable models, more advanced applications of SEM, such as growth curve analysis (Irvine et al., 1999) and multisample longitudinal analysis (Redmond et al., 1999), were utilized.

As a journal devoted to assessment, it is not surprising that *PA* publishes many instrument validation studies using CFA models. In fact, all studies involving SEM published in *PA* in both 1989 and 1999 evaluated CFA models. In 1989 only 3 of 56 empirical articles in *PA* reported results of SEM analyses. These involved CFA models estimated with LISREL, including studies investigating measurement invariance across groups (Golding and Aneshensel, 1989; Lanyon et al., 1989) and comparisons of multiple factor models (Tracey and Kokotovic, 1989). By 1999 a wide range of CFA strategies was applied in 11 of 40 empirical studies. These included consideration of multiple fit indices (Bowden, Carstairs, and Shores, 1999), exploratory strategies for modifying unsatisfactory models (Bowden, Carstairs, and Shores, 1999; Sanford, Bingham, and Zucker, 1999), and, for nonnormal data, item parcels (Osman et al., 1999; Sanford, Bingham, and Zucker, 1999) and alternative estimation methods (Long and Brekke, 1999).

Others have noted a similar trend in the prevalence of SEM in psychological research. Hoyle (1994) conducted a review of statistical methodologies employed by clinical researchers, tallying methods used in *JCCP* articles for the years 1972, 1982, and 1992. He found no mention of SEM in 1972 and 1982, while 8.7 percent of articles published in 1992 utilized SEM.

Perhaps due to improved user-friendliness of SEM software, increasing accessibility of instructive SEM texts (e.g. Kline, 1998; Maruyama, 1998), and inclusion of SEM in graduate curricula, SEM is slowly becoming a useful data-analytic strategy for clinical researchers. Clinical psychologists are using SEM to address an increasingly wider range of research hypotheses, including multiple group comparisons and growth curve models. Further, there is an increasing awareness of analysis options such as procedures for handling nonnormal data and for conducting specification searches.

Overview of SEM

In SEM researchers hypothesize a model and then assess whether the model is consistent with the data. In many applications the data are the variances and covariances among the measured variables. A model fits well if it statistically accounts for the variances and covariances among the measured variables. In other applications the data are not only the variances and the covariances, but also the means of the measured variables. For these applications a model fits well if it accounts for the means, variances, and covariances.

A model consists of model parameters: variances and covariances among the independent variables and weights that are used to create linear combinations of variables to predict outcome variables in the model. In specifying a model a researcher typically imposes constraints on model parameters, usually by restricting some of the parameters to be equal to zero or by constraining some of the parameters to be equal to each other. If the

Table 8.1 Covariance matrix for coping and adjustment example

	Behavioral coping (BC) scales				Emotional coping (EC) scales				Immediate adjust. (IA) scales		Long-term adjust. (LTA) scales	
	1	*2*	*3*	*4*	*1*	*2*	*3*	*4*	*1*	*2*	*1*	*2*
BC 1	2.80											
BC 2	0.40	0.98										
BC 3	0.36	0.18	2.07									
BC 4	0.35	0.17	0.16	1.58								
EC 1	0.75	0.42	0.28	0.27	2.38							
EC 2	0.83	0.58	0.21	0.20	1.38	1.84						
EC 3	0.74	0.64	0.28	0.26	1.65	1.35	3.06					
EC 4	0.24	0.07	0.06	0.05	0.68	0.56	0.67	1.51				
IA 1	0.76	0.38	0.34	0.33	0.77	0.63	0.76	0.31	3.16			
IA 2	0.79	0.39	0.36	0.34	0.80	0.65	0.78	0.32	1.44	2.80		
LTA 1	0.87	0.43	0.39	0.38	1.35	1.10	1.32	0.55	1.13	1.17	3.27	
LTA 2	1.15	0.57	0.92	0.50	1.80	1.46	1.76	0.73	1.50	1.55	2.51	4.41

constrained parameters are not consistent with the data, the model does not fit. Model parameters that are not constrained are estimated to maximize fit to the data. Estimated parameters do not produce lack of fit with the data; therefore, one model will fit as well or better than a second model if the first model has additional, freely estimated parameters.

We will illustrate the process of model specification, estimation, and testing in the context of the following hypothetical research scenario. A researcher is interested in studying the relationships among emotional and behavioral coping approaches and immediate and long-term adjustment. She collects data from 500 participants consisting of scores on four behavioral coping scales, four emotional coping scales, two immediate adjustment scales, and two long-term adjustment scales. The distributional properties of these measures are assessed and they are judged to meet approximately the multivariate normality assumption. The covariance matrix for the twelve measures is presented in table 8.1. In the following sections we use these data to specify and evaluate three types of models: confirmatory factor analysis, full latent variable, and path analytic models.

A confirmatory factor analysis model
With CFA, researchers hypothesize that a certain number of factors underlie measures and various measures are linked to particular factors. To illustrate a CFA model using data from the research scenario presented above, suppose the researcher hypothesizes that two correlated factors underlie the eight coping measures: one factor for the four behavioral coping scales and a second factor for the four emotional coping scales. The model can be represented by a path diagram, as shown in figure 8.1. Several types of model parameters are estimated in this model. Weights are estimated that relate the behavioral coping factor to the behavioral coping measures and the emotional coping

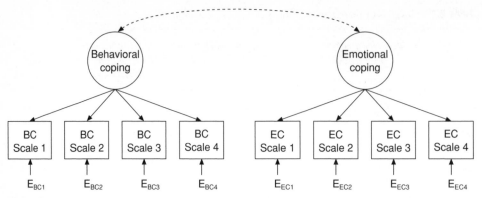

Figure 8.1   Confirmatory factor analytic model for coping example. In our path diagrams circles are factors or latent variables, squares are measured variables, directed arrows are directional relationships, and curved bidirectional arrows are nondirectional relationships.

factor to the emotional coping measures (indicated by arrows). In addition to the weights, the variances of the measurement errors (variances of the *E*s) and the covariance between the two factors (depicted as a dotted curve) are estimated parameters. The hypothesized model also implies that a number of parameters are constrained to zero in this model. As indicated by the lack of arrows, the weights between the behavioral coping factor and the emotional coping measures and the weights between the emotional coping factor and the behavioral coping measures are model parameters that have been constrained to zero. In addition, the covariances among the measurement errors have been constrained to zero.

The unconstrained parameters are estimated to maximally fit the data, the *covariance matrix among measured variables* as shown at the top of table 8.2 (note that this matrix consists of the first eight rows of the matrix in table 8.1). The model fits the data imperfectly because of the constraints imposed on some of the model parameters. The *reproduced covariance matrix* based on the model with its constrained and estimated parameters is shown in the middle of table 8.2. A *residual matrix* is calculated by subtracting the reproduced covariance matrix based on the hypothesized model from the covariance matrix among measured variables. Because not all of the values in the residual matrix are zeros, the model does not statistically account perfectly for the covariance matrix among the measured variables. The global fit indices reported by SEM software assess the degree to which the model fits the data matrix (i.e., the values in the residual matrix are close to zero).

A global fit index typically reported is the chi square statistic. The null hypothesis associated with this statistic is that the residual covariance matrix in the population contains all zeros; that is, the model fits perfectly in the population. For our example, the chi square statistic is statistically significant, $\chi^2(19, N = 500) = 57.56, p < .001$, implying that the model does not fit perfectly in the population. The results of the chi square must be interpreted cautiously, regardless of its outcome. First, if the hypothesis is rejected, as it is in our example, we do not necessarily want to reject the model. The

Table 8.2 Covariance matrix, reproduced covariance matrix, and residual covariance matrix for uncorrelated factors

	Behavioral coping (BC) scales				*Emotional coping (EC) scales*			
	1	*2*	*3*	*4*	*1*	*2*	*3*	*4*
				Covariance matrix				
BC 1	2.80							
BC 2	0.40	0.98						
BC 3	0.36	0.18	2.07					
BC 4	0.35	0.17	0.16	1.58				
EC 1	0.75	0.42	0.28	0.27	2.38			
EC 2	0.83	0.58	0.21	0.20	1.38	1.84		
EC 3	0.74	0.64	0.28	0.26	1.65	1.35	3.06	
EC 4	0.24	0.07	0.06	0.05	0.68	0.56	0.67	1.51
				Reproduced covariance matrix				
BC 1	2.80							
BC 2	0.45	0.98						
BC 3	0.27	0.17	2.07					
BC 4	0.25	0.17	0.10	1.58				
EC 1	0.80	0.52	0.31	0.29	2.38			
EC 2	0.71	0.47	0.27	0.26	1.38	1.84		
EC 3	0.82	0.54	0.32	0.30	1.59	1.42	3.06	
EC 4	0.32	0.21	0.12	0.12	0.63	0.56	0.64	1.51
				Residual covariance matrix				
BC 1	0.00							
BC 2	−0.05	0.00						
BC 3	0.09	0.01	0.00					
BC 4	0.10	0.00	0.06	0.00				
EC 1	−0.05	−0.10	−0.03	−0.02	0.00			
EC 2	0.12	0.11	−0.06	−0.06	0.00	0.00		
EC 3	−0.08	0.10	−0.04	−0.04	0.06	−0.07	0.00	
EC 4	−0.08	−0.14	−0.06	−0.07	0.05	0.00	0.03	0.00

chi square statistic is a function of not only the residual matrix, but also sample size. Accordingly, the test statistic will be significant if the lack of fit is trivial in the population and the sample size is sufficiently large. In addition, the chi square statistic tends to be inflated unless the measured variables are normally distributed and the sample size is sufficiently large ($N > 200$ for many applications; Boomsma, 1985, 1987). Second, if the hypothesis is not rejected, we do not want to conclude that the model fits in the population. In fact, it is unlikely that any constrained model fits perfectly in the population. Even if the hypothesized model is far from correct, lack of significance may be due to a lack of power resulting from an insufficient sample size. MacCallum, Browne, and Sugawara (1996) show that very large sample sizes may be necessary (e.g., $N > 1000$) to reject some incorrect hypotheses.

Because the chi square statistic is influenced by sample size, it is important to report global fit indices that are not. Two such indices are the comparative fit index (CFI; Bentler, 1990) and the root mean square error of approximation (RMSEA; Steiger and Lind, 1980). For our example, the CFI is .96, while the RMSEA is .06 (RMSEA 90 percent confidence interval of .04 to .08). Based on these results, the fit is good, but not jump-up-and-down great. Commonly accepted cutoffs for good fit are .90 or higher for the CFI and .05 or lower for the RMSEA. Recently, Hu and Bentler (1999) recommended somewhat different cutoffs: .95 or higher for the CFI and .06 or less for the RMSEA. Exact values for cutoffs are arbitrary and, as stated by Steiger (2000) in referring to a cutoff for RMSEA, "should not be taken too seriously" (p. 161).

Ideally in SEM, a series of *a priori* models is assessed and compared rather than assessing only a single model (Jöreskog, 1993). In our example, an alternative model might be the same as the first model, except with the behavioral and emotional coping factors being uncorrelated (i.e., removing the dotted curve from the path diagram in figure 8.1). This model fits much worse than the previous model, CFI = 0.81, RMSEA = .13 (RMSEA 90 percent confidence interval of .11 to .15), $\chi^2(20, N = 500) = 183.66$, $p < .001$. The only difference between the two models is whether the covariance between factors is estimated or constrained, and consequently the constraint of this parameter accounted for the diminished performance of the second model. More specifically, the constrained factor covariance of the second model, in addition to the other imposed constraints, forced the reproduced covariances between the behavioral coping measures and the emotional coping measures to be all zeros and, in so doing, failed to account for the sample covariances between the measures for the two factors.

The results of the significance tests for the individual models fail to address directly the hypothesis about the difference between the models. An approximate chi square difference test can be calculated to assess whether constraints imposed on one model to produce a second model yield poorer fit in the population. This chi square test is conducted by comparing the chi squares and the degrees of freedom for the two models. For our example, the resulting chi square difference is 126.10 ($183.66 - 57.56 = 126.10$) with 1 degree of freedom ($20 - 19 = 1$) and a p-value that is less than .001.

All too often researchers pay attention only to global fit indices and fail to examine the individual parameters to ensure they make sense in the context of the problem. In our example, the parameters for the first model with correlated factors are sensible given our theory: all the weights are positive and the covariance between the factors is positive. In addition, all the model parameters differ significantly from zero.

Given that the first model fits the data reasonably well, is it appropriate to interpret the results of this model within a causal framework even if the study is a "correlational design?" The direct paths of the model (i.e., the arrows in the diagram) indicate a causal flow from the factors to the measures and not in the opposite direction. However, in contrast to an experimental study, many other models may fit these data almost as well, as well, or better. Consequently, we must be very cautious in our interpretation unless we can rule out these other models on the basis of the design or theory. We will discuss these issues more extensively in the section on equivalent models.

A full latent variable model

CFA models are sometimes called measurement models because the focus is on the direct paths between constructs (i.e., factors) and the variables that measure them. CFA models may include covariances among factors, but these covariances leave unspecified the causal connections among the factors. On the other hand, full latent variable (FLV) models include not only a measurement component specifying direct paths between factors and measured variables, but also a structural component specifying direct paths among the factors. Researchers typically are most interested in the structural component of FLV models because the direct paths of this component address the validity of cause-and-effect relationships of psychological theories. However, researchers must also be concerned about the measurement component of FLV models because misspecification in the measurement component can lead to incorrect estimates of parameters in the structural part of models. More generally, misspecification in any one part of a model can lead to inaccurate parameter estimates in other parts of the model that are correctly specified.

To illustrate FLV models, we examine a simple coping theory. According to this theory, behavioral and emotional coping affect immediate adjustment and long-term adjustment. This theory can be translated into a FLV model, as depicted in figure 8.2.

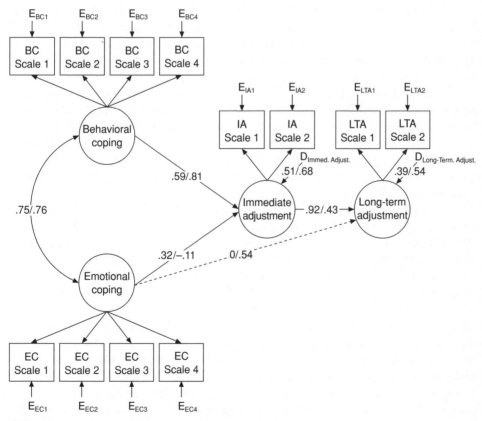

Figure 8.2 Full latent variable model for coping example.

The measurement component includes the paths relating the factors and the measurement errors (*E*s) to the measured variables, while the structural part includes the paths among the factors as well as structural disturbances (*D*s). The researchers investigating the coping theory are likely to be interested primarily in the paths between the coping and adjustment factors, but must guard against incorrect constraints imposed on all model parameters.

In FLV models researchers can assess direct, indirect, and total effects of one variable on another variable. A direct effect of one variable on another variable is specified by including a direct path or weight linking the two variables. Factors have direct effects on measured variables in the measurement part of FLV models as well as in CFA models, while factors also have direct effects on other factors in FLV models. In FLV models a variable can have an indirect effect on another variable through one or more mediating variables. An indirect effect is computed by multiplying the direct effects involved in a causal chain, that is, by multiplying a direct effect between a causal variable and a mediating variable, direct effect(s) between the mediating variables (if any), and a direct effect between a mediating variable and the effected variable. The sum of direct and indirect effects of one variable on another variable is the total effect.

For our coping data, two FLV models are hypothesized and depicted in figure 8.2: the fully mediated model and the partially mediated model. For the fully mediated model, behavioral and emotional coping directly affect immediate coping, and immediate coping has a direct effect on long-term coping. These direct effects imply indirect effects of emotional and behavioral coping on long-term adjustment through the mediating variable of immediate adjustment. The indirect effect of emotional (or behavioral) coping on long-term adjustment is the product of the direct effect of emotional (or behavioral) coping on immediate adjustment and the direct effect of immediate adjustment on long-term adjustment. The partially mediated model includes all of the effects of the first model, but also a direct effect of emotional coping on long-term adjustment, as indicated by the dotted arrow. In other words, the effect of emotional coping on long-term adjustment is both direct and mediated through immediate adjustment. The total effect of emotional coping on long-term adjustment is the sum of the direct effect and indirect effect of emotional coping on long-term adjustment.

We estimate the parameters of the fully mediated model and assess its fit based on the covariance matrix among the twelve measured variables presented in table 8.1. The chi square statistic is statistically significant, $\chi^2(50, N = 500) = 153.52$, $p < .001$, so we reject the null hypothesis that the model fits perfectly in the population. However, other global fit indices suggest a reasonably good fit, CFI = 0.94, RMSEA = .06 (RMSEA 90 percent confidence interval of .05 to .08). We proceed to examine the magnitude and direction of the standardized parameter estimates. Standardized estimates of the direct effects between factors are shown as the first set of estimates (before the slash) on figure 8.2. Although there are parameter estimates associated with the measurement part of the model, we display and focus our discussion here only on the paths between factors. All direct effects between factors are positive and statistically significant at the .05 level; however, the direct effect of emotional coping on immediate adjustment (.32) is somewhat weaker than the direct effect of behavioral coping on immediate adjustment (.59). The two indirect effects of emotional and behavioral coping on long-term adjustment are also positive and statistically significant: .29 (= .32 × .92) for emotional coping on long-term adjustment and .54 (= .59 × .92) for behavioral coping on long-term adjustment.

We also fit the partially mediated model to the data and compare its fit to the fully mediated model. Although the lack of fit for the partially mediated model is statistically significant, $\chi^2(49, N = 500) = 98.94$, $p < .001$, the model demonstrates very good fit, CFI = 0.97, RMSEA = .04 (RMSEA 90 percent confidence interval of .03 to .06). Further, the difference in chi square statistics is statistically significant, indicating the partially mediated model that includes one additional direct effect between emotional coping and long-term adjustment fits significantly better than the fully mediated model, $\chi^2_{\text{difference}}(1, N = 500) = 54.58$, $p < .001$. The standardized path coefficients for this model are shown after the slash in figure 8.2. The direct effect of emotional coping on long-term adjustment is positive, relatively large in magnitude (.54), and statistically significant, indicating that greater emotional coping leads to improved long-term adjustment. In contrast, the indirect effect of emotional coping on long-term adjustment through immediate adjustment is small and negative ($-.05 = -.11 × .43$). Although we cannot make an inference to the population about the indirect effect because it is nonsignificant, the results indicate that in the sample emotional coping has a small negative effect on long-term adjustment through immediate adjustment, but a positive direct effect on long-term adjustment. Overall, the total effect of emotional coping on long-term adjustment is .49, the sum of the direct and the indirect effects (.54 + −.05). In comparison, behavioral coping has an indirect effect (and total effect) on long-term adjustment of .35 (= .81 × .43).

The relative importance of emotional and behavioral coping on long-term adjustment differed for the fully mediated and partially mediated models. For the fully mediated model, behavioral coping had a stronger effect on long-term coping, while for the partially mediated model, emotional coping had a stronger effect on long-term coping. These results make it clear that the interpretation of FLV models is highly dependent on what parameters are constrained or freely estimated in a model. Misspecification of a model produces biased and, potentially, meaningless parameter estimates. Consequently, although the terms used to describe SEM results denote causation (e.g., direct, indirect, and total effects), we must be very cautious in our support of causal conclusions based solely on SEM analyses.

A path analytic model

With path models, researchers hypothesize causal relationships among measured variables, assuming the measured variables are perfect representations of the constructs. Instead of having multiple measured variables as indicators for a construct, a single measure is used to represent each construct and the focus is on the causal relations between these measured variables. As with FLV models, the results of a path analysis are interpreted by assessing fit of the overall model and evaluating the direct, indirect, and total effects of the variables in the model. Researchers may turn to path analysis if multiple measures are not available for the constructs of interest. For our example, we could specify and test path analytic models consistent with the researcher's mediation hypotheses above by using a single measure to represent each construct.

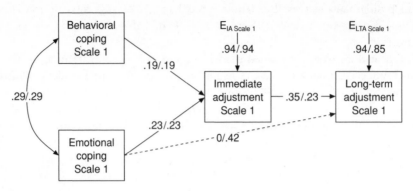

Figure 8.3   Path analytic model for coping example.

Figure 8.3 shows a path diagram for a path analysis model utilizing the first measured variable for each factor.

As with the FLV models, we will first test the fully mediated model where behavioral and emotional coping variables only affect long-term adjustment through the immediate adjustment variable. The model fits very poorly, $\chi^2(2, N = 500) = 110.34$, $p < .001$, CFI = 0.60, and RMSEA = .33 (RMSEA 90 percent confidence interval of .28 to .38). Parameter estimates are shown in figure 8.3 (before the slash). All direct effects and indirect effects are positive and statistically significant, but should not be interpreted due to the poor fit of the model.

The second path analytic model we fit is a partially mediated model that includes one additional estimated parameter, the direct effect of emotional coping on long-term adjustment. The fit of this model is very good according to the CFI of .97, but the chi square statistic is significant, $\chi^2(1, N = 500) = 8.99$, $p = .003$, and the RMSEA of .13 (RMSEA 90 percent confidence interval of .06 to .21) suggests inadequate fit. The RMSEA may have suggested a poorer fit because this index is sensitive to the fit of the model in relationship with its parsimony (as assessed by a model's df). Also, the RMSEA evaluates absolute fit, while the CFI assesses fit of the model in comparison with fit of a simple, null model. (See Rigdon, 1996, for further discussion of these indices.) The chi square difference test is statistically significant, with $\chi^2_{\text{difference}}(1, N = 500) = 101.35$, $p < .001$, indicating the addition of the direct effect of emotional coping on long-term adjustment did improve the fit to the covariance matrix. All direct and indirect effects are positive and statistically significant. The standardized effects suggest a positive mediated relationship between emotional coping and long-term adjustment through the intervening variable of immediate adjustment, in addition to the positive direct effect of emotional coping on long-term adjustment observed in both models.

The assumption that the measured variables used in a path analysis are perfect representations of the constructs they purportedly represent is worrisome. Results for these models vary substantially if different measured variables from table 8.1 are used to represent the constructs of interest. Path analysis demands that researchers cross their fingers and hope the measurement error associated with their measures is sufficiently small that the results apply to the constructs the measures are intended to represent. We encourage researchers to use a full latent variable approach, rather than a path analytic model, whenever possible, so measurement error can be included in the model.

Now that we have completed our brief overview of SEM, we discuss coefficient alpha and SEM, the first of the five topics that we consider.

Coefficient alpha and SEM

Coefficient alphas (Cronbach, 1951) are commonly reported by researchers to support the psychometric quality of measures used in their studies. Based on our review of articles published in *Psychological Assessment*, researchers tend to report coefficient alphas using one of two approaches. The first approach reports coefficient alpha as an index of internal consistency:

> The problem categories were internally consistent across the five situations within one interview, with alphas of .96 for latency, .82 for number of plans, .79 for quality of best response, and .81 for quality of overall response. (Carrol et al., 1999: 79)

> Cronbach's (1951) alpha was computed to examine the internal consistency of the ASIQ and LRFL. The Cronbach alpha for the 23-item ASIQ was high and acceptable, $\alpha = .98$; the alpha for the six items was .96. (Osman et al., 1999: 117)

The second approach reports coefficient alpha not as an internal consistency estimate *per se*, but as an internal consistency estimate of reliability:

> The FACES III exhibited good internal reliability in the present sample ($\alpha \geq 0.82$ for both the adaptability and cohesion subscales for SA and mothers). (Rotheram-Borus et al., 2000: 1085)

The first approach of reporting coefficient alpha offers the reader an incorrect interpretation of coefficient alpha, while the second method may yield misleading conclusions if the scales on which the alphas were computed do not meet certain assumptions. Further, we observed in our review of articles in *JCCP* and *PA* that some authors simply reported the values for coefficient alpha, perhaps commenting that the values were adequate. In so doing, they left it to the reader to decide what coefficient alpha represents. In the following sections we discuss why these reporting approaches are problematic, how confirmatory factor analysis can be used to improve investigation of internal consistency, and what reliability estimates can be computed as alternatives to coefficient alpha. We also discuss at length how coefficient alpha should be interpreted because coefficient alpha, probably "the most popular reliability coefficient in social science research" (Bollen, 1989: 215), is frequently presented as the only index to support a test's internal consistency and reliability, and is often misapplied.

Internal consistency and coefficient alpha
Internal consistency assesses the degree to which the items of a measure reflect a single factor or dimension. A measure is unidimensional if each of its items is a function of a

single factor plus error. In theory, a measure is either unidimensional or is not (McDonald, 1981). In practice, a measure is never precisely unidimensional, but is a function of not only the factor of interest, but also irrelevant content and method factors (Stout, 1990). Nevertheless, an index of internal consistency should yield a perfect value if items on a measure assess a single factor, close to a perfect value if items are primarily a function of a single factor and slightly affected by other factors, and should yield a low value if items are strongly affected by multiple factors.

Coefficient alpha should not be interpreted as an index of internal consistency considering that a multidimensional measure does not necessarily have a lower coefficient alpha than a unidimensional measure (e.g., Cortina, 1993; Green, Lissitz, and Mulaik, 1977). A measure can be multidimensional and yield a very high alpha or can be unidimensional and yield a very low alpha. Despite the lack of sensitivity of coefficient alpha to multidimensionality, it continues to be used as an indicator of internal consistency. For example, Hoyle and Smith (1994) address the interpretation of coefficient alpha as an index of internal consistency in their article on SEM in *JCCP*. After discussing the use of structural equation modeling for assessing internal consistency, they state, "A more common approach to evaluating internal consistency involves computing coefficient alpha, an approach that we advocate unless all of one's analyses are to be carried out in a structural equation modeling context" (p. 431). Contrary to their conclusion, we believe statistical methods specifically designed to explore a measure's dimensionality, such as confirmatory factor analysis (i.e., SEM) or exploratory factor analysis, are required to evaluate unidimensionality.

In table 8.3 we present coefficient alphas for measures that have one factor or two uncorrelated factors, have 6, 12, 24, or 48 items, and have items that have low factor weights of .4 or high factor weights of .8. Many of the coefficient alphas associated with single-factor measures (i.e., perfectly internally consistent measures) are lower than those

Table 8.3   Coefficient alphas for hypothetical measures with simple structure and one or two factors

Number of items	Factor weights	Single factor	Two orthogonal factors
6 items	.4	.53	.29
12 items	.4	.70	.48
24 items	.4	.82	.67
48 items	.4	.90	.80
6 items	.8	.91	.67
12 items	.8	.96	.83
24 items	.8	.98	.91
48 items	.8	.99	.96

Note: The factor variances were always set to 1. For two-factor measures, half the items were associated with one factor and the other half were associated with the second factor, and the two factors were uncorrelated. The error variances were set such that the item variances were always equal to 1 (i.e., $\sigma_\varepsilon^2 = .84$ for items with a factor weight of .4 and $\sigma_\varepsilon^2 = .36$ for items with a factor weight of .8).

with two-factor measures. A major problem with coefficient alpha as an index of unidimensionality is that it is inappropriately influenced by the number of items on a measure.

Internal consistency should be evaluated by methods that assess dimensionality directly, such as CFA. If an item covariance matrix has a single underlying factor such that the variances are equal and the covariances are equal, the results of a CFA will show that a one-factor model perfectly fits the data. In other words, CFA allows us to reach the correct conclusion that single-factor measures like those in table 8.3 are perfectly internally consistent. The covariance matrices for the two-factor measures in table 8.3 have two sets of covariances: (a) covariances that are equal and nonzero among items within a factor and (b) covariances that are all zeros among items loading on different factors. CFAs that specify the appropriate two-factor model produce perfect fit for these data, while those that specify a one-factor model reveal some lack of fit. In contrast to coefficient alpha, these factor analytic results allow us to reach the correct conclusion that these measures with two underlying factors are not internally consistent.

Coefficient alpha as a reliability estimate
Coefficient alpha is an appropriate reliability index for a measure if its scale score is computed by summing item scores and if the items meet certain classical test theory assumptions. (See Crocker and Algina, 1986, and Novick and Lewis, 1967, for detailed discussions of these assumptions.) According to classical test theory an item score is a function of a true score and an error score, and for a population of examinees, the mean of error scores for an item is zero, and the error scores for an item are uncorrelated with the true scores and the error scores for any other item. In addition, items must be essentially tau equivalent: the true scores for any two items must be within a constant of each other for an examinee. Although coefficient alpha is an accurate assessment of reliability if the assumptions are met, alpha may underestimate or overestimate reliability – in some cases, very badly – if the assumptions are violated.

Most discussions about coefficient alpha indicate it is a lower-bound estimate of reliability if the assumption of essential tau equivalency is not met (e.g., Cortina, 1993; Crocker and Algina, 1986; Miller, 1995). This assumption is violated if a single factor underlies all items, but the factor weights differ across items. In most cases this type of violation probably does not cause a major underestimate of reliability (Raykov, 1997a). The assumption is also violated if multiple factors underlie the items on a measure and, in this instance, the underestimate can be quite severe. For example, if the weights for the first three items are .8 for factor 1 and 0 for factor 2 and the weights for the second three items are 0 for factor 1 and .8 for factor 2, coefficient alpha is .67, as shown in table 8.3. However, the reliability for this six-item measure is actually .84, markedly higher than the alpha coefficient.[1]

Coefficient alphas may also produce inaccurate estimates of reliability if the errors for items are correlated (e.g., Fleishman and Benson, 1987; Green and Hershberger, 2000; Maxwell, 1968; Raykov, 1998; Rozeboom, 1966, 1989; Zimmerman, Zumbo, and Lalonde, 1993). Rozeboom (1966) used colorful psychometric language in concluding that coefficient alpha may be a poor estimate of reliability if errors are correlated:

> Hence the apparent power of internal-consistency reliability estimates is largely illusory, and however pleasant a mathematical pastime it may be to shuffle through the internal

statistics of a compound test in search of a formula which gives the closest estimate of the test's reliability under conditions of uncorrelated errors, this is for practical applications like putting on a clean shirt to rassle a hog. (Ibid: 415)

When items on a measure are administered on a single occasion, errors among items are likely to be positively correlated and yield spuriously high coefficient alphas.

We could optimistically assume the negative bias associated with violating the essential tau equivalency assumption will offset any positive bias associated with violating the uncorrelated errors assumption. Fortunately, this blind faith is unnecessary in that researchers can evaluate these assumptions using SEM techniques, although they may encounter problems in their analyses, such as inadequate sample size, nonnormality of item data, and model equivalency (Green and Hershberger, 2000; Miller, 1995; Raykov, 1998). At a minimum, researchers who report alpha as a reliability coefficient for a measure should present results suggesting that all items are primarily a function of a single factor plus uncorrelated errors.

SEM estimates of reliability

A number of SEM methods have been suggested to compute internal consistency estimates of reliability (Green and Hershberger, 2000; Miller, 1995; Raykov, 1997b, 1998). We discuss a method described by Raykov and Shrout (in press) that is a generalization of the other approaches and makes fewer restrictive assumptions than coefficient alpha. We illustrate the method for a hypothetical, six-item measure.

Step 1. Researchers hypothesize a factor analytic model for a measure. If the model fits the data, they proceed to step 2. If researchers use exploratory methods to achieve good fit, they should obtain a second sample to ensure that the good fit replicates before proceeding to step 2. For our example, let's assume the model that fits the data has two correlated factors. Items 1 through 4 are a function of factor 1 with weights of L_1, L_2, L_3, and L_4, and items 3 through 6 are a function of factor 2 with weights of L_5, L_6, L_7, and L_8.

Step 2. A model is developed that includes not only the construct factors underlying the items of a measure, but also two supplemental factors. One supplemental factor is the total score for the measure. For our example, and as shown in figure 8.4, factor 4 is the sum of the six items (with unit weights). The second supplemental factor is the true component of the total score. It is computed by producting each item–factor weight by the factor associated with that weight and summing the products. For our example, and as shown in figure 8.4, factor 3 is the true component:

$$F_3 = L_1F_1 + L_2F_1 + L_3F_1 + L_4F_1 + L_5F_2 + L_6F_2 + L_7F_2 + L_8F_2$$

When specifying this model using SEM software, the weight between factor 3 and each construct factor (1 or 2) is constrained to be equal to the sum of weights relating that construct factor to its respective items.

Step 3. Reliability is the ratio of the variance of the true score component to the variance of the total score for a measure or, in the context of the model specified in step 2, the variance of F_3 divided by the variance of F_4. Therefore, an internal consistency estimate can be computed by fitting the model developed in step 2, requesting the

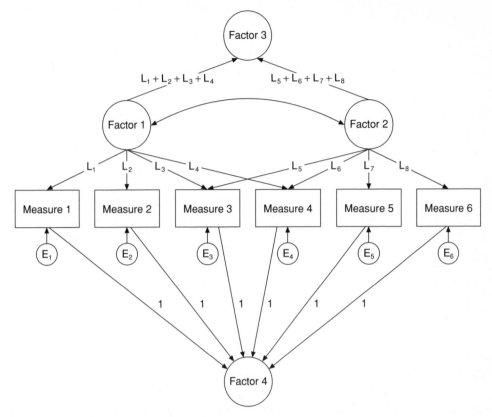

Figure 8.4 Model for estimating reliability.

estimated variances of F_3 and F_4, and dividing the estimated variance of F_3 by the estimated variance of F_4.

The above method makes fewer assumptions than coefficient alpha in that it can be applied to measures which are multidimensional and have correlated errors. Nevertheless, it is not a panacea. Perhaps most problematic is that the analyses are conducted on item data. We discuss the difficulties encountered when analyzing item data in the section "SEM analysis of nonnormal data." See Raykov and Shrout (in press) for other difficulties with applying this approach.

Conclusions
Coefficient alpha should not be used as an index of internal consistency and may or may not be a good estimate of reliability. Researchers should compute an internal consistency estimate of reliability like alpha only after assessing whether its assumptions have been met. Even then, they should consider the type of errors they are likely to encounter in using the scale of interest. For example, Becker (2000) argued that transient error is an important source of variability for many scales and can be assessed only by administering measures on two occasions, not by an internal consistency estimate of reliability.

Multivariate analyses of means

When faced with examining differences among groups on multiple dependent variables, clinical researchers routinely conduct a multivariate analysis of variance (MANOVA). If the MANOVA is statistically significant, they may conduct follow-up analyses, such as multiple analyses of variance (ANOVAs) on the dependent variables or discriminant analysis, to understand why the MANOVA yielded significance (Bray and Maxwell, 1985). MANOVA evaluates the omnibus hypothesis that the population means on all discriminant functions are the same across groups, and, consequently, discriminant analysis is the follow-up analysis most closely aligned to MANOVA. Nevertheless, researchers frequently conduct multiple ANOVAs rather than discriminant analysis after obtaining a significant MANOVA, probably because they find the results from ANOVAs more straightforward to interpret. In many clinical applications the difficulty with interpreting the results from discriminant analysis may not be the failure to understand the complexities of this multivariate technique, but rather the failure of the technique to produce results that address the questions posed by clinical researchers. This interpretational problem also applies to MANOVA. In many applications SEM analyses to examine group differences on multiple dependent variables may yield more meaningful results than MANOVA followed by discriminant analysis.

Choosing between MANOVA and SEM

Before presenting the methods used to conduct analyses of means with SEM, we consider in greater depth the decision between using a MANOVA and SEM to analyze the relationship between a grouping variable and multiple dependent variables. Initially in this discussion we ignore the grouping variable and focus on the relationship between the dependent variables and their associated dimensions. It should be noted that in our discussion we reserve the term "grouping variable" to refer to a variable that differentiates individuals into groups. Counter to the ANOVA/MANOVA literature, we reserve the term "factor" to describe dimensions associated with the dependent variables and not as a term to differentiate groups.

For both SEM and MANOVA approaches, models are investigated that link the dependent variables to factors (i.e., dimensions), but the type of link between the dependent variables and the factors differs for the two approaches. For SEM approaches, the links are arrows directed from the factors to the dependent variables, while for MANOVA the links are arrows directed from the dependent variables to the factors. It is crucial in deciding which analysis to conduct to distinguish between dependent variables that are affected by factors and dependent variables that produce factors. In SEM jargon the distinction is between dependent variables that are effect indicators versus those that are causal indicators. To choose between the two types of analyses, researchers must determine whether the measured variables are effect or causal indicators based on previous research and theory associated with measures.

Effect indicators. In most applications of SEM measured variables are hypothesized to be linear combinations of factors plus error; that is, arrows are directed from factors and errors to the measured variables. In these applications the measured variables are effect indicators within a latent variable system in that the indicators are affected by the factors (Bollen and Lennox, 1991; MacCallum and Browne, 1993). Measured variables that are effect indicators covary because they share common causes – the same underlying factors. The measurement model relating the effect indicators to factors can be validated by collecting data on the measured variables and conducting CFA. Clinical researchers routinely conceptualize human behaviors as effect indicators of underlying factors. For example, if individuals frown, make negative comments, and walk aimlessly, they do so because they are depressed. If other individuals smile, make positive statements, and walk purposefully, they do so because they are not depressed. The observable indicators are affected by the latent trait.

Causal indicators. In some applications researchers may hypothesize a factor to be a linear combination of measured variables. Under these conditions, measured variables cause the factor, and therefore these measured variables are referred to as causal indicators within an emergent variable system (Bollen and Lennox, 1991; MacCallum and Browne, 1993). Because causal indicators are not a function of factors, the indicators may or may not be correlated. Also, factors in an emergent variable system are not included in models to explain covariation among the causal indicators, but rather to explain the relationship between these indicators with other variables. Accordingly, factors in an emergent variable system are validated by examining their relationship with variables that are external to the system, potentially using SEM. Clinical researchers sometimes conceptualize behaviors as causal indicators that come together to form a factor, and the resulting factor takes on meaning in its relationship to other variables of interest. For example, individuals who have a flat tire on the way to the airport and find the parking lot congested and their plane delayed (i.e., causal indicators) might become stressed (i.e., high on the factor of stress) and subsequently act unmannerly toward airline personnel (i.e., variables external to the emergent variable system).

Choosing between MANOVA and SEM in practice. The distinction between effect and causal indicators is clear in theory, but may be murky in practice. Nevertheless, we must make this distinction in deciding whether to conduct a MANOVA or an SEM analysis in evaluating mean differences on multiple dependent variables. Based on our understanding of theory underlying clinical studies, we suspect SEM approaches should frequently be substituted for MANOVA for analyzing group differences.

For example, when conducting a two-group analysis with three measures of depression and three measures of self-efficacy, researchers may want to answer the question, "Do the two treatment groups differ on the constructs of depression and self efficacy?" They believe the therapies directly affect the constructs of self-efficacy and depression and that multiple measures are manifestations of these constructs. Given that the dependent measures are effect indicators of the two underlying constructs, as theorized, SEM is the appropriate analytical method. With SEM, researchers specify the factors of depression and self-efficacy and examine mean differences on these two factors. In contrast, MANOVA/discriminant analysis empirically defines a single factor that is the weighted combination of the six dependent variables that maximally differentiates the two groups. A test of differences on this factor would not address the research question. Only under very restrictive conditions are the results of MANOVA and SEM approaches likely to yield similar results (Cole et al., 1993).

Conducting SEM analyses of means

We very briefly outline two SEM methods that may be used to analyze mean differences on multiple measures: structured means and group coded methods. We hope to clarify some recommendations on applying these approaches in this section because the literature is confusing and somewhat contradictory. The literature on these methods continues to change, particularly for the structured means approach, so researchers wishing to conduct SEM analysis of means should examine the most recent writings and software applications. We recommend the articles by Aiken, Stein, and Bentler (1994) and Hancock (1997) for additional reading in this area.

The focus of both SEM methods is on evaluating differences in means of the factors underlying the dependent variables and not on the dependent variables themselves. We discuss approaches for comparing differences in means for two groups on three dependent variables, although they can be easily extended.

Structured means method. With this approach, data are required for each group. In contrast to the previous SEM applications we have discussed, the data include not only the variances and covariances among the measured variables, but also their means. All analyses are conducted using a multiple groups approach.

A model should have the same form (i.e., the same free parameters, although not necessarily the same values for these parameters) in each group. For our example, we specify a single factor underlying the three dependent variables. As shown at the top of figure 8.5, the model for each group in this instance looks similar to a standard CFA model except it includes a variable that takes on the value of 1 for all individuals. The

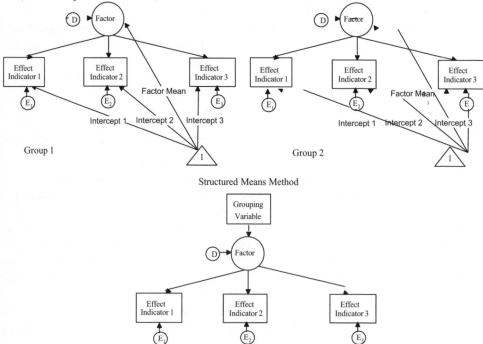

Figure 8.5 Path diagrams for structured means and group coded methods.

ones variable is represented in the figure by a triangle with a 1 inside. As in regression analysis, if a variable (the factor in figure 8.5) is a function of only a ones variable, the weight applied to the ones variable is a mean. If a variable (any of the effect indicators in figure 8.5) is a function of other variable(s) and a ones variable, the weight applied to the ones variable is an intercept.

A number of constraints must be imposed on the parameters for the multiple groups to obtain proper estimates and to test differences in factor means. In particular, the metric of the factor is arbitrary and must be assigned in each group. A standard approach is to fix the weight between each factor and one of its indicators to 1. For our example, we fix the weight between the first indicator and the factor to 1 in each group. In addition, the origin of the factor is arbitrary in one group. In our example, we may fix the mean of the factor in the first group to 0 to define its origin. At this point, the model is still not estimable unless at least one of the intercepts is constrained to be equal across the two groups. Generally speaking, it does not make much sense to have unequal factor weights and equal intercepts across groups. Consequently, because we have constrained the factor weights associated with the first indicator to 1 in both groups and thus equal to each other, we might constrain the intercept for the first indicator to be equal across groups. The minimal number of constraints has now been imposed on the model (i.e., the model is identified) and, given that the model fits the data, the factor mean associated with the second group can be estimated and tested to determine if it is significantly different from zero. If it is significantly different from zero, the means for the two groups differ significantly in that the factor mean for the first group was fixed to zero.

An argument can be made for requiring additional constraints on the model before testing differences in factor means. From an interpretational perspective, a measure might be considered biased if its intercepts differ between groups: individuals who have the same score on an underlying factor but are in different groups with different intercepts would have different scores on the measure. In addition, intuitively it would seem that a factor cannot be interpreted in the same way to the extent that its factor weights differ across groups. Accordingly, a number of authors have suggested that many or all of the intercepts and corresponding factor weights should be constrained to be equal across groups before tests of differences in factor means are meaningful. (See Hancock, Stapleton, and Berkovitz, 2001, for a complete discussion of this topic.)

If there are no differences in factor weights and intercepts between groups, the structured means approach is straightforward. To maximize power, researchers should constrain all intercepts and factor weights to be invariant across groups. However, if they choose to allow some of the intercepts and weights to be equal and others to differ between groups, they can still obtain good estimates of factor means and valid tests of differences in factor means, assuming the conditions required by the estimation procedure and significance test are met. In contrast, if not all factor weights and intercepts are equal in the population, researchers must be more cautious in choosing what parameter to constrain to be equal across groups. For example, if intercepts for a measure are not equal across groups in the population, but are constrained to be equal in the sample, SEM will yield, to some degree, inaccurate estimates of factor means and an invalid test of the differences in factor means. Further research is required to assess the robustness of this method.

The difficulty in applying the structured means approach is that we never know which parameters are equal and which are different across groups in the population and, therefore, it is unclear what equality constraints we should impose in our analyses. This problem appears to be a serious obstacle unless robustness studies tell us differently. For further discussion on this topic, see Hancock, Stapleton, and Berkovitz (2001).

Group-coded method. With the group-coded approach the data are the variances and covariances among the grouping variable and the dependent variables for the total sample rather than the means, variances, and covariance for the dependent variables for the separate groups. A single model is estimated for the combined groups that includes not only the factor model relating the factor(s) to the dependent variables, but also the effect of the grouping variable on the factor(s).

The model for the group-coded method for our example is presented at the bottom of figure 8.5. For this model, a ones variable is not included in the model because the means are not part of the dataset as they were for the structured means method. By combining samples and including the grouping variable in the analyses, we are able to assess the group mean differences directly by examining the relationship between grouping variable and the factor. In other words, the means on the factor differ as a function of the levels of the grouping variable if the grouping variable and the factor are related.

The implicit assumption underlying the group-coded method, at least as presented within figure 8.5, is that the same factor structure underlying the dependent variables holds for both groups. If this assumption is violated the group-coded method must be adapted or abandoned for the structured means method. However, if the assumption holds, the group-coded method is a simple approach to testing differences in factor means and can be customized to test more complex hypotheses, for example, mediational processes (Russell et al., 1998).

Conclusion

To evaluate group mean differences, clinical researchers have, from the 1970s to the 1990s, increasingly used MANOVA (Hoyle, 1994). Over the same period of time they almost never have applied SEM to assess mean differences. These researchers frequently design studies to examine whether groups differ on constructs assessed by effect indicators. SEM methods are a better match for these designs than MANOVA, although SEM methods are not problem free. It is interesting to note that researchers pay a price for using MANOVA with effect indicators. MANOVA is likely to have less power than SEM methods and, in some cases, substantially less (Hancock, Lawrence, and Nevitt, 2000).

SEM analysis of nonnormal data

The measured variables in SEM models hypothesized by clinical psychologists frequently consist of items or scales from psychological inventories or tests as well as behavioral assessments. Researchers wishing to use these data in structural equation models should consider whether the distributional assumptions have been met for the SEM estimation procedure they are using. The most frequently applied estimation method and the default option in most SEM software packages is maximum likelihood (ML).[2] ML estimation requires the measured variables to be multivariately normally distributed in the population and the sample size to be large. If measures fail to meet the normality assumption, results from ML estimation may be invalid and alternative estimation methods should be considered. In the following sections we briefly describe the distributional properties of measures commonly employed in clinical research, highlight the problems of ignoring the normality assumption, and describe some of the more promising methods for analyzing nonnormal data. Readers seeking a more comprehensive discussion of conducting SEM with nonnormal data are encouraged to read West, Finch, and Curran (1995); see also Bentler and Dudgeon (1996) and Kaplan (2000).

Nonnormality of data collected by clinical psychologists

In discussing the prevalence of nonnormality in clinical data it is convenient to define two types of measures: those that produce scores that are approximately continuous and those that yield a limited number of coarse categories. For simplicity, we will refer to the two types as continuous and coarsely categorized measures.

Continuous measures. We first consider continuous measures from cognitive tests and noncognitive measures. Micceri (1989) examined the distributional characteristics of 440 large datasets consisting of four types of data: ability, psychometric, criterion/mastery, and gain scores. He found a wide range of nonnormal distributions, with the most frequently observed distributions being characterized by mild to moderate asymmetry and moderate to extreme kurtosis. Micceri noted that psychometric measures, such as the Minnesota Multiphasic Personality Inventory (MMPI) subscales, interest inventories, and measures of anger and anxiety, tended to be lumpy and displayed greater asymmetry and heavier tails than ability measures.

Clinical psychologists are likely to focus on specific types of continuous measures. Of particular interest are those that assess constructs of psychopathology (e.g., depression, suicidal ideation, and obsessive-compulsive tendencies). Presumably, many of these measures are likely to be skewed in a variety of populations, regardless of whether they are scale scores from self-report paper-and-pencil measures, behavioral counts based on observational sampling, or summed ratings based on interviews.

Coarsely categorized measures. Items of most psychological inventories are coarsely categorized measures. Based on our review of the literature, clinical researchers frequently conduct factor analyses of items with dichotomous (e.g., MMPI–2 and California Psychological Inventory) or polytomous (e.g., Beck Depression Inventory and Positive and Negative Affect Schedule – Extended Version) response scales. On such measures, participants may be asked to indicate the extent to which they agree or disagree with a statement descriptive of their feelings or beliefs, or may be instructed to rate the relative frequency that they exhibit a particular behavior. Although their responses on items are limited to a small number of ordered categories, presumably a continuum of responses underlies them. Therefore, the scale points may be conceptualized as coarse categorizations imposed on a continuous latent distribution. Coarse categorization of item responses produces nonnormal data as well as invalidates the assumption that the measured variables are linearly related to the factors.

Coarsely categorized measures are not necessarily items from self-report inventories. For example, an outcome measure might be a 4-point therapist rating of client improvement in psychotherapy. In theory, underlying the therapists' judgments is a continuous dimension of improvement.

Consequences of violating distributional assumptions

When data are multivariate normal and the sample size is large, ML estimates of SEM parameters behave appropriately, and the likelihood ratio statistic closely follows a chi square distribution (Bollen, 1989). Because clinical psychologists frequently analyze data that are nonnormally distributed, it is important to consider the consequences of violating the normality assumption underlying ML estimation. The robustness of ML estimation to violation of this assumption is difficult to summarize succinctly because it is complexly affected by multiple factors, such as type of nonnormality present, sample size, model complexity, and number of scale points or thresholds for coarsely categorized measures. See West, Finch, and Curran (1995) for a summary of simulation studies on the robustness of normal-theory SEM.

For continuous measures, parameter estimates are not adversely affected by violation of the normality assumption. However, their standard errors are underestimated and, consequently, the z-tests associated with these parameters are too liberal. In addition, the chi square statistic for assessing model fit tends to be positively biased, resulting in inflated Type I error rates. Nonnormality resulting from coarse categorization also has serious consequences. The model parameter estimates tend to be biased, and the test statistics for the individual parameters and for the overall model may be inflated, even for relatively large samples. Problems are particularly severe when the measures have few categories and display differential skew.

Given that many psychological measures are nonnormally distributed and that non-normality has negative consequences, it is important to evaluate the multivariate normality assumption underlying ML estimation. Univariate and bivariate normality among measures can be examined; however, these are necessary but not sufficient conditions for multivariate normality. Researchers must also consider multivariate indices of skewness and kurtosis, outliers, and continuity of measurement scales.

Breckler (1990) found in a review of research in social psychology and personality that few researchers evaluate or even acknowledge the assumption of multivariate normality and proceed using ML estimation. However, in our review of more recent articles in *JCCP* and *PA*, it appears many clinical researchers are making a conscious effort to evaluate distributional assumptions and choose SEM methods accordingly (Long and Brekke, 1999; Osman et al., 1999; Sanford, Bingham, and Zucker, 1999). We now consider some of the more promising strategies available to researchers faced with continuous nonnormal measures and coarsely categorized measures.

SEM strategies for continuous nonnormal measures

A number of approaches have been proposed in the SEM literature for estimating and evaluating model fit with continuous nonnormal variables. We briefly discuss some of these methods next.

Transformations. If data are approximately multivariate normal and sample size is sufficient, ML estimates and tests are appropriate. If the measured variables are not multivariate normal, they may be transformed to attain more normally distributed scores.

A variety of standard transformations may be applied to reduce the skewness or kurtosis of individual measured variables. Shipley (2000) argued that kurtosis is a greater problem than skewness with ML and recommended the use of a modified power transformation to reduce kurtosis. Further research is required to determine how well ML methods will perform when this and other transformations are applied.

Robust ML method. Researchers may also consider correcting the inflated ML chi square statistic for nonnormality. The Satorra–Bentler scaled chi square test (SB test) adjusts the ML chi square downward as a function of the multivariate kurtosis (Satorra and Bentler, 1994). According to Curran, West, and Finch (1996), the SB test yields respectable Type I error rates even under severe departures from normality if sample size is at least moderate ($N \geq 200$). However, in planning SEM studies, sample size requirements might need to be adjusted to take into account the decrease in power of the SB test with an increase in multivariate nonnormality. Corrections for kurtosis can also be applied to obtain robust standard errors and tests of individual model parameters.

Distribution-free estimation methods. The development of asymptotic-distribution-free (ADF) estimation procedures (Browne, 1984) provided a hopeful alternative to normal theory methods. ADF methods have been implemented as weighted least squares in LISREL and arbitrary distribution generalized least squares in EQS. The ADF chi square test statistic may be quite inflated unless sample size is large. Minimal sample sizes may be 500 for simple models and 5,000 or greater for more complex models (Curran, West, and Finch, 1996; Hu, Bentler, and Kano, 1992). Accordingly, the utility of the original ADF estimation methods is limited for most clinical situations due to large sample requirements and reduced performance for larger models (Muthén and Kaplan, 1992).

Bentler and Yuan recently studied the performance of several model fit statistics with continuous normal and nonnormal distributions and across multiple sample sizes, with particular emphasis on alternative ADF methods (Bentler and Yuan, 1999; Yuan and Bentler, 1998). Using these results and considering the relative power of these statistics, they made several recommendations. Assuming the sample size is greater than the number of variances and covariances among the measured variables, the Yuan–Bentler corrected ADF chi square statistics may be used under nonnormal conditions to correct the inflated ADF chi square statistic (Yuan and Bentler, 1997). Alternatively, an *F*-statistic derived from the residual-based ADF statistic performs well for nonnormal (or normal) continuous data ranging from small to large sample sizes.

Bootstrapping. Bootstrapping techniques have also been suggested as an alternative approach to obtaining more appropriate estimates of standard errors and goodness-of-fit statistics under nonnormal data conditions (e.g., Bollen and Stine, 1992, 1993; Yung and Bentler, 1996). The empirical sampling distributions for the parameter estimates and fit statistics should yield more accurate results than normal theory methods when data are nonnormal. Studies are necessary to compare bootstrapping with adjusted ADF methods.

SEM strategies for coarsely categorized measures
Special methods are required for coarsely categorized measures (e.g., items) if categorization distorts the shape of the underlying distribution. In application it is more likely

distortion will occur with measures having a limited number of categories. Certainly, special techniques should be used if measures have only two or three options. We briefly describe the two most popular of these techniques below.

Categorical variable methodology. For models involving dichotomous or polytomous measures, categorical variable methodology (CVM; Muthén, 1984) can be used to estimate the structural equation model. With CVM the distributional assumption of multivariate normality applies to the latent distribution underlying the ordinally categorized measures. Simulation studies support the use of CVM when this assumption is met (Babakus, Ferguson, and Jöreskog, 1987; Muthén and Kaplan, 1985). However, the normality assumption for the underlying latent responses may not hold for measures assessing psychopathology in particular populations. Unfortunately, this assumption is difficult to assess, and CVM may not be robust to violations of this assumption, at least in terms of parameter estimation (Coenders, Satorra, and Saris, 1997).

Item parcels. Item parcels, also called testlets, are created by summing together scores for a set of items that assess the same factor. The parcels are then used as measured variables in the hypothesized model. Presumably the parcel scores approximate more closely multivariate normality than the original set of item scores and have a linear relationship with the underlying factors. A major risk with this ad hoc approach is obscuring the true factor structure underlying items. Recent examples of applying item parcels in the clinical literature we surveyed include Osman et al. (1999) and Sanford, Bingham, and Zucker (1999).

Conclusions

The literature on SEM analysis of nonnormal scale and item data is extensive and rapidly growing, as are the options available in SEM software packages. Our discussion will soon be outdated, so we encourage researchers faced with nonnormal data to seek the latest methods for analyzing nonnormal data. In considering various methods researchers should keep in mind that their performance is influenced by a number of factors, including type of nonnormality present, sample size, model complexity, and the number of scale points and the type of distribution underlying coarsely categorized measures.

Exploratory methods

When hypothesized models fail to fit adequately, exploratory procedures can be conducted to find revised models with improved fit. Although these methods may include the deletion of parameters, the primary focus is on the addition of parameters because addition rather than deletion of parameters improves model fit. One approach might be to revise a model based on a thoughtful, rational evaluation of parameters that could be added to or deleted from a model. Alternatively, a hypothesized model may be modified based on the results of empirically driven search methods or based on a mixture of rational and empirical modification procedures. We present three prototypes of situations in which researchers may combine different mixtures of rational and empirical approaches to seek a better fitting model:

The Minor Tune-Up. The hypothesized model demonstrates marginal fit, but needs a little tweaking to produce good fit. Researchers add some parameters and may delete a few others based on their understanding of the phenomena under investigation and, to a lesser extent, based on empirical search methods.

The Major Overhaul. The hypothesized model fits inadequately, but might be improved with substantial alterations. Researchers concentrate on the addition of parameters to improve fit and lean heavily on empirical search methods to determine what parameters need to be added to the model. The final model is likely to include a number of new parameters which presumably are theoretically defensible.

Trading in the Old Model for a New One. The hypothesized model fits very badly and must be abandoned for a whole new model. If researchers are evaluating a factor model, they may use exploratory factor analysis to define a new set of relationships between factors and observed measures. If researchers are assessing a complete latent variable model, they may initially use exploratory factor analysis to define a new set of factor–measure relationships and then use their understanding of the research area and empirical search methods to define relationships among factors.

These exploratory procedures confront us with interrelated questions: (a) "How much should one rely on rational versus empirical search methods?" (b) "What empirical methods work best?" (c) "Under what conditions can we most trust the results of searches?" We attempt to answer these questions in our discussion of exploratory methods.

Empirical searches with the LM test
Probably the most popular empirical search method involves adding parameters stepwise based on univariate Lagrange multiplier (LM) tests (also called modification indices; Jöreskog and Sörbom, 1989; Sörbom, 1989). Prior to conducting a search, researchers must define the search family, that is, the parameters that could potentially be added to the hypothesized model.[3] Parameters should be included in the search family only if they are meaningful within the context of the research study. In the first step of a search the LM test is used to identify the single parameter in the search family that would most improve model fit if included in the model. The researcher's model is respecified to include this parameter, and the respecified model is fitted to the data. In the second step the LM test is used to identify the parameter in the family (now excluding the previously selected parameter) that would maximally improve the fit of the respecified model, and then the model is respecified to include this additional parameter and fitted to the data. The specification search continues until the LM tests for all remaining parameters in the search family suggest minimal improvement in fit, which may be defined as a nonsignificant improvement in fit, perhaps at the .05 level.

SEM experts (Bentler and Chou, 1993; Chou and Bentler, 1993; Kaplan, 1990; Sörbom, 1989) argue convincingly that researchers should decide whether a parameter should be included in a model based not only on significance tests like the LM test, but also on statistics that assess expected change in a parameter estimate when that parameter is included in the model. Unless researchers are attentive to the expected change statistic they may dismiss relevant parameters due to a lack of power of significance tests or may add parameters that have trivial but statistically significant effects.

Errors with empirical searches

To understand the utility of empirical search methods we discuss briefly two types of errors that can be committed when parameters are added to models: errors due to sampling fluctuation and errors due to misspecification (Green, Thompson, and Poirer, 1999). An error due to sampling fluctuation occurs if a parameter is added to a model that improves fit in the sample, but is equal to zero in the population. Researchers are likely to commit this type of error to the extent that they define a large search family including many irrelevant parameters. An error due to misspecification occurs when a parameter is added to a model that increases model fit at a step in a search because the model fails to include all relevant parameters (i.e., a misspecified model), but would be unnecessary if the model were correctly specified. These errors occur even when searches are conducted on a population covariance matrix and, hence, they are distinguishable from errors due to sampling fluctuation.

Based on our understanding of errors due to sampling fluctuation and misspecification, researchers will have unsuccessful searches if they have a badly misspecified hypothesized model and have few relevant and many irrelevant parameters in their search family. Accordingly, researchers must carefully construct not only the hypothesized model, but also the search family based on best available theory and a thorough understanding of the empirical research literature. In addition, searches are likely to be more successful if sample size is large in order to minimize sampling error and produce stable parameter estimates. At any point in a search, many parameters in a search family may have nonzero values in the population because of the complexity of the human behavior and also due to model misspecification. Many of these parameter estimates are likely to be correlated and, therefore, unstable unless studies have large sample sizes. Based on exten-sive analyses of two large datasets, MacCallum et al. (1992) concluded that sample sizes of 1,200 or more may be needed to produce replicable empirical searches.

Other empirical search methods

The empirical search method we have previously described is a forward selection approach: parameters are added to a model one at a time to maximize incremental fit until the increase in fit is minimal. Other empirical search methods are possible. For example, with backward selection methods, all parameters in the search family are initially added to the hypothesized model and then these parameters are sequentially deleted so as to minimize loss in fit at each step until the decrease in fit is sizable. Sizable decrease may be defined as a significant decrease in fit, perhaps at the .05 level. If adding all parameters in a search family would yield an underidentified model, researchers could add as many plausible parameters as possible to the hypothesized model using a forward selection method and then sequentially delete these added parameters using backward selection. Green, Thompson, and Poirer (2001) argued that backward selection methods tend to do better than the more popular forward selection methods because backward selection methods are more likely to avoid errors due to misspecification by including all possible parameters initially in the model before evaluating the parameters in the search family. Some researchers (e.g., Marcoulides, Drezner, and Schumacker, 1998) have also suggested nonsequential methods, such as Tabu, which attempt to determine what combination of parameters would maximize model fit; however, currently these methods are applied very infrequently.

If sequential search methods are used, researchers should consider controlling for Type I errors across the multiple tests of parameters in a search family (Green and Babyak, 1997). Procedures for controlling familywise error rate are available for forward selection methods (Green, Thompson, and Babyak, 1998; Hancock, 1999) as well as backward selection methods (Green, Thompson, and Poirier, 2001). Researchers who use these methods are taking a conservative approach to model modification in that they are less likely to add parameters to hypothesized models. Accordingly, the likelihood of finding a model that fits adequately decreases; however, if researchers find a model that fits, they can feel more confident about their results. Also, researchers may be stimulated to narrow the family of parameters to be included in a search family to offset the loss of power brought about through the procedures used to control Type I error rate. Consequently, controlling Type I error rate encourages careful model development.

Conclusions

Based on our discussion of exploratory methods, we make some recommendations. Researchers should rely heavily on rational assessments of parameters in formulating their search family. Failing to make critical decisions will likely lead to inclusion of many irrelevant parameters in the model. Unfortunately, the resulting models can fit very well, and the errors go undetected. Further, controlling Type I errors in a search should encourage judicious limits on the size of the search families. Researchers who conduct empirical searches would probably obtain more meaningful models if they did not use the popular forward selection methods, but instead used backward selection or, if available, nonsequential search methods. Overall, due to the potential for capitalization on the chance characteristics of samples, good-fitting models should engender greater trust if they have not been modified or resulted from only minor tune-ups. Models that differ drastically from the initially hypothesized model should be viewed skeptically and not be considered seriously without fitting the modified model to data from a new sample. However, exploratory analyses can be a useful inductive exercise to challenge researchers to rethink their hypothesized models and potentially generate useful ideas for future research.

Equivalent models

Although structural equation modeling can be used to analyze the results from experimental studies (Russell et al., 1998), SEM is much more frequently applied to data from nonexperimental studies. The objective of these nonexperimental studies, in many applications, is the same as the objective of experimental studies: the assessment of cause-and-effect relationships. Psychologists tend to have a relatively rigid set of standards about what issues should be considered in discussing the validity of causal conclusions based on experiments. In contrast, no commonly accepted set of standards is routinely applied in evaluating causal conclusions based on SEM analyses of nonexperimental data.

In this section we briefly discuss some characteristics of experimental research and present a principle that underlies the ability of researchers to reach causal conclusions from experimental studies. We argue that this same principle should apply to reaching causal conclusions from SEM analyses of nonexperimental data. We then discuss problems with validating a hypothesized causal model using SEM when other models are equivalent to it. Finally, we suggest that researchers might find it provocative to propose equivalent models that are conceptually plausible but incompatible with the hypothesized model advocated by researchers.

Causal conclusions and experimental research

Experiments are designed to isolate the effect of the independent variable on the dependent variable. Well-designed experiments have the following characteristics: researcher's manipulation of the independent variable, the institution of controls to minimize the effects of variables other than the independent variable on the dependent variable, and precise measurement of the dependent variable (Kirk, 1995). Even with carefully designed experiments, researchers must consider explanations other than the independent variable causing the dependent variable. If researchers can make viable arguments against the alternative explanations, they may choose to present these arguments in the discussion section of their articles and conclude that the results are supportive of the effect of the independent variable on the dependent variable. On the other hand, if alternative explanations strongly rival the cause-and-effect hypotheses championed by researchers, they may consider conducting additional experiments to rule out these alternative explanations and describe these in multiple-study articles. Thus, the basic principle underlying the design, analysis, and interpretation of experimental studies is that the strength of a research conclusion is inversely related to the number and strength of rival hypotheses that can be generated as alternatives to the cause-and-effect hypothesis espoused by a researcher.

Equivalent models and causal conclusions

Models with different parameters are equivalent if they *must* yield the same reproduced covariance matrix for any sample covariance matrix.[4] It is possible for nonequivalent models to fit the data equally well for a particular dataset; however, equivalent models by definition must fit equally well for any dataset. When a proposed model is found that fits the data, models equivalent to the proposed model should be considered as rival hypotheses. A researcher cannot reach a strong conclusion about the hypothesized model to the extent that equivalent models are theoretically meaningful and consistent with the methods employed in the study.

For example, a researcher might propose that social anxiety in male adolescents can lead to fewer friends, then anger, and finally depression, as shown in the top part of figure 8.6. A cross-sectional study is conducted that requires boys between the ages of 15 and 18 to complete multiple measures to assess each factor in this mediational model. The researcher conducts SEM analyses, establishes that the proposed model fits the data very well, and concludes that the results support this model. However, without knowing

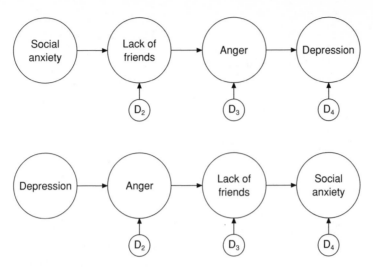

Figure 8.6   Equivalent mediated models.

what the data are, we also know that another mediational model, the one shown at the bottom of figure 8.6, must fit the data equally well and, in this sense, is also supported. This second model, which reverses the order of causation of the proposed model, is equivalent to the proposed model and acts as a potential rival hypothesis. To the extent that this second model is theoretically viable, it offers an alternative explanation for the results and weakens support for the researcher's model.

In this instance, the second model seems slightly less appealing conceptually in comparison with the proposed model. For example, we believe a better argument can be put forward for why anger leads to depression than for why depression leads to anger. Nevertheless, the second model cannot be ruled out on conceptual grounds. In addition, this model cannot be dismissed based on the methods employed in the study. In particular, no variables were manipulated, and the data were not collected across time. Accordingly, the second model is a tenable alternative explanation for the results and should, at a minimum, be presented in the discussion section of the article reporting this research. If the second model is ignored, some readers may think the data offer stronger support for the researcher's hypothesis than is warranted based on the SEM analysis.

A number of articles have been published describing methods for generating equivalent models (e.g., Lee and Hershberger, 1990; Raykov and Penev, 1999; Stelzl, 1986). These methods can be applied to models proposed by researchers to generate equivalent models. For our example, only one mediational model is equivalent to the researcher's model. Consequently, the viability of this equivalent model could be discussed. However, as shown by MacCallum, Wegener, Uchino, and Fabrigar (1993), models supported by data may, in practice, have many equivalent models and offer many alternative explanations for the results. Under these circumstances it might be argued that researchers could not possibly present all equivalent models in discussion sections and must, perhaps, instead rely on the sophistication level of readers to recognize that other explanations exist.

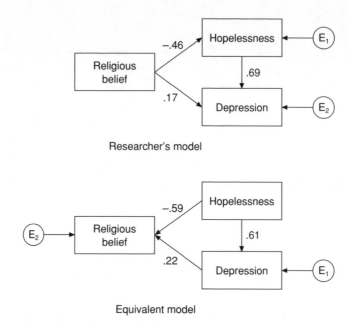

Figure 8.7   Equivalent models for religious belief example.

Alternatively, it could be argued it becomes even more important to make clear in discussion sections that support for the researcher's model is relatively weak because of the number of alternative explanations for the results. Rather than present all viable equivalent models, researchers might state that a number of viable equivalent models exist and discuss in depth one or two of these models, the ones that are defensible and most conceptually incompatible with the researcher's model. This discussion would make it apparent that the data do not offer strong support for the researcher's model.

For example, Murphy et al. (2000) conducted a path analysis among three variables: religious beliefs, hopelessness, and depression. As shown at the top of figure 8.7, they present a model with religious beliefs having a positive direct effect on depression, but having a stronger negative effect on depression through hopelessness. A number of models are equivalent to the presented model. Potentially the most conceptually incompatible model that is equivalent to the researchers' model is to reverse all the arrows, as shown at the bottom of figure 8.7. For this equivalent model, religious belief is not the causal variable, but the affected variable. Hopelessness has a negative direct effect on religious belief and has a weaker positive indirect effect on religious belief through depression.

Although the focus of this section is on equivalent models, the conclusions are relevant to a subclass of nonequivalent models. In practice, one or more nonequivalent models can frequently be found that fit almost as well, as well, or better than the researcher's model. If found, these nonequivalent models should be regarded as rival hypotheses to the researcher's model and should be treated similarly to equivalent models. Although researchers cannot be responsible for finding all possible good-fitting, nonequivalent models, other researchers should have the opportunity to find these models. They would have this chance if the data were made available by researchers who publish articles using SEM, as recommended by Hoyle and Panter (1995).

Conclusions

Applying SEM to data collected from multivariate field studies does not substitute for controlled experimentation, although it does permit us to take into account many of the complexities introduced by these studies (e.g., multivariate effects of measurement error). The acknowledgment of equivalent models and other good-fitting models in a discussion section of an article allows researchers to state in a clear and unambiguous fashion what we all know: the methods associated with field studies are insufficient to allow us to reach causal conclusions, and alternative explanations are available to explain the data. Discussion of alternative models is particularly important for readers unfamiliar with SEM who would then be able to better evaluate a study's worth.

Although we cannot reach firm causal conclusions from field studies, regardless of the statistical methods used, we can potentially further our understanding of phenomena by conducting these studies. By basing models on well-developed theory, it is less likely that equivalent or good-fitting non-equivalent models will be as interpretable and meaningful as the hypothesized model. Further, to the extent that hypothesized models are parsimonious, good fit is harder to achieve and fewer models are likely to be equivalent to the hypothesized model. These conditions strengthen support for a proposed model that fits the data well. A meaningful SEM study is one that not only supports a hypothesized model, but also allows us to discount alternative explanations for results – the same standard used to judge the worth of experimental studies.

Conclusions

The primary purpose of this chapter was to introduce five SEM topics that have important implications for the practice of clinical research. To achieve this goal, we attempted to discuss each of these topics in sufficient depth to allow us to reach a set of recommendations or conclusions. In the sections on coefficient alpha and multivariate analyses of means, we challenged the standard use of alpha and MANOVA and suggested alternative SEM approaches, recognizing that these alternative approaches are not problem free. In the sections on nonnormal data and exploratory analyses, we offered recommendations about how to conduct analyses based on current SEM theory and practice. For nonnormal data, the choice of estimation method is quite complex and is a function of factors such as the degree of nonnormality, the type of measures (e.g., Likert item versus summed scale score), model complexity, and sample size. With exploratory analyses, the search family of parameters should be based on the researcher's conceptual understanding of the investigation area, and the search should be conducted to minimize model misspecification. In the section on equivalent models, the recommendations concerned interpretation of results and stressed the importance of seeking alternative explanations for the data other than the model proposed by the researcher. We hope these sections not only encourage clinicians to read more on these issues, but also to explore other interesting topics in structural equation modeling.

Notes

1   Even though the reliability of a multidimensional measure might be reasonably high (in our example, .84), the results from it may be open to misinterpretation. A high overall score on a multidimensional measure might be due to high scores on all factors, very high scores on half of the factors and moderate scores on the other half of the factors, an extremely high score on a few factors and low scores on other factors, as well as other patterns of factor scores. However, to the extent that multiple factors underlying items are positively correlated and are a function of a higher-order factor, the results from a multidimensional measure are less open to misinterpretation. Under these conditions a person who obtains a high overall score on a measure is more likely to have scored high on all factors and high on the higher-order factor.

2   An alternative normal-theory technique is generalized least squares (GLS). We will not discuss GLS in this chapter because it is much less frequently applied, is asymptotically equivalent to ML, and, based on a recent study, produces more inaccurate parameter estimates and more often fails to reject incorrect models when compared to ML estimation (Olsson, Troye, and Howell, 1999).

3   For simplicity we describe the search family to include parameters that might be added to the hypothesized model. However, a more inclusive way to define the search family is as a subset of all constraints that are imposed on the hypothesized model. Some constraints may involve restricting parameters to zero and, accordingly, these parameters are not part of the hypothesized model. If one of these constraints is selected through a search, the parameter is allowed to be nonzero or, in other words, the parameter is added to the hypothesized model. However, other types of constraints may be included in the search family. For example, parameters that are part of the hypothesized model may be constrained to be equal to each other. If one of these constraints is selected in the search, the parameters are allowed to be unequal.

4   If the data include means as well as variances and covariances among the measured variables, models are equivalent if they yield the same reproduced covariance matrix and the same reproduced means for any dataset.

References

Aiken, L. S., Stein, J. A., and Bentler, P. M. (1994). Structural equation analyses of clinical subpopulation differences and comparative treatment outcomes: Characterizing the daily lives of drug addicts. *Journal of Consulting and Clinical Psychology, 62,* 488–99.

Atwood, R., Gold, M., and Taylor, R. (1989). Two types of delinquents and their institutional adjustment. *Journal of Consulting and Clinical Psychology, 57,* 68–75.

Austin, J. T., and Calerón, R. F. (1996). Theoretical and technical contribution to structural equation modeling: An updated annotated bibliography. *Structural Equation Modeling, 3,* 105–75.

Austin, J. T., and Wolfle, L. M. (1991). Annotated bibliography of structural equation modeling: Technical work. *British Journal of Mathematical and Statistical Psychology, 44,* 93–152.

Babakus, E., Ferguson, C. E., and Jöreskog, K. G. (1987). The sensitivity of confirmatory maximum likelihood factor analysis to violations of measurement scale and distributional assumptions. *Journal of Marketing Research, 24,* 222–8.

Becker, G. (2000). How important is transient error in estimating reliability? Going beyond simulation studies. *Psychological Methods*, 5, 370–9.

Bentler, P. M. (1990). Comparative fit indexes in structural models. *Psychological Bulletin*, 107, 238–46.

Bentler, P. M., and Chou, C.-P. (1993). Some new covariance structure model improvement statistics. In K. A. Bollen and J. S. Long (eds.), *Testing structural equation models* (pp. 235–55). Newbury Park, CA: Sage.

Bentler, P. M., and Dudgeon, P. (1996). Covariance structure analysis: Statistical practice theory, and directions. *Annual Review of Psychology*, 47, 563–92.

Bentler, P. M., and Yuan, K.-H. (1999). Structural equation modeling with small samples: Test statistics. *Multivariate Behavioral Research*, 34, 181–97.

Bollen, K. A. (1989). *Structural equations with latent variables*. New York: Wiley.

Bollen, K. A., and Lennox, R. (1991). Conventional wisdom on measurement: A structural equation perspective. *Psychological Bulletin*, 110, 305–14.

Bollen, K. A., and Stine, R. A. (1992). Bootstrapping goodness-of-fit measures in structural equation models. *Sociological Methods and Research*, 21, 205–29.

Boomsma, A. (1985). Nonconvergence, improper solutions, and starting values in LISREL maximum likelihood estimation. *Psychometrika*, 50, 229–42.

Boomsma, A. (1987). The robustness of maximum likelihood estimation in structural equation models. In P. Cuttance and R. Ecob (eds.), *Structural modeling by example: Applications in educational, sociological and behavioral research*. New York: Cambridge University Press.

Bowden, S. C., Carstairs, J. R., and Shores, E. A. (1999). Confirmatory factor analysis of combined Wechsler Adult Intelligence Scale – Revised and Wechsler Memory Scale – Revised scores in a healthy community sample. *Psychological Assessment*, 11, 339–44.

Bray, J. H., and Maxwell, S. E. (1985). *Multivariate analysis of variance*. Beverly Hills, CA: Sage.

Breckler, S. J. (1990). Applications of covariance structure modeling in psychology: Cause for concern? *Psychological Bulletin*, 107, 260–73.

Browne, M. W. (1984). Asymptotic distribution-free methods for the analysis of covariance structures. *British Journal of Mathematical and Statistical Psychology*, 37, 62–83.

Carrol, K. M., Nich, C., Frankforter, T. L., and Bisighini, R. M. (1999). Do patients change in the ways we intend? Assessing acquisition of coping skills among cocaine-dependent patients. *Psychological Assessment*, 11, 77–85.

Chou, C.-P., and Bentler, P. M. (1993). Invariant standardized estimated parameter change for model modification in covariance structure analysis. *Multivariate Behavioral Research*, 28, 97–116.

Coenders, G., Satorra, A., and Saris, W. E. (1997). Alternative approaches to structural modeling of ordinal data: A Monte Carlo study. *Structural Equation Modeling*, 4, 261–82.

Cole, D. A., Maxwell, S. E., Arvey, R., and Salas, E. (1993). Multivariate group comparisons of variable systems: MANOVA and structural equation modeling. *Psychological Bulletin*, 114, 174–84.

Cortina, J. M. (1993). What is coefficient alpha? An examination of theory and applications. *Journal of Applied Psychology*, 78, 98–104.

Crocker, L., and Algina, J. (1986). *Introduction to classical and modern test theory*. New York: Holt, Rinehart, Winston.

Cronbach, L. J. (1951). Coefficient alpha and the internal structure of tests. *Psychometrika*, 16, 297–334.

Curran, P. J., West, S. G., and Finch, J. F. (1996). The robustness of test statistics to nonnormality and specification error in confirmatory factor analysis. *Psychological Methods*, 1, 16–29.

Draucker, C. B. (1989). Cognitive adaptation of female incest survivors. *Journal of Consulting and Clinical Psychology*, 57, 668–70.

Fisher, J. D., Silver, R. C., Chinsky, J. M., Goff, B., Klar, Y., and Zagieboylo, C. (1989). Psychological effects of participation in a large group awareness training. *Journal of Consulting and Clinical Psychology*, 57, 747–55.

Fleishman, J., and Benson, J. (1987). Using LISREL to evaluate measurement models and scale reliability. *Educational and Psychological Measurement*, 47, 925–39.

Golding, J. M., and Aneshensel, C. S. (1989). Factor structure of the Center for Epidemiologic Studies Depression scale among Mexican Americans and non-Hispanic whites. *Psychological Assessment*, 1, 163–8.

Green, S. B., and Babyak, M. A. (1997). Control of Type I error with multiple tests of constraints in structural equation modeling. *Multivariate Behavioral Research*, 32, 39–52.

Green, S. B., and Hershberger, S. L. (2000). Correlated errors in true score models and their effect on coefficient alpha. *Structural Equation Modeling*, 7, 251–70.

Green, S. B., Lissitz, R. W., and Mulaik, S. (1977). Limitations of coefficient alpha as an index of text unidimensionality. *Educational and Psychological Measurement*, 37, 827–39.

Green, S. B., Thompson, M. S., and Babyak, M. A. (1998). A Monte Carlo investigation of methods for controlling Type I errors with specification searches in structural equation modeling. *Multivariate Behavioral Research*, 33, 365–84.

Green, S. B., Thompson, M. S., and Poirier, J. (1999). Exploratory analysis to improve model fit: Errors due to misspecification and a strategy to reduce their occurrence. *Structural Equation Modeling*, 6, 113–26.

Green, S. B., Thompson, M. S., and Poirier, J. (2001). An adjusted Bonferroni method for elimination of parameters in specification addition searches. *Structural Equation Modeling*, 8, 18–39.

Hancock, G. R. (1997). Structural equation modeling methods of hypothesis testing of latent variable means. *Measurement and Evaluation in Counseling and Development*, 20, 91–105.

Hancock, G. R. (1999). A sequential Scheffé-type respecification procedure for controlling Type I error in exploratory structural equation model modification. *Structural Equation Modeling*, 6, 158–68.

Hancock, G. R., Lawrence, F. R., and Nevitt, J. (2000). Type I error and power of latent mean methods and MANOVA in factorially invariant and noninvariant latent variable systems. *Structural Equation Modeling*, 7, 534–56.

Hancock, G. R., Stapleton, L. M., and Berkovitz, I. (2001). Loading and intercept invariance within multisample covariance and mean structure models. Unpublished manuscript.

Hoyle, R. H. (1994). Introduction to the special section: Structural equation modeling in clinical research. *Journal of Consulting and Clinical Psychology*, 62, 427–8.

Hoyle, R. H., and Panter, A. T. (1995). Writing about structural equation models. In R. H. Hoyle (ed.), *Structural equation modeling: Concepts, issues, and applications*. Thousand Oaks, CA: Sage.

Hoyle, R. H., and Smith, G. T. (1994). Formulating clinical research hypotheses as structural equation models: A conceptual overview. *Journal of Consulting and Clinical Psychology*, 62, 429–40.

Hu, L.-T., and Bentler, P. M. (1999). Cutoff criteria for fit indexes in covariance structure analysis: Conventional criteria versus new alternatives. *Structural Equation Modeling*, 6, 1–55.

Hu, L.-T., Bentler, P. M., and Kano, Y. (1992). Can test statistics in covariance structure analysis be trusted? *Psychological Bulletin*, 112, 351–62.

Irvine, A. B., Biglan, A., Smolkowski, K., Metzler, C. W., and Ary, D. (1999). The effectiveness of a parenting skills program for parents of middle school students in small communities. *Journal of Consulting and Clinical Psychology*, 67, 811–25.

Jöreskog, K. G. (1993). Testing structural equation models. In K. A. Bollen and J. S. Long (eds.), *Testing structural equation models* (pp. 294–316). Newbury Park, CA: Sage.

Jöreskog, K. G., and Sörbom, D. (1989). *LISREL 7: A guide to the program and applications* (2nd edn.). Chicago, IL: SPSS.

Kaplan, D. (1990). Evaluating and modifying covariance structure models: A review and recommendation. *Multivariate Behavioral Research*, 25, 137–55.

Kaplan, D. (2000). *Structural equation modeling: Foundations and extensions*. Thousand Oaks, CA: Sage.

Kirk, R. E. (1995). *Experimental design: Procedures for the behavioral sciences* (3rd edn.). Pacific Grove, CA: Brooks/Cole.

Kline, R. B. (1998). *Principles and practice of structural equation modeling*. New York: Guilford Press.

Lanyon, R. I., Dannenbaum, S. E., Wolf, L. L., and Brown, A. (1989). Dimensions of deceptive responding in criminal offenders. *Psychological Assessment*, 1, 300–4.

Lee, S., and Hershberger, S. (1990). A simple rule for generating equivalent models in covariance structure modeling. *Multivariate Behavioral Research*, 25, 313–34.

Long, J. D., and Brekke, J. S. (1999). Longitudinal factor structure of the Brief Psychiatric Rating Scale in Schizophrenia. *Psychological Assessment*, 11, 498–506.

MacCallum, R. C., and Austin, J. T. (2000). Covariance structure analysis: Statistical practice theory, and directions. *Annual Review of Psychology*, 51, 201–26.

MacCallum, R. C., and Browne, M. W. (1993). The use of causal indicators in covariance structure models: Some practical issues. *Psychological Methods*, 114, 533–41.

MacCallum, R. C., Browne, M. W., and Sugawara, H. M. (1996). Power analysis and determination of sample size for covariance structure modeling. *Psychological Methods*, 1, 130–49.

MacCallum, R. C., Roznowski, M., and Necowitz, L. B. (1992). Model modifications in covariance structure analysis: The problem of capitalization on chance. *Psychological Bulletin*, 111, 490–504.

MacCallum, R. C., Wegener, D. T., Uchino, B. N., and Fabrigar, L. R. (1993). The problem of equivalent models in applications of covariance structure analysis. *Psychological Bulletin*, 114, 185–7.

McDonald, R. P. (1981). The dimensionality of tests and items. *British Journal of Mathematical and Statistical Psychology*, 34, 100–17.

Marcoulides, G. A., Drezner, A., and Schumacker, R. E. (1998). Model specification searches in structural equation modeling using Tabu Search. *Structural Equation Modeling*, 5, 365–76.

Maruyama, G. M. (1998). *Basics of structural equation modeling*. Thousand Oaks, CA: Sage.

Maxwell, A. E. (1968). The effect of correlated errors on estimates of reliability coefficients. *Educational and Psychological Measurement*, 28, 803–11.

Micceri, T. (1989). The unicorn, the normal curve, and other improbable creatures. *Psychological Bulletin*, 105, 156–66.

Miller, M. B. (1995). Coefficient alpha: A basic introduction from the perspectives of classical test theory and structural equation modeling. *Structural Equation Modeling*, 2, 255–73.

Murphy, P. E., Ciarrocchi, J. W., Piedmont, R. L., Cheston, S., Peyrot, M., and Fitchett, G. (2000). The relation of religious belief and practices, depression, and hopelessness in persons with clinical depression. *Journal of Consulting and Clinical Psychology*, 68, 1102–6.

Muthén, B. (1984). A general structural equation model with dichotomous, ordered categorical, and continuous latent variable indicators. *Psychometrika*, 49, 115–32.

Muthén, B., and Kaplan, D. (1985). A comparison of some methodologies for the factor analysis of nonnormal Likert variables. *British Journal of Mathematical and Statistical Psychology*, 38, 171–89.

Muthén, B., and Kaplan, D. (1992). A comparison of some methodologies for the factor analysis of nonnormal Likert variables: A note on the size of the model. *British Journal of Mathematical and Statistical Psychology, 45,* 19–30.

Novick, M. R., and Lewis, C. (1967). Coefficient alpha and the reliability of composite measurements. *Psychometrika, 32,* 1–13.

Olsson, U. H., Troye, S. V., and Howell, R. D. (1999). Theoretic fit and empirical fit: The performance of maximum likelihood versus generalized least squares estimation in structural equation models. *Multivariate Behavioral Research, 34,* 31–59.

Osman, A., Kopper, B. A., Lineham, M. M., Barrios, F. X., Gutierrez, P. M., and Bagge, C. L. (1999). Validation of the Adult Suicidal Ideation Questionnaire and the Reasons for Living Inventory in an adult psychiatric inpatient sample. *Psychological Assessment, 11,* 115–23.

Raykov, T. (1997a). Scale reliability, Cronbach's coefficient alpha, and violations of essential tau-equivalence with fixed congeneric components. *Multivariate Behavioral Research, 32,* 329–53.

Raykov, T. (1997b). Estimation of composite reliability for congeneric measures. *Applied Psychological Measurement, 21,* 173–84.

Raykov, T. (1998). Coefficient alpha and composite reliability with interrelated nonhomogeneous items. *Applied Psychological Measurement, 22,* 375–85.

Raykov, T., and Penev, S. (1999). On structural equation model equivalence. *Multivariate Behavioral Research, 34,* 199–244.

Raykov, T., and Shrout, P. E. (in press). Reliability of scales with general structure: Point and interval estimation using structural equation modeling approach. *Structural Equation Modeling.*

Redmond, C., Spoth, R., Shin, C., and Lepper, H. S. (1999). Modeling long-term parent outcomes of two universal family-focused preventative interventions: One-year follow-up results. *Journal of Consulting and Clinical Psychology, 67,* 975–84.

Rigdon, E. E. (1996). CFI versus RMSEA: A comparison of two fit indices for structural equation modeling. *Structural Equation Modeling, 3,* 369–79.

Rotheram-Borus, M. J., Piacentini, J., Cantwell, C., Belin, T. R., and Song, J. (2000). The 18-month impact of an emergency room intervention for adolescent female suicide attempters. *Journal of Consulting and Clinical Psychology, 68,* 1081–93.

Rozeboom, W. W. (1966). *Foundations of the theory of prediction.* Homewood, IL: Dorsey.

Rozeboom, W. W. (1989). The reliability of a linear composite of nonequivalent subtests. *Applied Psychological Measurement, 13,* 277–83.

Russell, D. W., Kahn, J. H., Spoth, R., and Altmaier, E. M. (1998). Analyzing data from experimental studies: A latent variable structural equation modeling approach. *Journal of Counseling Psychology, 45,* 18–29.

Sanford, K., Bingham, C. R., and Zucker, R. A. (1999). Validity issues with the Family Environment Scale: Psychometric resolution and research application with alcoholic families. *Psychological Assessment, 11,* 315–25.

Satorra, A., and Bentler, P. M. (1994). Corrections to test statistic and standard errors in covariance structure analysis. In A. Von Eye and C. C. Clogg (eds.), *Analysis of latent variables in developmental research* (pp. 399–419). Newbury Park, CA: Sage.

Shipley, B. (2000). *Cause and correlation in biology? A user's guide to path analysis, structural equations and causal inference.* Cambridge: Cambridge University Press.

Sörbom, D. (1989). Model modification. *Psychometrika, 54,* 371–84.

Steiger, J. H. (2000). Point estimation, hypothesis testing, and interval estimation using the RMSEA: Some comments and a reply to Hayduk and Glaser. *Structural Equation Modeling, 7,* 149–62.

Steiger, J. H., and Lind, J. M. (1980, June). Statistically based tests for the number of common factors. Paper presented at the annual meeting of the Psychometric Society, Iowa City, IA.

Stelzl, I. (1986). Changing a causal model hypothesis without changing the fit: Some rules for generating equivalent models. *Multivariate Behavioral Research*, *21*, 309–31.

Stout, W. F. (1990). A new item response theory modeling approach and applications to unidimensionality assessment and ability estimation. *Psychometrika*, *55*, 293–325.

Swaim, R. C., Oetting, E. R., Edwards, R. W., and Beauvais, F. (1989). Links from emotional distress to adolescent drug use: A path model. *Journal of Consulting and Clinical Psychology*, *57*, 227–31.

Tracey, T. J., and Kokotovic, A. M. (1989). Factor structure of the Working Alliance Inventory. *Psychological Assessment*, *1*, 207–10.

West, S. G., Finch, J. F., and Curran, P. J. (1995). Structural equation models with nonnormal variables. In R. Hoyle (ed.), *Structural equation modeling: Concepts, issues, and applications* (pp. 56–75). Thousand Oaks, CA: Sage.

Yuan, K.-H., and Bentler, P. M. (1997). Mean and covariance structure analysis: Theoretical and practical improvements. *Journal of the American Statistical Association*, *92*, 767–74.

Yuan, K.-H., and Bentler, P. M. (1998). Normal theory based test statistics in structural equation modelling. *British Journal of Mathematical and Statistical Psychology*, *51*, 289–309.

Yung, Y.-F., and Bentler, P. M. (1996). Bootstrapping techniques in analysis of mean and covariance structures. In G. A. Marcoulides and R. A. Schumacker (eds.), *Advanced structural equation modeling: Issues and techniques* (pp. 195–226). Mahwah, NJ: Lawrence Erlbaum.

Zimmerman, D. W., Zumbo, B. D., and Lalonde, C. (1993). Coefficient alpha as an estimate of test reliability under violation of two assumptions. *Educational and Psychological Measurement*, *53*, 33–49.

CHAPTER NINE

Qualitative Methods in Psychological Research

Gloria L. Krahn and Michelle Putnam

Participant observation has been the *modus operandi* in the study of older hotel residents (single room occupancy hotels)... The initial phase of research in SRO hotels involved direct observation of the behavior of local residents in a variety of situations – hotels, hotel lobbies, restaurants, buses, parks. The basic assumption was that the subtleties of hotel life could only be gained through total immersion in the hotel milieu. Living in the hotel allowed me to observe dramatic events (e.g., hotel fires) that could not be anticipated in advance ... Since my monthly stipend check was equal to the average monthly income of persons in the hotel sample population, I worked out a budget and tried to live within the economic limits experienced by older residents. The role of "marginal native" provided flexibility and allowed relatively free movement among different sectors and social systems.

During the second phase of participant observation (from January to April), I was able to participate directly in the life of the study group ... In the desk clerk role I was able to establish relationships with several long-term hotel residents as well as to become acquainted with all the employees of the hotel. In this position I was able to observe, assess, and participate in transactions with the police, vice squad, community mental health workers, and other social service personnel. Additionally, it allowed me firsthand contact and experience with the many different types of persons using the south-of-Broadway turf. These various kinds of participation in the life of the SRO hotel residents allowed me to observe aspects of the hotel social structure and organization that would have been lost through use of nonparticipating methodologies.

Eckert (1980)

Qualitative Methods as Research Tools

Qualitative research methods can be an important part of a social scientist's research repertoire. When skillfully practiced, qualitative methods can provide a means to develop a context-rich description and understanding of phenomena. Qualitative methods are particularly appropriate when the researcher wants to gain a deeper understanding of a known phenomenon or desires to develop knowledge or theory in a new area. Qualitative research is interactive. The opportunity to speak one-on-one with an individual, interface with a group, or observe behavior in its naturally occurring context can be invaluable in helping develop an understanding of how people experience and interpret events. Its primary aim is to understand the meaning of the phenomena under study from the context or perspective of the individuals being studied. It provides a voice for study participants and allows research into complex phenomena that are not readily reduced to quantitative variables for inclusion in surveys or experimental designs (Murray, 1998).

Quantitative methods have been criticized for their narrow focus and inability to adequately capture the diverse array of experiences and contexts that often prevail in social science research. Qualitative designs can complement, enhance, or replace laboratory studies and experimental designs for some areas of study regarding the powerful set of forces at work in people's lives (Gergen, 1973, 1978; Harré and Secord, 1972; Rich and Ginsburg, 1999).

Adequate training in the knowledge and practice of qualitative research methods (e.g., focus groups, interviewing, observation) is critical for researchers to understand and to minimize the bias introduced by the researcher and the research process to the phenomenon under study. In qualitative research the researcher comes very close to the data, with the tools of qualitative methods bringing the data collector into close enough proximity to influence the data. Qualitative data collection is not protected by a structured protocol or established set of questions as it is in quantitative research. This makes the data vulnerable to the data collection process, and research procedures are needed to understand and minimize this likelihood. Good qualitative research is characterized by procedural rigor and based in sound understanding of the application of qualitative methodologies.

In our current work at the Center for Health and Wellness for Persons with Long Term Disabilities, for example, we are using qualitative methods to develop an initial understanding of the meaning of health and wellness to persons with diagnostic conditions like polio, multiple sclerosis, cerebral palsy, amputation, and spinal cord injury in order to inform the development of quantitative studies. Subsequent studies probe various theoretical, applied, and policy aspects of health and wellness practices among persons with disabilities, professionals who provide health promotion services, and the healthcare infrastructure that finances and regulates those services. Because health and wellness is a relatively new concept in its application to persons with long-term disabilities, we believe that qualitative inquiry into the phenomenon is the most effective way to ensure that our research reflects the experiences of persons living with disabilities in the community, thus helping to ensure the relevance and applicability of our findings.

This chapter presents a brief overview of the roots of qualitative methods in psychological research and describes a selection of popular qualitative techniques, highlights the practical applications of each, and presents resources for further exploration of each technique in depth. It then discusses sampling, qualitative data collection methods, qualitative data analysis, limitations of the qualitative approach, and suggestions for evaluating qualitative studies. It concludes by summarizing ethical considerations for the researcher in using qualitative research.

Types of Qualitative Methods

Qualitative research embodies a number of different research approaches, each with differing assumptions, intents, and methods. Historical trends in qualitative research show that as different types of phenomena have come under study (e.g., feminism, urban cultures, religiosity) there has been a tendency for different qualitative research paradigms and data collection methods (e.g., interviews, observation, focus groups) to dominate within areas of study. A number of reference texts are available that provide overviews of different approaches and their specific application to research (e.g., Grbich, 1999; Lincoln and Guba, 1985; Miles and Huberman, 1984, 1994; Patton, 1990, 1997; Strauss and Corbin, 1990; Taylor and Bogdan, 1998). These are valuable to both novices and experts in qualitative research. The interested reader is referred to these texts for more detailed background information on qualitative methods. As a brief introduction to qualitative research, the following section provides an overview of four of the most popular approaches.

Phenomenology

Phenomenology is the study of lived experiences through understanding the structure, essence, and context of the subjective experience of the individual (Beck, 1990). It is based in philosophy, and holds that experiences, or what have previously been referred to as phenomena, can be variously defined and studied. Phenomena can include such experiences as growing up within the inner city, experiencing first love, and living with HIV. The core principle of this approach is to study how individuals perceive and make sense of an experience and to determine the "essence" of that experience (Patton, 1990).

An example of the phenomenological approach is the work of Willard-Holt (1998), who studied the academic and personality characteristics of gifted students with cerebral palsy. The goal of the study was to understand how gifted students with developmental disabilities might be identified and appropriately served. She used the theoretical lens of phenomenology and methods of ethnography to describe both the characteristics of gifted students who were unable to communicate orally, and the ways in which they demonstrated their intellectual abilities. To explore this phenomenon, Willard-Holt used participant observation and interviewing as primary data collection techniques, and gathered supporting data through audiotapes, videotapes, transcripts of formal presentations by teachers, and documents that included school work, scholastic records, logs kept by aides, awards, and results of testing.

Grounded theory

Grounded theory is based on the philosophical foundation of symbolic interaction and has the purpose of developing new theory or refining existing theory directly from the raw data. It provides a prescribed, systematic process for analyzing qualitative data that may have been collected in a number of ways. Through the use of grounded theory researchers seek to provide plausible support for their theories through the following steps: (1) developing a rough definition of the phenomenon to be explained, (2) formulating a hypothesis about the phenomenon, (3) examining a single case to look for the fit between the data and the hypothesis, (4) revising the hypothesis or the definition of the phenomenon based on whether the data positively or negatively support the hypothesis, and (5) repeating with additional cases and proceeding until the hypothesis has been adequately revised and tested (Taylor and Bogdan, 1998). Throughout this process the researchers pay careful attention to the trustworthiness of the data, the development of the response categories, and the interpretation of findings into theory.

A number of researchers have used grounded theory approaches to develop models of treatment efficacy based on the perceptions of adults participating in the treatments. Recent studies have addressed participants' perceptions of mindfulness-based cognitive therapy (Mason and Hargreaves, 2001), nonpharmacological psychiatric treatment (Nelson, Lord, and Ochocka, 2001), chiropractic and exercise regimens (Yardley et al., 2001), and cognitive behavioral and relaxation procedures for cancer patients (MacCormack et al., 2001). Data collection methods rely heavily on interviews and focus groups. As in all qualitative methods, the relationship between process and resulting theory is very important. Glaser and Strauss (1967) contend that the adequacy of the theory generated by the grounded theory approach cannot be separated from the process by which it is generated.

Ethnography

Ethnography originated in the fields of anthropology and sociology as a qualitative method to develop a deeper or broader understanding of social groups. In particular, it has been used to study ethnic and cultural groups. Within this context the term "culture" is used to refer to an integrated pattern of human behaviors that include thoughts, communications, actions, and other behaviors (Cross et al., 1989). Through extensive fieldwork, ethnographers seek to become knowledgeable about cultural systems, components of the culture, and the rules that regulate the functioning of cultures. With increased attention to the cultural diversity within American society and efforts to increase cultural competence in provision of services (e.g., Anderson and Fenichel, 1989; Lynch and Hanson, 1992), ethnographic approaches can be a highly effective method to develop a better understanding of cultural contexts and behaviors. The quotation that opened this chapter is part of an ethnographic study by Eckert (1980) of single room occupancy (SRO) hotels in San Diego. Eckert both lived and worked in SRO hotels that allowed him unique access to long-term residents' culture.

Ecological psychology

Ecological psychology is set within an ecological systems perspective and views humans as interdependent with their settings. In his classic work, Bronfenbrenner (1979) applied an ecological psychology perspective to understand human behavior through consideration of its larger ecological context. Individuals are regarded as living and behaving within a series of nested ecological contexts. Ecological research seeks to determine the relationships between the behavior of humans and their environments. Environments may be interpreted as physical (e.g., space, climate, surroundings), interpersonal (e.g., who else is present? what do they say or do?), and social (what are the prevailing societal values? legally defined rights?).

Ecological psychology allows for the inference of intentionality in interpreting observed behavior. Data collection begins with detailed and comprehensive observations from a distanced, objective stance. These data are subsequently analyzed in terms of purposive, goal-directed action. As a method, ecological psychology gained prominence through the detailed, stream-of-behavior observations of Barker and Wright (1955) in describing one boy's day. This early work spawned a whole field of observational research in psychology that provided new insights into interpersonal interactions, particularly among family members that have spanned nearly half a century (e.g., Gottman, 1979; Jacob, Krahn, and Leonard, 1991; Mash and Terdal, 1997; Patterson, 1975). The ecological perspective can broaden the scope of contexts considered by researchers and policy analysts in their attempt to understand human behavior, moving from examining only immediate settings and interrelationships to considering the influences of broader community and societal factors.

The Selection of Population Samples in Qualitative Research

The selection of a population sample for qualitative research, as for quantitative research, is dependent on the purpose and scope of the study. However, unlike quantitative research, sampling in qualitative research is less concerned with randomness of sample selection and more with intent of the study. Patton (1990) outlines fifteen different types of sampling strategies that address different concerns. These include deviant case sampling, homogeneous sampling, typical case sampling, snowball sampling, theory-based sampling, purposeful random sampling, and politically important case sampling, among others.

For each method of data collection described below, there are various ways to select and structure a sample depending on the research questions under consideration. For example, a study may focus on homogeneous participants in order to describe how a particular phenomenon affects a specific subgroup of people. Such would be the case for research that studied the experience of commitment for detoxification and substance use treatment of homeless, young adult women in an inner-city setting. Another study may seek to deliberately include discrepant or extreme cases to gain the new information or insight that these participants can provide. Such heterogeneity of sample can be quite valuable when exploring previously unstudied phenomena and when seeking to gain an understanding of how events, behaviors, or concepts are perceived by a broad spectrum of people. A case in point would be the focus group research being undertaken in our own Center to gain a broader understanding of how people define health and wellness, including persons who vary on such factors as gender, age, nature of disability, and cultural background. In general, the recommendation for sampling in qualitative research is to continue sampling until no new information emerges or until the conceptual framework the researcher is working with becomes integrated, testable, and sufficiently explanatory of the phenomenon under study (Patton, 1990).

Overview of Qualitative Data Collection Methods

The qualitative approach to research is intended to develop a researcher's comprehension of a phenomenon through understanding its context and its meaning to the persons experiencing the phenomenon. The beginning point of qualitative research is asking questions, not establishing hypotheses. The process of data collection and data analysis is often dynamic, with the researcher being able to modify elements of the research design as needed to capture or explore new or previously unknown facets of the phenomenon during the research process. The following section provides a general overview of several popular qualitative data collection methods. For more detailed information on these methods and their application, the reader is referred to the general texts listed previously or to specific resources listed at the conclusion of this chapter.

In-depth interviews

The in-depth interview may be the most common of all qualitative methods of data collection. In practice, it is used in situations in which the interviewer wants to gain a better understanding of the individual's perception of a particular phenomenon by exploring a few general topics to help uncover the meaning of those topics to the individual. Despite its apparent simplicity, conducting an interview is often very challenging when the intent is to draw out all relevant perceptions of the respondent without influencing the reporting of these perceptions. There are many types of interviews, but data collection in qualitative research often relies on unstructured and semi-structured interviews. In the unstructured interview, there is no prescribed list of questions that are asked. The researcher carefully provides the topic and parameters for reporting, and attempts to gather information about the phenomena by conducting a more "stream of consciousness" discussion with the sample participants. An example would be "Tell me about the first time you fell in love?" Unstructured interviews are often used as pilot interviews to lend insight into how specific concepts should be defined or discussed and permit the researcher to become acquainted with these notions (Fielding, 1993). Semi-structured interviews, as the name implies, have more structure to them, often as a small set of open-ended questions. Their use requires that the researcher already have some understanding of the phenomena and a willingness to impose some preconceptions on the interview process. Semi-structured interviews contain open-ended questions that allow the respondent to describe his or her experiences in a broad way without the restraints that a more fully structured interview would create. Within both the unstructured and semi-structured interview, the interviewer seeks to clarify what the respondent is saying by probing responses with specific follow-up questions regarding the meaning attributed to specific events, or words used to describe those events (Seidman, 1998).

Key strategies for conducting successful qualitative interviews and developing a trust-worthy dataset include establishing rapport with the respondent, being consistent in the way interviewers ask questions across respondents, and recognizing and accounting for interviewer effects (Seidman, 1998). Interviewing is a mutually influencing process, with the interviewer role and the interview situation affecting the respondent's answers. When using the interview as a data gathering method it is important for the researcher to have a good understanding of who the respondents are, to practice the interview techniques before implementing for data collection, and to recognize the impact the interviewer may have on the data collection process. Several excellent resources are available that describe in greater detail the process of interviewing and the analysis of interview data (e.g., Seidman, 1998; Fielding, 1993).

The in-depth interview has been used effectively in many qualitative studies, particu-larly in areas where little is known about the topic of study and the researchers are engaging in exploratory work. Westgren and Levi (1999) conducted in-depth interviews with eight women about their sexual experiences after traumatic spinal cord injury. The researchers wanted to know how participants felt about their first sexual encounter after their injury, how the participant and her partner talked about the new situation in their sex life, and how the injury affected the participant's sex life. The interviews allowed the investigators to gain a better understanding of coping strategies, communication frustra-tions, and the need for particular rehabilitation information or assistance.

Focus groups

The focus group has gained enormous popularity as a data collection method over the past decade. This increased utilization may be attributed to the fact that focus groups are typically inexpensive, interactive, and a quick means of gathering information (Marshall and Rossman, 1995). Morgan (1993) recommends the use of focus groups for a number of situations: (1) when there is a gap in understanding between professionals and their target audience, (2) when the behavior and motivations being investigated are complex, (3) when one wants to learn more about the degree of consensus on a topic, and (4) when there are tensions or power differentials between different parties that make sur-veys or interviews inappropriate means for collecting information. What separates the focus group from the interview is its ability to create a dialogue among group participants that broadens and deepens the information gathered through the dynamics of discussion (Stewart and Shamdasani, 1990).

Typically, focus groups contain eight to twelve participants and last from one to two hours. Selection criteria for participants varies depending on the nature of the topic under study, but in all cases participants share certain characteristics or life experiences that are of interest to the study (Brotherson, 1994). In general, the interviewer develops a protocol with a series of open-ended questions intended to generate discussion on the topic by eliciting different opinions and points of view. Part of the uniqueness of this method is the fact that focus group members can comment on one another's point of view, modify their own opinions, and further develop their statements as the discussion evolves (Kidd and Parshall, 2000). Much like other forms of qualitative data collection, multiple focus groups are held until no new information is generated from the discussion process. Therefore, depending on the topic and the sample, the number of focus groups conducted during the data collection process can vary substantially.

Despite its flexible format the focus group method is a rigorous form of empirical inquiry when practiced well. Of particular importance to holding a successful focus group is the selection of participants. Researchers who use focus groups find that there can be significant bias in focus group research if only the most accessible members of a population are included in the research. For example, in their work on Mexican-American gang members in South Texas, Valdez and Kaplan (1999) discuss the importance of undertaking extensive field work to obtain information on gang structure, types of membership, and range of activities before determining whom to include in their research sample. They wanted participants that were homogeneous as gang members, but diverse enough to represent subtle variations within the gang population. Therefore, they sought to move beyond the traditional recruitment strategy of soliciting institutional referrals and instead gained access to gang members through actively volunteering in the community. In this instance, as in all qualitative research, selecting the appropriate sample was crucial to fulfilling the goals of the research study. The deliberateness of Valdez and Kaplan's sample selection indicates their awareness of the social dynamics of the group under study, and awareness that a more restricted sample may have resulted in substantial limitations of the study.

Similarly important in the focus group study is the role of the moderator during the group process itself. The central goal of the focus group is to enable spontaneous interaction between participants in order to lead to the discovery of deeper insights about the phenomenon (Kidd and Parshall, 2000). This goal is best achieved when the researcher or moderator is well trained in the focus group method and can actively avoid questions, actions, or reactions that inappropriately influence the comments or direction of the focus group discussion. A common error is to include excessive interaction between the moderator and participants, thereby reducing the independent nature of the comments produced and the "live" and immediate nature of the group discussion. The moderator (especially an unskilled or inexperienced one) may also bias results by providing cues about the desirability of answers by selectively responding to certain types of answers. Such errors can lead the researcher to put more faith in the findings than may be warranted (Stewart and Shamdasani, 1990).

Direct observation

Observation includes the systematic noting and recording of events and behaviors and the social, cultural, and physical environments in which they occur. The overall strategy is inductive, with the observer using initial observations as a starting point from which to formulate hypotheses (Waddington, 1994). Through observation, the researcher seeks to discover repeating patterns of behavior and the relationships between behaviors and particular environments (Marshall and Rossman, 1995; Taylor and Bogdan, 1998). Distinctions are made between two types of observation: participant and direct. In participant observation the researcher becomes an active player in the environment she or he is studying, purposefully engaging study participants in dialogue and assuming an active role. Direct observation involves the researcher acting as a bystander, watching the phenomena but maintaining a physical and psychological distance from it. Eckert's description of data collection in SRO hotels incorporated both direct and participant observation.

The steps involved in conducting observation include entering the field, recording data, analyzing data, and leaving the field. Initially, the researcher enters an environment of interest with some predetermined research questions. In this phase of the method, difficulty in gaining access to a particular organization or social situation will vary depending upon the nature of the phenomena under study. For example, in his research on strike behavior among brewery workers, Waddington (1994) progressed through several levels of both manufacturer and labor administration organizations in order to enter the brewery, and he then had to demonstrate allegiance to the strikers' cause in order to gain access to his population of interest – the strikers. In this case, his field notes served as the basis for development of a checklist that was used to develop categories and themes to explain behavior over time. Waddington left the field by breaking contacts with his informants at the end of the strike.

The main advantage of observational research is the opportunity to be a "fly on the wall" and observe the complex interactions of a particular social or physical setting. The drawbacks of observational studies include the length of time it may take a researcher to gain access to a community and the phenomena of interest, the time required to develop an understanding of the environment, and in the case of some types of participant observation, the personal commitment it may require to become part of a specific community (Taylor and Bogdan, 1998). Always of concern in observational research is the reactivity effect, the often-unknown degree to which the awareness of being observed influences the behaviors of interest. In some instances, observational data can be collected nonintrusively, although researchers need to be highly cognizant of ethical constraints on observing and recording behavior without prior informed consent by the study participants. Gardner (2000) provides a valuable and current overview of reactivity in direct observational studies of parent–child interactions.

Record review

Record review, or examination of extant documentation, can provide a valuable source of data for historical and discourse analyses. Examples of records that have been reviewed

include personal documentation such as diaries, journals, letters, films; formal documentation, like minutes of meetings, logs, announcements, formal policy statements; and official
documents, such as court records, marriage licenses, and other forms of archival data
(Grbich, 1999; Marshall and Rossman, 1995). All of these records can be useful in
developing a better understanding of the values, beliefs and, sometimes, status of the
population under study.

A typical method used to evaluate documents is content analysis, in which the documents are scrutinized in a systematic manner to search for patterns of thoughts or
behavior. A strength of content analysis is its unobtrusive nature, allowing the researcher
to investigate sensitive topics without altering the phenomena under study. A good
example of this is the study by Sobel et al. (2001) that retrospectively analyzed data from
a pediatric psychology clinic to determine the type of presenting problems and nature of
treatment. Analyzing 250 records (10 percent sample) they determined that the majority
of patients were boys (aged 2–12 years) presenting with externalizing behavior problems,
and referred for behavioral treatment. Similarly, Mills (1997) examined the medical files
of 53 inner-city SSI recipients who were previously on county general assistance and had
recently transferred to SSI. Using a case method approach, Mills conducted a complex
and extensive record review and found that almost 70 percent of the cases studied involved claimants with a history of violence, either as a victim or perpetrator of violence,
or both.

When and Where to Use Qualitative Research

Psychologists can use qualitative methods in many ways. They can be employed alone as
a means of exploring and describing a specific phenomenon, or they can be used in combination with quantitative methods as a way to clarify the researcher's understanding of
a specific phenomenon. The researcher may choose to use qualitative methods: (1) before
a study has begun to better understand the phenomenon under study; (2) during the course
of a longer research process as a means of primary data collection or to assist in interpretation of quantitative data prior to additional data collection; and (3) at the close of a
study to assist in understanding findings. Decisions can be made about when and where
to use qualitative methods depending on the researcher's intent and the nature of the study.

In general, qualitative data collection methods require a higher level of involvement with
respondents than do quantitative methods such as surveys. This is particularly evident
with participant observation when researchers join in family or community events to
observe and record events and to reflect on their own reactions and experiences. Unlike
quantitative research, where there is typically more personal distance between researchers
and research participants, qualitative research involves the investigator coming into closer
experiential proximity to the people and the issues involved. It is imperative that the
researcher has the ability to separate their observations from their reactions.

When this does not happen, numerous difficulties can arise. First, there can be a
problem with role confusion and possible role conflict in terms of the ethical responsibilities of researchers who become intimately familiar with the lives of their research

participants. The best way for the researcher to deal with this dilemma is to plan ahead and establish procedures to address such issues before the study begins. Precautionary steps to employ include training data collectors in procedures to follow and informing research participants of the "ground rules" for the research study early in the research process. This will help to reduce anxiety on the part of both data collectors and study participants. Second, qualitative data collection typically is not protected by a structured set of questions and response alternatives. This means that in cases where multiple researchers are employed to study the same phenomenon, data can become vulnerable to the biases of the investigators. For example, interviewers who probe the responses of particular interview questions but not others may bias the results. Protections can be built into the data collection methods by thoroughly training interviewers or observers, including training in self-awareness of biases. This training can minimize interviewer biases from influencing the reporting or recording of data, while, at the same time, keeping attention focused on the key phenomena under study.

An important trend in qualitative research over the past decade has been a growing appreciation for the use of multiple methods within the same study. Methodological pluralism is increasingly touted as a hallmark of good science (e.g., Sechrest and Sidani, 1995). Triangulation is the application of multiple data collection methods to the same research question in order to determine the convergence of information obtained through these multiple methods. The goal of triangulation is to broaden the perspective of the researcher and strengthen the stability of the study findings. Triangulation of qualitative and quantitative data has been applied in numerous studies addressing diverse research questions. The researcher is cautioned, however, that in resolving discrepancies of different methods and data types, use of multiple methods can pose notable challenges, particularly when the convergence of data types was not carefully planned for (e.g., Krahn, Hohn, and Kime, 1995).

As triangulation has become more widely accepted and used by researchers, attention and debate has shifted to the paradigms and premises of these new mixed-method designs. Through the application of triangulation, the multiple methods will intentionally or inadvertently combine different, and potentially conflicting, paradigms that represent differing assumptions about the nature of the social phenomena under study. Greene and Caracelli (1997) define three levels of decision-making to consider in mixed-method research design. These are the political level or purpose of the study, the philosophical (or paradigm) level, and the technical or methods level. While mixed methods at the technical level can often strengthen a study, mixing methods at the paradigm level can pose great difficulties. A common dilemma is mixing paradigms that allow for multiple "truths" to be held by different perspectives with a paradigm that is based in belief in a single interpretation of "truth."

Smith (1997) distinguishes paradigms from "crude mental models" and argues that it is these mental models that guide the actions of evaluators and researchers. She describes three types of mental models that researchers hold. The first model is based in the belief of a single reality that is separate from individuals' interpretations of it. Model I presumes that definitive knowledge is possible. This has been the presumption of a positivist and pragmatist perspective and would restrict the role of qualitative approaches. The second model presumes a real world that is beyond the interpretations of any single individual, but also one that cannot be studied free of individual perspective. In Model II qualitative and quantitative components must be conducted separately and simultaneously to avoid the bias of interdependence across methods. In the third mental model, the world is viewed as complex, contextually contingent, and mediated by individual interpretation. In Model III it is not possible to develop a definitive account of the phenomenon under study. The analysis of the data is the construction of the inquirer, and social processes are as important as structural variables. This model is at the heart of qualitative "knowing," but appreciation or acceptance of this model is difficult for adherents of a positivist and pragmatist perspective. Awareness and delineation of these crude mental models is helpful in understanding the sometimes-heated dialogue between qualitative and quantitative researchers.

Analyzing Qualitative Data

Perhaps the most universal experience with qualitative data analysis is that it is time intensive. Often the dataset is comprised of hundreds of pages of narrative text or complete books of field notes. The first task of the researcher is usually to sort and sift through the text, looking for commonalities of meaning, discrepancies across cases, and contextual variables of the experience. As themes begin to develop the researcher weaves together ideas, hypotheses, and emerging theories about the phenomenon, a process that allows for the reporting of findings and development of understanding regarding the nature of the phenomenon. If desired, these findings can be confirmed through further data collection. In approaches such as grounded theory (Glaser and Strauss, 1967; Strauss and Corbin, 1990), data collection is conducted conjointly with data analysis. Initially identified themes or constructs are checked against new data as they are collected and the constructs are revised accordingly, leading to a theory that has emerged from the data and is grounded in it.

A number of software packages are available today that assist researchers in analyzing their qualitative data. Qualitative analysis software is valuable in assisting the researcher to organize, store, and report data. It is not certain that software programs necessarily save researchers time in conducting their analyses. It is recommended that one ask colleagues for suggestions on programs they have used and had success with before selecting a software program. Popular programs on the market include NUDIST, Ethnograph, and Winmax. Each software program is structured differently and has its own unique qualities. Depending on the purpose of the research, one may be more suitable than others. For example, some software is better at developing models of grounded theory than others. Additionally, others have varied reporting features that may be of more use to some researchers than others. Given the current pace of software development for qualitative research, there is hope that the time investment required for qualitative data analyses will decline. Some researchers prefer to perform qualitative analysis by hand, using word-processing programs or cutting, pasting, and organizing note cards on large tack boards. Even as the technology increases, some individuals will prefer to conduct qualitative analysis in this tried and true manner.

Table 9.1 Lincoln and Guba (1985) criteria for evaluating qualitative research

Criteria	Meaning	Goal	Achieved through
Credibility	Confidence in the procedures and findings	To establish that the information being reported is the same as the informants' experiences	Triangulation; member checking (going back to the informants and determining whether the summarized information is consistent with the informants' experiences)
Transferability	The extent to which the findings are limited to their present context or are transferable to other groups or contexts	Provide description necessary to enable conclusion to be made about whether transfer is a possibility	Provide database that makes transferability judgments possible
Dependability	The extent of agreement in categorizing or coding the data or the reliability of the study's conclusions	Determine the acceptability of the process of inquiry and accuracy of product from that inquiry	Researchers need to demonstrate that the findings could be repeated using the same context and participants
Confirmability	The ability of the procedures to be formally audited and confirmed by independent review	Another researcher should be able to see the logic the researcher used to come to the final conclusions	Qualitative researchers should keep an audit trail using transcripts, field notes, observations and a journal of personal reactions throughhout the study so that the confirmability of the findings can be demonstrated

Analysis of narrative data involves developing a taxonomy of themes or categories in which to organize segments of narrative, revising these themes with additional data, and grouping narrative into these themes. The NUDIST program, for example, plots out themes and subthemes, developing a branching diagram of the coding taxonomy. Results are typically reported as quotations to illustrate these themes. Some researchers will report frequencies of theme usage as a measure of importance or salience, though there is some disagreement about such practices, particularly for focus group data where mention of a theme by one individual can provoke numerous additional comments that might not have arisen in an individual context.

Criteria for evaluating qualitative studies

As the frequency of qualitative studies increases, there is a corresponding and pragmatic need for established criteria by which to evaluate the rigor of their research methods. Two sets of criteria are presented here that are representative of a number of criterion sets in use at this time (e.g., Henwood and Pidgeon, 1992; Lincoln and Guba, 1985; Rennie, Phillips, and Quartaro, 1988). The first set of criteria is drawn from Lincoln and Guba (1985), who developed a set of criteria presented in table 9.1 that translate readily from quantitative approaches, and provide a transition into qualitative methods for quantitatively trained researchers, including most psychologists. The primary concept they propose is that of *trustworthiness*, a concept that is broadly analogous to reliability and validity in quantitative studies. In their framework, trustworthiness is determined by the four criteria of credibility, transferability, dependability, and confirmability.

A second set of criteria – that of Henwood and Pidgeon (1992) – more distinctly reflects the unique nature of qualitative methods. Because qualitative approaches do not rest on a norm of objectivity that assumes independence of the known from the knower, these criteria move beyond measures that reduce observer bias. Henwood and Pidgeon propose seven criteria as presented in table 9.2 to assess the merit of qualitative methods.

There are obvious similarities across these two sets of criteria, while their differences reflect the differing assumptions of their underlying models of research. The criteria of Lincoln and Guba provide a ready translation from criteria for assessing rigor of quantitative approaches. As researchers become increasingly accustomed to qualitative methods and readers become more familiar with these approaches, we anticipate that the criteria based in qualitative approaches (such as those of Henwood and Pidgeon) will be used increasingly.

Limitations of the Qualitative Approach

Traditionally, one of the most frequently discussed issues in both quantitative and qualitative research is the generalizability of a study's findings. In qualitative research, generalizability is heavily dependent upon the purpose and procedures of the study. Because the intent of qualitative approaches is to understand a phenomenon from the

Table 9.2 Henwood and Pidgeon (1992) criteria for evaluating qualitative research

Criteria	Meaning	Goal	Achieved through
Keeping close to the data	Being grounded in the data	Conceptual categories are summarized and labeled in ways that reflect their constituent data	Using comprehensive definitions summarizing why phenomena have been labeled in certain ways that allow both researcher and reader to evaluate the fit of data with the label assigned
Theory integrated at diverse levels of abstraction	Drawn from grounded theory, places importance on how the data are synthesized	To ensure that the theory at all levels of abstraction is related to the data in meaningful and integrated ways	Readily apparent connections should be evident between the data and both lower and higher levels of abstractions
Reflexivity	Keen awareness of the research procedures used	To be alert to the ways in which researchers' perspectives and biases influence the subject of study	Fully describing researchers' attitudes and values; keeping a "reflexive journal" recording the reflections of researcher's own role and values, daily schedule of the study, and the methodological decisions made
Documentation	Generating records of the values and assumptions of the researchers, definitions of categories, initial concerns, sampling decisions, observations about the context, data collection procedures, and ideas about the quality of the data	Build a paper trail of issues and decision-making that is open to audit by other researchers	Examples of documentation include research logs and records of classification
Theoretical sampling and negative case analysis	Describes broad and specific sampling that will develop or extend the theory, and includes seeking cases that are apparent exceptions to the theory	Corroborate the theory through selecting cases that challenge initial assumptions, categories, and theory	An example would be to sample broadly among families and explore the meaning of the differences presented by families who are "outliers" or exceptions to the rule
Sensitivity to negotiated realities	Refers to developing a shared interpretation of the findings through dialogue with research participants	To develop a shared understanding and interpretation between the researchers and participants	Negotiating joint reality between the perceptions of the participant and the observations and interpretations of the researcher
Transferability of findings	How clearly the context of the study is recognized and has been described and to what other contexts the obtained findings might apply	Awareness of contextual factors that influence how findings can or cannot be applied to other contexts	Providing detailed information about the contextual features of the study

frame of reference of the person living the experience, different experiences by different participants are valid and equally "true." Differing from quantitative approaches, qualitative approaches allow for the possibility that alternative and different perspectives could be derived, and that these alternative perspectives would be equally valid. These alternative perspectives may be particularly likely where sampling has included discrepant or extreme cases, and perhaps less likely in typical case sampling, where the purpose of the study has been to identify the common essence of experience. Concerns about generalizability tend to generate discomfort in researchers with a strongly quantitative perspective, or whose conceptual framework is based on a belief in a singular truth, more so than those who have some background or training in qualitative research (e.g., Clarke, 1992).

Qualitative methods have been fruitfully employed in exploring new phenomena to assist design of subsequent investigations, developing frameworks for understanding complex social situations such as culturally diverse perspectives which numeric data do not capture the essence of, and in interpreting findings of quantitative studies. Qualitative methods are not generally useful for hypothesis testing, or confirmation of preestablished theory or premises. Multiple-method designs are recommended for those research situations.

Ethical Considerations in Qualitative Research

Ethical considerations are a part of all research endeavors, whether qualitative or quantitative. Most universities and organizations that regularly engage in research have standing institutional review boards (IRBs) or human subjects committees that review research protocols for the protection of research participants. Their purpose is to identify and safeguard against any potential situations where physical or psychological harm could occur during the course of the study. Chapter 4 in this volume discusses these concerns. Common ethical issues include whether or not the participation of participants is voluntary; ensuring that informed consent to participate in the study has been obtained; ensuring that information and data collected are kept confidential and anonymous; requiring safeguard procedures to ensure the researcher's ability to protect participants from potential harm they could incur by participating in the study; and addressing concerns of deception by researchers to gain access to a study population.

Aside from these general concerns, particular ethical concerns can arise that are more specific to qualitative research. These stem from the close proximity of the researcher in relation to the phenomena under study and to the study participants. For example, researchers engaging in participant observation may face issues of role disclosure; interviewers discussing sensitive issues may find themselves in the uncomfortable dual role of therapist and scientist; and researchers involved in studies of traumatic phenomena such as domestic violence, terminal illness, and child poverty can experience substantial distress after repeatedly interviewing people and observing or reading accounts of these events (Cieurzo and Keitel, 1999; Russel, 1999; Urquiza, Wyatt, and Goodlin-Jones, 1997).

Beyond these ethical issues, many researchers have raised questions and expressed concerns about their legal responsibilities when conducting research on sensitive topics. For example, researchers who witness violence or illegal acts, like spouse abuse or theft, may consider whether or not they should report these activities to the proper authorities; and those who gain access to personal information regarding health or psychological status – such as whether or not a person with HIV is knowingly exposing others to the disease, or if a depressed individual is contemplating suicide – may need to take action to warn others.

Each of these scenarios generates different dilemmas. One set of arguments holds that researchers are not absolved of moral and ethical responsibility for their actions or inactions merely because they are conducting research. To act or to fail to act is to make an ethical or political choice (Taylor and Bogdan, 1998). Another set of arguments proposes that there should be no rigid imposition of standards and sanctions as to how qualitative researchers should approach moral and ethical issues. It holds that common sense and responsibility is the best approach, relying on university and organizational codes of conduct for guidelines (Punch, 1986). Despite the fact that there is no universal agreement on how to handle these issues, we believe that having the appropriate protocols in place *a priori* to address ethical, legal and moral questions, if and when they arise, is a good solution. Psychologists are bound to comply with the ethical code of conduct established by the American Psychological Association, and this applies for the conduct of research. We suggest reading some of the literature that addresses these topics (Kopala and Suzuki, 1999; Lee, 1993; Punch, 1986; Taylor and Bogdan, 1998).

The Role of Qualitative Methods in Psychological Research

Psychology as a discipline has been reluctant to include qualitative research methods in its repertoire of accepted research approaches. This reluctance is evident in the paucity of graduate programs providing training in these methods (Krahn and Eisert, 2000). Yet psychology students are increasingly using qualitative methods in their research, bringing in these approaches from other disciplines. This chapter has provided only a brief overview of the basics of qualitative methods and qualitative research. However, in our brief discussion we hope we have successfully conveyed the value of incorporating qualitative methods into the social scientist tool kit and practicing these methods with rigor and discipline. We have found qualitative methods to be a valuable resource in exploring our own areas of research and we encourage the pursuit of more advanced study into their use as a means of addressing research topics of interest in the field.

Additional Resources for Qualitative Methods

Barbour, R. S., and Kitzinger, J. (1999). *Developing focus group research: Politics, theory and practice* (pp. 64–78). London: Sage.

deMarrais, K. B. (1998). *Inside stories: Qualitative research reflections*. Mahwah, NJ: Lawrence Erlbaum Associates.

Dennis, R. M. (1993). Participant observations. In J. H. Stanfield, II, and R. M. Dennis (eds.). *Race and ethnicity in research methods*. Sage focus editions, vol. 157 (pp. 53–74). Newbury Park, CA: Sage.

Hodson, R. (1999). *Analyzing documentary accounts*. Newbury Park, CA: Sage.

Janesick, V. J. (1998). *"Stretching" exercises for qualitative researchers*. Thousand Oaks, CA: Sage.

Jorgensen, D. L. (1989). *Participant observation: A methodology for human studies*. Newbury Park, CA: Sage.

Kvale, S. (1996). *InterViews: An introduction to qualitative research interviewing*. Thousand Oaks, CA: Sage.

References

Anderson, P. P., and Fenichel, E. S. (1989). *Serving culturally diverse families of infants and toddlers with disabilities*. Arlington, VA: National Center for Clinical Infant Programs.

Barker, R. G., and Wright, H. F. (1955). *Midwest and its children*. New York: Harper and Row.

Beck, C. T. (1990). Qualitative research: Methodologies and use in pediatric nursing. *Issues in Comprehensive Pediatric Nursing*, *13*, 193–201.

Becker, H., Stuifbergen, A., and Tinkle, M. (1997). Reproductive health care experiences of women with physical disabilities: A qualitative study. *Archives of Physical Medicine and Rehabilitation*, *78*, S26–S33.

Bronfenbrenner, U. (1979). *The ecology of human development*. Cambridge, MA: Harvard University Press.

Brotherson, M. J. (1994). Interactive focus group interviewing: A qualitative research method in early intervention. *Topics in Early Childhood Special Education*, *14*, 101–48.

Cieurzo, C., and Keitel, M. (1999). Ethics in qualitative research. In M. Kopala and L. Suzuki (eds.), *Using qualitative methods in psychology* (pp. 63–5). Thousand Oaks, CA: Sage.

Clarke, L. (1992). Qualitative research: Meaning and language. *Journal of Advanced Nursing*, *17*, 243–52.

Cross, T. L., Bazron, B. J., Dennis, K. W., and Isaacs, M. R. (1989). *Towards a culturally competent system of care, Volume 1*. Available from the Georgetown University Child Development Center, 3307 M Street, NW, Washington, DC.

Eckert, J. K. (1980). *The unseen elderly: A study of marginally subsistent hotel dwellers*. San Diego, CA: Campanile Press.

Fielding, N. (1993). Qualitative interviewing. In N. Gilbert (ed.), *Researching social life*. (pp. 135–53). London: Sage.

Gardner, F. (2000). Methodological issues in the direct observation of parent–child interaction: Do observational findings reflect the natural behavior of participants? *Clinical Child and Family Psychology Review*, *3*, 185–98.

Gergen, K. (1973). Social psychology as history. *Journal of Personality and Social Psychology*, *26*, 309–20.

Gergen, K. (1978). Experimentation in social psychology. *European Journal of Social Psychology*, *8*, 507–27.

Glaser, B. G., and Strauss, A. L. (1967). *The discovery of grounded theory: Strategies for qualitative research*. New York: Aldine Press.

Gottman, J. M. (1979). *Marital interaction: Experimental investigations*. New York: Academic Press.

Grbich, C. (1999). *Qualitative research in health*. Thousand Oaks, CA: Sage.

Greene, J. C., and Caracelli, V. J. (1997). Defining and describing the paradigm issue in mixed-method evaluation. *New Directions for Evaluation*, *74*, 5–17.

Harré, R., and Secord, P. F. (1972). *The explanation of social behavior*. Oxford: Blackwell.

Henwood, K. L., and Pidgeon, N. F. (1992). Qualitative research and psychological theorizing. *British Journal of Psychology, 83*, 97–111.

Jacob, T., Krahn, G. L. and Leonard, K. (1991). Parent–child interactions in families with alcoholic fathers. *Journal of Consulting and Clinical Psychology, 59*, 1, 176–81.

Kidd, P., and Parshall, M. (2000). Getting the focus and the group: enhancing analytical rigor in focus group research. *Qualitative Health Research, 10*, 293–308.

Kopala, M., and Suzuki, L. (1999). *Using qualitative methods in psychology*. Thousand Oaks, CA: Sage.

Krahn, G. L., and Eisert, D. (2000). Qualitative methods in clinical psychology. In D. Drotar (ed.), *Handbook of research methods in pediatric and clinical child psychology* (pp. 145–64). New York: Plenum Press.

Krahn, G. L., Hohn, M. F., and Kime, C. (1995). Incorporating qualitative approaches in clinical child research. *Journal of Clinical Child Psychology, 24*, 2, 204–13.

Lee, R. (1993). *Doing research on sensitive topics*. Newbury Park, CA: Sage.

Lincoln, Y. S., and Guba, E. G. (1985). *Naturalistic inquiry*. Beverly Hills, CA: Sage.

Lynch, E. W., and Hanson, M. J. (1992). *Developing cross-cultural competence: A guide for working with young children and their families*. Baltimore, MD: Brookes.

MacCormack, T., Simonian, J., Lim, J., Remond, L., Roets, D., Dunn, S., and Butow, P. (2001). "Someone who cares": A qualitative investigation of cancer patients' experiences of psychotherapy. *Psycho-Oncology, 10*, 52–65.

Marshall, C., and Rossman, G. (1995). *Designing qualitative research* (2nd edn.). Thousand Oaks, CA: Sage.

Mash, E. J., and Terdal, L. G. (1997). Assessment of child and family disturbance: A behavioral-systems approach. In E. J. Mash and L. G. Terdal (eds.), *Assessment of childhood disorders* (3rd edn., pp. 3–70). New York: Guilford Press.

Mason, O., and Hargreaves, I. (2001). A qualitative study of mindfulness-based cognitive therapy for depression. *British Journal of Medical Psychology, 14*, 197–212.

Miles, M. B., and Huberman, A. M. (1984). *Qualitative data analysis*. Beverly Hills, CA: Sage.

Miles, M. B., and Huberman, A. M. (1994). *Qualitative analysis: An expanded sourcebook* (2nd edn.). Beverly Hills, CA: Sage.

Mills, L. G. (1997). Benefiting from violence: A preliminary analysis of the presence of abuse in the lives of the new SSI disability recipients. *Sexuality and Disability, 15*, 99–108.

Morgan, D. (1993). *Successful focus groups*. Newbury Park, CA: Sage.

Murray, J. (1998). Qualitative methods. *International Review of Psychiatry, 10*, 312–16.

Nelson, G., Lord, J., and Ochocka, J. (2001). Empowerment and mental health in community: Narratives of psychiatric consumer/survivors. *Journal of Community and Applied Social Psychology, 11*, 125–42.

Patterson, G. R. (1975). *Families: Applications of social learning to family life* (revd. edn.). Champaign, IL: Research Press.

Patton, M. Q. (1990). *Qualitative evaluation and research methods*. Newbury Park, CA: Sage.

Patton, M. Q. (1997). *Utilization-focused evaluation: The new century text* (3rd edn.). Thousand Oaks, CA: Sage.

Punch, M. (1986). *The politics and ethics of fieldwork*. Beverly Hills, CA: Sage.

Rennie, D. L., Phillips, J. R., and Quartaro, G. K. (1988). Grounded theory: A promising approach to conceptualization in psychology. *Canadian Psychology, 29*, 139–50.

Rich, M., and Ginsburg, K. (1999). The reason and rhyme of qualitative research: Why, when, and how to use qualitative methods in the study of adolescent health. *Journal of Adolescent Health, 25*, 371–8.

Russel, C. (1999). Interviewing vulnerable old people: Ethical and methodological implications of imagining our subjects. *Journal of Aging Studies*, *13*, 4, 403–17.

Sechrest, L., and Sidani, S. (1995). Quantitative and qualitative methods: Is there an alternative? *Evaluation and Program Planning*, *18*, 77–87.

Seidman, I. (1998). *Interviewing as qualitative research*. New York: Teachers College Press.

Smith, M. L. (1997). Mixing and matching: Methods and models. *New Directions for Evaluation*, *74*, 73–85.

Sobel, A. B., Roberts, M. C., Rapoff, M. A., and Barnard, M. U. (2001). Problems and interventions of a pediatric psychology clinic in a medical setting: A retrospective analysis. *Cognitive and Behavioral Practice*, *8*, 11–17.

Stewart, D., and Shamdasani, P. (1990). *Focus groups: Theory and practice*. Newbury Park, CA: Sage.

Strauss, A., and Corbin, J. (1990). *Basics of qualitative research*. Beverly Hills, CA: Sage.

Taylor, S., and Bogdan, R. (1998). *Introduction to qualitative research methods: A guidebook and resource*. Toronto: John Wiley and Sons.

Urquiza, A., Wyatt, G., and Goodlin-Jones, B. (1997). Clinical interviewing with trauma victims: Managing interviewer risk. *Journal of Interpersonal Violence*, *12*, 759–72.

Valdez, A., and Kaplan, C. (1999). Reducing selection bias in the use of focus groups to investigate hidden populations: The case of Mexican-American gang members from south Texas. *Drugs and Society*, *14*, 209–24.

Waddington, D. (1994). Participant observation. In C. Cassel and G. Symon (eds.), *Qualitative methods in organizational research: A practical guide*. London: Sage.

Westgren, N., and Levi, R. (1999). Sexuality after injury: Interviews with women after traumatic spinal cord injury. *Sexuality and Disability*, *17*, 309–19.

Willard-Holt, C. (1998). Academic and personality characteristics of gifted students with cerebral palsy: A multiple case study. *Exceptional Children*, *65*, 37–50.

Yardley, L., Sharples, K., Beech, S., and Lewith, G. (2001). Developing a dynamic model of treatment perceptions. *Journal of Health Psychology*, *6*, 269–82.

CHAPTER TEN

Basic Principles of Meta-Analysis

Joseph A. Durlak

Introduction

Meta-analysis is one method of reviewing a research literature and it is a pleasure to prepare this chapter because literature reviews usually do not receive the attention they deserve in methodology textbooks. For example, Jackson (1980) found that among the thirty-nine methodology texts he examined there was little discussion of how to conduct a scientifically rigorous review. This is unfortunate because reviews are becoming increasingly important in advancing scientific knowledge and understanding. Surveys suggest that up to 42 percent of scientists regularly read reviews as one way to keep abreast of developments in their field (Cooper and Hedges, 1994). Some reviews have become among the most widely cited documents in their field, and have exerted a strong influence on subsequent research and practice.

Conducting a literature review is as much a research strategy as conducting an individual experiment. The author poses a research question, selects a population to study, collects and analyzes data, and offers conclusions. Therefore, it is possible to discuss the basic principles that should be followed that will increase the validity of this research process.

History and Introduction to Meta-Analysis

Although techniques which would now be identified as meta-analysis appeared in scientific reports as far back as 1904, a few landmark reviews that appeared in the 1970s in the areas of psychotherapy, education, and industrial organizational psychology are generally credited with popularizing this approach to literature reviewing in the social sciences and education (Cooper and Hedges, 1994). Over three hundred meta-analyses appear annually in these fields and in medicine.

Meta-analysis is a method of reviewing research findings in a quantitative fashion by transforming the data from individual studies into what is called an effect size and then pooling and analyzing this information. The basic goal in meta-analysis is to explain why different outcomes have occurred in different studies. If different results were not obtained in a research field, there would be no need for the review in the first place because it would be common knowledge that almost all investigators have obtained the same results. This rarely happens.

This chapter focuses on treatment meta-analyses based on between-group designs, that is, designs in which an intervention or treatment of some type is compared to a control condition (which can be a no-treatment, waiting list, or attention placebo condition). This is the most common type of meta-analysis and produces what is called a standardized mean difference as the index of effect. However, meta-analyses can be done on other types of designs, such as one group pre–post designs, between treatment designs (when two different interventions are being compared), and single-subject designs. Effects from these different designs should not be combined in the same analysis because the designs on which they are based yield effects of different magnitudes (for explanations and examples, see Busk and Serlin, 1992; Cooper and Hedges, 1994; DuPaul and Eckert, 1997).

There are also other indices of effect such as the product moment correlation, r, and its variants, an odds ratio, and its variants, such as risk ratios and relative risk ratios. Several other sources (Cooper and Hedges, 1994; Hunter and Schmidt, 1990; Lipsey and Wilson, 2001; Rosenthal, 1991) offer good discussions and examples of these other indices. All indices of effect are simply different ways to express the magnitude of the relationship between variables; the choice of any index is made on the basis of the type of information contained in the reviewed studies. When most independent and dependent variables are continuous in nature, r is used; when most of the former are discrete or categorical (e.g., type of treatment or type of presenting problem) while outcomes are mostly continuous variables, standardized mean differences are used, but if the prime outcomes are largely categorical, then an odds ratio or one of its variants is used. For the most part, the basic principles of meta-analysis discussed in this chapter apply to reviews using all of these indices.

A standardized mean effect, which will be referred to as an effect size (ES) throughout this chapter (but which is alternatively abbreviated as d, $d+$, or g), is calculated by subtracting the mean of the control group from the mean of the treatment group and dividing by the pooled standard deviation (SD) of the two groups. Occasionally, reviewers only use the control group SD in this calculation, although most meta-analysts accept Hedges and Olkin's (1985) statistical justification that the pooled SD provides the best estimate of the true population effect. If the means and SDs are missing it is possible to estimate the ES from other information such as ns, r, t, or F values. Holmes (1984), Lipsey and Wilson (2001), and Wolf (1986) provide useful formulae for these circumstances.

The prime value of an ES is the advantage it gives the reviewer in quantifying the magnitude of an intervention, and expressing this magnitude in a common metric across studies. In other words, meta-analysis translates the unique data from each study into a standardized statistic (standardized because it is based on SD units) which permits information to be combined across studies and then analyzed. All else being equal, if two interventions each produce an ES of 0.50, then the interventions are equally powerful.

Most individual reports focus on the statistical significance of findings which is a very different issue than the magnitude of effect. In fact, suppose an investigator assessed the impact of treatment by conducting a *t*-test to see if twenty adult clients differed from a similar number of untreated controls on some outcome measure. If the results of the *t*-test fell short of statistical significance at the .05 level, the investigator might conclude the treatment was ineffective. Assuming a modest mean difference and pooled SD, however, the treatment could easily yield an ES anywhere between +0.66 and −0.66 (the latter could occur if the treatment was harmful to participants). In other words, there is no direct relationship between the statistical significance of outcomes and the ES that can be obtained from an individual report. A meta-analysis can provide a precise calculation of ESs in different studies and produce results that are not discernible when examining the findings from any one investigation.

Although an individual ES can be of any magnitude, those from between-group designs most typically fall between −0.50 and +1.50. When ESs are averaged across studies, however, it is customary to interpret ESs of around 0.20 as small in magnitude, those around 0.50 as moderate, and any > 0.80 as high in magnitude. This generally accepted convention was empirically confirmed by Lipsey and Wilson's (1993) summary of the results of 156 meta-analyses of interventions involving 9,400 studies and over a million participants. The overall mean ES from these meta-analyses was 0.47 with an SD of 0.27 (i.e., two-thirds of all intervention mean effects fell between 0.19 and 0.75).

Substantial procedural and statistical advances have been made in meta-analytic techniques during the 1980s, and it is now possible to describe the methodological standards that should be followed in a meta-analysis. These standards have been combined with those suggested for all types of literature reviews and are listed in table 10.1. Except when the special circumstances and purposes of a review suggest otherwise, the criteria listed in table 10.1 can be used to judge the scientific rigor of a meta-analysis. There are five major aspects to a meta-analysis. The more carefully each aspect of a meta-analysis is conducted and reported, the more valid is the final product, that is, the more confidence that can be placed in the data and conclusions. All aspects of the review process are important, however, and it is essential that the reviewer attend to the requirements of each phase of the meta-analysis.

Although the foregoing discussion should be helpful for both producers and consumers of meta-analyses, this brief chapter can only highlight the most important issues. For more depth and breadth of coverage, the best all-round resource is the handbook edited by Cooper and Hedges (1994); however, there are several other references that provide good introductions to meta-analysis, explain its technical aspects, and contain plenty of practical examples (Durlak, 1995, 2000; Durlak, Meerson, and Ewell-Foster, in press; Durlak and Lipsey, 1991; Lipsey and Wilson, 2001; Wolf, 1986). Rosenthal (1995) also offers an excellent guide on how to prepare a meta-analysis for publication. The following sections

Table 10.1   Useful criteria for judging the scientific rigor of a meta-analysis

Step 1: Formulating the research question	• The purpose of the review is clearly described • *A priori* hypotheses are offered • The research questions are reasonable, important, and testable
Step 2: Obtaining a representative study sample	• Specific inclusionary criteria are presented • Multiple search strategies are used to locate studies • Unpublished reports are evaluated
Step 3: Obtaining information from individual studies	• Methodological aspects of primary research are assessed • The extent of missing information is acknowledged • Adequate reliability was obtained for the coding procedures
Step 4: Conducting appropriate analyses	• One effect size was used per study per research question • Effects were weighted for analyses • Systematic model testing of hypotheses was performed • Plausible rival explanations for the results were evaluated
Step 5: Reaching conclusions and guiding future research	• The conclusions are appropriately qualified • Specific recommendations for future research are offered

Note: This evaluative scheme incorporates criteria specific to meta-analysis with criteria proposed for all types of reviews (e.g., Oxman, 1994).

discuss the most important elements that are part of each of the five major phases of a meta-analysis.

Step 1: Formulating the Research Question

It is difficult to accept the results of an individual experiment when there are no *a priori* hypotheses to guide the analyses. The situation is no different in a meta-analysis. "Rigorous hypothesis testing is as desirable in reviews as it is in primary research" (Jackson, 1980: 455). Good meta-analyses should begin with clearly formulated, specific research questions (i.e., hypotheses) that are important and testable. Otherwise, a meta-analysis can become nothing more than a post hoc fishing expedition in which multiple analyses will eventually produce a few significant findings of dubious value.

Good hypotheses usually come from an inspection of relevant research prior to the review. What theories or conceptualizations have been prominent in the research area? How might inconsistencies or controversies be resolved? What important variables bear examination? These are the types of questions that often lead to interesting hypotheses.

Step 2: Obtaining Representative Studies for Review

There is no such thing as a comprehensive review of all relevant research. There are over 20,000 outlets for published and unpublished scientific research (Cooper and Hedges, 1994), and a reviewer can never find every study that has been done on a particular topic. Therefore, the goal of a review is to obtain a representative study sample, that is, one that is not biased in its focus on published studies, on reports that are easy to obtain, or those located in some selective or restrictive way.

The literature search process begins with clear inclusionary criteria that describe the primary features of relevant studies. These criteria usually include the types of populations, interventions, and outcomes that are of interest. For example, a review may focus on individual treatments (as opposed to group therapy) for adults (as opposed to adolescents) who meet formal diagnostic criteria for depression (as opposed to those with milder problems or who have other types of difficulties). Authors can limit the scope of the review, as long as they provide a sufficient rationale or justification.

Once inclusionary criteria are developed, multiple search strategies are *essential* in finding relevant studies. The three most productive strategies are: (1) manual searches of journals (reading through the abstracts and procedure sections of all articles appearing in major journals over a designated time period), (2) examining the references of each obtained study and previous literature reviews, and (3) computer searches of different databases. Computer searches should *not* be relied on as the major search strategy, however, for several reasons. Computer databases do not include all possible sources of information, usually do not thoroughly sample books and book chapters, are modified over time (making a systematic search of the same database more difficult), exclude the most recent studies because of the time lag involved in their updating, and use their own terminology (i.e., glossary of search terms) that almost never corresponds exactly to the reviewer's interest. In some reviews less than 20 percent of the final study sample was located through computer searches, whereas the overwhelming majority of studies were identified using the first two procedures noted above (see Durlak, 2000).

Unpublished studies should be part of the review because of the possibility of publication bias, which is the tendency of authors not to submit and for journal editors not to accept reports containing negative results. Therefore, omitting unpublished work could underestimate the true effect size. Publication bias does not always occur, but its possibility should be examined, and the only way to do so is by including them in the review.

There are many different types of unpublished research, such as technical reports, dissertations and theses, convention papers, and so-called file drawer studies which are studies that researchers have conducted but for one reason or another have never published. Unpublished dissertations are a good choice for inclusion in a review because the incidence of relevant research can be estimated by examining *Dissertation Abstracts International*, and copies of dissertations can be obtained through interlibrary loan for inspection and analysis.

Step 3: Coding Studies for Important Information

The goal is to code all study features that might influence outcomes. In many cases attention is focused on various theoretical, practical, or clinical variables suggested by the research hypotheses. For instance, studies can be coded according to the theoretical orientation of the treatment, characteristics of the clients, presenting problems and outcome measures, and various parameters of the intervention such as its length, specific techniques employed, and who administered the treatment. It is also essential that the experimental quality of the studies is assessed in some way for two reasons: (1) the confidence one can place in a review's conclusions often depends on the quality of the reviewed research; and (2) methodological features may emerge as critical moderators of outcomes. These two points will be examined later.

Previous familiarity with the research area greatly aids the coding process. If the author is acquainted with how studies have been conducted and reported, then a coding scheme that captures these critical features can be developed. Reviewers usually offer copies of their coding schemes to interested readers on request, and these coding manuals contain definitions of each coded variable, and often explanations of how different coding issues or problems were resolved. Authors should report the reliability of coding procedures. The ways original studies are conducted and reported do not always make it easy to obtain all the desired information, and it is helpful to know if one can expect that the coding system used in the review can reasonably be reproduced with similar results by others. The exact methods used to estimate reliability in coding vary with the type of information that is obtained from studies (e.g., continuous versus categorical or discrete variables) and the number of coders used. Hartmann (1982) offers many useful suggestions about these matters.

It is now APA publication policy to list all the studies evaluated in a meta-analysis in the published report (American Psychological Association, 1994). In some cases published reviews have also provided details on exactly how each study was coded on each variable of interest and the values for ESs derived from each study (e.g., Irvin et al., 1999; Jaffe and Hyde, 2000). Such full disclosure of data is commendable, but not always possible because of editorial or page limitation pressures.

Step 4: Analyzing the Data Systematically

There are now customary procedures to follow when abstracting ESs from individual studies and combining results across studies that apply in most situations.

Using one effect per research question

The general principle to keep in mind is that each study should contribute one effect size in each analysis. This means that the ESs from interventions employing multiple

Table 10.2   Selected effect size outcomes from group therapy studies

			Type of outcome measure			
Study	Parent ratings	Teacher ratings	Achievement	Child report	Other	Mean ES per study
1				0.92		0.92
2		1.07	0.69	0.78	0.68	0.81
3	0.24	0.05	0.23	0.10	0.22	0.17
4		0.40	0.15	0.48		0.34
5	0.20	0.56				0.38
					Mean ES per study =	0.52

outcome measures should be averaged within each study when testing the impact of the intervention. For instance, table 10.2 contains some ESs from representative studies of the impact of group therapy for children and adolescents. Notice that the ESs from each study have been averaged in column 7 to yield one effect per study. These would be the data that would be analyzed if the reviewer were interested in the overall impact of group therapy. If the ESs within each study were not averaged, then the studies would contribute a different number of data points to the analysis. Study 3 has five ESs, whereas study 1 only has one.

In a subsequent analysis the reviewer can combine the ESs in a different way to investigate different research questions. For instance, to investigate if ESs vary according to the type of outcome measure, the reviewer would use the data that are separated according to this research question. ESs could be analyzed by averaging the data across studies for parent reports (two studies), for self-reports (three studies), and so on. Once again, each study should contribute only one ES in the analysis. If a study used multiple outcomes measures in the same category, such as two different parent rating scales, these data would be averaged within that study before being pooled with data from the other investigations.

Weighting effects prior to analysis

Before conducting any statistical analysis of ESs it is now recommended to weight the ES from each study by the inverse of its variance using Hedges and Olkin's (1985: 111) formula for this purpose. Basically, this formula gives more weight to studies with larger sample sizes, which makes sense since larger samples yield more accurate estimates of true population effects. Weighting is very important in clinical research, which is often plagued with small sample sizes. When authors have provided both types of information, unweighted effects have been up to 33 percent higher than weighted effects (see Durlak, 2000).

Statistical analysis of mean effects

Although SDs are sometimes presented, most meta-analyses provide confidence intervals (CIs) around mean effects (see Hedges and Olkin, 1985: ch. 5). CIs describe the range of effects one would expect at a specified probability level (e.g., .05) given chance and sampling error. CIs are useful for interpretative purposes; means whose CIs do not include zero differ significantly from zero and means whose CIs do not overlap differ significantly from each other.

Grouping studies for analyses

There are many different ways to divide a group of studies for analysis, in the sense that there are several theoretical, clinical, or methodological study features that might make a difference. Going back to table 10.2, how should the different study-level ESs (from 0.17 to 0.92) be explained? Was the most important factor the way studies were experimentally conducted (i.e., randomized vs. quasi-experimental studies?), the type of treatment used, characteristics of the presenting problem, or something else? All meta-analysts face the same basic dilemma and this issue is important because reviewers have made different choices at this point and the same data can yield different answers.

How studies are grouped for analysis has been the most controversial aspect of meta-analysis and has generated the so-called "apples and oranges" criticism frequently directed at meta-analysis. Critics contend that some reviewers have combined studies inappropriately for analysis. Studies that assess distinctly different constructs or processes should not be grouped together because combining such studies could produce misleading or inaccurate results by obscuring significantly different results produced by different subgroups of studies. For example, a review should not combine studies of behavioral therapy and psychotropic medication to assess the effects of treatment on depression or combine studies using drugs, exercise, or diet to help adults lose weight. While these examples are obvious, other situations are not so clear-cut. Researchers can reasonably disagree about how to divide a group of studies to analyze their outcomes. Fortunately, there are logical, systematic methods that can be used to justify one's approach in grouping studies for analysis.

These methods involve model testing, and there are three primary models that can be applied to effect size data: fixed effects, random effects, and mixed effects models. The decision to apply one model over another is based on what additional factors beyond sampling error are presumably influencing the variability of obtained effects. Some sampling error always occurs in a review because each study has only sampled from the total possible population of participants. Additional factors that might influence the variability of effects are: (a) systematic differences present in studies that it is hoped are captured by variables coded by the meta-analyst (so that a fixed effect model might be applied); (b) random differences across studies which cannot be identified (suggesting a random effects model should be used); and (c) a combination of unidentifiable random factors and systematic differences which could be identified (which would lead to a mixed effects model). Lipsey and Wilson (2001) offer a useful comparison of the different assumptions, applications, and statistical features of these three models. The following discussion explains fixed effects model testing, but regardless of which model is applied, the general aim is to determine to the extent possible why different studies are producing different effects.

Homogeneity testing (model testing) and the Q statistic

The basic procedure in the fixed effects approach is to test the outcomes of groups of studies for homogeneity using the Q statistic. The Q statistic is distributed as a chi square variable with its *df* equal to the number of tested studies minus one. Critical values for the Q are contained in tables (e.g., Hedges and Olkin, 1985: appendix B).

The Q statistic is also called a homogeneity test because it assesses if the variability in outcomes produced by a set of studies is greater than expected based on chance and sampling error. In other words, is it justified to put certain studies into the same group for analysis because they are all estimating the same common (homogeneous) effect? A *nonsignificant* Q value indicates homogeneity.

When the ESs from all reviewed studies are averaged together, one would expect *heterogeneity* in outcomes (because research studies typically yield different results). Thus, the critical value for the Q statistic for *all* studies should be *significant*. If the reviewer has a hypothesis (i.e., has a model in mind) concerning which variables moderate outcomes, however, this model can be statistically evaluated by subdividing the studies into different categories. The reviewer hopes that each subgroup of studies then yields a *nonsignificant* Q (i.e., the groups are homogeneous in outcomes) and that inspection of the means will indicate significant differences among the subgroups. This would confirm the reviewer's initial hypothesis or model.

The Q statistic is analogous to an ANOVA in the sense that a Q value for all the studies (i.e., a total Q) equals the sum of the Q for the different subgroup of studies (called Q-withins) plus a remaining value for Q-between. The Q-between tests whether the subgroups vary significantly in their effects.

Table 10.3 provides an example of the testing of two different hypotheses concerning which variables moderate the outcomes of group therapy studies. Hypothesis 1 was that the type of treatment administered would moderate outcomes and studies were divided according to whether behavioral, cognitive behavioral, or nonbehavioral forms of group therapy were conducted. In contrast, hypothesis 2 was that the severity of presenting problems would moderate outcomes and studies were divided into two groups: (1) those in which clients had mild, subclinical problems, and (2) those in which the problems were more serious and clinically significant. Both hypotheses were tested at the .05 probability level. (The reviewer would, of course, describe the coding of these hypothesized variables.)

The results indicated good support for hypothesis 1 and no support for hypothesis 2. The testing of each hypothesis begins with the total Q value for all 236 studies which was significant, but dividing studies according to type of treatment resulted in nonsignificant

Table 10.3 Illustration of model testing (hypothesis testing) using the Q statistic

Grouping of Studies	N	Q total	Mean	95% confidence interval
All studies	236	331.30	0.41*	0.27–0.55

Hypothesis 1: Type of treatment moderates outcomes: Q-between = 55.55*

	N	Q-withins	Mean	95% confidence interval
Type of treatment				
Behavioral	76	137.43*	0.56	0.49–0.64
Cognitive behavioral	80	74.64	0.38	0.31–0.44
Nonbehavioral	80	63.63	0.23	0.17–0.29

Hypothesis 2: Severity of presenting problem moderates outcomes: Q-between = 1.75

	N	Q-withins	Mean	95% confidence interval
Severity of problem				
Mild	129	184.16*	0.39	0.34–0.44
Moderate/severe	107	145.09*	0.45	0.38–0.51

Note: * = values of Q total, between, or within that are significant at .05.

Q-within values (which are desired) for two of the three groups and a significant Q-between (which is also desired). Inspection of the CIs for the three treatments indicated that each of the mean outcomes differed significantly from each other.

In contrast, dividing studies according to severity of presenting problem yielded significant Q-within values for both study groups and a nonsignificant Q-between (just the opposite of the findings for hypothesis 1). Consistent with such results, the CIs for the two means overlapped, which indicated there was no significant difference at the .05 level when clients with milder versus more serious problems were treated.

Weighted multiple regression procedures are also appropriate for identifying variables that explain effect size variability (see Lipsey and Wilson, 2001). Such analyses can be used in addition to, or as an alternative to, the model testing described above, and can be useful in examining the relative influence of multiple possible predictors of effect size, particularly if the predictors consist of both dichotomous and continuous variables (e.g., type of treatment and number of intervention sessions, respectively).

In summary, there are systematic model testing approaches that should be taken in meta-analysis that will statistically confirm or disconfirm whether the reviewer's model (i.e., grouping of studies) is justified. These approaches can effectively defend against an apples and oranges criticism of one's analyses. Notice, however, the essential value of *a priori* hypotheses and homogeneity testing. Model testing cannot occur without a model (*a priori* hypotheses), and it is certainly possible to obtain significantly different outcomes when groups of *heterogeneous* studies are compared. Under such circumstances it is hard to place much trust or confidence in the findings.

Hypotheses are never 100 percent confirmed in an individual experiment and it is not any different in a meta-analysis. Notice among the results in table 10.3 that findings for behavioral treatment indicated heterogeneity, not homogeneity of effects (the Q-within was significant). Contrary to popular opinion, it is possible to interpret findings from some heterogeneous study groups. In such cases, much depends on whether plausible rival explanations for the results can be ruled out. If none of the treatment Q-within values was homogeneous, however, such as for hypothesis 2 in table 10.3, it would be a different matter, and would indicate the hypothesis was simply incorrect.

Ruling out rival explanations

A meta-analyst should take advantage of the opportunity to use the information from studies to rule out other possible explanations for any findings. The most likely explanations for outcomes in a meta-analysis involve sampling error, study artifacts, methodological variables, and confounds among study characteristics. A check on sampling error is part of homogeneity testing via the Q statistic, so the other three categories are discussed below.

Study artifacts

Hunter and Schmidt (1990) discuss eleven different types of study artifacts, such as unreliability of outcome assessments and the failure to implement procedures correctly. Because study artifacts are basically sources of error that have crept into the original studies, it is usually not possible to correct them, but their possible existence should be noted by the reviewer. If most of the primary studies were seriously flawed by one or more artifacts, then the data should not be trusted no matter how many studies are available. Quantity is a poor substitute for quality.

Methodological features

As noted earlier, methodological features of reviewed studies should be coded, and this is because they may serve as a possible alternative explanation for the results. For instance, in table 10.3 it is possible that the way studies are designed could be a more important influence than the type of group treatment conducted. Somewhat surprisingly, meta-analysts have not reported consistent relationships between methodology and outcomes. In some cases well-conducted studies have produced higher ESs, and in others more poorly controlled investigations have. In other words, it is always an empirical question if and in what way methodological features might have influenced outcomes.

Reviewers can assess the influence of methodology in different ways. They might examine the impact of individual variables such as randomization to conditions or psychometric aspects of outcome measures. Alternatively, they might use multiple criteria to evaluate and categorize studies according to their overall design quality (e.g., low, medium, and high quality) and then compare the outcomes for studies in such categories. Both approaches have been used and have merit (Bangert-Drowns, Wells-Parker, and Chevillard, 1997). It is up to the meta-analyst to justify the approach taken when assessing method variables, which is usually based on prior research findings, results from other reviews, or the special requirements or circumstances of the particular research area.

Confounded variables

Study characteristics are not independently or randomly distributed in a research area. Sometimes clinical and methodological features are confounded (i.e., linked together) and sometimes different clinical features are. Confounds can certainly be a plausible alternative explanation for any results. For example, perhaps behavioral group therapy attained the best outcomes in table 10.3 because these were the most carefully controlled investigations and thus most sensitive to treatment effects. Perhaps more experienced group leaders were used to administering behavioral therapy, or better (i.e., more psychometrically adequate) outcome assessments were used.

To evaluate possible confounds, studies can be examined according to different variables and their outcomes assessed. Are there any outcome differences in the training and experience of leaders doing behavioral, cognitive behavioral, or nonbehavioral treatment? Are there any differences in the general methodology of studies using these different treatments, and so on? Much greater confidence can be placed in the results of a review if the author has been able to rule out the most likely alternative explanations for significant findings.

Step 5: Reaching Conclusions and Guiding Future Research

Tempering one's conclusions

Usually, authors have to qualify their conclusions in relation to one or more of the following factors: (1) the review's inclusionary criteria; (2) missing information among the studies; and (3) statistical power. For example, if certain types of problems, populations, or treatments were excluded in the search for relevant studies (e.g., individual therapy, interventions for adults), then the results cannot be generalized to these excluded areas. As elemental as this sounds, reviewers do not always keep their inclusionary criteria in mind when discussing their conclusions and their implications.

To my knowledge, there has never been a meta-analysis in which the author has noted that all the needed information was available in all the studies. Some data are always missing in a review. As a result, coding schemes routinely contain options for missing information and these missing data can preclude important analyses. For instance, in one case, we were unable to assess our hypothesis that the quality of program implementation would affect outcomes because virtually none of the examined reports contained any data on implementation (Durlak and Wells, 1997). Reviewers should acknowledge how the lack of relevant data in the study sample affected what analyses could be done and what conclusions could be reached.

Statistical power in a meta-analysis is based on the effect size one is expecting (small, medium, or large), the probability level of the analysis, and, when using standardized mean differences as effects, the number of studies being evaluated, *not* the number of participants in the studies. Therefore, to have 80 percent power to detect a medium effect size at the .05 level requires 64 studies *per group*. The analyses reported in table 10.3 have 80 percent power, but many analyses undertaken in reviews do not.

Statistical power is as important for negative findings as it is for positive results. Therefore, authors should distinguish between "evidence of no effect" versus "no evidence of effect" when reporting nonsignificant results (Oxman, 1994). In the former case, for example, a claim that treatments A and B achieve similar results (i.e., there are no significant differences in their outcomes) requires that a sufficient number of studies has evaluated each treatment providing sufficient statistical power to detect a treatment difference, if it indeed exists. "No evidence of effect" (or in this case no evidence of differential effects) means that not enough studies have been conducted on the two treatments to compare their outcomes in a fair or adequate way (i.e., with sufficient statistical power). The lack of sufficient studies is, of course, not the reviewer's fault, but it must be acknowledged if it occurs.

Offering guidelines for future research

A review serves a very useful purpose by connecting the past, the present, and the future. That is, in addition to evaluating prior work to reach some conclusions about the current status of research, a good review offers useful suggestions to improve the next generation of studies. Put another way, a review should conclude by telling the field what is known, what is unknown because of missing, confusing, or conflicting findings, and what should be done next.

A meta-analysis affords the opportunity to document various gaps and limitations in prior studies so they can be addressed in future studies. For instance, which issues, populations, interventions, or problems need more attention? Do models exist to study a particular phenomenon in a more rigorous or discerning way? How can current inconsistencies in findings be resolved? In other words, most areas do not simply need more research, they need *better* research, and reviewers are usually in a good position to offer recommendations to advance science and practice.

In sum, a meta-analysis can be a useful way to synthesize research findings and further progress in a field. This chapter has highlighted several steps that should be taken to increase confidence that the meta-analysis has been conducted systematically and carefully and its conclusions and implications can be accepted.

References

American Psychological Association (1994). *Publication manual of the American Psychological Association* (4th edn.). Washington, DC: American Psychological Association.

Bangert-Drowns, R. L., Wells-Parker, E., and Chevillard, I. (1997). Assessing the quality of research in narrative reviews and meta-analyses. In K. J. Bryant, W. Windle, and S. G. West (eds.), *The science of prevention: Methodological advances from alcohol and substance abuse research* (pp. 405–29). Washington, DC: American Psychological Association.

Busk, P. L., and Serlin, R. C. (1992). Meta-analysis for single-case research. In T. R. Kratochwill and J. R. Levin (eds.), *Single-case research design and analysis* (pp. 187–212). Hillsdale, NJ: Lawrence Erlbaum.

Cooper, H., and Hedges, L. V. (eds.) (1994). *Handbook of research synthesis*. New York: Russell Sage Foundation.

DuPaul, G. J., and Eckert, T. L. (1997). The effects of school-based interventions for attention deficit hyperactivity disorder: A meta-analysis. *School Psychology Review*, *26*, 5–27.

Durlak, J. A. (1995). Understanding meta-analysis. In L. G. Grimm and P. R. Yarnold (eds.), *Reading and understanding multivariate statistics* (pp. 319–52). Washington, DC: American Psychological Association.

Durlak, J. A. (2000). How to evaluate a meta-analysis. In D. Drotar (ed.), *Handbook of research in pediatric and clinical child psychology* (pp. 395–407). New York: Kluwer Academic/Plenum.

Durlak, J. A., and Lipsey, M. W. (1991). A practitioner's guide to meta-analysis. *American Journal of Community Psychology*, *19*, 291–332.

Durlak, J. A., and Wells, A. M. (1997). Primary prevention mental health programs for children and adolescents: A meta-analytic review. *American Journal of Community Psychology*, *25*, 115–52.

Durlak, J. A., Meerson, I., and Ewell-Foster, C. (in press). Conducting a scientifically rigorous meta-analysis. In J. C. Thomas and M. Hersen (eds.), *Understanding research in clinical and counseling psychology: A textbook*. Mahwah, NJ: Lawrence Erlbaum.

Hartmann, D. P. (ed.). (1982). *Using observers to study behavior: New directions for methodology of social and behavioral sciences*. San Francisco, CA: Jossey-Bass.

Hedges, L. V., and Olkin, I. (1985). *Statistical methods for meta-analysis*. New York: Academic Press.

Holmes, C. T. (1984). Effect size estimation in meta-analysis. *Journal of Experimental Education*, *52*, 106–9.

Hunter, J. E., and Schmidt, F. L. (1990). *Methods of meta-analysis: Correcting error and bias in research findings*. Newbury Park, CA: Sage.

Irvin, J. E., Bowers, C. A., Dunn, M. E., and Wang, M. C. (1999). Efficacy of relapse prevention: A meta-analytic review. *Journal of Consulting and Clinical Psychology*, *67*, 563–70.

Jackson, G. B. (1980). Methods for integrative reviews. *Review of Educational Research*, *50*, 438–60.

Jaffe, S., and Hyde, J. S. (2000). Gender differences in moral orientation: A meta-analysis. *Psychological Bulletin*, *126*, 703–26.

Lipsey, M. W., and Wilson, D. B. (1993). The efficacy of psychological, educational, and behavioral treatment: Confirmation from meta-analysis. *American Psychologist*, *48*, 1181–209.

Lipsey, M. W., and Wilson, D. B. (2001). *Practical meta-analysis*. Thousand Oaks, CA: Sage.

Oxman, A. D. (1994). Checklists for review articles. *British Medical Journal*, *309*, 648–51.

Rosenthal, R. (1991). *Meta-analytic procedures for social research* (revd. edn.). Newbury Park, CA: Sage.

Rosenthal, R. (1995). Writing meta-analytic reviews. *Psychological Bulletin*, *118*, 183–92.

Wolf, F. M. (1986). *Meta-analysis: Quantitative methods for research synthesis*. Beverly Hills, CA: Sage.

PART III

Topics of Research

CHAPTER ELEVEN

Research Methods for Developmental Psychopathology

Eric M. Vernberg and Edward J. Dill

Developmental psychopathology offers an evidence-based developmentally oriented conceptual framework for understanding the nature of problematic behavior throughout childhood and adolescence. Central tenets of developmental psychopathology provide structure for organizing and understanding the growing body of research on child populations. These include the need for comprehensive, integrative conceptualizations of psychopathology at multiple levels of ecological complexity and attention to developmental pathways leading to the emergence, intensification, or desistance of psychopathology. Overt signs of an underlying form of psychopathology often change with age, leading to interest in possible core deficits or vulnerabilities that give rise to a predictable set of symptoms at different ages. Different etiologies may produce a final common set of symptoms (*equifinality*), and developmental outcomes deriving from a common etiological factor often vary, influenced both by organismic features and the environment (*multifinality*) (Cicchetti and Rogosch, 1996). Commitment to these principles poses a number of challenges for research. This chapter describes core research issues that follow from this perspective.

Research Tasks for Developmental Psychopathology

Specify "mechanisms" which mediate risk of psychopathology

Mechanisms in the context of developmental psychopathology refer to basic mental and biological processes that drive dysfunctional behavior. These mechanisms are thought to exert influence directly and pervasively by affecting fundamental cognitive or physiological functions involved in interpreting and interacting with the environment (Dodge,

1993). Models for explaining the emergence of several specific disorders have been proposed and partially validated, with an emphasis on the linkages between behavioral episodes and the emergence of cognitive and biological architectures that eventually produce characteristic responses to environmental stimuli (Brodsky and Lombroso, 1998; Perry et al., 1995; Vernberg and Varela, 2001).

Social-cognitive mechanisms

Formulation of psychopathology models from a mechanisms perspective requires integration of information from multiple disciplines and research traditions. Dodge (1993) drew from cognitive science, attachment theory, and clinical developmental research on psychopathology to propose social-cognitive mechanisms for the emergence of conduct disorder and depression. His model links early social experiences with the development of knowledge structures, conceptualized as latent mental structures (e.g., schemas, working models, beliefs) that guide information processing in specific encounters in the social environment. These knowledge structures become important foci for research because they are thought to drive information processing, which in turn directly influences thoughts and behavior in specific situations. For example, low self-esteem and a negative self-schema are viewed as knowledge structures leading to social information qualities characteristic of depression, such as filtering out positive cues, hopeless expectations, and poverty of response accessing (Dodge, 1993). These features of information processing are posited to contribute to depressed mood, heightened sensitivity to cues of failure or rejection, and reduced activity level.

Specification of social-cognitive mechanisms allows greater precision in selecting measures and methods by identifying key constructs that must be assessed carefully to test hypothesized linkages among experiences, underlying cognitive structures, information processing, and behavior. Models specifying mechanisms also help organize seemingly disparate pieces of evidence into a more coherent, integrated organizational system.

Genetic mechanisms

Interest in possible genetic influences on the emergence of psychopathology has increased as advances in molecular science have enabled new techniques for studying gene–behavior relationships (Goldsmith, Gottesman, and Lemery, 1997). At the highly technical end of behavioral genetics research, genetic probes now allow searches for chromosomal regions associated with specific behavioral patterns. "Knockout genetics" enables animal researchers to inactivate specific genes and then observe the effects of these manipulations.

In their recent review of behavior genetics in the context of developmental psychopathology research, Goldsmith, Gottesman, and Lemery (1997) argue that the expression of most forms of psychopathology is influenced to some extent by genetics. For many disorders, individuals with the same diagnostic label likely receive genetic influences from different combinations of genetic material. Although a limited number of developmental disorders are linked to single gene mutations, most psychiatric disorders appear to be influenced by multiple genes, in complex interaction with each other and environmental influences (Brodsky and Lombroso, 1998). Identification of distinct developmental trajectories is important for research in behavioral genetics in the possible identification of specific subtypes with more homogeneous genetic contributors.

From this perspective, it is extremely important to gather information on family patterns of psychopathology and genetically influenced aspects of child-rearing environments (e.g., Reiss, 1995) in prospective longitudinal studies. More precise, direct measures of key environmental processes (observational and multiple informant data rather than exclusive reliance on self-report) and behavioral or physiological responses to a variety of stimuli are also essential to permit researchers to gain a clearer picture of the interplay between genetic and environmental influences in the development of psychopathology (Boyce et al., 1998).

Biological mechanisms
Whether influenced by genetics, environment, or a combination of genes and environment, there is keen interest in biological mechanisms involved in psychopathology (Quay, 1993). The formation of neural connections is determined in part by experience and environmental stimulation, and models have been proposed linking environmental events, psychobiological functioning, and specific forms of psychopathology. For example, extreme experiences in childhood, such as repeated, severe maltreatment, have been proposed to alter brain chemistry and architecture, leading to long-standing disturbances in affect regulation and arousal characteristic of posttraumatic stress disorder and other trauma-related disturbances (Perry et al., 1995; van der Kolk, 1997). Measurement advances, such as brain imaging and neurotransmitter technology, show promise in developing more complete models to explain the psychobiology of child psychopathology, in turn offering hope for more effective pharmacological, psychological, and environmental treatments for chronic disorders.

Measure continuity and transformation over time

Adopting a developmental perspective toward psychopathology focuses attention on continuity and transformation over time. This research task often involves tracking moving targets, in the sense that observable symptoms of specific forms of psychopathology may change according to developmental level. Consider, for example, difficulties encountered in attempting to measure depression across the lifespan (Kazdin, 1990; Weiss and Weisz, 1988). If, as some have proposed, depressive disorders are marked by an irritable mood in younger children but by a more clearly dysphoric mood in adolescence and adulthood, different measures are needed at different ages to tap these constructs. With regard to self-report measures, language must be tailored to several age ranges. However, if different measures are used with the same individuals over the course of a longitudinal study to measure a single construct (e.g., a depressive disorder), the measurement of developmental change becomes extremely difficult. Even if summary scores such as percentiles are compared, one must first determine if the measures are indeed measuring the same construct (e.g., slightly different variations in wording can often drastically change the meaning of an item). One solution is to use a battery of measures that assess several constructs at all ages studied (e.g., irritability *and* depressive affect). Nevertheless, if two measures do assess the same construct (e.g., lack of interest in daily activities) at different developmental periods, one is then faced with the original issue of whether or not the emergence of a psychological disorder (e.g., depression) should be based upon the same underlying factors or symptoms at various ages.

A related issue concerns the measurement of symptoms and disorders when psychopathology represents the extremes of a normal–abnormal continuum. In the measurement of overactivity in the context of Attention Deficit Hyperactivity Disorder (ADHD), for instance, the typical level of motor activity expected in settings such as classrooms or work settings tends to decrease with age. Clinicians adjust "critical cutoff" scores for clinical levels of overactivity based on age and gender, yet entirely different measures may be needed to take into account age related quantitative changes in motor activity and possible qualitative changes in the expression of overactivity. For example, obvious overactivity in middle childhood has been proposed to be replaced by subjective feelings of restlessness in adolescence, as individuals with chronic ADHD gradually become more capable of inhibiting overt behavior (Cantwell, 1996). When planning longitudinal studies to assess the development of psychopathology, researchers must choose measures with extreme care in order to balance the occasionally conflicting requirements of construct validity and continuity of measurement.

Prospective, longitudinal designs are crucial to answering certain questions related to continuity and change over time; yet the time, expense, and effort required for these designs forces psychological researchers to rely on mixed retrospective–prospective, accelerated longitudinal, and cross-sectional designs to build a sufficient knowledge base to warrant long-term longitudinal research. Experiments, whether embedded in longitudinal designs or carried out at a single measurement point, remain important as a means of identifying defining features of psychopathology, testing hypotheses about mechanisms underlying dysfunction, and gauging the impact of treatment and prevention efforts.

Cross-sectional designs

Cross-sectional designs, which gather data at only one time point, set the stage for longitudinal research. These designs offer a relatively inexpensive means for addressing some important concerns of developmental psychopathology, such as outlining the presentation of symptoms at different ages, gauging cohort-, gender-, or age-related differences in incidence and prevalence of mental disorders, and examining whether hypothesized patterns of association among variables can be documented. Cross-sectional studies can also be used to conduct initial tests of possible causal factors, especially when combined with "natural experiments" in which children vary in their level of exposure to an event or experience presumed to alter adaptation (Rutter, 1994). For example, a cross-sectional study of children's adjustment following a natural disaster found evidence consistent with a dose–response relationship among degree of exposure to life-threatening experiences, ongoing disruptions, and intensity of posttraumatic stress symptoms (Vernberg et al., 1996). Hypothesized relationships between additional elements of the conceptual model were also evaluated, such as the linkage between social support and symptomatology.

Rutter (1994) argued against the premature use of longitudinal designs, noting that justification for these designs often rests on strong cross-sectional evidence on the plausibility of the conceptual framework for the study, the psychometric integrity for measures, and risk or protective factors influencing the emergence or progression of psychopathology. The research base is not evenly developed for all forms of child psychopathology. Disruptive behavior disorders and Attention Deficit Hyperactivity Disorder, for example, appear to have a sufficient research base to warrant fully prospective, long-term longitudinal designs. Research on other forms of child psychopathology, including most internalizing disorders, has reached a level of sophistication where cross-sectional or brief longitudinal designs remain necessary.

Longitudinal designs

Longitudinal research designs are useful for tracking the natural history of child psychopathology, addressing critical issues such as onset, duration, persistence, escalation, and decay of symptoms (Loeber and Farrington, 1994). Gathering information from the same group of children at various times helps researchers trace sequences and paths of development, gauge the effects of life experiences during sensitive developmental periods, and evaluate the significance of possible risk or resiliency (protective) factors.

Retrospective longitudinal designs are often used to compare individuals who develop psychopathology with normal peers. Information about early development is gathered through self-recollections, the recollections of others (e.g., mothers' reports of their child's temperament as an infant), or through other means such as school or medical records. Although retrospective research can link early factors with later outcomes, the accuracy of retrospective reports is often questionable, being influenced by knowledge of later developmental events or other influences on memory (Briere, 1992; Willett, Singer, and Martin, 1998). Retrospective research can be strengthened by techniques employed to enhance the accuracy of retrospective recall, such as using administrative records to reconstruct event histories more accurately and to provide anchors for life history calendars (Friedman et al., 1988). Providing or eliciting information about the context surrounding key events also appears to increase the accuracy of retrospective reports (Bradburn, Rips, and Shevell, 1987; Friedman et al., 1988).

Prospective longitudinal designs track one or more cohorts of children forward in time, allowing researchers to document the emergence and course of psychopathology. These designs are especially useful for evaluating the predictive validity of potential indicators of future functioning and tracking the progression of mechanisms thought to underlie psychopathology. Unlike retrospective designs, which often rely on recall or records gathered originally for other purposes, suspected mechanisms or signals of dysfunction can be measured carefully and consistently over time, and sequences of events can be considered.

Prospective studies avoid questions about the validity of retrospective data, but are vulnerable to changes in methodology, instrumentation, or policy concerns over the course of the study (Loeber and Farrington, 1994). Participants are often lost as families move away or lose interest, and families who are experiencing greater difficulties often drop out. To minimize participant loss it is advisable to gather extensive identifying information on participants and their families during the first contact and obtain permission to search future records (e.g., legal, financial, educational) to help locate participants later (Loeber and Farrington, 1994). Financial incentives, respect and consideration toward the participants, and stability within the research team may also prevent drop outs.

Many prospective studies in developmental psychopathology begin data collection at an age just prior to a notable increase in the incidence and prevalence of a specific disorder or problem behavior (e.g., Gjerde and Westenberg, 1998; Loeber et al., 1998). In *mixed retrospective–prospective designs* information on earlier developmental periods is gathered from records or recall, and participants are then followed prospectively for months or years. When retrospective data are of high quality, these designs offer numerous practical advantages and provide strong scientific evidence of predictive factors and the life course of psychopathology.

Accelerated longitudinal designs, also referred to as cohort-sequential designs or mixed longitudinal designs, offer another strategy for studying developmental questions in a shorter time period than that required by fully longitudinal designs (Willett, Singer, and Martin, 1998). In these designs two or more age cohorts are followed simultaneously long enough for the younger cohort to reach the same age as the older cohort at the beginning of the study. For example, in a study of aggression and victimization in middle childhood, a sample of children born between 1988 and 1993 was assessed initially in 1999, yielding cross-sectional data covering years 6 through 11 (Twemlow, Fonagy, and Vernberg, 2001). By adding new cohorts of 6 year olds and continuing to track previously enrolled children through age 11, it is possible to piece together developmental trajectories for aggression and victimization for ages 6 through 11 using only a three-year study period. Comparisons of birth cohorts from different years (e.g., 1988 and 1990) when they reach the same age (e.g., 11 years old) helps separate age-related trends in development from cohort-specific effects.

Advocates of this approach cite efficiencies in cost and time relative to single-cohort long-term longitudinal studies (Farrington, 1991; Loeber and Farrington, 1994). Others advise using accelerated longitudinal designs when resources are unavailable for a long-term study and when the research questions focus on short-term developmental issues rather than longer-term developmental trajectories (Willett, Singer, and Martin, 1998). It is important to note that accelerated designs can be problematic in communities with higher levels of in- or out-migration by making it more difficult to gather different age cohorts that are similar in demographic characteristics and contextual backgrounds (Willett, Singer, and Martin, 1998).

Experimental designs

Experimental designs involve manipulation of a key variable with the intention of producing a predictable result on other variables of interest. In the context of developmental psychopathology two primary forms of experimental designs predominate. In *intervention trials* the independent variable (treatment condition) may take weeks, months, or even years to deliver, and follow-up assessments of treatment effects create a longitudinal–experimental design (e.g., Burchinal et al., 1997).

In contrast, *performance-based* experimental designs examine differences in response to experimenter-controlled stimuli by individuals with specific forms of psychopathology. These designs often provide critical tests of basic cognitive, physiological, and behavioral processes believed to contribute to specific forms of psychopathology (e.g., Oosterlaan and Sergeant, 1998).

Behavior genetic designs

One of the most controversial debates in developmental psychopathology concerns the relative contributions of genetics, shared environmental influences, and nonshared environmental influences to the development of psychopathology. On the positive side, accurate understanding of these three forces may lead to more effective prevention and treatment of psychopathology. Within a developmental systems perspective even the expression of psychological attributes that are highly influenced by genetics should be influenced by environmental manipulations that are timed appropriately.

Twin and adoption studies are most often used in behavior genetics designs. By comparing characteristics and behaviors of monozygotic and dizygotic twins (both reared together and separately), and by contrasting traits children share with their biological versus adoptive parents, it is possible to estimate effects for genetics, shared environmental influences, and nonshared environmental influences. However, finding enough pairs of twins willing to take part in a study (especially if one is looking for individuals with a specific trait or disorder), or obtaining access to adoption records in order to study both biological and adoptive parents, is a formidable challenge. One alternative, the step-family design, makes recruitment an easier task, but separating the genetic and environmental components for members of these families (e.g., step-siblings) is particularly difficult (O'Connor and Plomin, 2000). For example, the relative degree of shared and nonshared environmental effects varies depending upon the amount of time before divorce and remarriage and the amount of time each child spends with each biological parent after remarriage. Advances in understanding the human genome and in biological bases of psychopathology make it likely that behavior genetic designs will become even more important in the next generation of research on developmental psychopathology.

Maintain a focus on the individual

The majority of published psychological research involves the comparison of groups by analyzing overall means on target variables. Although the relationships among several variables may be examined in these *variable-oriented* studies (e.g., how gender or ethnicity affect the relationship among the primary set of variables), this approach does not entirely satisfy the *person-centered* orientation of a systems or interactionistic perspective in which the individual is seen as more than a collection of several defining characteristics (Bergman, 1998; Magnusson, 1995). Group means may fail to reflect any one individual's actual functioning, and the developmental significance of measured values on a single variable (e.g., aggressiveness in early adolescence) may depend on other factors (e.g., the co-occurrence of other severe behavior problems) (Magnusson, 1995). Statistically significant differences between groups may have little practical significance in studies with large samples, or may not be found due to limitations in statistical power in studies with smaller samples. Variability within groups may be large, and group means may be less meaningful than finer-grained subgroupings within larger categories.

A person-centered approach attempts to take into account the differing patterns of individual and environmental characteristics that determine actual behavioral responses and psychological processes by making the *person* rather than the *variable* the unit of analysis. Individuals can be represented by many related factors, each interacting in a complex manner with the others, and a particular *state* is defined by the entire configuration of these factors at one point in time (Bergman and Magnusson, 1997). Development is conceptualized as a continuous shifting of this overall configuration. However, while this progression is partially unique to each person, some *patterns* of factors tend to be more common than others, as certain combinations of characteristics and behaviors have more adaptive value in terms of the overall functioning of the total organism. Because these optimal patterns appear frequently within an individual's course of development, as well as within different individuals, a developmental research approach should attempt to identify these overarching patterns of functions and to explain the psychological phenomena (e.g., various forms of psychopathology, successful coping processes) that are associated with such patterns.

Attend to sampling issues

When collecting data on children and adolescents, researchers face the basic obstacle of obtaining a sufficient number of participants for their study. Large groups of children are often difficult to recruit into psychological research. Schools are the greatest source of a representative sample of children; however, school districts must protect the interests of their students and are often reluctant to allow psychological research unless they or the students receive benefits in return. Recruiting clinical samples of children with identified psychopathology is no easier task. Tracking children with psychological disorders is complicated by the fact that family dysfunction, parental distress, and concerns about uncovering and reporting child maltreatment can reduce motivation to join or remain in a study. Recruiting participants through newspapers, local organizations, or churches may be problematic because of selection bias.

In addition, the pattern of development of psychopathology is often influenced by contextual factors such as socioeconomic status or adversity, and personal characteristics such as health and cognition. Each of these factors presents its own sampling issues. For example, low-income families facing high adversity may have greater residential instability, making longitudinal data collection difficult. However, psychologists cannot ignore these significant influences if research findings are used to direct public policy, psychological treatment, and the general understanding of human psychological processes. Researchers should challenge themselves to work with media, community organizations, government agencies, schools, and hospitals to garner support for research efforts requiring access to selected samples of difficult-to-reach populations.

Confront ethical considerations

As in all areas of psychological research, ethical principles of working with human participants apply to the domain of developmental psychopathology. However, studying the emergence of psychopathology among children and adolescents poses special challenges. When a clinical or high-risk sample is used in a study, or when psychological disturbance is detected in a child of a nonclinical sample, it is important to consider whether diagnostic information or appropriate treatment can be withheld in order to study the development of psychopathology. When conducting prospective longitudinal investigations (e.g., concerning risk and resiliency factors with regard to the development of psychological distress), researchers may uncover sensitive information such as evidence of unhealthy coping strategies, harmful parental practices, or involvement with antisocial peers. While legal standards generally require suspected abuse or neglect to be reported to local authorities, researchers should also acknowledge previous research indicating the deleterious effects of other risk factors. Even if a particular situation is not causing physical harm to a child, psychologists are obligated to attempt to prevent psychological and emotional suffering when an evidence-based intervention may improve a research participant's condition. An additional consideration is that the early detection and treatment of a problem when it is just emerging is often more productive than attempting to intervene after a psychological disorder is fully developed. While a developmental psychopathology perspective is based upon the progression along the continuum from what is healthy development to what is abnormal, ethical considerations must place a critical limit upon this type of inquiry. In some cases a retrospective longitudinal design or a prospective design including treatment may be the only ethical solution. Finally, in research with children, adolescents, and families, issues regarding informed consent rise to the forefront. Even when written consent is obtained from a parent or guardian, the child's verbal or written assent often must also be obtained. This may pose a problem when working with clinical populations or individuals with low cognitive functioning, because the child's mental or emotional state may limit motivation to participate. Also, information provided by the child respondent could require the researcher's disclosure of confidential information, such as suicidality or maltreatment, to parents or social services. The balance between benefits of research in developmental psychopathology must be carefully weighed against disclosing or withholding sensitive information and offering or withholding treatment in intervention trials.

Selected Issues in Measurement and Analysis

Measurement considerations

Given questions of continuity and change in psychopathology among individuals who are also experiencing remarkable growth in cognitive, physical, and social capabilities, it is a challenge to select attributes that can be tracked throughout the developmental period of interest. Moreover, many research questions require attention to a broad range of factors, ranging from molecular processes to cultural forces. Multiple sources of information are needed to address most research questions, as is careful attention to the measurement of key social contextual variables.

Multiple informants

The use of multiple informants is widely encouraged in research in developmental psychopathology. Although the child's perspective is of great interest, other reporters are needed to make an informed assessment. Children may not be able to remember or accurately describe important information regarding their symptoms (Emslie and Mayes, 1999). Particularly at very early ages, researchers rely on the reports of adults in children's environments. Parents and teachers are often in a better situation to report on the precursors to certain child behaviors and to describe the specific behaviors themselves. In addition, trained observers may be used to gather objective information about the child and the environments in which the behaviors occur. As children develop, their reports become more reliable and they can be asked to report on themselves (Edelbrock et al., 1985). Self-report is especially valuable when personal information about internal states, attitudes, or covert activities is needed (Edelbrock et al., 1986; O'Donnell et al., 1998). Questionnaires and interviews are two common ways to gather information directly from the child. In addition to adult and self-report, children's peers may be asked to provide information about the participants. Various peer-report measures such as the Pupil Evaluation Inventory (Pekarik et al., 1976) and peer nomination instruments (Crick and Bigbee, 1998; Perry, Kusel, and Perry, 1988) have been used to gather information about children's behaviors, especially overt and relational aggression.

Reports from children, parents, teachers, observers, and peers often show only low to moderate agreement (Canino et al., 1995; Edelbrock et al., 1985; Huddleston and Rust, 1994). Differences between parental and child reports in particular have been shown to vary according to the child's age (Edelbrock et al., 1985), gender (Offord, Boyle, and Racine, 1989; Valla et al., 1993), and level of acculturation (Rousseau and Drapeau, 1998). These low levels of agreement may indicate a lack of reliability of certain reporters (Edelbrock et al., 1985); however, low correlations among informants do not necessarily reflect a shortcoming of any of the methods of data collection. The differences among informants may attest to the different vantage points the reporters have concerning a particular problem. Information on internalizing symptoms differs in level of accessibility to the different informants. Although people in the children's environments can witness some behaviors, children will be more knowledgeable about their feelings or fears. It is not surprising, then, that parent–child agreement on internalizing symptoms is much lower than that for externalizing symptoms (Edelbrock et al., 1986; Herjanic and Reich, 1982). Children's behavior also varies in different settings; thus, discrepancies between teacher and parent reports are likely to reflect these differences in behavior instead of a lack of reliability.

In some cases the lack of agreement among reporters may indicate biases of the reporters or a desire to give a socially appropriate picture of the situation (Rousseau and Drapeau, 1998). In complex family situations, such as domestic violence, gaining perspectives from everyone involved is encouraged as a way to improve the reliability of reports of behavior (Sternberg, Lamb, and Dawud-Noursi, 1998). Likewise, in cases involving families from different cultures, gathering data from numerous sources can help clarify the degree to which the expression or reporting of symptoms differs by culture (Chang, Morrissey, and Kaplewicz, 1995; Weisz, Suwanlert, Chaiyasit, Weiss, and Walter, 1987).

Integrating conflicting data from multiple informants can be burdensome, yet it results in a richer view of children and the factors related to their behaviors.

Performance-based measures

Performance-based measures, which involve measuring a child's performance or response to a specific, experimenter-controlled stimulus or task presented in a standardized format, offer a valuable source of information to complement information gained from rating scales, questionnaires, and observational data. These measures may be used to demonstrate the presence of a specific asset or deficit, to track change over time due to treatment or maturation, or to test theory-based hypotheses regarding mechanisms underlying various forms of psychopathology. Although performance-based measures offer many advantages, several considerations enter into their selection and use (Frick, 2000). Many performance-based measures were originally designed to test specific hypotheses concerning a particular disorder, and as hypotheses are adapted, so are the measures used to test them. Hence, psychometric data are often limited, and it becomes difficult to use these procedures to compare children from different samples. The ecological validity of many of these procedures can be called into question since they are purposefully designed to measure the behaviors of children in response to standardized laboratory situations rather than natural settings. Most performance-based measures have been developed primarily for use in research paradigms and not in clinical settings, and there is not much evidence at this time to suggest that these techniques supply data which direct psychological interventions any more effectively than less costly approaches (Frick, 2000). However, indirect effects, such as increased understanding of the factors underlying disorders, can aid clinicians in providing therapy. Some of these procedures attempt to elicit behaviors or psychological responses which are generally unacceptable (e.g., aggressive behavior, cheating, stealing), and researchers and clinicians must be vigilant to the possibility that experimenter-induced actions may influence behavior outside of the laboratory. These practical and ethical considerations must be kept in mind as psychologists explore these procedures in more detail and attempt to employ them in clinical as well as research settings. While many obstacles must be overcome in applying these methods to clinical populations, the ideal remains of being able to objectively assess a child's behavioral and psychological responses to a standard set of stimuli and to link these responses to particular underlying mechanisms of disorders.

An example of a laboratory and performance-based measure with regard to conduct disorders is provided by Frick and Loney (2000). In the study of covert conduct problems (e.g., cheating, stealing, property destruction), a temptation provocation paradigm is helpful because children are not likely to self-report such activities, and parents and other raters are unlikely to directly observe such behaviors taking place. In one variation on this theme children were left alone in a room with attractive toys and small amounts of money visible while they were supposed to be working on an academic task (in addition, the answer key to the assignment was left partly exposed). Aggressive and non-aggressive children with ADHD differed in stealing and property destruction frequencies in this simulated laboratory situation. Procedures such as this may prove to be helpful in some aspects of assessment and diagnosis. However, especially with regard to provocation paradigms, relevant ethical and therapeutic issues must be considered.

Specialized analytic methods

Concern for reciprocal interactions among multiple systems (e.g., cognitive, biological) and inclusion of person-centered analyses and variable-oriented research has led developmental psychopathology towards an expanded set of analytic techniques. Principal aspects of several of these methods are presented briefly.

Cluster and pattern approaches

Cluster and pattern analyses present an opportunity to apply a person-oriented approach by categorizing individuals based on *profiles* of values on key measures, rather than on single indicators. Profiles can be based on theory (*model-based*), or they may be *descriptive*, based on identification of frequently occurring profiles within the set of all possible profiles (Bergman, 1998). Bergman advocated using a descriptive approach, which requires fewer assumptions about the properties of data and is more flexible, in developmental research when theory and measurement are less well-developed. Factors included in the generation of profiles typically represent personal characteristics believed conjointly to contribute to an important aspect of functioning (e.g., social competence, academic success). The number of profiles represented could equal the number of participants; however, the more typical goal is to identify profiles shared by multiple participants. Individuals often are categorized or grouped together based on a shared profile, and participants with various profiles are compared on other indicators of outcome or performance. It is possible to use longitudinal data gathered at multiple ages in generating profiles, although it appears more practical and useful to identify profiles within a single age range, and to study how profile class membership changes over time (Bergman, 1998). This *snapshot and linking* approach attempts to understand how patterns of characteristics change (or remain stable) for individuals over time.

Many methods and statistical packages are available for identifying clusters or profiles, and the selection of an approach depends on the measurement properties of variables, the research aim, and the specificity of theories or conceptual models being investigated (for more detailed discussion and references, see Bergman, 1998; Bergman and Magnusson, 1997). The validity and reliability of clusters should be evaluated on several criteria. These include (a) the match between profile membership and raw data, (b) examination of cluster membership for pairs of participants who fall in the same category on a "true" or criterion classification, and (c) replication of categories with different samples (Bergman, 1998).

Individual growth curve analysis

Individual growth curve (IGC) models attempt to describe change in the expression of an important characteristic (e.g., capacity for emotional regulation, cognitive skills) as a continuous process (Francis, Schatschneider, and Carlson, 2000). Change on a key characteristic is represented for each individual separately, and individuals who share similar change trajectories can be grouped together. Correlates of different change trajectories, including interventions, personal characteristics, or environmental factors, can then be examined (Francis, Schatschneider, and Carlson, 2000).

Individual growth curve methods allow for the inclusion and analysis of at least four levels of information: (a) distinct patterns of development determined by specific individuals' intercepts (developmental starting points) and slopes (rates of growth); (b) the influence of predictor variables (i.e., personal and environmental characteristics) on individual differences in starting points and rates of growth; (c) overall development at a group level if the comparison of individual growth patterns warrants such an analysis; and (d) the incorporation of data from multiple sources and multiple populations (Stoolmiller, 1995). Advocates for the use of IGC note numerous advantages over measures of incremental change, such as difference scores between measures obtained at two or more points in time. These include increased information about the rate of change, greater tolerance for missing data and variable time intervals between measurements, and greater parsimony (Francis, Schatschneider, and Carlson, 2000).

Three waves of data are a minimal number for identifying the shape of individual developmental trajectories, and greater numbers of data collection points improve the measurement of growth trajectories (Willett, Singer, and Martin, 1998). Each additional wave collected increases the reliability of individual change trajectories, with sharp increases in reliability as the number of waves increases from three to seven. Willett and colleagues argue that researchers should collect extra waves of data at all costs, even if this means fewer children will be followed.

Hierarchical linear regression
Hierarchical linear regression methods can also be used to produce individual growth curves and to investigate the correlates of change (Francis, Schatschneider, and Carlson, 2000; Raudenbush, 1995). Using these statistical methods, two or three levels of models are typically tested for their goodness-of-fit with the available data. For illustration, consider a hypothetical effort to measure the development of depressive symptoms through childhood and adolescence, tracking 100 participants longitudinally. At the first level of analysis, individual growth curves for each participant could be computed (i.e., 100 separate curves). These curves could include constant, linear, quadratic, or higher-order polynomial terms in order to model the curves that best fit the available data. For instance, it may be determined that the following equation is the best possible approximation of the data: (depression variable) = constant + B_1 (age) + B_2 (age)^2 + error. Each participant in the study could have a different constant and different slopes (B weights) depending on their particular growth trajectories.

After identifying the level 1 equation that best fits the data, attention would focus on level 2, or the specification of group-level variables that may influence developmental trajectories (e.g., socioeconomic status, the presence or absence of a particular diagnosis, treatment group membership). Continuing with the present example, the presence or absence of an ADHD diagnosis could be proposed to have an impact on the growth trajectories with regard to depressive symptoms. In building a level 2 model the sample would be divided into those children with ADHD and those without ADHD. The parameters (constant and slopes) of the level 1 equation would be used as the dependent variables in the level 2 equations, which allows the researcher to determine the constant values and slopes for each of the level 2 parameters (e.g., ADHD diagnosis status). One such level 2 equation would use the constant term from the level 1 equation as the dependent variable: (level 1 constant) = B_1 (ADHD diagnosis status) + (level 2 constant) + error. Hence, the term "hierarchical" linear modeling describes this multilevel set of equations where the parameters of one equation are used as the dependent variables in an additional set of equations. The magnitude of the slopes (B weights) in the level 2 equations would be used to determine whether group membership has a statistically significant effect upon the parameters in the individual growth curve equations. For instance, it may be that children with ADHD in general exhibit a slightly faster rate of growth with regard to depressive symptoms. If one wanted to continue exploring the data by determining if gender, for example, moderates the contribution of ADHD group membership upon the equation parameters, a third level of equations could be employed in the same manner as with level 2 (except that the parameters of the level 2 equations would be used as the dependent variables in the third level of equations). It is also possible to test several predictor variables (e.g., gender and socioeconomic status) in one level of the analysis, depending upon the specific hypotheses of the study. Therefore, by using hierarchical sets of equations, growth trajectories for both individuals and groups can be modeled, and this information may be used to determine whether group-level analyses are warranted based upon patterns in the data.

Latent growth curve modeling

When one wishes to incorporate multiple sources of data in explaining psychological phenomena (as is suggested in clinical research), individual growth curves can be analyzed using structural equation modeling techniques in a process termed *latent growth curve modeling* (Stoolmiller, 1995). Because one should not assume that any one measure can capture a psychological construct without error, and because multiple measures of the same construct should be correlated to some extent, the use of "latent" variables in equations is recommended when obtaining several measures of the same underlying construct. There are several important differences between latent growth curve modeling and the hierarchical regression approach described above; however, a detailed statistical explanation of such differences is beyond the scope of this chapter. One must first have a good grasp of the procedures underlying structural equation modeling (see chapter 8, this volume), and then one should consult a text that specifically deals with latent variable analysis within developmental (longitudinal) designs (e.g., Little, Schnabel, and Baumert, 2000; von Eye and Clogg, 1994).

Survival analysis

Much research in developmental psychopathology includes time as an independent variable, e.g., asking how profiles, individual characteristics, or behaviors change as an individual matures. However, time can also be analyzed as a dependent variable in survival analysis to represent the duration of treatment effects (e.g., relapse risk) or the emergence of key markers of functioning (e.g., inpatient psychiatric hospitalization in children treated for serious emotional disturbance) (Singer and Willett, 1994; Willett and Singer, 1995).

Survival analysis consists of two complementary aspects: the survivor function and the hazard function. While the traditional terms of "survivor" and "hazard" were developed in the context of medical research on symptom remission or health following treatment, these analytic techniques can also be used to address research questions framed in the direction of improvement, as opposed to deterioration. The survivor function is simply a plot of the percentage of children who have reached or maintained a certain criterion (e.g., had not been hospitalized) at each data collection point. A particularly important value easily derived from this function is the *median lifetime*, which is the time at which at least 50 percent of individuals have reached the specified goal. In addition, a hazard function plots the hazard (a mathematically determined probability) of an individual beginning to exhibit symptoms at each data collection point, assuming that he or she was symptom-free until that time (Willett and Singer, 1995).

In the context of developmental psychopathology research, survival analysis can indicate effects of treatments, personal characteristic profiles, or environmental risks on outcomes such as length of time before relapse or progression to more severe psychopathology. For example, a hazard function could define the probability that an individual would develop a key symptom or demonstrate an important competency, provided that he or she had not reached that level previously. In this way, researchers can determine which points in development are particularly risky for symptom escalation or especially promising for the attainment of a skill. In addition, the median lifetimes can be compared for various groups of individuals. Finally, statistical models can then be built much like linear regression models, where predictor variables are multiplied by slope parameters and added to a baseline hazard level (a constant which is multiplied by a value describing time) to determine the hazard level for a member of a particular group or condition at particular times during development.

Qualitative analyses

In addition to the traditional quantitative approaches employed in psychopathology research, qualitative methods are slowly reappearing in the literature as tools for examining phenomena in a somewhat broader light (chapter 9, this volume). These methods, while being borrowed primarily from the fields of anthropology and sociology, were once heavily relied upon in the field of psychological research in the form of introspection. More recently, clinical child psychologists have used naturalistic observations, tape recordings, and open-ended interviews to probe cultural and phenomenological (subjective) aspects of psychological experiences. Researchers divide qualitative responses (e.g., from an interview) into several categories in order to separate out specific themes. As one looks at each new response one determines statistically if the current set of categories is sufficient, or if a different arrangement (e.g., the addition or consolidation of categories) would be more appropriate. In this way theories and hypotheses are slowly formed through the analysis of themes evident in large amounts of qualitative data, which is usually collected across many individuals. An example of this approach within the field of developmental psychopathology might be relected in the study of how children and adolescents from various cultural backgrounds cope with the death of same-age peers. Naturalistic observations and personal interviews with a large number of children and adolescents from different cultural groups could capture the subtleties of behavior, cognition, and emotional response that could not be derived from self- or other-report quantitative measures. Responses from interviews and notes from observations could then be categorized under different themes reflecting coping attempts, after which one could identify differences in the responses of children from various groups.

Krahn, Hohn, and Kime (1995) propose the use of both quantitative and qualitative methods in the same investigation, and suggest that this "triangulation" of methods will serve to validate empirical findings (with the use of two methods instead of one) and elucidate divergent results from the two approaches that may be worthy of further study. These authors mention several practical ways to combine what may seem to be incompatible strategies. Although both quantitative and qualitative methods may be used concurrently, other designs include: (a) using qualitative analyses to identify theories to be tested with traditional quantitative methods, and (b) using qualitative methods to follow up on results obtained from quantitative procedures (i.e., to explore purely "numerical" results more deeply). However, qualitative methods currently suffer from several drawbacks. First, lengthy observation or narrative reports are difficult to code reliably, and this tedious process requires large amounts of time and resources to complete. In addition, some psychologists are concerned about generalizing psychological processes from an analysis of data that is confounded with individual behavioral idiosyncrasies and subjective understandings of experience. Limitations such as these often deter researchers from employing qualitative methods in their studies; however, a heightened effort to include such methods in broad-scale investigations may prove to illuminate pertinent research questions and to more accurately capture individuals' psychological experiences, a consequence well suited to a developmental trajectory approach.

Conclusions

Research in developmental psychopathology requires a broad range of methods, measures, and analytic techniques. The ambitious task of integrating information from more specialized lines of inquiry, such as psychobiology, cognitive science, and cultural studies, into a comprehensive framework for understanding normal and abnormal development involves collaboration across disciplines and synthesis of seemingly incongruous information. Linking contextual factors to basic cognitive and biological processes is an important goal, as is finding a way to reconcile a holistic, person-centered view of human functioning with the more microanalytic, reductionist procedures characteristic of many fields of scientific endeavor. Research in psychology and related fields has become an increasingly influential force in both clinical practice and social policy, as greater attention has been paid to such issues as ecological validity and the influence of social ecology on virtually all aspects of human development.

References

Bergman, L. R. (1998). A pattern-oriented approach to studying individual development. In R. B. Cairns, L. R. Bergman, and J. Kagan (eds.), *Methods and models for studying the individual* (pp. 83–121). Thousand Oaks, CA: Sage.

Bergman, L. R., and Magnusson, D. (1997). A person-oriented approach in research on developmental psychopathology. *Development and Psychopathology, 9,* 291–319.

Boyce, W. T., Frank, E., Jensen, P. S., Kessler, R. C., Nelson, C. A., Steinberg, L., and the MacArthur Foundation Research Network on Psychopathology and Development (1998). Social context in developmental psychopathology: Recommendations for future research from the MacArthur Network on Psychopathology and Development. *Development and Psychopathology*, *10*, 143–64.

Bradburn, N. M., Rips, L. J., and Shevell, S. K. (1987). Answering autobiographical questions: The impact of memory and inference on surveys. *Science*, *236*, 157–61.

Briere, J. (1992). Methodological issues in the study of sexual abuse effects. *Journal of Consulting and Clinical Psychology*, *60*, 196–203.

Brodsky, M., and Lombroso, P. J. (1998). Molecular mechanisms of developmental disorders. *Development and Psychopathology*, *10*, 1–20.

Burchinal, M. R., Campbell, F. A., Bryant, D. M., Wasik, B. H., and Ramey, C. T. (1997). Early intervention and mediating processes in cognitive performance of children of low-income African-American families. *Child Development*, *68*, 935–54.

Canino, G., Bird, H. R., Rubio-Stipec, M., and Bravo, M. (1995). Child psychiatric epidemiology: What we have learned and what we need to learn. *International Journal of Methods in Psychiatric Research*, *5*, 79–92.

Cantwell, D. P. (1996). Attention deficit disorder: A review of the past 10 years. *American Academy of Child and Adolescent Psychiatry*, *35*, 978–87.

Chang, L., Morrissey, R. F., and Kaplewicz, H. S. (1995). Prevalence of psychiatric symptoms and their relation to adjustment among Chinese-American youth. *Journal of the American Academy of Child and Adolescent Psychiatry*, *34*, 91–9.

Cicchetti, D., and Rogosch, F. A. (1996). Equifinality and multifinality in developmental psychopathology. *Development and Psychopathology*, *8*, 597–600.

Crick, N. R., and Bigbee, M. A. (1998). Relational and overt forms of peer aggression: A multi-informant approach. *Journal of Consulting and Clinical Psychology*, *66*, 337–47.

Dodge, K. A. (1993). Social-cognitive mechanisms in the development of conduct disorder and depression. *Annual Review of Psychology*, *44*, 559–84.

Edelbrock, C., Costello, A. J., Dulcan, M. K., Calabro-Conover, N., and Kalas, R. (1986). Parent–child agreement on child psychiatric symptoms reported via structured interview. *Journal of Child Psychology and Psychiatry*, *27*, 181–90.

Edelbrock, C., Costello, A. J., Dulcan, M. K., Kalas, R., and Calabro-Conover, N. (1985). Age differences in the reliability of the psychiatric interview of the child. *Child Development*, *56*, 265–75.

Emslie, G. J., and Mayes, T. L. (1999). Depression in children and adolescents. *CNS Drugs*, *11*, 181–9.

Farrington, D. P. (1991). Longitudinal research strategies: Advantages, problems, and prospects. *Journal of the American Academy of Child and Adolescent Psychiatry*, *30*, 369–74.

Francis, D. J., Schatschneider, C., and Carlson, C. D. (2000). Introduction to individual growth curve analysis. In D. Drotar (ed.), *Handbook of research in pediatric and clinical child psychology: Practical strategies and methods* (pp. 51–73). New York: Kluwer Academic/Plenum.

Frick, P. J. (2000). Laboratory and performance-based measures of childhood disorders: Introduction to the special section. *Journal of Clinical Child Psychology*, *29*, 475–8.

Frick, P. J., and Loney, B. R. (2000). The use of laboratory and performance-based measures in the assessment of children and adolescents with conduct disorders. *Journal of Clinical Child Psychology*, *29*, 540–54.

Friedman, D., Thornton, A., Camburn, D., Alwin, D., and Young-DeMarco, L. (1988). The life-history calendar: A technique for collecting retrospective data. *Sociological Methodology*, *18*, 37–68.

Gjerde, P. F., and Westenberg, P. M. (1998). Dysphoric adolescents as young adults: A prospective study of the psychological sequelae of depressed mood in adolescence. *Journal of Research on Adolescence*, 8, 377–402.

Goldsmith, H. H., Gottesman, I. I., and Lemery, K. S. (1997). Epigenetic approaches to developmental psychopathology. *Development and Psychopathology*, 9, 365–87.

Herjanic, B., and Reich, W. (1982). Development of a structured psychiatric interview for children: Agreement between child and parent on individual symptoms. *Journal of Abnormal Child Psychology*, 10, 307–24.

Huddleston, E. N., and Rust, J. O. (1994). A comparison of child and parent ratings of depression and anxiety in clinically referred children. *Research Communications in Psychology, Psychiatry and Behavior*, 19, 101–12.

Kazdin, A. E. (1990). Childhood depression. *Journal of Child Psychology and Psychiatry*, 31, 121–60.

Krahn, G. L., Hohn, M. F., and Kime, C. (1995). Incorporating qualitative approaches into clinical child psychology research. *Journal of Clinical Child Psychology*, 24, 204–13.

Little, T. D., Schnabel, K. U., and Baumert, J. (eds.) (2000). *Modeling longitudinal and multilevel data: Practical issues, applied approaches and specific examples.* Mahwah, NJ: Lawrence Erlbaum.

Loeber, R., and Farrington, D. P. (1994). Problems and solutions in longitudinal and experimental treatment studies of child psychopathology and delinquency. *Journal of Consulting and Clinical Psychology*, 62, 887–900.

Loeber, R., Farrington, D. P., Stouthamer-Loeber, M., Moffitt, T. E., and Caspi, A. (1998). The development of male offending: Key findings from the first decade of the Pittsburgh Youth Study. *Studies on Crime and Crime Prevention*, 7, 141–71.

Magnusson, D. (1995). Individual development: A holistic, integrated model. In P. Moen, G. H. Elder, Jr., and K. Luscher (eds.), *Examining lives in context: Perspectives on the ecology of human development* (pp. 19–60). Washington, DC: American Psychological Association.

O'Connor, T. G., and Plomin, R. (2000). Developmental behavioral genetics. In A. J. Sameroff, M. Lewis, and S. M. Miller (eds.), *Handbook of developmental psychopathology* (2nd edn., pp. 217–235). New York: Kluwer Academic/Plenum.

O'Donnell, D., Biederman, J., Jones, J., Wilens, T. E., Milberger, S., Mick, E., and Faraone, S. V. (1998). Informativeness of child and parent reports on substance use disorders in a sample of ADHD probands, control probands, and their siblings. *Journal of the American Academy of Child and Adolescent Psychiatry*, 37, 752–8.

Offord, D. R., Boyle, M. H., and Racine, Y. (1989). Ontario child health study: Correlates of disorder. *Journal of the American Academy of Child and Adolescent Psychiatry*, 28, 856–60.

Oosterlaan, J., and Sergeant, J. A. (1998). Effects of reward and response cost on response inhibition in AD/HD, disruptive, anxious, and normal children. *Journal of Abnormal Child Psychology*, 26, 161–74.

Pekarik, E. G., Prinz, R. J., Liebert, D. E., Weintraub, S., and Neale, J. M. (1976). The pupil evaluation inventory: A sociometric technique for assessing children's social behavior. *Journal of Abnormal Child Psychology*, 4, 83–97.

Perry, B. D., Pollard, R. A., Blakely, T. L., Baker, W. L., and Vigilante, D. (1995). Childhood trauma, the neurobiology of adaptation, and "use dependent" development of the brain: How "states" become "traits." *Infant Mental Health Journal*, 16, 271–91.

Perry, D. G., Kusel, S. J., and Perry, L. C. (1988). Victims of peer aggression. *Developmental Psychology*, 24, 807–14.

Quay, H. C. (1993). The psychobiology of undersocialized aggressive conduct disorder: A theoretical perspective. *Development and Psychopathology*, 5, 165–80.

Raudenbush, S. W. (1995). Hierarchical linear models to study the effects of social context on development. In J. M. Gottman (ed.), *The analysis of change* (pp. 165–201). Mahwah, NJ: Lawrence Erlbaum.

Reiss, D. (1995). Genetic influence on family systems: Implications for development. *Journal of Marriage and the Family, 57*, 543–60.

Rousseau, C., and Drapeau, A. (1998). Parent–child agreement on refugee children's psychiatric symptoms: A transcultural perspective. *Journal of the American Academy of Child and Adolescent Psychiatry, 37*, 626–9.

Rutter, M. (1994). Beyond longitudinal data: Causes, consequences, changes, and continuity. *Journal of Consulting and Clinical Psychology, 62*, 928–40.

Singer, J. D., and Willett, J. B. (1994). Modeling duration and the timing of events: Using survival analysis in long-term follow-up studies. In S. L. Friedman and H. C. Haywood (eds.), *Developmental follow-up: Concepts, domains, and methods* (pp. 315–30). San Diego, CA: Academic Press.

Sternberg, K. J., Lamb, M. E., and Dawud-Noursi, S. (1998). Using multiple informants to understand domestic violence and its effects. In G. W. Holden and R. Geffner (eds.), *Children exposed to marital violence: Theory, research, and applied issues* (pp. 121–56). Washington, DC: American Psychological Association.

Stoolmiller, M. (1995). Using latent growth curve models to study developmental processes. In J. M. Gottman (ed.), *The analysis of change* (pp. 103–38). Mahwah, NJ: Lawrence Erlbaum.

Twemlow, S., Fonagy, P., and Vernberg, E. M. (2001). *Annual report on the Creating a Peaceful School Learning Environment (CAPSLE) project*. Topeka, KS: Menninger Clinic.

Valla, J. P., Bergeron, L., Breton, J. J., Gaudet, N., and Berthiaume, C. (1993). Informants, correlates and child disorders in a clinical population. *Canadian Journal of Psychiatry, 38*, 406–11.

van der Kolk, B. A. (1997). The complexity of adaptation to trauma: Self-regulation, stimulus, discrimination, and characterological development. In B. A. van der Kolk, A. C. McFarlane, and L. Weisaeth (eds.), *Traumatic stress: The effects of overwhelming experience on mind, body, and society* (pp. 182–213). New York: Guilford Press.

Vernberg, E. M., and Varela, R. E. (2001). Posttraumatic stress disorder: A developmental perspective. In M. W. Vasey and M. R. Dadds (eds.), *The developmental psychopathology of anxiety* (pp. 386–406). New York: Oxford University Press.

Vernberg, E. M., La Greca, A. M., Silverman, W. K., and Prinstein, M. J. (1996). Prediction of posttraumatic stress symptoms in children after Hurricane Andrew. *Journal of Abnormal Psychology, 105*, 237–48.

von Eye, A., and Clogg, C. C. (eds.) (1994). *Latent variables analysis: Applications for developmental research*. Thousand Oaks, CA: Sage.

Weiss, B., and Weisz, J. R. (1988). Factor structure of self-reported depression: Clinic-referred children versus adolescents. *Journal of Abnormal Psychology, 97*, 492–5.

Weisz, J. R., Suwanlert, S., Chaiyasit, W., Weiss, B., and Walter, B. R. (1987). Over and undercontrolled referral problems among children and adolescents from Thailand and the United States: The wat and wai of cultural differences. *Journal of Consulting and Clinical Psychology, 55*, 719–26.

Willett, J. B., and Singer, J. D. (1995). Investigating onset, cessation, relapse, and recovery: Using discrete-time survival analysis to examine the occurrence and timing of critical events. In J. M. Gottman (ed.), *The analysis of change* (pp. 203–59). Mahwah, NJ: Lawrence Erlbaum.

Willett, J. B., Singer, J. D., and Martin, N. C. (1998). The design and analysis of longitudinal studies of development and psychopathology in context: Statistical models and methodological recommendations. *Development and Psychopathology, 10*, 395–426.

VIGNETTE

Research Methods for Developmental Psychopathology

Anne K. Jacobs

Loeber, R., Stouthamer-Loeber, M., and White, H. R. (1999). Developmental aspects of delinquency and internalizing problems and their association with persistent juvenile substance use between ages 7 and 18. *Journal of Clinical Child Psychology*, *28*, 322–32.

Loeber and his colleagues analyzed longitudinal data from a sample of boys participating in the Pittsburgh Youth Study. Specifically, these investigators examined the co-occurrence of persistent substance use with other externalizing and internalizing symptoms. Several aspects of this article make it an exemplary study of developmental psychopathology, as described by Vernberg and Dill (chapter 11, this volume). For example, the authors attended to several sampling concerns that tend to plague developmental psychopathology research (e.g., a diverse sample large enough to reflect the specific psychopathology of interest). The participants were randomly selected from the 2,550 boys who began the Pittsburgh Youth Study while in the first, fourth, and seventh grades. For the present study, 500 boys were chosen for each of the three grade levels, 250 identified through structured diagnostic interviews as the most antisocial in each grade, and 250 randomly selected from the remainder of the boys. Data for the youngest sample were collected at screening and at each of the assessment waves in six-month intervals over the next four years. The sample reflected ethnic diversity, with African-American boys making up half of participants. Retention of subjects is often a concern in longitudinal research, but the authors reported very high participation rates, averaging 95.5 percent across the three grade samples.

Measurement instruments were reliable and valid, and all measures were completed by multiple informants, including caregivers, teachers, and the boys themselves. A well-validated structured interview was used to assess child psychopathology, specifically Attention Deficit Disorder (ADD) and Oppositional Defiant Disorder (ODD). The measures of delinquency and substance use were judged to be age-inappropriate for the younger boys so shorter, developmentally appropriate scales were developed. The number of participants was large enough to accommodate several analyses within each age sample. Results indicated the prevalence of different subtypes of persistent substance users. Odds ratios were presented to reflect the strength of association between problem behaviors and logistic regressions were used to predict persistent substance use from delinquency and externalizing or internalizing problems.

The authors found that preadolescent, persistent substance users tended to be persistent delinquents as well, and half of this comorbid group also had persistent internalizing problems. In adolescents a third of the persistent substance users did not have any other persistent problems. Boys who manifested only persistent internalizing problems were the least common subtype of substance users regardless of age. Persistent substance use in adolescence was predicted by persistent delinquency only, while persistent substance use in preadolescence was also predicted by internalizing problems. ODD predicted persistent substance use co-occurring with persistent delinquency in middle childhood, while persistent internalizing problems predicted such a combination in middle-to-late childhood. ADD did not predict persistent substance use or persistent delinquency. By using a prospective longitudinal design, the authors provided information that will be helpful in creating developmental models for boys with multiple problems. The strengths of the Loeber et al. (1999) article include:

- Longitudinal design
- High retention rate of participants
- Diverse participant group
- Large sample size enabling complex analyses
- Use of reliable and valid measures
- Modification of measures to make them age-appropriate
- Use of information from multiple informants

CHAPTER TWELVE

Adult Experimental Psychopathology

John P. Kline, Steven D. LaRowe, Keith F. Donohue, Jennifer Minnix, and Ginette C. Blackhart

Psychopathology curricula are an essential part of graduate training in clinical psychology. While the investigation of psychopathology addresses the classification and assessment of mental disorder, it must also include exploration of the relationships between environmental, cognitive, affective, and biological processes that underlie mental suffering. This is the domain of experimental psychopathology. As the name implies, this research is rooted in basic experimental psychology, and as such, garners information through experimental methods.

The last two decades have been exciting times for this field, largely because of the development of methods and technologies that enable the exploration of previously inaccessible processes. This chapter will review some of these applications, and while it is impossible to represent all areas of experimental psychopathological inquiry within a single chapter, we will illustrate how some of the methods from cognitive psychology, social psychology, and psychophysiology have been applied to the study of depression, anxiety, alcohol consumption, and psychological defensiveness.

Although we provide examples of basic work employing specific methods, we have also chosen to provide a more integrative context, which is probably best described as "multilevel." The basic approach to research embodied in this work involves the examination of phenomena across multiple levels of analysis, from basic brain systems to complex cognitive/affective processes. It also emphasizes the integration of data from multiple indicators of the relevant constructs, including physiological, self-reports, and behavioral measures. We believe that experimental psychopathology should encourage an integrative approach to analysis that considers multiple determinants for outcomes, reciprocal interaction between systems that operate on different levels of organization, and dynamic, context-contingent relationships. All this, of course, adds complexity to an already challenging field of research. However, it also offers an important perspective from which to find answers that are sufficiently elaborate for the questions to which they are addressed.

Issues for Multilevel Analysis

Cognitive, emotional, and physiological constructs are part and parcel of psychopathological inquiry, yet translations among these seemingly disparate levels of analysis pose a formidable challenge. Some biological theories often do little more than point to transmitter systems and neural structures that differ in some systematic way between patient and control groups, or between different patient groups. Some cognitive theories of psychopathology pay little attention to biological variables, in favor of "dysfunctional mechanisms" such as attention or memory. The inclusion of methodologies and conceptualizations from cognitive science, psychophysiology, and cognitive neuroscience has made for some very exciting advances. Yet with these advances have come some potential inferential pitfalls that need to be kept in mind.

The level of analyses conundrum

The ability to study biological dependent variables as they relate to more molar organismic behaviors (or as they are related to subjective experience, for that matter) poses a bit of a conundrum: just how molecular should an investigator get in order to relate biology, as both independent and dependent variable, to behavior and experience? While this is a complex issue, we believe that, in many instances, it may be a mistake to attempt to translate molecular biological variables directly into molar mental disorders. As we hope to illustrate, intermediate levels of analysis, i.e., of the functions of more grossly observable neural structures, constitute a very important step that should not be ignored. The problem, which we will call the *level of analysis conundrum*, is knowing just how deeply to delve into the biological underpinnings of a psychological phenomenon in order to arrive at a complete explanation. Kolb and Whishaw (1996: 153) have constructed a parable that illustrates this problem quite nicely:

> Mr. Higgins decided he should learn French so that he could enjoy French literature. After a year's intensive study Higgins was almost fluent in French, but it became clear to him that to really understand French, he was going to have to study Latin. Higgins had always been interested in Latin and so he plunged into it, only to find after a year's intense study that to master Latin, he really must study old Greek. Higgins was determined to learn French, and so he began a serious study of Greek. Alas, after a year's intense study of Greek, Higgins determined that he must now learn Sanskrit if he were to really appreciate Greek. This posed a problem, for there were few scholars of Sanskrit, but with a few months' effort, he managed to locate an old man in India who was a true scholar of Sanskrit. Excited at the possibility of soon learning French, Higgins moved to India to begin his study of Sanskrit. After six months the old man died. Demoralized because he did not yet have a good knowledge of Sanskrit, Higgins returned home and concluded that it was not possible to really learn French.

Clearly, biology is relevant to psychopathology, so an understanding of the basic structure and organization of the brain's affective and cognitive systems is essential to the understanding of how affective and cognitive states are produced and represented, as well as how disordered states differ from "normal" psychological function. Knowing where to begin, and where to stop, is less clear.

Integrating levels of analysis

Once the sophisticated bits of the behavioral and physiological data are compiled, combining them into coherent theories poses yet another problem. Which level wins out? Is a given form of psychopathology tantamount to a hardware or a software problem, i.e., is it "caused" by biology, is it caused by dysfunctional thought and emotion, or is it caused by the environmental contingencies that shape pathological behaviors? This sort of question, although intuitively appealing, may be misguided. Surely causes exist that are best understood as predominantly biological, some at psychological levels, and still others exist that are best understood in terms of environmental contingencies. It might also be possible to identify mediating causes, dysfunctional cognitive biases for example, which in themselves are in need of explanation.

No one of these "causes" at any level of analysis will explain every instance of any class of psychopathology. Even if, for example, it could be determined that x amount of genetics and y amount of environmental influence produced z amount of a particular class of psychopathology, this estimate would only constitute an average, and would not necessarily describe any given case in the population. Furthermore, such additive formulations do not take into account gene–environment interactions. Finally, "biology" and "genetics" are not synonymous: the examination of more proximate biological relations with identified psychopathology (e.g., neurotransmitter functioning in schizophrenia or depression) is by far the most prevalent variant of biology/psychopathology research. Although it might seem obvious that it is fallacious to assume that such biology–psychopathology relations are static and hardwired, such reasoning still seems to be relatively common among psychologists.

Methods for experimental psychopathology that take a multilevel perspective, thus placing molecular and intermediate-level physiological measures within a molar cognitive/affective context, may provide an especially powerful tool for the explication of psychopathological states. Just as it is not the best strategy to try to learn French by way of studying Sanskrit, more intermediate levels of analysis may result in theories that are more coherent and comprehensive than the ones that are currently favored. That being said, we turn now to examples of specific methods applied to theories of psychopathology. We begin with cognitive methods, followed by psychophysiological ones. Finally, we give examples of multilevel analysis employing both behavioral and psychophysiological dependent variables.

Cognitive Paradigms: Examples from Anxiety and Depression Research

Anxiety and attention

Considerable evidence suggests that individuals high in trait or clinical anxiety have attentional biases for threatening information. In other words, they tend to detect and process threatening stimuli more readily than those with little or no anxiety (see MacLeod, 1996, for a review). This bias for processing anxiety-related information is hypothesized to lead to a number of relevant outcomes, not the least of which is the maintenance of an anxious state. The role of this "processing bias" in maintaining anxious states has been investigated in a variety of studies using varied methodologies, including dichotic listening tasks (e.g., Burgess et al., 1981; Foa and McNally, 1986), dot probe tasks (e.g., MacLeod, Mathews, and Tata, 1986; Mogg, Mathews, and Eysenck, 1992), and the emotional Stroop paradigm (e.g., Mathews and MacLeod, 1985; MacLeod and Hagan, 1992; Mogg et al., 1993). Examples of these methods are presented in some detail below.

Dichotic listening studies

The dichotic listening task provides a means of assessing selective attention (Cherry, 1953), as well as a measure of hemispheric asymmetries in the selective processing of information (Dawson and Schell, 1982, 1983). Although auditory neural pathways do not completely cross, there is a slight tendency for contralateral connections to be somewhat stronger. As such, there tends to be a left ear (i.e., right hemisphere) advantage for nonverbal processing (e.g., musical passages, vocal prosody), and a right ear (i.e., left hemisphere) advantage for verbal processing (King and Kimura, 1972).

A "typical" dichotic listening task involves the simultaneous presentation of a separate passage of prose to each ear, while participants "shadow" (i.e., repeat aloud) the content from one ear and ignore the content from the other. Target words or phrases are embedded within the prose passages of both ears and participants are required to make a response when they detect the target. Participants generally detect target words within the shadowed passage fairly well, but have difficulty detecting target words embedded within the ignored passage. Researchers have adapted this paradigm for the study of the anxiety-related processing bias by comparing responses to target words that are either neutral (e.g., bone, wire) or threatening in nature (e.g., cancer, injury). If highly anxious individuals do, in fact, have a greater tendency to scan for and detect anxiety-related information than their low-anxious counterparts, then it is reasonable to hypothesize that the anxious individuals will be more likely to detect anxiety-related words in the "unattended" passage. Several studies have provided support for this hypothesis.

For instance, Burgess et al. (1981) studied four agoraphobic and two socially phobic individuals who were participating in a phobia treatment program, along with a group of psychology student comparison participants. These psychology students completed the Fear Survey Schedule (FSS; Wolpe and Lang, 1964). Items on the FSS relating to agoraphobia and social phobia were identified. Students that endorsed having "much" or "very much" fear for these items were identified as analogue phobic individuals. Remaining participants who did not endorse the specified fear-related items were assigned to a control group. The dichotic listening task involved simultaneously playing two passages of prose to each ear. Two different types of target words were embedded in the prose passages consisting of either a neutral word, or words associated with the fear-related items of the FSS (e.g., examination, seminar, shopping, and other such words related to either social phobia or agoraphobia). The participants were informed of the target word through the use of flashcards. While they shadowed the ear corresponding to their dominant hand, participants were instructed to tap a ruler if the target word appeared at any time in either passage presented in either ear. No differences for word detection were observed when the words appeared in the shadowed passage. However, phobics detected significantly more fear-relevant targets in the unattended (nonshadowed) passage than did the controls, suggesting that the phobics demonstrated a heightened sensitivity to information semantically related to their reported fears.

Foa and McNally (1986) presented individuals meeting DSM-III criteria for Obsessive Compulsive Disorder (OCD) with neutral targets compared to threatening OCD-relevant words (e.g., urine, feces, etc.). The procedure was administered both before and after treatment. Results of the pretreatment administration indicated no differences in word detection between threatening OCD-relevant and neutral words in the attended passage. In contrast, OCD participants detected threatening OCD-related target words more frequently than neutral targets in the unattended passage. During the posttreatment administration no significant differences were found for the detection of threatening OCD-relevant target words relative to neutral words. These results suggest that the pretreatment group differences in the detection of threat words were a result of the untreated anxiety disorder, rather than a result of mere familiarity with OCD-related words. Overall, the results suggest that individuals with OCD exhibit vigilance for threat-relevant stimuli.

Wexler et al. (1986) extended dichotic listening methods in order to study hemispheric asymmetries of emotional word perception in both anxiety and "repressive coping" as defined by Weinberger, Schwartz, and Davidson (1979). To this end, they presented participants with fused, rhymed pairs of negative-neutral, positive-negative, negative-positive, and positive-negative words in a counterbalanced order, such that each type of word pair was presented both left-right and right-left. The pairs of words were synchronized such that participants reported hearing only one of the two words in each pair. Individuals scoring both low on anxiety and high on the Marlowe Crowne Social Desirability Scale (i.e., "repressors"), reported hearing the fewest negative words, especially when the negative words were presented to the left ear. This finding is consistent with the hypothesis that repressive/defensive individuals have a bias against the processing of distressing material.

Although space limitations preclude a full study of all forms of psychopathology that have been studied with the dichotic listening paradigm, it should be noted that a rich literature on dichotic listening and schizophrenia also exists (see Bruder et al., 1999; Loberg, Hugdahl, and Green, 1999). In these studies, schizophrenics tend not to show the expected right ear advantage for the processing of verbal stimuli. Furthermore, other evidence suggests that positive symptoms, such as hallucinations and delusions, are associated with this diminished laterality (Malaspina et al., 2000). Through use of neuroimaging in conjunction with behavioral data (more will be said about such multilevel analyses later), Malaspina et al. (2000) have also found evidence that the decreased right ear advantage in schizophrenics may be driven by an overactive right temporal lobe.

Dot probe studies

The dot probe paradigm provides another method for investigating attentional biases in anxiety. In this paradigm word pairs are presented toward the center of a video screen, with one word placed above the center of the screen and the other below it. One of the words is periodically followed by a dot (a.k.a. the "probe"). Participants are required to indicate that they detected the dot by pressing a button. If, for some reason, participants are attending to the word that is eventually followed by the dot, they should detect the dot faster as indicated by a shorter response latency. However, if they are attending to one word but the unattended word is followed by the dot, then they will take longer to detect that dot, as indicated by greater response latency. Investigators have modified this method for use in anxiety research by using words that are either anxiety-related or neutral. In the studies that use these methods the hypothesis is that highly anxious individuals will detect dots that are preceded by anxiety-related words more quickly than they will detect dots preceded by neutral words. The opposite pattern is generally expected for low-anxious individuals. In general, highly anxious individuals show shorter probe detection latencies when the dot probes are preceded by anxiety-related words.

MacLeod, Mathews, and Tata (1986) used the dot probe paradigm to examine the attentional biases of individuals being treated for anxiety; low-anxious psychology students served as a comparison group. The study employed 288 word pairs, 96 of which were followed by a dot probe. On 48 of the 96 dot probe presentations, the word pairs consisted of a threatening word (e.g., opposed, humiliated, injury, ambulance, etc.) and a neutral word. Dots followed either type of word with equal frequency. On the remaining 48 presentations, both words of the pair were neutral. When pairs were followed by the dot probe, the dot remained on the computer screen until the response was made. The main dependent variable was response latency (i.e., the time between the onset of the dot and the button press), which was also measured by computer. Anxious individuals detected dots preceded by threat words significantly more rapidly than dots preceded by neutral words. Conversely, the comparison group detected probes more rapidly when preceded by neutral words than when preceded by threatening words. MacLeod, Mathews, and Tata (1986) concluded that anxious individuals shifted their attention toward threat words, resulting in reduced detection latencies. Controls, on the other hand, tended to shift attention away from threatening information. This finding has been replicated by Mogg, Mathews, and Eysenck (1992; as cited in MacLeod, 1996).

Although the dot probe paradigm has been examined most extensively in anxiety, it has also been examined in other applications. One such application is the delineation of basic processes maintaining anxious or depressive states. To this end, Bradley, Mogg, and Lee (1997) employed a technique called masking, where a target stimulus was subsequently "covered up" by another stimulus, referred to as a mask. The stimulus onset asynchrony, i.e., the time between the onset of the target and the onset of the mask, can be varied, such that low durations (14–50 msec) are not consciously processed, whereas higher durations (e.g., 100–1000 msec) are. Using this technique, Bradley, Mogg, and Lee (1997) found that anxiety was associated with a preconscious attentional bias toward threat words, whereas depression was associated with vigilance for depression-relevant words that are consciously, but not unconsciously, presented.

The emotional Stroop paradigm

The classic Stroop paradigm (1935) has been modified for use in emotion research, and has provided interesting data on anxiety-related attentional bias for threatening information. The classic version of the paradigm presents the written names of colors, some of which do not correspond to the printed color of the words. Participants are required to identify the color of the letters without reading the words that the letters spell. However, inasmuch as reading relies on relatively automatic processes, readers must actively inhibit the dominant response of reading the spelled word. Errors are made, and color identification is slowed relative to conditions in which the words are nonsensical or congruent with the printed colors. This phenomenon is known as the classic Stroop effect.

The modified Stroop paradigm presents words in color, but the letters spell out emotion-related words. Thus, if a word is emotionally salient, it will draw attention away from the color naming task, leading to increased errors and reaction times. As might be expected, anxious individuals typically show greater slowing of color naming when the content of the words is fear-relevant. Slowed color naming in anxious individuals is often explained as a result of allocation of more attentional resources to the processing of anxiety-related words.

A number of studies have provided evidence of the emotional Stroop effect in clinically anxious individuals. For instance, Mathews and MacLeod (1985) conducted a study involving a patient group consisting of individuals who had been referred for anxiety management training and a control group consisting of medical school employees. The investigators presented threatening words that were chosen on the basis of their relevance to cognitive content in generalized anxiety disorders, with the content of these words falling into either physical threat or social threat categories. Each content category was printed on two separate cards. Two control cards were printed as well with control words matched for length. All cards were presented to the participants and times to complete the color task for each card were measured. Anxious individuals showed slower color naming responses on all cards relative to controls. In addition, anxious participants with health concerns showed slower color naming to "physical threat" cards than to "social threat" cards. It seems reasonable to conclude that the observed slower color naming among anxious individuals reflected an attentional bias for threatening information.

As with other cognitive tasks, the Stroop paradigm has also been studied in other forms of psychopathology, most notably, depression. For example, Gilboa and Gotlib (1997) found that previously dysphoric and never dysphoric participants did not differ with respect to their performance on the emotion Stroop task. In contrast, previously dysphoric participants demonstrated significantly better memory for negative stimuli than did never dysphoric participants. Affect dysregulation and memory biases of previously dysphoric participants outlasted their dysphoric episode. These findings suggest that memory biases and affect regulation style may play a causal role in susceptibility to depression.

Implicit memory paradigms

Explicit and implicit memory paradigms have been used to study further those negative biases that have been associated with depression, and that may contribute to the maintenance of depressive states. *Explicit memory* typically refers to conscious attempts to remember previously learned material, while *implicit memory* typically refers to evidence of memory that is retrieved without conscious effort to do so (see Schacter, Church, and Treadwell, 1994). As will be discussed below, conscious/unconscious distinctions are not so easy to make, and implicit cognition is probably more parsimoniously described in operational language, e.g., "cognition demonstrated by an indirect test" (word stem completion, masked priming, reaction time facilitation or inhibition in a lexical decision task, etc.). Similarly, explicit cognition may be better described as cognition demonstrated through direct assessment (e.g., multiple choice, free recall, cued recall).

As its name implies, Mood-congruent memory (MCM) refers to a tendency to recall information congruent to one's current mood (Watkins et al., 1996). In depression, these memories are often negative and may be partly responsible for the sustained negative mood often seen in depressed individuals. Such a memory bias may help depressed patients maintain a negative world view, making disconfirming evidence less salient (Watkins et al., 1996). Watkins, Martin, and Stern (2000) contend that this bias is partly unconscious, i.e., that depressed individuals may unintentionally associate new situations with negative memories, yielding them an unfavorable overall view of life.

To study MCM in explicit memory, Watkins and colleagues have presented participants (both depressed and nondepressed) with a series of words that are viewed for 10 seconds each. These words are typically associated with positive emotions, negative emotions, or no emotion (neutral). After a distracter task, participants are asked to complete a cued recall task, e.g., cued by word stems containing the first few letters of a word (cf. Watkins et al., 1992). Participants are asked, for example, to complete the stems using the words that they learned previously. Depressed individuals tend to recall more negatively valenced words, relative to controls, who tend to recall more positively valenced words (Watkins et al., 1992).

These studies (Watkins et al., 1992, 1996; Watkins, Martin, and Stern, 2000) provide evidence that depressed individuals tend to retain more information biased towards their mood, in this case, predominantly negative information. The debatable aspect of this research, as will be discussed below, is the degree to which these findings are due to conscious or unconscious processes. "Unawareness" is inferred through a debriefing interview, in which participants are simply asked to say whether or not they were consciously trying to retrieve a word, whether they were "aware" of producing primed words, etc. The lack of mention of the experiment's intent, the participant's retrospective report, and priming to negative words is taken as evidence that participants are unaware that they had previously learned the words, and that the implicit memory so demonstrated must therefore be unconscious.

Although widely accepted and intuitively appealing, the characterization of "implicit" memories as perforce "unconscious" is problematic. The logic is based on what has been termed the "dissociation" paradigm for demonstrating implicit cognition (Merikle, 1992).

It necessitates that a measure of "awareness" exhibit null sensitivity, i.e., "without aware-ness" implies that the nonexistence of awareness has been demonstrated. Furthermore, the paradigm necessitates that another measure is sensitive to unconscious, but not to conscious, influences.

While a review of the pitfalls of inferences about unconscious processes is beyond the scope of this chapter, suffice it to say that inferences about unconscious perception are painfully difficult to make. For example, it is difficult at best to exhaustively demonstrate null awareness, while demonstrating unconscious sensitivity exclusive of awareness (see Cheesman and Merikle, 1986; Merikle, 1992; Merikle and Reingold, 1991; Merikle, Joordens, and Stolz, 1995; Reingold and Merikle, 1988). In other words, showing that something is *un*conscious necessitates the demonstration of a null proposition. This is like trying to prove that you did not scratch your nose last night while you were asleep, or that you did not just think an unhappy thought.

We do not mean to imply that unconscious influences on cognition cannot be and have not been demonstrated. It is only to say that the putative demonstrations of "unconscious" memory biases in depressed individuals by Watkins and colleagues do not conclusively accomplish that objective. Although it might be valid to say that a person can only report that which is in awareness, it is not valid to say that everything that is not reported is unconscious. Awareness of these biases may be a transient phenomenon, for example, that is not sensitive to measures on the time scale employed (e.g., being asked "were you aware" at the end of the experiment). However, research that ignores its own inferential limits provides us with an excellent example to underscore a crucial point: that it behooves students of psychopathology to be mindful of extant literature in basic psychological science, and to scrutinize their assumptions thoroughly.

A "directed rumination" task

Depressed individuals often evince what is referred to as a "ruminative response style" (Roberts, Gilboa, and Gotlib, 1998), which is characterized by excessive focus of atten-tion on depressive symptoms and on the causes, meanings, and consequences of those symptoms (Nolen-Hoeksema, 1991). Nolen-Hoeksema and colleagues have conducted a series of studies showing that a ruminative response style can increase an already dysphoric mood, and can actually prolong a depressive mood episode. For example, in two differ-ent studies, Lyubomirsky and Nolen-Hoeksema (1995) divided participants into dysphoric or nondysphoric groups based on scores on the short form of the Beck Depression Inventory (BDI-SF). Participants completed a mood questionnaire to rate their present mood state (i.e., levels of sadness and depression), on a 9-point Likert scale ranging from not at all (1) to extremely (9). Participants then engaged in either a directed rumination or a directed distraction task. For both tasks, participants were presented with 45 items on which they were asked to focus their attention and think about carefully. The rumination task items were designed to bring participants to focus on themselves, and included items such as "think about what your feelings might mean," "think about why you react the way you do," and "think about the kind of person you are." The distrac-tion task, on the other hand, was designed to bring participants' focus away from themselves, and included items such as "think about a boat slowly crossing the Atlantic," "think about a lone cactus in the desert," and "think about the layout of the local post office." Each condition lasted 8 minutes. After the tasks, participants again completed the same mood questionnaires that they had filled out earlier. Dysphoric individuals who had been instructed to ruminate became significantly more dysphoric, while dysphoric participants in the distraction condition became significantly less dysphoric. Nondysphoric participants showed no mood changes in either condition.

While Nolen-Hoeksema and her colleagues have studied the process of rumination and its effect on mood by using self-report mood questionnaires, others have studied similar processes using other measures, such as the electroencephalogram (EEG). For example, Carter, Johnson, and Borkovec (1986) found that trait worriers exhibited more overall cortical activation as well as relatively greater left hemispheric activation. Nitschke et al. (1999) examined EEG in an anxious arousal and an anxious apprehension (worry) group. Unlike Carter, Johnson, and Borkovec (1986), they found that the anxious apprehension group did not exhibit significant EEG asymmetry. More will be said about the use of EEG asymmetry measures later.

Psychophysiological Methods

Psychophysiological researchers often employ physiological measures for the purpose of assessing cognitive and emotional processes that people cannot or will not report. Through such methods researchers may assess memory (Allen, Iacono, and Danielson, 1992), emotional responses, and sometimes attitudes that are not necessarily readily observable or quantifiable (see Hugdahl, 1995). Since a comprehensive discussion of these methods is beyond the scope of this chapter, the interested reader is referred to Hugdahl (1995) for an excellent overview. Here we provide some illustrative examples of how psychophysiological methods have been used to study relevant emotional and cognitive processes.

Emotion and the startle reflex

Researchers often use measures of heart rate, skin conductance (a measure of hand perspiration), and facial muscle activity in the study of emotion. Not surprisingly, these response systems have been studied extensively in the context of disordered emotion. While heart rate and skin conductance are often used to index emotional arousal, increases in these indices occur regardless of whether a person's emotional arousal is positively or negatively valent. People have faster heartbeats and sweat more regardless of whether they are afraid, nervous, or sexually aroused.

Measures of facial muscle activity have been particularly useful in the study of emotional states. Of particular interest is the activity of the orbicularis oculi muscle. This muscle is located directly below the eyeball and is an integral component of the brainstem startle reflex in humans and other species. The startle reflex is an extremely useful measure in the study of negative emotional states, largely because of the relatively direct connections between the amygdala (i.e., an almond-shaped structure in the anterior temporal lobe that is involved with fear processing) and pontine nuclei that mediate aspects of the startle reflex. The startle reflex is thereby enhanced (i.e., made much larger) when an individual is in a negatively arousing emotional state (as anyone who has been "startled" while watching a scary movie will attest).

The startle reflex involves a "forward thrusting of the head and a descending flexor wave reaction, extending through the trunk to the knees" (Lang et al., 1993: 164). This response can be elicited using a high-intensity stimulus with a rapid rise time. This stimulus, commonly referred to as a "startle probe," may take the form of a flash of light, a puff of air, or a blast of sound. For example, when using a blast of sound, it is common to use a very brief (50 msec), loud blast of "white noise" (e.g., the sort of "static" noise that a TV would make if the cable service fails while the volume is at maximum).

The "blink" component of the startle reflex has been identified as one of its most involuntary and reliable components (Landis and Hunt, 1939), and is reflected in the activity of the orbicularis oculi muscle described above. Electromyographic (EMG) recordings of the blink response are obtained using two sensors, placed side-by-side just below the eye on the obicularis oculi muscle. Information from the two sensors is integrated using a microcomputer and yields output that is comprised of a single line which fluctuates during obicularis (i.e., blink) activity, and which remains flat when the orbicularis muscle is inactive. Startle blinks often result in an output that appears as a "peak" relative to baseline data. By measuring the height of the peak relative to baseline, researchers are able to identify the magnitude of the startle response blink.

Modulation of the startle response

As suggested above, emotional processes systematically influence the magnitude of the startle reflex. Brown, Kalish, and Farber (1951) first demonstrated the utility of startle as a measure of emotional states in studies of classical conditioning. These researchers found that fear-conditioned rats produced larger startle responses than did nonconditioned controls, suggesting that the startle response is potentiated by fear.

The startle response is also potentiated by fear in humans. For example, studies consistently demonstrate that humans show potentiated startle responses when threatened with electric shock (e.g., Curtin et al., 1998). In fact, human participants need not actually receive shocks to show potentiated startle, but merely need to be led to believe that they *might* be shocked during the course of an experiment. Potentiation of the startle response is observed even when no shock is administered throughout the course of an experiment.

Affective picture presentation also modulates the magnitude of the startle response. People tend to show larger startles while viewing negative pictures (e.g., mutilated bodies, guns, and knives) than they do while viewing neutral pictures (e.g., hair dryers, plates, and glasses). Similarly, people tend to show smaller startles while viewing positive pictures (e.g., erotica, puppies, and babies) than while viewing neutral pictures (see Vrana, Spence, and Lang, 1988; Bradley, Lang, and Cuthbert, 1993).

Among other things, this methodology has been used in the study of criminal psychopaths. Noting that psychopaths tend to show a deficit in emotion, specifically fear, Patrick, Bradley, and Lang (1993) used the revised version of the Psychopathy Checklist (PCL-R; Hare, 1991) to divide a sample of 54 incarcerated sexual offenders into three groups: psychopaths, nonpsychopaths, and a group of "mixed" psychopaths whose PCL-R scores fell between the other two groups. Twenty-seven IAPS slides were selected for presentation. Nine of these slides depicted pleasant scenes, 9 depicted neutral scenes, and 9 depicted unpleasant scenes. Slides were presented in balanced blocks of 9, with 3 of each category represented in each block. Slides were displayed for 6 seconds each, with an inter-slide interval ranging from 10–20 seconds. Startle probes were administered during 18 of the 27 slide presentations and this was balanced across the three categories (6 of the 9 pleasant, neutral, and unpleasant slide presentations contained startle probes). Startle probes consisted of a 50 msec burst of 95 dB white noise with probe onset occurring at either 3.5s, 4.5s, or 5.5s after slide onset. Startle responses were scored and averaged for each category within each group. The nonpsychopath and mixed psychopath groups showed a "typical" startle response pattern. That is, startle responses elicited during unpleasant slides were the largest, startle responses elicited during pleasant slides were the smallest, with responses elicited during neutral slides falling somewhere in between. Of most interest, however, was the pattern produced by the psychopath group. While this group showed a "typical" pattern with regard to pleasant and neutral slides (i.e., smaller startle responses elicited during pleasant slides were relative to neutral), the startle magnitudes elicited during unpleasant slides were *smaller* and tended to resemble the magnitude of responses elicited during the viewing of pleasant slides! Psychopathy had no effect on autonomic or self-report responses to slides. Levenston et al. (2000) recently extended this work, reporting that, for psychopaths, startle was inhibited during victim scenes and only weakly potentiated during threat. Furthermore, psychopaths showed more reliable blink inhibition across pleasant contents than did nonpsychopaths. The results are consistent with a heightened threshold for processing aversive stimuli in psychopaths that is not necessarily accessible to self-report. Furthermore, psychopaths may in fact process some aversive stimuli as intensely interesting or appetitive.

The use of the startle probe to examine fear in the criminal psychopath is but one application of this methodology. The startle response has also been used to examine the development of fear conditioning in normative groups (Hamm and Vaitl, 1996), and has served as an outcome measure in individuals with phobic disorders (Vrana, Constantine, and Westman, 1992). For a comprehensive review of the startle response, the interested reader is referred to Lang (1995).

Emotion and cerebral asymmetry

The experience of positive, approach-related emotion has been associated with relative left frontal and anterior-temporal lobe (both cortical and subcortical) activation, while the experience of negative, withdrawal-related emotion has been associated with higher relative activation of the right frontal and anterior-temporal regions. Observations of victims of left and right frontal strokes and patients undergoing unilateral hemispheric anesthesia during the intracarotid sodium amobarbitol (Wada) test have lent support to this model (see Liotti and Tucker, 1995, for a review). Perhaps the most extensive literature supporting this model, however, concerns relationships between emotional responses, emotional style, and anterior activation of the electroencephalogram (EEG; see Davidson, 1995, for a review).

EEG can be recorded from electrodes placed on the scalp, and provides a gross measure of regional brain activation. It can only tell us roughly where some types of brain activity originated – it cannot provide precise localization. However, EEG provides excellent *temporal* resolution, and some measures of event-related brain potentials are resolved with a time scale on the order of milliseconds (see Hugdahl, 1995, for an overview). Here we will consider one gross measure of regional brain activation, i.e., decreases in power in the *alpha* (8–13 Hz) band. *Decreases* in alpha power are used as an index of *increased* regional activation.

EEG has been used to evaluate the hypothesis that resting anterior asymmetry is associated with a stylistic tendency toward emotional reaction that is present during infancy and early childhood (Davidson and Fox, 1989; Fox et al., 1995). Accordingly, left frontal activation has been related to decreased vulnerability to depression (Tomarken and Davidson, 1994; Kline, Allen, and Schwartz, 1998; Kline, Blackhart, and Schwartz, 1999), whereas relative left frontal hypoactivation is associated with increased vulnerability to depression (Henriques and Davidson, 1991; Davidson, 1995). Tomarken, Davidson, and Henriques (1990) reported that research participants with greater relative right frontal EEG activation at baseline reported more negative emotions in response to viewing negatively valenced films. Other work has documented desirable psychometric properties in resting anterior asymmetry (RAA). For instance, RAA has been shown to have reasonable temporal stability (test–retest reliability) in both nondepressed (Tomarken et al., 1992) and depressed (Hitt, Allen, and Duke, 1995) individuals, and has been found to distinguish depressed from nondepressed individuals during both episode and remission (Allen et al., 1993; Bell et al., 1998; Henriques and Davidson, 1991), although this relation may not be entirely robust (cf. Reid, Duke, and Allen, 1998).

Although anterior asymmetry exhibits the psychometric reliability and validity characteristic of a trait, it can also change in response to manipulations of affective state. Davidson and Fox (1982) exposed infants to videotaped positive and negative facial expressions while tracking EEG asymmetry. They found that infants showed greater relative left frontal activation in response to happy expressions. Fox and Davidson (1986) presented infants with pleasant and unpleasant tastes, and found that a pleasant taste (i.e., sugar water) was associated with increased left sided activation compared to an unpleasant taste (citric acid) or water. Kline, Blackhart, et al. (2000) extended this work to elderly adults presented with pleasant (vanilla), unpleasant (valerian), and neutral (water) odors, and found increased left frontal activation for vanilla compared to water or valerian. Similar observations have been made during the *expression* of disgust and happiness by adults (Davidson et al., 1990) and in response to reward and punishment (Sobotka, Davidson, and Senulis, 1992).

In addition to the valence-dependent changes in asymmetric anterior EEG activation reviewed above, arousal involves different patterns of asymmetric posterior activation

(Heller, 1990, 1993). In this domain, changes in cortical and autonomic arousal are associated with corresponding shifts in activation of the right parietal and posterior temporal regions, relative to the left, irrespective of the valence of the perceived emotion. Patients with posterior right brain damage have shown decreased electrodermal responses compared to normal controls and patients with left hemispheric brain damage. Conditioned electrodermal responses have also been shown to be larger and more robust when the conditional stimulus is presented to the right as opposed to the left hemisphere (see Heller, 1993, for a review). Furthermore, increased anxious arousal is associated with increased relative right posterior cortical activation (Heller et al., 1997; Nitschke et al., 1999).

Activity in the right parietotemporal region of the brain has also been assessed by a vision task that can elicit a left hemispatial bias, implying right hemispheric activity. This measure, called the Chimeric Faces Task (CFT), consists of a 36-page booklet with two split faces on each page. The faces are photographs of the same person, with half of the face smiling and half of the face not smiling. The two faces on each page are mirror images of each other. The participant is instructed to assess which face is happier, the top or the bottom. Relative to nondepressed controls, depressed individuals typically show a reduced left hemispatial bias, indicating less activity in the right parietotemporal region (Heller, Etienne, and Miller, 1995). Interestingly, such findings may not be apparent when anxiety symptoms are comorbid with depression. Other paradigms used to assess activity in this region, such as dichotic listening or tachistoscopic tasks, have also found reduced activity for depressed individuals. This evidence has been corroborated by studies involving cerebral blood flow, EEG, and ERP (see Heller and Nitschke, 1997, for a review).

The finding that depressed individuals may have deficits in the functioning of the parietotemporal region of the brain may have many consequences for these individuals. Studies of brain-damaged patients with deficiencies in the right hemisphere have shown deficits in emotional processing, which may be highly related to social functioning (Heller and Nitschke, 1997).

While the links between frontal brain asymmetry and emotion have been replicated in numerous studies, there are also some notable failures to replicate this phenomenon. For instance, Hagemann et al. (1998) demonstrated the impact of methodological variations on the relationship between frontal alpha asymmetry and affective style. Reid, Duke, and Allen (1998) failed to confirm the hypothesis of left frontal hypoactivation in depression. Debener et al. (2000) reported that frontal asymmetry was not test–retest reliable in clinically depressed patients. Finally, Hagemann et al. (1999) found that trait negative affect was related to relative left-sided cortical activation. Investigators are currently investigating possible reasons for these inconsistencies, focusing on issues such as EEG recording and quantification methods, state and trait influences, and contextual factors.

Psychophysiological studies of alcohol and emotion

Alcohol is among civilization's oldest drugs and certainly one of its most popular. Throughout history, people have drunk alcoholic beverages to attenuate stress, enhance celebration, honor accomplishments, and mourn losses (for an excellent social history of drinking, see Barr, 1999). Across all of these diverse applications the ability of alcohol to alter the drinker's mood or perception of the world is a common element (Kuhn et al., 1998). Efforts to understand relationships between alcohol use and emotional response have driven investigators to address a number of key questions about drinking behavior and its consequences (see Stritzke, Lang, and Patrick, 1995): Can alcohol intoxication reduce general distress and decrease reactivity to aversive stimuli? Can it stimulate euphoria and enhance pleasure? Or could it do either, depending on such factors as dose, circumstances, time of assessment, and individual differences in responses to alcohol? By embracing a multidimensional–multilevel approach to understanding the construct of emotion and its mediators, and by assessing activity pertinent to the relevant brain substrates, research in experimental psychopathology has suggested some answers to these questions. Perhaps more importantly, this research has begun to illuminate the mechanisms and psychological processes that underlie these phenomena.

Early models of alcohol's effects on emotions were dominated by the assumption that alcohol acts primarily and specifically on the aversive motivational systems that underlie the experience of negative emotions. In this connection, the idea that drinking can diminish sensitivity to threats and aversive stimuli, an effect termed stress-response dampening (SRD; e.g., Sher and Levenson, 1982), stimulated excitement and enjoyed some empirical support during the 1990s. However, upon further scrutiny it became clear that this model has some shortcomings. The first of these is evident in the inclination of many proponents of SRD to equate decreased autonomic arousal with decreased negative affect, an assumption inconsistent with contemporary models of emotion (e.g., Lang, 1995). Specifically, research on SRD has used nonspecific indicators of arousal, such as heart rate, without a clear demonstration of the presumed valence of the underlying motivational system. Second, the SRD model seems to neglect the possibility that alcohol's apparent ability to reduce response to stressful situations might, in part, actually reflect augmentation of positive affect (cf. Marlatt, 1987). Overall, the SRD suggests a relatively mechanistic view of alcohol intoxication. In other words, it proposes a single, direct cause relationship between alcohol intoxication and emotional reactivity, and does not specify other factors or processes that might be relevant, such as the context in which intoxication and elicitation of emotional response take place, and individual differences in sensitivity to alcohol and/or affective stimuli (for a discussion of mechanistic and contextual models, see Schwartz, 1984).

More contemporary models for alcohol's effects on emotions incorporate a multi-dimensional system of emotionality. One such model posits two emotion/motivation systems, each with a distinct behavioral significance: a positive, appetitive system that governs approach behavior, and a negative, aversive system that governs withdrawal behavior (see Lang, 1995, for a review). Furthermore, there is growing support for a multilevel model in which alcohol may not act selectively on either of these motivation systems, but rather produces its effects *through* alteration of higher-level information processing systems that interact with them (see Lang, Patrick, and Stritzke, 1999, for a review).

Several alternative multilevel models, incorporating the potential interaction of cortical and subcortical brain systems, have been advanced to characterize this effect. The appraisal disruption model (Sayette, 1993) proposes that alcohol interferes with the initial appraisal of stressful information by constraining the spreading activation of associated information in long-term memory, and that this shallower processing of threatening information renders it less aversive. This model predicts that individuals who consume alcohol *before* they become aware of an impending stressor should show more stress-response dampening than those who began drinking *after* being informed about the stressor. The attention allocation model (Steele and Josephs, 1988, 1990) also suggests that alcohol's effects on information processing systems are primarily responsible for its effects on emotions. This approach proposes that alcohol impairs the brain's capacity to execute controlled, complex processing and thereby limits its attention to the most salient stimuli. Thus, the extent to which alcohol intoxication reduces an anxiety response is thought to depend upon the combined effects of compromised attentional capacity and the presence and nature of other demands that compete for cognitive resources that would ordinarily be available to process the stressor fully. In the absence of competing demands, moderate intoxication is not predicted to attenuate stress responding (Steele and Josephs, 1990).

Multilevel analyses of alcohol and emotion

The appraisal disruption and attention allocation models involve a more contextual view of alcohol intoxication and its effects. In other words, these models suggest that the emotional consequences of drinking arise from the interaction between relevant stimuli in the environment and alcohol-induced cognitive impairments that influence the way these stimuli are apprehended or processed. Research using the startle response elicited by aversive acoustic probes as an index of affective disposition has supported models for these relatively nonspecific, indirect effects of alcohol on emotional processes. In the first of these studies, Stritzke, Lang, and Patrick (1995) manipulated negative and positive affect state by intermittently presenting emotionally valenced photographic slides from the International Affective Picture System. Participants received either a moderate dose of alcohol or no alcohol prior to viewing a series of pleasant, neutral, and unpleasant images. Eye blink reactions to the probe were used to index the valence of the emotional response produced by the slides. Facial EMG activity was used to assess changes in emotional valence, and electrodermal activity was included to index arousal. In addition, changes in heart rate were recorded during a window surrounding image presentations. The results of this study indicated that alcohol diminished the *overall magnitude* of startle, regardless of the valence of the foreground images, but failed to alter affective modulation of startle response used to index emotional reactivity. A similar valence effect was also found for corrugator EMG.

These results run contrary to the key prediction of the SRD model of alcohol intoxication (viz., that alcohol would selectively reduce reactions to aversive images). Instead, only a nonspecific suppressant effect of alcohol on overall startle and skin conductance reactivity was observed, suggesting that the response dampening effects of alcohol might occur across a range of stimulus valences. It could be argued that the lack of support for the SRD model in these studies was due to the relative insensitivity of the startle paradigm for detection of the predicted effect. However, research by Patrick, Berthot, and Moore (1996) using the same paradigm to test effects of an established anxiolytic drug, diazepam, indicates that this is not the case. Unlike alcohol, diazepam did not dampen general startle reactivity; but it did produce the dose-related reduction in fear-potentiated startle predicted by the specific direct-cause SRD model. This suggests that alcohol's effects on emotional processes are more complicated than those of anxiolytic drugs. Whereas diazepam produces a direct and selective effect on negative emotional responsivity, alcohol apparently produces an effect that is more complex and varied, perhaps due to context.

This issue was explored in more recent work (Curtin et al., 1998) where participants were exposed to a situation in which both stress and competing stimuli were manipulated. Sober or moderately intoxicated participants were presented with cues that indicated either that an electric shock could be delivered (threat), or that the shock would not be delivered (safety). In some trial blocks participants were also exposed periodically to pleasant images that competed for their attention, whereas in others there were no such distractions. Startle probes were delivered at unpredictable times during the threat and safety intervals. The expected increase in startle magnitude during the threat condition and nonspecific attenuation of startle for participants who had received alcohol were observed. However, startle reactivity was reduced by alcohol only during blocks of trials in which the threat interval coincided with a pleasant distracter. The researchers reasoned that these intervals placed the highest cognitive demands on the participants, and that alcohol's apparent anxiolytic effects might be attributable to alcohol-induced limitations of cognitive capacity available to process complex stimulus contexts. These results are consistent with the predictions derived from the multidimensional–multilevel model proposed by Lang, Patrick, and Stritzke (1999). They essentially suggest that the anxiolytic effects of alcohol depend upon the diminished ability of participants in the alcohol condition to evaluate threat fully in contexts made complex by the presence of competing stimuli.

Subsequent research by Curtin and colleagues has expanded on this finding by more specifically addressing the relationship between cognitive processes, emotional reactivity, and behavioral response during alcohol intoxication (Curtin et al., 2001). As in the previous study, sober and intoxicated participants were exposed to a series of visual cues that signaled whether or not an electric shock could be delivered. The trials that made up this experiment were further divided into "threat focused" blocks, in which the participant was shown only the cue of threat or safety, and "divided-attention" blocks that included both the cue and a concurrent, competing reaction time task. In all types of blocks the cues for threat or safety were categories of words presented on a computer screen, but for the divided attention blocks the participants were instructed to attend primarily to the color of the words (green or red), which determined whether they were to execute a button press as quickly as possible to evaluate their reaction time. In this way the cognitive resources of the participants during the divided-attention blocks were divided between the threat information conveyed by the word category and the task information conveyed by the word color.

In addition to recording the latency of the button press, the researchers also recorded startle magnitude to probes presented in both blocks of trials, and the P3 component of event-related brain potentials (ERPs). P3, a positive, parietal-focused component of the ERP, was chosen because it is associated with attention to stimuli (Halgren, Squires, and Wilson, 1982; Knight, 1996; Kramer and Spinks, 1991). Analyses indicated that both startle and P3 amplitude were attenuated for intoxicated participants during the divided-attention block, but not in the threat-focus block. In addition, intoxicated participants showed relatively smaller decreases in reaction time during the divided-attention tasks than during the threat-focused task.

These results again demonstrated an alcohol-induced impairment of participants' ability to attend to the threat cue and develop the associated negative emotional reaction and behavioral inhibition. This outcome is also consistent with an interaction between brain systems such as the amygdala and hippocampus that underlie the mediating effect of attention and context on emotional reactivity during intoxication. Animal research has clearly implicated the hippocampus in spatial and contextual learning (LeDoux, 1995; Matthews et al., 1996; Melia et al., 1994), and human research indicates that it is involved in the attentional processes associated with the P3 (Kramer and Spinks, 1991). Curtin et al. (2001) emphasized the importance of using emotional processing paradigms that draw upon specific cognitive processes with known neurobiological substrates, and their work clearly demonstrates the utility of this approach. By including startle response, ERP, and reaction time components in their study, Curtin and colleagues were able to gather real-time information about the interaction of emotional, cognitive, and behavioral processes that would be impossible to obtain by observation or self-report. By simultaneously assessing and integrating these psychophysiological data, they were able to present a more complete model for the effects of alcohol intoxication on emotional response.

Multilevel analysis: An example from repressive/defensiveness research

Kline et al. (1998) have employed word masking and EEG recordings in order to assess the operation of self-deception and impression management in defensiveness. Defensiveness, or the tendency to present oneself in an overly favorable light by denying likely but negative self-attributes, while endorsing unlikely but desirable ones, is an important component of what has come to be known as the "repressive style" (Weinberger, Schwartz, and Davidson, 1979). Repressive/defensive individuals may be less prone to overt psychopathology (cf. Lane et al., 1990), but they appear to be more vulnerable to physical illnesses, likely through stress-compromised immunocompetence (see Esterling et al., 1993). While substantial research had shown that repressors evince increased physiological reactivity in the face of lower self-reported distress (see Kline, Knapp-Kline, et al., 2000, for a review), attempts to study the mechanisms behind this process are relatively rare.

Kline et al. (1998) examined detection accuracies, confidence ratings, and EEG activation in response to masked pleasant, unpleasant, neutral, and sexual words. Six words of each category were presented in random order in ascending durations ranging from 16.7 msec to 100.2 msec, sandwiched between 50.1 msec random letter masks. Masking allows for initial presentation and registration of words, followed immediately by a "mask," in this instance a random letter string, that interrupts processing of the word. Typically, words presented for approximately 50 msec or less do not appear to be processed consciously.

Kline et al. (1998) presented participants with two tasks, given in the following order: (a) a word identification task designed to elicit impression management (i.e., by requiring participants to say sexual words aloud), and (b) a word detection task designed to assess perceptual sensitivity (i.e., by having participants quietly choose from among words from the same category). EEG was recorded during the identification task during "subliminal" and "supraliminal" presentations. Individuals who wish to manage impressions would obviously wish to be absolutely sure before saying the sexual words. Indeed, sexual words did appear to elicit impression management (i.e., increased identification thresholds for sexual compared to other emotional words). This effect did not differ between groups; those scoring high on defensiveness showed just as much impression management as did those scoring low.

Patterns of detection accuracy for the various emotional word categories differed for high and low defensive participants, such that high defensiveness was associated with increased unconscious sensitivity (in response to < 50.1 msec durations) for emotional words, and lower conscious accuracy for sexual words as they were presented for higher durations up to 100.2 msec. The behavioral responses were paralleled by EEG responses. In general, defensive individuals showed EEG activation in the back of the head during the unconsciously presented emotional words, which suggests that the increased sensitivity, or "bias," influenced perceptual responding. However, when words were presented at higher durations, and high-defensive individuals became less accurate for the sexual words, their EEGs became more activated over the entire scalp, especially in the right frontal region (a brain region associated with behavioral inhibition). This finding suggests that defensiveness may be associated with early vigilance and then active inhibition of threat, a result that has since been replicated in many respects using other cognitive measures (Calvo and Eysenck, 2000).

Multilevel analysis and neuroimaging

The general logic of multilevel analyses can be applied to other physiological measures, including metabolic imaging methods such as Positron Emission Tomography (PET) and Magnetic Resonance Imaging (MRI). In designing and evaluating such research, it should be kept in mind that science is not technology: the inferences that can be made from an experiment are only as good as the experimental design and the integrity of the variables examined. A pretty picture of a MRI scan from a poorly designed study makes that study none the more scientific. When properly designed, studies employing self-report or behavioral observation measures can be scientifically superior to studies employing "hard" measures such as physiology. Despite the fact that MRI and PET provide better spatial resolution than the psychophysiological measures that we reviewed here, MRI and PET suffer from many of the same inferential limitations, and introduce a few of their own. However, PET and MRI have a distinct advantage over traditional psychophysiological methods; namely, better spatial resolution. On the other hand,

EEG affords researchers better temporal resolution, as well as a less restrictive, and perhaps less stressful, recording environment. As such, *converging operations*, or findings that have been replicated with more than one such methodology, add confidence to the validity of research findings.

For example, George et al. (2001) used MRI to study brain activation during alcohol cue exposure in ten alcoholics and ten social drinking controls. Participants gave alcohol craving ratings before and after a sip of alcohol, and after a 9-minute randomized presentation of pictures of alcoholic beverages and control pictures. Alcoholics reported more craving throughout the procedures than did controls. Alcoholics also showed evidence of greater activation of anterior paralimbic regions during cue exposures. After a sip of alcohol and while viewing alcoholic beverage cues, alcoholics showed increased activity in the left dorsolateral prefrontal cortex (DLPC) and the anterior thalamus. Social drinkers exhibited specific activation only while viewing control beverage pictures.

The results of Kline, Donohue, and Lang (2000) are consistent with those of George et al. (2001), in that both studies suggest that greater appetitive motives for drinking are reflected in greater left frontal activation. Kline, Donohue, and Lang (2000) extended the findings of George et al. (2001), in that similar phenomena took place over the normal range of social drinking, and similar brain activity effects were apparent in the EEG. Kline, Donohue, and Lang (2000) examined individual differences in motivational and emotional aspects of drinking during an alcohol challenge in social drinking participants across the range of "normal" drinking. Participants were given a moderate dose of alcohol (i.e., a peak of .06 gm/100 ml) verified by breath test. EEG was recorded from 19 leads referenced to linked ears. EMG was recorded from zygomatic and corrugator regions. In addition, self-report measures of subjective stimulation/sedation, positive/negative affect, alcohol craving, drinking motives (social, coping, enhancement), and drinking frequency/quantity were taken. Two clusters of participants were evident, and could be explained on the basis of motivational dispositions and emotional responses to drinking. Compared to Cluster 2, Cluster 1 showed greater relative left midfrontal (on a portion of the skull over the left DLPC) activation in the alpha (8–13 Hz) band and less corrugator activity while drinking. Cluster 1 reported less sedation than stimulation, increased craving, more frequent drinking episodes, and a greater number of drinks consumed per week. Cluster 1 appeared to show stronger appetitive responses to drinking, experience less sedation than stimulation, decreased corrugator activity, and increased alcohol craving compared to Cluster 2.

Taken together, the results of George et al. (2001) and Kline, Donohue, and Lang (2000) are consistent with the hypothesis that left frontal regions of the brain are involved with appetitive motives, and that such motives are activated during alcohol cue exposure and intoxication. Furthermore, both studies show once again the utility of multilevel analysis, i.e., in their inclusion of both subjective and neurophysiological measures. Finally, the juxtaposition of these studies illustrates the utility of converging operations, in that EEG and MRI both implicate the DLPC activity in appetitive motives for drinking. Having used EEG, Kline, Donohue, and Lang (2000) cannot make solid inferences about the DLPC *per se* – only about relative left frontal activation. On the other hand, EEG is less expensive to obtain than MRI, so Kline, Donohue, and Lang (2000) were able to examine a range of social drinkers, and a larger number of participants. Furthermore, Kline, Donohue, and Lang (2000) were able to examine activity during intoxication as well as drinking, and did so in a less restrictive, relatively neutral environment than what is typically associated with MRI. Finally, both studies are limited in that neither can speak conclusively to the role of the left DLPC in these appetitive motives: Is the relation representational, or is it regulatory? Does the left DLPC instantiate appetitive motivation, or is it somehow involved with the regulation of such motivation once it is elicited? Do these differences reflect diatheses, experiences, or some combination/interaction of the two? These questions do not reflect limitations in neuroimaging methods. Indeed, they may some day yield to cleverly designed experiments.

Conclusions

We have provided an overview of only a small portion of the vast literature on experimental psychopathology. Our overview is by no means comprehensive. We chose our examples to illustrate the manner in which methods from experimental psychology can be applied to the study of psychopathology. Although we focused mostly on depression, anxiety, emotional responses to alcohol, and defensiveness, these techniques can be, should be, and are used to study other forms of psychopathology. Our hope is that students and researchers will see the value of the use of multiple measures, and especially of multilevel, integrative analyses.

References

Allen, J. J., Iacono, W. G., and Danielson, K. D. (1992). The identification of concealed memories using the event-related potential and implicit behavioral measures: A methodology for prediction in the face of individual differences. *Psychophysiology*, 29, 504–22.

Allen, J. J., Iacono, W. G., Depue, R. A., and Arbisi, P. (1993). Regional electroencephalographic asymmetries in bipolar seasonal affective disorder before and after exposure to bright light. *Biological Psychiatry*, 33, 642–6.

Barr, A. (1999). *Drink: A social history of America*. New York: Carroll and Graf Publishers.

Bell, I. R., Schwartz, G. E., Hardin, E. E., Baldwin, C. M., and Kline, J. P. (1998). Differential resting quantitative electroencephalographic alpha patterns in women with environmental chemical intolerance, depressives, and normals. *Biological Psychiatry*, 43, 376–88.

Bradley, B. P., Mogg, K., and Lee, S. C. (1997). Attentional biases for negative information in induced and naturally occurring dysphoria. *Behaviour Research and Therapy*, 35, 911–27.

Bradley, M. M., Lang, P. J., and Cuthbert, B. N. (1993). Emotion, novelty, and the startle reflex: Habituation in humans. *Behavioral Neuroscience*, 107, 970–80.

Brown, J. S., Kalish, H. I., and Farber, I. E. (1951). Conditioned fear as revealed by magnitude of startle response to an auditory stimulus. *Journal of Experimental Psychology*, 41, 317–28.

Bruder, G., Kayser, J., Tenke, C., Amador, X., Friedman, M., Sharif, Z., and Gorman, J. (1999). Left temporal lobe dysfunction in schizophrenia: Event-related potential and behavioral evidence from phonetic and tonal dichotic listening tasks. *Archives of General Psychiatry*, 56, 267–76.

Burgess, I. S., Jones, L. M., Robertson, S. A., Radcliffe, W. N., and Emerson, E. (1981). The degree of control exerted by phobic and nonphobic verbal stimuli over the recognition behaviour of phobic and nonphobic subjects. *Behaviour Research and Therapy*, *19*, 233–43.

Calvo, M. G. and Eysenck, M. W. (2000). Early vigilance and late avoidance of threat processing: Repressive coping versus low/high anxiety. *Cognition and Emotion*, *14*, 763–87.

Carter, W. R., Johnson, M. C., and Borkovec, T. D. (1986). Worry: An electrocortical analysis. *Advances in Behaviour Research and Therapy*, *8*, 193–204.

Cheesman, J. and Merikle, P. M. (1986). Distinguishing conscious from unconscious perceptual processes. *Canadian Journal of Psychology*, *40*, 343–67.

Cherry, E. C. (1953). Some experiments in the recognition of speech with one and with two ears. *Journal of the Acoustical Society of America*, *25*, 975–9.

Curtin, J. J., Lang, A. R., Patrick, C. J., and Stritzke, W. G. K. (1998). Alcohol and fear-potentiated startle: The role of competing cognitive demands in the stress-reducing effects of intoxication. *Journal of Abnormal Psychology*, *107*, 547–65.

Curtin, J. J., Patrick, C. P., Lang, A. R., Cacioppo, J. T., and Birbaumer, N. (2001). Alcohol affects emotion through cognition. *Psychological Science*, *12*, 527–31.

Davidson, R. J. (1995). Cerebral asymmetry, emotion, and affective style. In R. J. Davidson and K. Hugdahl (eds.), *Brain asymmetry* (pp. 361–87). Cambridge, MA: MIT Press.

Davidson, R. J., and Fox, N. A. (1982). Asymmetrical brain activity discriminates between positive and negative affective stimuli in human infants. *Science*, *218*, 1235–7.

Davidson, R. J., and Fox, N. A. (1989). Frontal brain asymmetry predicts infants' response to maternal separation. *Journal of Abnormal Psychology*, *98*, 127–31.

Davidson, R. J., Ekman, P., Saron, C. D., and Senulis, J. A. (1990). Approach–withdrawal and cerebral asymmetry: Emotional expression and brain physiology: I. *Journal of Personality and Social Psychology*, *58*, 330–41.

Dawson, M. E., and Schell, A. M. (1982). Electrodermal responses to attended and nonattended significant stimuli during dichotic listening. *Journal of Experimental Psychology: Human Perception and Performance*, *8*, 315–24.

Dawson, M. E., and Schell, A. M. (1983). Lateral asymmetries in electro-dermal responses to nonattended stimuli: A reply to Walter and Ceci. *Journal of Experimental Psychology: Human Perception and Performance*, *9*, 148–50.

Debener, S., Beauducel, A., Nessler, D., Brocke, B., Heilemann, H., and Kayser, J. (2000). Is resting anterior EEG alpha asymmetry a trait marker for depression? Findings for healthy adults and clinically depressed patients. *Neuropsychobiology*, *41*, 31–7.

Esterling, B. A., Antoni, M. H., Kumar, M., and Schneiderman, N. (1993). Defensiveness, trait anxiety, and Epstein–Barr viral capsid antigen titers in healthy college students. *Health Psychology*, *12*, 132–9.

Foa, E. G., and McNally, R. J. (1986). Sensitivity to feared stimuli in obsessive-compulsives: A dichotic listening analysis. *Cognitive Therapy and Research*, *10*, 477–86.

Fox, N. A., and Davidson, R. J. (1986). Taste-elicited changes in facial signs of emotion and the asymmetry of brain electrical activity in human newborns. *Neuropsychologia*, *24*, 417–22.

Fox, N. A., Rubin, K. H., Calkins, S. D., Marshall, T. R., Coplan, R. J., Porges, S. W., and Long, J. M. (1995). Frontal activation asymmetry and social competence at four years of age. *Child Development*, *66*, 1770–84.

George, M. S., Anton, R. F., Bloomer, C., Teneback, C., Drobes, D. J., Lorberbaum, J. P., Nahas, Z., and Vincent, D. J. (2001). Activation of prefrontal cortex and anterior thalamus in alcoholic subjects on exposure to alcohol-specific cues. *Archives of General Psychiatry*, *58*, 345–52.

Gilboa, E. and Gotlib, I. H. (1997). Cognitive biases and affect persistence in previously dysphoric and never-dysphoric individuals. *Cognition and Emotion*, *11*, 517–38.

Hagemann, D., Naumann, E., Becker, G., Maier, S., and Bartussek, D. (1998). Frontal brain asymmetry and affective style: A conceptual replication. *Psychophysiology*, *35*, 372–88.

Hagemann, D., Naumann, E., Luerken, A., Becker, G., Maier, S., and Bartussek, D. (1999). EEG asymmetry, dispositional mood and personality. *Personality and Individual Differences*, *27*, 541–68.

Halgren, E., Squires, N. K., and Wilson, C. L. (1982). Brain generators of evoked potentials: The late (endogenous) components. *Bulletin of the Los Angeles Neurological Society*, *47*, 108–23.

Hamm, A. O. and Vaitl, D. (1996). Affective learning: Awareness and aversion. *Psychophysiology*, *33*, 698–710.

Hare, R. D. (1991). *The Hare Psychopathy Checklist – Revised*. Toronto: Multi-Health Systems.

Heller, W. (1990). The neuropsychology of emotion: Developmental patterns and implications for psychopathology. In N. Stein, B. L. Leventhal, and T. Trabasso (eds.), *Psychological and biological approaches to emotion*, vol. 1 (pp. 67–211). Hillsdale, NJ: Lawrence Erlbaum Associates.

Heller, W. (1993). Gender differences in depression: Perspectives from neuropsychology. *Journal of Affective Disorders*, *29*, 129–43.

Heller, W. and Nitschke, J. B. (1997). Regional brain activity in emotion: A framework for understanding cognition in depression. *Cognition and Emotion*, *11*, 637–61.

Heller, W., Etienne, M. A., and Miller, G. A. (1995). Patterns of perceptual asymmetry in depression and anxiety: Implications for neuropsychological models of emotion and psychopathology. *Journal of Abnormal Psychology*, *104*, 327–33.

Heller, W., Nitschke, J. B., Etienne, M. A., and Miller, G. A. (1997). Patterns of regional brain activity differentiate types of anxiety. *Journal of Abnormal Psychology*, *106*, 376–85.

Henriques, J. B., and Davidson, R. J. (1991). Left frontal hypoactivation in depression. *Journal of Abnormal Psychology*, *100*, 535–45.

Hitt, S. K., Allen, J. J. B., and Duke, L. M. (1995). Stability of resting frontal alpha asymmetry in major depression. *Psychophysiology*, *32*, S40.

Hodgins, D. C., el-Guebaly, N., and Armstrong, S. (1995). Prospective and retrospective reports of mood states before relapse to substance use. *Journal of Consulting and Clinical Psychology*, *63*, 400–7.

Hugdahl, K. (1995). Classical conditioning and implicit learning: The right hemisphere hypothesis. In R. J. Davidson and K. Hugdahl (eds.), *Brain asymmetry* (pp. 235–67). Cambridge, MA: MIT Press.

King, F. L., and Kimura, D. (1972). Left-ear superiority in dichotic perception of vocal nonverbal sounds. *Canadian Journal of Psychology*, *26*, 111–16.

Kline, J. P., Allen, J. J. B., and Schwartz, G. E. R. (1998). Is left frontal brain activation in defensiveness gender specific? *Journal of Abnormal Psychology*, *107*, 149–53.

Kline, J. P., Blackhart, G. C., and Schwartz, G. E. R. (1999). Gender specificity of resting anterior electroencephalographic asymmetry and defensiveness in the elderly. *Journal of Gender-Specific Medicine*, *2*, 35–9.

Kline, J. P., Donohue, K. F., and Lang, A. R. (2000). A multilevel analysis of drinking's appetitive motives and consequences. *Psychophysiology*, *38*, S57.

Kline, J. P., Knapp-Kline, K., Schwartz, G. E. R., and Russek, L. G. S. (2000). Anterior asymmetry, defensiveness, and perceptions of parental caring. *Personality and Individual Differences*, *31*, 1135–45.

Kline, J. P., Schwartz, G. E., Allen, J. J. B., and Dikman, Z. V. (1998). Perceptual and electroencephalographic registration of masked emotional words in defensiveness: An exploratory study. *Personality and Individual Differences*, *24*, 499–512.

Kline, J. P., Schwartz, G. E., Fitzpatrick, D. F., and Hendricks, S. E. (1998). Repressive/defensive coping and identification thresholds for pleasant and unpleasant words. *Imagination, Cognition, and Personality, 17*, 283–91.

Kline, J. P., Blackhart, G. C.,Woodward, K. M., Williams, S. R., and Schwartz, G. E. R. (2000). Anterior electroencephalographic asymmetry changes in elderly women in response to a pleasant and an unpleasant odor. *Biological Psychology, 52*, 241–50.

Knight, R. T. (1996). Contributions of human hippocampal region to novelty detection. *Nature, 383*, 256–9.

Kolb, B., and Whishaw, I. Q. (1996). *Fundamentals of human neuropsychology* (4th edn.). New York: W. H. Freeman.

Kramer, A., and Spinks, J. (1991). Capacity views of human information processing. In J. R. Jennings and M. G. H. Coles (eds.), *Handbook of cognitive psychophysiology: Central and autonomic nervous system approaches* (pp. 179–249). Chichester: John Wiley and Sons.

Kuhn, C., Swartzwelder, S., Wilson, W., Wilson, L. H., and Foster, J. (1998). *Buzzed: The straight facts about the most used and abused drugs from alcohol to ecstasy.* New York: W. W. Norton.

Landis, C. and Hunt, W. A. (1939). *The startle pattern.* New York: Rarrer and Rinehart.

Lane, R. D., Merikangas, K. R., Schwartz, G. E., Huang, S. S., and Prusoff, B. A. (1990). Inverse relationship between defensiveness and lifetime prevalence of psychiatric disorder. *American Journal of Psychiatry, 147*, 573–8.

Lang., A. R., Patrick, C. J., and Stritzke, W. G. (1999). Alcohol and emotional response: A multidimensional–multilevel analysis. In K. E. Leonard and H. T. Blane (eds.), *Psychological theories of drinking and alcoholism* (2nd edn., pp. 328–71). New York: Guilford Press.

Lang, P. J. (1995). The emotion probe: Studies of motivation and attention. *American Psychologist, 50*, 372–85.

Lang, P. J., Bradley, M. M., Cuthbert, B. N., and Patrick, C. J. (1993). Emotion and psychopathology: Startle probe analysis. In L. Chapman and D. Fowles (eds.), *Progress in experimental personality and psychopathology research*, vol. 16. New York: Springer.

LeDoux, J. E. (1995). Emotion: Clues from the brain. *Annual Review of Psychology, 46*, 209–35.

Levenston, G. K., Patrick, C. J., Bradley, M. M., and Lang, P. J. (2000). The psychopath as observer: Emotion and attention in picture processing. *Journal of Abnormal Psychology, 109*, 373–85.

Liotti, M., and Tucker, D. M. (1995). Emotion in asymmetric corticolimbic networks. In R. J. Davidson and K. Hugdahl (eds.), *Brain asymmetry* (pp. 389–423). Cambridge, MA: MIT Press.

Loberg, E., Hugdahl, K., and Green, M. F. (1999). Hemispheric asymmetry in schizophrenia: A "dual deficits" model. *Biological Psychiatry, 45*, 76–81.

Lyubomirsky, S., and Nolen-Hoeksema, S. (1995). Effects of self-focused rumination on negative thinking and interpersonal problem solving. *Journal of Personality and Social Psychology, 69*, 176–90.

MacLeod, C. (1996). Anxiety and cognitive processes. In I. G. Sarason, G. R. Pierce, and B. R. Sarason (eds.), *Cognitive interference: Theories, methods, and findings. The LEA series in personality and clinical psychology* (pp. 47–76). Mahwah, NJ: Lawrence Erlbaum Associates.

MacLeod, C., and Hagan, R. (1992). Individual differences in the selective processing of threatening information, and emotional responses to a stressful life event. *Behaviour Research and Therapy, 30*, 151–61.

MacLeod, C., Mathews, A., and Tata, P. (1986). Attention bias in emotional disorders. *Journal of Abnormal Psychology, 95*, 15–20.

Malaspina, D., Bruder, G., Furman, V., Gorman, J. M., Berman, A., and Van Heertum, R. (2000). Schizophrenia subgroups differing in dichotic listening laterality also differ in neurometabolism and symptomatology. *Journal of Neuropsychiatry and Clinical Neurosciences*, *12*, 485–92.

Marlatt, G. A. (1987). Alcohol, the magic elixir: Stress, expectancy, and the transformation of emotional states. In E. Gottheil, K. A. Druley, et al. (eds.), *Stress and addiction. Brunner/Mazel psychosocial stress series, No. 9* (pp. 302–22). Philadelphia, PA: Brunner/Mazel.

Marlatt, G. A., and Gordon, J. R. (1985). *Relapse prevention: Maintenance strategies in the treatment of addictive behaviors*. New York: Guilford Press.

Mathews, A., and MacLeod, C. (1985). Selective processing of threat cues in anxiety states. *Behaviour Research and Therapy*, *23*, 563–9.

Matthews, D. B., Best, P. J., White, A. M., Vandergriff, J. L., and Simson, P. E. (1996). Ethanol impairs cognitive spatial processing: New behavioral and electrophysiological findings. *Current Directions in Psychological Science*, *5*, 111–15.

Melia, K., Corodiman, K., Ryabinin, A., Wilson, M., and LeDoux, A. (1994). Ethanol (ETHO) pretreatment selectively impairs classical conditioning of contextual cues: Possible involvement of the hippocampus. *Society for Neuroscience Abstracts*, *24*, 1007.

Merikle, P. M. (1992). Perception without awareness: Critical issues. *American Psychologist*, *47*, 792–5.

Merikle, P. M., and Reingold, E. M. (1991). Comparing direct (explicit) and indirect (implicit) measures to study unconscious memory. *Journal of Experimental Psychology: Learning, Memory, and Cognition*, *17*, 224–33.

Merikle, P. M., Joordens, S., and Stolz, J. A. (1995). Measuring the relative magnitude of unconscious influences. *Consciousness and Cognition: An International Journal*, *4*, 422–39.

Mogg, K., Mathews, A., and Eysenck, M. W. (1992). Attentional bias to threat in clinical anxiety states. *Cognition and Emotion*, *6*, 149–59.

Mogg, K., Bradley, B. P., Williams, R., and Mathews, A. (1993). Subliminal processing of emotional information in anxiety and depression. *Journal of Abnormal Psychology*, *102*, 304–11.

Nitschke, J. B., Heller, W., Palmieri, P. A., and Miller, G. A. (1999). Contrasting patterns of brain activity in anxious apprehension and anxious arousal. *Psychophysiology*, *36*, 628–37.

Nolen-Hoeksema, S. (1991). Responses to depression and their effects on the duration of depressive episodes. *Journal of Abnormal Psychology*, *100*, 569–82.

Patrick, C. J., Berthot, B. D., and Moore, J. D. (1996). Diazepam blocks fear-potentiated startle in humans. *Journal of Abnormal Psychology*, *105*, 89–96.

Patrick, C. J., Bradley, M. M., and Lang, P. J. (1993). Emotion in the criminal psychopath: Startle reflex modulation. *Journal of Abnormal Psychology*, *102*, 82–92.

Regier, D. A., Narrow, W. E., and Rae, D. S. (1990). The epidemiology of anxiety disorders: The Epidemiologic Catchment Area (ECA) experience. *Journal of Psychiatric Research*, *24 (Supplement 2)*, 3–14.

Reid, S. A., Duke, L. M., and Allen, J. J. B. (1998). Resting frontal electroencephalographic asymmetry in depression: Inconsistencies suggest the need to identify mediating factors. *Psychophysiology*, *35*, 389–404.

Reingold, E. M., and Merikle, P. M. (1988). Using direct and indirect measures to study perception without awareness. *Perception and Psychophysics*, *44*, 563–75.

Roberts, J. E., Gilboa, E., and Gotlib, I. H. (1998). Ruminative response style and vulnerability to episodes of dysphoria: Gender, neuroticism, and episode duration. *Cognitive Therapy and Research*, *22*, 401–23.

Sayette, M. A. (1993). An appraisal-disruption model of alcohol's effects on stress responses in social drinkers. *Psychological Bulletin*, *114*, 3, 459–76.

Schacter, D. L., Church, B., and Treadwell, J. (1994). Implicit memory in amnesic patients: Evidence for spared auditory priming. *Psychological Science*, *5*, 20–5.

Schwartz, G. E. (1984). Psychobiology of health: A new synthesis. In B. L. Hammonds and C. J. Scheirer (eds.), *Psychology and health. Master lecture series*, vol. 3. (pp. 149–93). Washington, DC: American Psychological Association.

Sher, K. J., and Levenson, R. W. (1982). Risk for alcoholism and individual differences in the stress-response dampening effect of alcohol. *Journal of Abnormal Psychology, 91*, 350–67.

Sobotka, S. S., Davidson, R. J., and Senulis, J. A. (1992). Anterior brain electrical asymmetries in response to reward and punishment. *Electroencephalography and Clinical Neurophysiology, 83*, 236–47.

Steele, C., and Josephs, R. (1988). Drinking your troubles away II: An attention allocation model of alcohol's effect on psychological stress. *Journal of Abnormal Psychology, 97*, 196–205.

Steele, C., and Josephs, R. (1990). Alcohol myopia: Its prized and dangerous effects. *American Psychologist, 45*, 921–33.

Stritzke, W. G. K., Lang, A. R., and Patrick, C. J. (1995). Alcohol and human emotion: A multidimensional analysis incorporating startle-probe methodology. *Journal of Abnormal Psychology, 104*, 114–22.

Stroop, J. R. (1935). Studies of interference in serial verbal reactions. *Journal of Experimental Psychology, 18*, 643–62.

Tomarken, A. J., and Davidson, R. J. (1994). Frontal brain activation in prepressor and nonrepressors. *Journal of Abnormal Psychology, 103*, 339–49.

Tomarken, A. J., Davidson, R. J., and Henriques, J. B. (1990). Resting frontal brain asymmetry predicts affective responses to films. *Journal of Personality and Social Psychology, 59*, 4, 791–801.

Tomarken, A. J., Davidson, R. J., Wheeler, R. E., and Doss, R. C. (1992). Individual differences in anterior brain asymmetry and fundamental dimensions of emotion. *Journal of Personality and Social Psychology, 62*, 676–87.

Vrana, S. R., Constantine, J. A., and Westman, J. S. (1992). Startle reflex modification as an outcome measure in the treatment of phobia: Two case studies. *Behavioral Assessment, 14*, 279–91.

Vrana, S. R., Spence, E., and Lang, P. J. (1988). The startle problem response: A new measure of emotion? *Journal of Abnormal Psychology, 97*, 487–91.

Watkins, P. C., Martin, C. K., and Stern, L. D. (2000). Unconscious memory bias in depression: Perceptual and conceptual processes. *Journal of Abnormal Psychology, 109*, 282–9.

Watkins, P. C., Mathews, A., Williamson, D. A., and Fuller, R. D. (1992). Mood-congruent memory in depression: Emotional priming or elaboration? *Journal of Abnormal Psychology, 101*, 581–6.

Watkins, P. C., Vache, K., Verney, S. P., and Mathews, A. (1996). Unconscious mood-congruent memory bias in depression. *Journal of Abnormal Psychology, 105*, 34–41.

Weinberger, D. A., Schwartz, G. E., and Davidson, R. J. (1979). Low-anxious, high-anxious, and repressive coping styles: Psychometric patterns and behavioral and physiological responses to stress. *Journal of Abnormal Psychology, 88*, 369–80.

Wexler, B. E., Schwartz, G. E., Warrenburg, S., and Servis, M. (1986). Effects of emotion on perceptual asymmetry: Interactions with personality. *Neuropsychologia, 24*, 699–710.

Wolpe, J., and Lang, P. J. (1964). A fear survey schedule for use in behavior therapy. *Behavior Research and Therapy, 2*, 27–30.

VIGNETTE

Adult Experimental Psychopathology

Anne K. Jacobs

Lang, A. R., Pelham, W. E., Atkeson, B. M., and Murphy, D. A. (1999). Effects of alcohol intoxication on parenting behavior in interactions with child confederates exhibiting normal or deviant behaviors. *Journal of Abnormal Child Psychology*, *27*, 3, 177–89.

Lang and colleagues used experimental analogue methods to examine the effects of acute alcohol intoxication on parenting behaviors in interactions with child confederates who displayed either friendly and cooperative behaviors, or showed acting out behaviors consistent with Attention Deficit Disorder (ADHD), Conduct Disorder (CD), and Oppositional Defiant Disorder (ODD). The study was solid in its experimental design and data analysis. All of the 192 participating parents had a son aged 5 to 12 and half of the participants had a son diagnosed with an externalizing disorder. Multiple measures were used to ascertain the presence of a child Axis I diagnosis. In addition to its inclusion of married mothers, the study stands out in its inclusion of married fathers and single mothers. Within each of these three parenting groups, half of the parents had sons who received a diagnosis. Participants completed extensive self-report measures of demographic characteristics, alcohol-related habits, personality/emotional traits, life stresses, family environments, and marital satisfaction (if applicable). These variables were utilized as covariates in primary study analyses. Participants were randomly assigned to an alcohol or nonalcohol consumption condition.

Due to the nature of research on the effects of alcohol, special consideration needs to be given to the ethical aspects of such an investigation. Lang and colleagues took care to detail the manner in which they attended to these ethical concerns. They excluded parents who had drinking problems, who were trying to curtail alcohol use for any reason, or who had any medical or psychiatric condition that would make drinking alcohol unsafe. Before giving female participants alcohol, they first screened for pregnancy. Transportation was provided to and from the experiment site, and participants who received alcohol were detained until their blood alcohol levels were at .04 percent or less and declining on two successive tests.

Experimenters who gave the participants directions for the child interactions and those who coded the videotapes were blind to the participants' alcohol condition. The child confederates were rigorously trained and were assessed as having an 87.3 percent accuracy rate for their portrayal of either externalizing or cooperative children. High interrater reliability was achieved for most of the coded parent behaviors. The few behaviors with low occurrences or low reliabilities were not used in the analyses. Participants' mood scores at baseline were controlled for in analyses of mood at times 2 and 3. Because a large number of measures and multiple correlated tests were used, the authors set a conservative alpha level ($\alpha = .01$) for their analyses; the influence of this decision on statistical power (i.e., reducing it) was also discussed.

The authors found that intoxicated parents rated the externalizing child confederates as less deviant than did parents in the nonalcohol condition. Furthermore, alcohol intoxication was related to all parent groups showing less attention, less productive work, and using more commands, indulgences, and off-task talk in their interactions with the children. Regardless of their level of alcohol consumption, participants who interacted with the externalizing child confederates reported significant increases in feelings of anxiety, depression, and hostility. The authors recognized and discussed the limitations of their statistical power, but overall, the findings made an important contribution to both the clinical and scientific literature regarding acute alcohol intoxication and parenting. The strengths of the study conducted by Lang and colleagues include:

- Randomized design
- Raters kept blind to experimental condition
- Inclusion of married mothers and fathers and single mothers
- Attention to ethical concerns associated with studies using alcohol
- Multiple measures used to screen for ADHD, CD, and ODD in parents' offspring
- High degree of accuracy for child confederates
- Multilevel analyses examining influence of alcohol and environmental stimuli
- Used conservative alpha level due to large number of measures and tests used
- Controlled for baseline differences in analyses of changes in mood
- Acknowledged possible limitations in power when discussing results
- Results important for clinical applications and scientific literature

CHAPTER THIRTEEN

Child and Adolescent Assessment and Diagnosis Research

Paul J. Frick and Amy H. Cornell

Introduction

There has been much discussion in clinical psychology and other applied areas of psychology about the importance of integrating research and practice. Perhaps nowhere is the importance of such integration as great, and its failure as evident, as in the area of psychological assessment and diagnosis (Frick, 2000a). Psychological testing involves the assessment of clinically important constructs in an effort to understand the psychological functioning of a child or adolescent, typically to make important treatment decisions (Kamphaus and Frick, in press). As such, these efforts are critically dependent on the most current knowledge of the psychological constructs being assessed, be they personality traits, psychological disorders, cognitive styles, dimensions of family functioning, or many other psychosocial constructs that may be relevant for understanding a child's psychological adjustment. Unfortunately, this natural and important integration of research and practice often does not take place. Instead, there is a substantial discrepancy between measures that are being used in research to assess these constructs to study and understanding them and those that are being used in practice to make important decisions about individual children and adolescents.

There are a number of reasons for this wide gap between research and practice in psychological assessment and diagnosis, but most are related to two overriding issues (Frick, 2000a). First, the choice of methods used in the practice of psychological assessment has often been driven more by an allegiance to a particular theoretical orientation, or even more problematically, by an allegiance to a particular assessment technique, rather than being based on research concerning the nature of the psychological construct that is being assessed (Kamphaus and Frick, in press). Second, psychological assessment research is often conducted in such a way that its usefulness for the practicing psychologist is quite limited. That is, the wide gap between research and practice is not simply the failure of practicing psychologists to remain current on the psychological research and integrate this research in their practice of assessment and diagnosis. Equally problematic for this integration is the fact that the methods and goals of much of the research being conducted make it difficult to translate the findings from research into meaningful applications for the practicing psychologist.

The content and organization of this chapter are designed to highlight these central issues and to suggest research goals and methods that may better facilitate an integration between science and practice in the areas of assessment and diagnosis. Specifically, we focus on some important psychometric considerations in the development of assessment techniques and in establishing diagnostic procedures for childhood psychopathology that have important implications for the types of interpretations that are typically made by the practicing psychologist. Furthermore, we summarize several topics for assessment research that are very relevant to practice but have not been the focus of much systematic research. The overriding theme, however, is on issues that have the potential for having research better inform the practice of psychological assessment and diagnosis.

Important Psychometric Issues

Reliability and validity

The concepts of reliability and validity are two of the most basic concepts in measuring psychological constructs. Most psychology students, even at the undergraduate level, can provide a general description of these concepts, with reliability referring to the consistency of the scores provided by an assessment procedure and validity referring to the evidence that the procedure measures what it is purported to measure. Given these basic definitions, one might assume that establishing the reliability and validity of an assessment technique is quite simple and that this process would not be a critical focus of much research beyond the original development of an assessment technique. This view is widespread but incorrect. In fact, all assessment and diagnosis research is in some way related to these two basic concepts.

To understand the importance of these concepts it is critical to expand on the basic definitions of reliability and validity. For example, reliability and validity are not characteristics of tests or assessment procedures. They are characteristics of *specific interpretations* made from *specific scores* of the test within *specific populations*. As a result, some interpretations can be made reliably and validly from the scores of an assessment technique, whereas other interpretations may not be valid. For example, the Child Symptom Inventory-IV (CSI-IV; Gadow and Sprafkin, 1998) is a parent and teacher rating scale designed to assess the symptoms of some of the major disorders of childhood included in the *Diagnostic and Statistical Manual of Mental Disorders*, 4th edition (DSM-IV; American Psychiatric Association, 1994). As such, scores from the CSI-IV were designed to provide an approximation of clinician diagnoses. There is evidence that, for many disorders, scores on the CSI-IV are moderately to strongly associated with clinician diagnoses of DSM-IV disorders (Gadow and Sprafkin, 1998). However, because its purpose was to be used as a screening tool for DSM diagnoses, a large normative sample of children was not collected for the CSI-IV. Thus, although scores from the CSI-IV do indicate risk for certain DSM disorders, it is impossible to determine how deviant a child's score is from a normative sample.

To expand the concepts of reliability and validity even more, the optimal methods of establishing reliability and validity of an assessment procedure are not universal. Instead, they may vary depending upon the characteristics of the construct being measured. For example, establishing the stability of a measure over time is more important for measures assessing some constructs (e.g., personality traits) than others (e.g., state anxiety, episodic depression). Similarly, the optimal external criteria to validate various assessment procedures will also be construct dependent. For example, in the field trials for the DSM-IV, different outcomes were used to validate the criteria for Attention Deficit Hyperactivity Disorder (e.g., school work completion; Lahey, Applegate, McBurnett, et al. 1994) compared to the outcomes used to validate the criteria for Conduct Disorder (e.g., police contacts; Lahey, Applegate, Barkley, et al. 1994). In short, establishing the reliability and validity of other assessment procedures must be conducted within a clear theoretical context which clearly specifies the important dimensions along which the measure should and should not be evaluated (Frick, 2000b; Morey, 1991).

Another important characteristic of validating a test or assessment procedure is the continuous nature of this process. It is an ongoing process of accumulating more and more evidence for the validity of certain interpretations and defining the samples and settings in which these interpretations are most appropriate. An important implication of this dynamic view of validity is that the information which is available in the manual of a test, or any single review of a test, is limited to the information which was available and gathered at the time it was published. Therefore, an assessor must be aware of the current state of the research on a measure to interpret it appropriately. This dynamic and continuous view of validity also illustrates the importance of having a significant body of research on each assessment technique in order to inform users of the technique. There are many types of research that can contribute to this process by increasing the number and quality of interpretations that can be made from an assessment technique. Unfortunately, many forms of validation research that could provide important information for practice are rarely undertaken. These common limitations and implications for future assessment and diagnosis research are summarized in table 13.1.

Typical limitations in the validation process

First, many assessment techniques used to study psychological constructs are not used consistently across studies. That is, many assessment techniques used in research are designed for a particular study to address the specific goals of that study. The procedures may then be changed in subsequent studies to reflect different goals of research (Frick, 2000a). This methodology allows for revision of assessment methods based on the findings of one or more studies, rather than continuing to use the same method of

Table 13.1 Common limitations in the validation of techniques used in the assessment and diagnosis of children and adolescents

Limitation	Typical existing research	Goals for future research
Lack of systematic validation using the same version of the assessment technique across samples	Technique is changed to address specific research questions involving the construct of interest	Strike a balance between changing our assessment procedures as our knowledge of a construct advances with systematic validation to allow for well-justified applied uses
There is often little evidence for whether interpretations made from an assessment technique have comparable validity for children with differing characteristics	Technique is typically standardized and validated on mixed samples of children	Need to systematically test validity across gender, developmental level, ethnicity, socioeconomic status, and other relevant characteristics
Little information is typically available as to what information provided by one technique adds to the information provided by other techniques	Assessment techniques are typically validated in isolation from other comparable techniques or their validity is compared to that of other techniques	Need to provide more tests of the incremental validity of the information provided by one test within a battery of tests for predicting clinically important criteria
The validation of most assessment techniques provides little evidence for the direct clinical utility of the technique	Validation studies typically focus on increasing our understanding of the construct being assessed (i.e., indirect clinical utility)	Greater attention needs to be paid to validating interpretations that have direct clinical utility, such as enhancing diagnosis, selecting the most appropriate treatment, or monitoring treatment effects

assessment, despite evidence that it can be improved in some way. However, this methodology often results in assessment techniques that are not systematically developed and tested across multiple samples and settings, thereby limiting their usefulness in applied settings.

Second, many tests and procedures used in the assessment of children and adolescents lack any systematic examination of whether or not their validity is generalizable across gender, developmental level, socioeconomic status, and ethnicity (Kamphaus and Frick, in press). Much of the validation research done on assessment techniques utilizes group data using heterogeneous samples. For example, in developing a test, the authors may provide evidence that certain scales are associated with important clinical outcomes (e.g., risk for a psychiatric diagnosis) within a large sample that has substantial representation of various ethnic minority children. This type of research does not indicate whether or not the validity of the scales for predicting risk for a psychiatric diagnosis is equivalent across all ethnic groups included in the sample. Such conclusions require additional tests to determine whether there is evidence that the validity of certain interpretations is equivalent for each group separately.

Third, much validation research studies a technique in isolation from other potential ways of assessing the same psychological construct. Since techniques are rarely used in practice in isolation, but are often combined with other methods of assessing the same construct, an equally important question involves a technique's "incremental utility." That is, how much does a certain technique contribute to making clinically important interpretations *over and above* the information provided by other techniques? For example, Barkley (1991) reviewed research on the use of laboratory and performance based measures of attention (e.g., continuous performance tasks) for making a diagnosis of ADHD. Numerous studies demonstrated that scores from laboratory measures differentiate children with ADHD from control children and are sensitive to the effects of stimulant medication (see also Rapport et al., 2000). However, the correlations between the laboratory measures with parent and teacher reports of ADHD symptoms tend to be low to moderate. Further, teacher and parent ratings are more "ecologically valid," in that they assess a child's behavior in his or her natural settings. So the important question, one that is not addressed directly in this research, is whether or not the laboratory measures add any clinically useful information (e.g., predict the need for treatment or potential response to medication) to these more ecologically valid measures of behavior.

Fourth, validation research has often failed to provide information that is directly relevant to many clinical interpretations. Vasay and Lonigan (2000) distinguish between the indirect clinical utility and direct clinical utility of an assessment technique. Indirect clinical utility is evidence that an assessment technique adds to an understanding of the construct that is being assessed, such as helping to define subtypes of a disorder that may have different causal and maintaining factors or that may predict a particularly severe and stable manifestation of the disorder (e.g., Frick, Barry, and Bodin, 2000). In contrast, direct clinical utility is evidence that information provided by an assessment technique directly leads to improved clinical decision-making, such as by enhancing the diagnosis of a disorder, or improving the ability to match persons to optimal treatments, or aiding in the monitoring of treatment efficacy. Unfortunately, much of the validity evidence that is available for most assessment techniques is for their indirect clinical utility and not for their direct clinical utility.

In summary, the basic concepts of reliability and validity are critical for guiding most assessment and diagnosis research. Another critical psychometric issue, especially for the assessment of children and adolescents, is the ability of assessment techniques to provide normative information. Given that children and adolescents are rapidly progressing through many developmental stages and given that behaviors that are normative at one stage may be indicative of pathology at another, it is critical that assessments of youth include techniques that allow for normative comparisons. Therefore, the development and validation of norm-referenced scores are a critical focus of assessment and diagnosis research for youth.

Norm-referenced scores: Types of standard score transformations

Most assessment techniques provide some index of a child's performance, called the child's raw scores (e.g., sum of the items on a rating scale, number of errors on a measure of sustained attention, number of aggressive responses on a projective storytelling technique). However, raw scores generally offer little information about how a child's performance compares with the performance of other children of a similar age, gender, ethnicity, or other relevant characteristics. "Norm-referenced" scores are designed to provide such information. These scores involve converting a child's raw score to a standardized score, reflecting where the child's score falls in the distribution of scores from some comparison sample of children. One of the most commonly used metrics for standard scores is the T-score, which has a mean of 50 and a standard deviation of 10. Using the T-score metric, if a child receives a standard score of 60, this indicates that his or her score falls at one standard deviation above the sample mean of the comparison sample.

While this basic definition of norm-referenced standard scores appears quite straight-forward, there are a number of important considerations for interpreting these standard scores that are often ignored in many applied settings. For example, there are potentially important variations in how the distribution of scores in the comparison sample is used to form standard scores, a process called the "standard score conversion." Some techniques create a distribution of scores in the comparison sample that approximates a normal curve, others use a linear transformation that maintains the shape of the raw score distribution, even if it is not normally distributed. There are other methods of creating standard scores as well (Tellegen and Ben-Porath, 1992) and each could affect the interpretation of the resulting norm-referenced score (see Frick and Kamphaus, 2000).

As a result, assessment and diagnosis research can be critical for addressing many of the issues involved in selecting the most appropriate conversion method for an assessment technique. First, since the most appropriate transformation should be based on the characteristics of the construct being assessed (e.g., inattention, depression), research is needed to determine how the construct is distributed in the general population to determine if deviations in a comparison sample are a sampling artifact or if they reflect actual differences in how the trait is manifested in the population. Second, research is needed to directly compare the effects of different types of transformation to determine if the differences are trivial and have little impact on the validity of the interpretations made from the standard score.

Norm-referenced scores: Types of samples

Another important issue for interpreting norm-referenced scores is the quality of the comparison sample from which the standard scores were derived. Judging the "quality" of the comparison sample is difficult because the most important characteristics of the sample may differ depending on the specific interpretation. One of the most common interpretations concerns how "normative" a child's score is compared with scores obtained by other children of the same age. In this case, the sample on which the scores are based should be representative of the general population of children within a certain age group and large enough within this age group to provide a distribution of scores that are representative. There is great variation in how large and representative standardization samples are for assessment techniques used with children and adolescents (see Kamphaus and Frick, in press, for a more complete review). For example, some standard scores are based on large samples (e.g., $n = 3{,}483$ children between the ages of 4 and 18) that were collected to approximate the United States census on variables such as gender, race, and socioeconomic status (Reynolds and Kamphaus, 1992), whereas other scores are based on relatively small samples ($n = 200$ children between the ages of 6 and 15) with very questionable representation of children from diverse backgrounds (e.g., children were from three school districts in southern California; McArthur and Roberts, 1982). Because of such variation in normative samples, assessors must evaluate these comparison samples and determine if they are appropriate for the interpretations that are to be made from the test. However, this evaluation can be guided by assessment and diagnosis research. For example, research can help to determine if the distributions on which the standard scores are based are stable across diverse samples (e.g., Sandberg, Meyer-Bahlburg, and Yager, 1991).

Another important issue for interpreting norm-referenced scores concerns whether or not the comparison group is a "normative" sample or a "normal" sample. A normal sample is one that may exclude children who have received mental health services or who had been placed in special education classes (e.g., Achenbach, 1991). If children with potential problems in adjustment are excluded, it is quite likely that the upper end of the distribution of scores on the assessment technique is eliminated or severely truncated. A normative sample, however, is representative of the general population, not only by ensuring adequate representation across demographic categories, but also by virtue of including children with problems in adjustment at a rate that is typical for the population of children of interest (e.g., Reynolds and Kamphaus, 1992). As a result of the type of sample used, a child's score may appear more deviant when compared to scores from a "normal" sample in which the upper end of the distribution is eliminated but appear less deviant when compared to scores from a "normative" sample in which the upper end of the distribution is maintained.

A related issue is whether or not norm-referenced scores should be based only on children of the same gender. That is, should a girl's score reflect how she falls in the distribution of scores for girls only, or for a combined sample of all children? This is a critical issue because many types of emotional and behavior problems experienced by children and adolescents show clear sex differences in their prevalence. In essence, using sex-specific comparisons equates for these differences in prevalence. Although sex-specific comparison groups are probably the most commonly used for most assessment techniques (see Kamphaus and Frick, in press), the theoretical rationale for such gender-specific norms is debatable. For example, if one has a scale assessing impulsive and overactive behaviors in children, boys are quite likely to be rated higher on these behaviors than girls. Using sex-specific norms this difference in prevalence is "removed" because a child is considered to have an elevated level of behavior if his or her scores are deviant compared with others of the same sex. If these differences reflect true sex differences in the trait being assessed in the normal population, the rationale for removing them is unclear.

To inform assessors on the most appropriate normative comparison group, a critical question is whether girls who reach a normative cutoff relative to other girls, but not compared to a mixed sample which includes boys, show characteristics that one wishes to predict with the score (e.g., impaired social functioning, risk for school failure). This is an important focus of assessment and diagnosis research that has not received much attention, but which has very immediate implications for assessing children and adolescents. Furthermore, a similar issue could be raised in determining whether children should only be compared to samples that are homogeneous with respect to ethnicity, socioeconomic status, region, or many other demographic characteristics.

Empirically derived cutoffs

Implicit in this discussion of norm-referenced cutoffs is the fact that norm-referenced scores provide an index of where a child's score is located within some reference group and cutoffs for considering a score to be "clinically significant" (e.g., a T-score of 70 or the 98th percentile) are based solely on normative considerations. Another method for determining clinically meaningful cut scores involves developing empirically derived cutoffs. For example, scores would be considered significant based on how well they predict some clinically important criterion (e.g., risk for recidivism after release from an institution, risk for a psychiatric diagnosis), irrespective of how rare or common a score is in the general population. Obviously, this requires a substantial amount of systematic research to establish such cut scores and to determine how well these cutoffs predict the criterion of interest across multiple samples with different characteristics. Unfortunately, this type of systematic research is lacking for most assessment techniques.

There are two notable examples of this type of research. First, the Children's Depression Inventory (CDI; Kovacs, 1992) is a self-report rating scale designed to assess depression in children. The manual for the CDI (ibid: 40–1) provides information on the percentage of children with clinical diagnoses of depression at various CDI scores. Based on this information the manual provides several recommended "cut-points" on the CDI that seem to be optimal points for predicting the presence of a diagnosis of depression. Second, Lahey, Applegate, Barkley, et al. (1994) evaluated the symptoms of Conduct Disorder in a large sample ($n = 440$) of clinic-referred children to determine at what level the symptoms predicted various indicators of impairment. They found that children with one or two symptoms of Conduct Disorder did not tend to show significantly more impairment (e.g., police contacts) than those with no symptoms. However, at three symptoms there was a noticeable increase in the level of impairment that steadily increased with the presence of additional symptoms. This led to the recommended cutoff of three symptoms for the diagnostic threshold in making a diagnosis of Conduct Disorder.

Both of these examples illustrate the use of empirically derived cutoffs for assessment techniques. Since many interpretations made from assessment techniques focus on the prediction of clinical criteria (e.g., need for treatment), it is unfortunate that more assessment and diagnosis research has not focused on establishing empirically derived cutoffs for various assessment techniques. One argument that has been raised in using empirically derived cutoff scores is that any cutoff will be somewhat arbitrary in that many scores are best considered as being "continuous" with no clear distinction between when something is normative or pathological (Achenbach, 1995). As such, deriving cutoffs creates an illusion of a very clear break between normative and pathological scores on an assessment technique and, therefore, clinicians should simply interpret the range of scores on a test without trying to place a child or adolescent into some arbitrary category. This argument illustrates the importance of not placing undue meaning on scores around the cutoff of any assessment technique. However, this argument ignores the fact that there may be some constructs that are best considered to be qualitatively distinct (e.g., resulting from different causal factors) from normal variations of the trait being assessed (Kagan and Snidman, 1991). More practically, it ignores the fact that most decisions made from clinical assessments are by nature categorical, such as deciding whether or not a child is in need of treatment or deciding what type of treatment approach for a child might have the best chance of success. Therefore, it is important to provide data that is most relevant for these types of clinical decisions.

Predictive utility estimates

Unfortunately, much of the research on the association between scores on assessment techniques and clinically important outcomes has not been conducted in a way that provides information that directly relates to these categorical clinical decisions. For example, much research simply provides group-level data, such as showing that scores from an assessment technique differentiate nonreferred children from children in a specific diagnostic group or showing that scores from a technique are correlated with treatment outcome. These data do not indicate how likely any individual child with a given score would be to show the outcome of interest.

More informative statistics for these purposes are conditional probability estimates (Kraemer, 1992; Waldman and Lilienfeld, 1991). Two of the more commonly used conditional probability estimates are sensitivity and specificity rates. Sensitivity rates are the proportion of children with a given outcome (e.g., disorder) who score above a certain point on an assessment technique (e.g., T-score of 70 on a rating scale), thereby showing how "sensitive" scores on the technique are for the outcome. In contrast, specificity refers to the proportion of children without the outcome that score below a certain point on an assessment technique, thereby showing how many children with the outcome would be left unclassified by the assessment technique. Although sensitivity and specificity are the most commonly used conditional probability indices, they were primarily developed for epidemiological research to determine optimal methods for detecting diseases (Kraemer, 1992). They do not provide the conditional probabilities that are most relevant for most clinical decisions. In most clinical settings an assessor typically has the score from an assessment technique and wishes to estimate the probability of an outcome (e.g., a diagnosis being present) for the person being assessed, rather than knowing the outcome and determining which score best predicts it.

This has led to the increasing use of the conditional probability estimates of positive predictive power (PPP) and negative predictive power (NPP). Like sensitivity and specificity rates, PPP and NPP indices are directly related to the proportion of "true positives" (i.e., those with the high scores on a test that have the outcome of interest) and "true negatives" (i.e., those below the cutoff on the test who do not have the outcome of interest) within a sample. However, PPP is the proportion of those who score high on a test who have the outcome, and NPP is the proportion of those who score below the cutoff on a test who do not have the outcome of interest. As a result, PPP and NPP provide the conditional probability estimates that directly relate to the type of decisions made in clinical practice and, therefore, are the more relevant statistics for most assessment and diagnosis research.

However, there are two important issues in the use of PPP and NPP indices (or any conditional probability estimate). First, these indices are highly influenced by the base rate of the outcomes being predicted (Frick et al., 1994). Therefore, the PPP and NPP of an assessment technique may be different if one is predicting a diagnosis of Conduct Disorder in a community sample, where the base rate is likely to be quite low, than if one is predicting the same diagnosis in a juvenile institution, where the base rate of the diagnosis is quite high. As a result, it is necessary to examine these indices across a wide variety of settings and samples to provide the most useful information to guide clinical assessments (Frick et al., 1994; Waldman and Lilienfeld, 1991; Widiger et al., 1984). Second, since all of the conditional probability estimates are also dependent on the base rate of elevations on a scale, moving a cut score on a measure will affect the conditional probability estimates. More importantly, moving the cut score up or down on a measure will typically have differential effects on the various conditional probability estimates. Specifically, as one moves the cut score on a measure higher and thereby decreases the number of children who cross the cutoff, one typically increases the proportion of children above the cutoff who have the outcome of interest (PPP), but one decreases the proportion of children below the cutoff who do not have the outcome of interest (NPP). One typically has the opposite trade-off in terms of relative magnitude of NPP and PPP when one lowers the cutoff. The natural question then is, given the trade-off between NPP and PPP rates, what is the best method for determining an "optimal" cut score for predicting a certain outcome using these indices?

What is optimal is dependent on the purpose of prediction and the specific outcome to be predicted. For example, in developing an appropriate screening cutoff to determine inclusion in a relatively benign school-based prevention program for depression, one may not be concerned with including a relatively large number of children who may be at somewhat low risk for actually developing depression and, therefore, a fairly lenient cutoff that leads to a relatively high rate of potential false positive cases (i.e., low PPP rates) may be used. In contrast, if one is wanting to determine an appropriate cut score for inclusion in a drug trial for a new antidepressant medication, one may want a more stringent (higher) cutoff on the measure to ensure that only the most at-risk children receive the more intensive treatment, even if this leads to a relatively high rate of false negative cases (i.e., low NPP rates).

To aid in this decision-making, there is a method of statistical analysis that allows one to model the increasing and decreasing PPP and NPP values across the various potential cut scores on an assessment measure to make some determination of optimal cutoffs for predicting certain outcomes. These techniques are based upon the Receiving Operating Characteristics (ROC) model, a test evaluation process derived from signal detection theory (Kraemer, 1992). In these procedures a graph of PPP and NPP values is plotted showing the relative trade-off between the probability indices at various cut points. This graph is an "ROC plane" and it provides geographical means of determining at which scores the conditional probability points are optimized. An example of this procedure is the study by Mota and Schachar (2000) which used an ROC procedure to determine the optimal points at which ADHD symptoms predicted psychosocial impairment as a method of evaluating the appropriate diagnostic threshold for this disorder.

While conceptually the use of the ROC model is relatively straightforward and easily understood by most researchers, the statistical underpinnings are somewhat complex. This complexity has limited the widespread use of the ROC model in assessment and diagnosis research. Further, limitations in the conditional probability estimates that form the basis for the ROC analyses also limit the interpretations one can make from these analyses. Specifically, since the conditional probability estimates are contingent on the base rates of the outcomes in the sample on which the estimates are based, so too are the results of the ROC (see Kraemer, 1992, for methods of controlling for base rates). Additionally, as with any validity index, the optimal cutoff determined by the ROC analysis is not solely a function of the assessment technique itself. It is also dependent on the specific outcome to be predicted. That is, one cutoff score from a test may be optimal for predicting a particular outcome (e.g., diagnosis of Attention Deficit Hyperactivity Disorder), whereas another cutoff may be optimal for predicting a second type of outcome (e.g., response to treatment). Despite these cautions, the use of conditional probability indices to derive meaningful cutoffs has become a critical focus of assessment and diagnosis research.

Issues in Interpreting Comprehensive Batteries

To this point, we have reviewed a number of critical psychometric issues in the development and use of assessment techniques with children and adolescents. These issues are critical for guiding assessment and diagnosis research in a way that fosters a better integration between research and practice. However, all of these issues focus on individual techniques. In practice, no meaningful decision (e.g., diagnosis, recommendation for treatment) should ever be made based on a single assessment technique. There are many reasons for this practice. First, rarely is there any single technique that is without flaws for assessing a construct. Every technique has some limitation in the quality of information provided (e.g., behavioral ratings being potentially biased by the current mood of the rater, Frick and Kamphaus, 2000). Second, most psychological constructs are multifaceted, requiring different assessment techniques to assess the various facets of the construct, such as the cognitive, behavioral, and psychophysiological aspects of depression (Garber and Kaminski, 2000). Third, one of the most consistent findings within developmental psychopathology research is that children with problems in one area of adjustment (e.g., conduct problems) often have problems in many other areas as well (e.g., peer rejection, learning disabilities) and there is no assessment technique that is optimal for assessing all constructs (Kamphaus and Frick, in press). Fourth, another consistent finding from developmental psychopathology research is the need to understand the various important contexts (e.g., family, school, peer) in which a child functions to adequately understand his or her psychosocial functioning. Therefore, assessments must not only assess important individual differences within the child, but must also assess important aspects of his or her psychosocial context.

As a result, most assessments require information on many aspects of a child's psychosocial functioning, as well as information on the important contexts that can influence his or her development, all assessed by multiple methods. Because of this need for comprehensive batteries, one of the most critical steps in the assessment process is the integration of information across various tests and techniques to make valid interpretations from the assessment results. Unfortunately, this critical aspect of the assessment process has been neglected by most assessment and diagnosis research. As a result, interpretations based on multiple sources of information have typically been left to the intuition of the assessor, and such intuition can be influenced by a number of potential biases (Nezu and Nezu, 1993). Because of these biases, even if the interpretations made from the individual tests are well supported, the manner in which they are integrated to make clinical decisions may lack validity. While sparse, there are a few areas of research that have begun to inform this stage of the assessment process.

Lack of agreement among informants

It is not difficult to explain the often low correlations between different assessment techniques, such as between projective tests and behavioral observations, because these techniques typically focus on very different aspects of a child's functioning (Finch and Belter, 1993). Also, it is clear that the needed research to inform clinical decision-making across different techniques is a comparison of the incremental utility of the different approaches for making certain interpretations, such as making a diagnosis of major depression (e.g., Ball et al., 1991) or determining the role of impulsivity in explaining antisocial behavior (e.g., White et al., 1994).

However, a more difficult conceptual issue is why different informants, who are reporting on the same aspects of a child's adjustment, do not provide highly correlated information. In a seminal review of this research, Achenbach, McConaughy, and Howell (1987) showed that, across 119 studies, the average correlation among different informants reporting a child's behavioral or emotional adjustment (i.e., parent, teacher, peer, mental health worker, trained observer, self-report) was $r = .30$, ranging from .20 between teacher and self-report to .44 between teacher and peer report. Based on these moderate correlations, discrepancies between sources of information are the rule rather than the exception in the assessment of childhood psychopathology. The most obvious practical implication of this low level of agreement among informants is the need to collect multiple sources of information, in order to obtain an adequate assessment of a child's adjustment (Kamphaus and Frick, in press). However, another implication is that it is essential for assessment and diagnosis research to uncover the reasons for this low rate of multi-informant agreement. There are several areas of research that have begun to address this issue and these are summarized in table 13.2.

One area of research has shown that at least part of the reason for the low correlations between different informants is that these informants observe children in different situations. As a result, the modest correlations among their reports may reflect real situational variability in children's behavior across settings. For example, in the Achenbach, McConaughy, and Howell (1987) review, the average correlation between similar informants (e.g., two parents, two teachers) was .64, which was much higher than the .30 average cross-informant correlation. Similarly, Duhig et al. (2000) provided a review of sixty studies and reported that the average correlation between two parents' ratings of their children's adjustment was .46 for emotional problems and .66 for behavioral problems.

Research has also implicated several factors within the child's family context which can affect the level of agreement between reporters on children's adjustment. Specifically, the level of interparental agreement has been shown to be lower in families experiencing high levels of distress (Christensen, Margolin, and Sullaway, 1992) and in families experiencing impoverished living conditions (Duhig et al., 2000). There have been a number of studies suggesting that parental adjustment, such as parental depression, can increase the rate of disagreement between the disturbed parent and other raters in reporting on children's adjustment (see Richters, 1992, for a review). In addition to documenting this association between parental adjustment and level of agreement in ratings of children's behavior, several studies have begun to test substantive reasons for the effect of parental adjustment on level of agreement. For example, some studies have found that parental depression leads to overreporting of many different types of problems, suggesting that the emotional distress in parents may make them less tolerant of their children's behavior (Briggs-Gowan, Carter, and Schwab-Stone, 1996). Alternatively, there is evidence that parental anxiety may be specifically related to overreporting of their children's anxiety, but not of their behavior problems, suggesting that they may over-interpret or project anxiety in their report of their children's anxiety (Frick, Silverthorn, and Evans, 1994).

The level of agreement between informants also may vary as a function of the age of the child being assessed. For example, very young children may not be reliable reporters of their own emotions and behavior (e.g., Edelbrock et al., 1985) or of their family context (Shelton, Frick, and Wootton, 1996) using very structured assessment techniques. However, the reliability of their self-report and, concomitantly, its agreement with other sources of information, seems to increase with age (Cantwell et al., 1997). In contrast, the reliability and validity of teacher report of child behavioral and emotional problems may decrease with age, possibly due to the fact that, as a child approaches

Table 13.2 Research relevant for combining information from different informants

Research focus	Summary of findings	Exemplar studies
Compare correlation of informants who see the child in similar contexts (e.g., two parents, or two teachers) and different contexts (e.g., parent and teacher)	Informants who see the child in similar contexts typically show higher correlations in their report of the child's adjustment than those who do not, suggesting that some of the poor multi-informant agreement is due to true situational variability in children's behavior	Achenbach et al. (1987)
Test the potential influence of contextual variables on the degree of multi-informant agreement on ratings of children's adjustment	Multi-informant agreement tends to be lower in families experiencing a high degree of distress and conflict and in families experiencing poverty	Christensen et al. (1992); Duhig et al. (2000)
Correlate indices of parental adjustment with discrepancies in the parental report of their children's adjustment to the information provided from other sources	Depressed parents may overstate and overgeneralize many types of problems in their children. Anxiety in parents may show a more specific relation to overreporting of anxiety in their children	Frick et al. (1994)
Compare the agreement among informants at various developmental levels	Agreement of child self-report with other sources of information often increases with age, whereas the agreement of teacher report decreases, especially as the child enters adolescence	Achenbach et al. (1987); Edelbrock et al. (1985)
Compare the validity of different informants for different domains of child adjustment	Clinicians judge teachers as more important informants for inattention/hyperactivity, parents for conduct problems, and parents and children for emotional problems. Teacher report of inattention/hyperactivity is the strongest predictor of later impairment, whereas parent report of conduct problems is the strongest predictor of later impairment	Loeber et al. (1990); Loeber et al. (1991); Verhulst et al. (1994)

adolescence, teachers tend to have less contact with a child over the school day and may be less able to report on their adjustment (Reynolds and Kamphaus, 1992).

Each of these areas of research has documented important influences on the level of informant agreement and are relevant for interpreting the information gathered from multiple sources in clinical assessments. They provide the assessor with information on some areas in which low levels of agreement are especially likely (e.g., self-report and teacher report for adolescents) and some potential explanations for the disagreement (e.g., lack of teacher contact with the student). However, none of these aforementioned areas of research test directly the differential validity of the various informants on children's adjustment. That is, there has been very little research determining if information provided by one informant has better clinical utility (e.g., predicting clinical diagnosis, predicting outcome, predicting response to treatment) than another. There are, however, several notable exceptions that illustrate this type of research.

As a first example, Loeber, Green, and Lahey (1990) conducted a survey of 105 psychologists and psychiatrists and asked them to rate how useful they viewed information provided by mothers, teachers, and children for assessing 44 different behaviors in pre-adolescent children (ages 7–12). They reported several systematic differences in how useful different informants were judged by diagnosticians. Specifically, teachers were rated as more useful than parents or children for assessing inattentive and hyperactive behaviors, whereas parents were rated as more useful than teachers or children for assessing severe antisocial and aggressive behaviors. Both parents and teachers were rated as more useful than children for assessing oppositional and defiant behaviors. For assessing emotional problems, parents and children were rated as more useful than teachers, with parents being rated as somewhat more useful than children.

These findings are important for understanding the current standard of practice and expert clinical opinions as to the validity of different informants. However, Loeber et al. (1991) actually compared parent, teacher, and children's report of behavior problems in 6–13-year-old boys for predicting clinically important indices of impairment (e.g., school suspensions, police contacts, grade retention, special education placement) one year after the ratings were obtained. Consistent with expert opinion, teachers' reports of inattentive and hyperactive behaviors were the best predictors of impairment one year later. For conduct problems, parent report was somewhat superior to both teacher and child report, although both teacher and child report had some utility in predicting later impairment as well. Importantly, although child report seemed to have the poorest predictive utility, this was likely due to the relatively young age of the sample (i.e., pre-adolescent) and due to the sole focus on behavioral problems.

Models for integrating information

Another important area of research for guiding the integration of information from comprehensive assessment batteries is to test different "models" or frameworks for integrating multiple sources of information. Some researchers have attempted to develop very systematic "algorithms" that explicitly weigh certain sources of information over others based on the existing literature. For example, Riech and Earls (1987) developed a systematic method for weighing information for each of the major types of childhood disorders. They developed a system in which teacher information was weighed more heavily for making diagnoses of attention deficit disorder, whereas child self-report was weighed more heavily in making diagnoses of depression. As another example of this type of research, Bird, Gould, and Stagheeza (1992) developed a method of weighing information that was empirically derived from logistic regression analyses. Different weights were assigned to each source of information based on the relative contributions of each assessment method for predicting an outcome (i.e., a diagnosis) from the regression analyses.

Piacentini, Cohen, and Cohen (1992) point out some important limitations in both of these approaches. They suggest that the method of providing "clinical guidelines" still leaves a great deal of interpretation to the subjectivity of the assessor. In addition, the method of empirically determining weights for each assessment source is greatly dependent on the characteristics of the sample from which the weights were derived and, thus, may not generalize across samples. Instead, Piacentini, Cohen, and Cohen (1992) provide evidence that a simple method for weighing information that eliminates subjective clinical decisions and does not rely on complex and sample dependent weights is most likely to provide the most valid interpretations. Specifically, they recommend that assessors use an "either–or" rule to weigh information from different sources. In their approach, a significant result (e.g., elevation on a given rating scale) is considered important if it is present from any source, even if it is not significant from all sources. The rationale for this model for clinical decision-making rests on the assumption that "false positives" from assessment instruments (e.g., indicating the presence of diagnosis when it is in fact not present) are much rarer than "false negatives" (e.g., not showing the presence of a disorder that is in fact present). Such an assumption may be quite appropriate for some assessment situations, such as making a diagnosis when there is no compelling reason for the informants to intentionally distort information. However, there may be many situations in which there are compelling reasons for some sources of information to be biased toward providing a more pathological picture of a child's adjustment (e.g., custody decisions). Further, there are some assessment techniques that may provide more false positives (e.g., higher rates of pathology) than others (Lilienfeld, Wood, and Garb, 2000).

As a result, there is no single agreed model for integrating assessment information from comprehensive batteries of tests to guide clinical decisions. Most recommended procedures try to combine some objective guidelines to limit subjectivity and potential for bias, but still allow for some level of clinical decision-making in recognition of the complexity of the process (see Kamphaus and Frick, in press; Nezu and Nezu, 1993). However, it is critical that assessment and diagnosis research continue to develop and test different models to guide this process. It is an excellent example of a type of clinical research that has very immediate and important applications.

Conclusions

The goal of this chapter was to highlight several critical issues that are important for guiding research on the assessment and diagnosis of youth. The particular research topics reviewed in this chapter were chosen because they have immediate relevance to the diagnostic and assessment process. The topics ranged from some basic aspects of establishing the reliability and validity of various assessment techniques in order to guide clinically important interpretations, to more advanced topics related to developing and testing models for integrating multiple sources of assessment information.

Perhaps nowhere is the promise, and failure, of integrating research and practice greater than in the failure to systematically develop and validate meaningful cutoffs from assessment measures. Many, if not most, decisions made from clinical assessments are categorical decisions that make some predictive interpretation from the scores of an assessment technique or test battery (e.g., does the child need treatment and if so, what type? Is the child at risk to others if released from an institution?). Unfortunately, the validity of scores from most assessment techniques for making such decisions is rarely tested and, when it is tested, it is rarely replicated across samples with different characteristics to determine how generalizable they may be. Even when such research is conducted, the results are reported in such a way that their usefulness is limited for guiding interpretations of an individual child's score.

In short, although there has been a recent emphasis on improving the link between research and treatment in child psychology (Lonigan, Elbert, and Johnson, 1998), a similar emphasis is needed for improving the science and technology of assessment and diagnosis of childhood psychopathology (Frick, 2000a). Even more importantly, the success of these endeavors is intertwined. To use the most current knowledge of a psychological construct (e.g., depression) to improve treatment, it is necessary to have measurement strategies that can be used in both research and practice. As a result, the overriding goal of this chapter has been to outline various methods and strategies that can begin to bridge the gap between assessment methods used in research and those used in practice.

References

Achenbach, T. M. (1991). *The child behavior checklist – 1991*. Burlington, VT: University of Vermont Press.

Achenbach, T. M. (1995). Empirically based assessment and taxonomy: Applications to clinical research. *Psychological Assessment, 7*, 261–74.

Achenbach, T. M., McConaughy, S. H., and Howell, C. T. (1987). Child/adolescent behavioral and emotional problems: Implications of cross-informant correlations for situational specificity. *Psychological Bulletin, 101*, 213–32.

American Psychiatric Association (1994). *The diagnostic and statistical manual of mental disorders – 4th edn*. Washington, DC: American Psychiatric Association.

Ball, J. D., Archer, R. P., Gordon, R. A., and French, J. (1991). Rorschach depression indices with children and adolescents: Concurrent validity findings. *Journal of Personality Assessment, 57*, 465–76.

Barkley, R. A. (1991). The ecological validity of laboratory and analogue assessment methods of ADHD. *Journal of Abnormal Child Psychology, 19*, 149–78.

Bird, H. R., Gould, M. S., and Stagheeza, B. (1992). Aggregating data from multiple informants in child psychiatry epidemiological research. *Journal of the American Academy of Child and Adolescent Psychiatry, 31*, 78–85.

Briggs-Gowan, M. J., Carter, A. S., and Schwab-Stone, M. (1996). Discrepancies among mother, child, and teacher reports: Examining the contributions of maternal depression and anxiety. *Journal of Abnormal Child Psychology*, 24, 749–65.

Cantwell, D. P., Lewinsohn, P. M., Rohds, P., and Seeley, J. R. (1997). Correspondence between adolescent report and parent report of psychiatric diagnostic data. *Journal of the American Academy of Child and Adolescent Psychiatry*, 36, 610–19.

Christensen, A., Margolin, M., and Sullaway, M. (1992). Interparental agreement on child behavior problems. *Psychological Assessment*, 4, 419–25.

Duhig, A. M., Renk, K., Epstein, M. K., and Phares, V. (2000). Interparental agreement on internalizing, externalizing, and total behavior problems: A meta-analysis. *Clinical Psychology: Science and Practice*, 7, 435–53.

Edelbrock, C., Costello, A. J., Dulcan, M. K., Kalas, R., and Conover, N. C. (1985). Age differences in the reliability of the psychiatric interview of the child. *Child Development*, 56, 265–75.

Finch, A. J., and Belter, R. W. (1993). Projective techniques. In T. H. Ollendick and M. Hersen (eds.), *Handbook of child and adolescent assessment* (pp. 224–38). Boston, MA: Allyn and Bacon.

Frick, P. J. (2000a). Laboratory and performance-based measures of childhood disorders. *Journal of Clinical Child Psychology*, 29, 475–8.

Frick, P. J. (2000b). The problems of internal validation without a theoretical context: The different conceptual underpinnings of psychopathy and the disruptive behavior disorders criteria. *Psychological Assessment*, 12, 451–6.

Frick, P. J. and Kamphaus, R. W. (2000). Behavior rating scales in the assessment of children's behavioral and emotional problems. In C. E. Walker and M. C. Roberts (eds.), *Handbook of clinical child psychology*, 3rd edn. (pp. 190–204). New York: Wiley.

Frick, P. J., Barry, C. T., and Bodin, S. D. (2000). Applying the concept of psychopathy to children: Implications for the assessment of antisocial youth. In C. B. Gacono (ed.), *The clinical and forensic assessment of psychopathy* (pp. 3–24). Mahwah, NJ: Erlbaum.

Frick, P. J., Silverthorn, P., and Evans, C. S. (1994). Assessment of childhood anxiety using structured interviews: Patterns of agreement among informants and association with maternal anxiety. *Psychological Assessment*, 6, 372–9.

Frick, P. J., Lahey, B. B., Applegate, B., Kerdyck, L., Ollendick, T., Hynd, G. W., Garfinkel, B., Greenhill, L., Biederman, J., Barkley, R. A., McBurnett, K., Newcorn, J., and Waldman, I. (1994). DSM-IV field trials for the disruptive behavior disorders. *Journal of the American Academy of Child and Adolescent Psychiatry*, 33, 529–39.

Gadow, K. D., and Sprafkin, J. (1998). *Child symptom inventory – 4: Screening manual*. Stony Brook, NY: Checkmate Plus.

Garber, J., and Kaminski, K. M. (2000). Laboratory and performance-based measures of depression in children and adolescents. *Journal of Clinical Child Psychology*, 29, 509–25.

Kagan, J., and Snidman, N. (1991). Temperamental factors in human development. *American Psychologist*, 46, 856–62.

Kamphaus, R. W., and Frick, P. (in press). *Clinical assessment of children's personality and behavior*, 2nd edn. New York: Allyn and Bacon.

Kovacs, M. (1992). *Children's depression inventory (CDI)*. Toronto: Multi-Health Systems.

Kraemer, H. C. (1992). *Evaluating medical tests: Objective and quantitative guidelines*. Newbury Park, CA: Sage Publications.

Lahey, B. B., Applegate, B., Barkley, R. A., Garfinkel, B., McBurnett, K., Kerdyck, L., Greenhill, L., Hynd, G. W., Frick, P. J., Newcorn, J., Biederman, J., Ollendick, T., Hart, E. L., Perez, D., Waldman, I., and Shaffer, D. (1994). DSM-IV field trials for oppositional defiant disorder and conduct disorder in children and adolescents. *American Journal of Psychiatry*, 151, 1163–71.

Lahey, B. B., Applegate, B., McBurnett, K., Biederman, J., Greenhill, L., Hynd, G. W., Barkley, R. A., Newcorn, J., Jensen, P., Richters, J., Garfinkel, B., Kerdyck, L., Frick, P. J., Ollendick, T., Perez, D., Hart, E. L., Waldman, I., and Shaffer, D. (1994). DSM-IV field trials for attention-deficit/hyperactivity disorder in children and adolescents. *American Journal of Psychiatry, 151,* 1673–85.

Lilienfeld, S. O., Wood, J. M., and Garb, H. N. (2000). The scientific status of projective techniques. *Psychological Science, 11,* 27–66.

Loeber, R., Green, S. M., and Lahey, B. B. (1990). Mental health professionals' perception of the utility of children, mothers, and teachers as informants on childhood psychopathology. *Journal of Clinical Child Psychology, 19,* 136–43.

Loeber, R., Green, S. M., Lahey, B. B., and Stouthamer-Loeber, M. (1991). Differences and similarities between children, mothers, and teachers as informants on disruptive child behavior. *Journal of Abnormal Child Psychology, 19,* 75–95.

Lonigan, C. J., Elbert, J. C., and Johnson, S. B. (1998). Empirically supported psychosocial interventions for children: An overview. *Journal of Clinical Child Psychology, 27,* 138–45.

McArthur, D. S., and Roberts, G. E. (1982). *Roberts apperception test for children.* Los Angeles, CA: Western Psychological Services.

Morey, L. (1991). Classification of mental disorder as a collection of hypothetical constructs. *Journal of Abnormal Psychology, 100,* 289–93.

Mota, V. L., and Schachar, R. J. (2000). Reformulating Attention-Deficit/Hyperactivity Disorder according to Signal Detection Theory. *Journal of the American Academy of Child and Adolescent Psychiatry, 39,* 1144–51.

Nezu, A. M., and Nezu, C. M. (1993). Identifying and selecting target problems for clinical interventions: A problem-solving model. *Psychological Assessment, 5,* 254–63.

Piacentini, J. C., Cohen, P., and Cohen, J. (1992). Combining discrepant diagnostic information from multiple sources: Are complex algorithms better than simple ones? *Journal of Abnormal Child Psychology, 20,* 51–63.

Rapport, M. D., Chung, K. M., Shore, G., Denney, C. B., and Isaacs, P. (2000). Upgrading the science and technology of assessment and diagnosis: Laboratory and clinic-based assessment of children with ADHD. *Journal of Clinical Child Psychology, 29,* 555–68.

Reynolds, C. R., and Kamphaus, R. W. (1992). *Behavior Assessment System for Children (BASC).* Circle Pines, MN: American Guidance Services.

Richters, J. E. (1992). Depressed mothers as informants about their children: A critical review of the evidence of distortion. *Psychological Bulletin, 112,* 485–99.

Riech, W., and Earls, F. (1987). Rules for making psychiatric diagnoses in children on the basis of multiple sources of information: Preliminary strategies. *Journal of Abnormal Child Psychology, 15,* 601–16.

Sandberg, D. E., Meyer-Bahlburg, H. F. L., and Yager, T. J. (1991). The child behavior checklist nonclinical standardization samples: Should they be utilized as norms? *Journal of the American Academy of Child and Adolescent Psychiatry, 30,* 124–34.

Shelton, K. K., Frick, P. J., and Wootton, J. (1996). The assessment of parenting practices in families of elementary school-aged children. *Journal of Clinical Child Psychology, 25,* 317–27.

Tellegen, A., and Ben-Porath, Y. S. (1992). The new uniform T-scores for the MMPI-2: Rationale, derivation, and appraisal. *Psychological Assessment, 4,* 145–55.

Vasay, M. W., and Lonigan, C. J. (2000). Considering the clinical utility of performance-based measures of childhood anxiety. *Journal of Clinical Child Psychology, 29,* 493–508.

Verhulst, F. C., Koot, H. M., and Ende, J. V. (1994). Differential predictive value of parents' and teachers' reports of children's problem behaviors: A longitudinal study. *Journal of Abnormal Child Psychology, 22,* 531–46.

Waldman, I. D. and Lilienfeld, S. O. (1991). Diagnostic efficiency of symptoms for Oppositional Defiant Disorder and Attention-Deficit Hyperactivity Disorder. *Journal of Consulting and Clinical Psychology, 59*, 732–8.

White, J. L., Moffitt, T. E., Caspi, A., Bartusch, D. J., Needles, D. J., and Stouthamer-Loeber, M. (1994). Measuring impulsivity and examining its relation to delinquency. *Journal of Abnormal Psychology, 103*, 192–205.

Widiger, T. A., Hurt, S. W., Frances, A., Clarkin, J. F., and Gilmore, M. (1984). Diagnostic efficiency and DSM-III. *Archives of General Psychiatry, 41*, 1005–12.

VIGNETTE

Child and Adolescent Assessment and Diagnostic Research

Anne K. Jacobs

Carrion, V. G., Weems, C. F., Ray, R., and Reiss, A. L. (2002). Toward an empirical definition of pediatric PTSD: The phenomenology of PTSD symptoms in youth. *Journal of the American Academy of Child and Adolescent Psychiatry, 41,* 2, 166–73.

Carrion and colleagues have conducted an investigation of pediatric PTSD which has a number of characteristics that makes it a strong example of assessment and diagnostic research. The authors examined the relationship between the frequency and intensity of childhood PTSD symptoms and the child's overall impairment. They assessed the diagnostic requirement of having to meet DSM-IV symptom criteria on each of three symptom clusters, and looked at the aggregation of PTSD symptom clusters across developmental stages. While the number of participants, 59 7–14-year-old children, was not large, it was sufficient to answer the research questions and reflected a great deal of diversity in gender, ethnicity, and socioeconomic status. The authors recruited participants from local social service departments and mental health clinics, thus reflecting a population of children and adolescents likely encountered by clinicians. All participants had been exposed to interpersonal trauma, and had experienced a trauma at least six months before referral to the research project. The authors screened out children with a history of neurological disorders or alcohol/drug use or dependence in order to avoid contamination with the variables of interest.

The measures used by the authors included self- and caretaker-report, and study measures were reported to be reliable, valid, and developmentally sensitive. As one measure of reliability, the authors reported obtaining an intraclass correlation coefficient of .97 on a subsample of interviews with one of the originators of the Clinician-Administered PTSD Scale for Children and Adolescents (CAPS-CA). To measure children's physical maturation level the authors had participants rate their pubertal development based on drawings and written descriptions reflecting the five Tanner stages (i.e., instead of choosing an arbitrary age to reflect puberty). The authors also assessed PTSD symptoms and other behavioral and social problems, and used a brief intelligence screening. Often research is criticized for using participants who do not generally reflect the complexity of cases seen in clinics, but the authors nicely addressed this issue by assessing for disorders co-occurring with PTSD and including comorbid participants in study analyses.

Analyses were appropriate for both the sample size and the questions the authors were investigating. The authors used linear regression to examine the relationship between each symptom's frequency, intensity, and PTSD diagnosis and overall clinical impairment. They used the standard alpha level of $p < .05$ and focused on variables that accounted for at least 10 percent of the dependent variable variance. Subgroups were created for (a) children meeting all three DSM-IV PTSD symptom cluster criteria, (b) children who met two, and (c) children who only met the criteria for one cluster. Differences were examined between the three subgroups in demographics, time since trauma, type of trauma, comorbidity, distress, impairment, and pubertal status using ANOVAs and chi square analyses. Appropriately, the Fisher least-significant-difference procedure was employed for multiple comparisons between group means as a method to control for possible inflation of Type I error inherent in multiple comparisons.

The researchers found support for distinguishing between the frequency and intensity of PTSD symptoms in children and adolescents. For example, the intensity of the avoidance (e.g., of feelings, thoughts, and conversations) associated with the trauma and distress at exposure to trauma-linked cues predicted functional impairment. The intensity of difficulty concentrating, avoidance, and feelings of trauma recurrence were predictive of PTSD diagnosis. Impairment and distress in children with subthreshold criteria did not differ significantly from that observed in children who met all three cluster criteria. This high level of impairment in subthreshold children was not due to comorbidity. Furthermore, symptom clusters occurred together more frequently in the later stages of puberty. The authors acknowledged the power limitations inherent with having a relatively small sample size and using a cross-sectional design. For their efforts, however, the authors reported a number of findings of interest to both researchers and clinicians. The strengths of the Carrion et al. article include:

- Participant diversity
- Appropriate statistics used for sample size and research questions
- Participants reflective of typical clinical samples
- Developmentally sensitive, reliable, and valid measures
- Use of multiple informants for providing research data
- Examined possible effects of comorbidity
- Results add to scientific literature and are useful to clinicians

CHAPTER FOURTEEN

Adult Clinical Assessment and Diagnosis Research: Current Status and Future Directions

Thomas E. Joiner, Jr., and Jeremy W. Pettit

At the heart of all clinical assessment and diagnosis one finds the same thing: a test, or evaluation instrument. A test, as defined by Kaplan and Saccuzzo (1997: 7), is a "measurement device or technique used to quantify behavior or aid in the understanding and prediction of behavior." Clinical assessment and diagnosis involve the application of one or more tests toward the evaluation of behaviors and mental activities that are considered relevant to human functioning and mental health.

While assessment as it is currently known has developed primarily since Sir Francis Galton began his studies of individual differences in the mid-to-late nineteenth century, various methods of assessing human behavior have been used for millennia. The Chinese employed oral examinations for civil service selection as early as 2000 BC (DuBoise, 1970). Likewise, an account in the biblical book of Judges, dating back prior to 1000 BC, indicates that the Hebrew military leader Gideon used behavioral observation to select an elite group of soldiers: soldiers were accepted or rejected based upon the manner in which they drank from a spring (Judges 7: 5–7).

Clinical assessment and diagnosis (i.e., assessment of psychopathology) finds its roots largely in the pioneering work of Emil Kraepelin (1912). Kraepelin, who founded the German Institute for Psychiatric Research, was among the first to develop tests for evaluating emotionally distressed people. Since that time, clinical assessment and diagnosis has progressed through various stages wherein different perspectives guided the process of assessment. Objective, structured personality tests flourished in the first half of the twentieth century, followed by surges in projective tests, "dustbowl empiricism," applied behavior analysis, and self-report symptom scales that measure mental disorders and a host of related conditions. As assessment and diagnosis have matured, so has the field's conceptualization of mental disorders and its statistical repertoire for constructing and evaluating assessment tools. Indeed, the intricacies of current techniques for constructing, validating, administering, and interpreting measures may appear daunting.

Despite the apparent complexities inherent in the clinical assessment and diagnosis of mental states, the process is actually straightforward and mechanical. Why then does assessment so frequently appear such an ominous task for the clinician? There are two main reasons for the uncertainty associated with clinical assessment and diagnosis. First, there is often a paucity of scientific knowledge regarding the true nature of the phenomena being assessed. That is, constructors and administrators of assessment devices often do not possess a thorough understanding of the construct they wish to measure by means of a given assessment instrument. Second, threats to the reliability and validity of the measurement process may bias the assessment in some manner, thereby producing inaccurate or equivocal results.

Accordingly, the statement presented in the opening sentence of the preceding paragraph may be rephrased as follows: clinical assessment and diagnosis of mental states is a straightforward and mechanical process, *if* (a) the deep nature of the phenomena being assessed is well characterized and *if* (b) threats to the psychometric adequacy of the measurement process are identified and minimized. In the field of mental disorders, however, neither of these criteria is routinely met. The latter criterion is adequately handled in certain cases, but the former will likely plague assessment and diagnosis until the adoption of an alternative approach to understanding psychopathology.

In this chapter we survey assessment and diagnostic techniques with reference to these two issues (as well as some others). We highlight the features and problems of three common approaches to clinical assessment and diagnosis: structured clinical interviews, symptom scales, and projective tests. In addition, we end the chapter with a discussion of a promising candidate for an alternative approach to studying psychopathology.

Structured Clinical Interviews

In structured clinical interviews the interviewer presents patients with a standardized set of questions in a particular order. Probe questions, which serve to elicit more information on a given topic, are similarly presented in a standardized manner. A trademark, therefore, of structured clinical interviews is the systematization of stimulus presentation to interviewees, as well as the reduction of the role of clinical judgment (Groth-Marnat, 1999).

The systematized approach of structured interviews offers increased reliability over less structured approaches. By delineating clear, explicit criteria for category inclusion and exclusion, structured interviews reduce the level of error inherent in unstructured interviews, which rely to a greater extent upon clinical judgment. Past empirical work demonstrates (poignantly, at times) the shortcomings of clinical judgment and the superiority of standardized, actuarial decision-making (e.g., Dawes and Corrigan, 1974; Garb, 1998; Meehl, 1954; Nisbett and Ross, 1980). Citing numerous empirical investigations (e.g., Chapman, 1967; Chapman and Chapman, 1967, 1969), Nisbett and Ross (1980) cogently argue that clinicians' evaluations of covariation, cause, and prediction are commonly plagued by biases in judgment. Such errors in clinical judgment often arise from failure to recognize a number of factors relevant to assessment, including base-rate frequencies, primacy effects, confirmatory bias, hindsight bias, attribution type, and dissimilarities between the clinician and the patient (Garb, 1998). In their review, Nisbett and Ross further demonstrate that actuarial methods consistently outperform clinical judgment. Not only do *optimal* actuarial methods typically outperform clinical judgments; almost *any* actuarial method outperforms clinical judgment due to the superior reliability of actuarial formulas alone!

Clearly, the standardized approach of the structured clinical interview helps yield more reliable diagnoses than may be obtained during an unstructured interview. Nonetheless, structured interviews differ in the extent to which they require clinical judgment, and some situations require flexible, less rigorous approaches in order to adequately obtain required information (Groth-Marnat, 2000). Among structured interviews, reliability decreases as the amount of clinical judgment involved increases (as would be expected given that actuarial formulas have higher reliabilities). The reliability of structured interviews also depends on the specificity of the diagnosis sought after (Groth-Marnat, 1999). Global assessments that seek only to establish the presence or absence of psychopathology typically have high reliabilities, as do interviews that assess overt behaviors. In contrast, interviews that seek to assess specific syndromes or pathological phenomena (e.g., obsessions, worries) demonstrate lower reliabilities.

Another feature of structured clinical interviews is that they are typically scored rapidly and easily, which allows for the development of standardized norms, against which scores may be compared. In general, cutoff scores are applied so that a specific score represents the presence or absence of a given condition (Kaplan and Saccuzzo, 1997). This represents one advantage of structured clinical interviews over less structured approaches to assessment. That is, they identify subsets of the population who meet accepted criteria for specific disorders (i.e., nosological purity or sensitivity), who do *not* meet accepted criteria for other disorders (i.e., diagnostic specificity), and whose symptoms noticeably set them apart from other people (i.e., symptom severity).

On the basis of their relative "nosological purity" one would expect such structured interviews to yield accurate diagnostic classification, but only to the extent that the assessed mental disorders are genuinely categorical in nature. Structured clinical interviews, typically based upon the DSM classification system, *assume* that disorders are indeed categorical in nature. At present, however, this assumption is premature, as the dimensional vs. categorical debate regarding mental disorders has not yet been empirically resolved (e.g., Lilienfeld and Marino, 1999; Wakefield, 1999). Our current understanding of mental disorders does not allow us to conclusively know which disorders (if any) are categorical (i.e., either fully present or absent) and which disorders (if any) fall upon a dimensional continuum (i.e., everyone possesses the condition of interest to differing degrees, based upon the number or severity of symptoms present). Thus, assessment tools stemming from this underlying taxonic assumption are valid only to the extent that the assumption itself is valid.

The categorical assumption inherent in structured clinical interviews may also introduce other difficulties into the assessment process. While the structured interview approach addresses whether nosologically defined disorders are comorbid with one another (i.e., diagnostic specificity; e.g., see Lewinsohn, Rohde, Seeley, and Hops, 1991; Rohde,

Lewinsohn, and Seeley, 1991), comorbidity of nosologically defined disorders with *syndromally* defined symptom clusters is not taken into account. Put differently, diagnostic specificity, but not symptom specificity, is addressed. It is quite possible that a given individual may not meet diagnostic criteria for a particular category of disorder, but may nonetheless suffer from many of the symptoms which comprise the category. An easily imaginable example is an anxiety disordered patient who, while not meeting full criteria for Major Depression, experiences considerable and clinically significant depressive symptomatology (see Katon and Roy-Byrne, 1991, for a discussion of mixed anxiety-depression). This is a natural outgrowth of a categorical approach to measurement: to say whether a diagnostic category is present or absent is not necessarily to say whether dimensionally defined, syndromal symptom clusters are present or absent.

One might argue that the presence or absence of a diagnostic category should be highly correlated with the presence or absence of syndromal symptoms. "Should" is the operative word here, as the findings of Rudd and Rajab (1995) attest. Rudd and Rajab administered questionnaires to several groups of participants selected on the basis of structured clinical interviews (i.e., NIMH Diagnostic Interview Schedule; Robins, Helzer, Cottler, and Goldring, 1989). Three of the diagnostic groups are particularly relevant to the present discussion: mood disordered, anxiety disordered, and comorbid for mood and anxiety disorders. The three groups scored quite similarly on measures of depression (BDI; Beck and Steer, 1987), hopelessness (Beck Hopelessness Scale; Beck and Steer, 1988), and anxiety (Millon Clinical Multiaxial Inventory Anxiety). The mood disordered group did not differ from the other groups on the depression and hopelessness measures, and the anxiety disordered group did not differ from the other two groups on the measure of anxiety. This study demonstrates the potential for considerable *homogeneity* in syndromal symptoms *across* diagnostic categories. A study by Hollon, Kendall, and Lumry (1986) highlights a related problem: *heterogeneity* in syndromal symptoms *within* a diagnostic category. Within Hollon, Kendall, and Lumry's sample of 29 substance abuse disordered patients, a subgroup of 12 carried chart diagnoses of depression, and on the average, scored in the clinical range on the BDI, but did not meet criteria for DSM-III Major Depression. Assuming for the moment that the questionnaires (e.g., BDI) in these studies were valid, reliance on diagnostic categories would have obscured the important observations that (1) there may be considerable similarity across diagnostic groups in syndromal symptoms; and (2) there may be considerable variation within a diagnostic group in syndromal symptoms.

Accordingly, it is not difficult to imagine that a study designed to compare diagnostic groups on a variable hypothesized to be specific to depression may find no differences. Indeed, precisely this situation obtained in the Hollon, Kendall, and Lumry (1986) study, which found that nosologically defined groups did not differ on measures of depressive dysfunctional attitudes and negative automatic thoughts, whereas syndromally defined groups did.

It is the rare theory of depression which would venture that its tenets apply *only* to nosologically defined depression and *not* to the syndromal depressed symptoms experienced by those with other disorders. Measurement of both nosologic *and* syndromal depression, therefore, seems necessary for the thorough testing of any theory of depression. The same principle likely holds for a large majority of mental disorders, and represents a limitation of an exclusively categorical approach in general, and structured clinical interviews in particular.

Another potential limitation of structured interviews is that there are times when such interviews appear to be less accurate than other forms of measurement. For instance, self-report inventories sometimes outperform clinician-assessed symptoms in accurately assessing mental states. Joiner, Rudd, and Rajab (1999) reported such findings in an investigation of clinician vs. patient ratings of suicidality (see also Jobes et al., 1997). The authors compared clinician ratings based upon a semi-structured interview (Modified Scale for Suicidal Ideation; Miller et al., 1986) and self-reported ratings of suicidality among 328 patients referred to a suicide treatment project. A discrepancy in assessed level of suicidality arose in approximately one-half of this sample, such that clinicians viewed the patients as at high risk for suicide, whereas the patients viewed themselves as at low risk. Over 6-, 12-, and 18-month follow-ups, self-reported ratings more accurately predicted subsequent levels of suicidality. In fact, patients rated as high risk by clinicians, but low self-reported risk, eventually resembled those who were initially rated as low risk by both clinician and self-report. In contrast, patients with initial high risk ratings by both clinician and self-report emerged as a more chronic, severe group than those with discrepant ratings.

The findings of Joiner, Rudd, and Rajab (1999) give credence to the notion that patients may assess themselves more accurately than clinicians do. Although their study does not address the actuarial vs. clinical judgment question, it is likely that an actuarial formula would have also outperformed the clinician ratings due to a factoring in of base rates. The base rate for suicide is quite low, even among individuals experiencing suicidal ideation. Thus, even among the sample of patients referred for treatment of suicidality, one would not expect 89 percent (the percentage designated by clinicians as "high risk" in Joiner, Rudd, and Rajab, 1999) to truly be at high risk for suicide. However, given the magnitude of the consequences of a false negative (i.e., suicide among a patient designated as low risk), the clinicians' overcautious approach is understandable. The goal, nonetheless, is to maintain a cautious stance while reducing the number of incorrectly classified patients.

Lastly, a number of pragmatic issues may serve as drawbacks for structured clinical interviews. Such interviews lack flexibility, and they can be quite lengthy, particularly if the interviewer is unable to focus on selected subsets of the interview. They also require the cooperation of the interviewee, which can be difficult when dealing with emotionally distressed or psychotic patients (Kaplan and Saccuzzo, 1997). When one is dealing with a particularly distressed or uncooperative patient, less structured methods of assessment may produce superior results or an increased likelihood that the patient will subsequently participate in a structured interview.

Commonly used structured clinical interviews

The Structured Clinical Interview for the DSM-IV (SCID-I; First et al., 1995b) is perhaps the most commonly used structured clinical interview. The SCID is a comprehensive interview used to make Axis I diagnoses for the DSM-IV, and as such it closely conforms to the DSM-IV diagnostic decision trees. A companion interview, the SCID-II (First et al., 1994), is available to derive Axis II personality disorder diagnoses.

Computerized versions for the SCID (Mini-SCID; First et al., 1995) and the SCID-II (AutoSCID-II; First et al., 1996) have also been developed.

The SCID is designed for use by a trained professional. Its format includes a number of open-ended queries and item skip structures, thereby requiring a moderate degree of clinical judgment. Due to the SCID's comprehensive nature, length of administration time may be of concern. However, selection of appropriate modules (e.g., based on an initial screen) may be used instead of administering the entire schedule.

Reliability estimates for the different versions of the SCID vary considerably, and unfortunately, few studies have examined the reliability of the most recent version of the SCID. However, interrater agreement indices from earlier versions and the current version have yielded estimates ranging from .40 to the high .90s, and most estimates fall above .60 or .70 (First et al., 1995; First, Spitzer, et al., 1995a, b; Maffei et al., 1997; Reich and Noyes, 1987; Riskind et al., 1987). Test–retest reliability and internal consistency coefficients likewise appear to be adequate, with estimates from approximately .70 to .95 (Dressen and Arntz, 1998; Maffei et al., 1997; Oumitte and Klein, 1995). Procedural validity has generally been assumed because the SCID parallels the DSM-IV. Limited support exists for the SCID's concurrent validity (Maziade et al., 1992), as measured by correlation with psychiatrists' diagnoses and with related measures, but it remains to be convincingly demonstrated (Renneberg et al., 1992; Steiner et al., 1995).

A second commonly used structured clinical interview is the Diagnostic Interview Schedule (DIS; Robins et al., 1981; Robins et al., 1989). The DIS was originally developed by the National Institute of Mental Health to be administered by nonprofessional interviewers for epidemiological studies (Helzer and Robins, 1988). Consistent with this mission, results with the DIS appear to be similar across clinicians and nonprofessional interviewers alike (Helzer, Spitznagel, and McEvoy, 1987; Robins et al., 1981). Like the SCID, the DIS uses verbatim item wording and specific guidelines concerning administration and progression of questions.

The DIS may be used to generate diagnoses based upon the DSM-IV and Research Diagnostic Criteria (RDC; Spitzer, Endicott, and Robins, 1978). This is accomplished through questions that focus primarily on the interviewee's overall life picture, with additional questions about symptoms occurring during the past year, 6 months, 1 month, and 2 weeks. Administration time runs approximately 60–90 minutes, and a computerized version generally requires an additional 30–45 minutes.

The sensitivity of the DIS varies across diagnoses, with a mean of 75 percent. The DIS is quite accurate at identifying individuals who do not meet criteria for a disorder, with a mean specificity of 94 percent (Groth-Marnat, 1999). These sensitivity and specificity values were obtained by comparison with psychiatrist-assigned diagnoses. Test–retest reliabilities appear to be modest, ranging from the mid .30s to mid .40s (Vandiver and Sher, 1991).

Symptom Scales

Symptom scales are among the most commonly utilized assessment methods. Not coincidentally, they also constitute the most economical means of assessment. Whereas structured clinical interviews require lengthy one-on-one interactions between patient and clinician, self-report symptom scales can often be completed by the patient alone in a matter of minutes. Furthermore, scoring and interpretation is likewise easy, given the availability of standardized cutoff scores and norms.

Critics of self-report symptom measures often claim that the measures lack specificity. The argument is usually made with regard to "high-end" scores. That is, high scores may not be specific to a single nosologic category, such as depression or anxiety, but may represent elevations in symptoms which span diagnostic categories (see Kendall et al., 1987, for discussion of the issue; see also, Gotlib, 1984; Tanaka-Matsumi and Kameoka, 1986).

This position has merit. For example, Rudd and Rajab (1995) recently demonstrated that mood and anxiety disordered subjects were not easily discriminable on measures of depression and anxiety. This is consistent with Kendall et al.'s (1987) caution that individuals scoring high on the BDI should not be labeled "clinically depressed" unless they also meet criteria based on a structured diagnostic interview – a recommendation that is, in turn, consistent with the scale's original purpose (Beck, Steer, and Garbin, 1988: 79).

Four approaches to addressing the high-end specificity problem of self-report symptom scales have been proffered. First, and perhaps most simply, symptoms of depression and anxiety may be measured, and it may be determined whether hypothesized effects apply to depression specifically or to psychological distress more generally (i.e., to both depression and anxiety). For example, Metalsky and Joiner (1992) reported that specific components of the hopelessness theory of depression (Abramson, Metalsky, and Alloy, 1989) were operative with respect to depressive but not to anxious symptoms. Second, a similar – but perhaps more rigorous – strategy involves the statistical covariance of anxious and depressive symptoms from one another (see Kendall and Ingram, 1989). If hypothesized effects apply to depression when anxiety is statistically controlled (i.e., the effects apply to the variance associated with depression but not with anxiety), but do not apply to anxiety when depression is controlled, an argument for depression symptom specificity can be made (e.g., Stark, Schmidt, and Joiner, 1996). A third strategy arises from consideration of the work of Clark and Watson (1991), who argue that the specific component of depression is anhedonia, whereas the specific component of anxiety is physiological hyperarousal. If hypothesized effects hold for the former (e.g., as measured by low positive affectivity scores on the Positive and Negative Affect Schedule (PANAS); Watson, Clark, and Tellegen, 1988), but not the latter (e.g., as measured by the BAI), depression symptom specificity can be said to obtain (e.g., Joiner and Metalsky, 1995). A fourth and final strategy for addressing the high-end specificity problem is to compare the self-report scores of relatively pure cases of depression and anxiety (i.e., non-comorbid cases) with each other and with comorbid cases of depression and anxiety. Group differences in symptom scale scores may suggest that specificity is not a problem for a particular measure.

Thus, the symptom scale approach presents difficulties regarding issues of nosologic purity and diagnostic specificity (i.e., convergent and discriminant validity), but procedures exist to address such problems. The remaining "gold standard" criterion, symptom severity, also presents problems for the symptom scale approach. In one sense, this should be the easiest criterion for symptom scales to meet, because most are designed as measures of symptom severity (e.g., Beck, Steer, and Garbin, 1988: 79). Nonetheless, because the scales are dimensional, considerable uncertainty exists regarding the designation of optimal cutoff points denoting the presence of clinical disorders or clinically significant symptomatology (e.g., Kendall et al., 1987). Obviously, the structured clinical interview approach, with its categorical classification system, easily deals with this issue.

A limitation of both structured clinical interviews and self-report symptom scales, however, is that they rely exclusively on the respondent as the source of diagnostic information. In other words, they assume the respondent has a capacity for self-observation and for providing honest, candid answers to personal questions (Kaplan and Saccuzzo, 1997). Regrettably, not all patients are honest and candid in assessment settings, and those who are not typically fall in the "low-end" range of self-report symptom scales. Recently, the "low-end specificity" of symptom measures has emerged as a measurement and methodological issue (e.g., Hooley and Richters, 1992; Kendall et al., 1987; Swann et al., 1992). Kendall et al. (1987) raised this issue, arguing that people who score low on such measures may not necessarily be nonsymptomatic, but may be " 'Pollyannas,' professional daredevils, incipient hypomanics, and the kind of people who want to talk to you when you sit next to them on an airplane" (p. 294). Hammen (1983) had earlier voiced concern that low-end subjects may be best characterized *not* by the absence of symptoms, but by the presence of other forms of psychopathology (e.g., psychopathy, hypomania). And earlier still, there were concerns that self-report symptom measures were particularly susceptible to the effects of faking and social desirability (Beck, 1972; Beck and Beamesderfer, 1974; Langevin and Stancer, 1979).

Three recent studies have empirically examined the issue of low-end specificity. Joiner, Schmidt, and Metalsky (1994) found that a disproportionate number of undergraduates who scored at the low end (0–9) of the BDI were elevated in MMPI-Lie and F-K scores, suggesting a tendency to deny symptoms and to attempt to appear in a favorable light. Also, the proportion of "denial" subjects among very low scorers (0–1) was higher than among other (2–9) low-end subjects. Similarly, Rudd and Rajab (1995) found that many subjects who scored at the low end (0–9) of the BDI nonetheless received psychiatric diagnoses, such as anxiety and substance use disorders. It therefore appears that the low-end specificity of the BDI is indeed problematic, as many have suggested (e.g., Hammen, 1983; Kendall et al., 1987). Joiner, Schmidt, and Schmidt extended these findings to children and adolescents. Inpatient youngsters who scored at the low end of the Children's Depression Inventory (CDI; Kovacs, 1980/1981, 1992) also scored more highly than depressed youngsters on the Lie scale of the Revised Children's Manifest Anxiety Scale (RCMAS; Reynolds and Richmond, 1985), which measures one's tendency to present oneself in a favorable light and to deny flaws and weaknesses, including symptoms. Moreover, this pattern did not hold for anxiety symptoms (i.e., low-end scores on the RCMAS did not correspond to higher scores on the Lie scale), a finding which suggests that defensive denial may be specific to certain forms of psychopathology. Taken together, the results of these three studies imply that extremely low scores on self-report depression scales may indicate defensive self-enhancement among children, adolescents, and adults. Hence, the diagnostic specificity of these measures may be compromised among low-end scores. The sensitivity of other types of self-report symptom scales (especially those symptoms which carry a social stigma) awaits investigation.

Examples of symptom scales

Symptom scales are seemingly innumerable, with new scales appearing (literally) each day. In order to illustrate the strengths and limitations of the symptom scale approach to assessment, we review three well-known and widely used scales utilized in the assessment of depression and anxiety. We begin with an anxious symptom scale, the State–Trait Anxiety Inventory (STAI; Spielberger, 1968; Spielberger, Gorusch, and Lushene, 1970).

The STAI is based on Spielberger's theory of state and trait anxiety. *State anxiety* refers to current feelings of apprehension and arousal of the autonomic system, whereas *trait anxiety* represents a stable, more enduring personality characteristic of responding to stress with anxiety (Nixon and Steffeck, 1977). The STAI consists of two 20-item scales: the A-State scale and the A-Trait scale. The A-State scale asks respondents to report feelings of anxiousness at the time they complete the questionnaire, and the A-Trait asks respondents to report how they generally feel.

Both scales of the STAI have demonstrated high internal consistencies, with alpha coefficients in the high .80s and low .90s (Knight, Waal-Manning, and Spears, 1983). Test–retest reliability of state anxiety is generally low, as would be expected (Joesting, 1975, 1976, 1977; Knight, Waal-Manning, and Spears, 1983). Test–retest reliability estimates of trait anxiety have varied, with some finding acceptable levels (from .66 to .84; Joesting, 1975, 1976, 1977; Spielberger, Gorusch, and Lushene, 1970), and others finding low levels (.29 to .54; Nixon and Steffeck, 1977). Despite this discrepancy, the more well-designed studies tend to support the reliability of the trait anxiety measure. Convergent validity has been provided by high correlations with other measures of anxiety (e.g., Multiple Affect Adjective Checklist Anxiety Scale; Dobson, 1985). Consistent with other findings regarding the overlap of anxious and depressive symptoms, the STAI trait scale correlates moderately to highly (r ranges from .50 to .70) with depressive symptom scales (e.g., BDI, Self-Rated Depression Scale, MMPI Depression Scale, Multiple Affect Adjective Check List Depression Scale; Dobson, 1985; Knight, Waal-Manning, and Spears, 1983). Hence, discriminant validity is a concern when using the STAI.

A second commonly used self-report symptom scale is the Beck Depression Inventory (BDI; Beck et al., 1979; Beck and Steer, 1987). The most frequently used symptom scale for depression, the BDI is a 21-item self-report inventory that typically requires 5–10 minutes to complete. Respondents are asked to rate the severity of each of the 21 symptoms on a scale from 0–3. Thus, scores may range from 0 to 63. Scores below 10 are generally considered nonclinical, scores from 10–19 correspond to mild depressive symptoms, scores of 20–8 correspond to moderate depression, and scores above 28 represent severe depression (Beck and Steer, 1987). Consistent with the findings of Joiner, Rudd, and Rajab (1999) regarding denial, scores below 4 may represent denial or an attempt to present oneself in an overly favorable manner. In contrast, scores above 40 are rare, even among severely depressed persons, and may represent an exaggeration of symptoms.

The BDI measures six of the nine criteria for a DSM-IV diagnosis of major depressive disorder (MDD), and its content was rationally derived by expert consensus of depressive symptoms. Although the BDI is not indicative of the full clinical syndrome of depression, it has been well validated as a measure of severity of depressive symptoms (Beck, Steer, and Garbin, 1988). Moreover, a limited amount of evidence suggests that the BDI may be as sensitive to major depressive disorder as structured clinical interviews, at least in community samples (Stukenberg, Dura, and Kiecolt-Glaser, 1990). While it possesses utility as a screening instrument, it should not be used alone to diagnose depression spectrum disorders (Marton et al., 1991). Concurrent validity has been established through moderate-to-high correlations with other depression symptom scales (e.g., .76 with the MMPI Depression Scale, .76 with the Zung Self Reported Depression scale; Beck, Steer, and Garbin, 1988; Brown, Schulberg, and Madonia, 1995). Similarly, correlations with clinician ratings and a structured interview-based diagnosis of major depression have been moderate to high, ranging from .55 to .96 (Beck, Steer, and Garbin, 1988; Marton et al., 1991). The BDI has demonstrated discriminant validity *vis-à-vis* a number of relevant conditions (e.g., Dysthymic Disorder vs. MDD; Steer, Beck, Brown, and Berchick, 1987; psychiatric vs. nonpsychiatric populations; Marton et al., 1991), but not anxiety disorders (Rudd and Rajab, 1995).

The BDI has yielded adequate reliability estimates, with results from a meta-analysis reporting a mean internal consistency of .86 (Beck, Steer, and Garbin, 1988). Test–retest reliabilities vary according to the time interval between retesting and the sample being studied. Estimates of test–retest reliability have traditionally fallen between .40 and .90 (Beck, Steer, and Garbin, 1988). Given a sufficient interval between testing sessions, relatively low test–retest correlations are to be expected, inasmuch as the BDI asks respondents to report symptoms occurring only in the last two weeks and depressive symptoms fluctuate considerably over time.

Overall, the BDI appears to be a reliable and valid measure of depressive symptoms. Its clinical utility is limited somewhat by poor diagnostic specificity and its susceptibility to "faking good." As described above, however, procedures exist to help account for both of these limitations.

Another frequently used self-report symptom scale, the Positive and Negative Affect Schedule (PANAS; Watson, Clark, and Tellegen, 1988), is superior at distinguishing depression and anxiety. The PANAS is based upon the original *tripartite model* of depression and anxiety (Clark and Watson, 1991). The original tripartite model asserted that (a) depression is specifically characterized by anhedonia (low positive affect), (b) anxiety is specifically characterized by physiological hyperarousal, and (c) general negative affect is a nonspecific factor associated with both depression and anxiety. The model has been somewhat modified, however, on the basis of empirical work conducted over the past decade (see Mineka, Watson, and Clark, 1998). Briefly, the updated model maintains that both depression and anxiety disorders are characterized by a shared, nonspecific factor of general negative affect, and that each disorder includes a specific, nonshared component (e.g., depression is distinguished by low positive affect). The primary modification of the model is that physiological hyperarousal is no longer viewed as an attribute of all anxiety disorders; rather, it serves as a specific marker for panic disorder (e.g., Brown et al., 1998). Analogously, each of the other Axis I anxiety disorders is characterized by its own unique component in addition to negative affect.

Consistent with the original tripartite model, the PANAS includes two 10-item scales of adjectives describing mood states: one for Positive Affect (PA; the extent to which a person feels enthusiastic, active, and alert) and one for Negative Affect (NA; the extent to which a person experiences subjective distress such as anger, disgust, guilt, and fear). Each item is rated on a scale from 1 ("very slightly or not at all) to 5 ("very much"); thus, scores for PA and NA may range from 10 to 50 each. The two scales are largely uncorrelated, with estimates ranging from −.12 to −.23 (Watson, Clark, and Tellegen, 1988). They also display high internal consistency, with coefficient alpha ranging from .84 to .91 among psychiatric and nonpsychiatric populations. Test–retest reliability over a 2-month period is adequate, and suggests that the scales may be used as state and trait measures, depending on the instructions given to respondents. The PANAS scales also display expected patterns of convergent and discriminant validity with other measures of affect and with measures of distress and psychopathology (e.g., BDI, STAI-A, Hopkins Symptom Checklist). For more information on reliability and validity of the PANAS, see Watson, Clark, and Tellegen (1988) and Watson, Clark, and Carey (1988).

In sum, the PANAS offers a reliable, valid measure of either state or trait affect, and is useful in differentiating depression from anxiety. Nevertheless, the sensitivity and the specificity of the PANAS as a diagnostic instrument are not yet known. Like other self-report symptom scales, the PANAS is open to the denial bias. To our knowledge, no studies have investigated whether extremely low scores on the PANAS may be indicative of underreporting or exaggerating symptoms.

Projectives

The projective hypothesis, as espoused by Frank (1939), maintains that a person's interpretation of an ambiguous stimulus represents his or her thought processes, feelings, experiences, needs, and previous experiences. Projective assessment instruments developed largely out of the clinical observation that people may impose meaning upon ambiguous stimuli. In addition, projectives became attractive because they were hypothesized to circumvent problems inherent in interviews and self-report, such as the "denial" bias discussed in the section on symptom scales.

Of course, projectives have long been a source of controversy. Proponents maintain that they provide valuable, relevant clinical information that is not afforded by other assessment approaches. Critics, however, note the often poor psychometric properties of projective instruments, and argue for a discontinuation in their application as diagnostic tools.

An advantage of projective techniques is their ease and speed of administration. Nonetheless, the ease of administration is countered by complex and lengthy scoring and interpretation procedures. A second advantage of projectives is that they do not rely upon the respondent to provide accurate, self-evaluative reports. As such, they are not as susceptible to the "faking" or "denial" problems that hinder structured interviews and symptom scales.

Unfortunately, projective techniques have not stood up well under the test of empirical scrutiny. Their questionable validity (e.g., Chapman and Chapman, 1967; Garb, Wood, and Nezworski, 2000; Groth-Marnat and Roberts, 1998; Halperin and McKay, 1998; Petot, 2001; Wood et al., 2000b) raises serious concerns about what exactly projective tests measure, and if such information is germane to clinical assessment and diagnosis. In addition (and as is the case with structured clinical interviews and self-report symptom scales), the validity of projective techniques remains in doubt until the resolution of larger classification issues regarding the nature of mental disorders.

Commonly used projectives

The best known, researched, and widely used projective instrument is the Rorschach Inkblot Test (Rorschach, 1921). The Rorschach consists of ten bilaterally symmetrical inkblots that are presented visually in a serial fashion. Examinees are asked to tell the examiner what each inkblot reminds them of (the actual verbal prompt upon presentation of each inkblot is, "what might this be?"). Responses are scored according to the location on the inkblot where the examinee focused, the properties of the inkblot used to make the response (determinants; e.g., shape, color), and the category of objects that the response belongs to (content; e.g., human, animal, architecture).

The Rorschach was originally designed as a measure of personality structure and dynamics (Weiner, 2000). Despite its intended purpose, however, it has been commonly utilized as a psychopathology diagnostic tool for decades (Wood et al., 2000a), with numerous researchers emphasizing its diagnostic utility (e.g., Exner, 1991; Meloy and Gacono, 1995; Levin, 1993; Weiner, 1997). Further, its proponents argue that its assessment of personality strengths and weaknesses provides useful information for treatment planning (e.g., Weiner, 2000).

In contrast, a recent review of empirical research conducted on the Rorschach since 1980 suggests that the instrument does not possess adequate validity as a diagnostic tool (Wood et al., 2000b). Of primary concern, Wood et al. (2000b) draw attention to several methodological limitations that plague much of the research on the Rorschach. These methodological flaws include comparing diagnostic groups to normative data, basing criterion diagnoses on Rorschach procedures (rather than on clinical interviews), failing to appropriately blind individuals involved in the research process, and failing to use appropriate statistical tests and controls.

After a comprehensive review of studies with acceptable methodologies, Wood et al. (2000b) conclude that only a small number of Rorschach scales have a well-demonstrated relationship to psychiatric disorders (see also Hiller et al., 1999). Four disorders, schizophrenia, schizotypal personality disorder, borderline personality disorder, and bipolar disorder, all display associations with "deviant verbalizations," and three of the four are related to "bad form" responses. Not coincidentally, these disorders are all characterized to varying degrees by disordered, at times bizarre, thoughts. Wood et al. (2000b) make the argument that these disorders may be diagnosed more efficiently using other methods of assessment, such as structured clinical interviews and the Minnesota Multiphasic Personality Instrument – Second Edition (MMPI-2).

Beyond these four disorders, the Rorschach has yet to demonstrate valid, replicable associations with specific psychological disorders. Nevertheless, proponents of the instrument argue to the contrary. For instance, Exner (1991, 1993) maintains that the Depression Index (DEPI) serves as a sensitive and specific measure of depression. A plethora of empirical evidence stands in stark contrast to Exner's claim (see Wood et al., 2000b; Jorgensen, Andersen, and Dam, 2000). Similar patterns of findings have emerged with posttraumatic stress disorder and other anxiety disorders, conduct disorder, dissociative identity disorder, dependent personality disorder, narcissistic personality disorder, and antisocial personality disorder. To our knowledge, the relationships which exist between other DSM-IV disorders and the Rorschach have not yet been empirically investigated.

On the basis of a large body of empirical data, we suggest that the Rorschach has yet to prove itself as a valuable diagnostic tool. Perhaps it possesses other properties that may be of value to mental health professionals, but its use in arriving at DSM-IV diagnoses appears unfounded.

In addition to the Rorschach, projective tests requiring the respondent to draw various objects are frequently used. For example, Joiner, Schmidt, and Barnett (1996) report that the "House-Tree-Person" (H-T-P; Buck, 1948; Burns, 1987; Van Hutton, 1994) drawing test is used almost as frequently as well-established child assessment measures such as the MMPI-A and the Child Behavior Checklist, and far more often than measures like the Personality Inventory for Children. Other commonly used projective drawing techniques include the Draw-A-Person (DAP; Koppitz, 1968, 1984; Mitchell, Trent, and McArthur, 1993), Kinetic Family Drawing (KFD; Burns, 1982; Burns and Kaufman, 1972), and Kinetic-School Drawing tests (KSD; Knoff and Prout, 1985; Prout and Phillips, 1974).

Interrater reliability of global ratings of projective drawings is generally high, and test–retest reliability based upon global ratings appears to be adequate (Kahill, 1984; Naglieri, 1988). The majority of the empirical literature, however, has not supported the validity of projective drawing techniques as personality assessment tools (e.g., Chapman and Chapman, 1967; Motta, Little, and Tobin, 1993; Roback, 1968; Smith and Dumont, 1995; Stawar and Stawar, 1989; Wanderer, 1969). Projective drawing techniques have received limited support as measures of the presence of sexual abuse, as screening instruments for children with low cognitive abilities, and as measures of self-concept among mentally retarded children (Ottenbacher, 1981; Scott, 1981; Van Hutton, 1994). However, contradictory evidence exists for each of the aforementioned uses (e.g., Castilla and Klyczek, 1993; Groth-Marnat and Roberts, 1998; Palmer et al., 2000).

In a recent study of projective drawing tools, Joiner, Schmidt, and Barnett (1996) determined the relation between basic drawing indices (e.g., size, line heaviness, and detail) and established measures of depression and anxiety symptoms. The drawing indices demonstrated high reliability, with interrater agreement approaching perfection (1.0). However, the indices were unrelated to other emotional distress indices, thereby showing no concurrent validity. Remarkably enough, the indices were not even related to each other!

Nevertheless, if one were to assume the veridicality of the projective hypothesis (i.e., projectives detect emotional distress in people who otherwise would not or could not express it), this pattern of findings could be held to occur because "deniers" score low on self-report measures and high on projective measures. This potential pattern would deflate the correlations between projective and self-report measures. Joiner, Schmidt, and Barnett (1996) tested this prospect by excluding the "deniers" (i.e., those with elevated Lie Scale scores) and found identical results – the projective drawing indices were unrelated to standard self-report measures of depression and anxiety such as the Revised Children's Manifest Anxiety Scale (RCMAS; Reynolds and Richmond, 1985) and the Children's Depression Inventory (CDI; Kovacs, 1980/1981, 1992).

In conclusion, evidence for the validity of projective drawing techniques is sparse, despite their widespread use. As Rorschach proponents argue (e.g., Weiner, 2000), *perhaps* projective drawing tools receive little empirical support for assessing psychopathology because they were not originally intended to do so. The obvious question, then, is "why are they commonly used in assessment and diagnosis of psychopathology?" Kaplan and Saccuzzo (1997) reflect upon this phenomenon as follows: "If there is a tendency to overinterpret projective test data without sufficient evidence, then projective drawing tests are among the worst offenders" (p. 460).

Conclusions

In this chapter we have reviewed three major approaches to assessment and diagnosis, commented on their basic features and limitations, and provided relevant examples of these approaches. Structured clinical interviews, often considered the "gold standard" of assessment, offer the advantages of nosologic purity, diagnostic specificity, and symptom severity. In addition, their systematized approach increases reliability by reducing room for human error and clinical judgment. Symptom scales offer a more economical approach than structured interviews, and at times even outperform structured interviews. Nevertheless, they are subject to the "denial" bias and lack diagnostic specificity unless steps are taken to control for other disorders. Projectives provide a means of avoiding the "denial" bias, yet are plagued by poor psychometric properties.

At various points in this chapter we have alluded to the most fundamental problem facing assessment and diagnosis: a poor understanding of the deep nature of mental disorders. The mental health field has traditionally adopted a medical model approach to conceptualizing mental disorders, viewing disorders as discrete categories rather than dimensions. Indeed, our current nosological system is based upon this categorical assumption. This assumption does not find roots in empiricism; rather, it derives from committee decision-making. We maintain that the dearth of empirical knowledge concerning the nature of mental disorders will continue to call into question the validity of clinical assessment and diagnosis. But how do we go about solving this dilemma? That is, how do we determine whether and to what extent disorders are categorical or dimensional?

A promising approach (and currently the only viable approach) is through the application of taxometrics to psychopathology. Briefly, *taxometrics* refers to a group of statistical procedures that can be used to discern categories from continua, and to establish the true indicators of presumed categories. Waller and Meehl (1998: 4) define a *taxon* as "a non-arbitrary class, a natural kind" – the words "category" and "type" also capture the meaning of the term. The DSM-IV *assumes* that disorders are taxa. One either meets criteria for Major Depressive Disorder or one doesn't; there is no in-between, no "partial MDD." Within the presumed taxon of MDD, however, a severity continuum exists such that a patient may be considered "mild," "moderate," or "severe." In addition, the patient may be rated on the Global Assessment of Functioning (GAF), another dimensional continuum within the presumed taxon of MDD. Despite these dimensional continua within MDD, the disorder presumably remains a taxon (according to DSM-IV).

Taxometrics may be applied to MDD (or any other disorder, for that matter) to determine whether it indeed stands apart as a unique, natural category, or whether it is more accurately viewed as a dimensional continuum. Furthermore, after a taxon has been established, taxometrics allows for investigation of the validity of taxon indicators. In our example of MDD, the taxon indicators would be symptoms of MDD. A straightforward approach to indicator validity is to assess the simple difference between taxon members' score on the indicator (i.e., symptom) versus non-taxon members' score on the indicator (Joiner and Schmidt, in press). For instance, to assess whether anhedonia is a valid indicator of MDD, we would compute the difference in anhedonia scores between persons meeting criteria for MDD (taxon members) and those not meeting criteria for MDD (non-taxon members). We will not go further into the specifics of taxometrics here, but refer readers to Meehl (1992, 1995, 1997), Meehl and Yonce (1996), Waller and Meehl (1998), and Joiner and Schmidt (in press) for in-depth discussions of its theory and procedures.

Obviously, learning and applying a taxometric approach require a substantial investment of time and energy. We argue, nonetheless, that it is a necessary investment if real progress in nosology is to be made. The probable impact of the application of taxometrics to psychopathology has been aptly described by Joiner and Schmidt (in press):

> When this general approach is widely and systematically applied to various psychopathological syndromes, the upshot is likely to be a thorough-going revision of the current diagnostic scheme – some categories will become continua, some diagnostic criteria will be eliminated, others introduced, and so on.

Obviously, such changes would have a dramatic impact upon clinical assessment and diagnosis. They would permit us to know with confidence that the diagnostic phenomena being assessed really exist, and would facilitate their correct identification based upon empirically validated indicators.

References

Abramson, L. Y., Metalsky, G. I., and Alloy, L. B. (1989). Hopelessness depression: A theory-based subtype of depression. *Psychological Review, 96*, 358–72.

Beck, A. T. (1972). Measuring depression: The depression inventory. In T. A. Williams, M. M. Katz, and J. A. Shields (eds.), *Recent advances in the psychobiology of the depressive illnesses* (pp. 299–302). Washington, DC: US Government Printing Office.

Beck, A. T., and Beamesderfer, A. (1974). Assessment of depression: The depression inventory. In P. Pichot (ed.), *Modern problems in pharmacopsychiatry* (pp. 151–69). Basel: Karger.

Beck, A. T., and Steer, R. A. (1987). *Manual for the revised Beck Depression Inventory*. San Antonio, TX: Psychological Corporation.

Beck, A. T., and Steer, R. A. (1988). *Beck Hopelessness Scale Manual*. San Antonio, TX: Psychological Corporation.

Beck, A. T., Steer, R. A., and Garbin, M. (1988). Psychometric properties of the Beck Depression Inventory: 25 years of evaluation. *Clinical Psychology Review, 8*, 77–100.

Beck, A. T., Rush, A. J., Shaw, B., and Emery, G. (1979). *Cognitive therapy of depression*. New York: Guilford Press.

Brown, C., Schulberg, H. C., and Madonia, M. J. (1995). Assessing depression in primary care practice with the Beck Depression Inventory and the Hamilton Rating Scale for Depression. *Psychological Assessment, 7*, 59–65.

Brown, T. A., Chorpita, B. F., and Barlow, D. H. (1998). Structural relationships among dimensions of the DSM-IV anxiety and mood disorders and dimensions of negative affect, positive affect, and autonomic arousal. *Journal of Abnormal Psychology, 107*, 2, 179–92.

Buck, J. N. (1948). The H-T-P technique, a qualitative and quantitative scoring manual. *Journal of Clinical Psychology, 4*, 317–96.

Burns, R. C. (1970). *Kinetic Family Drawings (KFD): An introduction to understanding children through kinetic drawings*. New York: Brunner/Mazel.

Burns, R. C. (1982). *Self-growth in families: Kinetic Family Drawings (KFD): Research and application*. New York: Brunner/Mazel.

Burns, R. C. (1987). *Kinetic House-Tree-Person (KHTP)*. New York: Brunner/Mazel.

Burns, R. C., and Kaufman, S. H. (1972). Action, styles, and symbols in Kinetic Family Drawings (KFD). New York: Brunner/Mazel.

Castilla, L. M., and Klyczek, J. P. (1993). Comparison of the Kinetic Person Drawing Task of the Bay Area Functional Performance Evaluation with measures of functional performance. *Occupational Therapy in Mental Health, 12*, 2, 27–38.

Chapman, L. J. (1967). Illusory correlation in observational report. *Journal of Verbal Learning and Verbal Behavior, 6*, 1, 151–5.

Chapman, L. J., and Chapman, J. P. (1967). Genesis of popular but erroneous psychodiagnostic observations. *Journal of Abnormal Psychology, 72*, 3, 193–204.

Chapman, L. J., and Chapman, J. P. (1969). Illusory correlation as an obstacle to the use of valid psychodiagnostic signs. *Journal of Abnormal Psychology, 74*, 3, 271–80.

Clark, L. A., and Watson, D. (1991). Tripartite model of anxiety and depression. Psychometric evidence and taxonomic implications. *Journal of Abnormal Psychology, 100*, 316–36.

Dawes, R. M., and Corrigan, B. (1974). Linear models in decision making. *Psychological Bulletin, 81*, 2, 95–106.

Dobson, K. (1985). An analysis of anxiety and depression scales. *Journal of Personality Assessment, 49*, 5, 522–7.

Dressen, L., and Arntz, A. (1998). Short-interval test–retest interrater reliability of the Structured Clinical Interview for DSM-III-R Personality Disorders (SCID-II) in outpatients. *Journal of Personality Disorders, 12*, 2, 138–48.

DuBoise, P. H. (1970). *A history of psychological testing*. Boston, MA: Allyn and Bacon.

Exner, J. E. (1991). *The Rorschach: A comprehensive system. Volume 2: Interpretation* (2nd edn.). New York: Wiley.

Exner, J. E. (1993). *The Rorschach: A comprehensive system. Volume 1: Basic Foundations* (3rd edn.). New York: Wiley.

First, M. B., Gibbon, M., Williams, J. B., and Spitzer, R. L. (1995). *Users manual for the Mini-SCID (for DSM-IV-version 2)*. North Tonewanda, NY: Multi-Health Systems/American Psychiatric Association.

First, M. B., Gibbon, M., Williams, J. B., and Spitzer, R. L. (1996). *Users manual for the AutoSCID-II (for DSM-IV)*. North Tonewanda, NY: Multi-Health Systems/American Psychiatric Association.

First, M. B., Spitzer, R. L., Gibbon, M., and Williams, J. B. (1995a). The Structured Clinical Interview for DSM-III-R Personality Disorders (SCID-II): II. Multisite test–retest reliability study. *Journal of Personality Disorders, 9*, 2, 92–104.

First, M. B., Spitzer, R. L., Gibbon, M., and Williams, J. B. (1995b). Structured Clinical Interview for DSM-IV Axis I Disorders – patient edition. (SCID-I/P, Version 2.0). New York: Biometrics Research Department, New York State Psychiatric Institute.

First, M. B., Spitzer, R. L., Gibbon, M., Williams, J. B. W., and Benjamin, L. (1994). Structured Clinical Interview for DSM-IV Axis II Personality Disorders. (SCID-II, Version 2.0). New York: Biometrics Research Department, New York State Psychiatric Institute.

Frank, L. K. (1939). Projective methods for the study of personality. *Journal of Psychology, 8*, 343–89.

Garb, H. N. (1998). *Studying the clinician: Judgment research and psychological assessment*. Washington, DC: American Psychological Association.

Garb, H. N., Wood, J. M., and Nezworski, M. T. (2000). Projective techniques and the detection of child sexual abuse. *Child Maltreatment: Journal of the American Professional Society on the Abuse of Children, 5*, 2, 161–8.

Gotlib, I. H. (1984). Depression and general psychopathology in university students. *Journal of Abnormal Psychology, 93*, 19–30.

Groth-Marnat, G. (1999). *Handbook of psychological assessment* (3rd edn.). New York: Wiley.

Groth-Marnat, G. (2000). Visions of clinical assessment: then, now, and a brief history of the future. *Journal of Clinical Psychology, 56*, 349–65.

Groth-Marnat, G., and Roberts, L. (1998). Human Figure Drawings and House Tree Person drawings as indicators of self-esteem: A quantitative approach. *Journal of Clinical Psychology, 54*, 2, 219–22.

Halperin, J. M., and McKay, K. E. (1998). Psychological testing for child and adolescent psychiatrists: A review of the past 10 years. *Journal of the American Academy of Child and Adolescent Psychiatry, 37*, 6, 575–84.

Hammen, C. L. (1983). *Cognitive and social processes in bipolar affective disorders: A neglected topic*. Paper presented at the convention of the American Psychological Association, Anaheim, California.

Helzer, J. E., and Robins, L. N. (1988). The Diagnostic Interview Schedule: Its development, evolution, and use. *Social Psychiatry and Psychiatric Epidemiology, 23*, 6–16.

Helzer, J. E., Spitznagel, E. L., and McEvoy, L. (1987). The predictive validity of lay Diagnostic Interview Schedule diagnoses in the general population: A comparison with physician examiners. *Archives of General Psychiatry, 44*, 1069–77.

Hiller, J. B., Rosenthal, R., Bornstein, R. F., Berry, D. T. R., and Brunnell-Neuleib, S. (1999). A comparative meta-analysis of Rorschach and MMPI validity. *Psychological Assessment, 11*, 278–96.

Hollon, S. D., Kendall, P. C., and Lumry, A. (1986). Specificity of depressotypic cognitions in clinical depression. *Journal of Abnormal Psychology, 95*, 52–9.

Hooley, J. M., and Richters, J. E. (1992). Allure of self-confirmation: A comment on Swann, Wenzlaff, Krull, and Pelham. *Journal of Abnormal Psychology, 101*, 307–9.

Jobes, D. A., Jacoby, A. M., Cimbolic, P., and Hustead, L. A. T. (1997). Assessment and treatment of suicidal clients in a university counseling center. *Journal of Counseling Psychology, 44*, 368–77.

Joesting, J. (1975). Test–retest reliabilities of State–Trait Anxiety Inventory in an academic setting. *Psychological Reports, 37*, 1, 270.

Joesting, J. (1976). Test–retest reliabilities of State–Trait Anxiety Inventory in an academic setting: Replication. *Psychological Reports, 38*, 1, 318.

Joesting, J. (1977). Test–retest correlations for the State–Trait Anxiety Inventory. *Psychological Reports, 40*, 2, 671–2.

Joiner, T., and Metalsky, G. (1995). A prospective test of an integrative interpersonal theory of depression: A naturalistic study of college roommates. *Journal of Personality and Social Psychology, 69*, 778–88.

Joiner, T. E., Jr., and Schmidt, K. L. (1997). Drawing conclusions – or not – from drawings. *Journal of Personality Assessment, 69*, 3, 476–81.

Joiner, T. E., Jr., and Schmidt, N. B. (in press). Taxometrics can "do diagnostics right" (and isn't quite as hard as you think). In M. Malik and L. Beutler (eds.), *Alternatives to DSM*. Washington, DC: American Psychiatric Association.

Joiner, T. E., Jr., Rudd, M. D., and Rajab, M. H. (1999). Agreement between self- and clinician-rated suicidal symptoms in a clinical sample of young adults: Explaining discrepancies. *Consulting and Clinical Psychology, 67*, 2, 171–6.

Joiner, T. E., Jr., Schmidt, K. L., and Barnett, J. (1996). Size, detail, and line heaviness in children's drawings as correlates of emotional distress: (More) negative evidence. *Journal of Personality Assessment, 67*, 1, 127–41.

Joiner, Jr., T. E., Schmidt, K. L., and Metalsky, G. I. (1994). Low-end specificity of the Beck Depression Inventory. *Cognitive Therapy and Research, 18*, 55–68.

Jorgensen, K., Andersen, T. J., and Dam, H. (2000). The diagnostic efficiency of the Rorschach Depression Index (DEPI) and the Schizophrenia Index (SCZI): A review. *Assessment, 7*, 3, 259–80.

Kahill, S. (1984). Human figure drawings in adults: An update of the empirical evidence, 1967–1982. *Canadian Psychology, 25*, 269–90.

Kaplan, R. M., and Saccuzzo, D. P. (1997). *Psychological testing: Principles, applications, and issues* (4th edn.). Pacific Grove, CA: Brooks/Cole Publishing.

Katon, W., and Roy-Byrne, P. (1991). Mixed anxiety and depression. *Journal of Abnormal Psychology, 100*, 337–45.

Kendall, P. C., and Ingram, R. E. (1989). Cognitive-behavioral perspectives: Theory and research on depression and anxiety. In P. C. Kendall and D. Watson (eds.), *Anxiety and depression: Distinctive and overlapping features* (pp. 27–53). San Diego, CA: Academic Press.

Kendall, P. C., Hollon, S. D., Beck, A. T., Hammen, C. L., and Ingram, R. E. (1987). Issues and recommendations regarding use of the Beck Depression Inventory. *Cognitive Therapy and Research, 11*, 289–99.

Knight, R. G., Waal-Manning, H. J., and Spears, G. F. (1983). Some norms and reliability data for the State–Trait Anxiety Inventory and the Zung Self-Rating Depression scale. *British Journal of Clinical Psychology, 22*, 245–9.

Knoff, H. M., and Prout, H. T. (1985). The Kinetic Drawing System: A review and integration of the kinetic family and school drawing techniques. *Psychology in the Schools, 22*, 50–9.

Koppitz, E. M. (1968). *Psychological evaluation of children's human figure drawings*. Yorktown Heights, NY: Psychological Corporation.

Koppitz, E. M. (1984). *Psychological evaluation of human figure drawings by middle school pupils*. New York: Grune and Statton.

Kovacs, M. (1980/1981). Rating scales to assess depression in school-aged children. *Acta Paedopsychiatrica, 46*, 305–15.

Kovacs, M. (1992). *Children's depression inventory manual.* Los Angeles: Western Psychological Services.

Kraepelin, E. (1912). *Lehrbuch der psychiatrie.* Leipzig: Barth.

Langevin, R., and Stancer, H. (1979). Evidence that depression rating scales primarily measure a social undesirability response set. *Acta Psychiatrica Scandinavica, 59,* 70–9.

Levin, P. (1993). Assessing posttraumatic stress disorder with the Rorschach projective technique. In J. P. Wilson and B. Raphael (eds.), *International handbook of traumatic stress syndromes* (pp. 189–200). New York: Plenum Press.

Lewinsohn, P. M., Rohde, P., Seeley, J. R., and Hops, H. (1991). Comorbidity of unipolar depression: I. Major depression with dysthymia. *Journal of Abnormal Psychology, 100,* 205–13.

Lilienfeld, S. O., and Marino, L. (1999). Essentialism revisited: Evolutionary theory and the concept of mental disorder. *Journal of Abnormal Psychology, 108,* 3, 400–11.

Maffei, C., Fossate, A., Agostoni, I., Barraco, A., Bagnato, M., Deborah, D., Namia, C., Novella, L., and Petrachi, M. (1997). Interrater reliability and internal consistency of the Structured Clinical Interview for DSM-IV Axis II Personality Disorders (SCID-II), Version 2.0. *Journal of Personality Disorders, 11,* 3, 279–84.

Marton, P., Churchard, M., Kutcher, S., and Korenblum, M. (1991). Diagnostic utility of the Beck Depression Inventory with adolescent psychiatric outpatients and inpatients. *Canadian Journal of Psychiatry, 36,* 428–31.

Maziade, M., Roy, A. A., Fournier, J. P., Cliche, D., Merette, C., Caron, C., Garneau, Y., Montgrain, N., Shriqui, C., Dion, C., Nicole, L., Potvin, A., Lavallee, J. C., Pires, A., and Raymond, V. (1992). Reliability of best-estimate diagnosis in genetic linkage studies of major psychoses. *American Journal of Psychiatry, 149,* 1674–86.

Meehl, P. E. (1954). *Clinical vs. statistical prediction: a theoretical analysis and a review of the evidence.* Minneapolis: University of Minnesota Press.

Meehl, P. E. (1992). Factors and taxa, traits and types, differences of degree and differences of kind. *Journal of Personality, 60,* 117–74.

Meehl, P. E. (1995). Bootstrap taxometrics. *American Psychologist, 50,* 266–75.

Meehl, P. E. (1997). Credentialed persons, credentialed knowledge. *Clinical Psychology: Science and Practice, 4,* 91–8.

Meehl, P. E. (1999). Clarifications about taxometric method. *Applied and Preventive Psychology, 8,* 165–74.

Meehl, P. E., and Yonce, L. (1996). Taxometric analysis: II. Detecting taxonicity using covariance of two quantitative indicators in successive intervals of a third indicator (MAXCOV procedure). *Psychological Reports, 78,* 1091–1227.

Meloy, J. R., and Gacono, C. B. (1995). Assessing the psychopathic personality. In J. N. Butcher (ed.), *Clinical personality assessment* (pp. 410–22). New York: Oxford University Press.

Metalsky, G. I., and Joiner, Jr., T. E. (1992). Vulnerability to depressive symptomatology: A prospective test of the diathesis-stress and causal mediation components of the Hopelessness Theory of Depression. *Journal of Personality and Social Psychology, 63,* 667–75.

Metzger, R. L. (1976). A reliability and validity study of the State–Trait Anxiety Inventory. *Journal of Clinical Psychology, 32,* 2, 276–8.

Miller, I. W., Norman, W. H., Bishop, S. B., and Dow, M. G. (1986). The modified scale for suicidal ideation: Reliability and validity. *Journal of Consulting and Clinical Psychology, 54,* 724–5.

Mineka, S., Watson, D., and Clark, L. A. (1998). Comorbidity of anxiety and unipolar mood disorders. *Annual Review of Psychology, 49,* 377–412.

Mitchell, J., Trent, R., and McArthur, R. (1993). *Human Figure Drawing Test: An illustrated handbook for interpretation and standardized assessment of cognitive impairment.* Los Angeles, CA: Western Psychological Services.

Motta, R., Little, S., and Tobin, M. (1993). The use and abuse of human figure drawings. *School Psychology Quarterly*, 8, 162–9.

Naglieri, J. A. (1988). *Draw A Person: A quantitative scoring system*. San Antonio, TX: Psychological Corporation.

Nisbett, R., and Ross, L. (1980). *Human inference: strategies and shortcomings of social judgment*. Englewood Cliffs, NJ: Prentice-Hall.

Nixon, G. F., and Steffeck, J. C. (1977). Reliability of the State–Trait Anxiety Inventory. *Psychological Reports*, 40, 357–8.

Ottenbacher, K. (1981). An investigation of self-concept and body image in the mentally retarded. *Journal of Clinical Psychology*, 37, 415–18.

Oumitte, P. C., and Klein, D. N. (1995). Test–retest stability, mood–state dependence, and informant–subject concordance of the SCID-Axis II Questionnaire in a nonclinical sample. *Journal of Personality Disorders*, 9, 2, 105–11.

Palmer, L., Farrar, A. R., Valle, M., Ghahary, N., Panella, M., and DeGraw, D. (2000). An investigation of the clinical use of the House-Tree-Person projective drawings in the psychological evaluation of child sexual abuse. *Child Maltreatment: Journal of the American Professional Society on the Abuse of Children*, 5, 2, 169–75.

Petot, J. (2001). Interest and limitations of projective techniques in the assessment of personality disorders. *European Psychiatry*, 15 (Supplement 1), 11–14.

Prout, H. T., and Phillips, D. D. (1974). A clinical note: The Kinetic School Drawing. *Psychology in the Schools*, 11, 303–6.

Reich, J. H., and Noyes, R. (1987). A comparison of DSM-III personality disorders in acutely ill panic and depressed patients. *Journal of Anxiety Disorders*, 1, 123–31.

Renneberg, B., Chambless, D. L., Dowdall, D. J., and Fauerbach, J. A. (1992). The Structured Clinical Interview for DSM-III-R, Axis II and the Millon Clinical Multiaxial Inventory: A concurrent validity study of personality disorders among anxious outpatients. *Journal of Personality Disorders*, 6, 2, 117–24.

Reynolds, C. R., and Richmond, B. O. (1985). *Revised Children's Manifest Anxiety Scale (RCMAS) manual*. Los Angeles, CA: Western Psychological Services.

Riskind, J. H., Beck, A. T., Berchick, R. J., Brown, G., and Steer, R. A. (1987). Reliability of *DSM-III* diagnoses for major depression and generalized anxiety disorder using the Structured Clinical Interview for *DSM-III*. *Archives of General Psychiatry*, 44, 817–20.

Roback, H. B. (1968). Human figure drawings: Their utility in the clinical psychologist's armamentarium for personality assessment. *Psychological Bulletin*, 70, 1–19.

Robins, L., Helzer, J., Cottler, L., and Goldring, E. (1989). National Institute of Mental Health Diagnostic Interview Schedule, Version III Revised (DIS-III-R). St. Louis, MO: Washington University Press.

Robins, L. N., Helzer, J. E., Croughan, J. L., and Ratcliff, K. S. (1981). National Institute of Mental Health Diagnostic Interview Schedule. *Archives of General Psychiatry*, 38, 381–9.

Rohde, P., Lewinsohn, P. M., and Seeley, J. R. (1991). Comorbidity of unipolar depression: II. Comorbidity with other mental disorders in adolescents and adults. *Journal of Abnormal Psychology*, 100, 214–22.

Rorschach, H. (1921). *Psychodiagnostik*. Bern: Bircher (Hans Huber Verlag, trans. 1942).

Rudd, M. D., and Rajab, M. H. (1995). Specificity of the Beck Depression Inventory and the confounding role of comorbid disorders in a clinical sample. *Cognitive Therapy and Research*, 19, 51–68.

Scott, L. H. (1981). Measuring intelligence with the Goodenough–Harris Drawing Test. *Psychological Bulletin*, 89, 483–505.

Smith, D., and Dumont, F. (1995). A cautionary study: Unwarranted interpretations of the Draw-A-Person test. *Professional Psychology: Research and Practice*, 26, 298–303.

Spielberger, C. D. (1968). *Self-evaluation questionnaire. STAI Form X–2*. Palo Alto, CA: Consulting Psychologists Press.

Spielberger, C. D., Gorusch, R. L., and Lushene, R. E. (1970). *Manual for the State–Trait Anxiety Inventory*. Palo Alto, CA: Consulting Psychologists Press.

Spitzer, R. L., Endicott, J., and Robins, E. (1978). Research diagnostic criteria: Rationale and reliability. *Archives of General Psychiatry*, *35*, 773–82.

Stark, K., Schmidt, K., and Joiner, T. (1996). Parental messages and automatic self-statements among depressed and anxious children. *Journal of Abnormal Child Psychology*, *24*, 615–32.

Stawar, T. L., and Stawar, D. E. (1989). Kinetic Family Drawings and MMPI diagnostic indicators in adolescent psychiatric inpatients. *Psychological Reports*, *65*, 143–6.

Steer, R. A., Beck, A. T., Brown, G., and Berchick, R. J. (1987). Self-reported depressive symptoms that differentiate recurrent-episode major depression from dysthymic disorders. *Journal of Clinical Psychology*, *43*, 2, 246–50.

Steiner, J. L., Tebes, J. K., Sledge, W. H., and Walker, M. L. (1995). A comparison of the Structured Clinical Interview for DSM-III-R and clinical diagnoses. *Journal of Nervous and Mental Disease*, *183*, 6, 365–9.

Stukenberg, K. W., Dura, J. R., and Kiecolt-Glaser, J. K. (1990). Depression screening validation in an elderly, community-dwelling population. *Psychological Assessment*, *2*, 134–8.

Swann, W. B., Wenzlaff, R. M., Krull, D. S., and Pelham, B. W. (1992). Allure of negative feedback: Self-verification strivings among depressed persons. *Journal of Abnormal Psychology*, *101*, 293–305.

Tanaka-Matsumi, J., and Kameoka, V. A. (1986). Reliabilities and concurrent validities of popular self-report measures of depression, anxiety, and social desirability. *Journal of Consulting and Clinical Psychology*, *54*, 328–33.

Vandiver, T., and Sher, K. J. (1991). Temporal stability of the diagnostic interview schedule. *Psychological Assessment*, *3*, 277–81.

Van Hutton, V. (1994). *House-Tree-Person and Draw-A-Person as measures of abuse in children: A quantitative scoring system*. Odessa, FL: Psychological Assessment Resources.

Wakefield, J. C. (1999). Evolutionary versus prototype analyses of the concept of disorder. *Journal of Abnormal Psychology*, *108*, 3, 374–99.

Waller, N., and Meehl, P. E. (1998). *Multivariate taxometric procedures*. Thousand Oaks, CA: Sage.

Wanderer, Z. W. (1969). Validity of clinical judgments based on human figure drawings. *Journal of Consulting and Clinical Psychology*, *33*, 143–50.

Watson, D., Clark, L. A., and Carey, G. (1988). Positive and negative affectivity and their relation to anxiety and depressive disorders. *Journal of Abnormal Psychology*, *97*, 346–53.

Watson, D., Clark, L. A., and Tellegen, A. (1988). Development and validation of brief measures of positive and negative affect: The PANAS scales. *Journal of Personality and Social Psychology*, *54*, 1063–70.

Weiner, I. B. (1997). Current status of the Rorschach Inkblot Method. *Journal of Personality Assessment*, *68*, 5–19.

Weiner, I. B. (2000). Using the Rorschach properly in practice and research. *Journal of Clinical Psychology*, *56*, 3, 435–8.

Wood, J. M., Lilienfeld, S. O., Garb, H. N., and Nezworski, M. T. (2000a). Limitations of the Rorschach as a diagnostic tool: A reply to Garfield (2000), Lerner (2000), and Weiner (2000). *Journal of Clinical Psychology*, *56*, 3, 441–8.

Wood, J. M., Lilienfeld, S. O., Garb, H. N., and Nezworski, M. T. (2000b). The Rorschach test in clinical diagnosis: A critical review, with a backward look at Garfield (1947). *Journal of Clinical Psychology*, *56*, 3, 395–430.

VIGNETTE

Adult Clinical Assessment and Diagnosis

Anne K. Jacobs

Ruscio, J., and Ruscio, A. M. (2000). Informing the continuity controversy: A taxometric analysis of depression. *Journal of Abnormal Psychology*, *109*, 3, 473–87.

It is natural that in a description of how mental illness is assessed and diagnosed, a discussion would ensue concerning the DSM classification system, which is characterized principally by categorical diagnostic constraints. Joiner and Pettit (chapter 14, this volume) addressed the dimensional versus categorical debate regarding the current state of diagnosis and advocated the application of taxometric statistical procedures to psychopathology as a means of clarifying the degree to which currently employed diagnostic labels truly represent discrete categorical entities. A clear example of such an application can be found in the work of Ruscio and Ruscio, who analyzed two large clinical samples, each with a high base rate of depression and a wide range of symptom severity levels, using innovative taxometric procedures, MAXCOV (Maximum Covariance) and MAMBAC (Mean Above Minus Below A Cut) (Meehl, 1995).

While the samples had high base rates of depression, individuals nonsyndromal for major depression were also included in both studies. Participants in the first study were 996 male veterans who completed both the Beck Depression Inventory and the Self-Rating Depression Scale. The measurement scales on these two measures had items with too few levels to serve as input indicators, so the authors constructed appropriate input indicators using three different approaches: (a) summing a set of raw items from the same questionnaire, (b) summing items from the same questionnaire in pairs, and (c) creating cross-measure composite indicators. Nuisance covariance between resulting indicators was low.

The sample from the second study comprised Minnesota Multiphasic Personality Inventories (MMPI) scale scores obtained at the University of Minnesota Hospitals from 8,045 females and 5,662 males. Analyses were performed for the total sample, then separately for men and women to account for established gender differences in depression.

Three composite indicators were compiled from the MMPI items reflecting: (a) somatic/vegetative content, (b) depressed mood and anhedonia, and (c) feelings of worthlessness/guilt, impaired concentration and decision-making. All nuisance correlations between scales fell within the appropriate limits for taxometric procedures.

The results from both sets of analyses failed to support a depression taxon and pointed instead to the dimensionality of depression. The authors addressed the limitations of their study, the influence the results could have on the conceptualization of depression, and discussed the pros and cons of using a taxometric approach in assessment/diagnostic research. The strengths of the study conducted by Ruscio and Ruscio include:

- Application of taxometric procedures to a diagnostic category
- Use of large clinical samples with a broad range of ages
- Inclusion of both inpatient and outpatient samples
- Inclusion of participants with and without major depression
- Sample had high base rates of major depression and a wide range of symptom severity levels
- Analyzed three widely used measures with established reliability and validity
- Low nuisance covariance
- Analyzed men and women separately due to gender differences in depression literature
- Results challenge the manner in which the diagnostic category of depression is conceived

Reference

Meehl, P. E. (1995). Bootstraps taxometrics: Solving the classification problem in psychopathology. *American Psychologist, 50,* 266–75.

CHAPTER FIFTEEN

Therapy and Interventions Research with Children and Adolescents

Ric G. Steele and Michael C. Roberts

Psychotherapy with children and families involves a complex set of elements reflecting the multiple and interacting systems within which children function. Equally complex is the corpus of clinical research into whether psychotherapy and interventions benefit children, adolescents, and their families, and into the processes by which psychological change occurs. In this chapter we will provide the context for evaluating and conducting research into the processes and effects of child psychotherapy. The range of what is considered child psychotherapy includes the following:

1 Child–adolescent interventions (including individual psychotherapy, group psychotherapy, play therapy, behavioral and cognitive behavioral interventions, skills training, and psychopharmacology).
2 Parent interventions (including consultation and education/training).
3 Family interventions (including family therapy and systems, family empowerment/support).
4 School and community interventions (including consultation with social services, the legal system, and medical settings). (Roberts et al., 1998: 296)

Within these domains of child psychotherapy, Kazdin (1988) identified over 230 published forms of child therapy. Given this diversity of approaches and the complexity of the processes, the empirical foundations for psychotherapy become even more important. Based on Gordon Paul's (1967) axiom about psychotherapy, Saxe, Cross, and Silverman (1988) asserted that research into therapy for children should be oriented to establishing: "(a) what therapy [works], (b) under what conditions, (c) for which children, (d) at which developmental level, (e) with which disorders, (f) under what environmental conditions, and (g) with which concomitant parental, familial, environmental, or systems intervention" (p. 803). Fortunately, methodologies are similar for investigating these numerous and overlapping issues.

Early Studies of Child Psychotherapy Outcomes

The history of evaluation of child psychotherapy has been one of increasing sophistication in conceptualization and research methodology. Hans Eysenck (1952) provided a narrative review of the scientific and professional literature and concluded that child psychotherapy (typically psychoanalytically based at that time) did not improve children's functioning compared to children who were in no-therapy control groups. Levitt (1957, 1963) came to similar conclusions in later reviews. The early literature on child psychotherapy also contained many reports of case studies and experimental studies with small numbers of patients, using poorly constructed assessment instruments, lacking diagnostic rigor, with inadequate controls and comparisons. Advances in methodology have been made over time with the contributions of experimental psychology. The introduction of behavioral (and later cognitive-behavioral) techniques to develop a clinical psychology methodology for therapeutic outcomes, applicable regardless of the clinical researcher's theoretical orientation, also enhanced scientific methods. Current research is characterized by attention to the types of questions raised by Saxe, Cross, and Silverman (1988), with increased rigor in conceptualization, design, measurement, and analysis.

Empirically Supported Treatments

Of considerable importance has been the recent movement toward "empirically supported treatments." This increased interest derives from a variety of influences, including (a) a strong desire on the part of psychologists oriented to the scientist-practitioner model to enhance the scientific base for clinical practice (Calhoun et al., 1998; Davison, 1998); (b) a focus on accountability in both practice and research (Weisz et al., 2000); and (c) the policies of managed care organizations, which increasingly provide financial reimbursements only to those therapies and interventions with established utility. Other professional disciplines, such as medicine and social work, have also increased their reliance on evidence-based practice. ·

The Society of Clinical Psychology (Division 12) of the American Psychological Association initiated a project to identify psychological treatments that have empirical support for improving the functioning of those who receive the therapy (Chambless et al., 1996, 1998). The treatments were evaluated for the list of empirically supported treatments (ESTs) in order to improve the specificity of treatments for specific problems (Chambless and Ollendick, 2001). The criteria required (a) increased detail on the participant samples included in the research studies, (b) randomized clinical trials and/or single-case designs, (c) delineation of the therapy approach, typically through treatment manuals, and (d) replication by independent research teams. The EST reviewers place the treatments into two major categories: "well-established" and "probably efficacious" based on prescribed criteria. The initial and subsequent efforts on this project focused primarily on therapies for adult clients (Chambless et al., 1996, 1998). Applications of the template were extended to treatments for children, adolescents, and families in the activities of other groups, including the Society of Clinical Child and Adolescent Psychology (Division 53; Lonigan, Elbert, and Johnson, 1998), the Society of Pediatric Psychology (Division 54; Spirito, 1999), and the Hawaii Empirical Basis to Service Task Force (Chorpita et al., 2002). Chambless and Ollendick (2001) provided a fairly comprehensive summary of the EST reviews. The identification of ESTs is a process designed to find the most effective treatments for specific mental health problems and to help practitioners select which approaches to take with particular clients. The explicit delineation of acceptable methodological criteria is also helping increase the quality of treatment outcome research. The published summaries and periodic updates expose what has and what has not been established adequately.

The EST movement has been met with some controversy, in which opponents have raised concerns about the approach and implications for the practice of clinical psychology (e.g., Goldfried and Wolfe, 1996). Critics have suggested that EST criteria promote over-dependence on randomized clinical trials (RCTs) to establish efficacy and effectiveness (Blatt, 2001; Goldfried and Wolfe, 1996; Chambless and Ollendick, 2001), and that EST summaries create a separation between treatment outcomes research and clinical work as practiced in the "real world" (Blatt, 2001; Goldfried and Wolfe, 1996), such that there is a dilemma of interpretability and RCT generalization (Goldfried and Wolfe, 1996). We will not attempt to resolve this debate here, except to emphasize the contribution of strong research methodology in establishing the worth and utility of psychotherapy for children and adolescents – regardless of the theoretical underpinnings of any given intervention. The EST movement continues to evaluate (and improve) psychotherapeutic interventions. The APA Committee on Accreditation now includes training in ESTs in its program accreditation guidelines.

Consistent with Simons and Wildes (chapter 16, this volume), we will examine issues related to sample and treatment selection, comparison conditions, and outcome measures. However, given some of the unique characteristics of therapy and intervention among children, a number of additional concerns must be addressed. For example, the involvement of parents and/or third parties as participants or informants requires additional considerations involving selection and/or outcome measures. Further, developmental and contextual differences between therapy with adults and therapy with children require that some of the common issues of research design must be adapted. Thus, while we recognize that some aspects of research design are universal, this chapter will highlight research design and methodology that has potential to add to the knowledge base about what works in treating children and adolescents. Finally, to better illustrate the application of research methodology to child and adolescent populations, we will provide specific examples of investigations in order to illustrate some of the conceptual issues presented in this chapter.

Efficacy–Effectiveness

A distinction of conceptualizations of particular relevance in outcomes research has been that between *efficacy* and *effectiveness* (Chambless and Ollendick, 2001; Nathan, Stuart, and Dolan, 2000). Efficacy research measures outcomes of very well specified interventions with specific disorders or problems. Efficacy studies include (a) random assignment of participants who are carefully screened to increase similarity of problems, (b) clinical trial methodology, often with double blind designs, and (c) manualized treatments to increase specificity of therapy and treatment integrity.

Effectiveness research applies those therapeutic techniques found to be efficacious in preceding investigations to a broader population and in clinical service settings other than lab-based research clinics. Despite their more naturalistic settings, effectiveness studies still require methodological rigor and careful controls, including restricted specificity of diagnosis and treatments. Although most attention has been given to efficacy and effectiveness research issues (Nathan, Stuart, and Dolan, 2000), the Clinical Treatment and Services Research Workgroup of the National Institute of Mental Health (1998) has categorized two additional domains of treatment research as "practice research" and "service system research" (Street, Niederehe, and Lebowitz, 2000). Practice research examines "how and which treatments or services are provided to individuals within service systems and evaluates how to improve treatment or service delivery" (Clinical Treatment and Services Research Workgroup, 1998: 11). Service system research investigates how quality of care and treatment effects might be affected by different characteristics and structures of mental health service systems. Clinical child and pediatric psychology has not yet conducted adequate research into the efficacy and effectiveness of most of its widely practiced interventions, and much less in practice and service systems issues (Roberts, Brown, and Puddy, 2002).

Sample Selection

Sample selection lies at the very heart of research design for treatment outcome studies in child and adolescent populations, bearing upon both internal and external validity. With regard to internal validity, sample selection determines, in part, whether one may assume a causal relationship between treatment conditions and a given outcome (Lonigan, Elbert, and Johnson, 1998). That is, internal validity provides a mechanism for ascertaining the *efficacy* of a treatment (e.g., that treatment *A* is superior to treatment *B*, or to no treatment at all). Sample selection is equally important when one considers external validity, or the extent to which one may generalize research findings beyond the study sample. Unfortunately, in any intervention outcome study, internal validity and external validity are at odds with one another: limiting the variance within and across groups necessarily improves the clinical researcher's ability to demonstrate treatment effects (internal validity). However, such limitations also limit the degree to which one may generalize findings to a larger population with a greater range of variability (Goldfried and Wolfe, 1998).

Analog samples: Internal validity

A chief concern within the child treatment outcome literature is the degree to which outcome study samples resemble actual clinical patients as they present in the "real world" (Chorpita et al., 1998; Sifers et al., 2002). Often this concern is cast in terms of "analog" (i.e., participants who demonstrate some symptoms of a disorder, but who have not identified a need for therapy) versus "clinical" samples (i.e., those participants who have presented to a clinic for treatment of the identified condition). Because of obvious recruitment advantages, studies frequently employ analog samples to demonstrate the clinical efficacy of interventions. For example, participants are often recruited via newspaper advertisement or means other than self-initiated referral to a clinic. As noted by Kaslow and Thompson (1998), much of the literature in support of psychotherapy for children with "depression" is based on research conducted on children with "depressive symptoms" rather than syndrome-level depression. More recently, Asarnow, Jaycox, and Tompson (2001) reiterated this concern. Beyond recruitment advantages, the use of analog samples has the additional benefit of a decreased probability of comorbid or competing diagnostic conditions that may reduce or mask treatment effects.

Unfortunately, the use of recruited (or analog) samples may be significantly associated with reduced severity of presenting problems, thereby decreasing the external validity of the investigations. In fact, in a meta-analysis of treatment outcome studies among children, Weisz, Donenberg, et al. (1995) reported that clinical severity (i.e., analog vs. clinical sample) moderated the effect size of clinical outcomes. Studies conducted with analog samples demonstrated medium effect sizes, while studies conducted with clinical samples demonstrated smaller effect sizes. Weisz, Donenberg, et al. (1995) also noted that severity and setting were correlated, such that more severe cases tended to present to (and be recruited from) clinical settings, whereas less severe cases (i.e., analog samples) tended to be recruited in research settings. One implication of this finding is that studies conducted with analog samples may offer "inflated" estimates of therapeutic benefit (especially regarding the proportion of treated individuals who achieve recovery criteria by treatment termination), relative to what should be expected in clinical samples (Kazdin and Weisz, 1998).

"Real world" samples: External validity

The obvious – but obviously challenging – solution to the issue of poor external validity is to conduct treatment outcome studies with participants/clients who have identified a need for intervention. As one example of a study with strong external validity, Kaminer et al. (1998) examined the relative effectiveness of two modalities of outpatient group therapy designed to decrease the risk of relapse among dually diagnosed adolescents with substance abuse recruited from a partial hospital program. Similarly, several studies by Kendall and colleagues (e.g., Kendall, 1994; Kendall et al., 1997) demonstrated that intervention outcome research could be conducted with extremely high external and ecological validity without compromising experimental control across treatment conditions (i.e., generating all of their clients/participants from community referrals without recruitment or advertisement).

Comorbid problems

One concern that has been offered regarding the use of clinical samples is the fact that comorbid conditions (i.e., those diagnosed in addition to the presenting problem) may mitigate treatment effects for the symptoms or syndrome identified for treatment (Kendall et al., 1997). Further, Kazdin and Weisz (1998) noted that identifying cases for inclusion in treatment outcome studies with children is often more difficult than among adults due to the likelihood of comorbid problems being overlooked by referral parties (e.g., parents). This may be particularly true when an identified condition is particularly obvious (e.g., oppositional behavior) and potential comorbid conditions are less apparent (e.g., depressive symptoms).

Alternatively, because of the possibility of the comorbid conditions having untoward effects on treatment, individuals with identified comorbid conditions are often excluded from RCTs involving clinical samples. For example, in an investigation of three treatment approaches for adolescent depression, Brent et al. (1997) excluded individuals with comorbid conditions, including ongoing pharmacological therapy due to suicidal ideation, substance abuse, or ongoing sexual or physical abuse. As noted by these authors, the extent to which empirically supported therapies translate into practice settings, where the presentation of comorbid conditions is the norm rather than the exception, is often unknown.

Research conducted among clinical samples, rather than analog samples, and in which comorbidities are assessed and reported (rather than used as exclusionary criteria), is needed to strengthen the link between treatment outcome studies and clinical practice (Ollendick and King, 1998). For example, in a follow-up investigation of their 1997 findings, Brent et al. (1998) examined predictors of treatment efficacy in their clinical trial of three psychosocial treatments for depressive symptoms. Log-linear analyses indicated differential treatment outcome as a function of comorbid anxiety symptoms at the beginning of therapy, with anxious and depressed adolescents evidencing greater depressive symptoms at the end of therapy than adolescents who started therapy with depression alone. Further analyses revealed differences in treatment efficacy as a function of anxiety symptoms.

Reporting sample characteristics and analyses

With regard to the balance between internal and external validity, the detailed reporting of sample characteristics is tantamount to the issues of sample selection and recruitment. However, as noted by Chorpita et al. (1998), this balance may be more challenging within the child literature than within the adult literature because of the numerous parameters that remain "free to vary" (p. 7) in the child's environment. For example, Kazdin (1995) and Kazdin and Weisz (1998) noted that children receive psychological interventions in contexts that vary widely with respect to parental psychopathology and adjustment, as well as family functioning and characteristics (e.g., socioeconomic status; SES), and that these variations may influence treatment effects. The psychopharmacological literature provides an intriguing example of such an interaction: Yaryura-Tobias et al. (2000) reported on the differential efficacy of fluvoxamine for the treatment of obsessive-compulsive disorder (OCD) among (a) children with a parent who also had OCD versus (b) children with a parent with another Axis-I disorder or (c) children of parents with no diagnosed disorder. Results suggested greater treatment efficacy of fluvoxamine among the group of children with a parent with OCD, relative to the group with another or no parental psychopathology.

The extent to which moderators of treatment effects can be identified determines the degree to which the clinical researcher may understand differential effectiveness across samples (Kazdin, 1995; Kazdin and Weisz, 1998). Of particular note in the treatment outcome literature is the lack of information pertaining to cultural and/or racial differences within study samples (Chambless et al., 1996; US Department of Health and Human Services, 2001; Kaslow and Thompson, 1998; Sue, 1990). As a result, the current literature is characterized by a paucity of findings that address the relative therapeutic benefits of psychotherapies for children of color. Bernal and Scharrón-Del-Río (2001) recommend efficacy and effectiveness studies within specific ethnic groups, rather than the use of comparative approaches (across ethnic groups) because of methodological weaknesses – including poor conceptualization (e.g., "why should ethnicity matter?") – as well as reliance on the "deficit" model.

Obviously, many investigations will lack the necessary power to detect moderator effects (e.g., treatment by race interactions), and will be unable to investigate therapies within specific ethnic minority populations. Nevertheless, the reporting of sample characteristics provides the necessary information for analyses of aggregated results across samples (e.g., meta-analyses) to investigate such interactions (see Weisz, Weiss, et al., 1995, for an example of such an investigation). Sifers et al. (2002) noted that although age, gender, and ethnicity (or race) are frequently reported within the child and pediatric literature (≥ 63 percent of investigations sampled), other characteristics such as SES, attrition, and location were reported less frequently (i.e., < 50 percent of investigations sampled). These findings were consistent with those of Brestan and Eyberg (1998), who observed that fewer than half of studies reviewed (within the conduct problem treatment literature) reported the SES or racial/ethnic breakdown of the samples. Currently, the relatively poor reporting of specific sample characteristics limits the usefulness of meta-analytic studies designed to answer the question "What works, and for whom?" (Brestan and Eyberg, 1998; Weisz and Hawley, 1998; Weisz, Weiss, et al., 1995). As Kaslow and Thompson (1998) quipped, "there are no disadvantages to informing the reader of the client characteristics" (p. 153). Conversely, the advantages of accurate and complete reporting of sample characteristics may be substantial.

Treatment Selection

Given the existence of over 230 published therapies (Kazdin, 1988), the selection of which treatment to employ with a particular client becomes a difficult concern, and one with great importance for clinical research. Although the literature contains supportive research for behavioral interventions, in surveys of psychologists over time, clinicians have more frequently identified themselves as aligned with a "traditional" or "eclectic" treatment orientation rather than behavioral or cognitive-behavioral orientations (Kazdin, Siegel, and Bass, 1990; Koocher and Pedulla, 1977; Tuma and Pratt, 1982). Therapeutic outcomes investigators have noted the rift between clinical research and clinical practice (Kazdin et al., 1990; Weisz, Weiss, and Donenberg, 1992). Some commentators have interpreted the results of meta-analyses of therapeutic outcomes (e.g., Casey and Berman, 1985) as indicating that no one form of psychotherapy is proven more effective than another, although psychotherapy in general is found to be effective. This interpretation is also present in the adult psychotherapy literature, which led Luborsky (1995) to award the "dodo prize" (from *Alice in Wonderland*), in which the declaration is made that "everyone has won so all shall have prizes" (p. 106). Later meta-analyses of child, adolescent, and family therapy outcomes have indicated that children who receive therapy function better on average than do those who have not received needed interventions. Specifically, however, behavioral treatments have obtained stronger support in the research literature than have nonbehavioral treatments (Kazdin et al., 1990; Weisz et al., 1987; Weisz, Weiss, et al., 1995). (See chapter 10, this volume, for a discussion of meta-analytical procedures.)

Clearly, increasing the clinical relevance of the research designs and the basis of results from clinical settings (i.e., real-world clinics) will help close the gap between research and practice, as will the "aging out" of practitioners trained earlier in traditional techniques that have not received empirical support. As Shirk and Phillips (1991) emphasized, selection of a treatment for a child in need of service should be based on the potential for effecting change, not on the clinician's allegiance or loyalty to a theory or therapeutic modality.

Manualized Treatment

The use of a treatment manual is one of the hallmarks of EST criteria. As noted by Lonigan, Elbert, and Johnson (1998: 141),

> treatment manuals provide a means of specifying the intervention procedures conducted during the course of therapy. Manualized treatments can be as prescriptive as those that specify session-by-session activities, or they can simply represent a codified framework for a treatment approach in which the clinician chooses which techniques to apply to what issues in what session.

Manuals also detail the procedures and processes of therapy for other clinicians and researchers to conduct replication studies, to train novice therapists, and to disseminate protocols to other settings. The specificity in a manual is important to guide the therapeutic approach, as well as to enhance the clinician's ability to evaluate the fidelity to the manual. That is, fidelity checks are assessments that the treatment was delivered as specified by the investigators: a process that is easier if outlined in a manual. Fidelity should be a fundamental consideration in designing a therapeutic outcomes research project.

"Manualization" of treatment has been criticized because therapy is seen as more of an "art" and the manuals are viewed as too structured, restrictive, and inflexible (e.g., Strupp, 2001). Kendall (2001a, b; Kendall and Hudson, 2001) observed that manuals are not typically applied inflexibly, and that they serve as models of treatment, rather than rigid protocols that require no clinical judgment or skills. He demonstrated how treatment fidelity could be achieved with flexibility built into the model. Indeed, most EST manuals convey the fact that clinicians may change the procedures as indicated by the circumstances of a given case. In designing therapeutic outcomes research projects, the researcher needs to develop manuals (or models of intervention) and to assess actual treatment fidelity with the specified therapeutic approach. Some excellent examples of treatment manuals include parent–child interaction therapy (Hembree-Kigin and McNeil, 1995), children's anxiety disorders (Kendall et al., 1992), and multisystemic treatment for antisocial behavior (Henggeler et al., 1998).

Treatment Integrity/Fidelity

An important consideration for therapeutic outcomes research is that the study be conducted using methods that allow reliable replication of the treatment or intervention (Chambless and Hollon, 1998). Because of the assurance that therapy components *can* be reliably replicated by other clinicians, manualized treatment strategies and strategies that implement behavioral or cognitive behavioral components appear to be favored in the adult EST literature (Chambless and Ollendick, 2001). However, the use of manualized treatment strategies has received less universal endorsement within the child and pediatric literature as a necessary criterion for "well-established" or "probably efficacious" treatments (Lonigan, Elbert, and Johnson, 1998). This may reflect the reality that clients' development levels often vary considerably across samples and that, due to these developmental and contextual differences, treatments may use well-known behavioral or social learning principles that must be modified for each client (Kendall and Hudson, 2001). As discussed by Kendall (2001a, 2001b) and Wells et al. (2000), the use of a manualized intervention does not prevent flexibility within the goals and strategies outlined by the intervention manual.

Nevertheless, when a manualized treatment program is evaluated within the clinical literature, assurance of treatment integrity contributes to the level of confidence that may be placed in the intervention (Chorpita et al., 1998; Lonigan, Elbert, and Johnson, 1998). That is, demonstration that a particular therapy among children is more effective than another therapy (or no therapy) is predicated on the certainty that the therapy that was *performed* actually corresponds to the therapy *described* in the report or manual. Thus, not only is the researcher responsible for elucidating the form of therapy used; he or she is also accountable for providing evidence of treatment integrity for the given intervention(s).

Unfortunately, methods of demonstrating treatment integrity among child and adolescent samples vary both with regard to their clinical utility and the conclusions that one may draw. A common practice within the clinical child literature is to simply report the nature and quantity of supervision received by the study therapists. As noted by

Ingram and Riley (1998), information regarding the training and supervision of study therapists is of value, but objective evidence that the treatment administered corresponds with the treatment described in the manual or report is "more powerful" (p. 758). For example, Barkley et al. (2001) reported on the efficacy of a treatment strategy addressing parent/child communication among adolescents with ODD and ADHD. The authors indicated that training and supervision of therapists was provided before and during the treatment phase (respectively) and that audiotapes of a percentage of therapy sessions were reviewed to ensure treatment fidelity. Although the authors reported a mechanism by which treatment validity could be established, the reporting of the degree of adherence to the protocol would have been preferable.

Examples of treatment integrity measurement

Schumann et al. (1998) provided an excellent example of such reporting in their investigation of the efficacy of parent–child interaction therapy (PCIT). These authors reported that a primary observer randomly observed 50 percent of the sessions, and recorded each element of the therapy covered in each session. A second observer randomly selected 50 percent of the observed videotapes, to provide inter-observer reliability. Schumann et al. (1998) reported that accuracy of the therapy delivered was 97 percent with the treatment protocol, and average inter-observer reliability was 96 percent. Because of the method of ensuring and reporting treatment integrity, the clinical researcher can be relatively sure that the therapy evaluated by Schumann et al. (1998) was the same therapy reported in the PCIT manual (Eyberg and Durning, 1994). The employment of primary and secondary observers, and the reporting of inter-observer reliability, were particularly valuable in this case.

Other methods of adequately ensuring treatment fidelity exist as well. For example, in the Multimodal Treatment Study of Children with ADHD (MTA; Wells et al., 2000) the authors reported that study personnel that implemented behavioral and classroom procedures received ongoing supervision throughout the study period. Further, treatment algorithms designed to guide clinical decision-making were developed to reduce the effects of "site drift" across the multiple study locations. As noted by Wells et al. (2000), the development of such algorithms protected both the internal and external validity of the findings. These algorithms ensured that therapists across sites were administering equivalent forms of the therapies, and thus increase the confidence that can be placed in the assertion that the therapy itself was responsible for the observed change (i.e., internal validity). Likewise, adequate reporting of clinical decision-making criteria used in the study increases the likelihood that nonstudy personnel will administer an equivalent form of the therapy in clinical settings (i.e., generalizability).

Participant adherence to treatment

Beyond the assurance that the therapy delivered is the therapy described, questions of treatment adherence (i.e., participant adherence) must also be addressed to help ascertain the clinical significance of the results. Within treatment outcome studies, differential attrition across treatment conditions represents a significant threat to the internal validity of the investigation (Chambless and Hollon, 1998). Further, if sizable treatment effects were obtained for a sample with 80 percent attrition, questions regarding the generalizability of those findings would be suspect. As noted by Kazdin (1996), a significant number of children and families discontinue therapy before treatment goals can be sufficiently met. However, treatment termination and study attrition itself can be investigated to determine causes, correlates, and outcomes (e.g., Sobel et al., 2001).

Unfortunately, Chorpita et al. (1998) suggested that some of the steps taken to ensure internal validity of a study (e.g., monitoring, assessment, alternative treatment and control conditions) may reduce the likelihood of families remaining adherent to treatment or assessment protocols. This detrimental effect may be particularly problematic within families in which the child's symptoms are exceptionally challenging. That is, parents of children with severe symptoms may be less willing to remain in a waitlist control condition, or to remain in a treatment protocol that they perceive as inferior to other options (Chorpita et al., 1998). Such attrition may compromise internal or external validity. Research reports that include details of differential attrition (e.g., by treatment assignment, or by symptom severity) provide an advantage to the reader with regard to interpretation of findings (e.g., Barkley et al., 2001).

Further, efforts to obtain follow-up assessments from nonadherent families (i.e. "intent to treat" model; Flick, 1988) may address some issues of validity that result from attrition or exclusionary criteria. Specifically, inclusion of all randomized participants at follow-up, regardless of compliance with the treatment protocol, may protect clinical findings against possible bias due to differential attrition or to participant exclusion on the basis of comorbid conditions (Pocock, 1983). For example, in the analysis of treatment effects on symptoms of depression, Brent et al. (1997) included follow-up data from all randomized participants.

Comparison Conditions

A hallmark feature of research-supported psychotherapy is the demonstration of superiority to placebo or to other treatment conditions (Lonigan, Elbert, and Johnson, 1998). However, as noted by Chambless and Hollon (1998), empirical support for a therapy may be accomplished in a number of ways, including randomized control trials, controlled single-case experiments, or other time-sample designs. Each of these design models has strengths and weaknesses with regard to intervention research with children. Ultimately, the decision of which experimental design to use may determine the extent to which internal or external validity (i.e., efficacy vs. effectiveness) can be demonstrated (Lonigan, Elbert, and Johnson, 1998; Heard, Dadds, and Conrad, 1992).

With regard to the demonstration of treatment efficacy (i.e., "Does the therapy work?"), the argument is frequently made that RCTs are an "absolute" criterion (e.g., Lonigan, Elbert, and Johnson, 1998). Stated briefly, in RCT methodology, participants from a single population are randomly assigned to one of at least two differing treatment conditions. Random assignment to treatment conditions and equivalency of groups before treatment improves the likelihood that any observed treatment effects are due to differences in treatment conditions, rather than to inherent differences in the groups or to maturation effects.

However, whether an investigation demonstrates treatment efficacy or treatment effectiveness is determined in part by the comparison condition employed (Chambless and Hollon, 1998; Lonigan, Elbert, and Johnson, 1998). Specifically, Lonigan and colleagues suggested that studies comparing a treatment condition to a placebo or waitlist control demonstrate the efficacy of an intervention, whereas studies comparing multiple treatments tend to be more rigorous, and potentially demonstrate treatment effectiveness. Chambless and Hollon (1998) further noted that studies comparing a treatment to a placebo or to a no-treatment condition may help establish an intervention as efficacious, but that comparisons with other treatments may help clarify mechanisms by which therapies work. For example, Keating et al. (1983) randomly assigned thirty children with nocturnal enuresis to one of three treatment conditions or a waitlist control to determine the efficacy of the therapies for the reduction of bedwetting. No group differences (i.e., differences across treatment conditions) were observed, but all three treatment conditions did significantly better than the no-treatment control.

Rather than comparing treatment conditions to waitlist controls or to no therapy, Doleys et al. (1977) examined the relative effectiveness of two forms of therapy (dry-bed training vs. retention control training) for nocturnal enuresis. Unlike placebo-controlled studies, which demonstrate efficacy of treatments, investigations such as Doleys et al. (1977) provide evidence for the superiority of one therapy over another. Studies such as these may evidence greater external validity, because clients who present to actual clinics would probably not be assigned to a waitlist control. As such, these comparisons may reflect relative advantages between two therapies that would actually be used in the clinical setting.

Beyond distinguishing between efficacy and effectiveness studies, Kaslow and Thompson (1998) have recommended the use of *multi-component analyses* (often referred to as "dismantling" studies) to determine the specific aspects of therapies that effect change. Echoing this idea, Ollendick and King (1998) noted that the identification of the critical components of therapy may allow further refinement and development of interventions for children and adolescents. For example, Bollard and Nettlebeck (1982) examined the effectiveness of various components of therapy for nocturnal enuresis (e.g., urine alarm alone, urine alarm plus waking schedule, urine alarm plus retention control training). Similarly, Barkley et al. (2001) examined the effects of behavior management therapy (BMT) alone and BMT followed by problem-solving communication therapy (PSCT) on the amelioration of parent–adolescent conflict.

For many child intervention investigations, random assignment to treatment conditions is not possible. As treatment conditions approach those seen in an actual clinic, the pressure to assign a client to a known efficacious therapy (i.e., rather than placebo or waitlist control) increases. Thus, research conducted in clinical settings may not have the option of assigning clients to waitlist control conditions, or of random assignment to conditions. For example, Schiff et al. (2001) examined the effects of an intervention designed to reduce procedural pain among children with HIV-infection. For both pragmatic (i.e., small population) as well as ethical reasons (i.e., concerns about withholding treatment from children in pain) the authors utilized a single-group repeated measures design to examine treatment effectiveness. As a further example, Barkley et al. (2001) employed a quasi-random method of assigning families to one of two treatment conditions for parent–adolescent conflict management: sequentially referred or recruited families were assigned to treatment conditions in waves until both treatment conditions were filled.

As noted by Chambless and Hollon (1998), nonexperimental or quasi-experimental designs (e.g., Barkley et al., 2001; Schiff et al., 2001) are frequently more useful in determining effectiveness among empirically validated studies (i.e., does it work in the clinic?) than they are at demonstrating efficacy (i.e., does the therapy work under "ideal" conditions?). Nevertheless, efforts must be made to ensure internal validity (i.e., to demonstrate that treatment results are caused by the intervention). For example, studies employing quasi-experimental approaches or quasi-random assignment to groups must adequately demonstrate equivalency of groups prior to treatment. Barkley et al. (2001) examined pretreatment characteristics of families assigned to each of the two treatment conditions, and found no significant differences with regard to family composition, number of symptoms of ADHD or ODD, or parental report of inattention or aggressive behaviors (CBCL). However, slight differences between groups with regard to age of adolescent, grade in school, and IQ were reported and addressed by the authors. When such differences are found it is incumbent upon the researcher to address the possible confounding effects of these differences on the results.

For studies employing nonexperimental designs (e.g., Schiff et al., 2001), steps must be taken to demonstrate that the effects observed (i.e., change from pre- to posttreatment) are the result of the intervention and not due to maturation, history, or exposure. Such methods include adequate establishment of baseline (pretreatment) functioning, as well as demonstration of sustained posttreatment improvements in functioning. For example, Schiff et al. (2001) assessed observed distress, child-reported pain, and parental anxiety during HIV-related medical procedures at baseline, and again at three time-points post-intervention (scheduled procedure visits). Analyses included repeated measures ANOVAs for all three measures between baseline and each assessment session. (Single-case design methodology is discussed in greater detail in chapter 5, this volume.)

Outcome Measure Selection

Reporters of information

Perhaps more so than other aspects of methodology, outcome measure selection among children and adolescents may differ significantly from adult methodology. Owing primarily to the nature of referral and therapy for children, a fundamental distinction between selection of outcome measures among adults and children is "who to ask?"

Unlike adults, who generally refer themselves to psychotherapy, children are typically brought to therapy by a concerned caregiver or other adult. However, children and caregivers often do not agree on the nature of the referral problem. Yeh and Weisz (2001) reported that the majority of a large sample of outpatient parent–child pairs failed to agree on a single referral problem. Further, when problems were grouped into categories, more than one-third of pairs failed to agree on a single problem area. These results suggest that outcome measures that fail to take into account both parent and child perspectives may miss a significant source of variance within the sample. As noted by Kendall (1994), treatment outcome investigations that make use of multiple measures are preferable to those that utilize only one assessment measure. For example, in their investigation of a behavioral treatment for simple phobias in children, Heard, Dadds, and Conrad (1992) utilized self- and parent-report measures of symptomatology, as well as structured and nonstructured interviews, to assess treatment outcome.

Timing of measurement

A second methodological concern related to outcome measure selection is the timing of outcome assessment. Kazdin and Weisz (1998) have noted that the current literature tends to focus on assessments that occur immediately posttreatment. While information pertaining to post-therapy gains is informative, the degree to which there is maintenance of these gains over time is of at least equal concern. Further, longer-term assessment of outcomes may elucidate developmental trajectories of children who demonstrate short-term improvements following interventions (Pelham, Wheeler, and Chronis, 1998). As a rather extreme example, Long et al. (1994) examined the long-term (14-year) effects of a behavioral intervention given to noncompliant children between the ages of 2 and 7 and their mothers. Although selection bias may have had some impact on the findings, results indicated that in late adolescence/young adulthood the treatment sample was functioning as well as an age-matched nonclinical control group.

Criteria for treatment outcomes

Beyond timing of posttreatment assessment and follow-up is the question of exactly what constitutes improvement. That is, by what criteria is treatment outcome judged? One criticism with the current literature on child psychotherapy outcomes is the reliance on statistical significance rather than clinical significance (Kazdin and Weisz, 1998). That is, a therapy may prove statistically superior to placebo, and yet have little relevance to clinical practice (i.e., by virtue of producing very small, but statistically significant, improvements on target problems). Investigations of studies that have the potential to demonstrate clinically significant results are clearly superior to those that do not. For example, Kendall (1994) examined the efficacy of CBT for anxiety compared to a waitlist control group, and found that 64 percent of treated children, versus 5 percent of the waitlist control group, no longer met diagnostic criteria for a disorder at the end of therapy. However, the use of clinically relevant outcome criteria may still be less meaningful than indicators of improved functioning in the "real world" (i.e., functional improvement; Kazdin and Weisz, 1998).

One general model addressing outcome measures was advanced by Hoagwood et al. (1996) and addresses many of the issues noted above. This model categorizes measures of outcomes into five domains: symptoms, functioning, consumer perspectives, environmental contexts, and systems (SFCES). *Symptoms* include behavioral or emotional problems and diagnoses in terms of "number, type, frequency, or duration of specific symptoms" (p. 1060). *Functioning* includes adaptation of capacity to various settings (e.g., home, school, peer group) on a continuum of competence to impairment. The *consumer perspective* includes the subjective experiences of the child and family in treatment regarding quality of care and satisfaction, both generally and specifically. *Environment* refers to how the settings in which children function are modifiable. This intervention outcome may be the result of a direct targeting of the environment to change, as well as the side effects in these settings resulting from therapeutic changes in the child and family. *Systems* refers to the manner in which the care of children is organized and delivered, how various service components interact and change. Most outcome research can be placed into one of the SFCES domains. Jensen, Hoagwood, and Petti (1996) applied the SFCES model to review the literature in children's mental health research (and noted its sparseness). Roberts, Brown, and Puddy (2002) outlined a more detailed and inclusive model for categorizing (and guiding) outcomes and services delivery research, including seventeen categories of dependent measures for this type of research.

Conclusions

The recent impetus toward empirically supported interventions among children has received some criticism within the psychological community. However, the EST movement has the potential to bring a number of benefits to the child psychotherapy literature, including more ecologically and culturally valid treatment approaches. For such promises to be realized, however, future research into child and adolescent treatments must adhere to sound principles of research design. Of particular concern to the child literature is adequate description of study samples, including "standard" demographic information, as well as potential moderators of treatment effects. In addition, future child outcome studies must incorporate carefully chosen measures that translate into clinically relevant, if not functionally keyed, outcomes. Given the unique situation of children, who do not generally refer themselves to therapy, such outcomes will necessarily reflect child-reported as well as caregiver-reported changes in functioning. Relatedly, these outcome assessments should reflect not only immediate post-therapy gains, but also longer-term changes in maladaptive trajectories. Finally, investigations of the effectiveness of therapies among children and adolescents of color are sorely needed. Although examining race or culture as a moderator of treatment gains may be useful, specific efficacy and effectiveness studies within non-Caucasian samples may provide more ecologically valid results.

References

Asarnow, J. R., Jaycox, L. H., and Tompson, M. C. (2001). Depression in youth: Psychosocial interventions. *Journal of Clinical Child Psychology, 30*, 33–47.

Barkley, R. A., Edwards, G., Laneri, M., Fletcher, K., and Metevia, L. (2001). The efficacy of problem-solving communication training alone, behavior management training alone, and their combination for parent–adolescent conflict in teenagers with ADHD and ODD. *Journal of Consulting and Clinical Psychology, 69*, 926–41.

Bernal, G., and Scharrón-Del-Río, M. R. (2001). Are empirically supported treatments valid for ethnic minorities? Toward an alternative approach for treatment research. *Cultural Diversity and Ethnic Minority Psychology, 7*, 328–42.

Blatt, S. J. (2001). The effort to identify empirically supported psychological treatments and its implications for clinical research, practice, and training: Commentary on papers by Lester Luborsky and Hans H. Strupp. *Psychoanalytic Dialogues, 11*, 633–44.

Bollard, J., and Nettlebeck, T. (1982). A component analysis of dry-bed training for treatment of bedwetting. *Behaviour Research and Therapy, 20*, 383–90.

Brent, D. A., Kolko, D. J., Birmaher, B., Baugher, M., Bridge, J., Roth, C., and Holder, D. (1998). Predictors of treatment efficacy in a clinical trial of three psychosocial treatments for adolescent depression. *Journal of the American Academy of Child and Adolescent Psychiatry, 37*, 906–14.

Brent, D. A., Holder, D., Kolko, D., Birmaher, B., Baugher, M., Roth, C., Iyengar, S., and Johnson, B. A. (1997). A clinical psychotherapy trial for adolescent depression comparing cognitive, family, and supportive therapy. *Archives of General Psychiatry, 54*, 877–85.

Brestan, E. V., and Eyberg, S. M. (1998). Effective psychosocial treatments of conduct-disordered children and adolescents: 29 years, 82 studies, and 5,272 kids. *Journal of Clinical Child Psychology, 27*, 180–9.

Calhoun, K. S., Moras, K., Pilkonis, P. A., and Rehm, L. P. (1998). Empirically supported treatments: Implications for training. *Journal of Consulting and Clinical Psychology, 66*, 151–62.

Casey, R. J., and Berman, J. S. (1985). The outcome of psychotherapy with children. *Psychological Bulletin, 98*, 388–400.

Chambless, D. L., and Hollon, S. D. (1998). Defining empirically supported therapies. *Journal of Consulting and Clinical Psychology, 66*, 7–18.

Chambless, D. L., and Ollendick, T. H. (2001). Empirically supported psychological interventions: Controversies and evidence. *Annual Review of Psychology, 52*, 685–716.

Chambless, D. L., Sanderson, W. C., Shoham, V., Johnson, S. B., Pope, K. S., Crits-Christophe, P., Baker, M., Johnson, B., Woody, S. R., Sue, S., Beutler, L., Williams, D. A., and McCurry, S. (1996). An update on empirically validated therapies. *Clinical Psychologist, 49*, 5–18.

Chambless, D. L., Baker, M. J., Baucom, D. H., Beutler, L. E., Calhoun, K. S., Crits-Christophe, P., Daiuto, A., DeRubeis, R., Detweiler, J., Haaga, D. A. F., Johnson, S. B., McCurry, S., Mueser, K. T., Pope, K. S., Sanderson, W. C., Shoham, V., Stickle, T., Williams, D. A., and Woody, S. R. (1998). Update on empirically validated therapies II. *Clinical Psychologist, 51*, 3–16.

Chorpita, B. F., Barlow, D. H., Albano, A. M., and Daleiden, E. L. (1998). Methodological strategies in child clinical trials: Advancing the efficacy and effectiveness of psychosocial treatments. *Journal of Abnormal Child Psychology, 26*, 7–16.

Chorpita, B. F., Yim, L. M., Donkervoet, J. C., Arendorfer, A., Amundsen, M. J., McGee, C., et al. (2002). Toward large-scale implementation of empirically supported treatments for children: A review and observations by the Hawaii Empirical Basis to Services Task Force. *Clinical Psychology: Science and Practice*, *9*, 165–90.

Clinical Treatment and Services Research Workgroup, the National Advisory Mental Health Council, National Institute of Mental Health (1998). Bridging science and service. Bethesda, MD: National Institutes of Health. Retrieved: December 22, 2000 from http://nimh.nih.gov/research/bridge.htm.

Davison, G. C. (1998). Being bolder with the Boulder model: The challenge of education and training in empirically supported treatments. *Journal of Consulting and Clinical Psychology*, *66*, 163–7.

Doleys, D. M., Ciminero, A. R., Tollison, J. W., Williams, C. L., and Wells, K. C. (1977). Dry-bed training and retention control training: A comparison. *Behavior Therapy*, *8*, 541–8.

Eyberg, S. M., and Durning, P. (1994). Parent–child interaction therapy: Procedures manual. Unpublished manuscript, University of Florida.

Eysenck, H. J. (1952). The effects of psychotherapy: An evaluation. *Journal of Consulting Psychology*, *16*, 319–24.

Flick, S. N. (1988). Managing attrition in clinical research. *Clinical Psychology Review*, *8*, 499–515.

Goldfried, M. R., and Wolfe, B. E. (1996). Psychotherapy practice and research: Repairing a strained alliance. *American Psychologist*, *51*, 1007–16.

Goldfried, M. R., and Wolfe, B. E. (1998). Toward a more clinically valid approach to therapy research. *Journal of Consulting and Clinical Psychology*, *66*, 143–50.

Heard, P. M., Dadds, M. R., and Conrad, P. (1992). Assessment and treatment of simple phobias in children: Effects on family and marital relationships. *Behaviour Change*, *9*, 73–82.

Hembree-Kigin, T. L., and McNeil, C. B. (1995). *Parent–child interaction therapy*. New York: Plenum.

Henggeler, S. W., Schoenwald, S. K., Borduin, C. M., Rowland, M. D., and Cunningham, P. B. (1998). *Multisystemic treatment of antisocial behavior in children and adolescents*. New York: Guilford Press.

Hoagwood, K., Jensen, P. S., Petti, T., and Burns, B. J. (1996). Outcomes of mental health care for children and adolescents: I. A comprehensive conceptual model. *Journal of the American Academy of Child and Adolescent Psychiatry*, *35*, 1055–63.

Ingram, J. C., and Riley, G. (1998). Guidelines for documentation of treatment efficacy for young children who stutter. *Journal of Speech, Language, and Hearing Research*, *41*, 753–70.

Jensen, P. S., Hoagwood, K., and Petti, T. (1996). Outcomes of mental health care for children and adolescents: II. Literature review and application of a comprehensive model. *Journal of the American Academy of Child and Adolescent Psychiatry*, *35*, 1064–77.

Kaminer, Y., Blitz, C., Burleson, J. A., Kadden, R. M., and Rounsaville, B. J. (1998). Measuring treatment process in cognitive-behavioral and interactional group therapies for adolescent substance abusers. *Journal of Nervous and Mental Disorders*, *186*, 407–13.

Kaslow, N. J., and Thompson, M. P. (1998). Applying the criteria for empirically supported treatments to studies of psychosocial interventions for child and adolescent depression. *Journal of Clinical Child Psychology*, *27*, 146–55.

Kazdin, A. E. (1988). *Child psychotherapy: Developing and identifying effective treatments*. Elmsford, NY: Pergamon Press.

Kazdin, A. E. (1995). Scope of child and adolescent psychotherapy research: Limited sampling of dysfunctions, treatments, and client characteristics. *Journal of Clinical Child Psychology*, *24*, 125–40.

Kazdin, A. E. (1996). Dropping out of child psychotherapy: Issues for research and implications for practice. *Clinical Child Psychology and Psychiatry*, *1*, 133–56.

Kazdin, A. E., and Weisz, J. R. (1998). Identifying and developing empirically supported child and adolescent treatments. *Journal of Consulting and Clinical Psychology, 66*, 19–36.

Kazdin, A. E., Siegel, T. C., and Bass, D. (1990). Drawing on clinical practice to inform research on child and adolescent psychotherapy: Survey of practitioners. *Professional Psychology: Research and Practice, 21*, 189–98.

Kazdin, A. E., Bass, D., Ayers, W. A., and Rodgers, A. (1990). Empirical and clinical focus of child and adolescent psychotherapy research. *Journal of Consulting and Clinical Psychology, 60*, 733–47.

Keating, J., Butz, R., Burke, E., and Heimberg, R. (1983). Dry-bed training without a urine alarm: Lack of effect of setting and therapist contact with child. *Journal of Behaviour Therapy and Experimental Psychiatry, 14*, 109–15.

Kendall, P. C. (1994). Treating anxiety disorders in children: Results of a randomized clinical trial. *Journal of Consulting and Clinical Psychology, 62*, 100–10.

Kendall, P. C. (2001a). President's message: Pros and cons of manual-based treatments. *Clinical Child and Adolescent Psychology Newsletter, 16*, 1, 1–3.

Kendall, P. C. (2001b). President's message: Flexibility within fidelity. *Clinical Child and Adolescent Psychology Newsletter, 16*, 2, 1–3, 5.

Kendall, P. C., and Hudson, J. L. (2001). President's message: Working with families, flexibility. *Clinical Child and Adolescent Psychology Newsletter, 16*, 3, 1–2, 10.

Kendall, P. C., Flannery-Schroeder, E., Panichelli-Midel, S. M., Southam-Gerow, M., Henin, A., and Warman, M. (1997). Therapy for youths with anxiety disorders: A second randomized trial. *Journal of Consulting and Clinical Psychology, 65*, 366–80.

Kendall, P. C., Chansky, T. E., Kane, M. T., Kim, R., Kortlander, E., Ronan, K. R., Sessa, F. M., and Siqueland, L. (1992). *Anxiety disorders in youth: Cognitive-behavioral interventions.* Needham Heights, MA: Allyn and Bacon.

Koocher, G. P., and Pedulla, B. M. (1977). Current practices in child psychotherapy. *Professional Psychology, 8*, 275–87.

Levitt, E. E. (1957). The results of psychotherapy with children: An evaluation. *Journal of Consulting Psychology, 32*, 286–9.

Levitt, E. E. (1963). Psychotherapy with children: A further evaluation. *Behavior Research and Therapy, 60*, 326–9.

Long, P., Forehand, R., Wierson, M., and Morgan, A. (1994). Does parent training with young noncompliant children have long-term effects? *Behaviour Research and Therapy, 32*, 101–7.

Lonigan, C. J., Elbert, J. C., and Johnson, S. B. (1998). Empirically supported psychosocial interventions for children: An overview. *Journal of Clinical Child Psychology, 27*, 138–45.

Luborsky, L. (1995). Are common factors across different psychotherapies the main explanation for the Dodo bird verdict that "Everyone has won so all shall have prizes"? *Clinical Psychology: Science and Practice, 2*, 106–9.

Nathan, P. E., Stuart, S. P., and Dolan, S. L. (2000). Research on psychotherapy efficacy and effectiveness: Between Scylla and Charybdis? *Psychological Bulletin, 126*, 964–81.

Ollendick, T. H., and King, N. J. (1998). Empirically supported treatments for children with phonic and anxiety disorders: Current status. *Journal of Clinical Child Psychology, 27*, 156–76.

Paul, G. L. (1967). Outcome research in psychotherapy. *Journal of Consulting Psychology, 31*, 109–18.

Pelham, W. E., Wheeler, T., and Chronis, A. (1998). Empirically supported psychosocial treatments for attention deficit hyperactivity disorder. *Journal of Clinical Child Psychology, 27*, 190–205.

Pocock, S. J. (1983). *Clinical Trials: A practical approach.* New York: John Wiley and Sons.

Roberts, M. C., Brown, K. J., and Puddy, R. W. (2002). Service delivery issues and program evaluation in pediatric psychology. *Journal of Clinical Psychology in Medical Settings, 9,* 3–13.

Roberts, M. C., Carlson, C. I., Erickson, M. T., Friedman, R. M., La Greca, A. M., Lemanek, K. L., Russ, S. W., Schroeder, C. S., Vargas, L. A., and Wohlford, P. F. (1998). A model for training psychologists to provide services for children and adolescents. *Professional Psychology: Research and Practice, 29,* 293–9.

Saxe, L., Cross, T., and Silverman, N. (1988). Children's mental health: The gap between what we know and what we do. *American Psychologist, 43,* 800–7.

Schiff, W. B., Holtz, K. D., Peterson, N., and Rakusan, T. (2001). Effect of an intervention to reduce procedural pain and distress for children with HIV infection. *Journal of Pediatric Psychology, 26,* 417–28.

Schumann, E. M., Foote, R. C., Eyberg, S. M., Boggs, S. R., and Algina, J. (1998). Efficacy of Parent–Child Interaction Therapy: Interim report of a randomized trial with short-term maintenance. *Journal of Clinical Child Psychology, 27,* 34–45.

Shirk, S. R., and Phillips, J. S. (1991). Child therapy training: Closing gaps with research and practice. *Journal of Consulting and Clinical Psychology, 59,* 766–76.

Sifers, S. K., Puddy, R. W., Warren, J. S., and Roberts, M. C. (2002). Reporting of demographics, methodology, and ethical procedures in journals in pediatric and child psychology. *Journal of Pediatric Psychology, 27,* 19–25.

Sobel, A. B., Roberts, M. C., Rayfield, A., Bernard, M. U., and Rapoff, M. A. (2001). Evaluating outpatient pediatric psychology services in a primary care setting. *Journal of Pediatric Psychology, 26,* 395–405.

Spirito, A. (1999). Introduction: Special series on empirically supported treatments in pediatric psychology. *Journal of Pediatric Psychology, 24,* 87–90.

Street, L. L., Niederehe, G., and Lebowitz, B. D. (2000). Toward a greater public health relevance for psychotherapeutic intervention research: An NIMH workshop report. *Clinical Psychology: Science and Practice, 7,* 127–37.

Strupp, H. S. (2001). Implications of the empirically supported treatment movement for psychoanalysis. *Psychoanalytic Dialogues, 11,* 605–19.

Sue, D. W. (1990). Culture-specific strategies in counseling: A conceptual framework. *Professional Psychology: Research and Practice, 21,* 424–33.

Tuma, J. M., and Pratt, J. M. (1982). Clinical child psychology practice and training: A survey. *Journal of Clinical Child Psychology, 11,* 27–34.

US Department of Health and Human Services (2001). *Mental health: Culture, race, and ethnicity – A supplement to mental health: A Report of the Surgeon General.* Rockville, MD: US Department of Health and Human Services, Public Health Service, Office of the Surgeon General.

Weisz, J. R., and Hawley, K. M. (1998). Finding, evaluating, refining, and applying empirically supported treatments for children and adolescents. *Journal of Clinical Child Psychology, 27,* 206–16.

Weisz, J. R., Weiss, B., and Donenberg, G. R. (1992). The lab versus the clinic: Effects of child and adolescent psychotherapy. *American Psychologist, 47,* 1578–85.

Weisz, J. R., Donenberg, G. R., Han, S. S., and Weiss, B. (1995). Bridging the gap between laboratory and clinic in child and adolescent psychotherapy. *Journal of Consulting and Clinical Psychology, 63,* 688–701.

Weisz, J. R., Weiss, B., Alicke, M. D., and Klotz, M. L. (1987). Effectiveness of psychotherapy with children and adolescents: A meta-analysis for clinicians. *Journal of Consulting and Clinical Psychology, 55,* 542–9.

Weisz, J. R., Hawley, K. M., Pilkonis, P. A., Woody, S. R., and Follette, W. C. (2000). Stressing the (other) three Rs in the search for empirically supported treatments: Review procedures, research quality, relevance to practice and the public interest. *Clinical Psychology: Science and Practice, 7*, 243–58.

Weisz, J. R., Weiss, B., Han, S. S., Granger, D. A., and Morton, T. (1995). Effects of psychotherapy with children and adolescents revisited: A meta-analysis of treatment outcome studies. *Psychological Bulletin, 117*, 450–68.

Wells, K. C., Pelham, W. E., Kotkin, R. A., Hoza, B., Abikoff, H. B., Abramowitz, A., Arnold, L. E., Cantwell, D. P., Conners, C. K., Carmen, R. D., Elliott, G., Greenhill, L. L., Hechtman, L., Hibbs, E., Hinshaw, S. P., Jensen, P. S., March, J. S., Swanson, J. M., and Schiller, E. (2000). Psychosocial treatment strategies in the MTA Study: Rationale, methods, and critical issues in design and implementation. *Journal of Abnormal Child Psychology, 28*, 483–505.

Yaryura-Tobias, J. A., Grunes, M. S., Walz, J., and Neziroglu, F. (2000). Parent obsessive-compulsive disorder as a prognostic factor in a yearlong fluvoxamine treatment in childhood and adolescent obsessive compulsive disorder. *International Clinical Psychopharmacology, 15*, 163–8.

Yeh, M., and Weisz, J. R. (2001). Why are we here at the clinic? Parent–child (dis)agreement on referral problems at outpatient treatment entry. *Journal of Consulting and Clinical Psychology, 69*, 1018–25.

VIGNETTE

Therapy and Interventions Research with Children, Youth, and Families

Anne K. Jacobs

Kendall, P. C., Flannery-Schroeder, E., Panichelli-Mindel, S. M., Southam-Gerow, M., Henin, A., and Warman, M. (1997). Therapy for youths with anxiety disorders: A second randomized clinical trial. *Journal of Consulting and Clinical Psychology*, 65, 3, 366–80.

Kendall and colleagues conducted a methodologically exemplar study that illustrates many of the recommendations for conducting research on therapy with children, youth, and family described by Steele and Roberts (chapter 15, this volume). This investigation was a replication study and extension of a manualized treatment program for children with anxiety disorders. The participants were children aged 9–13 years who received a primary diagnosis of generalized anxiety disorder, social phobia, or separation anxiety disorder. Participants were referred through clinics, counselors, and media descriptions and all met DSM-IV diagnostic criteria for a primary anxiety disorder. Children with comorbid disorders were included, thus making the sample more reflective of children typically seen in clinic settings. Study children were randomly assigned to a cognitive-behavioral treatment group or a waiting-list control group, and assessments were conducted following treatment and at one-year follow-up. The retention rate was high, with over 90 percent of the original sample participating at the follow-up. The sample of children with complete data was diverse in terms of ethnicity and family socioeconomic level. Efforts were taken to control for any effects of outside treatment, as children in the control group were not included in the sample if their parents had secured alternative treatment.

Kendall and his colleagues expanded the scope of outcome measures beyond mere self-report of behavior. Multimethod assessment was employed, using feedback from the children, their parents, teachers, and videotapes of child behaviors during an anxiety-provoking task. The researchers used well-established measures (e.g., Child Behavior Checklist, Children's Depression Inventory) that were appropriate for the age of the children. In addition to the various measures of child behavior, children rated their relationship with their therapists and therapists rated the amount, degree, and nature of parental involvement. The cognitive-behavioral treatment manual was used in a flexible manner that was sensitive to client age, intellectual ability, and family factors. In reference to treatment integrity, two experienced cognitive-behavioral therapists listened to 15 percent of the audiotaped sessions and found 100 percent adherence to session goals.

A series of ANOVAs and MANOVAs run to examine treatment outcomes was appropriate both for the number of participants and the study research questions. Possible moderators of treatment effects were hypothesized and explored. Treatment effects were discussed in terms of both statistical and clinical significance. In addition to comparing pretreatment and posttreatment scores, Kendall and his colleagues compared the posttreatment scores of the treatment group to those of children randomly assigned to a waitlist control group. Statistically significant difference emerged for behavior observations and self-, parent-, and teacher-reports. Not only did posttreatment scores in the treatment condition show substantial improvement over pretreatment scores, but posttreatment scores were significantly better than postwaiting-list scores. Outcome measures were administered again one year after posttreatment to examine the durability of treatment effects. Posttreatment and follow-up scores for child-report measures did not differ significantly. Similar maintenance of treatment effects was shown for parent-report measures. Comorbid status did not emerge as a moderator of treatment outcomes or one-year follow-up scores. Other factors that may influence outcomes, such as children's ratings of the therapeutic relationship and therapist ratings of parental involvement, did not significantly influence treatment gains or maintenance scores. This study by Kendall and his colleagues stands out as an exemplar work of therapy research with children based upon the following considerations:

- Participants presented with comorbid disorders, reflecting more typical clinical samples
- Developmentally sensitive, reliable, and valid measures
- Use of multiple informants and methods of assessment
- Use of a manualized treatment in a flexible manner
- Reported treatment integrity data
- Appropriate statistics used for sample size and research questions
- Tested possible moderators of treatment effects
- Comparison to a control group
- One-year follow-up of treatment effects with high retention rate of participants
- Results add to scientific literature and are useful in a clinic setting

CHAPTER SIXTEEN

Therapy and Interventions Research with Adults

Anne D. Simons and Jennifer E. Wildes

Introduction

The history of psychotherapy research is relatively brief. Though there may be some disagreement regarding its exact date of origin, a reasonable date of birth might be the publication of Hans Eysenck's groundbreaking "The Effects of Psychotherapy: An Evaluation" (Eysenck, 1952). This article reviewed data from 24 studies of 7,000 patients receiving various forms of psychotherapy in order to address the question, does psychotherapy work? The importance of this article (and subsequent follow-up pieces in 1960 and 1969) cannot be overstated. It represented the first time anyone had attempted to use even quasi-empirical methods to evaluate the effects of psychotherapy. Eysenck's answer to the "does it work?" question was for the most part negative. Indeed, in the 1960 article, Eysenck wrote, "the therapeutic effects of psychotherapy are small or non-existent"; he recommended that psychologists not be trained in an activity of such doubtful value. Eysenck's articles did not go unnoticed. Critics charged that his methods were flawed, his interpretations were biased, and that he failed to include some of the psychotherapies which were new on the scene (especially those based on learning theory which were achieving better results than classic psychoanalytic therapies) (Bergin, 1971; Garfield, 1981). Criticisms of his methods notwithstanding, Eysenck's article posed a very real challenge to devotees of psychotherapy to prove its worth.

Fifty years after Eysenck, the psychotherapy research picture is quite different. Eysenck's review covered psychoanalysis, nondirective psychotherapy, eclectic psychotherapy, and treatment by general practitioners. The patients in the review were primarily diagnosed as "neurotic." Today, it is estimated that there are about 400 different types of psychotherapy, many of which were only beginning to emerge in Eysenck's day, and the old

DSM designation of "neurosis" has been replaced in DSM-IV by a number of related diagnostic categories. In other words, neither the therapies nor the patients are the same as those included in Eysenck's review. Further, Eysenck's rough and subjective categorization of patient outcomes (i.e., uncured, improved, very much improved, and cured) has been supplanted by sophisticated assessment measures of clinical outcomes and advanced statistical procedures for analyzing change (Jacobson et al., 1999). Finally, the field has become far more knowledgeable about what constitutes an appropriate control condition against which to compare various forms of psychotherapy. One of the strongest criticisms of Eysenck's work concerns his estimate of the rate of spontaneous remission. Eysenck put this number, representing the proportion of patients who would improve without treatment, at 66 percent. For most disorders, of course, the number is now rarely estimated to be more than half that (i.e., a spontaneous remission rate of about one-third). Certainly, today's clinical researchers possess information that is more reliable than Eysenck's ballpark estimates regarding the untreated course of relevant clinical disorders.

Although much has changed since Eysenck's day, one thing has remained quite constant: an urgent need for evidence that psychotherapy is effective. A prominent voice in the psychotherapy research community, Sol Garfield, has suggested that we have now entered an "age of accountability" for psychotherapy, and has proposed that the rallying cry for this age could be, "let scientific evaluation make determinations about what treatments, provided by whom, are best applied to what types of client problems" (Garfield, 1994). Current students of psychotherapy may not find this suggestion particularly noteworthy, inasmuch as many have come of age in the current era of managed healthcare, in which practice guidelines and training include an emphasis on empirically supported treatments. However, in the not-so-distant past it was far more common for nonempirical criteria to serve as the major determinants of what students were taught and what clinicians practiced. As pointed out by Beutler and Davison (1995), two of the most common criteria traditionally used to judge therapies have been *face validity* (i.e., "it looks good and is logical") and *consensual validity* ("everyone knows it's true"). A variation on such themes is reference to one's own experience ("I do this therapy and I know it works"). As Garfield (1994) wryly observed, "In the past, few psychotherapists ever questioned the efficacy of psychotherapy, that is, they never questioned the efficacy of their own therapy, although they may have had doubts about the therapy of others!"

The historical antecedent for this anti-research stance towards psychotherapy is fully captured in a letter that Talley, Strupp, and Butler (1994) reproduced in their book *Psychotherapy: Research and Practice*. This was a letter dated February 2, 1934 from Sigmund Freud to Sol Rosenzweig. Rosenzweig had written Freud to share with him the results of studies he had conducted on some of the basic tenets of psychoanalytic theory. Freud's response?

> I have examined your experimental studies for the verification of psychoanalytic propositions with interest. I cannot put much value on such confirmation because the abundance of reliable observations on which these propositions rest makes them independent of experimental verification. Still, it can do no harm.

The situation has changed dramatically. Today, there is a very real demand for results – for *accountability* – from a wide range of stakeholders, including insurance companies, funding agencies, policy planners, researchers, therapists, and most importantly, patients. Simply put, there is a demand for "proof" that psychotherapy works.

Eysenck began with the deceptively simple question of whether psychotherapy is any more effective than no treatment. Over time, his seminal question (*does it work?*) has been revealed as overly simplistic and overly broad. Hans Strupp provides a useful analogy to illustrate why this question cannot meaningfully guide research. When evaluating the effects of surgery, one would never ask, "does a knife work?" Rather, one would need to know the answer to a host of additional questions. In whose hands? Does training matter? Does it work better or worse with patients receiving appendectomies or those with lower back pain? And so on. As applied to psychotherapy, this analogy suggests that Eysenck's query must be rewritten into a number of smaller and more specific questions. And this is exactly what has happened. Gordon Paul penned one of the first rewrites, rephrasing the *does it work?* question as, "what treatment, by whom, is most effective for this individual, with that specific problem, under what set of circumstances?". And while it would be difficult (if not impossible) to fully address this multipart question with a single study, the question provides a more differentiated, and thus more useful, framework for thinking about psychotherapy research.

There are several other questions that psychotherapy research can, does, and should address. Once research has demonstrated that a particular psychotherapy does have an impact (it works), the mechanisms and processes through which these effects are achieved can be investigated (*how* and *why* does this particular therapy work?), the conditions under which effectiveness is increased or decreased (what are the moderators of therapeutic change?) and the duration of effects can be determined (*how long* do the effects last?). Therapy research can also contribute to our knowledge about both adaptive and maladaptive human functioning in general. This chapter is dedicated to a presentation and discussion of these and other questions for psychotherapy research as well as the methodology required for addressing these questions.

Evaluating Outcomes: Does it Work?

Implicitly embedded in the claim, *Psychotherapy X works*, is the clause, "better than nothing." In other words, patients who receive Psychotherapy X will be better off (as indicated by measures of meaningful outcomes) than they would be if they did not receive this therapy. However, testing this claim is not so straightforward, in part because the same patients clearly cannot both receive and *not* receive Psychotherapy X. Therefore, the research design requires the use of two nonoverlapping groups of patients, one which receives the intervention and the other which does not. The null hypothesis in this design could be stated as "measures of outcome will not differ between patients who receive Psychotherapy X and those who do not"; likewise, the experimental hypothesis is that "measures of outcome *will* differ between the patients who receive Psychotherapy X and those patients who do not." One critical assumption implicit in such a design is the supposition that patients treated with Psychotherapy X and the patients not treated with Psychotherapy X are identical with respect to all other factors that might influence treatment outcomes (e.g., diagnosis, severity, etc.).

Obviously, however, all patients are not identical. Individual differences on variables that are known (or hypothesized) to influence clinical outcomes – such as positive treatment expectancy, co-occurring diagnoses, degree of impairment (or symptom severity), clinical history, and so forth – are all to be expected. Why is this a problem? Consider the following: in a study of the sort just described, patients who received Treatment X were observed to look better, at the end of the study period, than those who do not. One is tempted to sing the praises of the treatment and claim that "it works." However, unless steps were taken to ensure that the two groups of patients were equivalent in all meaningful respects upon study entry, the degree to which the superior outcomes should be attributed to the treatment, or perhaps to the possibility that patients who received Treatment X inadvertently happened to have higher expectations for improvement (or significantly lesser severity of illness, or more benign clinical history, etc.), would remain unclear. One approach to addressing individual differences among patients is random treatment assignment, the *sine qua non* (literally translated: "without which, not," i.e., the *essential component*) of what are known as randomized clinical trials (RCTs). Random treatment assignment means that every patient entering the study has an equal chance of being assigned to a given treatment condition. The rationale for this practice is that any preexisting differences that might influence outcomes will be approximately evenly distributed across all groups. So, even though individual outcomes might vary (because no two patients are identical) within the different treatment groups, any *mean* differences between the groups beyond those attributable to chance will be due to the different treatments. It is important to note that random treatment assignment does not guarantee group equivalence, especially if the groups are small. Therefore, it is good practice to check to determine (e.g., by means of between-group comparisons on relevant variables) that randomization "worked." Random treatment assignment obviously also controls for biases such as self-selection, as well as powerful inadvertent biases that may be introduced when clinicians themselves decide on the particular treatment for each patient.

Designing an investigation of the effect of a given therapy involves a series of interrelated design and methodological decisions regarding (1) the therapy, (2) the comparison condition(s), (3) the patients, and (4) the study outcome measures. For almost all of these decisions, there is no one correct answer. Rather, there are a number of possible approaches, each one carrying its own set of advantages and disadvantages. The following section will highlight some of the more important considerations that pertain in each of these four primary domains in which sound methodological decision-making is crucial.

The therapy

If the researcher's aim is to determine the effects of a particular psychotherapy, then the therapy must be carefully specified. While this statement may appear gratuitous, the history of psychotherapy research is filled with reports of the effects of treatments referred to only by a theoretical label such as "humanistic" or "client centered" or "eclectic." While such labels *suggest* what may be transpiring over the course of therapy, they do not provide useful information about what is actually being performed under a given theoretical label. Similarly, how is one to know whether Therapist A's interpretation of a given psychotherapy approach approximates Therapist B's? Indeed, a prominent cognitive therapist and trainer, Christine Padesky, once commented on the variations in therapists' understanding of cognitive therapy by saying that some people think that they are doing cognitive therapy as long as they periodically ask their clients, "what are you thinking?" (Padesky, 1996). While cognitive therapists do indeed focus on the content of patients' thinking, they do so guided by a specific theoretical conceptualization of the patient's problems and a formulation of the strategy for change that guides *how* and *when* to ask for thoughts and *what to do* with them once they are elicited.

The need to standardize treatment interventions to ensure that they are being implemented as intended has resulted in a "small revolution" in psychotherapy research (Luborsky and DeRubeis, 1984). This revolution is marked by a proliferation of treatment manuals, which provide sufficiently detailed descriptions of interventions so that other clinicians can replicate them. Manuals now exist for treatments as diverse as interpersonal psychotherapy (Klerman et al., 1984), exposure and response prevention (Steketee, 1993), cognitive therapy (Beck et al., 1979), and behavioral marital therapy (Jacobson and Margolin, 1979), and for disorders ranging from panic disorder to bulimia and binge eating (Agras and Apple, 1997). (See Woody and Sanderson, 1998, for an updated listing of manuals and training resources; see also Najavits, 1998, for guidelines on writing a treatment manual.) These manuals range from being very specific to very broad. They also vary in the amount of structure and standardization of how and when interventions are to be introduced. Some provide session-by-session outlines of interventions, whereas others provide a more general overview of the manner in which problems are conceptualized and the principles used for treatment planning and decision-making. Few manuals are designed for stand-alone use; rather, supplemental training and supervision are typically recommended.

The advantages of treatment manuals for the conduct of RCTs are obvious. Indeed, consensus on this point is strong enough that manuals now are considered an absolute necessity for such trials. Because RCTs are adaptations of the experimental method, the RCT treatment manual may be thought of as providing a means of operationalizing the independent variable. They allow researchers to conduct a "manipulation check" to ensure that the independent variable is implemented appropriately, and they also allow for replication by different researchers at different sites. Treatment manuals also facilitate the training of therapists. With the treatment model and intervention strategies clearly described, therapists can more easily learn new treatment strategies and broaden the range of treatments which they can skillfully deliver (Calhoun et al., 1998). Therefore, it could be argued that treatment manuals encourage the dissemination of newly developed treatments (Addis, 1997). Such advantages notwithstanding, the current emphasis among clinical researchers on manualized treatments has been not universally applauded within the field, and practicing clinicians as a group seem to have been slow to embrace this development (Persons, 1995). Critics have argued that manuals (1) undermine the "art" of clinical work, (2) fail to fit for the kind of patients who typically present in nonresearch settings (i.e., those with multiple problems as opposed to carefully selected homogeneous research samples), (3) promote "one therapy fits all" thinking and "schoolism," and (4) discourage innovation. However, several clinical researchers have thoughtfully addressed such criticisms (Addis et al., 1999; Wilson 1996). They argue that manuals indeed can be used creatively and flexibly, offer suggestions for individualizing treatment, and argue that manual-based treatment is not necessarily incompatible with treatment innovation. As for the criticism that manuals do not translate well into nonresearch settings, there are emerging data demonstrating that community therapists can use manuals effectively. Wade, Treat, and Stuart (1998) trained clinicians in a community mental health center to use Barlow and Craske's protocol, *Mastery of Your Anxiety and Panic*, to treat patients with a primary diagnosis of panic disorder. The results suggested that this panic control treatment could indeed be transported to a CMHC setting, with outcomes equivalent to those obtained in more standard research settings.

The advent of treatment manuals has spawned another important development in psychotherapy research: the construction of scales to assess the related constructs of therapy *adherence* and *competence*. Adherence is the term generally used to refer to the degree to which the therapist followed the therapy procedures and interventions. The most basic measure of adherence is simply rating the absence or presence of specific therapist behaviors or interventions. In a sophisticated presentation of issues around the assessment of adherence, Waltz et al. (1993) recommend that adherence measures include four types of items. The first type of item assesses therapist behaviors that are specific to the treatment and considered to be essential elements of the therapy under consideration. An example for behavior therapies might be *setting an agenda*. This is a required element for behavior therapies, but does not typically occur in other protocols (e.g., analytically oriented therapies). The second sort of item is therapist behaviors that are essential to the specific treatment but not unique to it. An example of such an item might be *development of a therapeutic alliance*. Such an alliance is essential to behavior therapies, but certainly not unique to them since most schools of therapy see this as an essential feature. The third type of item is one that is acceptable within a given treatment modality but not considered necessary. An example of this type of item for behavioral therapies might be exploration of childhood events. Finally, the fourth type of item assesses behaviors that are considered to fall outside of the treatment – behaviors that would be considered a violation of the treatment model. An example of this would be the use of *interpretation of resistance* in behavioral therapies.

Adherence measures that include all four types of items allow the researcher to determine the occurrence of both prescribed and proscribed therapist behaviors. When more than one therapy is being investigated, the researcher can investigate whether the treatments are really discriminable (e.g., DeRubeis et al., 1982) and how much overlap has occurred in the different therapy conditions. This approach to checking treatment integrity was used, for example, by Hill and colleagues regarding the Treatment of Depression Collaborative Research Program (TDCRP) (Hill, O'Grady, and Elkin, 1992), a multisite comparative outcome study which compared four different treatments for depression (interpersonal psychotherapy, cognitive behavior therapy, pharmacotherapy, and placebo plus clinical management). Such information regarding treatment adherence can often be crucial to the interpretation of a study. For example, one may consider the situation in which no difference in outcome was found between Therapy A and Therapy B. Adherence ratings might reveal that the therapists delivering Therapy A were including many of the interventions proscribed from Therapy A but considered essential to Therapy B. Conversely, adherence ratings could reveal very little overlap between therapist behaviors in Therapy A and Therapy B. The interpretation of the "no difference" in outcome would be quite different in the two scenarios. In the first scenario the absence of difference between treatments might simply be due to the fact that Therapy A and Therapy B included the same interventions. In the second scenario the finding of no difference in outcomes would more likely be seen as due to the operation of common factors that cut across different treatments.

Measures of adherence also can be used to investigate questions related to change processes in therapy. For example, it has been shown that the patient's level of homework compliance is positively associated with favorable outcomes in cognitive behavior therapy for depression. However, there has historically existed very little published information about what therapist behaviors promote homework compliance. Using a measure of therapy protocol adherence, Bryant and Simons (1999) recently addressed this question and found that adherence to the item "checking on previously assigned homework" was the best predictor of patient compliance.

Competence refers to how skillfully the therapist delivers the treatments. Competence obviously assumes adherence to the therapy protocol as specified in the treatment manual. In order to rate how well an intervention was delivered, the behavior has to have occurred. However, competence is a far more difficult assessment to make than the occurrence/nonoccurrence ratings for adherence. Competence assessments require expert judges who evaluate therapist behaviors in the context of the theory of change specified by the treatment model, the procedures described in the treatment manual, the stage of therapy, and the overall conceptualization of the client's presenting problems. Such scales have been developed for a number of different treatments, including cognitive therapy (the Cognitive Therapy Scale; Young and Beck, 1980) short-term supportive expressive dynamic therapy (Barber and Crits-Christoph, 1996), interpersonal psychotherapy (Klerman et al., 1984), and addiction treatment (Carroll et al., 2000).

Competency ratings are useful for a variety of research purposes. First and foremost, they are essential for quality assurance purposes (i.e., to ensure that the therapy is being competently delivered). In order for a therapy to be given a fair test, a certain level of therapist competence has to be achieved. If Therapy A fails to achieve the desired results, competency ratings will help determine whether the poor showing of the therapy is due to the therapy itself, or the fact that it was inadequately delivered. Competency ratings are also helpful in studies that compare the effects of different treatments, primarily as a means of disentangling the effects due to the treatments, *per se*, from those that may be due to differential competence in the delivery of the treatments. Imagine the situation in which two psychotherapies are compared. Therapy A yields better outcomes than Therapy B. In one case, therapists conducting Therapy A and Therapy B each achieved acceptable competency ratings. In the other case, therapists delivering Therapy A maintained a competent level of performance but therapists delivering Therapy B failed to do so. The interpretation of the finding of better outcomes for Therapy A would be very different in these two scenarios. A third research question that calls for competency ratings concerns the relationship between competency and outcome. Interestingly, the few studies that have addressed this issue have not overwhelmingly supported the expected relationship between competency and clinical outcome (Barber, Crits-Christoph, and Luborsky, 1996; Shaw et al., 1999). It is possible that these weaker than expected findings are due to shortcomings in the competency measures themselves. For example, both Whisman (1993) and Shaw et al. (1999) have suggested that the CTS (the competency scale for cognitive therapy) may not capture critical components of the therapy. It may also be that aspects of scoring lessen the scale's validity. For example, the eleven items of the scale all carry equal weight in the overall scoring even though some of the items clearly tap into bigger and theoretically more meaningful "chunks" of therapist performance. On the other hand, it is also possible that the specific therapist behaviors assessed by the different scales do not contribute to the outcomes obtained. This is the so-called *common factors* view, which holds that all of the different specific types of psychotherapy achieve their results through a common core of processes, rather than via behaviors that are specific to particular forms of treatment. Because competency scales typically assess both common and specific factors, they can in principle be used to further investigate the controversial *common factors* position.

Up until this point in our discussion of competency, it has been assumed that it is possible to determine an acceptable level of therapist competence. However, this seemingly straightforward objective is not so easy to achieve. How does one determine what constitutes an acceptable level of competence? Should this decision be made at the level of the full course of treatment or on a session-by-session basis? Must every session in a course of treatment be rated? Should competency raters have access to all of the clinical contextual information while making ratings? How should the variable of "patient difficulty" be handled? Where should the threshold for competence be set? These questions need to be addressed by clinical researchers without falling into the tempting trap of looking to patient outcome for guidance. In other words, while it is tempting to conclude that if the patient gets better then the therapy was competently delivered, such thinking represents a potential error of logic (since patient recovery could be due to any number of other factors). Tests of the relationship between therapist competence and patient outcome, therefore, have to keep these two variables separate, and subject them to separate analyses. However, it may sometimes prove difficult for the clinical investigator to clearly separate these two variables, inasmuch as therapist and patient behaviors are clearly reciprocally related.

The comparison condition(s)

One of the first issues confronted by an investigator planning to evaluate the impact of a specific form of psychotherapy is the choice of a comparison condition. As stated before, in order to assert that a therapy "works," the researcher must include a comparison condition. However, there is no "one size fits all" comparison condition. The decision rests on the scientific objectives of the study, what previous research has already been conducted, the feasibility and acceptability of the comparison condition, and ethical considerations. Perhaps the most important consideration is the specific research question. For example, if one has a newly developed treatment to be tested, the question is likely to be "does my new treatment work better than no treatment?" If there are other treatments that have already been shown to "work," one might want to ask the question, "does my treatment achieve better results than already documented bona fide treatments?" Each of these questions would require a different comparison group.

Waitlist or no treatment comparisons are commonly used in the early stages of the investigation of a treatment. These comparisons offer a number of methodologic advantages over an uncontrolled study. If change occurs in the therapy condition, the investigator can rule out factors such as repeated testing, history, and statistical regression to the mean as explanations for such change *if comparable* change has failed to occur in the no treatment condition. This type of comparison condition is particularly useful when little is known about the effects of a treatment and the investigator wishes to determine "is this treatment better than nothing?" The waitlist comparison group was appropriately used in one of the very first investigations of CBT for depression (Shaw, 1977). At the time, very little was known about the effects of CBT (or any psychosocial treatment) on depression; therefore, a waitlist comparison was suitable. However, there are a number of disadvantages, both subtle and obvious, to no treatment or waitlist comparison designs. First, for many disorders there is already some empirical evidence for the benefits of a particular psychotherapy. In these cases, the demonstration that a treatment is superior to no treatment has no clear pragmatic implications for choosing one therapy over another. Second, such a demonstration says nothing about what *specifically* is helpful about the therapy, nor whether the therapy's theory of change is valid. Third, in certain clinical situations (e.g., patients at risk for suicide or other self-injurious behavior), withholding treatment is ethically problematic. Beyond the ethical concerns, a pure no treatment condition may simply not be practical. Once patients have self-identified as in need (by virtue of volunteering for a research study), they may actually avail themselves of other forms of help (self-help books, videos, websites, pastoral counseling, support groups, etc.) after being assigned to the no treatment condition. Finally, waitlists can be seen as stacking the deck against the psychotherapy. Distressed patients may not be willing or able to wait out the waitlist period, and those who remain may represent a less severely ill group. This would stack the deck against the psychotherapy, since final "no treatment" scores for the waitlist group would be artificially "healthy." Alternatively, the deck may be stacked for the psychotherapy. Those receiving no treatment would have a negative expectation of gain (or an expectation of no gain), whereas the therapy group might show benefits simply due to expectation of improvement.

A treatment as usual (TAU) condition circumvents some of the problems associated with no treatment and waitlist conditions. In TAU patients are free to seek whatever other treatment is *usual* in the community. Therefore, concerns about withholding treatment from those in need and concerns about expectation effects are eliminated. In their initial investigation of Dialectical Behavior Therapy, Linehan and colleagues effectively used this design for women with chronic parasuicidal behavior, a group for whom withholding treatment would have certainly been ill-advised (Linehan et al., 1991). One disadvantage of this choice however, is that TAU represents an ill-defined set of procedures. So in the case of Linehan's study one is left with the finding that DBT is superior to TAU but with very little information about what TAU represents. In some cases TAU may be a very heterogeneous collection of treatments. In others, TAU may be more standardized. For example, Teasdale, Williams, and Segal (2000) used a relatively fixed treatment protocol for the TAU condition in their investigation of mindfulness-based cognitive therapy (MBCT) and its efficacy in decreasing the risk of relapse and recurrence in depression.

In any given treatment situation there are a number of factors that may influence the outcome of the treatment. In medicine, these factors are often conceptualized as either *specific* or *incidental*. Usually the specific factors are the actual chemicals in the drug or the actual procedure (e.g., removal of the inflamed appendix), and the results due to these specific factors are considered to be specific effects. Incidental factors include passage of time, attention from a caring professional, expectations of gain, belief in the treatment, and so on. Effects due to these incidental aspects of the treatment situation are seen as incidental effects. When these effects are positive they are often referred to as *placebo effects*, meaning effects that are not attributable to a known active ingredient but to one or more of these "context" variables. The term placebo has a number of connotations, many of them negative, and yet the original term was not pejorative. It literally means "I shall please." The history of medicine is full of examples of remedies that "worked," but were subsequently shown not to have any true active ingredient. Consequently, the therapeutic effects are most appropriately interpreted as due to some combination of the incidental features of treatment. In other words, the outcome represents a placebo effect.

In medical research, investigating whether the effects of treatment are due to specific or incidental factors is possible because these effects can be logically and experimentally disentangled. This is accomplished by comparing a medical treatment with another treatment that is identical in all respects except that the second treatment does not include the specific ingredient of the medical treatment. This is usually accomplished by using a pill placebo under double-blind conditions. The pill looks, tastes, and smells like the real medication but simply does not include the chemical compounds thought to be beneficial for the problem being treated. The double blind refers to the fact that neither the patient nor the researcher knows which patients are taking real medication and which patients are taking pill placebos. Some researchers take the design of the pill placebo a step farther and use an *active* placebo. These are pill placebos that leave out the putative therapeutic agents but include other chemicals that will simulate side effects similar to those of the real medicine (see Murphy, Simons, Wetzel, and Lustman, 1984, for an example of the use of an active placebo taken from depression research). The logic behind an active placebo is that savvy patients, especially those who have been on the active medication before, often figure out whether they are taking real medicine or a pill placebo based on their experience of side effects. Side effects can also tip off clinicians and evaluators to the placebo versus active medication status of patients. Indeed, there is data to suggest that the "blind" in pharmacotherapy studies is often broken (Greenberg et al., 1992). This obviously defeats the purpose of a placebo condition (i.e., to control for all of the incidental effects of the treatment situation in order to get a clearer picture of the specific effects of the pharmacologic agent).

The thinking behind placebo conditions in pharmacotherapy studies is reasonably straightforward. Patients are randomly assigned to either Medication A or pill placebo, the double blind is maintained, and patients are treated equally in all other respects (e.g., same number of appointments, same doctors, etc.). If Medication A achieves better effects than pill placebo, it makes sense to conclude that the better outcome was due to the specific ingredient(s) in the medication. Psychotherapy researchers interested in disentangling specific effects and incidental effects have tended to borrow from medicine and to use placebo designs. However, as straightforward as this approach is in medicine, it does not translate smoothly to studies of psychotherapy. As comprehensively discussed by Parloff (1986), the use of placebos in psychotherapy research requires (1) a placebo intervention that *lacks* the specific components of the experimental therapy, (2) a placebo that is *credible* to patients and therapists alike, and (3) therapist and patient blindedness regarding the placebo treatment. These requirements present conceptual and practical problems. First of all, there is no general agreement that cuts across different treatment modalities and orientations as to the determination of specific and incidental psychotherapy factors. Indeed, different therapies, derived from different theories, would yield different classifications. In other words, "what is considered specific, active, and essential by advocates of one school of psychotherapy may be classed as nonspecific, inert, and incidental by another" (Parloff, 1986: 83). Indeed, it is exactly the incidental or common factors of various psychotherapies that some see as responsible for the positive outcomes of psychotherapy (Wampold, 2001). The second and third problems for a placebo are also problematic for psychotherapy research. In order for a treatment to be credible, the therapist needs to be able to gain the patient's confidence, present a sensible rationale for the treatment, and generate some enthusiasm and expectation of improvement. But how can a therapist do this if he or she knows that the intended treatment was designed to be inert? These and other problems have led to a call for the abandonment of placebo comparisons in psychotherapy research and a search for alternative designs to address the question of specificity of effects (DeMarco, 1998; Seligman, 1995; Parloff, 1986; Wampold, 2001).

One of these alternatives is the so-called *dismantling* study. The logic of this design is that once a treatment has been shown to be effective, it can be taken apart or dismantled to see which of the components or ingredients of the treatment is responsible for the effects. Practically, this means comparing a treatment that has been shown to achieve good outcomes with the *same* treatments *minus* one or more ingredients. An example of this type of study is Feske and Goldstein's (1997) study of eye movement desensitization and reprocessing (EMDR) for panic disorder. EMDR had been shown to be more effective than a number of different comparison conditions. However, it has not been clear whether or not the eye movement component in EMDR was essential. Therefore, Feske and Goldstein randomly assigned patients to receive EMDR, EMDR *without* the eye movements, or a waiting list control. Their results failed to support the purported essential role of eye movements in this treatment, a conclusion that has been replicated in other dismantling studies (Cahill, Carrigan, and Frueh, 1999; Davidson and Parker, 2001). The opposite of dismantling, *additive* designs can also be used to investigate the unique contribution of a specific treatment component or ingredient. In this design a particular treatment component is *added* (rather than subtracted as in a dismantling study) to an existing treatment. If such an addition results in better outcomes, it suggests that the particular component that was added is responsible for the superior results. Michelson et al. (1996) investigated whether anything was gained by adding cognitive interventions or relaxation training to graded exposure treatment for panic disorder. They compared graded exposure alone, graded exposure plus relaxation, and graded exposure plus cognitive therapy. Their results indicated that, indeed, the addition of cognitive therapy to graded exposure led to improved short-term and long-term outcomes. *Parametric variation* designs are still another choice. These studies isolate a particular parameter thought to be important (e.g., number of sessions, degree of therapist self-disclosure, amount of homework) and set up treatment conditions that vary only with respect to this parameter.

Comparisons with bona fide treatments represent still another choice in treatment evaluation research. In the typical case, two or more treatments that have already been through the initial stages of evaluations (in other words, have already been shown to be superior to no treatment or treatment as usual) are compared. Examples of this approach are abundant in the psychotherapy research literature. A recent example is found in the work of Agras et al. (2000), who compared interpersonal psychotherapy with cognitive behavior therapy in the treatment of 220 outpatients with bulimia. They observed that patients who received CBT were more likely than those who received interpersonal psychotherapy to stop binging and purging by the end of the 20 weeks of treatment. Such comparative outcome studies are often conducted as *multi-site* studies, meaning that the same study is executed at two or more sites. One of the major reasons for this is that when comparing two treatments that have already been shown to be effective (i.e., bona fide treatments) the difference in outcomes between the two treatments is likely to be rather small. This is in contrast to a comparison of a treatment with a waitlist or similar control condition, in which one typically expects a moderate-to-large difference between the two conditions. The smaller the difference in effects, the larger the size of the sample needs to be. Obtaining large clinical samples at a single site can be quite challenging. This is not an insignificant concern. Kazdin and Bass (1989) reviewed comparative outcome studies conducted between 1986 and 1989 and found that the vast majority failed to include sufficient numbers of patients to detect the expected small to medium effect sizes.

Multisite studies have been presented as the answer to problems of statistical power (or the extent to which a study can detect differences between treatment groups). As power is in part a function of sample size (as well as the actual size of the effect and the criterion for statistical significance), increasing sample size is a conceptually (if not practically) simple solution. By conducting the same study at several different sites, one can recruit greater numbers of patients. This is especially true if the base rate of the problem being studied is low. Another advantage of multisite studies is that the findings may be more generalizable, inasmuch as recruiting patient samples from several different geographic locations should increase clinical and socioeconomic diversity of the overall sample. Multisite studies also have the potential to clarify so-called *allegiance effects*. It is well known that the therapies often perform better at some sites than others in outcome trials. These *site differences* may be due to a number of different factors, and they greatly complicate the interpretation of results from multisite studies. Between-site differences are sometimes seen as a reflection of the loyalty and enthusiasm a given site and its staff may have for a particular form of treatment (Luborsky et al., 1999). The exact nature of this effect is somewhat controversial, as it may be that allegiance is a stand-in for competence and expertise which would be expected to be correlated with outcome (Thase, 1999). Also, the effect seems to be particularly relevant during the first years after the introduction of a new therapy (Gaffan, Tsaousis, and Kemp-Wheeler, 1995). If several sites, especially those with presumably different preferences and allegiances, come together and implement the same treatment protocol(s) under the aegis of the same study, such allegiance effects should either be clarified or ruled out altogether.

Multisite studies are not without their potential problems, however. It is administratively challenging to keep all sites "on the same page." Further, if there are problems in the study, their impacts are likely to be serious. Because so much effort and so many resources are required to launch and complete multisite studies, they tend to be extremely visible and their results tend to carry disproportionate weight in the literature. For example, it has been argued that one such study, the NIMH Treatment of Depression Collaborative Research Program (Elkin et al., 1989), has been too heavily relied upon by developers of practice guidelines as a source of relevant information regarding the relative efficacy of psychosocial versus pharmacological interventions (DeRubeis et al., 1999; Jacobson and Hollon, 1996).

The patients

An important research issue concerns the patients who participate in psychotherapy studies. The most usual scenario is one in which patients are recruited and screened to determine whether they meet previously determined inclusion and exclusion criteria. Typically, inclusion criteria include a DSM diagnosis and a specified level of severity assessed by a standardized measure. Exclusion criteria often include other diagnoses and medical conditions, which might interfere with, or contraindicate, treatment. For example, in a recent comparison of exposure-plus-ritual-prevention (EX/RP) versus cognitive-behavior therapy for obsessive compulsive disorder, participants were required to meet criteria for a DSM-IV diagnosis of primary OCD, have a minimum symptom duration of one year, be between 18 and 65 years of age, and be fluent in written and spoken English (McLean et al., 2001). Patients were excluded if they evidenced active thought disorder, mental retardation or organic mental disorder, use of psychotropic medication or psychological treatment, or any physical illness that would prevent completion of the treatment protocol.

Although diagnosis and severity have the advantage of being explicit and reasonably standardized these are not the only, or necessarily the most appropriate, index to use for psychotherapy studies. It has been argued that the DSM lacks sufficient reliability and validity to use with any confidence. Further, DSM diagnoses are atheoretical by design. In other words, the system is agnostic. This is both a strength and a weakness. It is a strength in that the DSM allows clinical researchers of various orientations to communicate with a common language, regardless of their beliefs about the etiology and maintenance of various disorders. The weakness of the DSM, as it pertains to psychotherapy research, is that it may make it difficult to identify which problems respond best to which treatments. Many psychopathological processes may cut across diagnoses. For example, excessive rumination is a symptom of many different diagnoses, including obsessive compulsive disorder, forms of schizophrenia, and depression. Similarly, social withdrawal is associated with social phobia, depression, and other diagnoses. It may be that particular treatments are quite effective for processes that cut across multiple disorders. However, this would not get identified in studies in which patients are selected by diagnosis.

Another issue involved in clinical trials concerns the representativeness of patients who participate in psychotherapy trials. First of all, inclusion and exclusion criteria typically are designed to yield a relatively homogeneous group of patients. It is not unusual for more patients to be rejected than accepted into such trials, which may mean these study samples are clinically different from patients presenting for treatment in the community. Of particular concern is the fact that study samples often consist of individuals with a single diagnosis, whereas patients in the community often present with multiple problems and diagnoses. Given these differences, it has been argued that research conducted with "pure" samples fails to inform work with more complicated community cases. A second source of selection bias derives from the conditions of participation in a psychotherapy trial. To be sure, there are some incentives for patients to participate in such trials – particularly for those who may not have other treatment options. In clinical trials, treatment is usually free and patients can be assured that their treatment is carefully monitored. However, the burden of participation is also quite high. First, many potential participants refuse due to the risk of being assigned to a control condition, or even to a bona fide treatment that may not fit with their preferences and assumptions about what will be helpful (Addis and Jacobson, 1996). Further, standard trials currently include easily one to two days of assessments, including lengthy interviews and self-report schedules. Increasingly, investigators embed other assessments designed to uncover potential moderators of change (in other words, the conditions which may increase or decrease the effects of therapy) and/or investigate basic questions regarding the psychopathology in question. Such additional and frequently burdensome assessments often do not directly inform treatment; however, they are essential for increasing our knowledge about treatment effects and the processes by which they are obtained.

It remains unclear whether the above factors introduce a bias of selection into psychotherapy research and thereby vitiate the results of such trials (Persons and Silberschatz, 1998). Franklin et al. (2000) recently took up this question as it pertains to exposure-and-ritual-prevention (EX/RP) treatment of obsessive compulsive disorder. In this study none of the typical exclusion criteria for studies of OCD were used. Rather, those older than 65 and those with concurrent Axis I or II diagnoses, medical problems, psychotropic medication, etc., were included. Patients were treated with EX/RP on an outpatient fee for service basis. Using a *benchmarking* strategy (Wade, Treat, and Stuart, 1998), results were compared to those obtained in randomized clinical trials with more homogeneous patient samples. Study patients achieved comparable reductions in their OCD symptomatology, which suggests that the benefits of EX/RP are not limited to highly selected patients.

Outcome measures

The conceptualization of clinical outcomes and their measurement has undergone a great deal of change since the beginning of psychotherapy research. Whereas Eysenck used crude and subjective (and controversial) categorizations of "uncured, improved, very much improved, and cured," current practice is guided by two important considerations. One concerns the *coverage* of outcome assessments, while the other concerns the *limitations of statistical comparisons* between groups of treated patients.

With respect to coverage, an assessment of the target symptoms and problems is the minimum requirement. For example, if a study is evaluating the effects of a treatment for alcoholism, the assessment battery must include alcoholism-relevant variables (e.g., drinking frequency and quantity), whether or not DSM criteria for alcohol abuse are still met. These variables should be assessed through reliable and valid self-report measures, as well as through other informants if possible. The value of multiple informants depends on the nature of the problem. For example, it is essential to ask someone other than the patient about conduct disordered behavior but it may not be so essential to ask multiple informants about behavior that is essentially subjective (e.g., depressed mood). Depending on the problem, collateral measures (e.g., blood alcohol level) might also be used.

Increasingly, it has been argued that diagnosis and symptom-based assessments are insufficient, and that assessments of multiple other domains – such as social and occupational functioning, quality of life, utilization of services – should be included. Logically, these different indices would appear to be correlated. For example, if someone is drinking less, one might reasonably expect that absenteeism from work would also be reduced. Similarly, if one is less depressed, it might be expected that his or her social activity level would increase. Interestingly, however, this is not always the case. Symptom reduction and functioning do not always show equivalent change in response to treatment. For example, treatment may help an individual function more adaptively with the symptoms he or she has. The result would be no change in symptoms but significant change in functioning (Kazdin, 1994), an outcome that may well be important. Further, different treatments may vary in terms of which domains they are most likely to influence. Two treatments may be equivalent with respect to acute change on symptom measures, but one of the treatments may surpass the other with respect to subsequent service utilization.

Coverage also includes measures that may not pertain to outcome *per se*, but may be informative for elaborating our understanding of "why treatment leads to change, how the changes come about, and what processes must be activated within treatment and the client to achieve change" (Kazdin, 2001). This includes processes that likely cut across different treatments (e.g., therapeutic alliance; Martin, Garske, and Davis, 2000), as well as those that are theoretically tied to a particular form of treatment (e.g., change in cognitions in cognitive therapy; DeRubeis et al., 1990; Whisman, 1993). In addition, the identification of processes that can be shown to produce (or *mediate*) a treatment effect, as well as factors that may influence the strength of (or *moderate*) treatment results, adds important information of real potential usefulness. (For a classic article on mediation and moderation in social psychological research, see Baron and Kenny, 1986.)

The second issue, limitations of statistical comparisons between groups of treated individuals, concerns the standard practice of calculating mean scores for different treatment groups on a measure of interest (e.g., a symptom severity measure), comparing these mean scores, and then concluding that one treatment is "better" than another (or that there is no difference in effects of the different treatments). The primary limitation of this practice is the fact that these group means tell us little about individual patients, or even about the proportion of patients who responded well versus those who did not. Just as serious is the problem that these means may lack meaning! In other words, a treatment may produce a statistically significant reduction on some outcome measure but this reduction may not translate into something clinically meaningful. A weight loss of 5 pounds (e.g., as the result of a weight reduction intervention) may be statistically significant, but if the person still weighs 295 pounds posttreatment, the *clinical significance* of this treatment effect is questionable. There are many ways to define and operationalize clinical significance. Some approaches are statistical (use of *effect size*) and ask the question, "is the amount of change large enough?" Others focus on comparisons with normative samples and ask, "has the patient returned to normal functioning?" A full treatment of these issues can be found in a special issue of *Journal of Consulting and Clinical Psychology* (Vol. 67, No. 3, 1999).

In addition to statistically significant change and clinically significant change, there are other indices that are important when evaluating psychotherapies. *Acceptability* asks the question of whether people will accept the treatment. A treatment may be 100 percent effective but if the demands on the patient (be they physical, psychological, financial, side effects, or something else) are too great and no one completes the treatment, its worth is questionable. Related to acceptability is the issue of *attrition*. The loss of patients over the course of a psychotherapy study has serious implications due to the fact that it can undo the effects of random treatment assignment (i.e., random distribution of individual differences that may impact therapy outcome). For example, suppose that random assignment "worked" and that the level of severity was equivalent at pretreatment for Therapy A and Therapy B. Subsequently, however, many of the patients with severe symptoms drop out of Therapy A (but not Therapy B). At the end of treatment, Therapy A patients show greater improvement on various outcome indices than those who received Therapy B. One might be tempted to conclude that Therapy A is superior. However, the patients in Therapy A and Therapy B are no longer equivalent due to the differential attrition. Probably the best way to deal with attrition is to understand its causes and work to prevent it in the first place. When this is not possible (or feasible), one may employ various statistical procedures, which use end point data from the drop outs and attempt to estimate the biases that may have been introduced by attrition.

Durability of effects is a concept that refers to how long the effects of treatment are sustained. The maintenance of improvement following termination of therapy is important to the overall assessment of the costs and benefits of different treatments, especially treatments for recurring and relapsing disorders (e.g., addictions, depression). The assessment of such long-term outcomes requires *follow-up studies*, research that is difficult to conduct due to a number of conceptual and methodologic issues. Among the questions with which researchers need to grapple are: "How are relapse and recurrence defined?" "If a person returns to treatment, does this count as a recurrence or might it reflect different thresholds for treatment seeking?" "How long a follow-up period is scientifically sufficient?" This last question requires knowledge of the naturalistic course of a particular problem so that one can be sure that the follow-up period covers the period of highest risk for relapse and recurrence. Further, when comparing long-term effects of different treatments, the possibility of a *differential sieve* needs to be considered. Like the problem of attrition mentioned earlier, different treatments may differentially "graduate" patients into the follow-up phase of treatment such that initial randomization of factors that may be important to relapse and recurrence is undone.

Two final indices that deserve consideration in the evaluation of treatment are *disseminability* and *cost effectiveness*. Briefly summarized, a therapy may achieve extremely good results, but may nonetheless require intensive and expensive training for therapists, making it unavailable to most clinicians (and patients) in the community. This issue has been a source of much debate as therapies that have been shown to be effective in research settings have been slow to make their way into the community (Persons, 1995). Part of the reason for this may be the aforementioned sentiment that the results of tightly controlled randomized clinical trials (often referred to as *efficacy studies*) do not apply to the majority of clinicians' practices. In other words, overreliance on studies that use random assignment and manualized therapies may lead us to worthless or inaccurate conclusions about the nature of psychotherapy and its effects. A number of specific arguments along these lines have been raised. For example, while random assignment ("the prettiest of the methodological niceties in efficacy studies"; Seligman, 1995) is considered the *sine qua non* of efficacy studies, some have suggested that it may undercut one of psychotherapy's most powerful effects – remoralization – by denying patients choice and control over the kind of therapy they receive and the therapist with whom they work. Similarly, the recent identification of therapies as "empirically supported" (Task Force on Promotion and Dissemination of Psychological Procedures, 1995; Chambless and Hollon, 1998; Chambless and Ollendick, 2000; DeRubeis and Crits-Christoph, 1998) is based on unrepresentative studies and samples.

A cursory review of the above-cited references reveals what might be considered an over-representation of behavioral and cognitive-behavior therapy. However, it is difficult to say that this is a bias. Rather, it most likely reflects the fact that behavioral and cognitive-behavioral clinical researchers are typically "raised" in environments that value (and conduct) the kinds of randomized clinical trials that form the basis for identification of ESTs (by way of contrast, some theoretical orientations have been characterized by a tendency to dismiss clinical trial methodology, as well as the DSM system around which the EST effort has operated; DeRubeis and Crits-Christoph, 1998). Further, it is indisputable that these forms of therapy are easier to "manualize," a requirement for identification as an EST. Finally, the short-term nature of behavioral and cognitive-behavioral therapies renders them well-suited for research.

Sample unrepresentativeness refers to the unfortunate fact that only a very few studies include ethnic minorities in their samples, in spite of the fact that ethnic minorities now make up nearly 30 percent of the US population and experience equivalent (in some cases *higher*) rates of mental disorder. Miranda (2001) recently completed a review of the vast literature on the psychosocial treatment of depression, and found that in all of these studies there was a combined total of only 150 African-Americans (and the vast majority of these were in a single study) (Brown et al., 1999). Clinical researchers are according increased attention to this issue. However, until more such work is conducted, the degree to which our current understanding of ESTs applies to ethnic minorities will remain unclear (Hall, 2001).

One of the solutions suggested by those who criticize the EST effort is to support more *effectiveness* studies *that report on the results of psychotherapy as it is actually conducted in the field with those patients who actually seek it*. In such studies, inclusion criteria are broad, randomization is not required, treatment is typically conducted in a nonresearch setting, and there may or may not be a control comparison group. The goal is to determine if an intervention is efficacious *under conditions of customary clinical practice*. There are many examples of such studies, one of the most visible being the Consumer Report study (Seligman, 1995). They have the advantage of maximizing both ecological and external validity, but at the sacrifice of internal validity – arguably too high a price to pay. In a cogent analysis of this situation, Kraemer (2001) states that efficacy and effectiveness studies are often discussed as if they were antonyms, or "opposite extremes on a complex multi-dimensional continuum of decision-making in research design" (Kraemer, 2001). She goes on to note that another way to view these two approaches is to think of "extreme efficacy studies" as high in internal validity but low on external validity, and "extreme effectiveness studies" as high on external validity and low in internal validity. Kramer argues that this dichotomy leads to the "distressing situation in which only the right answers to the wrong questions (extreme efficacy studies) and the wrong answers to the right questions (extreme effectiveness studies) [will be] found" (Kraemer, 2001)

In an effort to depolarize the controversy, there have been calls for methodologic diversity and reminders that different studies are best equipped to answer different questions (Chambless and Hollon, 1998). Further, it may be useful to turn away from conceptualizing efficacy and effectiveness studies as occupying a continuum. A continuum is actually only one step removed from the antonym view; it still pits efficacy and effectiveness trials against each other. Rather, it may be productive to return to the dimensions of internal and external validity and think of how studies occupy all four quadrants (see figure 16.1). Extreme efficacy and effectiveness studies are located at the extremes of high internal validity/low external validity and high external validity/low internal validity. However, it is possible to design "hybrid" studies whose characteristics would place them elsewhere on the grid. Consider, as an example, TADS (Treatment of Adolescent Depression Study), a current NIMH-funded multisite study designed to investigate different treatments for depression in teens. The study design incorporates features of both efficacy and effectiveness trials. It uses random treatment assignment, even a pill placebo, but it also has very broad inclusion criteria (teens with comorbid conditions, even those being treated for ADHD) and a range of aims and outcome assessments, including cost-effectiveness and other indices mentioned earlier in this chapter. These characteristics would place TADS on the grid somewhere in the space between efficacy and effectiveness studies. Such hybrid studies are designed to maintain

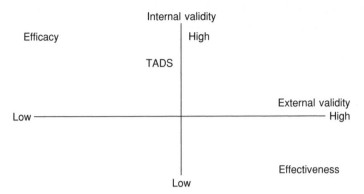

Figure 16.1 Efficacy, effectiveness, and validity.

acceptable levels of internal and external validity so that there will be "right" answers to the "right" questions.

Conclusions

This chapter has provided an overview of some of the methods, issues, and trends in contemporary psychotherapy research. Clearly, the questions posed, the methods used, the data analytic strategies employed, and the sheer amount of clinical research activity have all evolved such that there is now a sizable, quality literature on many forms of psychotherapy and the mechanisms of change. And while further research continues to be needed, psychotherapy research has developed considerably since the initial attempts to determine whether it "works."

References

Addis, M., and Jacobson, N. (1996). Reasons for depression and the process and outcome of cognitive-behavioral psychotherapies. *Journal of Consulting and Clinical Psychology, 64,* 1417–24.

Addis, M. E. (1997). Evaluating the treatment manual as a means of disseminating empirically validated psychotherapies. *Clinical Psychology: Science and Practice, 4,* 1–11.

Addis, M. E., Hatgis, C., Soysa, C. K., Zaslavsky, I., and Bourne, L. S. (1999). The dialectics of manual-based treatment. *The Behavior Therapist, 22,* 130–3.

Agras, W. S., and Apple, R. F. (1997). *Overcoming eating disorders: A cognitive behavioral treatment for bulimia nervosa and binge-eating disorder.* San Antonio, TX: Psychological Corporation.

Agras, W. S., Walsh, T., Fairburn, C., Wilson, G., and Kraemer, H. (2000). A multicenter comparison of cognitive-behavioral therapy and interpersonal psychotherapy for bulimia nervosa. *Archives of General Psychiatry, 57,* 459–66.

Barber, J. P. and Crits-Christoph, P. (1996). Development of a therapist adherence/competence rating scale for supportive-expressive dynamic psychotherapy: A preliminary report. *Psychotherapy Research*, *6*, 81–94.

Barber, J. P., Crits-Christoph, P., and Luborsky, L. (1996). Effects of therapist adherence and competence on patient outcome in brief dynamic therapy. *Journal of Consulting and Clinical Psychology*, *64*, 619–22.

Baron, R. M., and Kenny, D. A. (1986). The moderator–mediator variable distinction in social psychological research: Conceptual, strategic, and statistical considerations. *Journal of Personality and Social Psychology*, *6*, 1173–82.

Beck, A. T., Rush, A. J., Shaw, B. F., and Emery, G. (1979). *Cognitive therapy for depression*. New York: Guilford Press.

Bergin, A. E. (1971). The evaluation of therapeutic outcomes. In A. E. Bergin and S. L. Garfield (eds.), *Handbook of psychotherapy and behavior change: an empirical analysis* (pp. 217–70). New York: Wiley.

Beutler, L. (2000). David and Goliath: When empirical and clinical standards of practice meet. *American Psychologist*, *55*, 997–1007.

Beutler, L., and Davison, E. (1995). What standards should we use? In S. Hayes, V. Follette, R. Dawes, and K. Grady (eds.), *Scientific standards of psychological practice*. Reno, NV: Context Press.

Brown, C., Schulberg, H., Sacco, D., Perel, J., and Houck, P. (1999). Effectiveness of treatments for major depression in primary medical care practice: A post hoc analysis of outcomes for African American and white patients. *Journal of Affective Disorders*, *53*, 185–92.

Bryant, M. J., and Simons, A. D. (1999). Therapist skill and patient variables in homework compliance: Controlling an uncontrolled variable in cognitive therapy outcome research. *Cognitive Therapy and Research*, *23*, 381–99.

Cahill, S., Carrigan, M., and Frueh, B. (1999). Does EMDR work? and if so, why?: A critical review of controlled outcome and dismantling research. *Journal of Anxiety Disorders*, *13*, 5–33.

Calhoun, K., Moras, K., Pilkonis, P., and Rehm, L. (1998). Empirically supported treatments: Implications for training. *Journal of Consulting and Clinical Psychology*, *66*, 151–62.

Carroll, K. M., Nich, C., Sifry, R., Nuro, K., Frankforter, T., Ball, S., Fenton, L., and Rounsaville, B. (2000). A general system for evaluating therapist adherence and competence in psychotherapy research in the addictions. *Drug and Alcohol Dependence*, 225–38.

Chambless, D., and Hollon, D. (1998). Defining empirically supported therapies. *Journal of Consulting and Clinical Psychology*, *66*, 7–18.

Chambless, D., and Ollendick, T. (2000). Empirically supported psychological interventions: Controversies and evidence. *Annual Review of Psychology*, *52*, 685–716.

Davidson, P., and Parker, K. (2001). Eye movement desensitization and reprocessing (EMDR): A meta-analysis. *Journal of Consulting and Clinical Psychology*, *69*, 305–16.

DeMarco, C. (1998). On the impossibility of placebo effects in psychotherapy. *Philosophical Psychology*, *11*, 207–27.

DeRubeis, R., and Crits-Christoph, P. (1998). Empirically supported individual and group psychological treatments for adult mental disorders. *Journal of Consulting and Clinical Psychology*, *66*, 37–52.

DeRubeis, R., Gelfand, L., Tang, T., and Simons, A. (1999). Medications versus cognitive behavior therapy for severely depressed outpatients: Mega analysis of four randomized comparisons. *American Journal of Psychiatry*, *156*, 1007–13.

DeRubeis, R., Hollon, S., Evans, M., and Bemis, K. (1982). Can psychotherapies for depression be discriminated? A systematic investigation of cognitive therapy and interpersonal therapy. *Journal of Consulting and Clinical Psychology*, *50*, 744–56.

DeRubeis, R., Evans, M., Hollon, S., Garvey, M., Grove, W., and Tuason, V. (1990). How does cognitive therapy work? Cognitive change and symptom change in cognitive therapy and pharmacotherapy for depression. *Journal of Consulting and Clinical Psychology*, 58, 862–9.

Dobson, K. (1989). A meta-analysis of the efficacy of cognitive therapy for depression. *Journal of Consulting and Clinical Psychology*, 57, 414–19.

Elkin, I., Shea, M. T., Watkins, J., Imber, S., et al. (1989). National Institute of Mental Health Treatment of Depression Collaborative Research Program: General effectiveness of treatments. *Archives of General Psychiatry*, 46, 971–82.

Eysenck, H. J. (1952). The effects of psychotherapy: An evaluation. *Journal of Counseling Psychology*, 16, 319–24.

Feske, U., and Goldstein, A. (1997). Eye movement desensitization and reprocessing treatment for panic disorder: A controlled outcome and partial dismantling study. *Journal of Consulting and Clinical Psychology*, 65, 1026–35.

Franklin, M., Abramowitz, J., Kozak, M., Levitt, J., and Foa, E. (2000). Effectiveness of exposure and ritual prevention for obsessive-compulsive disorder: Randomized compared with nonrandomized samples. *Journal of Consulting and Clinical Psychology*, 68, 594–602.

Gaffan, E., Tsaousis, J., and Kemp-Wheeler, S. (1995). Researcher allegiance and meta-analysis: The case of cognitive therapy for depression. *Journal of Consulting and Clinical Psychology*, 63, 966–80.

Garfield, S. L. (1981). Psychotherapy: A 40 year appraisal. *American Psychologist*, 36, 174–83.

Garfield, S. L. (1994). Eclecticism and integration in psychotherapy: Developments and issues. *Clinical Psychology – Science and Practice*, 1, 123–37.

Greenberg, R. P., Bornstein, R. F., Greenberg, M. D., and Fisher, S. (1992). A meta-analysis of antidepressant outcome under "blinder" conditions. *Journal of Consulting and Clinical Psychology*, 60, 664–9.

Hall, G. (2001). Psychotherapy research with ethnic minorities: Empirical, ethical, and conceptual issues. *Journal of Consulting and Clinical Psychology*, 69, 502–10.

Hill, C. E., O'Grady, K. E., and Elkin, I. (1992). Applying the collaborative Study Psychotherapy Rating Scale to rate therapist adherence in cognitive behavior therapy, interpersonal therapy, and clinical management. *Journal of Consulting and Clinical Psychology*, 60, 73–9.

Jacobson, N., and Christensen, A. (1996). Studying the effectiveness of psychotherapy: How well can clinical trials do the job? *American Psychologist*, 51, 1031–9.

Jacobson, N., and Hollon, S. (1996). Cognitive-behavior therapy versus pharmacotherapy: Now that the jury's returned its verdict, it's time to present the rest of the evidence. *Journal of Consulting and Clinical Psychology*, 64, 74–80.

Jacobson, N., Roberts, L., Berms, S., and McGlinchey, J. (1999). Methods for defining and determining the clinical significance of treatment effects: Description, application and alternatives. *Journal of Consulting and Clinical Psychology*, 67, 300–7.

Kazdin, A. (1994). Methodology, design and evaluation in psychotherapy research. In A. E. Bergin and S. Garfield (eds.), *Handbook of psychotherapy and behavior change* (4th edn.). New York: John Wiley and Sons.

Kazdin, A. (2001). Progression of therapy research and clinical application of treatment require better understanding of the change process. *Clinical Psychology – Science and Practice*, 8, 143–51.

Kazdin, A., and Bass, D. (1989). Power to detect differences between alternative treatments in comparative psychotherapy outcome research. *Journal of Consulting and Clinical Psychology*, 57, 138–47.

Klerman, G. L., Weissman, M. M., Rounsaville, B. J., and Chevron, E. S. (1984). *Interpersonal psychotherapy of depression*. New York: Basic Books.

Kraemer, H. (2001). Pitfalls of multisite randomized clinical trials of efficacy and effectiveness. *Schizophrenia Bulletin*, *26*, 533–41.

Linehan, M. M., Armstrong, H. E., Suarez, A., Allmon, D., and Heard, H. (1991). Cognitive-behavioral treatment of chronically parasuicidal borderline patients. *Archives of General Psychiatry*, *48*, 1060–4.

Luborsky, L., and DeRubeis, R. (1984). The use of psychotherapy treatment manuals: A small revolution in psychotherapy research style. *Clinical Psychology Review*, *4*, 5–14.

Luborsky, L., Diguer, L., Seligman, D., Rosenthal, R., Krause, E., Johnson, S., Halperin, G., Bishop, M., Berman, J., and Schweizer, E. (1999). The researcher's own therapy allegiances: A "wild card" in comparisons of treatment efficacy. *Clinical Psychology – Science and Practice*, *6*, 95–106.

McLean, P., Whittal, M., Sochting, I., Koch, W., Paterson, R., Thordarson, D., Taylor, S., and Anderson, K. (2001). Cognitive versus behavior therapy in the group treatment of obsessive compulsive disorder. *Journal of Consulting and Clinical Psychology*, *609*, 205–14.

Martin, D., Garske, J., and Davis, M. (2000). Relation of the therapeutic alliance with outcome and other variables: A meta-analytic review. *Journal of Consulting and Clinical Psychology*, *68*, 438–50.

Michelson, L., Marchione, K., Greenwald, M., Testa, S., and Marchione, N. (1996). A comparative outcome and follow-up investigation of panic disorder with agoraphobia: The relative and combined efficacy of cognitive therapy, relaxation training, and therapist-assisted exposure. *Journal of Anxiety Disorders*, *10*, 297–330.

Najavits, L. M. (1998). How to write a treatment manual. *Behavior Therapist*, *21*, 177–8.

Padesky, C. (1996). *Mind over mood*. Workshop presentation, Portland, Oregon.

Parloff, M. B. (1986). Placebo controls in psychotherapy research: A sine qua non or a placebo for psychotherapy research? *Journal of Consulting and Clinical Psychology*, *54*, 79–87.

Persons, J. (1995). Why practicing psychologists are slow to adopt empirically validated treatments. In S. Hayes, V. Follette, R. Dawes, and K. Grady (eds.), *Scientific standards of psychological practice*. Reno, NV: Context Press.

Persons, J. B., and Silberschatz, G. S. (1998). Are results of randomized controlled trials useful to psychotherapists? *Journal of Consulting and Clinical Psychology*, *66*, 126–35.

Seligman, M. (1995). The effectiveness of psychotherapy: The *Consumer Reports* study. *American Psychologist*, *50*, 965–74.

Shaw, B. F. (1977). Comparison of cognitive therapy and behavior therapy in the treatment of depression. *Journal of Consulting and Clinical Psychology*, *45*, 543–51.

Shaw, B. F., Elkin, I., Yamaguchi, J., Olmsted, M., Vallis, T. M., Dobson, K. S., Lowery, A., Sotsky, S. M., Watkins, J. T., and Imber, S. D. (1999). Therapist competence ratings in relation to clinical outcome in cognitive therapy of depression. *Clinical Psychology – Science and Practice*, *6*, 10–32.

Steketee, G. (1993). *Treatment of obsessive compulsive disorder*. New York: Guilford Press.

Talley, P., Strupp, H., and Butler, S. (eds.) (1994). *Psychotherapy research and practice: Bridging the gap*. New York: Basic Books.

Task Force on Promotion and Dissemination of Psychological Procedures (1995). Training in and dissemination of empirically validated psychological treatments: Report and recommendations. *Clinical Psychologist*, *48*, 2–23.

Teasdale, J., Segal, Z., Williams, J., Ridgeway, V., Soulsby, J., and Lau, M. (2000). Prevention of relapse/recurrence in major depression by mindfulness-based cognitive therapy. *Journal of Consulting and Clinical Psychology*, *68*, 615–23.

Thase, M. (1999). What is the investigator allegiance effect and what should we do about it? *Clinical Psychology – Science and Practice*, *6*, 113–15.

Vallis, T. M., Shaw, B. F., and Dobson, K. S. (1986). The Cognitive Therapy Scale: Psychometric properties. *Journal of Consulting and Clinical Psychology*, *54*, 381–5.

Wade, W., Treat, T., and Stuart, G. (1998). Transporting an empirically supported treatment for panic disorder to a service clinic setting: A benchmarking strategy. *Journal of Consulting and Clinical Psychology*, *66*, 231–9.

Waltz, J., Addis, M., Doerner, K., and Jacobson, N. (1993). Testing the integrity of a psychotherapy protocol: Assessment of adherence and competence. *Journal of Consulting and Clinical Psychology*, *61*, 620–30.

Wampold, B. (2001). *The great psychotherapy debate: Model, methods, and findings*. New York: Lawrence Erlbaum Associates.

Whisman, M. (1993). Mediators and moderators of change in cognitive therapy of depression. *Psychological Bulletin*, *114*, 248–65.

Wilson, G. T. (1996). Manual based treatments: The clinical application of research findings. *Behavior Research and Therapy*, *34*, 295–314.

Wilson, T. (1995). Empirically validated treatments as a basis for clinical practice. In S. Hayes, V. Follette, R. Dawes, and K. Grady (eds.), *Scientific standards of psychological practice*. Reno, NV: Context Press.

Woody, S., and Sanderson, W. (1998). Manuals for empirically supported treatments: 1998 update. *Clinical Psychologist*, *51*, 17–21.

Young, J., and Beck, A. T. (1980). Cognitive Therapy Scale rating manual. Unpublished manuscript, University of Pennsylvania, Philadelphia.

VIGNETTE

Therapy and Interventions Research with Adults

Anne K. Jacobs

Edinger, J. D., Wohlgemuth, W. K., Radtke, R. A., Marsh, G. R., and Quillian, R. E. (2001). Cognitive behavioral therapy for treatment of chronic primary insomnia: A randomized controlled trial. *Journal of the American Medical Association, 285*, 1856–64.

Several aspects of the article by Edinger and colleagues make it an exemplar article of therapy and interventions research as described by Simons and Wildes (chapter 16, this volume). The study was a randomized, double-blind, behavioral placebo-controlled clinical trial. Prestudy power calculations were done to determine the sample size sufficient to permit detection of treatment effects of the magnitude observed in a pilot study, even in light of anticipated drop-out rates. Seventy-five adults presenting with chronic primary insomnia were randomly assigned to either cognitive-behavioral therapy, progressive muscle relaxation, or a quasi-desensitization (placebo) condition. Assignment to therapist was also random. Potential participants were excluded if they could not abstain from sleep aids, or if they used a psychotropic medication. Other sleep disorders, as well as mental and physical illnesses, were ruled out. Outcome measures included subjective self-reports and objective physiological measurements. Adequate internal consistency was reported for the measures. Treatment credibility and participants' perceptions of therapists' warmth and competence were also measured across the three conditions. Elements of the three treatment conditions were clearly specified.

Statistical analyses, a series of ANOVAs and ANCOVA, were appropriate based on the sample size and research questions. The authors examined differences between participants who completed the study and those who dropped out. At the beginning of treatment the three conditions did not differ in ratings of treatment credibility or therapist warmth and competence. All therapy sessions were tape-recorded, and a subset of sessions was randomly selected to check treatment integrity; participants' compliance with treatment was also measured and reported to be adequate. Analyses were initially run excluding drop-outs, then again including drop-outs and using midtreatment questionnaires as projected end points. Subjective and objective reports indicated that participants who received cognitive behavioral therapy showed greater improvement in their insomnia than did the other two groups. These improvements held through a 6-month follow-up. The significance of the results was reported in terms of both statistical and clinical significance. As an ethical note, the authors did not ask participants who had been assigned to the placebo condition to complete the 6-month follow-up; instead, these participants were debriefed and given either cognitive behavioral therapy or relaxation training.

Through its design addressing several aspects of treatment efficacy, the present study by Edinger and his colleagues stands out as an exemplary work of therapy research with adults due to:

- Strong randomized, well-blinded research design
- Comparison of target treatment to both alternative treatment and behavioral placebo
- Use of subjective and objective measures
- Use of clearly specified treatments
- Reported treatment credibility, integrity, and compliance data
- Measured participants' perceptions of therapists' warmth and competence
- Appropriate statistics used for sample size and research questions
- Six-month follow-up of treatment effects reported
- Results were discussed in terms of statistical and clinical significance

CHAPTER SEVENTEEN

Research in Prevention and Promotion

George C. Tremblay and Barbara Landon

Prevention and promotion have played a fitful role in the history of clinical psychology. Prevention advocates were among the pioneers of our science; examples include Binet's "mental orthopedics" to improve education for low-intelligence children (Binet and Heisler, 1975), Lewin's (1946) wartime action research to enhance safety and productivity in factories, and Skinner's (1948) exploration of the principles for a utopian community. Throughout the post-World War II era, though, the prevention agenda has been repeatedly overwhelmed by a burgeoning demand for treatment of acute and chronic dysfunction. Even as public policy has flirted periodically with prevention, such demands have fueled the growth of clinical psychology toward provision of mental health services to persons diagnosed with mental illness.

The history of public health provides compelling evidence for the relative efficiency of preventive versus reparative interventions. No disease or disorder has ever been eliminated primarily by treating those who have it; success stories in public health involve preventive victories such as eradicating smallpox and polio, halting epidemics of cholera and dysentery, and dramatically reducing infant mortality (Price et al., 1988). There will never be a sufficient number of trained clinicians to provide treatment for all diagnosable cases of mental disorders, estimated at 29.5 percent of the US population (Kessler et al., 1994). The case for preventive efforts in mental health thus rests on practical, as well as ideological, considerations (e.g., Cowen, 1994), yet the burden of proof for demonstrating the efficacy of preventive mental health interventions falls to social scientists.

There are indications that psychological research is beginning to meet that burden. In the early 1990s the US Congress directed the National Institutes of Mental Health (NIMH) and the Institute of Medicine (IOM) to generate a comprehensive review of mental health prevention, intended to guide public policy and allocation of federal support for research (Munoz, Mrazek, and Haggerty, 1996). An agenda emerged for the progress of "prevention science" that explicitly favors interventions aimed at reducing incidence of discrete, DSM-defined disorders, over programs "driven . . . by a focus on the enhancement of well-being" (Mrazek and Haggerty, 1994: 27). Formal adoption of this agenda has exacerbated a longstanding tension between conceptions of prevention that are organized around models of discrete disease, versus those that focus on the development of competence or "wellness" for its own sake (Cowen, 1994), and/or on locating pathology in social institutions rather than individuals (Albee, 1996; Perry and Albee, 1994). Although we shall have occasion to revisit differences between the models for illness prevention and wellness promotion, they share much in the way of research methodology. We begin by introducing the developmental perspective that underlies both traditions.

Developmental Framework for Prevention

Risk and protective factors

The foundation for prevention and promotion research is the identification of malleable characteristics of individuals or environments that influence developmental trajectories toward mental health or distress. Risk factors are associated with greater incidence or severity of distress, whereas protective factors foster competence, well-being, and/or resilience under stressful circumstances. The study of developmental pathways and associated risk and protective factors has intensified over the past three decades, coalescing into the discipline of developmental psychopathology (Cicchetti, 1984; Sroufe and Rutter, 1980). Key contributions of developmental psychopathology to understanding mental health are: (1) mutually informed study of normal and abnormal development (Sroufe, 1990); (2) explicit attention to the fluid, unfolding nature of developmental trajectories, viewing health or maladjustment as a function of cumulative influences; (3) acknowledgment of interplay between nature and nurture over time (Rutter et al., 1997); and (4) recognition that risk and protective factors are rarely specific to a given outcome; that is, diverse pathways can lead to the same outcome ("equifinality"), and the influence exerted by a given developmental component will depend heavily on the broader risk constellation ("multifinality") (Cicchetti and Rogosch, 1996).

Risk and protective factors for a given developmental pathway range from biological dispositions such as temperament (Caspi et al., 1995; Kagan, 1989; McBurnett, 1992), to socioeconomic status (National Center for Children in Poverty, 1990), cultural/political conditions (e.g., war), stressful experiences (Rutter, 1996), academic achievement (Patterson, DeBaryshe, and Ramsey, 1989), or peer relations (Putallaz and Dunn, 1990). The impact of these factors typically varies across development, concentrating at critical junctures (many fetal teratogens are most toxic during the first trimester of pregnancy, for example, and the potency of peer influences escalates in adolescence). Developmental psychopathology is not a main effects enterprise: individual characteristics interact with environmental features to form a risk constellation (Rutter et al., 1997). One form that such an interaction might take is illustrated by the stress-diathesis model of psychopathology, in which a person may carry a disposition to react poorly to certain stressors, yet that disposition is only "activated" if a stressor occurs (Nicholson and Neufeld, 1992). Thus, the study of risk and protective factors is complicated by diversity of influences, the salience of timing, and person–environment interactions.

Risk and protective factors versus mechanisms

Establishing a reliable association between individual or environmental features and later outcomes is sufficient to identify a risk or protective factor, but it does not necessarily explain the actual mechanism by which risk or protection is conferred (Gore and Eckenrode, 1996). Low socioeconomic status (SES), for example, surfaces as a risk factor for a broad range of negative outcomes (National Center for Children in Poverty, 1990). The mechanism by which SES operates may be fairly straightforward when, for example, a child contracts an illness for which immunization is available because the family did not have access to affordable primary care. In other contexts SES may function instead as a marker for more proximal influences on, say, child conduct problems, such as exposure to lead paint or other neurotoxins (Loeber, 1990), inadequate parenting, or antisocial models (Patterson, DeBarysye, and Ramsey, 1989; Rutter, 1996).

   Biological risk and protective factors also illustrate the importance of understanding mechanisms of developmental influence. Behavior genetic research currently supports the conclusion that many, if not most behavioral characteristics have a substantial heritable component (Plomin and Rutter, 1998). Technological and ethical obstacles might tempt one to dismiss the realm of genetic influences as outside the reach of intervention. Such a conclusion fails to appreciate the range of mechanisms through which biology is expressed. A child's early intellectual endowment, for example, is predictive of educational and occupational achievement only in part because cognitive ability confers performance advantages; it is also associated with opportunity advantages. A bright child is likely to be presented with more opportunities for educational and occupational achievement by virtue of both brighter parents and active pursuit of environments that offer greater challenges (Rutter et al., 1997). If society cannot readily improve a child's inborn cognitive capacities, it can still provide children with some of the opportunities that are critical and proximal elements of the developmental path toward success (e.g., Head Start; Zigler and Muenchow, 1992).

   Distinguishing true risk and protective processes from mere marker variables is critical for effective prevention. Such distinctions can only be made through theory-driven research. A risk or protective mechanism constitutes a mediated effect, whereby some independent variable exerts its influence on an outcome (dependent variable) by means of a specified process. Theory-driven research must evaluate not only covariation between independent and dependent variables, but also demonstrate the intervening process that accounts for this covariation. Exploration of mediating relationships can take place in the context of correlational or experimental research.

   Notwithstanding the axiomatic caution in introductory research courses against inferring causation from correlation, a family of essentially correlational techniques has contributed a great deal to elucidating developmental pathways. This contribution rests on the ability to partition variance in the criterion variable(s) among multiple predictor variables, thereby testing hypotheses about their unique covariation with the phenomenon of interest. One way to evaluate mediational models is through a series of regression analyses (Holmbeck, 1997). To return to our example of SES influencing child conduct problems, confirmation of a mediating role for inadequate parenting would require a series of four regression analyses, demonstrating (1) a significant relationship between SES and parenting; (2) a significant relationship between SES and child conduct; (3) a significant relationship between parenting and child conduct; and (4) a significant *reduction* in the strength of the relationship between SES and child conduct, when the parenting variable is controlled for (i.e., entered prior to SES in the regression equation).

Structural equation modeling (SEM) can provide an alternative means of testing mediational hypotheses involving correlational data (Holmbeck, 1997). Among the benefits of SEM are the ability to test an entire path model simultaneously, the ability to specify measurement error in the path model, and "degree of fit" statistics that help the investigator to evaluate how well the entire hypothesized model accounts for the data. SEM is most useful when applied to relatively large samples, and when the investigator has access to more than one measured indicator of each latent construct in the model.

Experimental trials, whether single case or large scale, can target hypothesized mediating variables for intervention, and in so doing, simultaneously test the malleability of the intervention target, and the strength of the theory linking it to the outcome of interest.

A prototype for prevention research

Prevention research begins with a focus on a developmental outcome (disorder for the "illness prevention" model, resilience in the face of adversity from the "wellness promotion" perspective), and proceeds through an ordered sequence of steps (Mrazek and Haggerty, 1994; Reiss and Price, 1996). Epidemiological and developmental research enables investigators to establish patterns of prevalence for the outcome of interest, and to draft a "map" of pathways to (and around) it. Common landmarks on this map are identified as potential risk and protective factors, and theories about their operation are proposed. Pilot studies, such as small *n* or single-case designs, evaluate the "efficacy" of the intervention, that is, the extent to which it brings about change in the hypothesized mediating process, and to which such change covaries with the outcome of interest. Larger-scale clinical trials follow, in order to evaluate the operation of the theory under less controlled, more typical conditions ("effectiveness" research). The final phase of this model is investigation of effective strategies for dissemination, and ongoing evaluation of the program in the broader community.

Linking Preventive Research and Intervention

Classifying preventive efforts

Reiss and Price (1996) summarized three general approaches to prevention, mapping most directly onto the illness prevention model. The first, aimed at reducing the incidence of classifiable mental disorders, targets relevant risk and protective mechanisms among populations who have yet to demonstrate any symptoms of the disorder. The second approach aims to reduce the severity of disorder, through identification of prodromal cases and interruption of the trajectory toward more severe manifestations. The third approach aims to reduce secondary diagnoses among persons who already meet criteria for a mental disorder. This framework, similar to classic public health typology (Caplan, 1964; Commission on Chronic Illness, 1957, cited in Mrazek and Haggerty, 1994), specifies prevention that is primary (incidence reducing, targeting whole communities), secondary (prevalence reducing, targeting high risk groups), or tertiary (impairment reducing, targeting identified cases). Wellness promotion researchers have employed the first two categories of the public health typology as well, to distinguish between interventions offered to the entire public, versus to groups at risk for some problematic outcome.

Controversy concerning claims of more "preventive" status than is warranted (e.g., Cowen, 1996) contributed to adoption by the IOM of a more restrictive prevention classification, based on weighing potential risk of disorder (and thus potential gain from intervention), against the cost of participating in a preventive intervention (Gordon, 1983, in Mrazek and Haggerty, 1994). *Universal* interventions are deemed to offer a favorable risk/benefit ratio to everyone in a population. The addition of iodine to table salt to prevent goiter, or offering prenatal classes to all pregnant couples to prevent parent–child distress, are examples of universal preventive measures. The benefits of *selective* interventions outweigh the costs only for subgroups of the population who are at elevated risk of developing a disorder. Individuals targeted by selective interventions are presumed to demonstrate no risk manifestations other than membership in a risk group. Examples would be flu innoculations for hospital employees, by virtue of their greater exposure to pathogens and their potential for infecting vulnerable populations, or school-based support groups for children of divorce. *Indicated* preventive measures are suitable for individuals who are currently asymptomatic, but who present some individual-level characteristic associated with high risk of developing a disorder. This risk renders the intervention justified, even if associated costs are relatively high. Widespread screening for persistent dieting by adolescents of normal weight, with referral of high risk individuals for further assessment and counseling, constitutes an indicated intervention for the prevention of eating disorders (except where it identifies diagnosable cases). The target of indicated prevention is not an early symptom of a disorder, because there is no assurance that the risk factor will develop into disorder; this is what distinguishes indicated prevention from early treatment. Thus, the IOM definition, unlike the classic public health definition, restricts the domain of prevention to intervention with individuals who are not symptomatic.

Strategies for preventive intervention

The aforementioned classifications provide the first broad strokes in defining the realm of prevention. In this section we progress to more molecular issues in intervention and related research design. We have grouped these issues into three categories: (1) selecting intervention targets; (2) selecting intervention tactics, including scope and timing of intervention; and, because prevention programs are frequently delivered on a large scale, (3) working in communities.

Selecting targets

Intervention targets refer to the specific elements of the risk constellation – intersection of individual persons, families, and environments – that the intervention most directly aims to alter. One of the challenges in identifying efficient intervention targets is distinguishing risk mechanisms from marker variables (cf. Coie et al., 1993; Gore and Eckenrode, 1996; Munoz, Mrazek, and Haggerty, 1996; Rutter, 1996), which can function as decoy intervention targets. Obesity, for example, has long been associated with heart disease, lending justification for an extraordinary investment of resources in weight loss efforts in the United States and elsewhere. Recently, it has been argued that focusing on weight may obscure more important risks (e.g., level of physical activity) that are (1) not necessarily addressed by weight loss, (2) more amenable to influence than weight status, and (3) less fraught with iatrogenic risks to physical and psychological well-being (Garner and Wooley, 1991; Wadden, Anderson, and Foster, 1999; Wei et al., 1999). As empirical support for this view of cardiac risk accumulates, a few promising interventions are drawing attention away from weight status, and seeking instead to enhance physical activity, decouple self-esteem from weight, and reduce eating pathology (including repetitive dieting; cf. Burgard and Lyons, 1994; McFarlane, Polivy, and McCabe, 1999).

The choice of intervention targets should derive, then, from efforts to first define the nature of risk, and then to identify the most potent and malleable risk component. The potency of risk at a given node in the causal model can be represented by the question, "What increment of change would shift the outcome of interest?" The malleability of risk can be assessed by asking, "How much effort will it take to change this risk or protective factor?" Combined, these two estimates yield a ratio of impact to intervention effort, or "bang for the buck," so to speak.

We began this section with a reference to "risk constellations," or the intersection of various risk and protective factors. The breadth of potential candidates for inclusion in the risk constellation depends partly on professional training (e.g., medical versus sociological) and theoretical orientation. Bronfenbrenner (1977) proposed an ecological model in which human development is subject to simultaneous influence from concentric levels of the environment. The microsystem (immediate setting, such as family or classroom) is most proximal to the individual, with the exosystem (community and institutional practices) and macrosystem (larger social conditions and rules) levels setting the context within which individuals and families function. To illustrate these more distal levels of influence, Cicchetti, Toth, and Rogosch (2000) identified cultural acceptance of corporal punishment as an exosystem risk factor for child maltreatment, and active community and neighborhood programs as an exosystem protective factor. At the macrosystem level a shortage of affordable child care increases the risk for neglect, whereas a prosperous economy with a high rate of employment reduces that risk.

The distinction between micro-, exo-, and macrolevels of influence spans the discussion of intervention targets and tactics. The choice of intervention level is likely to be influenced as much by the perspectives and expertise of the professionals involved, as by "objective" features of the developmental process of interest. Many clinical psychologists have elected not to operate within exo- and macrosystem perspectives, but rather to target risk and protective factors that are considered to operate within individuals. Community oriented psychologists are steeped in an ideology that emphasizes systemic over individual influences on behavior (Albee, 1996; Elias, 1987), and often prefer to target the norms, structures, and practices of organizations or social units. Quite apart from ideological considerations, preventionists might intervene on a systems level on the basis of the "bang for the buck" calculation. Preventive processes that demand proactive changes in the behavior of individuals frequently require a high degree of persuasion in order to be successful. Modifications of the environment, by contrast, are not so dependent on individual motivation and compliance (although substantial persuasion may be required to institute them in the first place; cf. Tremblay and Peterson, 1999). The dimension of "active versus passive" preventive interventions reflects a continuum of effort demanded from the persons whose behavior is ultimately of interest.

Other considerations aside, requiring smaller effort of participants may yield greater likelihood of implementation (Tremblay and Peterson, 1999). If, for example, preventionists wish to reduce teen smoking, the theoretical model might incorporate contributions to smoking behavior from teens' attitudes about smoking, as well as from the availability of cigarettes. The teens' attitudes could be targeted (individual level variable; perhaps via advertisements designed to reduce the appeal of smoking), as could the availability of cigarettes (macrosystem variable; perhaps through removing cigarette vending machines or raising cigarette taxes). The bang for the buck calculation suggests that macrosystem intervention might be more effective, provided that the community is prepared to accept such restrictions. There are many demonstrations of large effects wrought by passive interventions aimed at efficient targets. To name only two, the Poison Prevention Packaging Act of 1970 dramatically reduced the incidence of child poisonings by mandating child resistant caps and limiting the quantity of medication that could be placed in a single container (Walton, 1982), and the Refrigerator Safety Act has virtually eliminated children's suffocation in refrigerators simply by requiring that refrigerator doors be operable from the inside (Robertson, 1983). One would have been hard pressed to achieve effects of this magnitude by educating children regarding the dangers of ingesting pills or playing in refrigerators.

Given that multiple domains and levels are implicated in most risk pathways, it seems plausible that the most powerful and enduring effects would be obtained by targeting more than one of them (Coie et al., 1993). The FAST Track program to prevent conduct disorders (Conduct Problems Prevention Research Group, 1992) offers an example of a multicomponent preventive intervention that is remarkable in many respects, including the clarity of its theoretical foundation, the incorporation of both universal and selected prevention elements, and the scope of its ongoing assessment process. The universal component of the intervention consists of a classroom-based interpersonal problem-solving curriculum, beginning in grade one. The selected compon-ent, offered to a subset of children identified during kindergarten as at high risk for the persistence of conduct problems, adds much more intensive parent groups, child social skills training, case management, and academic tutoring. In its most comprehensive form, the intervention targeted six domains: (1) disruptive behavior at home, (2) aggressive and off-task behavior at school, (3) social cognitions and affect regulation skills, (4) peer relations, (5) academic skills, and (6) the family's relationship with the school. It involved multiple agents (child, parents, teachers, and peers) across home and school settings. Early reports show positive effects on parenting and on children's academic and social skills, peer relations, and disruptive behavior for the high risk sample, and on classroom behavior and peer relations for the universal intervention (Conduct Problems Prevention Research Group, 1999a; 1999b).

By contrast, the educational reform efforts of Felner and his colleagues (Project HiPlaces; Felner, 2000) target exosystem variables and the promotion of educational effectiveness for adolescents. The theoretical model underlying Project HiPlaces specifies protective mechanisms such as "establishing small personalized learning communities," "empowering decision-making at each of the appropriate system levels," and "holding high expectations and opportunities that promote success for all students" (pp. 293–4). Like FAST Track, Project HiPlaces involves intervention in multiple domains, but with more direct attention to modifying educational environments than the individuals who occupy them.

Selecting tactics

If targets are the risk or protective processes that an intervention aims to alter, tactics describe the means by which the intervention is delivered to its intended target, or the vehicle used for disseminating the intervention. In this section we discuss the scope and strategic timing of preventive interventions.

The universal/selected/indicated typology, described above, addresses the scope of intervention, from population-wide to narrowly focused, based on the distribution of risks within the population of interest. Risks that are considered to be evenly distributed across the population suggest interventions of universal scope, whereas risks that are concentrated within identifiable subgroups of the population call for interventions of narrower scope (selected or indicated). Wellness promotion programs, for example, often target protective mechanisms (e.g., competence, resilience, empowerment; Cowen, 1994) thought to reduce a broad array of risks, and thus to be beneficial to everyone. These programs employ universal intervention tactics, such as integrating coping skills education into school environments (cf. Elias and Weissberg, 2000), that are feasible if the intervention is relatively inexpensive and/or acceptable to the entire community. When interventionists seek to prevent problems that occur at a relatively low base rate, and among certain subgroups of the population, selective interventions with high risk groups are more efficient. High risk populations may be readily identifiable, as are children of divorce (Pedro-Carroll, 1997), or they may be less obvious, such as maltreated children (Cicchetti, Toth, and Rogosch, 2000), or adolescents with body image concerns.

The importance of timing in intervening with risk and protective processes has received increased attention with accumulating scholarship in developmental psychopathology. A circumstance that poses a threat during some stressful life transition or sensitive period of maturation, may be either irrelevant or fully entrenched at another juncture. If a preventive intervention is to fall on fertile ground, it should occur after the presence of a risk process predicts a problematic outcome, but before it has been allowed to exert significant influence (Coie et al., 1993). Both the potency and malleability of a risk mechanism may be compromised outside this window of opportunity. Even identifying high risk samples (for interventions of narrow scope) is complicated when the predictive validity of the risk factor is low. Under these conditions a sample selected on the basis of the risk factor will include people who would not have gone on to suffer problematic outcomes (false positives) and fail to include people who would (false negatives), both of which may represent inefficient use of intervention resources.

Two related developmental concepts are relevant to identifying windows of opportunity for prevention or promotion: maturation and transition. Risks may accumulate around particular periods of development (i.e., maturation), and/or around changes in an individual's surroundings that demand adaptation. The risk for physical harm from child maltreatment, for example, has been shown to peak during two periods of maturation: preschool years, when the demands and frustrations of caring for children are great and their capacity for self-care and protection is small, and again at puberty, when the adolescent's struggle for individuation frequently antagonizes parents (Wolfe and St. Pierre, 1989). Just prior to either of these periods represents an optimal time to offer strategies for coping with parent–child conflict. An example of a transitional risk is entailed in Patterson, DeBaryshe, and Ramsey's (1989) model for the development of conduct disorder. Children with conduct problems often emerge from families in which coercive behavior functions to terminate aversive interactions (i.e., such behavior is negatively reinforced). Under such conditions, coercive behavior may be considered adaptive. In the school environment, however, coercive behavior is not the most adaptive pattern of responding to situational demands (it tends to be punished). The task of transitioning from the contingencies of the home environment to those of the school environment thus represents a node of concentrated risk in the developmental trajectory toward academic failure, peer rejection, and diversification of conduct problems. Intervention aiming to divert this trajectory should take place before or during the transition into school, before conflict in school initiates a cascade of failure outside the home.

A third example invites consideration of both maturational and transitional elements in defining windows of opportunity. The threat of ingesting household poisons is concentrated when children are old enough to explore their environment but still young enough to impulsively swallow substances they encounter. Maturation considerations alone, then, might tempt one to intervene toward the middle of the child's first year, to encourage safe storage of household chemicals. Christophersen (1993) observed, however, that the most effective time to introduce infant safety measures appears to be during the prenatal period, after parents are attuned to the issue but before they have had the opportunity to develop a false sense of security from engaging in unsafe practices that their children have been fortunate enough to survive unscathed. Maximal potency of the risk process, defined by the child's capacities, would fall late in the first year of life, but maximal malleability is achieved during the transition to parenthood.

Working in communities
Communities play an important role in prevention and promotion at several levels. First, the concept of community – some circumscribed population of individuals who share certain characteristics – helps to establish the reach of a given risk. Features shared

by members of a community, in other words, are themselves important sources of risk and protection; the very act of defining communities is a necessary step in developing an understanding of risks faced by their inhabitants (Kellam and Van Horn, 1997). Definitions of community usually imply a geographic boundary, but may, for some purposes, derive from other shared characteristics such as ethnicity, sexual orientation, or the experience of a traumatic event.

Second, as Reiss and Price (1996) observed, "Prevention research begins and ends in communities" (p. 1113). At minimum, one must negotiate with a community to arrange access for basic and applied prevention research. Beyond logistical considerations, community psychology ideals encourage empowering stakeholders and adapting to local needs (cf. Elias, 1987; Heller, 1996). If prevention work is to have lasting impact, researchers must either build long-term relationships with host communities, or offer them ownership in the project so that the intervention remains in place after the investigators have vacated the community with their data.

Psychology researchers are acutely aware of the challenges of recruiting and retaining individuals to participate in interventions, yet the recruitment of *communities* to support prevention is an underdeveloped aspect of research methodology (Capaldi et al., 1997). Biglan (1995) has proposed a scientific framework for identifying the contextual variables that influence cultural practices – in effect, an extension of functional analysis to Bronfenbrenner's exosystem level. Just as there is now a strong body of evidence that supports shaping the behavior of individuals to promote better mental health, there is also a growing empirical basis for preferring some cultural practices (e.g., educational methods) over others. Nonetheless, "effective behavior change methods are seldom adopted simply because they have been shown to work" (Biglan 1995: 15). Observing that public policy and dissemination are themselves behavioral phenomena, Biglan asserts that clinical psychology is well equipped to incorporate these processes into its explicit domain of study, and to deliberately shape the adoption of empirically supported cultural practices.

Finally, features of the community define "boundary conditions" for the generalization of findings in prevention research. Both illness prevention and wellness promotion models call for a progression from efficacy research, in the form of relatively controlled clinical trials, to effectiveness research in more representative community contexts, in order to evaluate the external validity of an intervention and its underlying theory. It is incumbent on investigators to specify and deliberately sample theoretically relevant setting (community) characteristics.

Selected Methodological Topics in Prevention Research

Ethical considerations

Americans have often been wary of large-scale efforts to influence their behavior, particularly, it seems, when the rationale invokes science (although they are much more complacent about influence by advertisers). This suspicion is not without basis, of course; there have been horrific abuses perpetrated in the name of science (e.g., human experimentation by the Nazis, the notorious Tuskegee study on the natural course of syphilis), and less flagrant infringements on the rights of research participants have been, and continue to be, more common than acceptable. Indeed, the risk that a scientist's power and prestige might be abused is so constant, even for conscientious investigators, that research institutions routinely subject scientific proposals to independent review to safeguard the welfare of participants. In the spirit of such self-monitoring, we offer a few comments concerning ethical challenges highlighted by prevention research.

Preventive interventions are not always evident to the persons whose behavior is targeted for modification. An intervention may not involve any direct contact whatsoever, much less an explicit informed consent procedure between researcher and participant. To the extent that prevention research targets systems-level variables, or individual-level variables without a participant's awareness, researchers risk exacerbating the public's mistrust of science. Influence attempts that are overt, such as those of the advertising industry or the legal system, are broadly accepted. Efforts of behavioral scientists to "engineer" healthy behaviors, or to eradicate unhealthy ones, can be perceived as paternalistic manipulations (cf. Chomsky's (1971) attack on Skinner's reinforcement of desirable behaviors).

In view of the historical tendency for humans to exploit and otherwise coerce one another, Biglan (1995) has suggested six practices to promote ethical social change research. The first stipulates that minimizing coercion and punishment should be the highest priority. Although these methods of influence can be used legitimately and appropriately by military or police organizations to prevent crime or violence, social scientists do not and should not have such license. A second recommendation involves voluntary informed consent. Traditional, individualized informed consent is rarely practical in large-scale prevention research, but prevention researchers can nevertheless provide public information so that citizens can make informed choices about program participation or implementation in their communities. The third suggestion is to submit intervention proposals to review by disinterested parties, much like the institutional review process for laboratory-based behavioral research, to ensure that the risks and benefits of research are appropriately distributed and communicated. A fourth recommendation is to involve target populations in the design of the research itself. The involvement of stakeholders can improve participation as well as outcome (Mertens, 1998), and relates to Biglan's fifth principle, which is to maintain awareness of power imbalances among researchers, policy makers, and target populations.

Biglan's sixth practice guideline is an emphatic reminder that all efforts should be based on data. There are numerous instances of prevention efforts whose proponents have either ignored or failed to provide empirical data. Self-esteem programs for children, for example, have squandered tremendous resources because well-meaning educators assumed, mistakenly, that poor self-esteem is the cause, rather than the effect, of school failure or social rejection (Biglan, 1995). Likewise, there are hundreds of programs that rest on their face validity rather than evaluation of their efforts (for a large-scale example, consider Project DARE, instituted in over half of the nation's school districts despite consistent evidence of minimal impact on drug use) (e.g., Ennet et al., 1994; Lynam et al., 1999). The failure to evaluate change efforts has been compared to a hospital abandoning the monitoring of vital signs on heart surgery patients "because the last 100 operations have been a success" (Biglan, 1995: 196). Prevention and promotion efforts that are committed to and based on empirical evidence are more likely to succeed, and to address the problems that incur the greatest social costs.

Measurement issues

The purpose of this section is not to offer an overview of program evaluation, but to draw attention to special challenges of measurement in prevention. Both of these challenges are a function of the community context in which prevention and promotion research typically takes place. One involves levels of measurement and statistical analysis, and a second involves what has been termed the ecological validity of measures.

Levels of measurement

Throughout this chapter we have discussed person versus systems levels of conceptualization. We noted that risk constellations consist of person characteristics interacting with environment (systems) characteristics. We noted that intervention targets and tactics may focus on individuals or systems, or both. A logical extension of this pattern might be to offer person versus systems levels of measurement and statistical analysis, or better still, a strategy for measuring and analyzing relationships of persons to systems (cf. the Fort Bragg study, which measured utilization of systems by individuals), or systems to each other. Unfortunately, a technology for measuring systems-level relationships has yet to be widely promulgated.

Shinn (1990) argued that most research in community psychology is, or ought to be, cross-level in nature, examining relations between people and their settings. Instead, researchers articulate an interest in cross-level relationships, such as empowerment or person–environment fit, *which they subsequently measure with indicators of individual psychological variables* (e.g., locus of control, satisfaction). Thus, there is frequently a mismatch between level of conceptualization, on the one hand, and level of data collection and analysis, on the other. The validity of measuring extraindividual phenomena by eliciting the opinions or experiences of individuals is open to question. Shinn proposes two reasons for the persistence of this practice: "confusion between the consciously perceived environment and the functionally significant environment, and relative poverty of psychological theory at extraindividual levels" (p. 122).

The problem of subjective responses is attenuated by the use of multiple informants and methods, but measurement of the phenomenon remains fundamentally indirect (Shinn, 1990). One risk of extrapolating from an individual level of analysis to a systems level of conceptualization is that relationships discovered at one level may be irrelevant to the other. Shinn offers the example of homelessness, which is likely to have entirely different determinants at the levels of cities and of individuals. Aggregated effects are a function of central tendency (e.g., employment rates), whereas individual outcomes are determined by deviations from central tendency (lack of employment skills). There have been attempts to address the levels of measurement versus conceptualization issue with statistical techniques, but they are complex and not readily accessible for most researchers. Adding to the chorus favoring theoretically driven prevention research, Shinn (1990) emphasizes the search for functionally significant, rather than merely accessible (to awareness) intervention targets, and construct validation of measures.

Ecologically valid measurement

Related to levels of measurement is the concept of ecological validity, which distinguishes between the assessment of (intraindividual) subjective well-being, and of person–environment fit (Kellam and Van Horn, 1997). When researchers investigate a subject's mental state, they assess well-being. To evaluate person–environment fit it is necessary to first define the social demands to which a subject is responding, and then determine how well the subject is meeting those demands. The appropriate informants for this investigation are "natural raters" in the various social contexts in which the subject functions. Natural raters' judgments of the subject's performance are referred to as "social adaptational status" measures (Kellam and Van Horn, 1997: 181). Kellam and Van Horn propose that social adaptational status and psychological well-being are distinct components of mental health.

Seeking performance information from sources other than the subject is not unique to community psychology or prevention, of course. It comes naturally to clinicians working with children or substance abusers, for example, both populations whose need for treatment is frequently determined by the judgments of others. Ecological validity is salient for prevention research precisely because this work is frequently aiming for broader goals than the amelioration of current subjective distress for participants (who are, by definition, not "symptomatic"). Interventions that aim to empower community members have been criticized on the basis that they are public relations exercises rather than meaningful improvements (Stufflebeam, 1994). As in all instances, ecological validity is best served by measuring theoretically determined, prevention-relevant constructs.

Priorities for Future Research

The field of prevention has been blessed with several spirited and informative manifestos during the past decade (e.g., Coie et al., 1993; Cowen, 1994; Mrazek and Haggerty, 1994; Reiss and Price, 1996), and as a result suffers no shortage of recommendations for future progress. We offer a sampling of those most relevant to the issues highlighted in this chapter.

Development of measurement and analytic expertise

As indicated in the previous section, prevention research contends with devilishly complex measurement issues. Prevention science sits astride the intersection of life-span development, epidemiology, and clinical or community psychology (Kellam and Van Horn, 1997; Reiss and Price, 1996). This position is usually touted as a source of synergistic perspectives, but if the field has benefited from their combined strengths, it has also inherited their collective complications. Longitudinal modeling, sampling challenges, the problem of levels of analysis, combining data from multiple informants, skewed data and small effect sizes (cf. Durlak and Wells, 1997) – all call for sophisticated measurement and analytic techniques. Coping with these problems, where strategies have been developed at all, frequently requires skills that exceed the methodological repertoire of the average clinical researcher. Recognizing this deficit, both the NIMH (Coie et al., 1993) and IOM (Munoz, Mrazek, and Haggerty, 1996) panels recommended the allocation of resources to train entry-level and mid-career scientists in prevention research methodology. If some of these resources are directed to disseminating prevention methodology into doctoral-level curricula, more clinical psychology researchers may be in a position to contribute to prevention research.

Multidisciplinary efforts

The inherent complexity of prevention research threatens to make it the exclusive province of specialists. One alternative to demanding unrealistic expertise from any who would wade into the fray, is inviting contributions from multiple disciplines (e.g., psychology, epidemiology, medicine), and also from both sides of the scientist–practitioner divide (Reiss and Price, 1996). To be sure, multidisciplinary collaboration brings its own set of challenges – disparate professional languages, traditions, and techniques – but it is precisely this diversity that is needed to apprehend the layered contexts of community research. Federal funding agencies are increasingly encouraging large, longitudinal, multisite, and/or multidisciplinary efforts (the FAST Track program is one of these) which concentrate resources to develop powerful and exciting studies.

More wellness promotion

This chapter began by describing the prevention movement's struggle for priority on the public policy agenda. Among many speculations regarding the reasons for that struggle, we focus on two that have particular relevance for wellness promotion. First, the costs of treatment for illness are usually assessed against the immediate beneficiary of that treatment, or some entity with a contractual obligation to the beneficiary. By contrast, the costs of prevention and promotion programs are typically borne by society at large, rather than individuals or third party payers (Albee and Gullotta, 1997). Taxpayers are more likely to resist expenditures for intervention efforts as perceived urgency of the service diminishes. This brings us to our second point, which is that humans are, by nature, tempted to grant causal primacy to proximal events (Gilovich, 1991) and to equate proximity of cause and effect with urgency (Cowen, 2000). This presents a problem for prevention, and particularly for wellness promotion: early intervention programs are at risk of being perceived as either inefficient (if for risk prevention), or outright frills (if for wellness enhancement).

Wellness promotion advocates find themselves waging a campaign on two fronts. On one hand, they insist that there is more to quality of life than absence of disease, and that our society should invest in competence and positive subjective states solely on their own merits (Seligman and Csikszentmihalyi, 2000). At the same time, they muster strong arguments in favor of wellness promotion *as an illness prevention strategy*. In response to arguments that the conceptualization, measurement, and determinants of psychological well-being remain too vague at present to merit priority in the public policy agenda (Munoz, Mrazek, and Haggerty, 1996), wellness advocates (e.g., Cowen, 2000) counter that disease-driven developmental models fail to appreciate the global impact of positive states on mental health. Promoting wellness, they assert, constitutes disease prevention *par excellence*, offering protection against numerous problematic outcomes (cf. multifinality; Cicchetti and Rogosch, 1996) as a *byproduct* of enhancing competence (Zigler, Taussig, and Black, 1992). Furthermore, wellness promotion interventions are potent, demonstrating effect sizes as strong as disease prevention programs (Durlak and Wells, 1997). Cowen's (2000) objection to a disease-focused definition of prevention science underscores this theme: "Moreover, should it turn out that some types of disorder reduction can better be realized by a wellness enhancement than by a risk–disease prevention approach, exclusive emphasis on the latter will act to obscure the former's potential for cutting down the flow of the very adverse conditions that a frontal disease-prevention strategy seeks to eradicate" (p. 495).

Conclusions

Throughout the history of clinical psychology in the US, prevention efforts have struggled to compete for priority in the public health agenda. The past decade has seen a resurgence of interest, as an expanding body of evidence has changed the complexion of prevention from a visionary campaign – rooted primarily in compelling ideology – to a science with a strong empirical basis. Developmental psychopathology has helped to clarify the connection between early life experiences and later functioning. The central insights of developmental psychopathology have revolved around the relationship between normal and abnormal development, the interplay between nature and nurture over time, and the convergences among developmental trajectories, such that there are few unique correspondences between early events and later outcomes.

The unique challenges of research in prevention and promotion arise in no small part simply from the elapsed time between hypothesized causes and effects. Temporal contiguity is one of the intuitive cues by which humans infer causal relationships, because the complexities introduced by longer spans of time stretch our cognitive capabilities. Theory is so important to the enterprise of prevention research because it guides investigators across these long spans of time. Theory enables teasing out active ingredients from confounding variables (e.g., risk mechanisms from marker variables) in the primordial soup of developmental influences. Theory permits measurement of distal indicators of the outcome of interest, when the outcome itself is inaccessibly distant in the future.

Prevention research identifies theoretically relevant risk and protective mechanisms, which then become potential targets for intervention. Intervention may aim to prevent discrete illnesses (the illness prevention model), or to promote broad competencies (the wellness promotion model). Important prevention design considerations include the scope of the intervention (universal, selected, or indicated), the level of the target variable (individual or micro-, exo-, or macrosystem), and the timing of intervention, so as to maximize the potency and malleability of the risk process. Communities are important elements in the definition of risk factors and high risk populations. They serve as the context for most preventive interventions, so researchers must learn to navigate within communities, and to serve local needs.

Methodological issues addressed in this chapter included the ethics of broad-scale interventions, challenges of measurement, and multidisciplinary collaboration. Because preventive interventions frequently are not evident to the individuals whose behavior they attempt to modify, some special ethical considerations arise. Social scientists can safeguard the rights of participants by minimizing coercive methods of influence, involving the public in choices about program implementation, and carefully evaluating prevention programs. The measurement of systems-level variables, and especially of relationships between individual and systems-level constructs, is both conceptually and technically complex. Experts have identified dissemination of prevention methodology and analysis as a high priority for the progress of prevention research. Multidisciplinary collaboration is one means for engaging expertise from various traditions in behavior change efforts.

Prevention has been a "hard sell" in part because people tend to attach little urgency to distal causes, and in part because the public is generally asked to pay for preventive interventions, whereas affected individuals often assume more of the burden for treatment of acute distress. Wellness promotion is arguably the most proactive variant of prevention, magnifying both its promise and its burden of attracting a constituency.

References

Albee, G. W. (1996). Revolutions and counterrevolutions in prevention. *American Psychologist*, *51*, 1130–3.

Albee, G. W., and Gullotta, T. P. (1997). Primary prevention's evolution. In G. W. Albee and T. P. Gullotta (eds.), *Primary prevention works* (vol. 6, pp. 3–21). Thousand Oaks, CA: Sage Publications.

Biglan, A. (1995). *Changing cultural practices: A contextualist framework for intervention research*. Reno, NV: Context Press.

Binet, A., and Heisler, S. (trans.) (1975). *Modern ideas about children*. Menlo Park, CA: Suzanne Heisler.

Bronfenbrenner, U. (1977). Toward an experimental ecology of human development. *American Psychologist*, *32*, 513–31.

Burgard, D., and Lyons, P. (1994). Alternatives in obesity treatment: Focusing on health for fat women. In P. Fallon, M. A. Katzman, and S. C. Wooley (eds.), *Feminist perspectives on eating disorders* (pp. 212–30). New York: Guilford Press.

Capaldi, D. M., Chamberlain, P., Fetrow, R. A., and Wilson, J. E. (1997). Conducting ecologically valid prevention research: Recruiting and retaining a "whole village" in multimethod, multiagent studies. *American Journal of Community Psychology*, *25*, 471–92.

Caplan, G. (1964). *Principles of preventive psychiatry*. New York: Basic Books.

Caspi, A., Henry, B., McGee, R., Moffitt, T. E., and Silva, P. A. (1995). Temperamental origins of child and adolescent behavior problems: From age three to fifteen. *Child Development*, *65*, 55–68.

Chomsky, N. (1971). The case against B. F. Skinner. *The New York Review of Books*, December 31, 18–24.

Christophersen, E. R. (1993). Improving compliance in childhood injury control. In N. A. Krasnegor, L. Epstein, S. B. Johnson, and S. J. Yaffe (eds.), *Developmental aspects of health compliance behavior* (pp. 219–31). Hillsdale, NJ: Erlbaum.

Cicchetti, D. (1984). The emergence of developmental psychopathology. *Child Development*, *55*, 1–7.

Cicchetti, D., and Rogosch, F. A. (1996). Equifinality and multifinality in developmental psychopathology. *Development and Psychopathology*, *8*, 597–600.

Cicchetti, D., Toth, S. L., and Rogosch, F. A. (2000). The development of psychological wellness in maltreated children. In D. Cicchetti, J. Rappaport, I. Sandler, and R. P. Weissberg (eds.), The Promotion of Wellness in Children and Adolescents (pp. 395–426). Washington, DC: Child Welfare League of America.

Coie, J. D., Watt, N. F., West, S. G., Hawkins, J. D., Asarnow, J. R., Markman, H. J., Ramey, S. L., Shure, M. B., and Long, B. (1993). The science of prevention: A conceptual framework and some directions for a national research program. *American Psychologist*, *48*, 1013–22.

Commission on Chronic Illness (1957). *Chronic illness in the United States* (Vol. 1). Cambridge, MA: Harvard University Press.

Conduct Problems Prevention Research Group (1992). A developmental and clinical model for the prevention of conduct disorder: The FAST Track program. *Development and Psychopathology*, *4*, 509–27.

Conduct Problems Prevention Research Group (1999a). Initial impact of the fast track prevention trial for conduct problems: I. The high risk sample. *Journal of Consulting and Clinical Psychology*, *67*, 631–47.

Conduct Problems Prevention Research Group (1999b). Initial impact of the fast track trial for conduct problems: II. Classroom effects. *Journal of Consulting and Clinical Psychology*, *67*, 648–57.

Cowen, E. L. (1994). The enhancement of psychological wellness: Challenges and opportunities. *American Journal of Community Psychology*, *22*, 149–79.

Cowen, E. L. (1996). The ontogenesis of primary prevention: Lengthy strides and stubbed toes. *American Journal of Community Psychology*, *24*, 235–49.

Cowen, E. L. (2000). Psychological wellness: Some hopes for the future. In D. Cicchetti, J. Rappaport, I. Sandler, and R. P. Weissberg (eds.), *The promotion of wellness in children and adolescents* (pp. 477–503). Washington, DC: Child Welfare League of America.

Durlak, J. A., and Wells, A. M. (1997). Primary prevention mental health programs for children and adolescents: A meta-analytic review. *American Journal of Community Psychology*, *25*, 115–52.

Elias, M. (1987). Establishing enduring prevention programs: Advancing the legacy of Swampscott. *American Journal of Community Psychology*, *15*, 539–53.

Elias, M. J., and Weissberg, R. P. (2000). Wellness in schools: The grandfather of primary prevention tells a story. In D. Cicchetti, J. Rappaport, I. Sandler, and R. P. Weissberg (eds.), *The promotion of wellness in children and adolescents* (pp. 243–70). Washington, DC: Child Welfare League of America.

Ennet, S. T., Tobler, N. S., Ringwalt, C. L., and Flewelling, R. L. (1994). How effective is Drug Abuse Resistance Education? A meta-analysis of Project DARE outcome evaluations. *American Journal of Public Health*, *84*, 1394–1401.

Felner, R. (2000). Educational reform as ecologically based prevention and promotion: The project on high performance learning communities. In D. Cicchetti, J. Rappaport, I. Sandler, and R. P. Weissberg (eds.), *The promotion of wellness in children and adolescents*. Washington, DC: Child Welfare League of America.

Garner, D. M., and Wooley, S. C. (1991). Confronting the failure of behavioral and dietary treatments for obesity. *Clinical Psychology Review, 11*, 729–80.

Gilovich, T. (1991). *How we know what isn't so: The fallibility of human reason in everyday life*. New York: Free Press.

Gore, S., and Eckenrode, J. (1996). Context and process in research on risk and resilience. In R. J. Haggerty, L. R. Sherrod, N. Garmezy, and M. Rutter (eds.), *Stress, risk, and resilience in children and adolescents: Processes, mechanisms, and interventions* (pp. 19–63). New York: Cambridge University Press.

Heller, K. (1996). Coming of age of prevention science. *American Psychologist, 11*, 1123–7.

Holmbeck, G. N. (1997). Toward terminological, conceptual, and statistical clarity in the study of mediators and moderators: Examples from the child clinical and pediatric psychology literatures. *Journal of Consulting and Clinical Psychology, 65*, 599–610.

Kagan, J. (1989). Temperamental contributions to social behavior. *American Psychologist, 44*, 668–74.

Kellam, S. G., and Van Horn, Y. V. (1997). Life course development, community epidemiology, and preventive trials: A scientific structure for prevention research. *American Journal of Community Psychology, 25*, 177–88.

Kessler, R. C., McGonagle, K. A., Shanyang, Z., Nelson, C. B., Hughes, M., Eshleman, S., Wittchen, H., and Kendler, K. S. (1994). Lifetime and 12-month prevalence of DSM-III-R psychiatric disorders in the United States: Results from the National Comorbidity Survey. *Archives of General Psychiatry, 51*, 8–18.

Lewin, K. (1946). Frontiers in group dynamics, part 2: Channels of group life: Social planning and action research. *Human Relations, 1*, 143–53.

Loeber, R. (1990). Development and risk factors of juvenile antisocial behavior and delinquency. *Clinical Psychology Review, 10*, 1–41.

Lynam, D. R., Milich, R., Zimmerman, R., Novak, S. P., Logan, T. K., Martin, C., Leukefeld, C., and Clayton, R. (1999). Project DARE: No effects at 10-year follow-up. *Journal of Consulting and Clinical Psychology, 67*, 590–3.

McBurnett, K. (1992). Psychobiological approaches to personality and their applications to child psychopathology. In B. B. Lahey and A. E. Kazdin (eds.), *Advances in clinical child psychology* (vol. 14, pp. 107–64). New York: Plenum Press.

McFarlane, T., Polivy, J., and McCabe, R. E. (1999). Help, not harm: Psychological foundation for a non-dieting approach toward health. *Journal of Social Issues, 55*, 261–76.

Masten, A. S., Best, K. M., and Garmezy, N. (1990). Resilience and development: Contributions from the study of children who overcome adversity. *Development and Psychopathology, 2*, 425–44.

Mertens, D. (1998). *Research methods in education and psychology: Integrating diversity with quantitative and qualitative approaches*. Thousand Oaks, CA: Sage Publications.

Mrazek, P. J., and Haggerty, R. J. (eds.) (1994). *Reducing risks for mental disorders: Frontiers for preventive intervention research*. Washington, DC: National Academy Press.

Munoz, R. F., Mrazek, P. J., and Haggerty, R. J. (1996). Institute of Medicine report on prevention of mental disorders: Summary and commentary. *American Psychologist, 51*, 1116–22.

National Center for Children in Poverty (1990). *Five million children*. Washington, DC: National Center for Children in Poverty.

Nicholson, I. R., and Neufeld, R. W. J. (1992). A dynamic vulnerability perspective on stress and schizophrenia. *American Journal of Orthopsychiatry, 62*, 117–30.

Patterson, G., DeBaryshe, B., and Ramsey, E. (1989). A developmental perspective on antisocial behavior. *American Psychologist, 44*, 329–35.

Pedro-Carroll, J. (1997). The children of divorce intervention program: Fostering resilient outcomes for school-aged children. In G. W. T. P. G. Albee (ed.), *Primary prevention works* (pp. 213–38). Thousand Oaks, CA: Sage Publications.

Perry, M. J., and Albee, G. W. (1994). On "the science of prevention." *American Psychologist, 49*, 1087–8.

Plomin, R., and Rutter, M. (1998). Child development, molecular genetics, and what to do with genes once they are found. *Child Development, 69*, 1223–42.

Price, R. H., Cowen, E. L., Lorion, R. P., and Ramos-McKay, J. (eds.) (1988). *14 ounces of prevention*. Washington, DC: American Psychological Association.

Putallaz, M., and Dunn, S. E. (1990). The importance of peer relations. In M. Lewis and S. M. Miller (eds.), *Handbook of developmental psychopathology* (pp. 227–36.). New York: Plenum.

Reiss, D., and Price, R. H. (1996). National research agenda for prevention research: The National Institute of Mental Health Report. *American Psychologist, 51*, 1109–15.

Robertson, L. S. (1983). *Injuries: Causes, control strategies, and public policy*. Lexington, MA: Lexington Books.

Rutter, M. (1996). Stress research: Accomplishments and tasks ahead. In R. J. Haggerty, L. R. Sherrod, N. Garmezy, and M. Rutter (eds.), *Stress, risk, and resilience in children and adolescents: Processes, mechanisms, and interventions* (pp. 354–85). New York: Cambridge University Press.

Rutter, M., Dunn, J., Plomin, R., Simonoff, E., Pickles, A., Maughan, B., Ormel, J., Meyer, J., and Eaves, L. (1997). Integrating nature and nurture: Implications of person–environment correlations and interactions for developmental psychopathology. *Development and Psychopathology, 9*, 335–64.

Seligman, M. E. P., and Csikszentmihalyi, M. (2000). Positive psychology: An introduction. *American Psychologist, 55*, 5–14.

Shinn, M. (1990). Mixing and matching: Levels of conceptualization, measurement and statistical analysis in community research. In P. Tolan, C. Keys, F. Chertok, and L. Jason (eds.), *Researching community psychology* (pp. 111–26). Washington, DC: American Psychological Association.

Skinner, B. F. (1948). *Walden Two*. New York: MacMillan.

Sroufe, L. A. (1990). Considering normal and abnormal together: The essence of developmental psychopathology. *Development and Psychopathology, 2*, 335–47.

Sroufe, L. A., and Rutter, M. (1980). The domain of developmental psychopathology. *Child Development, 55*, 17–29.

Stufflebeam, D. L. (1994). Empowerment evaluation, objectivist evaluation, and evaluation standards: Where the future of evaluation should not go and where it needs to go. *Evaluation Practice, 15*, 321–38.

Tremblay, G., and Peterson, L. (1999). Prevention of childhood injury: Clinical and public policy challenges. *Clinical Psychology Review, 4*, 415–34.

Wadden, T. A., Anderson, D. A., and Foster, G. D. (1999). Two-year changes in lipids and lipoproteins associated with the maintenance of a 5% to 10% reduction in initial weight: Some findings and some questions. *Obesity Research, 7*, 170–8.

Walton, W. W. (1982). An evaluation of the Poison Prevention Packaging Act. *Pediatrics, 69*, 363–70.

Wei, M., Kampert, J. B., Barlow, C. E., Nichaman, M. Z., Gibbons, L. W., Paffenbarger, R. S., and Blair, S. N. (1999). Relationship between low cardiorespiratory fitness and mortality in normal-weight, overweight, and obese men. *Journal of the American Medical Association, 282*, 1547–53.

Wolfe, D. A., and St. Pierre, J. (1989). Child abuse and neglect. In T. H. Ollendick and M. Hersen (eds.), *Handbook of child psychopathology* (pp. 377–98). New York: Plenum.

Zigler, E., and Muenchow, S. (1992). *The inside story of Head Start*. New York: Basic Books.

Zigler, E., Taussig, C., and Black, K. (1992). A promising preventative for juvenile delinquency. *American Psychologist, 47*, 997–1006.

VIGNETTE

Research in Prevention and Promotion

Anne K. Jacobs

Coyle, K., Basen-Engquist, K., Kirby, D., Parcel, G., Banspach, S., Harrist, R., Baumler, E., and Weil, M. (1999). Short-term impact of Safer Choices: A multicomponent, school-based HIV, other STD and pregnancy program. *Journal of School Health, 69*, 5, 181–8.

The Safer Choices program is a theoretically driven, multicomponent program designed to target several domains related to unsafe adolescent sexual behavior. The authors of the above-cited investigation detailed the features of the five program components: school organization, curriculum and staff development, peer resources and school environment, parent education, and school–community linkages. The authors' findings regarding the program's short-term impact are strengthened by their methodologically sound study design and the use of a comparison program. A total of twenty schools in California and Texas were randomly assigned to the intervention condition or to a comparison condition in which the students received a standard, knowledge-based HIV prevention program. Data were collected at baseline and at a seven-month follow-up. The authors reported a 66 percent participation rate, and provided statistics describing the reasons for student nonparticipation, as well as attrition analyses. While multiple informants were not used in data collection, the authors described steps taken to ensure confidentiality and to help increase the accuracy of the self-report measures used.

The final sample of 3,864 was ethnically diverse and large enough to allow for several complex analyses. The authors were careful to articulate the power limitations in examining between-school differences in light of the small number of schools. Detailed psychometric information was provided on the study measures and reported coefficient alphas on all attitude/belief and behavior measures were indicative of adequate internal consistency. Coyle and colleagues employed a multilevel model of analyses examining the clustering of individuals within schools, in addition to using individuals as the unit of analysis. In this way, variations between schools and correlations within schools between students were examined. Demographic covariates of outcome scores and baseline differences were controlled for in analyses of change scores (i.e., from baseline to seven-month assessment) between the two conditions. Possible between-state effects were also examined, as well as group-by-location interactions.

The authors found that students who received the Safer Choices program showed significant change in the desired directions on nine of the thirteen study psychosocial variables, as well as self-reported risk behaviors. One group-by-location interaction was found to be significant which indicated greater effects in Texas than in California in reducing unprotected intercourse. The results were encouraging, but the authors were careful to recognize the possible lack of generalizability of study findings to students who are frequently absent from school or those who drop out. In addition to the 7-month follow-up described in this article, the authors plan to conduct additional follow-ups at 19 and 31 months post-baseline. The strengths of the Coyle et al. article include:

- Multicomponent prevention program
- Well-detailed features of program components
- Randomized design
- High retention rate of participants
- Ethnically diverse participant group
- Large sample size enabling complex analyses
- Use of a standard prevention program as a comparison
- Took steps to help increase truthfulness of self-reports
- Multilevel model of analyses to account for clustering of individuals within schools
- Controlled for baseline differences between intervention and comparison schools
- Plan to have two additional follow-ups at 19 months and 31 months after baseline

CHAPTER EIGHTEEN

Research in Ethnic Minority Communities: Cultural Diversity Issues in Clinical Psychology

Yo Jackson

Over the past twenty years, psychological science has experienced an increased dialogue regarding the importance of ethnicity in clinical and developmental research. Aware of the USA's ever growing population of people of color, psychology has responded by discussing relevant issues and developing panels of experts to generate and advocate a new consciousness in the discipline. By examining the mainstream focus in past research, this new awareness has called upon scientists and practitioners to increase their use and practice of cultural competence. This is especially true in the methodological approaches in clinical psychology science. As with many revolutions, the constructs and behaviors suggested have not met with universal applause. Rather, it has been outspoken minorities of psychologists who have led the call to direct changes in the way the profession manages its scientific research.

Currently, it is unclear if the majority of scientific practitioners are simply unaware of the need for revising their approaches to research and treatment, or if they lack information about how to align their approaches to reflect cultural sensitivity. However, professional conduct changes are clearly necessary, because past research has consistently indicated the failure of traditional treatments to meet the needs of people of color (American Psychological Association, 1993; Dana, 1993; Sue et al., 1991).

The field of multicultural competence and ethnic diversity is a rather new, but compelling area, providing clear and feasible guidelines for alterations in academic, clinical, and research practice (Sue, Arredondo, and McDavis, 1995). Unfortunately, little comprehensive study has focused on the internal and external validity of research methods and treatment approaches for people of color (Sue, 1999). In some ways researchers appear to have left the task of understanding ethnicity to the domain of cross-cultural psychology, segregated from mainstream clinical research (Graham, 1992). Perhaps because people of color are often not considered to be part of society's mainstream, it has been relatively easy for theorists and scientists to ignore the psychological needs of this segment of the population (Jackson, 1995).

To this point, the majority of research on psychotherapy outcomes has been conducted on white, middle economic status people (Graham, 1992). When research is limited to white, middle economic status samples, the ability to inform the public regarding mental health behaviors of people of color is undermined.

People of Color in Clinical Research

Because people of color are underrepresented in clinical psychology research, up-to-date knowledge regarding the effectiveness of psychotherapy practices is absent. Examinations of the contents of scientific journals in psychology demonstrate the neglect of ethnicity and culture. For example, Graham (1992) found only 3.6 percent of empirical articles from six APA journals from 1970 to 1989 focused on African-Americans. Similarly, Loo, Fong, and Iwamasa (1988) found in their survey of twenty years of publication in community psychology journals that only 11 percent were about people of color. Moreover, meta-analytic reviews suggest that over a 20-year period from 1970 only 15 experimental or quasi-experimental studies of Hispanic-Americans in therapy exist. The majority of those were on children only (Navarro, 1993). Surveys of publications on the epidemiology of psychological disorders have indicated that the inclusion of people of color has decreased over time in the published research, while the number of articles on Anglo-American populations has increased (Jones, LaVeist, and Lillie-Blanton, 1991). Because the rate of growth for people of color is faster than the rate for Anglo-Americans, this finding is especially problematic. The current lack of accurate information regarding the mental health and well-being of people of color is likely to increase along with the total population.

The goal of this chapter is to bridge the gap and address the conceptual and methodological issues relevant for research on people of color. Furthermore, the information is presented here to help clinical psychology researchers improve the methodology and utility of their work by enhancing awareness of culturally relevant research issues.

Conceptual Concerns

Science is only as useful as its ability to define its terms. Controversy over meaning is the nature of science; however, when terminology is debated or interchanged, less understanding and knowledge results. This is the case with the use of terms in ethnic minority research. The debate stems from whether people should be classified as traits or as states. Without being cognizant of the implications of their behavior, researchers have often grouped together and labeled people based on traits (physical attributes) and on states (cultural values). The problem, however, is that sorting people by physical traits leads to different grouping or sampling depending on the trait being studied.

Increased immigration of people of color to the United States over the past ten years is primarily responsible for population growth among people of color. Therefore, increased mobility to and within the United States makes it likely that any sample of people of color will contain an intermingling of people, including more people of mixed ethnic descent. The practice of grouping individuals based on racial status is no longer logical. Psychological researchers must accept that cultural differences found within ethnic and racial groups are real.

The degree to which an individual connects or ascribes to a particular culture is not something necessarily reflected in racial background status or in perceived physical attributes. However, because culture has been closely linked with constructs such as race, ethnicity, and social class, confusion between constructs has been a barrier to progress (Brislin, 1983; Jahoda, 1984; Rohner, 1984). The pressure is on psychologists to accept a general definition of culture, or at least to specify the definition used in each study of people of color. Generally, most definitions of culture follow the notions suggested by Triandis et al. (1986), suggesting that the subjective conceptualization of culture reflects the social norms, beliefs, roles, and values of a person or community.

Misuse of terms

To enhance knowledge on multicultural issues in clinical research, the definition of key terms is necessary. Often it is here, at this basic level, that researchers often interchange and misuse conceptually different terms. One fundamental criticism of research with people of color is the ever-present confusion over terms such as "race," "ethnicity," and "culture," along with other demographic confounding variables (Kurasaki et al., 2000).

In hindsight, one of the earliest errors was in the use of the term "race" as an explanatory construct for differences in results. Recent researchers have clearly indicated that race is not a biological construct and, therefore, grouping participants by their racial category is likely to misrepresent psychological processes (Beutler et al., 1996; Heath, 1991; Zuckerman, 1990). Alvidrez, Azocar, and Miranda (1996) suggested that race no longer be included in research. Instead, investigators are called upon to work toward understanding and explaining differential outcomes for people of color, rather than assume the results are explained by race.

Ethnicity

Ethnicity has recently been defined as broad groupings based on race (Phinney, 1996). Unfortunately, it is assumed in most research that people with the same ethnicity or race also share similar personality characteristics. However, individual people do not identify equally with their respective ethnic groups (Dana, 1988). Ethnicity generally refers to group membership, often based on physical attributes or country of origin (Betancourt and Lopez, 1993). The most common practice in research is for investigators to use ethnicity as a descriptive or demographic variable; a way of categorizing subgroups within a sample of people. Although this is a common practice, it is fraught with problems.

The first problem arises because when ethnicity is used in this way, the strict sense of ethnicity is violated. That is, ethnicity also encompasses a sense of shared values and beliefs, often called culture. Yet as a demographic or grouping variable, this notion of ethnicity then ignores the degree to which those grouped together actually share a common culture. Within-group differences abound and are more relevant for explaining outcomes than between-group cultural differences (Dana, 1988, 1993; Greene, 1987; Suzuki and Kugler, 1995). Moreover, these data are often based on participants' self-report of ethnicity, or worse, investigator assumption of ethnicity, and in either case there is no evidence that the people so identified are actually grouped accurately. Even genetic studies have supported this notion, often demonstrating that greater variance is accounted for by within-group differences than between-group differences (Latter, 1980). Significant differences in behavior between people of color and others in research, possibly due to cultural influence, should be considered *a priori*, then defined and measured. Moreover, the mechanism within cultures should be explored for its possible explanatory power for the phenomenon under investigation.

For example, in their study on the influence of HIV status on sexual risk-taking behavior among Hispanic women, Carmona, Romero, and Loeb (1999) also attended to the cultural influence of gender roles within the Hispanic community. In a discussion of possible cultural considerations they provide several possible *a priori* explanations of potential correlates for their results. Furthermore, they add a measure designed to assess how "Hispanic-identified" each participant is, so that they might get a better sense of within-group differences.

Unfortunately, past research has too often failed to include culture as a possible influential construct from the beginning, and instead attributed differences in the results to differences in the racial make-up of the sample. Researchers must acknowledge the limitations of categorizing people based on ethnic category. The lack of attention to possible errors in self-identification and more importantly the lack of attention to culture and within-group differences make a significant portion of research on people of color less than useful. External validity in these studies is diminished if there is no effort to ensure that the people of color in the sample are actually *culturally* similar, not just *ethnically* similar (Sue, 1999).

In contrast, Casas, Ponterotto, and Sweeney (1987) provide a superb example of participant description where they report distinctive information about their sample, moving beyond ethnic categories. For example, the authors report that

> subjects for the study consisted of 45 Mexican American couples from low-income neighborhoods in the Santa Barbara, California area. The sample ranged in age from 28–46 with a mean age of 38 . . . 28 spoke Spanish in the home and 17 spoke English. In all, 43 were born in the United States and 47 were born in Mexico . . . 48 describe themselves as Mexican, 22 as Mexican-American, 10 as Chicano, 2 as Americans, 1 as Latino, and 1 as other. (p. 48)

Although this level of detail is not expected in all studies, it does provide a good target. The description goes a long way in informing the public regarding generalizability of the findings over simply reporting that the sample was comprised of "Hispanics." In this way, the informed reader is able to get a sense of how identified with the culture of origin the sample was and can make more accurate comparisons when attempting to apply the findings or replicate the results.

Some researchers have attempted to address ethnic differences by matching individuals on other demographic variables such as socioeconomic status, age, or gender. However, most demographic variables are confounded with ethnic group status and cultural practices. Moreover, matching cannot control for other influential incidents, such as discrimination experiences and racism (Phinney, 1996).

Socioeconomic status

One consistent confounding variable in clinical research is socioeconomic status (SES), because the majority of people designated as ethnic minorities usually reside in the lower economic classes. For example, Frerichs, Aneshensel, and Clark (1981) found that when SES was controlled, previously documented differences between Latinos, Anglos, and African-Americans in reported levels of depressive symptoms disappeared. It is possible then, when the influence of SES is not considered, to misattribute economic differences to cultural differences.

La Greca et al. (1996) appreciated this notion when they examined the symptoms of posttraumatic stress in school-age children after Hurricane Andrew. The authors included over 400 children in their study, about half of whom were children of color. Furthermore, the non-Caucasian group was evenly separated into African-American and Hispanic-American subgroups and the between-group differences were tested. The authors made clear and compelling predictions about the role of ethnicity *a priori* and reflected on the financial limitations associated with ethnic minority status as one of the possible explanations for some of the between-group differences.

However, Betancourt and Lopez (1993) suggest that because more people of color are classified in the lower strata of economic status, in the practice of controlling for SES, variance associated with culture will also be removed. That is, a significant overlap is likely between culture and SES, given the history of discrimination against people of color, such that the lines between what is an ethnicity-based cultural difference and what is a culture of poverty differences gets blurred. It is possible that some cultural practices (e.g., beliefs, norms, behaviors) are common to a particular segment of the social class structure (Sobal and Stunkard, 1989).

Cultural differences

Research exploring the relation between minority group status and culture has clearly suggested behavioral and psychological differences among ethnic groups (LaFromboise, 1990; Leong, Wagner, and Tata, 1995; Sodowsky, Kwan, and Pannu, 1995). This is less clear when participants are also classified as Americans, as this often means an interconnection between culture of origin and American culture. For example, Chinese-Americans are people who may have available to them two distinct and different cultures on which to base and guide their behavior and beliefs. Therefore, research that includes a population of Chinese-Americans must take steps to determine how much similarity between individuals exists in the sample.

Although influential, cultural differences, however, are not generally viewed positively in society (Jones, 1988). It is possible that cultural differences may lead some to conclude that difference is equal to deficiency (Okazaki and Sue, 1995). The "either–or" mentality that pervades American culture has historically assumed that anything outside of the majority norm must be deviant and therefore inferior. Perhaps in an effort to appeal to a broad audience and to avoid such misleading implications, theoretical perspectives in mainstream psychology usually exclude cultural variables and assume that the psychological principles developed, tested, and applied in the United States with mostly Caucasian subjects are universal.

As an improvement, Betancourt and Lopez (1993) suggest a multilevel research approach incorporating an application of cultural findings to other cultures and adding cultural components to psychological theoretical domains. By beginning the research endeavor with the understanding that the universal approach is not generally useful for explaining outcomes among people possessing diverse cultural attachments, researchers are more likely to uncover the mechanisms behind behavior, not simply record differences between individuals.

However, even when culture is included in research and differences are found, researchers often fail to explore what it is about the culture variable that contributes to the projected outcome. This requires some kind of assessment, not simply a descriptive detail of the ethnicities of the participants of the sample under study. When measured, the influence of culture on behavior and outcomes has been demonstrated repeatedly. However, as a descriptive term, it provides no new or likely accurate information.

Methodological Issues

A typical study on people of color is often designed as follows. A researcher is interested in comparing responses or behaviors between groups on some variable. Sometimes controls are included to restrict the influence of SES, age, and other demographic variables. If differences between the groups are found, the conclusion is often that the difference in scores on the variable of interest reflects the difference between the two ethnic groups. Conclusions like these can and may be correct, but they can also be dangerous, as there is no context for the outcome.

Historically, this kind of difference on the part of the person of color group has usually been viewed as deviance. The field has grown to appreciate the need for caution before assuming deviance on behalf of an entire group of people and has begun to appreciate the influence of culture on an individual's behavior. However, culture or cultural factors are rarely if ever directly measured in clinical psychology research. Without a direct measure of culture it is not possible to conclude that cultural differences are at work on the variable of interest.

Furthermore, it is important that researchers explicitly describe the participants in the sample and clearly present the definition of ethnicity grouping used in the study (Sifers et al., 2002). Within-group differences cannot be ignored, and to this point investigators are obliged to provide more information on as many descriptors as possible (e.g., the country of origin, parents' ethnicity). Given the general trend toward mixed ethnic status it is likely too large a task to account for all possible within-group differences in a sample. However, research must include information on how subgroups were identified and defined. Any differences then found between subgroups could be fertile ground for replication and meaningful comparison of the research to later studies.

Culture and Group Differences

With improved definitions and descriptions of samples, researchers may be left with the task of explaining differences between and among groups. Operational definitions of ethnicity are best constructed to reflect the distal nature of this variable. Other more proximal variables such as socioeconomic status, acculturation, and cultural factors can be used to explain both within-group and between-group differences (Aldwin and Greenberger, 1987; Leaf et al., 1987; Takeuchi, Leaf, and Kuo, 1988).

Instead of avoiding the possible measurement confusion regarding culture, researchers are encouraged to develop *a priori* hypotheses on the function of culture in particular studies. Researchers are urged to learn about the influence of culture on behavior and cognitions and consult with more learned colleagues of a particular culture and collaborate on research projects. Alvidrez, Azocar, and Miranda (1996) also suggested that researchers include focus groups composed of the population from which they plan to sample to inform hypotheses and measure development. It is important that all future research consider how culture will be operationally defined so that meaningful comparisons and replications of research can be accomplished.

For example, it is clear that regardless of ethnic culture, there exists a separate culture of economic status. People with fewer economic resources are likely to have similar attitudes and behaviors consistent with the limitations of their life circumstances. Research has documented that economically poorer people often have an external locus of control and locus of responsibility (Heller, Quesada, and Chalfant, 1983; Neighbors et al., 1983). Because a greater number of people of color occupy lower economic status groups, it is possible that socioeconomic factors can be responsible for differences between Anglo and ethnic minority populations.

When cultural factors are mistaken for economic factors, research becomes less useful for explaining behavior. For example, a common assumption is that people of color are crisis-oriented and nonintrospective in therapy, and therefore less likely to benefit from insight-oriented treatments. However, the daily stressors experienced by those with less economic resources are likely to be associated with a crisis-oriented perspective toward life, regardless of cultural background. Without a measure of the influence of economic status, confounds like this one are inevitable.

Although a common practice, when middle economic status Anglo-Americans are compared to lower economic status people of color, the confusion is made worse. The desire to include people of color and study cultural influences on psychological process will add to knowledge in the field, but this aspiration cannot be achieved with unequal comparisons of people based primarily on ease of availability. That is, researchers must strive to ensure that all groupings of sample members are clearly defined and soundly justified.

Unfortunately, the profession has failed to consistently hold researchers accountable for describing and justifying the organization of their samples and subsamples (Sifers et al., 2002). To avoid this problem journal editors should require that all studies considered for publication include a detailed definition and justification for how the sample was collected and the ethnic and socioeconomic strata of the study sample. Furthermore, researchers should attempt to include stratified samples, especially focused on including middle and upper economic status people of color in research.

Acculturation and Enculturation

The final issue for improving methodology in clinical research is the use of acculturation and enculturation as a substitute variable for culture. *Acculturation* is the degree to which an individual adheres to the cultural values and practices of the dominant culture. *Enculturation*, however, represents the adherence to culture of origin or traditional culture. The operational use of these terms, however, actually represents four possible outcomes of classification in a given sample of people of color. Besides adhering to majority culture (acculturation) or culture of origin (enculturation), people of color can also take part in several cultures at once, or behave bi-culturally. In contrast, individuals can also be classified as marginal, or attaching to no particular ethnic culture. Acculturation, then, is best conceptualized as orthogonal dimensions, not places on a single continuum (Felix-Ortiz, Newcomb, and Myers, 1994; Oetting and Beauvais, 1991). Although one's placement in a particular category is not static and can change in time, without measurement of this construct researchers risk not knowing how participants in their studies identify with various cultures.

When ethnic groups are compared and within-group difference is not considered, the researcher does not know if the differences in the results are due to an actual difference between the groups or if the differences in scores reflect differences in culture "saturation." This would be especially problematic for study variables that might be more sensitive or salient to cultural issues (e.g., family behavior, childrearing). Moreover, if there are no group differences on the study variables, the researcher does not know if the lack of significant differences is due to the fact that the people of color group in the sample was simply very acculturated and therefore much more likely to respond like a Caucasian comparison group. By having a measure of acculturation a researcher may be able to aid in the interpretation of group differences by accounting for influence of acculturation (or enculturation) as a potential moderator variable.

Including a measure of the degree to which participants are aligned with mainstream culture versus their culture of origin is a good start, but it is not without limitations. Because the items on acculturation measures are often behavior-focused (e.g., language usage, eating habits) it is not clear that a high score on these measures actually indicates low adherence to original ethnic culture. At best, acculturation measures are circuitous indices of adherence to cultural values, suggesting that the better practice would be to directly measure more proximal and specific aspects of cultural practices. This consideration is important because the comparison of people of color to Caucasians is not always the focus of clinical psychology research.

Researchers have to consider three factors when including people of color in research: (1) recruitment of the sample, (2) adaptation of measures and interventions, and (3) modifying the conceptualization of ethnicity to increase knowledge of cultural factors and psychological process (Alvidrez, Azocar, and Miranda, 1996).

Selecting participants

A general sense of pessimism pervades commentaries and research studies regarding the feasibility of recruiting and retaining people of color in clinical psychology research. Failing to explain how the researchers were able to recruit participants makes future replication and additions to the field of clinical research and people of color difficult. The majority of research neglects to explain the pragmatic details of the procedures for recruitment and retention of ethnic minority subjects. This practice makes forming judgments about a particular study difficult and fails to assist other researchers toward improving sampling procedures.

One notable exception is a recent study by Thompson, Neighbors, Munday, and Jackson (1996), where the authors detailed a specified procedure used to recruit African-American psychiatric patients in a large-scale research study. In the end, the results did not support the notion that researchers and subjects need to be matched based on ethnicity (African-American and Anglo) – overall an unexpected but positive outcome of the project. The authors suggested that to get people of color – specifically African-Americans – to participate in research, investigators must take time to interact with the population. Immersion in the community not only provides an opportunity to learn more about the facets of cultures present in the population, but also allows investigators to ask about some of the possible barriers to research participation. Inclusion of a research project by investigators known to members of the community allows for part-ownership of the project by the ethnic community.

Also, having investigators who are similar to the population in ethnicity may enhance the legitimacy or reduce the potential threat posed by research projects. By following these guidelines, the authors were able to report a 78 percent response and retention rate, clearly eliminating some of the barriers for people of color in research.

Of these barriers, institutional racism has likely been the primary reason for a dearth in participation of African-Americans in clinical research (Thomas and Sillen, 1972). A legacy of bias in representing African-Americans as mentally ill and inferior has fostered negative perceptions of psychiatric research by African-Americans. It should be no surprise then that researchers often find little interest among African-Americans to trust researchers, especially Anglo-American researchers.

Cultural barriers include the differential way that mental illness is conceived in traditional African-American culture. Negative attitudes toward psychotherapy are another possible impediment. Traditional African-American culture dictates that those in need of help for emotional difficulties should consult informal resources, such as clergy and extended family members (Neighbors, 1988). The result of these various impediments is often small and inadequate populations from which to sample for clinical research.

The approach used by Thompson et al. (1996) was made up of several components. First, the investigators sought to collect a pool of research assistants or interviewers who were familiar with both mental illness and low-income African-Americans. Second, interviewers underwent extensive training on how to present the study. Third, cultural sensitivity was indirectly addressed by matching the ethnic status of the interviewer to that of the potential participants. When that was not possible, the researchers took advantage of the opportunity to test for possible differential outcomes when the interviewer was Anglo-American and the potential participant was African-American.

Miranda et al. (1996) provided several good examples for recruiting and retaining Hispanic people in research. Their studies include an individualized approach. Contact with participants was frequent and personal to the needs of the family. Conveying a sense of warmth and caring toward the participants was also important and culturally sensitive. Furthermore, the researchers provided bilingual assistants for participants whose first language was Spanish. Transportation was provided to participants when necessary to make appointments with the investigators. Many of the assessments were conducted at the homes of the participants.

A general sense of personal connection and interest in the well-being of the participants appears to be key to recruiting and retaining some, likely more, enculturated Hispanic people in research. Investigators who seek to focus on one or more of the cultural groups represented in the Hispanic population may find these suggestions useful in planning research designs. Specifically, attention to the barriers that prevent participation may require providing childcare and transportation, while speaking Spanish and forming a respectful, warm relationship with individual participants will be critical. If no such serious efforts are made to include Hispanic participants it will mean that future research will have to exclude people and cultures that currently comprise over 12 percent of the US population. In turn, this is likely to lead to questionable scientific practice.

Given the historical legacy of genocide, discrimination, loss, and bias that is consistent across tribes in the United States, clinicians are also likely to see multiple needs for study of the Native-American population. To this end, Norton and Mason (1996) outlined some important procedures for projects focused on inclusion of Native peoples. The authors suggested that tribes and tribal leaders are becoming more intense in their scrutiny of proposals for research among members of the tribe. In the past, after giving consent, several tribes have been hurt by the carelessness of researchers, who often ignored important cultural differences (American Indian Law Center, 1994). In order to obtain consent for a research project investigators should be prepared for the significant time and expense required. A dialogue with tribal leaders about the utility of the project is just one of the steps researchers will have to take. Too often, the research question of interest to clinical psychology is not consistent with the primary concerns of the tribe.

It is likely that researchers will have to adjust their investigations to include work directed toward answering questions that the tribal members request, in addition to the original research issues. According to Norton and Mason (1996), researchers who become invested in the community and demonstrate a commitment to the people of the tribe are likely to receive more cooperation and support for their research (not dissimilar to suggestions for research within other groups and communities).

Norton and Mason also suggested that to recruit Native-Americans communication with tribal leaders and tribal councils is critical regarding the nature of informed consent procedures and confidentiality. Researchers must ensure that all forms are written in a language that is easily understood by members of the tribe, for whom English may not be a first language. Confidentiality concerns could possibly arise from the collective nature of the culture in most tribes and a desire not to share information with those perceived to be "outsiders." In contrast, some tribal members may prefer to be interviewed by other Native-Americans, especially those from another tribe.

Measurement Problems

Measurement of psychological constructs is the bedrock of clinical research. Psychometrically sound measures are vital to advancement of the field and understanding what treatments or interventions are effective. When measures are developed, often the resulting assessment instrument falls short of what it should be. For example, measures that previously included few or inadequate numbers of people of color are often revised to a new version and tested on samples that are reported to match the census data. Census counts referenced are often ten years old by the time the measure is published. A newer, more diverse norming sample is seen as an improvement. Unfortunately, external validity is assumed when measures match the number in the United States census. This is inadequate because the comparison group is not likely to be representative or include sufficient numbers to make reasonable comparisons and conclusions regarding scores and outcome.

Furthermore, if people of color are not included in the testing of an intervention or the development of a new assessment tool, the consequences for the field of psychology could be profound. For example, if an investigator included a majority of Anglo-Americans and did not test the intervention or assessment measure in particular ethnic minority populations, the measure is likely to be invalid for important segments of the populations. It is the use or application of a measure and not the measure itself that may be considered invalid. Testing the efficacy of the measure or intervention would likely produce poor estimates or greater standard error rates among people for whom the measure was not tested.

In contrast, one of the best examples of assessment research with people of color is a study by Zvolensky et al. (2001). The authors examined the utility of the Anxiety

Sensitivity Index with a Native Americans-only sample and a Caucasian-only sample. With a rather large sample (N = 282) of Native people, the authors were able to provide evidence for the relevance of this measure across cultural groups. Furthermore, to ensure some of the cultural homogeneity of their sample, the authors recruited participants from an all-Native American university where tribe specificity could be determined.

The same issue is relevant for descriptive research. Psychologists are likely to get a skewed representation of how an intervention operates on a target population when cultural factors are ignored. Context of behavior has long been considered an important variable in services and intervention research. However, failure to appreciate cultural differences means that investigators risk misunderstanding how culture can dictate how people interpret and react to psychological symptoms (Guarnaccia, Rubio-Stipec, and Canino, 1989). Cultural differences influence help-seeking behaviors and the use of alternative modes of care (Hohmann et al., 1990).

Need for Change

Mandates for paradigm shifts in research are evident from several professional sources. The American Psychological Association in its *Ethical Principles for Psychologists and Code of Conduct* (APA, 1992) indicated that researchers are to ensure that group differences are accounted for when using measures normed on white populations.

Another directive came in 1994 from the National Institutes of Health, which required researchers to formulate specific intentions and methods for including women and people of color in research projects. Ratings for funding are now organized, in part, on how well researchers can meet this requirement. The National Institutes of Health fortified their commitment to ethnic minority populations by developing a policy for all funded research.

NIH policy requires that, for all research involving human subjects and human tissues, applicants must include in study populations appropriate representation of both genders, minorities, and children (21 years of age and under). The purpose of this policy is so that research findings can benefit all individuals at risk for the disease, disorder, or condition under study. This policy is intended to apply to males and females of all ages. If both genders, minorities, or children are not included or are inadequately represented in the research plan, a clear and compelling rationale must be provided in the application.

Assessment of scientific and technical merit of applications must include an evaluation of the proposed composition of the study population and its appropriateness for the scientific objectives of the study. If representation of gender, minorities, or children in the study design is inadequate to answer the scientific question(s) addressed *and* justification for the selected study population is inadequate, the reviewer should consider this to be a scientific weakness or deficiency in the study design and must consider this weakness in assigning a numerical rating (National Institutes of Health, 1994).

Clinical research must appreciate the diversity of the populations in the United States and demonstrate via practice its understanding of the heterogeneity of people. In this policy the NIH recognized the definition of "ethnic minority groups" used by the Office of Management and Budget (OMB), which designated four groups of heterogeneous people; Black/African-American, American Indian/Alaska Native, Asian/Pacific Islander, and Hispanic. Although these categories are currently debated and possibly under revision by the OMB, the definition attends to the diversity within these populations by including the phrase "and their subpopulations" to help researchers appreciate the within-group differences among the four broad groups. For NIH purposes, it is sufficient to include members from any of these groups and no requirement is made that every funded study includes members from each of the four groups. Researchers are encouraged to pay particular attention to their plan for recruitment and retention of subjects, as justification is required for funding.

Furthermore, *The Diagnostic and Statistical Manual*, fourth edition (DSM-IV; American Psychiatric Association, 1994) includes many changes from previous versions, but a major change is seen in the new focus on possible cultural issues that may explain behavior over psychopathology. In three places the DSM-IV cautions the user to remember that behavior has a basis in traditional cultural practices and therefore should not always be considered pathological.

Next, the APA has published *Guidelines for Culturally Competent Psychological Researchers* (1993) for psychologists who are professionally involved in serving people of color. Fundamental for any clinical researcher, the information is written such that any investigator seeking to include people of color in research would benefit from following these rules. Representing general principles, the content is intended to serve as suggestions for anyone working with people from culturally diverse populations.

Application of the Mandates

Although with good intentions, advocates for these directives often provide little in the way of information as to *how* scientist-practitioners are to apply these mandates. Indeed, trends and practices are slow to change in psychology and perhaps a shift toward accounting for culture poses unique and difficult problems. For example, the degree of identification with a particular culture is generally considered to be one's ethnic identity. However, currently, there is no consistently accepted method to measure ethnic identity. Although several rating scales have been developed, these often are only preliminary to what might later become psychometrically sound measures. Moreover, few of the scales on these measures have been designed to measure ethnic identity across an ethnically diverse sample (Kohatsu and Richardson, 1996; Sabnani and Ponterotto, 1992). Still problematic is the issue of *how* to apply the mandates. Specifically, how are researchers to account for the influence of culture when including or focusing research questions on populations of color?

To aid researchers, the APA recently published *Guidelines for Research in Ethnic Minority Communities*, written jointly by the Council of National Psychological Associations for the Advancement of Ethnic Minority Interests (2000). The Council represents organizations including the Society for the Psychological Study of Ethnic Minority

Issues (Division 45 of APA), the National Hispanic Psychological Association, the Society of Indian Psychologists, the Asian American Psychological Association, and the Association of Black Psychologists. The leadership of each organization developed and wrote guidelines for conducting research for each ethnic group, respectively. Specific and detailed, the document appears to be the first directive for research including people of color disseminated by a national psychological organization. Decisions on sample selection, measures, methods, and interpretation of results are considered for studies including African-American, Asian-American, Hispanic-American, and Native-American populations. Moreover, the rationale for why research must be retooled to appreciate culturally dissimilar people is presented. This represents the first set of rules for researchers to follow when conducting investigations that focus on or simply include people of color. The guidelines are clear and specialized and provide powerful rationales for changing practice in clinical psychology research.

For example, the model for conducting research with Hispanic populations proposes three stages: conceptualization, methods/procedures, and interpretation/dissemination. In the conceptualization phase the authors suggest a rigorous definition of the population, in that researchers need to define the Hispanic population they are drawing from in terms of race/ethnicity, country of origin, level of acculturation, educational background, and socioeconomic status. The language ability of the researcher and research assistants is key and the English/Spanish receptive and expressive fluency and the implications of this information for the study should also be considered. The use of translators should be considered, along with the availability of translated measures if necessary. The psychometric soundness of the measures for the Hispanic population should also be considered. Next, the relevance of acculturation to the study should be considered, as well as whether the variables of interest are culturally salient, cross-culturally or generalizable to Hispanic only.

In the next stage of the model the authors recommend that researchers determine the appropriate methodology and measures. However, they go on to suggest that researchers also need to consider culturally sensitive steps for entry into the community to ensure access to the populations of interest. It is important to make sure that the language skills of the researchers are adequate to administer the study measures and that the researchers have the cultural knowledge and background to interact with the participants in a culturally appropriate manner.

Finally, in the last stage, the authors suggest that researchers should request reviews of the results and interpretations from ethnic and nonethnic colleagues. Also, the researchers are encouraged to consider alternative explanations for their interpretations. The models for conducting research with the other ethnic minority groups follow a fairly similar format; however, they are tailored to the specific needs of the particular ethnic group.

Following these ideas will require a substantial paradigm shift for most clinical psychology researchers, who are accustomed to more straightforward methods designed to target the variables of interest. However, it is no longer possible to continue to conduct research as usual, knowing that within-group differences exist and that culture has an influence on an individual's behavior, without a clear and compelling justification for doing so. Researchers are going to have to explain to editors and reviewers why they did *not* account for or measure cultural factors when including people of color in research.

Clinical researchers are encouraged to follow the current mandates toward increasing the degree of cultural competence reflected in their research. Clinical research, however, may be harder to do in areas where the population is primarily composed of Anglo-Americans. Collaborating with other investigators and letters of support from members of the target population are some possible methods for addressing this procedural issue. Although cultural factors are not at issue in all studies, when they are relevant, it is clear that resources are beginning to emerge to aid those who are new to these approaches in making the necessary changes in their style of research.

Conclusions

Consistently emerging from the literature on ethnic minorities in clinical psychology is the need for epidemiological studies on the incidence and prevalence rates of mental health and mental illness within and between cultural groups. Data that can indicate where and for whom intervention is needed will be critical for the field to become timely and useful. Also, as the population of different cultures grows, so does the need for more research on bi-racial and multiracial individuals. The developmental process of growing up culturally pluralistic is unknown and requires further investigation. For the science of psychology to grow with the human population, it is important to expand previously held practices. To advance knowledge the scientific discipline of clinical psychology must progress in its understanding of culture and its role in the lives of individuals – not only for people of color, but for the majority of Anglo-Americans whose lives are also influenced by American culture. The result will be a more useful, ethical, and practical experience of discovery. Clinical psychology will then be able to produce tools useful to the growing needs of the American public and more sensitive to the reality and diversity of society and the world.

References

Aldwin, C., and Greenberger, E. (1987). Race, racism, and epidemiological surveys. *Hospital and Community Psychiatry*, *45*, 27–31.

Alvidrez, J., Azocar, F., and Miranda, J. (1996). Demystifying the concept of ethnicity for psychotherapy research. *Journal of Consulting and Clinical Psychology*, *64*, 903–8.

American Indian Law Center (1994). *The model tribal research code*. Albuquerque, NM: American Indian Law Center.

American Psychiatric Association (1994). *Diagnostic and statistical manual of mental disorders* (4th edn.). Washington, DC: American Psychiatric Association.

American Psychological Association (1992). Ethical principles of psychologist and code of conduct. *American Psychologist*, *47*, 1597–1611.

American Psychological Association Office of Ethnic Minority Affairs (1993). Guidelines for providers of psychological services to ethnic, linguistic, and culturally diverse populations. *American Psychologist*, *48*, 45–8.

Betancourt, H., and Lopez, S. R. (1993). The study of culture, ethnicity, and race in American psychology. *American Psychologist*, *48*, 629–37.

Beutler, L., Brown, M. T., Crothers, L., and Booker, K. (1996). The dilemma of factitious demographic distinctions in psychological research. *Journal of Consulting and Clinical Psychology*, *64*, 892–902.

Brislin, R. W. (1983). Cross-cultural research in psychology. *Annual Review of Psychology*, *34*, 363–400.

Carmona, J. V., Romero, G. J., and Loeb, T. B. (1999). The impact of HIV status and acculturation on Latinas' sexual risk taking. *Cultural Diversity and Ethnic Minority Psychology*, *5*, 209–21.

Casas, J. M., Ponterotto, J. G., and Sweeney, M. (1987). Stereotyping the stereotypes: A Mexican American perspective. *Journal of Cross Cultural Psychology*, *18*, 45–57.

Council of National Psychological Associations for the Advancement of Ethnic Minority Interests (2000). *Guidelines for research in ethnic minority communities*. Washington, DC: American Psychological Association. Retrieved March 23, 20002 from: http://www.apa.org/pi/oema/onlinebr.html.

Dana, R. H. (1988). Culturally diverse groups and MMPI interpretation. *Professional Psychology: Research and Practice*, *19*, 490–5.

Dana, R. H. (1993). *Multicultural assessment perspectives for professional psychology* (pp. 1–29). Boston, MA: Allyn and Bacon.

Felix-Ortiz, M., Newcomb, M. D., and Myers, H. (1994). A multidimensional measure of cultural identity for Latino and Latina adolescents. *Hispanic Journal of the Behavioral Sciences*, *16*, 99–115.

Frerichs, R. R., Aneshensel, C. S., and Clark, V. A. (1981). Prevalence of depression in Los Angeles County. *American Journal of Epidemiology*, *113*, 691–9.

Graham, S. (1992). Most of the subjects were White and middle class: Trends in published research on African Americans in selected APA journals, 1970–1989. *American Psychologist*, *47*, 629–39.

Greene, R. L. (1987). Ethnicity and MMPI performance: A review. *Journal of Consulting and Clinical Psychology*, *55*, 497–512.

Guarnaccia, P. J., Rubio-Stipec, M., and Canino, G. (1989). Ataques de nervios in the Puerto Rican Diagnostic Interview Schedule: The impact of cultural categories on psychiatric epidemiology. *Culture, Medicine, and Psychiatry*, *13*, 275–95.

Heath, D. B. (1991). Uses and misuse of the concept of ethnicity in alcohol studies: An essay in deconstruction. *International Journal of Addictions*, *25*, 607–28.

Heller, P. L., Quesada, G. M., and Chalfant, H. P. (1983). Class perceptions of disordered behavior, and suggestions for therapy: A tri-cultural comparison. *Sociology of Health and Illness*, *5*, 196–207.

Hohmann, A. A., Richeport, M., Marriott, B. M., Canion, G. J., and Rubio-Stipec, M. (1990). Spiritism in Puerto Rico: Results of a stratified island-wide community study. *British Journal of Psychiatry*, *156*, 328–35.

Jackson, M. L. (1995). Multicultural counseling. In J. G. Ponterotto, J. M. Casas, L. A. Suzuki, and C. M. Alexander (eds.), *Handbook of multicultural counseling* (pp. 3–16). Thousand Oaks, CA: Sage.

Jahoda, G. (1984). Do we need a concept of culture? *Journal of Cross-Cultural Research*, *15*, 139–51.

Jones, C. P., LaVeist, T. A., and Lillie-Blanton, M. (1991). "Race" in the epidemiologic literature: An examination of the *American Journal of Epidemiology*, 1921–1990. *American Journal of Epidemiology*, *134*, 1079–83.

Jones, J. M. (1988). Racism in black and white: A bicultural model of reaction and evolution. In P. A. Katz and D. A. Taylor (eds.), *Eliminating racism: Profiles in controversy* (pp. 117–35). New York: Plenum.

Kohatsu, E. L., and Richardson, T. Q. (1996). Racial and ethnic identity assessment. In L. A. Suzuki, P. J. Meller, and J. G. Ponterotto (eds.), *Handbook of multicultural assessment: Clinical, psychological and educational applications* (pp. 611–50). San Francisco, CA: Jossey-Bass.

Kurasaki, K. S., Sue, S., Chun, C., and Gee, K. (2000). Ethnic minority intervention and treatment research. In J. F. Aponte and J. Wohl (eds.), *Psychological intervention and cultural diversity* (2nd edn., pp. 234–49). Needham Heights, MA: Allyn and Bacon.

LaFromboise, T. (1990). Counseling intervention and American Indian tradition. *Counseling Psychologist, 18*, 628–54.

La Greca, A. M., Silverman, W. K., Vernberg, E. M., and Prinstein, M. J. (1996). Symptoms of Posttraumatic Stress in children after Hurricane Andrew: A prospective study. *Journal of Consulting and Clinical Psychology, 64*, 712–23.

Latter, B. (1980). Genetic differences within and between populations of the major human subgroups. *American Naturalist, 116*, 220–37.

Leaf, P. J., Bruce, M. L., Tischler, G. L., and Holzer, C. E. (1987). The relationship between demographic factors and attitudes toward mental health services. *Journal of Community Psychology, 15*, 275–84.

Leong, F. T. L., Wagner, N. S., and Tata, S. P. (1995). Racial and ethnic variations in help-seeking attitudes. In J. G. Ponterotto, J. M. Casas, L. A. Suzuki, and C. M. Alexander (eds.), *Handbook of multicultural counseling* (pp. 3–16). Thousand Oaks, CA: Sage.

Loo, C., Fong, K. T., and Iwamasa, G. (1988). Ethnicity and cultural diversity: An analysis of work published in community psychology journals. *Journal of Community Psychology, 16*, 332–49.

Miranda, J., Azocar, F., Organista, K. C., Munoz, R. F., and Lieberman, A. (1996). Recruiting and retaining low-income Latinos in psychotherapy research. *Journal of Consulting and Clinical Psychology, 64*, 868–74.

National Institutes of Health (1994). Guidelines on the inclusion of women and minorities as subjects in clinical research. 59, *Federal Register*, 14, 508 (Document no. 94–5435).

Navarro, A. M. (1993). The effectiveness of psychotherapy with Latinos in the United States: A meta-analytic review. *Interamerican Journal of Psychology, 27*, 131–46.

Neighbors, H. W. (1988). Needed research on the epidemiology of mental disorders in Black Americans. In O. Harrison, J. S. Jackson, C. Munday, and N. B. Bleiden (eds.), *A search for understanding: The Michigan Research Conference on Mental Health Services for Black Americans* (pp. 49–60). Detroit, MI: Wayne State University Press.

Neighbors, H. W., Jackson J. S., Bowman, P. J., and Gurin, G. (1983). Stress, coping, and Black mental health: Preliminary findings from a national study. *Prevention in Human Services, 2*, 3, 5–29.

Norton, I. M., and Mason, S. M. (1996). Research in American Indian and Alaska Native communities: Navigating the cultural universe of values and process. *Journal of Consulting and Clinical Psychology, 64*, 856–60.

Oetting, G. R., and Beauvais, F. (1991). Orthogonal cultural identification theory: The cultural identification of minority adolescents. *International Journal of the Addictions, 25*, 655–85.

Okazaki, S., and Sue, S. (1995). Cultural considerations in psychological assessment of Asian Americans. In J. N. Butcher (ed.), *Clinical personality assessment: Practical approaches* (pp. 107–19). New York: Oxford University Press.

Phinney, J. S. (1996). When we talk about American ethnic groups, what do we mean? *American Psychologist, 51*, 918–27.

Poortinga, Y. H., and Malpass, R. S. (1986). Making inferences from cross-cultural data. In W. Lonner and J. Berry (eds.), *Field methods in cross cultural research* (pp.17–26). Newbury Park, CA: Sage.

Rohner, R. P. (1984). Toward a conception of culture for cross-cultural psychology. *Journal of Cross-Cultural Psychology, 15,* 111–38.

Sabnani, H. B., and Ponterotto, J. G. (1992). Racial/ethnic minority-specific instrumentation in counseling research: A review, critique, and recommendations. *Measurement and Evaluation in Counseling and Development, 24,* 161–87.

Sifers, S. K., Puddy, R. W., Warren, J. S., and Roberts, M. C. (2002). Reporting of demographics, methodology, and ethical procedures in journals in pediatric and child psychology. *Journal of Pediatric Psychology, 27,* 19–25.

Sobal, J., and Stunkard, A. J. (1989). Socioeconomic status and obesity: A review of the literature. *Psychological Bulletin, 105,* 260–75.

Sodowsky, G. R., Kwan, K. K., and Pannu, R. (1995). Ethnic identity of Asian Americans in the United States. In J. G. Ponterotto, J. M. Casas, L. A. Suzuki, and C. M. Alexander (eds.), *Handbook of multicultural counseling* (pp. 3–16). Thousand Oaks, CA: Sage.

Sue, D. W., Arredondo, P., and McDavis, R. J. (1995). Multicultural counseling competencies and standards. In J. G. Ponterotto, J. M. Casas, L. A. Suzuki, and C. M. Alexander (eds.), *Handbook of multicultural counseling* (pp. 609–43). Thousand Oaks, CA: Sage.

Sue, S. (1999). Science, ethnicity, and bias: Where have we gone wrong? *American Psychologist, 54,* 1070–7.

Sue, S., Fujino, D. C., Hu, L. T., Takeuchi, D. T., and Zane, N. W. S. (1991). Community mental health services for ethnic minority groups: A test of the cultural responsiveness hypothesis. *Journal of Counseling Psychology, 59,* 533–40.

Suzuki, L. A., and Kugler, J. F. (1995). Intelligence and personality assessment: Multicultural perspectives. In J. G. Ponterotto, M. J. Casas, L. A. Suzuki, and C. M. Alexander (eds.), *Handbook of multicultural counseling* (pp. 493–515). Thousand Oaks, CA: Sage.

Takeuchi, D. T., Leaf, P. J., and Kuo, H. (1988). Ethnic differences in the perception of barriers to help-seeking. *Social Psychiatry and Social Epidemiology, 23,* 273–80.

Thomas, A., and Sillen, S. (1972). *Racism and psychiatry.* New York: Brunner/Mazel.

Thompson, E. E., Neighbors, H. W., Munday, C., and Jackson, J. S. (1996). Recruitment and retention of African American patients for clinical research: An exploration of response rates in an urban psychiatric hospital. *Journal of Consulting and Clinical Psychology, 64,* 861–7.

Triandis, H. C., Kashima, Y., Shimada, E., and Villareal, M. (1986). Acculturation indices as a means of confirming cultural differences. *International Journal of Psychology, 21,* 43–70.

Triandis, H. C., Bontempo, R., Betancourt, B., Bond, M., et al. (1986). The measurement of the etic aspects of individualism and collectivism across cultures. *Australian Journal of Psychology, 38,* 257–67.

US Department of Education (1982). A study of alternative definitions and measures relating to eligibility and service under Part A of the Indian Education Act. Unpublished report.

Zuckerman, M. (1990). Some dubious premises in research and theory on racial differences: Scientific, social and ethical issues. *American Psychologist, 45,* 1297–1303.

Zvolensky, M. J., McNeil, D. W., Porter, C. A., and Stewart, S. H. (2001). Assessment of anxiety sensitivity in young American Indians and Alaskan Natives. *Behaviour Research and Therapy, 39,* 477–93.

VIGNETTE

Research in Ethnic Minority Communities

Anne K. Jacobs

Bird, H. R., Canino, G. J., Davies, M., Zhang, H., Ramirez, R., and Lahey, B. B. (2001). Prevalence and correlates of antisocial behaviors among three ethnic groups. *Journal of Abnormal Child Psychology, 29*, 6, 465–78.

Jackson (chapter 18, this volume) identified the need for studies on the prevalence rates of mental illness between cultural groups. Bird and colleagues conducted a study which serves as a good example of such research. The authors examined the prevalence of Oppositional Defiant Disorder (ODD), Conduct Disorder (CD), and severity of anti-social behavior among three ethnic groups: Hispanics, African-Americans, and Mainland Non-Hispanic, Non-African American. Hispanics were further divided into Island Puerto Ricans and Mainland Hispanics. Psychosocial correlates of antisocial behavior within each ethnic group were also examined. The authors reported a high participation rate, 84.4 percent, among youth in the five chosen sites, resulting in data from 1,285 pairs of youth and parent/primary caretakers in Connecticut, Georgia, New York, San Juan, and Puerto Rico. The samples were not stratified by socioeconomic level. While this limited the authors' ability to control for the influence of socioeconomic level in their analyses, the samples were representative of each community.

All measures and interviews were offered in English or Spanish, and psychometric properties of measures were well described. Specifically, test–retest reliability, interrater reliability for diagnoses, and internal consistency for all scales were presented. The entire protocol was computer-assisted, thus aiding interviewer fidelity to the research protocol within and between sites. The authors decided to classify the Hispanic participants as Island Puerto Ricans or Mainland Hispanics, which resulted in reduced numbers of participants within the resulting groups. This decision reflected a quandary that is likely common in research: the decision to sacrifice either statistical power or the ability to examine some of the cultural differences that exist within ethnic groups. The authors did an excellent job of describing the limitations in their analyses due to relatively small group sizes once the Hispanic participant group was subdivided. The authors clearly acknowledged that some of the analyses were only exploratory in nature due to the constraints of the sample size.

These researchers found that there were significantly lower rates of antisocial behavior among children in Puerto Rico as compared to rates among other ethnic groups in the mainland United States. Out of the variables examined in the present study, this finding seemed to be linked to better reported relations between Puerto Rican children and their families as compared to the mainland ethnic groups. African-American youth had significantly higher rates of CD than did Puerto Rican youth and ODD rates among the three mainland ethnic groups were almost three times greater than that of Puerto Rican youth. African-American participants reported significantly poorer family relations while Mainland Hispanics and non-Hispanic, Non-African American family relation scores fell between those of Puerto Rican families and African-American families. The lack of variability in socioeconomic levels in the sample of families in Puerto Rico was presented as a limitation of the study. The findings, however, are especially impressive given that most families in the Puerto Rican sample were from low SES homes. Although this study could not answer longitudinal questions about the development of family relations and antisocial behaviors, it was an important step in beginning to look at the prevalence of particularly troubling behaviors among different ethnic groups. A summary of the strengths of the Bird et al. article includes:

- High participation rate
- Focus on differences between ethnic groups and within Hispanic participants
- Acknowledgment of limitations of sample size and use of appropriate statistics
- Reliable and valid measures, administered in language chosen by each participant
- Use of multiple informants
- Results reduce paucity of scientific literature on ethnic groups in general and on non-Mexican American Hispanics specifically

CHAPTER NINETEEN

Investigating Professional Issues in Clinical Psychology

Michael C. Roberts, Jodi L. Kamps, and Ephi J. Betan

Professional issues in clinical psychology include topics related to the research and practice activities of the professional discipline; its ethics, education and training; and associated concerns of credentialing and licensing, legal considerations, and accreditation. These issues are often discussed in the published literature without the benefit of a research framework. This literature includes, for example, anecdotal descriptions of the impact of managed care on clinical practice, logical and case analyses of ethical codes of conduct, or descriptions of specialty training programs or experiences. Fortunately, however, a vast amount of empirical research has also been conducted in order to establish a database for understanding systematically what clinical psychologists do, how they function as clinicians and scientists, what they believe, and what guides their behavior. Although both types of literature are useful, in this chapter we will focus on how researchers in clinical psychology empirically investigate training issues, clinical practice, research activities, professional ethics, and other related topics.

Clinical researchers investigate professional issues to gain an understanding of what is happening in the professional field, to examine problems and successes, and to validate ways for the profession to perform its functions better. The methodologies are similar across topics (e.g., the use of surveys and content analyses of clinical case files and journals), but may be adjusted to the topic under study to produce an interpretable empirical understanding. All of these approaches and topics combine to create a picture of clinical psychology in its variations of concerns, debates, activities, and specialties. In this chapter we will describe the range of research topics and types of research methodologies.

Research on Training Issues in Clinical Psychology

How a professional field trains its members is critical to its self-definition and status as a profession. Since the formation of clinical psychology, considerable attention has been given to education and training (e.g., scientist-practitioner model: Belar and Perry, 1990; Raimy, 1950; professional psychology model: Korman, 1974). Many conceptual pieces and commentaries have been published about general issues in, as well as specific elements of, training. Such topics include supervision, innovative curricula, and specialized training in specialties of neuropsychology, health psychology, geropsychology, and clinical child and pediatric psychology. However, these are not research-based, but are often the consensus of a conference or committee or the views of the authors. Numerous research articles have followed to investigate the efficacy of training in the specialized models and, in addition, to assess how the graduates of training do in their later clinical, research, and teaching positions. Although carefully assessed outcomes of training would appear to be the best measures for this research, rarely have these been employed. Aspects of professional training (and eventual functioning) have, to a large extent, been examined through surveys of trainers, the trainees and graduates, although occasionally objective data may be gathered to bear on a professional training issue.

Training processes and content

Measuring what goes on in programs has been accomplished through surveys of training directors, such as the biennial survey of members of the Council of University Directors of Clinical Psychology (CUDCP). The survey results are distributed within the organization, but not published. The survey results provide information to training directors about other programs for comparison. The accreditation criteria for the American Psychological Association (1996) also require that programs conduct self-studies of their goals and objectives, their process of training (i.e., how they attempt to accomplish their goals), and the outcomes of the training according to the goals. These self-studies contain a wealth of information to benefit the programs and assist the accreditation review, but are rarely made available publicly. Some parts of the documents are starting to appear on program websites, but not systematically.

Other sources of data on training process include a multitude of surveys completed by directors of clinical training. As one example, Hood, Ferguson, and Roberts (2000) surveyed training directors and graduate students representing APA-accredited clinical psychology training programs with regard to the amount of training offered on managed care. The researchers found that the directors and students agree that managed care issues were addressed in courses, but that training was not substantial. The student respondents indicated a desire for more training on managed care; on some questions, there were discrepancies between students' and directors' reports of training. Earlier, in a somewhat similar survey, Cantor and Moldawsky (1985) surveyed training programs to determine what kinds of training were being provided on managing an independent practice.

More recently, Crits-Christoph et al. (1995) conducted a survey of directors of clinical training and internship programs with regard to training in empirically supported treatments. Although most programs were found to teach empirically based treatments, the researchers found that a sizable number of programs (over 20 percent) failed to train their students even minimally from a research literature. These types of surveys have been conducted on whether training programs provide coverage on such topics as sexuality training (Wiederman and Sansome, 1999), geropsychology (Hinrichsen, Myers, and Stewart, 2000), projective testing (Rossini and Moretti, 1997), and prescription privileges for psychologists (Massoth et al., 1990).

A serious problem for surveys of this type has been the dwindling response returns to the surveys. Training directors report being deluged with questionnaires and frequently discard them uncompleted. The representativeness of the sample and generalizability of the results may be questioned when relatively few potential respondents participate. Additionally, response biases (over- and underreporting) may become involved when respondents want to demonstrate that their programs' training is adequate or is attentive to current issues.

Training outcomes

Assessing the outcomes of professional training in clinical psychology has typically taken three approaches: (1) examining the annual reports submitted by training programs for accreditation by APA; (2) analyzing objectively reported data from public domain resources; and (3) surveying graduates about their current functioning. Cherry, Messenger, and Jacoby (2000) examined the accreditation annual reports of clinical psychology doctoral programs to reveal training model outcomes. These researchers separated the programs according to their self-described orientations as clinical scientist, scientist-practitioner, or practitioner-scholar. By examining these outcome data, Cherry, Messenger, and Jacoby found that graduates spend different amounts of time in clinical and research activities differentiated by the philosophy of their training programs and were employed in different settings as well. An earlier study of training program reports indicated a longer time from admission to graduation (time to degree) for Ph.D. programs than for Psy.D. programs (Gaddy et al., 1995). Additionally, graduates' employment settings and research activities were found to be consistent with training models in the graduate programs. Generally, though, these training reports are not open for research scrutiny.

Utilizing publicly available information, Yu et al. (1997) provided mean scores of recent graduates on the Examination for Professional Practice in Psychology (EPPP; the national psychology licensing exam) according to the universities at which the test-takers matriculated. This analysis also computed types of programs and found that graduates from research-oriented universities tended to score higher than those from professional schools. Similar studies have been conducted using the EPPP results to compare clinical versus school and counseling psychology programs and university-based programs versus freestanding programs (e.g., Kupfersmid and Fiala, 1991; McGaha and Minder, 1993). In another analysis of public domain information, Maher (1999) used data from the National Research Council (NRC) study of doctoral departments. He examined reputational rankings and quantitative information to draw conclusions about the types of resources, training, and quality in professional-applied versus research-oriented programs. For example, Maher noted that, over time, more Ph.D.s have been graduated by universities with the lowest quality ranking in the NRC study. Robiner and Crew (2000) presented data gathered from state regulatory boards about the numbers of psychology licenses as well as from predoctoral and internship program reports. They drew conclusions from their analyses about the size of the workforce, what it should be, and what training programs have done and should do to produce the "right sized" workforce in professional psychology.

Also using quantitative information about training programs, Ilardi et al. (2000) determined which ones were more proficient in training students who later took faculty positions in APA accredited training programs. The variable of "placement of a graduate on a clinical psychology faculty," as defined by Ilardi et al. (2000), is one of several potential measures of a program's outcomes. The authors suggest that other measures of career and training outcomes could be gathered, such as successful independent practice, teaching at liberal arts colleges, medical center faculty, or public sector employment, among others (see also Ilardi and Roberts, 2002). In a similar training outcomes study more narrowly targeted, La Greca, Stone, and Swales (1989) surveyed pediatric psychologists to ascertain which doctoral and internship programs were producing the most specialists. It was noted that nearly 75 percent of those responding did not attend one of the top twelve programs, indicating that no set of programs has dominated training and that many programs seem to prepare for this specialty, at least historically.

Surveys of professionals have also been employed to determine whether their training was adequate and to suggest where changes might be made to improve education. For example, La Greca et al. (1988), in a survey of pediatric psychologists, determined where they were currently functioning, such as in medical centers, pediatricians' offices, and university departments. They also found that most respondents rated certain coursework and experiences as important for the specialty, such as child development and psychopathology, specific assessment and intervention techniques, and medical knowledge.

This is but a sampling of the issues in professional training of clinical psychology examined through a variety of research methodologies, although survey methodology seems to prevail. The *sine qua non* of a profession is its continual self-examination. Investigations into the education and training of clinical psychologists are central to this process.

Research into Clinical Practice in Clinical Psychology

A breadth of research exists examining the roles of clinical psychologists in clinical practice. Studies have covered diverse topics ranging from the practice activities of psychologists to the impact of managed care on clinical practice. Despite the wide array of topical areas, however, research about clinical practice of psychologists has primarily involved two types of research methodology: case analyses (both retrospective and prospective) and surveys.

Case analyses

Retrospective case analysis typically involves reviewing charts in order to evaluate past information and has frequently been used to elucidate descriptive information about the activities of clinical psychologists and their client populations. This method of obtaining information has been used by several individuals to evaluate their clinical practices in a variety of settings. For example, researchers have examined clinical psychology services offered in children's medical settings (Olson et al., 1988; Rodrigue et al., 1995; Singer and Drotar, 1989; Sobel, Roberts, Rapoff, and Barnard, 2001). Olson et al. (1988) conducted an archival evaluation of the types of referrals received by a pediatric psychology inpatient service over a period of years. Similarly, Singer and Drotar (1989) described consecutive referrals to a psychological consultation service over a two-year period in a pediatric rehabilitation hospital. Rodrigue et al. (1995) also conducted an archival examination of referrals to a health center-based pediatric psychology service. In a more recent case analysis, Sobel, Roberts, Rapoff, and Barnard (2001) delineated characteristics of 250 clients in a pediatric psychology clinic in a medical setting in a metropolitan area.

Other outpatient clinics have also been subjected to case analyses. An evaluation of successive contacts in an adolescent outpatient clinic was conducted in order to determine if client characteristics or referral processes were related to outcome indicators (Tolan, Ryan, and Jaffe, 1988). They found that inclusion of other family members in therapy and continuity of care were crucial variables in the adolescents' outcome. Similarly, Clement (1994) conducted a quantitative evaluation of his private practice spanning 26 years. His practice included individuals ranging in age from 6 months to 79 years and involved 86 DSM III-R diagnostic categories. He reported that 75 percent of his clients had improved at termination, although the success rate varied based on diagnosis. Interestingly, Clement (1994) found no relationship between phase of his career and treatment outcome.

One study, by Sobel, Roberts, Rayfield, Barnard, and Rapoff (2001), employed a prospective case analysis of an outpatient pediatric psychology service in a primary care setting. Enrolling patients as they began treatment, rather than reviewing files after treatment termination, the characteristics and outcomes of 100 patients were coded. This study found that the majority of clients were Caucasian boys between the ages of 2 and 12 years who were referred for school and behavior problems. Eighty-one percent of the sample also received brief (between one and five sessions), behaviorally oriented treatment. Similarly, an earlier prospective case analysis by Charlop et al. (1987) analyzed patient and problem characteristics of 100 consecutively referred families in a hospital-based pediatric psychology outpatient clinic. These investigators found that noncompliance, tantrums, and aggression were among parents' most pressing concerns, and that behavioral treatment approaches resulted in successful clinical outcomes as judged by therapists.

Surveys of clinical practice

Surveys have also been a helpful tool used by several researchers interested in exploring the practice activities of clinical psychologists. Similar to case analyses, surveys have explored a broad array of topics, ranging from therapists' views of treatment manuals (Najavits et al., 2000) and prescribing privileges (Klusman, 1998), to therapists' experience with custody evaluation practices (Ackerman and Ackerman, 1997), adult survivors of childhood sexual abuse (Polusny and Follette, 1996), psychotropic medication and psychotherapy (Wiggins and Cummings, 1998), and diagnostic decision-making with African-American and non-African American clients with schizophrenia (Trierweiler et al., 2000).

Several other topical areas have been the target of numerous surveys in clinical psychology. Such areas include descriptive information about psychologists in clinical practice, the impact of managed care on clinical practice, and insurance reimbursement. Tryon (1983) conducted a national survey of 165 full-time private practitioners and gathered information regarding practitioners' educational levels, orientations, hours, referral sources, patients, fees, consulting jobs, and organizational memberships. In a more comprehensive survey of psychologists' practice activities, the Committee for the Advancement of Professional Practice (CAPP) commissioned a survey of all licensed APA members (American Psychological Association Practice Directorate, 1996). Surveys were mailed to 47,119 licensed healthcare professionals and 15,918 completed surveys were returned, yielding a response rate of 33.8 percent. The major findings indicated: (a) younger practitioners (licensed after 1990) are less likely to go into solo private practice, a phenomenon which might be driven by market forces; (b) psychologists based in healthcare settings are more likely to use outcome measures in comparison with psychologists in solo practice; and (c) concerns about managed care transcend all settings in which psychologists practice.

With the increasing prevalence of managed care, several recent surveys have explored the implications of managed care on psychologists' clinical practice (Murphy, DeBernardo, and Shoemaker, 1998; Phelps, Eisman, and Kohout, 1998; Rothbaum et al., 1998; Russell et al., 2000). Overall, respondents of these surveys, which included members of the APA's Division of Independent Practice, licensed psychologists across the country, and psychologists from New Jersey and Iowa, indicated uniformly negative perceptions of managed care. Across surveys, respondents also indicated increased dependence on managed care companies for their income. With the increase of managed care, however, respondents reported increased ethical concerns, loss of control over clinical decision-making, decreased levels of job autonomy, and pressure to change clients' quality of care. Reimbursement for psychological services has also been the subject of surveys for psychologists in individual states. Sinnett and Holen (1993) surveyed psychologists in Kansas and found that insurance restrictions limited the length and type of treatment, and the determination of "medical necessity" represents an obstacle to utilization of services. Similarly, Bowers and Knapp (1993) surveyed psychologists in private practice in Pennsylvania about their difficulties with insurance reimbursement. Respondents indicated that, when working with managed care, they encountered increased paperwork and difficulty getting authorization for longer treatment.

A number of studies of clinical psychology practice have investigated how clinical services are perceived, delivered, and received. For example, treatment acceptability studies assess how clients and families, physicians, and school personnel perceive the usefulness and appropriateness of various psychological treatments for the presenting problem (Arndorfer, Allen, and Aljazireh, 1999; Calvert and Johnston, 1990). Another concept, client or consumer satisfaction, is often assessed as an outcome measurement after treatment termination, and serves to indicate whether clients found services useful. For example, Schroeder (1996) provided data on parent feedback for an innovative "Come-in/Call-in" service in a pediatric psychology unit. Sobel, Roberts, Rayfield, Barnard, and Rapoff (2001) assessed ratings of parent and referral sources to determine satisfaction with psychological services. In a study with adult clients, Pekarik and Wolff (1996) failed to find a positive relationship between client satisfaction and other psychotherapy outcomes. They concluded that while satisfaction is one variable assessing quality of services, it should not serve as a substitute for other measures of psychotherapy change.

Of course, there exists a rich corpus of research regarding treatment outcomes (efficacy and effectiveness). This research is reviewed in chapters on child therapy and interventions and adult therapy and interventions in this handbook. Related to this line of research are studies examining costs of providing mental health services, and specifically, whether there are any cost-savings resulting from psychological treatment when more expensive medical costs are reduced (medical cost-offset). Several studies have examined these cost effects for adult clinical services (e.g., Groth-Marnat and Edkins, 1996) and child and family services (e.g., Finney, Riley, and Cataldo, 1991).

The APA Practice Directorate is undertaking an Internet-based survey of psychological practice using Real-Time Behavioral Sampling (New internet-based surveys, 2001). This "PracticeNet" project will request information on a recently completed session of clinical practice by a large number of clinical practitioners. The aggregated results from these practitioners across the country will provide a picture of practice-related activities in clinical care, practice administration, or supervision.

Overall, studies of the clinical practice of psychologists have enabled important information to be accumulated about the characteristics of clinical psychologists, their clients, and their practices. By examining surveys over time, one may gather a picture of how the characteristics, beliefs, and practices of psychologists have changed (Watkins and Watts, 1995). Additionally, psychologists who evaluate their practices may hold a competitive edge over those that do not, especially with the advent of managed care (Clement, 1996; Roberts and Hurley, 1997).

Research on Research Activities in Clinical Psychology

Empirical research has also been conducted on clinical psychology's research enterprise itself. Such investigations have examined the variety of topics being studied in the profession, the manner in which research is conducted, who is doing the research, the degree to which the research meets professional standards, and the utility of the work for clinicians and other researchers.

Journal article content analyses

Journal articles are often considered the *sine qua non* of scientific information exchange, so examinations of publishing trends and analyses of article content provide objective information about the scientific activities of the profession of clinical psychology. Journal articles can be selected and coded for the presence of specific information, or for the details of study variables and findings. When coding journal articles for a content analysis, investigators must take care in the development of the categories and their definitions to support the validity, reliability, and meaningfulness of interpretation. For example, Elkins and Roberts (1988) analyzed ten years of publications in the *Journal of Pediatric Psychology* (and Roberts, 1992, did so for later years) by coding articles on categories of gender of senior author, affiliation, academic rank, theoretical orientation, population type, population age, article type (applied research, basic research, professional practice, literature reviews), and research purpose. These investigators found an increase in applied research, usually conducted in medical settings and on psychological aspects of medical problems, an increase in the proportion of women as senior authors, and a predominance of behavioral orientation in the research. A later content study of this journal's research found that many of the articles contained only minimal statements about the clinical utility or implications of the findings for the practicing clinician (Roberts et al., 1996).

While not focusing on a single journal, Fristad, Emery, and Beck (1997) conducted a content analysis of research articles in which childhood depression was assessed. They investigated whether a particular assessment measure, the Children's Depression Inventory (CDI), was used to diagnose the depression. Given limitations of this instrument, the authors also categorized the degree to which additional assessments were used (e.g., diagnostic interviews, other measures) and cautions noted in the publications. Fristad, Emery, and Beck (1997) found that half of the studies used the CDI and that a majority of these did not incorporate additional assessments, although the limitations of the instrument were often noted. Such findings have the potential to catalyze improvements in the overall caliber of inquiry into diagnosis and treatment of childhood depression. These findings parallel an examination of published articles by Haaga and Solomon (1993) into the use of the Beck Depression Inventory for diagnosing adults in research studies.

Other research utilizing scientific journals in clinical psychology has investigated the adequacy of research designs and methodological reporting. For example, Park, Adams, and Lynch (1998) studied the sociodemographic factors in research published in the journal *Health Psychology* over a twelve year period. They categorized the participant samples of the research, reported in terms of race, income, educational level, gender, and age. They found that information on these variables typically was included inconsistently in the articles. Betan, Roberts, and McCluskey-Fawcett (1995) conducted a content analysis of articles in two applied child psychology journals. They found that a majority of the articles did not provide adequate information about rates of participation and other characteristics. Similarly, Sifers et al. (2002) categorized information from four journals in pediatric and child psychology in order to identify potential problems in methodology reporting. They found that socioeconomic status was infrequently reported in published articles, although participants' gender, age, and ethnicity were included in general terms at moderate-to-high rates. They suggested that there was wide variability in reporting information important for the interpretation of study findings.

Such investigations of clinical psychology research have consistently indicated that the published literature omits important information that would allow a research consumer to draw conclusions about the representativeness of a studied sample and generalizability of the obtained findings – thereby limiting the utility of the research findings. Thus, research utilizing journal content analysis has the potential to highlight means by which the field of clinical psychology may improve its scientific foundations.

Citation impact

A different approach to investigating the science of clinical psychology has been to assess the impact of published research by examining the influence of journals and articles cited in further research. The citation impact factor for a journal reflects the average number of times an article in that particular journal is cited by articles published in other journals, with higher numbers representing journals that are more widely cited. For example, the SSCI citation impact factor for the *Journal of Consulting and Clinical Psychology* = 3.85, the *Journal of Clinical Psychology* = 0.46, *Behavior Therapy* = 2.49, *Clinical Psychology: Science and Practice* = 2.39, the *Journal of Abnormal Psychology* = 3.36, the *Journal of Pediatric Psychology* = 1.68, and the *Journal of Clinical Child and Adolescent Psychology* = 0.82. These indices measure the influence a journal has in the field (at least in terms of influencing other research that ends up in a publication). Such an index does not measure the impact of an article or journal in a clinical innovation or application. With the advent of electronic databases, most frequently accessed articles can be tracked (even if not eventually cited in a subsequent publication). Oxford University Press, for example, currently collects data for on-line versions of its journals to determine "most frequently read contents" (number of webpage "hits") and content usage (including some informa-tion on the person accessing the journal articles on-line). This capacity of electronic databases can help determine what is a hot topic or trendy within the profession and what has influenced others by tracking ideas as part of the network of scholarship. In a related vein, Cohen (1979) conducted a mail survey of clinical psychologists to ascertain whether clinicians read and utilize research articles. He found that between two and four articles were read per month by practicing clinicians, but that they regarded having dis-cussions with colleagues as the best (highest) source of information. Some might argue that citation counts measure quality, significance, and usefulness. A citation impact factor can also be calculated for an individual article, a specific researcher/author, or a collec-tion of authors in a department or university (Top universities, 1995). This information is available through the Social Science Citation Index (SSCI: Institute for Scientific Information; see www.isinet.com).

Research into Professional Ethics

A topic receiving considerable empirical attention in psychology is professional ethics, with regard to psychologists' ethical knowledge, practice, and violations, as well as to the effectiveness of ethics education.

Ethical knowledge, practice, and violations

Research on knowledge of professional ethics is concerned with what psychologists understand and believe about ethical standards in clinical practice, research practice, and teaching. This includes knowledge of the Code of Ethics of the American Psychological Association and principles, abilities to apply sound ethical decision-making to ethical dilemmas, and consensus regarding appropriate ethical resolutions, especially in the clinical field. There are two primary modes of investigation into ethical knowledge: hypothetical vignettes and surveys (e.g., of knowledge, attitudes, and behaviors). There are also a few studies in the literature using videotaped, scripted clinical interviews in which the actors portray clinical material with ethical implications; however, this is not a common method.

Hypothetical vignettes usually describe an ethical dilemma and place the research participant in the role of the psychologist who must respond. Vignettes have been used to assess awareness of ethical issues by asking participants to indicate if the vignettes contain ethical dimensions (Baldick, 1980). Vignettes have also been used to explore how psychologists deal with ethical dimensions. Hypothetical scenarios have been employed for this purpose to investigate ethical practice in research and teaching. For example, Costa and Gatz (1992) employed scenarios to assess how faculty members determine authorship credit and order when faculty and students collaborate.

Hypothetical vignettes are used to assess knowledge of ethical principles. In this case the respondents typically select a resolution from multiple-choice options provided. The results are reported in terms of the percentages of respondents selecting each option. When used to measure ethical knowledge these data reflect the percentage of participants who possess appropriate ethical knowledge or understanding. Such a measure of ethical knowledge is based on an assumption that one specific response is more accurate than others.

The studies of Bernard and colleagues became the model for using vignettes to research psychologists' knowledge and application of ethical principles (Bernard and Jara, 1986; Bernard, Murphy, and Little, 1987). They provided two vignettes and asked samples of graduate students and clinicians to respond to two questions: "According to the APA ethics code, what should you do?" and "What would you most likely do?" Using this research method, researchers replicated the finding that although the majority of participants knew what they *should* do in response to the hypothetical scenario, an average of 50 percent of the participants indicated they *would* select a less intrusive intervention. Given this result, researchers have been particularly interested in understanding the discrepancy between participants' appropriate knowledge of professional ethics (what they should do) but apparent unwillingness (what they would do) to follow through with an ethical resolution. Building on the use of hypothetical scenarios with follow-up questions to understand this ethical unwillingness, Haas, Malouf, and Mayerson (1988) explored personal and professional factors, Wilkins et al. (1990) investigated the effect of perceived closeness (friend or professional acquaintance) on willingness, and Smith et al. (1991) investigated clinicians' rationales and justifications for their indicated resolutions. More recently, Betan and Stanton (1999) examined how emotional responses and subjective concerns influence ethical decision-making and willingness to behave ethically. Buckloh and Roberts (2001) considered psychologists' reactions to managed care ethical dilemmas.

A related issue involves beliefs, attitudes, and consensus regarding ethical practice. Recognizing that few ethical dilemmas are clear-cut, researchers into professional ethics have been interested in establishing a standard of practice. Thus, researchers have provided scenarios and interpreted participants' chosen ethical responses in terms of consensus, i.e., if a majority of respondents chose a particular response as most ethically appropriate in a given situation, consensus regarding how to manage the ethical dilemma was assumed. Alternatively, Tymchuk et al. (1982) asked participants to indicate whether they agreed with the decisions made about ethical dilemmas outlined in the vignette and what criteria they considered relevant to the decision. Both studies found that psychologists show adequate agreement on issues that have received heightened attention in the field and media, but limited agreement on less highlighted issues.

Moving from assessing specific knowledge of ethical principles (as though there is one accurate response) to seeking consensus, research into ethical practice has shifted toward greater complexity in an effort to capture all the possibilities of ethical practice; that is, toward determining what ethical issues people actually experience and what they do to manage or respond to an ethical dilemma. Surveys are a primary tool in this type of research endeavor to understand. Malpractice and risk management surveys provide relevant information concerning this applied dimension of ethical practice. Researchers compile statistics provided by companies underwriting malpractice coverage in order to assess the incidence of malpractice claims and the chance of being sued (Bennett et al., 1990; Conte and Karasu, 1990; Pope, 1986). Empirical investigations of the events and activities associated with malpractice claims and litigation identified areas (therapist behaviors, client characteristics, and practice settings) requiring particular caution and guidelines for risk management (Conte and Karasu, 1990; Jobes and Berman, 1993; Pope, 1986, 1989; Roswell, 1988).

The identification of high risk areas and management guidelines raises questions about what clinicians actually experience in practice and how they manage the situations that may make them vulnerable to ethical violations or litigation. For example, Montgomery, Cupit, and Wimberley (1999) reported on a survey of professionals' awareness of malpractice and risk management issues, experiences of malpractice complaints and lawsuits, as well as practice activities to reduce worry and vulnerability. Seeking more specificity, other researchers have used surveys to generate an understanding of how psychologists manage particular issues that may result in ethical problems. As one illustration, Peruzzi and Bougar (1999) investigated how practicing psychologists assess suicide risk in order to identify which of the multitude of suicide risk factors identified in empirical research are most important to clinicians when they are treating a potentially suicidal patient.

Other researchers have surveyed topics such as ethical dilemmas encountered by psychologists (e.g., Pope and Vetter, 1992); beliefs regarding practice in psychotherapy (Pope, Tabachnick, and Keith-Spiegel, 1988); awareness of and opinions about fellow professionals' ethical misconduct (Wood et al., 1985); attitudes and practices regarding physical contact with patients (Holroyd and Brodsky, 1977); ethical considerations in the use of technology (McMinn et al., 1999); practices by researchers to ensure ethical conduct (e.g., McCrady and Bux, 1999); managing authorship decisions (Goodyear, Crego, and Johnston, 1992); and ethical issues in teaching practical courses (e.g., Rupert et al., 1999).

To more adequately address difficulties in professional ethics, clinical researchers need to examine actual violations. Underreporting may bias surveys of practitioners' self-reported involvement in ethical violations, but such surveys help document ethically questionable practice occurrences (e.g., Pope, Tabachnik, and Keith-Spiegel, 1987). Other data sources include reports to state and APA ethics committees, legal suits, and malpractice liability claims. Finally, in the effort to understand the factors that contribute to ethical violations, researchers are using *interviews*, or qualitative approaches. An example is Somer and Saadon's (1999) interviews with former victims of sexual boundary violations by psychotherapists to understand the process of exploitation.

Training in professional ethics

Because clinical psychology, as a field, must be committed to enhancing ethical practice among clinicians, researchers, and teachers in psychology, research into professional ethics identifies areas of concern of limited knowledge, and of limited ethical practice. The manner in which clinical psychology teaches ethics, therefore, has been another area of empirical focus, with attention to the modes and effectiveness of training in professional ethics. Methodology derives from the research question. Thus, researchers interested in whether psychologists receive ethics training and in what fashion typically use surveys of either psychologists or training program directors. The literature includes broad-based surveys of ethics training, i.e., does it exist and in what form (Newmark and Hutchins, 1981; Tymchuck et al., 1982; Vanek, 1990), as well as more discrete surveys of a specific facet of ethics, such as, for example, sexuality (Wiederman and Sansome, 1999) and sexual ethics (Housman and Stake, 1999). Data generated include the percentage of graduate programs surveyed providing the ethics training, the primary modes of teaching ethics during the educational process (in a formal course, as part of other courses, or in supervision), and the reported content of training. To evaluate the effectiveness of ethics training, investigators have used pre- and posttest measures or comparison control group designs. In illustration of a control group design, Gawthrop and Uhleman (1992) assessed the effectiveness of a 3-hour ethical decision-making workshop by comparing students' responses to a vignette containing an ethical dilemma. One group of students received the workshop, a second group received a handout on ethical decision-making, and the third group received only instructions on how to complete the measure. In comparison to the latter two groups, the group receiving the workshop training scored significantly higher on ratings of their ethical decision-making ability and quality. Using a pre- and posttest instrument, McGovern (1988) assessed changes in students' knowledge and understanding of the ethical principles following an ethics course. Baldick (1980) assessed effectiveness of training in ethics by measuring the ethical discrimination ability of psychology interns as a function of training. Another way to evaluate training involves psychologists' evaluation of the usefulness of graduate school training (Tyler and Clark, 1987). A considerable amount of attention in clinical psychology is devoted to this topic, because ethics in research and practice define the field as a profession.

Topics Related to Professional Issues

Research into other aspects of professional functioning of psychologists has included surveys into professional views regarding various aspects of the science and practice of the field, perceptions of clients/patients, diagnoses and treatment modalities, among other issues.

Attitudes and beliefs of clinical psychologists

In terms of professionals' attitudes, questionnaire-based surveys have examined such topics as psychologists' biases regarding premature infants or children with attention-deficit hyperactivity disorders, stereotypes of children and adults with cancer, attitudes toward gay and lesbian clients, beliefs about spanking as a form of discipline for children, and many others. Such studies investigate psychologists' particular beliefs that may interfere with appropriate assessment and treatment, and may be useful in identifying where training and continuing education need to focus to change negative biases. Surveys have also identified the theoretical orientations of clinical psychology practitioners, finding recently, for example, that 43 percent described themselves as relying on cognitive-behavioral theory, in comparison with 24 percent who accepted psychodynamic/analytic theories (Addis and Krasnow, 2000). Norcross, Karg, and Prochaska (1997) found similar results and were able to track changes in primary theoretical orientation in the membership of the APA Division of Clinical Psychology over time since 1960 by comparing their results to earlier surveys.

Other surveys of clinical psychologists' attitudes have examined perceptions of empirically supported treatments – a recent emphasis in the field (paralleled in other professions such as in medicine and social work with their focus on "evidence-based practice"). Addis and Krasnow (2000) conducted a national survey of practicing psychologists to determine their attitudes toward the recent promulgation of psychotherapy treatment manuals. They found considerable variability in acceptance and views about the content and appropriateness of these manuals. Frequently the respondents expressed negative views about the manuals. Additionally, the psychologists endorsed perspectives about manualized treatments that were somewhat divergent from the intent of the manual developers. Earlier surveys of clinical psychologists on the usefulness of various sources of information found that research articles and books were not perceived as particularly helpful (Cohen, 1979; Cohen, Sargent, and Sechrest, 1986; Morrow-Bradley and Elliott, 1986).

A new professional issue is reflected in organized efforts to obtain prescription authority or privileges for psychologists. This effort has not been without controversy. Surveys published in *Professional Psychology* (an APA journal) have found that clinical psychology graduate students, interns, and internship directors generally supported prescription privileges for psychologists (Ax, Forbes, and Thompson, 1997; Sammons et al., 2000; Tatman et al., 1997). These more recent findings contrast with earlier surveys, which found some resistance and lack of consensus regarding prescription privileges (Boswell and Litwin, 1992; Massoth et al., 1990).

In a more extensive examination of attitudes about important issues in psychology, Oakland (1994) reported on an APA-sponsored survey of members of the organization. A survey instrument requesting prioritization of 32 issues was distributed to APA governance and a random sample of the membership. Oakland analyzed the priority ratings according to the various constituencies. The highest ranking priorities were doctoral standards, psychology's public image, the public's understanding of psychology applications, science values and interests, and developing effective interventions.

Much as with opinion surveys of the general public, the validity and reliability of the surveys of clinical psychology professionals depend on the adequacy of the sampling and return rates, as well as the phrasing of questions. Over time, participation rates seem to be decreasing and the generalizability of the survey findings becomes more limited. The fact that the field may erroneously utilize such fallible information in decision-making about its future in terms of training, clinical practice, or policy also varies and even negative attitudes about a new development have rarely dissuaded its proponents.

Delphic surveys on the future of the profession

Opinions and ideas of a group, particularly leaders in a professional field, may also be systematically sampled through a process called the Delphic method. This technique is particularly useful for forecasting trends for the profession (San Tucker and Roberts, 1990). In a Delphic poll a panel of recognized experts is identified and surveyed repeatedly to obtain a consensus on certain issues through structured feedback about the responses. Unlike a one-time survey, Delphic participants react to each other's responses to shape further positions on the issues. Delphic polls have traditionally involved mailed questionnaires, although new Internet technologies increase the feasibility of gathering information on-line. The Delphic method, although involving some aspects of qualitative research, permits quantification of the written responses and ratings of issues. Comparison can be made between different groups on their statements. The Delphic procedure typically involves posing a question that calls for participants to identify critical issues for the future. When participants' responses are compiled, the names of the respondents are removed and the verbatim comments are randomly reorganized. The entire set is then returned to the participants for a second round in which they are asked to give ratings of importance. Often the top ten priority issues are sent back to the participants for a rank ordering in terms of their importance in answering the original question. These rankings are then averaged across participants to determine the consensus ranking of the top issues confronting the field. The Delphic method has been used in applied and professional psychology. For example, Prochaska and Norcross (1982) conducted a Delphic survey of practicing clinicians to predict what psychotherapy would be like in the future. At the time, the participants identified that there would be an increase in women and minority therapists, greater coverage under national health insurance, standard implementation of peer review, and a decrease in long-term individual treatment. (As a measure of its utility, it should be noted, many years later, some of these predictions have come to pass, although the participants could not have foreseen some aspects of the profession's future.)

Brown and Roberts (2000) surveyed pediatric psychologists in research and clinical practice to identify domains of importance to the future of pediatric psychology. The top three domains were concerned with the field's ability to demonstrate need for changes in the reimbursement system with managed care. The clinicians and researchers rarely differed in their rankings of the issues, perhaps indicating that this subspecialty has been much more integrated than other areas of clinical psychology. The Delphic method provides one way to systematically gather opinions and ideas from professionals.

Legal analyses

Clinical psychology has also examined legal issues related to the profession through analyses traditionally associated with the legal profession. These legal analyses are most frequently found in the journals *Law and Human Behavior, Psychology, Public Policy, and the Law* (PPPL), and less frequently in *Professional Psychology: Research and Practice*. For example, one issue of PPPL included articles analyzing the impact of a 1993 US Supreme Court ruling, *Daubert v. Merrell Dow Pharmaceuticals*, in presenting a new standard regarding the admissibility of scientific evidence in the courtroom (Shuman and Sales, 1999). This ruling would affect psychologists' testimony in the various types of cases for which they serve as expert witnesses (e.g., divorce and child custody, dangerousness evaluations, neuropsychology of injuries). In an analysis of the Supreme Court ruling in *Jaffee v. Redmond*, Shuman and Foote (1999) describe how the Court's recognition of the privilege between psychotherapist and patient might influence therapy and clinical practice. Such legal analyses constitute research endeavors of a different type than the ones discussed in this book and require expertise in legal issues beyond psychology (Dernbach et al., 1994; see also www.jurist.law.pitt.edu). Nonetheless, as a mechanism for developing understanding about professional issues in psychology, this research approach can be quite valuable to the field.

Surveys on employment and salaries of clinical psychologists

Surveys of doctoral training, employment trends, and salaries are also important indicants of professional issues. For example, the National Science Foundation surveys all people who have earned doctorates in the United States at the point of submission of their dissertations. The survey is used to objectively evaluate graduate education (Sanderson et al., 1999). Similarly, the American Psychological Association periodically surveys selected samples of its members to determine what professional employment positions psychologists are taking and what are the average salaries for various positions and settings (e.g., Kohout and Wicherski, 1996; Williams, Kohout, and Wicherski, 2000). This type of survey permits the identification of areas of concern and the tracking of trends over time to assist the association in its organizational support efforts and advocacy (e.g., Pion, Kohout, and Wicherski, 2000).

Conclusions

In this chapter we have highlighted several major areas that we believe directly relate to the definition of psychology as a *professional* discipline. Empirical research aids in identifying successful and problematic areas of this discipline and specialty of clinical psychology. We paid particular attention to the methods psychologists have used to date to empirically investigate psychologists' ethical conduct, academic training, clinical practice, and research activities. The monitoring and development of sound practice in these areas is vital to maintaining the integrity of clinical psychology as a profession. This review of research hopefully will serve as a stepping-stone toward sharpening the field's empirical investigations on professional matters in psychology. The more we as clinical psychologists understand about professional issues and work toward discovering modes of training and education that ensure professional practice and empirical foundations, the more we are in a position to preserve the status as a profession. As such, professions always involve self-monitoring and analysis. The research methodologies are the means by which this occurs.

References

Ackerman, M. J., and Ackerman, M. C. (1997). Custody evaluation practices: A survey of experienced professionals (revisited). *Professional Psychology: Research and Practice*, 28, 137–45.

Addis, M. E., and Krasnow, A. D. (2000). A national survey of practicing psychologists' attitudes toward psychotherapy treatment manuals. *Journal of Consulting and Clinical Psychology*, 68, 331–9.

American Psychological Association Committee on Accreditation (1996). *Guidelines and principles for accreditation of programs in professional psychology and accreditation operating procedures.* Washington, DC: American Psychological Association Committee on Accreditation.

American Psychological Association Practice Directorate (1996). *The Committee for the Advancement of Professional Practice (CAPP) practitioner survey.* Washington, DC: American Psychological Association Practice Directorate.

Arndorfer, R. E., Allen, K. D., and Aljazireh, L. (1999). Behavioral health needs for pediatric medicine and the acceptability of behavioral solutions: Implications for behavioral psychologists. *Behavior Therapy*, 30, 137–48.

Ax, R. K., Forbes, M. R., and Thompson, D. D. (1997). Prescription privileges for psychologists: A survey of predoctoral interns and directors of training. *Professional Psychology: Research and Practice*, 28, 509–14.

Baldick, T. (1980). Ethical discrimination ability of intern psychologists: A function of ethics training. *Professional Psychology: Research and Practice*, 11, 276–82.

412   *Roberts, Kamps, Betan*

Belar, C. D., and Perry, N. W. (1990). *Proceedings: National Conference on Scientist-Practitioner Education and Training for the Professional Practice of Psychology*. Sarasota, FL: Professional Resource Press.

Bennett, B. B., Bryant, B. K., VandenBos, G. R., and Greenwood, A. (1990). *Professional liability and risk management*. Washington, DC: American Psychological Association.

Bernard, J. L., and Jara, C. S. (1986). The failure of clinical psychology graduate students to apply understood ethical principles. *Professional Psychology: Research and Practice, 17*, 313–15.

Bernard, J. L., Murphy, M., and Little, M. (1987). The failure of clinical psychologists to apply understood ethical principles. *Professional Psychology: Research and Practice, 18*, 489–91.

Betan, E. J., and Stanton, A. L. (1999). Fostering ethical willingness: Integrating emotional and contextual awareness with rational analysis. *Professional Psychology: Research and Practice, 30*, 295–301.

Betan, E. J., Roberts, M. C., and McCluskey-Fawcett, K. (1995). Rates of participation for clinical child and pediatric psychology research: Issues in methodology. *Journal of Clinical Child Psychology, 24*, 227–35.

Boswell, D. L., and Litwin, W. J. (1992). Limited prescription privileges for psychologists: A 1-year follow-up. *Professional Psychology: Research and Practice, 23*, 108–13.

Bowers, T. G., and Knapp, S. (1993). Reimbursement issues for psychologists in independent practice. *Psychotherapy in Private Practice, 12*, 73–87.

Brown, K. J., and Roberts, M. C. (2000). Future issues in pediatric psychology: Delphic survey. *Journal of Clinical Psychology in Medical Settings, 7*, 5–15.

Buckloh, L. M., and Roberts, M. C. (2001). Managed mental health care: Attitudes and ethical beliefs of child and pediatric psychologists. *Journal of Pediatric Psychology, 26*, 193–202.

Calvert, S. C., and Johnston, C. (1990). Acceptability of treatments for child behavior problems: Issues and implications for future research. *Journal of Clinical Child Psychology, 19*, 6–74.

Cantor, D. W., and Moldawsky, S. (1985). Training for independent practice: A survey of graduate programs in clinical psychology. *Professional Psychology: Research and Practice, 16*, 768–72.

Charlop, M. H., Parrish, J. M., Fenton, L. R., and Cataldo, M. F. (1987). Evaluation of hospital-based outpatient pediatric psychology services. *Journal of Pediatric Psychology, 12*, 485–503.

Cherry, D. K., Messenger, L. C., and Jacoby, A. M. (2000). An examination of training model outcomes in clinical psychology programs. *Professional Psychology: Research and Practice, 31*, 562–8.

Clement, P. C. (1994). Quantitative evaluation of 26 years of private practice. *Professional Psychology: Research and Practice, 25*, 173–6.

Clement, P. C. (1996). Evaluation in private practice. *Clinical Psychology: Science and Practice, 3*, 146–59.

Cohen, L. H. (1979). The research readership and information source reliance of clinical psychologists. *Professional Psychology, 10*, 780–5.

Cohen, L. H., Sargent, M. M., and Sechrest, L. B. (1986). Use of psychotherapy research by professional psychologists. *American Psychologist, 41*, 198–206.

Conte, H. R., and Karasu, T. B. (1990). Malpractice in psychotherapy: An overview. *American Journal of Psychotherapy, 44*, 232–46.

Costa, M. M., and Gatz, M. (1992). Determination of authorship credit in published dissertations. *American Psychological Society, 3*, 354–7.

Crits-Christoph, P., Frank, E., Chambless, D. L., Brody, C., and Karp, J. F. (1995). Training in empirically validated treatments: What are clinical students learning? *Professional Psychology: Research and Practice, 26*, 514–22.

Dernbach, J. C., Singleton, R. V., Wharton, C. S., and Ruhtenberg, J. M. (1994). *Practical guide to legal writing and legal method*. Buffalo, NY: William S. Hein.

Elkins, P. D., and Roberts, M. C. (1988). *Journal of Pediatric Psychology*: A content analysis of articles over its first 10 years. *Journal of Pediatric Psychology, 13*, 575–94.

Finney, J. W., Riley, A. W., and Cataldo, M. F. (1991). Psychology in primary health care: Effects of brief targeted therapy on children's medical care utilization. *Journal of Pediatric Psychology, 16*, 447–61.

Fristad, M. A., Emery, B. L., and Beck, S. J. (1997). Use and abuse of the Children's Depression Inventory. *Journal of Consulting and Clinical Psychology, 65*, 699–702.

Gaddy, C. D., Charlot-Swilley, D., Nelson, P. D., and Reich, J. N. (1995). Selected outcomes of accredited programs. *Professional Psychology: Research and Practice, 26*, 507–13.

Gawthrop, J. C., and Uhleman, M. C. (1992). Effects of the problem-solving approach in ethics training. *Professional Psychology: Research and Practice, 23*, 38–42.

Goodyear, R. K., Crego, C. A., and Johnston, M. W. (1992). Ethical issues in the supervision of student research: A study of critical incidents. *Professional Psychology: Research and Practice, 23*, 203–10.

Groth-Marnat, G., and Edkins, G. (1996). Professional psychologists in general health care settings: A review of the financial efficacy of direct treatment interventions. *Professional Psychology: Research and Practice, 27*, 161–74.

Haaga, D., and Solomon, A. (1993). Impact of Kendall, Hollon, Beck, Hammen, and Ingram (1987). On treatment of the continuity issue in "depression" research. *Cognitive Therapy and Research, 17*, 313–24.

Haas, L. J., Malouf, J. L., and Mayerson, N. H. (1988). Personal and professional characteristics as factors in psychologists' ethical decision making. *Professional Psychology: Research and Practice, 19*, 35–42.

Hinrichsen, G. A., Myers, D. S., and Stewart, D. (2000). Doctoral internship training opportunities in clinical geropsychology. *Professional Psychology: Research and Practice, 31*, 88–92.

Holroyd, J., and Brodsky, A. M. (1977). Psychologists' attitudes and practices regarding erotic and nonerotic physical contact with patients. *American Psychologist, 32*, 843–9.

Hood, C. A., Ferguson, K. S., and Roberts, M. C. (2000). Clinical training for the millennium: How much on managed care? *The Clinical Psychologist, 53*, 1, 3–7.

Housman, L. M., and Stake, J. E. (1999). The current state of sexual ethics training in clinical psychology: Issues of quantity, quality, and effectiveness. *Professional Psychology: Research and Practice, 30*, 302–11.

Ilardi, S. S., and Roberts, M. C. (2002). Program proficiency in training graduate students for clinical faculty careers: Does program size matter? *Clinical Psychology: Science and Practice, 9*, 108–11.

Ilardi, S. S., Rodriguez-Hanley, A., Roberts, M. C., and Seigel, J. (2000). On the origins of clinical psychology faculty: Who is training the trainers? *Clinical Psychology: Science and Practice, 7*, 346–54.

Jobes, D. A., and Berman, A. L. (1993). Suicide and malpractice liability: Assessing and revising policies, procedures, and practice in outpatient settings. *Professional Psychology: Research and Practice, 24*, 91–9.

Klusman, L. E. (1998). Military health care providers' views on prescribing privileges for psychologists. *Professional Psychology: Research and Practice, 29*, 223–9.

Kohout, J. L., and Wicherski, M. (1996). Employment settings of psychologists. *Psychiatric Services, 47*, 809.

Korman, M. (1974). National conference on levels and patterns of professional training in psychology. *American Psychologist, 29*, 441–9.

Kupfersmid, J., and Fiala, M. (1991). Comparison of EPPP scores among graduates of varying psychology programs. *American Psychologist, 46*, 534–5.

La Greca, A. M., Stone, W. L., and Swales, T. (1989). Pediatric psychology training: An analysis of graduate, internship, and postdoctoral programs. *Journal of Pediatric Psychology, 14,* 103–16.

La Greca, A. M., Stone, W. L., Drotar, D., and Maddux, J. E. (1988). Training in pediatric psychology: Survey results and recommendations. *Journal of Pediatric Psychology, 13,* 121–39.

McCrady, B. S., and Bux, Jr., D. A. (1999). Ethical issues in informed consent with substance abusers. *Journal of Consulting and Clinical Psychology, 67,* 186–93.

McGaha, S., and Minder, C. (1993). Factors influencing performance on the Examination for Professional Practice in Psychology (EPPP). *Professional Psychology: Research and Practice, 24,* 107–9.

McGovern, T. V. (1988). Teaching the ethical principles of psychology. *Teaching of Psychology, 15,* 22–6.

McMinn, M. R., Buchanan, T., Ellens, B. M., and Ryan, M. K. (1999). Technology, professional practice, and ethics: Survey findings and implications. *Professional Psychology: Research and Practice, 30,* 165–72.

Maher, B. A. (1999). Changing trends in doctoral training programs in psychology. *Psychological Science, 10,* 475–81.

Massoth, N. A., McGrath, R. E., Bianchi, C., and Singer, J. (1990). Psychologists' attitudes toward prescription privileges. *Professional Psychology: Research and Practice, 21,* 147–9.

Montgomery, L. M., Cupit, B. E., and Wimberley, T. K. (1999). Complaints, malpractice, and risk management: Professional issues and personal experiences. *Professional Psychology: Research and Practice, 30,* 402–10.

Morrow-Bradley, C., and Elliott, R. (1986). Utilization of psychotherapy research by practicing psychotherapists. *American Psychologist, 41,* 188–97.

Murphy, M. J., DeBernardo, C. R., and Shoemaker, W. E. (1998). Impact of managed care on independent practice and professional ethics: A survey of independent practitioners. *Professional Psychology: Research and Practice, 29,* 43–51.

Najavits, L. M., Weiss, R. D., Shaw, S. R., and Dierberger, A. E. (2000). Psychotherapists' views of treatment manuals. *Professional Psychology: Research and Practice, 31,* 404–8.

New internet-based surveys capture snapshots of psychology practice (2001). *The APA/Division Dialogue* (January–February), 7, 8.

Newmark, C. S., and Hutchins, T. C. (1981). Survey of professional education in ethics in clinical psychology internship programs. *Journal of Clinical Psychology, 37,* 681–3.

Norcross, J. C., Karg, R. S., and Prochaska, J. O. (1997). Clinical psychologists in the 1990s: Part I. *Clinical Psychologist, 50,* 2, 4–9.

Oakland, T. (1994). Issues of importance to the membership of the APA. *American Psychologist, 49,* 879–86.

Olson, R. A., Holden, E. W., Friedman, A., Faust, J., Kenning, M., and Mason, P. J. (1988). Psychological consultation in a children's hospital: An evaluation of services. *Journal of Pediatric Psychology, 13,* 479–92.

Park, T. L., Adams, S. G., and Lynch, J. (1998). Sociodemographic factors in health psychology research: 12 years in review. *Health Psychology, 17,* 381–3.

Pekarik, G., and Wolff, C. B. (1996). Relationship of satisfaction to symptom change, follow-up adjustment and clinical significance. *Professional Psychology: Research and Practice, 27,* 202–8.

Peruzzi, N., and Bougar, B. (1999). Assessing risk for completed suicide in patients with major depression: Psychologists' views of critical factors. *Professional Psychology: Research and Practice, 30,* 576–80.

Phelps, R., Eisman, E. J., and Kohout, J. (1998). Psychological practice and managed care: Results of the CAPP practitioner survey. *Professional Psychology: Research and Practice, 29,* 31–6.

Pion, G., Kohout, J., and Wicherski, M. (2000). "Rightsizing" the workforce through training reductions: A good idea? *Professional Psychology: Research and Practice, 31*, 266–71.

Polusny, M. A., and Follette, V. M. (1996). Remembering childhood sexual abuse: A national survey of psychologists' clinical practices, beliefs, and personal experiences. *Professional Psychology: Research and Practice, 27*, 41–52.

Pope, K. (1986). New trends in malpractice cases and changes in APA liability insurance. *Independent Practitioner, 6*, 4, 23–6.

Pope, K. (1989). Malpractice suits, licensing disciplinary actions, and ethics cases: Frequencies, causes, and costs. *Independent Practitioner, 9*, 1, 22–6.

Pope, K., and Vetter, V. A. (1992). Ethical dilemmas encountered by members of the American Psychological Association. *American Psychologist, 47*, 397–411.

Pope, K., Tabachnik, B. G., and Keith-Spiegel, P. (1987). Ethics of practice: The beliefs and behaviors of psychologists as therapists. *American Psychologist, 42*, 993–1006.

Pope, K., Tabachnik, B. G., and Keith-Spiegel, P. (1988). Good and poor practices in psychotherapy: National survey of beliefs of psychologists. *Professional Psychology: Research and Practice, 19*, 547–52.

Prochaska, J. O., and Norcross, J. C. (1982). The future of psychotherapy: A Delphic poll. *Professional Psychology, 13*, 620–38.

Raimy, V. C. (1950). *Training in clinical psychology*. New York: Prentice-Hall.

Roberts, M. C. (1992). Vale dictum: An editor's view of the field of pediatric psychology and its journal. *Journal of Pediatric Psychology, 17*, 785–805.

Roberts, M. C., and Hurley, L. K. (1997). *Managing managed care*. New York: Plenum.

Roberts, M. C., McNeal, R. E., Randall, C. J., and Roberts, J. C. (1996). A necessary reemphasis on integrating explicative research with the pragmatics of pediatric psychology. *Journal of Pediatric Psychology, 21*, 107–14.

Robiner, W. N., and Crew, D. P. (2000). Rightsizing the workforce of psychologists in health care: Trends from licensing boards, training programs, and managed care. *Professional Psychology: Research and Practice, 31*, 245–63.

Rodrigue, J. R., Hoffmann, R. G., Rayfield, A., Lescano, C., Kubar, W., Streisand, R., and Banko, C. G. (1995). Evaluating pediatric psychology consultation services in a medical setting: An example. *Journal of Clinical Psychology in Medical Settings, 2*, 89–107.

Rossini, E. D., and Moretti, R. J. (1997). Thematic Apperception Test (TAT) interpretation: Practice recommendations from a survey of clinical psychology doctoral programs accredited by the American Psychological Association. *Professional Psychology: Research and Practice, 28*, 393–8.

Roswell, V. A. (1988). Professional liability: Issues for behavior therapists in the 1980s and 1990s. *Behavior Therapist, 11*, 163–71.

Rothbaum, P. A., Bernstein, D. M., Haller, O., Phelps, R., and Kohout, J. (1998). New Jersey psychologists' report on managed mental health care. *Professional Psychology: Research and Practice, 29*, 37–42.

Rupert, P. A., Kozlowski, N. F., Hoffman, L. A., Daniels, D. D., and Piette, J. M. (1999). Practical and ethical issues in teaching psychological testing. *Professional Psychology: Research and Practice, 30*, 209–14.

Russell, D. W., de la Mora, A., Trudeau, L., Scott, N. A., Norman, N. A., and Schmitz, M. F. (2000). Psychologists' reactions to Medicaid managed care: Opinion and practice change after 1 year. *Professional Psychology: Research and Practice, 31*, 547–52.

Sammons, M. T., Gorny, S. W., Zinner, E. S., and Allen, R. P. (2000). Prescriptive authority for psychologists: A consensus of support. *Professional Psychology: Research and Practice, 31*, 604–9.

San Tucker, H., and Roberts, M. C. (1990). Future issues in children's health care: Addressing psychosocial concerns. *Children's Health Care, 19*, 199–208.

Sanderson, A., Dugoni, B., Hoffer, T., and Selfa, L. (1999). *Doctorate recipients from United States universities: Summary report, 1998.* Chicago, IL: National Opinion Research Center (see website: www.nsf.gov/sbe/srs/srs00410/).

Schroeder, C. S. (1996). Mental health services in pediatric primary care. In M. C. Roberts (ed.), *Model programs in child and family mental health* (pp. 265–84). Mahwah, NJ: Lawrence Erlbaum Associates.

Shuman, D. W., and Foote, W. (1999). *Jaffee v. Redmond*'s impact: Life after the Supreme Court's recognition of a psychotherapist–patient privilege. *Professional Psychology: Research and Practice, 30,* 479–87.

Shuman, D. W., and Sales, B. D. (Guest Editors) (1999). Special theme issue: *Daubert*'s meanings for the admissibility of behavioral and social science evidence. *Psychology, Public Policy, and Law, 5* (Whole issue No. 1).

Sifers, S. K., Puddy, R. W., Warren, J. S., and Roberts, M. C. (2002). Reporting of demographics, methodology, and ethical procedures in journals in pediatric and child psychology. *Journal of Pediatric Psychology, 27,* 19–25.

Singer, L., and Drotar, D. (1989). Psychological practice in a rehabilitation hospital. *Journal of Pediatric Psychology, 14,* 479–89.

Sinnett, E. R., and Holen, M. C. (1993). The perceived influence of health insurance of psychological services. *Psychotherapy in Private Practice, 12,* 41–50.

Smith, T. S., McGuire, J. M., Abbott, D. W., and Blau, B. I. (1991). Clinical ethical decision making: An investigation of the rationales used to justify doing less than one believes one should. *Professional Psychology: Research and Practice, 22,* 235–9.

Sobel, A. B., Roberts, M. C., Rapoff, M. A., and Barnard, M. U. (2001). Problems and interventions of a pediatric psychology clinic in a medical setting: A retrospective analysis. *Cognitive and Behavioral Practice, 8,* 11–17.

Sobel, A. B., Roberts, M. C., Rayfield, A., Barnard, M. U., and Rapoff, M. A. (2001). Evaluating outpatient pediatric services in a primary care setting. *Journal of Pediatric Psychology, 26,* 395–405.

Somer, E., and Saadon, M. (1999). Therapist–client sex: Clients' retrospective reports. *Professional Psychology: Research and Practice, 30,* 504–9.

Tatman, S. M., Peters, D. B., Greene, A. L., and Bongar, B. (1997). Graduate students' attitudes toward prescription privileges training. *Professional Psychology: Research and Practice, 28,* 515–17.

Tolan, P., Ryan, K., and Jaffe, C. (1988). Adolescents' mental health service use and provider, process, and recipient characteristics. *Journal of Clinical Child Psychology, 17,* 229–36.

Top universities in psychology ranked by output and impact (1995). *APS Observer, 8* (5), 24, 28.

Trierweiler, S. J., Neighbors, H. W., Munday, C., Thompson, E. E., Binion, V. J., and Gomez, J. P. (2000). Clinician attributions associated with the diagnosis of schizophrenia in African American and non-African American patients. *Journal of Consulting and Clinical Psychology, 68,* 171–5.

Tryon, G. S. (1983). Full-time private practice in the United States: Results of a national survey. *Professional Psychology: Research and Practice, 14,* 685–96.

Tyler, J. D., and Clark, J. A. (1987). Clinical psychologists reflect on the usefulness of various components of graduate training. *Professional Psychology: Research and Practice, 18,* 381–4.

Tymchuk, A. J., Drapkin, R. S., Major-Kinsley, S. M., Ackerman, A. B., Coffman, E. W., and Baum, M. S. (1982). Ethical decision making and psychologists' attitudes toward training in ethics. *Professional Psychology: Research and Practice, 13,* 412–21.

Vanek, C. A. (1990). Survey of ethics education in clinical and counseling psychology. *Dissertation Abstracts International, 52,* 5797B (University Microfilms No. 91–14, 449).

Watkins, C. E., and Watts, R. E. (1995). Psychotherapy survey research studies: Some consistent findings and integrative conclusions. *Psychotherapy in Private Practice, 13*, 49–68.

Wiederman, M. W., and Sansome, R. A. (1999). Sexuality training for professional psychologists: A national survey of training directors of doctoral programs and predoctoral internships. *Professional Psychology: Research and Practice, 30*, 312–17.

Wiggins, J. G., and Cummings, N. A. (1998). National study of the experience of psychologists with psychotropic medication and psychotherapy. *Professional Psychology: Research and Practice, 29*, 549–52.

Williams, S., Kohout, J. L., and Wicherski, M. (2000). Salary changes among independent psychologists by gender and experience. *Psychiatric Services, 51*, 1111.

Wilkins, M. A., McGuire, J. M., Abbott, D. W., and Blau, B. I. (1990). Willingness to apply understood ethical principles. *Journal of Clinical Psychology, 46*, 539–47.

Wood, B. J., Klein, S., Cross, H. J., Lammers, C. J., and Elliott, J. K. (1985). Impaired practitioners: Psychologists' opinions about prevalence, and proposal for intervention. *Professional Psychology: Research and Practice, 16*, 843–50.

Yu, L. M., Rinaldi, S. A., Templer, D. I., Colbert, K. A., Siscoe, K., and van Patten, K. (1997). Score on the Examination for Professional Practice in Psychology as a function of attributes of clinical psychology graduate programs. *Psychological Science, 8*, 347–50.

VIGNETTE

Investigating Professional Issues in Clinical Psychology

Anne K. Jacobs

Zirkle, D. S., Jensen, M. A., Collins-Marotte, J., Murphy, R. J., and Maddux, C. (2002). Therapeutic practices and ethical beliefs of professionals working with adolescents in residential treatment. *Counseling and Values*, 46, 2, 108–17.

Roberts, Kamps, and Betan (chapter 19, this volume) addressed the need for clinical researchers to determine what ethical issues are actually experienced by practitioners, to gather information on practitioners' ethical beliefs, and to study ethical violations in practice. Zirkle and colleagues addressed these issues in the present article. The authors examined dual relationships, specifically those occurring at the time of discharge, between both direct care (e.g., childcare counselors) and professional staff (e.g., supervisory professionals, psychologists, and therapists) and adolescent clients in two residential treatment programs. Self-report measures of ethical beliefs and behaviors incorporated items from national ethics surveys and frequently occurring incidental behaviors that were noted during the clinical team meetings at the residential centers. The authors included items to detect social desirability responding and piloted the surveys to make sure they were easy to understand and appropriate for the two study settings. Staff reported frequencies of behaviors and beliefs regarding the degree to which the behaviors were ethical. The beliefs survey was administered 45 days after the behavior survey. The authors detailed the manner in which self-reports were kept confidential and reported a high return rate. They noted that no serious ethical infractions were reported by staff.

The authors analyzed their data using chi square analyses of staff category and ethical beliefs and behaviors, controlling for running multiple tests on the data. They found no statistically significant differences between direct care and professional staff on reported ethical behaviors. Significant between-group differences emerged for several ethical beliefs, such as the appropriateness of calling a former client, taking a client to a social outing, or introducing a former client to one's family. Direct care and professional staff did not agree regarding the ethics of three behaviors: (a) attending a special event of a former client, (b) purchasing an item from a client, and (c) hiring a client to work at your agency. Direct care staff were more likely to label these behaviors as "sometimes" to "always" ethical. While no dual sexual relationships or gross boundary infractions were reported, a few direct care staff reported having nonsexual friendships with clients following treatment termination and 20 percent of direct care staff felt these types of friendships were ethical. In addition to adding to clinical research, these results then guided staff development and written policies regarding ethical behavior (e.g., identifying and avoiding possible dual relationships) at these residential centers. Notable strengths of the study conducted by Zirkle and colleagues include:

- Collecting data from both direct care and professional staff
- Inclusion of frequently occurring behaviors discussed during clinical team meetings
- Use of survey items from prior national studies on ethics
- Surveys piloted to ensure understandability and appropriateness of items
- Measurement of both behaviors and beliefs
- Detailed steps taken to ensure confidentiality and improve truthfulness of self-reports
- High response rate and adequate sample size for analyses used
- Results were used to inform staff development opportunities and policies

CHAPTER TWENTY

Reflections on the Future of Clinical Psychological Research

Stephen S. Ilardi and Michael C. Roberts

Although the present volume has covered in some detail an array of methodological and statistical issues central to the design, implementation, and evaluation of clinical psychological research, we would like to conclude by reflecting on a research agenda for clinical psychology in the near future. In so doing, we concede at the outset that the judgment of history has usually proven unkind to so-called *futurists*, especially those with the temerity to offer highly specific predictions of distant events. In this chapter, therefore, we will try to refrain from engaging in unbridled speculations about the discipline of clinical psychology in the far-off future (after all, who would have predicted even thirty years ago that clinical psychologists would, by the year 2002, lobby successfully for the authority to prescribe psychotropic medications in New Mexico?). Rather, our aim in this chapter is to focus attention on a number of important windows of opportunity for scientific discovery in the discipline of clinical psychology in the years immediately ahead – areas of exploration which represent the extension of existing productive research programs in order to address a host of important unresolved questions regarding the "prediction and control" of psychological phenomena.

Interventions for Psychological Disorders

Evidence-based psychotherapy

As outlined by Steele and Roberts (chapter 15) and Simons and Wildes (chapter 16) in this volume, one of the field's more important developments over the past decade has been the explicit attempt on the part of the American Psychological Association's Society of Clinical Psychology (Division 12) to delineate a list of psychotherapy protocols of demonstrated efficacy in the treatment of specific psychological disorders. This is a laudable development, with clear potential to advance both the science and practice of clinical psychology. Indeed, one might even be led at first blush to predict that such an initiative would be universally applauded by clinical psychologists. After all, what psychologist would not be interested in knowing the degree to which there exists credible scientific evidence to support the efficacy of the myriad psychological interventions that he or she might wish to employ? Of course, the question cannot be framed adequately in such a straightforward fashion, and there are compelling reasons beyond mere obscurantism that may account for the initial resistance on the part of some clinical psychologists to jumping on board the evidence-based therapy bandwagon. For although there now exists a reasonably well-articulated set of evidentiary criteria requisite for a given treatment's being regarded as *empirically supported* (see Chambless and Hollon, 1998; Chambless and Ollendick, 2000), as well as a preliminary list of psychotherapy protocols which have received the *empirically supported* imprimatur, there remain a number of unresolved questions – both conceptual and pragmatic in nature – concerning the delineation of so-called "treatments that work." We believe the clarification of such outstanding questions, a few of which are outlined below, will constitute a fruitful and enormously important avenue of clinical psychological research in the years ahead.

One may ask, for example, what does the *empirically supported treatment* (EST) designation actually indicate about the clinical utility of a given therapy protocol? According to the most widely influential set of criteria employed to date (Chambless and Hollon, 1998; Chambless and Ollendick, 2000), such a label typically suggests only that there exist two or more randomized controlled trials (RCTs) in which individuals who received the designated treatment (delivered according to the specifications of a well-articulated manual) experienced statistically superior outcomes in comparison with those in a no-treatment (or waitlist) or other control condition. Although such information is certainly of some importance, it is perhaps even more informative to consider just how much this form of EST designation actually *fails* to indicate. The following unaddressed questions come immediately to mind:

1 What is the magnitude (i.e., effect size) of the typical improvement observed in treatment?

2 Is such improvement *clinically significant* or merely *statistically significant*? For example, one might consider a hypothetical treatment for panic disorder which reliably yields a mean reduction in the frequency of panic episodes that is 2 percent greater than that observed among untreated individuals. With a large enough sample size, such treatment-related improvement – although clinically insignificant – could be found to be statistically significant (even at $p < .001$!). Such a treatment would be regarded as empirically supported under the currently adopted EST designation criteria, but should it?

3 Is the treatment merely *better than nothing* (i.e., more efficacious than a no-treatment or waitlist control), or does it also outperform a credible placebo condition (as is typically required by the medical community for claims of efficacy regarding psychotropic medications)?

4 What is the level of variability across relevant studies in the observed effect size of treatment, and how many additional RCT trials of comparable sample size (if any)

would be required in order to establish the magnitude of the treatment effect within a reasonable confidence interval?

5   What proportion of individuals who receive this treatment may be expected to achieve full recovery from the targeted clinical syndrome by the posttreatment assessment?

6   How do outcomes in this treatment compare with those observed in other (rival) treatments for the same disorder/condition, and to what extent may this treatment be regarded as the "treatment of choice"?

7   What are the specific "active ingredients" in the treatment protocol (i.e., as determined on the basis of dismantling and component analysis studies)?

8   Via what actual *mechanism(s)* do the treatment's "active ingredients" produce their salubrious effects?

9   What proportion of the variance in treatment outcomes is accounted for by nonspecific (or *common factors*) effects (e.g., therapeutic alliance) versus specific treatment effects that occur only due to the distinctive "active ingredients" inherent in a given protocol?

10   When a therapist in the "real world" diverges from the manualized psychotherapy protocol (or merely tweaks it), will the treatment still be efficacious (the answer to this question would seem to be contingent in part on satisfactory resolution of the aforementioned "active ingredients" question)? If so, how much tweaking is permitted without the risk of compromising efficacy?

11   How generalizable are the observed treatment outcomes in the RCTs to outcomes observed in the "real world"? Does the treatment, for example, have the same level of efficacy with clients who fail to conform to the narrowly specified inclusion and exclusion criteria characteristic of RCTs?

12   What level of therapist training or experience is necessary in order for the treatment protocol to be delivered with maximally efficacious results?

13   Are there certain subsets of individuals (e.g., members of various ethnic minorities, individuals with or without certain comorbid diagnoses, etc.) for whom the treatment is less (or more) efficacious?

14   To what degree are therapists to be considered "interchangeable parts" in the implementation of any given intervention? Put differently, to what degree do there exist therapists who happen to engender particularly favorable (or toxic!) outcomes when implementing a given manualized therapy protocol "by the book"?

15   If such reliable intertherapist variations are found to exist (see Garfield, 1998, for a discussion of evidence in the affirmative), to what factors (e.g., nonverbal communication style, verbal prosody, physical appearance, conveyance of empathy, etc.) are they to be attributed?

The above list of questions is certainly far from exhaustive, but we believe it nonetheless highlights some of the more important topics that may serve as the focus of psychotherapy research in the years ahead. We also observe that there are still many psychological disorders – notably, nine of the ten personality disorders enumerated under the *Diagnostic and Statistical Manual of Mental Disorders*, 4th edition (DSM-IV) (borderline PD serves as the lone exception) – for which there are at present no treatments of established efficacy. As such, the efficacious treatment of Axis II personality pathology would appear to represent a genuine "frontier territory" of psychological interventions research.

Dissemination of efficacious interventions

On a related note, a compelling challenge for the field of clinical psychology at present concerns the effective dissemination and "marketing" of its psychotherapeutic interventions of well-demonstrated efficacy. Regrettably, both the lay public and healthcare policy makers remain, for the most part, poorly informed about the benefits of clinical psychological interventions. For example, there exists a short-term psychotherapeutic intervention for obsessive-compulsive disorder (OCD) – Exposure and Ritual Prevention (EX/RP) (Foa and Goldstein, 1978) – which appears, on the basis of compelling research evidence, to yield substantially superior treatment outcomes in comparison with those observed in pharmacotherapy (e.g., Kozak, Liebowitz, and Foa, 2000). And yet the overwhelming majority of patients who seek treatment for OCD will receive an intervention other than EX/RP (most will be treated pharmacologically). Indeed, it is doubtful that any more than a small percentage of such patients will ever be informed that an efficacious nonpharmacological treatment option for OCD even *exists*; an even smaller percentage will learn of research evidence regarding EX/RP's superior acute treatment outcomes in comparison with psychotropic meds and its lower posttreatment relapse risk.

Similar examples could be given regarding numerous other highly efficacious psychotherapy interventions which have remained a "well kept secret" – unknown even among those for whom they could be of great benefit. To what can this puzzling state of affairs be attributed? Interestingly, very little systematic research has ever been undertaken with the aim of addressing such a question (although the answer will likely be found to lie at least in part with the elephantine marketing budgets of pharmaceutical companies, and, by comparison, the relative paucity of resources available for the marketing and dissemination of psychosocial interventions). Moreover, we are aware of few investigations aimed at discovering the most effective means of improving upon the status quo, especially the degree to which: (a) the lay public is made aware of efficacious psychosocial alternatives to pharmacotherapy for various psychological disorders; (b) the medical community (especially primary practice providers, who often serve as "gatekeepers" for treatment utilization) is made aware of the same; (c) clinical psychologists are well trained in the delivery of such efficacious interventions; (d) nondoctoral-level practitioners are trained and supervised by clinical psychologists in order to make such interventions available on a less costly basis; and (e) insurance companies and managed care organizations utilize empirically derived information in deciding which mental health services to reimburse. At present the best means of achieving such desirable aims remain unknown, and would thus appear to constitute an important area of investigation for clinical psychologists in the years ahead.

Clinical psychologists prescribing psychotropic medications

At the time of writing, there is legislation pending in over a dozen states to grant prescriptive authority to "appropriately trained" clinical psychologists, and such authority has already been signed into law in the state of New Mexico. It may be difficult to overstate the magnitude of potential consequences to the field of clinical psychology inherent in this set of developments, especially if, as many observers seem to expect, there ensues a "domino effect" of numerous other states quickly moving to grant prescriptive authority to psychologists in the wake of the New Mexico decision. There will doubtless be numerous consequences to the field – including many which remain unforeseen at present – as the prescription privileges movement begins to achieve a modicum of success, and this development also appears likely to bring in its wake a set of important new research questions. We suspect that much of the initial research catalyzed by the advent of prescribing psychologists will be of the pragmatic variety, e.g., can psychologists be trained to prescribe psychotropic medications with resulting patient outcomes comparable to those observed in treatment provided by psychiatrists, or by general practice physicians (who do the lion's share of psychotropic prescribing), physician's assistants, or nurse practitioners? If so, what level of training (predoctoral or postdoctoral) for prescribing psychologists is *optimal*? Will prescription patterns differ among psychologists and MD practitioners? Which specific subsets of patients (e.g., those with severe comorbid medical complications) would be inappropriate for treatment by prescribing psychologists in light of their limited formal medical training? And so forth.

There exist other potential research questions in this domain of a more subtle nature, but which may prove equally significant to the field. For example, what impact (if any) will the advent of prescription privileges for psychologists have upon the extensiveness of training in psychosocial interventions which doctoral programs provide for their students? To what extent will graduate students entering classes of clinical psychology begin to differ in composition from their contemporary counterparts? Will it be the most competitive or least competitive students who flock to those programs which provide explicit training in psychopharmacology practice? What proportion of licensed prescribing psychologists will continue to provide psychosocial interventions (or combination treatment)? How effectively will they do so? Will prescribing psychologists, by virtue of their graduate training, be more likely than MD prescribers to educate patients regarding efficacious nonpharmacological treatment alternatives? Will they be more likely than MDs to refer appropriate patients for psychotherapeutic treatment? Will they be more or less likely to collaborate with their nonprescribing clinical psychologist colleagues in the implementation of psychotherapy-versus-medication outcome trials? Will they be more or less likely to have their practice decisions influenced by the "marketing" strategies (e.g., free meals, vacations, speaking fees, etc.) routinely employed by pharmaceutical companies? Clearly, there are numerous questions germane to the prescribing psychologist phenomenon which may prove worthy of investigation in the years ahead.

Empirically Supported Assessment

As recently observed by Larry Beutler (2000), "most of the theories and approaches that are used within the community of practitioners are unsupported by empirical evidence." This unfortunate fact is perhaps nowhere more evident than in the practice of psychological assessment. In fact, although most clinical psychologists would doubtless concur with the notion that only assessment measures of demonstrated psychometric adequacy (e.g., reliability and validity) should be utilized in clinical practice and research, it is the case that some of the most widely used methods of psychological assessment – for example, many of the key indices on the Rorschach inkblot test – are of questionable reliability and validity (e.g., Wood et al., 2000; Wood et al., 2001). In part, this situation may be attributed to the fact that there exists at present no widely agreed-upon set of evidentiary criteria against which the psychometric adequacy of any given assessment instrument may be evaluated. That is to say, the field at present has no consensus answer for the question: What is the minimum threshold of reliability (interrater, temporal, internal, etc.) and validity (criterion, convergent, discriminant, etc.) which is to be deemed acceptable for an instrument in widespread usage in clinical, research, and forensic settings? Similarly, how many independent corroborative investigations should be required in order to establish firmly the psychometric adequacy of any given assessment instrument? We believe that such questions – and the ensuing delineation of "empirically supported assessment instruments" derived from the answers thereto – may form the basis for a program of research of crucial importance to the science and practice of clinical psychology in the years ahead. Of course, were such a delineation to occur (and we believe it will in due course), one might predict considerable displeasure – perhaps even howls of protest – among the aficionados of each assessment instrument which fails to demonstrate psychometric adequacy sufficient for inclusion on "The List" of empirically supported measures.

Integration of Neuroscience: Theory and Methodology

There is perhaps no domain of scholarly inquiry which is currently experiencing a more dramatic pace of scientific discovery than that which now characterizes the neurosciences (Wilson, 1998). Because those engaged in neuroscience research "proceed on a daily basis to make the implicit explicit, and the internal observable," David Barlow (1997) has suggested that "biological factors must be integrated into any comprehensive model of human behavior and behavior change" (p. 447). Indeed, although still in its nascent stages, such a process of integration has already begun to occur within clinical psychology (cf. Ilardi, 2002), and we believe this process carries with it research opportunities of great potential significance to the field in coming years. A few of the more important developments on this front are outlined below.

Functional neuroimaging

Techniques of functional neuroimaging – functional magnetic resonance imaging (fMRI), positron emission tomography (PET), quantitative electroencephalography (QEEG), etc. – make possible the assessment of neurophysiological events in real time. Because there is compelling evidence to support the claim that such brain events proximally mediate the occurrence of psychological events (Ilardi and Feldman, 2001), the assessment of real-time brain events carries with it the potential to shed considerable light on neurophysiological processes associated with the occurrence of psychological disorders and the amelioration thereof. For example, clinical researchers at UCLA have recently utilized PET imaging with adult obsessive-compulsive disorder (OCD) patients to demonstrate both (a) that exposure-based behavior therapy for OCD produces salubrious changes in abnormal cortical and subcortical brain functioning comparable to those observed in SSRI pharmacotherapy (Schwartz, 1998); and (b) that PET scan data may be utilized pretreatment to identify the subset of OCD patients likely to evidence preferential treatment response to behavior therapy versus meds, and vice versa (Brody et al., 1998). It is perhaps difficult to overstate the potential clinical and conceptual importance of such findings, and we believe that we are witnessing in this form of integrative clinical neuroscience research merely the tip of the proverbial iceberg. "Because neuroimaging techniques will continue to become increasingly accurate (fine-grained), affordable, and widely available in the years ahead, we face the prospect in the not-too-distant future of clinical psychologists selecting and refining optimal psychosocial interventions, and even evaluating their moment-to-moment efficacy, on the basis of salient neurocomputational assessment data" (Ilardi, 2002). Indeed, we believe that the nascent integration of mainstream clinical psychology with functional neuroimaging methodology, itself informed by the neuroscience conceptual framework, carries with it the potential to catalyze an enormously fruitful period of scientific discovery regarding the neurophysiological underpinnings of pathological psychological processes and the optimal psychosocial means of addressing them. As described in the following section, it may also hold promise for advancing the field's nosology.

Categorization/classification of disorders

Although thoughtful critiques of the *Diagnostic and Statistical Manual for Mental Disorders* (DSM) abound (e.g., Carson, 1996), the DSM system is nevertheless the *de facto* diagnostic standard for the field of clinical psychology, as well as the functional *lingua franca* for communicating information about clinically relevant symptomatology across an array of mental health disciplines (e.g., psychiatry, social work, nursing, etc.). However, we note that each recent iteration of the DSM revision process (DSM-III in 1980, DSM-III-R in 1987, and DSM-IV in 1994) has been characterized by the refinement of diagnostic categories and subtypes, including the actual diagnostic algorithms for the delineation thereof, on the basis of relevant empirical research – much of which has been conducted by clinical psychologists.

An important opportunity for clinical psychological research is thus to be found in the inevitable revisions of the DSM system in the decades ahead. Such revisions will be required at least in part because the majority of DSM-IV-defined categories of disorder are characterized by the following limitations: (a) considerable within-category heterogeneity of symptomatology; (b) an absence of sensitive and specific objective (e.g., neurophysiological) markers of category membership; (c) seemingly arbitrary symptomatic severity thresholds requisite for categorization – e.g., "five or more of the following nine symptoms" (why not *six*?), "duration of at least two weeks" (why not *one*?), etc.; and (d) an absence of compelling empirical evidence to support the DSM system's assumption of *categorical* rather than *dimensional* diagnostic constructs. It is possible, of course, that great progress could occur on the aforementioned fronts simply on the basis of the assiduous collection of large N-samples of reliable and valid clinical symptomatic data and the subsequent application of sophisticated data analytic procedures well-suited to the detection and delineation of taxonic (i.e., categorical) constructs, e.g., Paul Meehl's (1995) innovative MAXCOV and MAMBAC procedures. However, even such an admirably empirical, "data driven" approach will be limited by the extent to which the underlying theory which drives the selection and measurement of symptoms to be included in each analysis is itself valid. In other words, there truly is no such thing as merely "letting the data speak," inasmuch as the act of measurement is always informed by theoretical considerations about what is worth measuring (i.e., what is to be regarded as "signal" and what is to be ignored as mere "noise").

The domain of neuroscience (or more precisely, *cognitive* neuroscience; cf. Cosmides and Tooby, 1999) supplies a precise and testable theory of psychopathology which may prove useful to clinical psychologists in the task of generating a more useful and valid system by which to classify psychological disorders. Specifically, from the vantage point of cognitive neuroscience, a psychological disorder may be regarded as the reflection of aberrant functioning on the part of one or more neurophysiological mechanisms which mediate adaptive psychological processes, i.e., disorder equals *harmful dysfunction* (Wakefield, 1999). For example, it appears that the left and right frontal cortical hemispheres function in tandem to regulate the valence (positive versus negative) of subjectively experienced emotion, with a relative decrease in left frontal activity resulting in dysphoria and reduced right frontal activity yielding positive affect (Heller and Nitscke, 1997). Chronically and severely depressed affect, such as might be observed in major depression, could thus be regarded within this framework as (at least in part) a reflection of dysfunction in frontal cortical affect regulation circuits (Davidson et al., 2002).

It has also been discovered that anxiously depressed individuals differ substantially from those with no co-occurring anxiety (i.e., so-called "pure" depressives) in their characteristic patterns of cortical dysfunction (Heller and Nitscke, 1998). Thus, these two subpopulations of depressed patients might warrant vigorous investigation as candidate taxonic (categorical) subtypes (no such anxious-depression subtypes are recognized within the current DSM-IV nosology). Such a neurophysiologically informed approach to classification could conceivably serve to catalyze discovery regarding other salient subtype differences in symptomatology, etiology, clinical course, optimal treatment, and so forth. By extension, we would suggest that ongoing neuroimaging advances in the precise cerebral localization of specific psychologically relevant functions (e.g., mood regulation, impulse inhibition, attentional regulation, initiation of approach behavior, perceptual organization, logical sequencing, anxious arousal, etc.) may provide both a conceptual and empirical foundation for substantially enhancing the validity of future classification systems of psychological disorder.

Enhanced psychological assessment

Clinically relevant psychological assessment is heavily dependent upon the use of self-report measures. Indeed, the investigation of individuals' thoughts and feelings might seem to entail few viable alternatives to asking each individual to provide some form of self-report. Yet such an approach, of course, is notoriously prone to many sources of measurement error, including an array of response biases attributable to overt presentation management (i.e., responding to an instrument's items based upon perceived social demand characteristics), erroneous recall, or even an absence of requisite metacognitive awareness (e.g., as would be necessary to answer a query such as, "How many times has your attention wandered in the past five minutes?"). We suggest, however, that the domain of neuroscience appears to provide a set of alternative approaches to the measurement of some important cognitive and affective processes – measurement approaches which are not as vulnerable as self-report questionnaires to the aforementioned sources of measurement error.

Electroencephalographic (EEG) event related potential (ERP) components (e.g., P300, N400, etc.) appear especially well suited for use in the measurement of cognitive phenomena, inasmuch as such ERP waveforms serve to signal the occurrence of very specific information processing events (i.e., cognitive events) in the brain that can be measured with great temporal accuracy (on the order of milliseconds). For example, the N400 component occurs when an individual reads a word in a sentence that is perceived as *semantically incongruent* (i.e., the word doesn't "fit" in its context); as such, this brainwave component may be used as an *objective* gauge of an individual's subjectively experienced semantic processing during a reading task. Ilardi and Atchley (2001) have recently capitalized on this fortuitous feature of the N400 component by pioneering its use to measure the occurrence of depressive self-deprecatory thoughts, and to do so in a fashion which does not rely on self-report. Depressotypic, self-deprecatory sentences (e.g., "I am a loser") were read by depressed and never-depressed participants, and were observed to elicit large-magnitude mean N400 responses only among individuals in the never-depressed group (i.e., only among never-depressed individuals was the word "loser" typically perceived as incongruent with self-concept). Because the N400 and other ERP components occur so quickly (fractions of a second) after the onset of each stimulus word, they cannot be consciously manipulated by participants, and so appear to be largely immune from many of the reporting biases (e.g., conformity with perceived social demand characteristics) which plague self-report cognitive measures.

The past several years have witnessed an enormous increase in the reported uses of this sort of objective, electrophysiologically informed approach to the real-time assessment of clinically relevant cognitive events, in part due to the clear advantages articulated in the preceding paragraphs. Indeed, to the extent that thoughts and feelings are reflected in a set of corresponding brain events, inevitable future improvements in the accuracy of measurement of such brain events (i.e., through advances in neuroimaging technology) will make possible the increasingly fine-grained objective (albeit indirect) measurement of such cognitive and affective events via the measurement of corresponding brain events. Such measurement, we believe, will serve to help establish the external validity of self-report cognitive and affective measures, and may hold promise in helping clinical investigators determine the differential degree to which various cognitive and affective constructs are fully amenable to accurate self-report. This envisioned process (i.e., that of enhancing the accuracy, objectivity, and overall construct validity of psychological assessment on the basis of conceptual and methodological integration with the domain of cognitive neuroscience) is one which entails significant opportunities for future research discovery on the part of clinical psychologists, especially for those who are willing and able to (a) obtain advanced training in cognitive neuroscience during graduate school or thereafter; and (b) collaborate across formal disciplinary boundaries with cognitive neuroscientists, a growing subset of whom are interested in bringing their expertise to bear upon research questions within the traditional purview of clinical psychology.

The Application of Novel Data Analytic Techniques

The foundational data analytic techniques which have received prominent coverage in this text (e.g., regression analysis, structural equation modeling (SEM), univariate and multivariate analysis of variance (ANOVA), *t*-tests for the comparison of group means, and so forth) will doubtless continue in widespread use among psychological researchers for the foreseeable future. Nevertheless, the set of sophisticated data analytic tools available to the clinical researcher continues to expand at a rapid pace, and the field is likely to witness the increased utilization of many relatively novel techniques for the analysis of clinical psychological data in the years ahead.

Although the full enumeration and explication of such emerging techniques is far beyond the scope of this chapter, we believe the following may serve as at least a partial listing of some more or less esoteric techniques that appear likely to come into increasingly widespread use in clinical psychological research in the near future:

1   *Latent growth curve models* (reviewed in McArdle and Bell, 2000), which are particularly well suited to the analysis of longitudinal clinical data, inasmuch as they estimate an individual trajectory of change over time (on one or more key variables) for each study participant and then utilize each individual's estimated temporal change function (i.e., growth curve) as the variable of interest in between-group comparisons.

2   *Hierarchical linear models* (reviewed in Raudenbush, 2000), which, in a fashion similar to latent growth curve models, are capable of illuminating population changes in variables over time on the basis of analyses of individual differences in temporal change trajectories.

3   *Item response models*, which confer important advantages over widely utilized multivariate techniques (e.g., exploratory factor analysis) in the development and refinement of psychometrically sound assessment measures, and which are now increasingly used by clinical researchers to evaluate the psychometric adequacy of existing instruments (e.g., the Beck Depression Inventory; Bedi, Maraun, and Chrisjohn, 2001).

4   *Latent class models*, a set of procedures well suited to the detection (or disconfirmation) of hypothesized categorical constructs – such as diagnostic categories – which are frequently held to underlie the occurrence of covariation patterns in a set of measured variables (e.g., symptom severity ratings).

5   *Simulations of neural network computation* (e.g., parallel distributed processing models), which are used to test hypotheses about a subset of the information processing operations of the brain's own neural arrays, and appear to have the potential to shed light on the phenomenology and etiology of psychological disorders ranging from depression (Matthews, Derryberry, and Siegle, 2000), to posttraumatic stress disorder (Tryon, 1999), to schizophrenia (Pelaez, 2000).

Although this is far from an exhaustive list of important "cutting-edge" quantitative tools, we believe that each of the aforementioned statistical techniques is useful by virtue of helping the clinical psychological researcher more effectively test hypotheses regarding the phenomenology, assessment, or treatment of psychological disorders.

Conclusions

Heraclitus famously suggested that the universe is in a state of continual flux, and that the only true constant is *change*. Although the legendary inspiration for this thesis was the philosopher's observation of running water – "you can't step in the same river twice" – Heraclitus might draw similar inspiration from the field of clinical psychology were he alive today. Change in the field's science and practice, a constant throughout the first century of clinical psychology's existence, is inevitable in the years that lie ahead. Indeed, the scientific process moves inexorably forward, and many of the most firmly held beliefs and cherished practices of the present day will doubtless be modified, enhanced, or even debunked, to be replaced by more useful theories, concepts, practices, and research methodologies. Rather than view this eventuality with a sense of apprehension or foreboding (change is rarely comfortable, after all), we are inclined to see it as an immense opportunity for scientific discovery on multiple fronts, as outlined in the present chapter. Some of the more important areas of research opportunity for the field include: (a) the formulation and dissemination of novel psychotherapeutic interventions of increasing efficacy, effectiveness, and efficiency; (b) the identification of specific (and/or nonspecific) *active ingredients* in each efficacious therapy intervention, and the most efficient means of delivery thereof; (c) clarification of the relative advantages and disadvantages (rate of recovery, dropout, relapse, aversive side effects, short-term and long-term cost, etc.) associated with pharmacological versus psychosocial interventions for each psychological disorder; (d) integration of neuroscience theory and method (e.g., neuroimaging) to elucidate etiological and ameliorative *mechanisms* that characterize psychological disorders; (e) the development of psychological assessment instruments of greater demonstrated validity and reliability; and (f) the further delineation and refinement of disorder constructs (and diagnostic algorithms) on the basis of sophisticated statistical analyses. It is our hope that the contemplation of such developments will provide some measure of inspiration to aspiring clinical psychological researchers, especially regarding the possibility of contributing to discoveries of immense importance in the advancement of the field's science and practice.

References

Barlow, D. (1997). It's yet another empirical question [Commentary]. *Behavior Therapy, 28,* 445–8.

Bedi, R. P., Maraun, M. D., and Chrisjohn, R. D. (2001). A multisample item response theory analysis of the Beck Depression Inventory-1A. *Canadian Journal of Behavioral Science, 33,* 176–85.

Beutler, L. (2000). Empirically based decision making in clinical practice. *Prevention and Treatment, 3,* Article 27. Available on the World Wide Web: http://journals.apa.org/prevention/volume3/pre0030027a.html.

Brody, A. L., Saxena, S., Schwartz, J. M., Stoessel, P. W., Maidment, K., Phelps, M. E., and Baxter, L. R. (1998). FDB-PET predictors of response to behavioral therapy and pharmacotherapy in obsessive-compulsive disorders. *Psychiatry Research, 84,* 1–6.

Carson, R. C. (1996). Aristotle, Galileo, and the DSM taxonomy: The case of schizophrenia. *Journal of Consulting and Clinical Psychology, 64,* 1133–9.

Chambless, D. L., and Hollon, S. D. (1998). Defining empirically supported therapies. *Journal of Consulting and Clinical Psychology, 66,* 7–18.

Chambless, D. L., and Ollendick, T. H. (2000). Empirically supported psychological interventions: Controversies and evidence. *Annual Review of Psychology, 52,* 685–716.

Cosmides, L., and Tooby, J. (1999). Toward an evolutionary taxonomy of treatable conditions. *Journal of Abnormal Psychology, 108,* 453–64.

Davidson, R. J., Pizzagalli, D., Nitscke, J. B., and Putnam, K. (2002). Depression: Perspectives from affective neuroscience. *Annual Review of Psychology, 53,* 545–74.

Foa, E. B., and Goldstein, A. (1978). Continuous exposure and complete response prevention of obsessive-compulsive neurosis. *Behavior Therapy, 9,* 821–9.

Garfield, S. L. (1998). Some comments on empirically supported treatments. *Journal of Consulting and Clinical Psychology, 66,* 121–5.

Heller, W., and Nitscke, J. B. (1997). Regional brain activity in emotion: A framework for understanding cognition in depression. *Cognition and Emotion, 11,* 637–61.

Heller, W., and Nitscke, J. B. (1998). The puzzle of regional brain activity in depression and anxiety: The importance of subtypes and comorbidity. *Cognition and Emotion, 12,* 421–47.

Ilardi, S. S. (2002). The cognitive neuroscience perspective: A brief primer for clinical psychologists. *Behavior Therapist, 25,* 49–52.

Ilardi, S. S., and Atchley, R. A. (2001). *Language processing biases in depression: A cognitive neuroscience perspective.* Presented in November at the annual meetings of the Association for Advancement of Behavior Therapy, Philadelphia, Pennsylvania

Ilardi, S. S., and Feldman, D. (2001). The cognitive neuroscience paradigm: A unifying metatheoretical framework for the science and practice of clinical psychology. *Journal of Clinical Psychology, 57,* 1067–88.

Kozak, M. J., Liebowitz, M. R., and Foa, E. B. (2000). Cognitive behavior therapy and pharmacotherapy for obsessive-compulsive disorder: The NIMH-sponsored collaborative study. In W. K. Goodman, M. V. Rudorfer, and J. D. Maser (eds.), *Obsessive-compulsive disorder: Contemporary issues in treatment. Personality and clinical psychology series* (pp. 501–30). New York: Lawrence Erlbaum Associates.

McArdle, J. J., and Bell, R. Q. (2000). An introduction to latent growth models for developmental data analysis. In T. D. Little, K. U. Schnabel, and J. Baumert (eds.), *Modeling longitudinal and multilevel data: Practical issues, applied approaches, and specific examples* (pp. 69–107). St. Paul, MN: Assessment Systems Corporation.

Matthews, G., Derryberry, D., and Siegle, G. J. (2000). Personality and emotion: Cognitive science perspectives. In S. E. Hampson (ed.), *Advances in personality psychology, Vol. 1* (pp. 199–237). New York: Psychology Press.

Meehl, P. E. (1995). Bootstraps taxometrics: Solving the classification problem in psychopathology. *American Psychologist, 50*, 266–75.

Pelaez, J. R. (2000). Towards a neural network based therapy for hallucinatory disorders. *Neural Networks, 13*, 1047–61.

Raudenbush, S. W. (2000). Comparing personal trajectories and drawing causal inferences from longitudinal data. *Annual Review of Psychology, 52*, 501–25.

Schwartz, J. M. (1998). Neuroanatomical aspects of cognitive-behavioral therapy response in obsessive-compulsive disorder: An evolving perspective of brain and behavior. *British Journal of Psychiatry, 173* (Supplement 35), 38–44.

Tryon, W. W. (1999). A bidirectional associative memory explanation of posttraumatic stress disorder. *Clinical Psychology Review, 19*, 789–818.

Wakefield, J. C. (1999). Evolutionary versus prototype analyses of the concept of disorder. *Journal of Abnormal Psychology, 108*, 374–99.

Wilson, E. O. (1998). *Consilience: The unity of knowledge.* New York: Knopf.

Wood, J. M., Lilienfeld, S. O., Garb, H. N., and Nezworski, M. T. (2000). The Rorschach test in clinical diagnosis: A critical review, with a backward look at Garfield (1947). *Journal of Clinical Psychology, 56*, 395–430.

Wood, J. M., Nezworski, M. T., Garb, H. N., and Lilienfeld, S. O. (2001). Problems with the norms of the Comprehensive System for the Rorschach: Methodological and conceptual considerations. *Clinical Psychology: Science and Practice, 8*, 397–402.

Index

AB design, 78
ABA design, 95
ABAB design, 79–80
abstracting services, 43
acceptability, therapy, 344, 401
accreditation criteria, APA, 397
acculturation, 383–4
Achenbach, T. M., 273–4
Adams, S. G., 403
ADD *see* Attention Deficit Disorder
added in order tests, 105
addiction
    studies of, 253
    treating, 335, 343, 344
Addis, M. E., 408
additive designs, 339–40
ADF methods *see* asymptotic-distribution-free
    methods
ADHD *see* Attention Deficit Hyperactivity
    Disorder
adherence *see* fidelity
adolescents *see* children and adolescents;
    diagnostic assessment, children and
    adolescents; therapy, children and
    adolescents
adoption studies, 219
Advancement of Behavior Therapy,
    Association for the, 34
Advancement of Professional Practice,
    Committee for the, 401

affective picture presentation, 244–5, 249
African-Americans
    attitudes to psychotherapy, 385
    including in samples, 384–5
    research guidelines, 388–9
    studies of, 346, 377, 380, 394–5, 401
Agras, W. S., 340
Aiken, L. S., 127, 128
alcohol
    effect on emotion, 247–51
    studies of effects, 253, 260–1
    treatment for addiction, 343
allegiance effects, 340–1
Allen, J. J. B., 247
alpha, coefficient, 119, 138, 149–53
alternating treatments design, 80–3
Alvidres, J., 378, 382
American Psychological Association (APA)
    accreditation criteria, 397
    ethics code, 52, 58, 60, 61, 64, 387
    and ethnic minority research, 387–8
    and meta-analyses, 201
    publishing guidelines, 33, 37–8, 44
    surveys of members, 401, 410–11
    web journals, 42
American Psychological Association: subbodies
    Committee on Accreditation, 309
    Society for the Psychological Study of
        Ethnic Minority Issues (Division 45),
        388–9

American Psychological Association: subbodies
(*cont'd*)
Society of Child and Adolescent
Psychology (Division 53), 309
Society of Clinical Psychology (Division 12),
34, 308–9, 408, 420–1
Society of Clinical Psychology (Division 12)
Task Force, 26–7
Society of Pediatric Psychology (Division 54),
309
American Psychologist, 34
analysis of covariance (ANCOVA), 106–8,
125–6, 352
ANCOVA with heterogeneous slopes, 107
analysis of variance (ANOVA), 25–6,
99–112, 134, 154, 328, 352
ANCOVA, 106–8, 125–6, 352
MANOVA, 108–10, 138, 154–5, 158,
328
one-way, 100–1, 102–4, 125
repeated measures, 110–12, 319
two-way, 104–6
ANCOVA *see* analysis of covariance
Anderson, Cynthia M., summary of chapter,
8
Aneshensel, C. S., 380
ANOVA *see* analysis of variance
antisocial behavior, studies of, 394–5
anxiety
child sufferers, 166–7, 315, 320, 327–8
design for hypothetical case, 74–6
diagnosing, 287, 290, 291, 292, 293–4,
296
state anxiety, 292
studies of, 236–40, 247, 320, 327–8
trait anxiety, 292
Anxiety Sensitivity Index, 386–7
APA *see* American Psychological Association
appetitive motivation, 253
Applegate, B., 269–70
applied clinical scientists, role, 4
appraisal disruption model, 249
approval, institutional, 55–6
ASAP (*Analysis of Social Issues and Public
Policy*), 42
Asarnow, J. R., 311
Asian American Psychological Association,
389
assessment *see* diagnostic assessment

Association for the Advancement of Behavior
Therapy, 34
Association of Black Psychologists, 389
assumptions
detecting and correcting violations, 131–4,
151–2
distributional, 160
asymptotic-distribution-free (ADF) methods,
161
Atchley, R. A., 428
Atkeson, B. M., 260–1
attention allocation model, 249
Attention Deficit Disorder (ADD), 232–3,
260–1
Attention Deficit Hyperactivity Disorder
(ADHD)
and covert conduct, 223
diagnosing, 264, 266, 272
measuring, 216
MTA, 316
research into, 217
treating, 316
attenuation, correcting for, 24–5
attrition, effect on test results, 17, 18, 317,
344
Australian Psychological Society
ethics code, 66
authorship, crediting, 60, 405, 407
Azocar, F., 378, 382

Baldick, T., 407
Banspach, S., 374–5
Barker, R. G., 180
Barkley, R. A., 266, 269–70, 316, 318, 319
Barlow, David, 425
Barnard, M. U., 400, 402
Barnett, J., 296, 297
Baron, R. M., 128, 344
Basen-Enquist, K., 374–5
Bass, D., 340
Bass, L. J., 66
Baumler, E., 374–5
BDI *see* Beck Depression Inventories
Beck, S. J., 403
Beck Depression Inventories (BDI), 292–3
administering, 16
reliability, 290, 291
research into, 403
response scales, 159, 305

Becker, G., 153
bedwetting, studies of, 318
behavior genetic designs, 219
behavior management therapy (BMT), 318
behavior therapies, 334
    behavior management therapy (BMT), 318
    behavioral marital therapy, 333
    Dialectical Behavior Therapy (DBT),
        337–8
    see also cognitive behavioral therapy
Behavior Therapy, 34, 404
behavioral marital therapy, 333
Behavioral Technology Today, 42
Belmont Report, 52
benchmarking, 342
Bentler, P. M., 144, 161
    SB test, 161
Bergman, L. R., 224
Bernal, G., 313
Bernard, J. R., 405
Berthot, B. D., 250
beta weights, 124
Betan, Ephi J., 403, 405–6
    summary of chapter, 10
Betancourt, H., 380, 381
Beutler, Larry, 330, 424
Biglan, A., 363, 364
Binet, A., 354
biology, and behavior *see* genetic influences,
        and behavior
bipolar disorder, diagnosing, 295–6
Bird, H. R., 277, 394–5
Black Psychologists, Association of, 389
Blackhart, Ginette C., 246
    summary of chapter, 9
blind review, 44–5
blinking, and emotion, 244, 245, 249
BMT *see* behavior management therapy
Bogdan, R., 192
Bolger, N., 129, 133
Bollard, J., 318
Bollen, K. A., 18
Bonferroni procedure, 103–4, 105, 109, 111
book reviews, publishing, 35
bootstrapping, 161
borderline personality disorder
    diagnosing, 295–6
    and ESTs, 422
Borkovec, T. D., 243

Bose, R. C., 109, 111
Bougar, B., 406
Boulder Conference (1949), 4
Bowers, T. G., 401
Box adjustment, 110–11
Bradley, B. P., 239–40
Bradley, M. M., 245
brain
    alcohol's effects, 247–51
    brain activity and mood, 243, 245–9, 251,
        252–4
    brain activity, and diagnosis, 428–9
    brain areas and their associations, 244,
        245–7, 251, 253–4, 427
    event-related brain potentials (ERPs), 251,
        428
    neuroimaging, 252–4, 425–6
    research opportunities, 425–9
Braver, L. S., 19
Braver, M. C. W., 19
Breckler, S. J., 160
Brent, D. A., 312, 317
Brestan, E. V., 313
brewery workers, studies of, 184
British Psychological Society, ethics code, 66
Bronfenbrenner, U., 180, 359
Brown, J. S., 244
Brown, Keri J., 321, 410
    summary of chapter, 8
Browne, M. W., 143–4
Bryant, M. J., 335
Buckloh, L. M., 406
bulimia, treating, 333, 340
Burgess, I. S., 237

California Psychological Inventory, 159
Campbell, D. T., 15, 27
Canadian Psychological Association, ethics
        code, 65–6
cancer patients, studies of, 179
Canino, G. J., 394–5
Canter, M. B., 58, 66
Cantor, D. W., 397
CAPP *see* Committee for the Advancement of
        Professional Practice
Caracelli, V. J., 186
Carmona, J. V., 379
Carrion, V. G., 282–3
Carter, W. R., 243

Casas, J. M., 379–80
case analyses, 400
case studies, publishing, 34
categorical predictors, 124–6
categorical variable methodology (CVM), 162
Cauchy distributions, 132
causal ambiguity, effect on test results, 17–18
causal conclusions
  and equivalent models, 166–7
  and experimental research, 166
CBT *see* cognitive behavioral therapy
CD *see* Conduct Disorder
CDI *see* Children's Depression Inventory
Center for Health and Wellness for Persons
    with Long Term Disabilities, 177, 181
cerebral activity *see* brain, brain activity
cerebral palsy, studies of, 178–9
CFA *see* confirmatory factor analysis
CFI *see* comparative fit indices
CFT *see* Chimeric Faces Task
Chambless, D. L., 309, 317, 318, 319
changing criterion design, 86–8
Charlop, M. H., 400
Chen, H. T., 27
Cherry, D. K., 398
chi square statistics
  in ADF, 161
  definition, 142
  and distributional assumption violation,
    160
  examples, 142–4, 146, 148
  SB test, 161
Child Behavior Checklist, 296, 328
Child Symptom Inventory-IV (CSI-IV),
    263–4
children and adolescents
  antisocial behavior, 394–5
  anxiety in, 166–7, 315, 320, 327–8
  assignment to test groups, 94
  brain activity, 246
  conduct disorder, 269–70, 362
  coping with death, 227
  covert conduct, studying, 223
  delinquency, 232–3
  depression in, 215, 311, 312, 346–7, 403
  education, 354, 356
  ethical issues, 220–1, 223, 319, 418–19
  food selectivity, 86–8
  HIV, 319

hyperactivity, 216, 217, 223, 264, 266, 272
injury control, 360, 362
interaction of depressives with, 274
journals about, 403, 404
mentally retarded, 296
natural disaster, reaction to, 216
nocturnal enuresis, 318
noncompliance, 320
obesity, 102–3
OCD, 313
parental interaction with, 184, 315, 316,
    318, 319
pediatric psychologists, training, 399
pediatric psychology, trend forecasting, 410
phobias, 320
psychology programs, 4
psychology services, research into, 185,
    400, 402
PTSD, 282–3
pubertal status, measuring, 282–3
research, 403
as research subjects, 62–4, 67, 220, 222,
    232, 310–11
risks to mental health, 356, 357, 362
self-esteem programs, 364
as self-reporters, 274, 276, 291, 319–20
substance use, 232–3
twin and adoption studies, 229
see also developmental psychopathology;
    diagnostic assessment, children and
    adolescents; therapy, children and
    adolescents
Children's Depression Inventory (CDI), 269,
    291, 328, 403
Chimeric Faces Task (CFT), 247
chiropractic regimens, studies of, 179
Chomsky, Noam, 364
Chorpita, B. F., 312, 317
Christopherson, E. R., 362
Cicchetti, D., 359
CIs *see* confidence intervals
citation impact/index, 38, 404
Clark, L. A., 290
Clark, V. A., 380
Clement, P. C., 400
client satisfaction, 401–2
clinical assessment *see* diagnostic assessment
Clinical Child and Adolescent Psychology,
    Society of, 309

clinical practice research, 310, 399–402
Clinical Psychology, Society of, 34, 308–9,
    408, 420–1
  Task Force, 26–7
Clinical Psychology: Research and Practice,
    404
Clinical Psychology: Science and Practice, 34
clinical scientists, role, 4
clinical services
  program evaluation, 6
  research into, 310
cluster analyses, 224
coefficient alpha, 119, 138, 149–53
Cognitive and Behavioral Practice, 34
cognitive behavioral therapy (CBT), 337,
    340, 341, 352–3, 408
  imaginary study using, 14–22
cognitive paradigms, and experimental
    psychopathology, 236–40
cognitive therapy, 333, 338, 340
  mindfulness-based cognitive therapy
    (MBCT), 179, 338
  studies of, 179
Cognitive Therapy Scale (CTS), 335, 336
Cohen, J., 23, 277
Cohen, L. H., 404
Cohen, P., 277
Cole, J. W. L., 111
Collins-Marotte, J., 418–19
Colombo, J., 56
comments, publishing, 34
Committee for the Advancement of
    Professional Practice (CAPP), 401
common factor analysis, 118
common factors view, 336
communities, and prevention, 362–3
comorbid problems, effect on research
    outcomes, 312
comparative fit indices (CFI)
  definition, 144
  examples, 144, 146, 147, 148
comparison conditions, 317–19, 336–41
compensation, for research participation, 58,
    63
competence, therapist, 335–6
computer programs *see* software
conditional probability estimates, 270–2
Conduct Disorder (CD), 260–1, 264,
    269–70, 362, 394–5

conference presentations
  publishing, 35
  reports, 4
confidence intervals (CIs), 203
confidentiality, 61–2, 410
confirmatory factor analysis (CFA), and SEM,
    139, 140, 141–4, 145, 151
Conrad, P., 320
consent, research subjects, 56–8, 63, 67
Consumer Report study, 346
consumer satisfaction, 401–2
Contemporary Psychology, 35
content analysis, 185
control groups, use of, 15–16, 22–3, 318,
    327, 337
  effect of reactions on experiments, 19
  ethical issues, 65
  non-randomized pretest–posttest control
    group design, 18
  pretest–posttest control group design,
    18–19
  Solomon four-group design, 19
  see also comparison conditions
convention presentations *see* conference
    presentations
Cook's D statistic, 131
Cooper, C. C., 67
Cooper, J. O., 77, 83
coping
  CFA model of, 141–4
  children coping with death, study of,
    227
  FLV model of, 145–7
  imaginary study of, 141–9
  path analytic model of, 147–9
copyright, of published articles, 44
  see also plagiarism
Cornell, Amy H., summary of chapter, 9
correlation matrices, 25, 118
correlational data, 115–37
correlational designs, 115–16
correlational group comparison, 17–18
Costa, M. M., 405
costs
  insurance reimbursement, 401
  surveys into, 402
Council of National Psychological
    Associations for the Advancement of
    Ethnic Minority Interests, 388–9

Council of University Directors of Clinical
    Psychology (CUDCP), 397
covariance, analysis of *see* analysis of
    covariance
covert conduct, studying, 223
Cowen, E. L., 368
Coyle, K., 374–5
Crew, D. P., 399
criminal psychopaths, studies of, 245
Crits-Christoph, P., 398
Cronbach, L. J., 27, 119
Cross, T., 307–8
cross-sectional designs, 216–17
CSI-IV *see* Child Symptom Inventory-IV
CTS *see* Cognitive Therapy Scale
CUDCP *see* Council of University Directors
    of Clinical Psychology
cultural diversity issues, 10, 222, 313, 376–93
    acculturation and enculturation, 383–4
    cultural differences, 380–1
    cultural differences and attitudes to
        psychotherapy, 387
    cultural influence, assessing, 382–3
    culture and ethnicity, 379, 381–3
    culture and SES, 380
    DSM's attitude, 388
    ethnography, 178, 179–80
    misuse of terms, 378
    NIH and APA policy guidelines, 387–90
    research vignette, 394–5
    see also ethnic minorities, research among
Cupit, B. E., 406
Curran, P. J., 160, 161
Curtin, J. J., 250, 251
custody evaluation procedures, and therapists,
    401
cutoffs, diagnostic, 269–72, 278, 286, 291
CVM *see* categorical variable methodology

Dadds, M. R., 320
DAP test *see* Draw-A-Person test
DARE, Project, 364
data
    baseline, 74–6
    protecting, 62
    sharing, 61
data analysis
    correlational (observational) data, 115–37
    developmental psychopathology, 224–8

diagnosis, 267–72
ethical issues, 58–61
future of, 429–30
group designs, 97–112
limitations of statistical comparisons, 344
model selection, 25–6
qualitative, 187–9, 190, 227–8
single-case designs, 88
statistical conclusion validity, 23–6
see also meta-analysis; regression analysis;
    software; structural equation modeling
Daubert v. Merrell Dow Pharmaceuticals, 410
Davidson, R. J., 246
Davies, M., 394–5
Davison, E., 330
death, studies of children coping with, 227
DBT *see* Dialectical Behavior Therapy
DeBaryshe, B., 362
Debener, S., 247
debriefing, 64, 67
deception, ethics of, 64–5
defensiveness, studies of, 251–2
definitions, developing operational, 74
Delaney, H. D., 107, 111
delinquency, studies of, 232–3
Delphic method, 409–10
dependence, detecting and correcting, 133–4
depression
    and brain areas, 246, 247, 427
    child sufferers, 215, 311, 312, 403
    diagnosing, 287, 290, 291
    diagnosing: neuroscience, 428
    diagnosing: projectives, 296
    diagnosing: research into, 403
    diagnosing: symptom scales, 292–4
    diagnosing: taxometrics, 298, 305–6
    explaining, 430
    imaginary therapy study, 14–23
    and interaction with children, 274
    and MBCT, 338
    measuring over time, 215–16
    and memory, 240–2
    studies of, 239–40, 242–3
    therapy research, 312, 334–5, 337, 346–7
descriptive analyses, 97–9
design
    additive designs, 339–40
    behavior genetic designs, 219
    correlational designs, 115–16

cross-sectional designs, 216–17
ethical issues, 53–8, 61–8
ethnic minority studies, 381–2
factorial design, 93, 96, 104
group designs, 92–6
longitudinal designs, 217–18
longitudinal research, 215–19
parametric variation designs, 340
qualitative research, 178–85
randomized block, 93
research into, 403
and validity, 13–30
see also experimental design and studies;
 quasi-experimental design; single-case
 design; structural equation modeling
developmental psychopathology, 9, 213–31
data analysis, 110–12, 224–8
ethical issues, 220–1, 223
importance, 355
and the individual, 219–20
measurement, 215–19, 221–3, 232–3
mechanisms, 213–15
research methods vignette, 232–3
risk and protective factors, 355–7
risk and time periods, 361–2
sampling, 220, 232
stress-diathesis model, 355–6
see also experimental psychopathology
*Diagnostic and Statistical Manual of Mental
 Disorders* (DSM)
criteria validation, 264
policy re: cultural issues, 388
potential revisions, 426–7
strengths and weaknesses, 341–2
diagnostic assessment, 9, 284–306
ethnic minorities, 386–7
history of, 284
nature of disorders, 286, 297–8
projectives, 294–7
research opportunities, 5, 424–5, 427–9
research vignette, 305–6
self-report inventories, 288, 427–8
single-case design, 74
structured clinical interviews, 285–9
symptom scales, 289–94
diagnostic assessment, children and
 adolescents, 262–81, 403
children as self-informants, 274, 276, 291
multiple informants, 222–3, 272–7

projectives, 296
reliability and validity, 263–7
research vignette, 282–3
scores, 267–72
Diagnostic Interview Schedule (DIS), 289
Dialectical Behavior Therapy (DBT), 337–8
diazepam, studies of, 250
dichotic listening studies, 237–8
Dill, Edward J., summary of chapter, 9
DIS *see* Diagnostic Interview Schedule
disabled
 as research subjects, 62–3
 studies of, 177, 178–9, 182, 296
dismantling studies *see* multi-component
 analyses
disorders
 classification of, 264, 341–2, 426–7
 nature of, 286, 297–8
dissertations, locating and obtaining, 200
distraction tasks, directed, 242–3
Division of Health Psychology, 34
Dodge, K. A., 214
Doleys, D. M., 318
Donenberg, G. R., 311
Donnelly, J. E., 102–3
Donohue, Keith F., 253–4
 summary of chapter, 9
dot probe studies, 237, 239–40
Draw-A-Person (DAP) test, 296
drawing tests, 296–7
Drotar, D., 50, 400
drugs
 pharmacotherapy studies, 338–9, 423
 psychotropic medication, 401
 substance use, studies of, 232–3, 287
 see also prescription privileges
DSM *see* Diagnostic and Statistical Manual of
 Mental Disorders
Duhig, A. M., 274
Duke, L. M., 247
Dunn procedure *see* Bonferroni procedure
durability of effects, 344–5
Durlak, Joseph A., summary of chapter, 9

Earls, F., 276–7
Eckert, J. K., 176, 180, 184
ecological psychology, 180, 359–60
 see also environment, and behavior
Edinger, J. D., 352–3

education
  effects of, 356
  studies of, 354
EEG *see* electroencephalogram
effect, indices of, 197
effect size (ES), 24, 197–8
  grouping, 203–6
  using, 201–2
effectiveness, 6
  and comparison conditions, 317–18
  and efficacy, 310
  and quasi-experimental designs, 319
  studies, 346–7
efficacy, 6
  and comparison conditions, 317–18
  and effectiveness, 310
  evaluating for single-case designs, 88–90
  and internal validity, 310
  and quasi-experimental designs, 319
  studies, 345, 346–7
Elbert, J. C., 314
elderly, studies of, 176, 180, 184, 246
  geropsychology training, 398
electroencephalogram (EEG)
  and alcohol studies, 253
  and defensiveness studies, 251–2
  and depression studies, 243
  and diagnosis, 428
  and emotion studies, 246–7
electromyograph (EMG), use of, 244, 249, 253
Elkins, P. D., 403
EMDR *see* eye movement desensitization and reprocessing
Emery, B. L., 403
EMG *see* electromyograph
emotion
  alcohol's effect, 247–51
  and brain patterns, 243, 245–9, 251, 252–4
  studies of, 243–51
emotional Stroop paradigm, 237, 240
empirically supported treatments (ESTs), 308–9
  improving, 420–3
  psychologists' attitudes to, 408
  representativeness, 321, 345–6
  training, 398
enculturation, 383–4

enuresis, studies of nocturnal, 318
environment, and behavior
  ecological psychology, 180, 359–60
  nature vs nurture, 219, 236
  person–environment fit, 366
  and risk and protective factors, 355–6
EPPP *see* Examination for Professional Practice in Psychology
EQS, 161
equifinality, 213, 355
ERPs *see* event-related brain potentials
error mean square (MSE), 100, 101
ES *see* effect size
ESTs *see* empirically supported treatments
ethical issues, 8, 52–70
  alcohol studies, 260–1
  child studies, 220–1, 223, 319, 418–19
  codes, APA, 52, 58, 60, 61, 64, 387
  codes, other, 65–6
  developmental psychopathology, 220–1, 223
  managed care, 67, 406
  and prevention, 363–5
  qualitative research, 191–2
  research into, 404–8
  research planning, 53–8, 61–8
  resolving dilemmas, 66–7
  and single-case designs, 80, 86
  training, 407–8
ethnic minorities, research among, 10, 313, 345–6, 376–93
  acculturation and enculturation, 383–6
  conceptual concerns, 377–81
  culture and group differences, 382–3
  design, 381–2
  measurement, 386–7
  NIH and APA policy guidelines, 387–90
  OMB groups, 388
  research vignette, 394–5
  sampling, 384–6
  and SES, 380, 382–3
ethnicity, and psychology, 378–80
ethnography, 178, 179–80
event-related brain potentials (ERPs), 251, 428
evidence-based psychotherapy *see* empirically supported treatments
Examination for Professional Practice in Psychology (EPPP), 398

exercise regimens, studies of, 179
Exner, J. E., 296
exosystem, influence on behavior, 359–60
experimental design and studies, 92–4, 116
  developmental psychopathology, 218
  performance-based, 218
  posttest control group design, 93, 94
  pretest–posttest control group design, 18–19, 93–4
  and SEM, 165
  Solomon four-group design, 19
  variables, 15
experimental psychopathology, 9, 234–59
  cognitive paradigms, 236–43
  issues, 235–6
  psychophysiological methods, 243–54
  research methods vignette, 260–1
experimenter expectations, effect on test results, 23
expert witnesses, acting as, 410
exposure and response prevention, 333
Exposure and Ritual Prevention (EX/RP), 341, 342, 423
Eyberg, S. M., 313
eye movement desensitization and reprocessing (EMDR), 339
eyes
  blinking, and emotion, 244, 245, 249
  orbicularis oculi muscle, 243–4
Eysenck, Hans, 308, 329–30
Eysenck, M. W., 239

Fabrigar, L. R., 167
factorial design, 93, 96, 104
families
  family relations, studies of, 394–5
  study attrition, 317
  test group assignment, 319
  see also children and adolescents; parenting
Farber, I. E., 244
FAST Track program, 360–1, 367
fear
  startle reflex, 243–5, 249–51
  see also anxiety; phobias, studies of
Fear Survey Schedule (FSS), 237–8
Felner, R., 361
Ferguson, K. S., 397
Feske, U., 339
fidelity, treatment, 314–15, 334–5

Finch, J. F., 160, 161
Finger, Michael S., 24
  summary of chapter, 7
Fisher least-significant-difference procedure, 283
fixed effects model testing, 203–6
Flannery-Schroeder, E., 327–8
fluvoxamine, studies of, 313
FLV models *see* full latent variable models
Foa, E. G., 238
focus groups, 182–3
  and assessment of culture's influence, 382
follow-up studies, 21, 344–5, 353, 375
Fong, K. T., 377
food selectivity, treating, 86–8
Foote, W., 410
formative analysis, 88
Fox, N. A., 246
Frank, L. K., 294
Franklin, M., 342
free random assignment, 93
frequency distributions, 97–8
Frerichs, R. R., 380
Freud, Sigmund, 330
Frick, Paul J., 223
  summary of chapter, 9
Fristad, M. A., 403
FSS *see* Fear Survey Schedule
full latent variable (FLV) models, and SEM, 145–7

GAF *see* Global Assessment of Functioning
Galton, Sir Francis, 284
gang members, studies of Mexican-American, 183
Gardner, F., 184
Garfield, Sol, 330
Gatz, M., 405
Gawthrop, J. C., 407
Geisser–Greenhouse lower bound correction, 110–11
gender, and norm-referenced scores, 268–9
general linear model (GLM) approach, 101–2
genetic influences, and behavior, 214–15, 219, 236, 356
George, M. S., 253
geropsychology training, 398
Gigerenzer, G., 23
Gilboa, E., 240

Glaser, B. G., 179
GLM approach *see* general linear model
    approach
Global Assessment of Functioning (GAF),
    298
global fit indices, 142–4
Goldsmith, H. H., 214
Goldstein, A., 339
Gotlib, I. H., 240
Gottesman, I. I., 214
Gottlieb, M. C., 67
Gould, M. S., 277
Graham, S., 377
Green, Samuel B., 164–5
    summary of chapter, 8
Green, S. M., 276
Greene, J. C., 186
Greenhoot, Andrea Follmer, summary of
    chapter, 8
Grizzle, J. E., 111
grounded theory, 179, 187
Guba, E. G., 188, 189

Haaga, D., 403
Haas, L. J., 405
Hagemann, D., 247
Hamdan, L., 75
Hammen, C. L., 291
Harrist, R., 374–5
Hawaii Empirical Basis to Service Task Force,
    309
Hawkins, R. P., 75
hazard function, 226, 227
Health and Wellness for Persons with Long
    Term Disabilities, Center for, 177, 181
Health Psychology, 403
Health Psychology, Division of, 34
Heard, P. M., 320
heart rate, and emotion, 243
Hedges, L. V., 197, 202
Henin, A., 327–8
Henriques, J. B., 246
Henwood, K. L., 189, 190
Heron, T. E., 77, 83
heterogeneous regressions model, 107
Heward, W. L., 77, 83
hierarchical linear regression, 225–6, 429
Hill, C. E., 334–5
HiPlaces, Project, 361

hippocampus, 251
Hispanic-Americans
    including in samples, 385
    research guidelines, 388–9
    studies of, 377, 379, 379–80, 394–5
history, effect on test results, 15–16, 18
HIV
    prevention programs, 374–5
    studies of behavioral influence, 379
    studies of sufferers, 319
Hoagwood, K., 321
Hohn, M. F., 228
Holen, M. C., 401
Hollon, S. D., 287, 317, 318, 319
Holmes, C. T., 197
homelessness, determinants of, 365
homogeneity testing, 204–6
homoscedasticity assumption, 130
Hood, C. A., 397
hopelessness, diagnosing, 287
hotels, single room occupancy, studies of,
    176, 180, 184
House-Tree-Person (H-T-P) test, 296
Howell, C. T., 273–4
Hoyle, R. H., 140, 150, 169
HSD, 104
H-T-P test *see* House-Tree-Person test
Hu, L.-T., 144
Hugdahl, K., 243
Hunter, J. E., 206
Huynh–Feldt adjustment, 110–11
hyperactivity *see* Attention Deficit
    Hyperactivity Disorder; children,
    hyperactivity

IAPS *see* International Affective Picture System
identity matrices, 25
IGC analysis *see* individual growth curve
    analysis
Ilardi, Stephen S., 399, 428
    summary of chapter, 10–11
independence, detecting and correcting
    violations, 133–4
Indian Psychologists, Society of, 389
indicators
    causal, 155
    effect, 154–5
individual growth curve (IGC) analysis,
    224–5

individuals
  and developmental psychopathology,
    219–20
  see also single-case design
inferential analyses, 99–112
informants *see* reporters
Ingram, J. C., 316
injury control, child, 360, 362
inkblot tests, 295–6, 425
insomnia, treating, 352–3
Institute of Medicine (IOM), 354–5, 358,
  367
Institutional Review Boards (IRBs), 55–6, 66,
  191
instrumental decay, effect on test results, 16,
  18
instrumentation, effect on test results, 16, 18
insurance reimbursement, surveys into, 401
interactions, modeling, 126–8
internal consistency, and coefficient alpha,
  149–53
International Affective Picture System (IAPS),
  245, 249
interpersonal psychotherapy, 333, 335, 340
interrupted time series designs, 95
intervention trials, 218
interventions
  preventive, 357–63
  selective, 358
  universal, 358
  see also therapy
interviews
  in-depth, 181–2
  structured clinical, 285–9
intracarotid sodium amobarbitol test, 246
inverse transformations, 133
IOM *see* Institute of Medicine
IRBs *see* Institutional Review Boards
item parcels, 162
item response modeling, 429
Iwasama, G., 377

Jackson, G. B., 196, 199
Jackson, J. S., 384, 385
Jackson, Yo, summary of chapter, 10
Jacoby, A. M., 398
Jaffe, C., 400
Jaffee v. Redmond, 410
Jaycox, L. H., 311

Jensen, M. A., 418–19
Jensen, P. S., 321
Johnson, M. C., 243
Johnson, S. B., 314
Joiner, Thomas E., Jr.
  on projective drawing tools, 296, 297
  on self-reporting inventories and symptom
    scales, 288, 290, 291
  summary of chapter, 9
  on taxometrics, 298
Journal of Abnormal Psychology, 404
Journal of Applied Behavior Analysis, 34
Journal of Clinical Child Psychology, 404
Journal of Clinical Psychology, 404
Journal of Consulting and Clinical Psychology,
  34, 139–40, 149, 404
Journal of Pediatric Psychology, 403, 404
journals
  circulation, 43
  citation impact, 404
  content analyses, 402–4
  electronic, 42–3, 404
  getting published in *see* publication
    procedures
Judd, Charles M., 128, 133, 134
  summary of chapter, 8

Kalish, H. I., 244
Kaminer, Y., 311
Kansas University, Clinical Child Psychology
  Program, 4
Kaplan, C., 183
Kaplan, R. M., 284
Karg, R. S., 408
Kashy, D. A., 129, 133
Kaslow, N. J., 311, 313, 318
Kazdin, A., 340
Kazdin, A. E., 74, 307, 312, 317, 320
Keating, J., 318
Kellam, S. G., 366
Kemps, Jodi L., summary of chapter, 10
Kendall, P. C.
  on diagnosis, 287, 290, 291
  on treatment manuals, 315
  on treatment outcome research, 311, 320,
    327–8
Kenny, D. A., 128, 129, 133, 134, 344
KFD test *see* Kinetic Family Drawing test
Kim, Christine, summary of chapter, 8

Kime, C., 228
Kinetic Family Drawing (KFD) test, 296
Kinetic-School Drawing (KSD) test, 296
King, N. J., 318
Kirby, D., 374–5
Kirk, R. E., 112
Kline, John P., 246, 251–2, 253–4
    summary of chapter, 9
Knapp, S., 401
Kolb, B., 235
Kraemer, H., 346
Kraepelin, Emil, 284
Krahn, Gloria L., 228
    summary of chapter, 8
Kramer, C. Y., 104
Krasnow, A. D., 408
KSD test *see* Kinetic-School Drawing test
kurtosis, 159, 161

La Greca, A. M., 380, 399
labor, studies of, 184, 354
Lagrange multiplier (LM) tests, 163–4
Lahey, B. B., 269–70, 276, 394–5
Landon, Barbara, summary of chapter, 10
Lang, A. R., 249, 250, 253–4, 260–1
Lang, P. J., 245
LaRowe, Steven D., summary of chapter,
    9
latent class modeling, 429
latent growth curve modeling, 226, 429
Lavin, B. D., 66
learning
    analyzing studies, 110–12
    and the hippocampus, 251
Lee, S. C., 239–40
legal analyses, 410
Lemery, K. S., 214
letters, publishing, 34
level of analysis conundrum, 235–6
Levenston, G. K., 245
levers, 131
Levi, R., 182
Levitt, E. E., 308
Lewin, K., 354
licensing, psychologists, 398–9
Lincoln, Y. S., 188, 189
Linehan, M. M., 337–8
Lipsey, M. W., 197, 198, 204
LISREL, 139, 140, 161

listening, dichotic listening studies, 237–8
literature reviews
    publishing, 32–3
    see also meta-analysis
LM tests *see* Lagrange multiplier tests
Loeb, T. B., 379
Loeber, R., 232–3
log transformations, 133
logit transformations, 133
Loney, B. R., 223
Long, P., 320
longitudinal designs, 217–18
longitudinal studies
    analyzing, 110–12
    developmental psychopathology, 215–19,
        232
Lonigan, C. J., 266, 314, 318
Loo, C., 377
Lopez, S. R., 380, 381
Luborsky, L., 314
Lumry, A., 287
Lynch, J., 403
Lyubomirsky, S., 142

MacCallum, R. C., 143–4, 164, 167
McClelland, G. H., 132, 134
McClusky-Fawcett, K., 403
McConaughy, S. H., 273–4
McGovern, T. V., 407
MacLeod, C., 239, 240
McNally, R. J., 238
macrosystem, influence on behavior, 359–60
Maddux, C., 418–19
Magnetic Resonance Imaging (MRI), 252–4
Maher, B. A., 398–9
Major Depressive Disorder (MDD), 298
Malaspina, D., 238
Malouf, J. L., 405
malpractice claims, surveys into, 406
MAMBAC *see* Mean Above Minus Below A
    Cut
managed care
    ethics of, 67, 406
    surveys on implications, 401
    training programs, 397
MANOVA *see* multivariate analysis of
    variance
manuals, treatment, 314–15, 327–8, 333–4,
    401, 408

marginal means, 98–9
Marlowe Crowne Social Desirability Scale, 238
marriage, behavioral marital therapy, 333
Marsh, G. R., 352–3
Martin, C. K., 241, 242
Martin, N. C., 225
masking, 239–40, 251–2
  masked review, 44–5
Mason, S. M., 385–6
matched random assignment, 93
Mathews, A., 239, 240
Matthews, J. R., 75
maturation, effect on test results, 16, 18
Maximum Covariance (MAXCOV), 305, 427
maximum likelihood (ML), 158–9, 160, 161
Maxwell, S. E., 107, 111
Mayerson, N. H., 405
MBCT *see* mindfulness-based cognitive therapy
MCM *see* Mood-congruent memory
MDD *see* Major Depressive Disorder
Mean Above Minus Below A Cut (MAMBAC), 305, 427
means, 98–9
  standardized mean difference, 197
means analyses, multivariate, 154–8
measurement and measurements
  adult psychotherapy research, 343–7
  child psychotherapy research, 215–19, 221–3, 232–3, 319–21, 327–8
  correlational data, specifying models for, 117–20
  developmental psychopathology, 215–19, 221–3, 232–3, 319–21
  ethnic minority research, 386–7
  longitudinal studies, 215–19
  measurement equivalence, 24
  and prevention, 365–6, 366–7
  reliability and test results, 24–5
measures
  coarsely categorized, 159–60, 161–2
  continuous, 159, 160–1
  laboratory, 266
  outcome, 319–21, 327–8, 343–7
  performance-based, 223, 266
  physiological, 243–54

mechanisms, and developmental psychopathology, 213–15
  biological, 215
  genetic, 214–15
  social-cognitive, 214
Medawar, P. B., 43, 49
median lifetime, 227
mediation, models of, 128–30
medication *see* drugs; prescription privileges
Medicine, Institute of, 354–5, 358, 367
Meehl, Paul E., 298, 427
memory
  analyzing studies, 110–12
  and depression, 240–2
  explicit, 241
  implicit, 241
  MCM, 241
  studies of, 243
mental disabilities, studies of, 296
Messenger, L. C., 398
meta-analysis, 8–9, 196–209
  ethical issues, 55
meta-analyses, results of
  MMPI, 24
  therapeutic outcomes, 313, 314
Metalsky, G. I., 290, 291
methodology
  effect on meta-analysis, 206
  research into reporting, 403–4
Mexican-American, studies of, 183, 379–80
Micceri, T., 159
Michelson, L., 340
microsystem, influence on behavior, 359–60
Mills, L. G., 185
mindfulness-based cognitive therapy (MBCT), 179, 338
Minnesota Multiphasic Personality Inventories (MMPI), 24–5, 159, 295, 305–6
Minnix, Jennifer, summary of chapter, 9
Miranda, J., 346, 378, 382, 385
mixed effects model testing, 203–4
ML *see* maximum likelihood
MMPI *see* Minnesota Multiphasic Personality Inventories
model comparison approach, 121–30
model equivalency, 139, 165–9
model selection, 25–6
modification indices *see* Lagrange multiplier tests

Mogg, K., 239–40
Moldawsky, S., 397
Montgomery, L. M., 406
mood
    and brain activity, 243, 245–9, 251,
        252–4
    diagnosing mood disorder, 287
    see also emotion
Mood-congruent memory (MCM), 241
Moore, J. D., 250
Mordock, J. B., 56
Morgan, D., 182
Morin, C. M., 83, 85
mortality *see* attrition, effect on test results
Mota, V. L., 272
motivation, appetitive, 253
MRI *see* Magnetic Resonance Imaging
MSE *see* error mean square
MST *see* treatment mean square
MTA *see* Multimodal Treatment Study of
    Children with ADHD
multi-component analyses, 318, 339–40
multifinality, 213, 355
multilevel analysis, 235–6, 252–4
multilevel modeling procedures, 134
Multimodal Treatment Study of Children
    with ADHD (MTA), 316
multiple baseline design, 83–6, 95
multiple treatment interference, 21, 83
Multitrait-Multimethod matrices, 118
multivariate analyses of means, and SEM,
    154–8
multivariate analysis of variance (MANOVA),
    108–10, 138, 328
    and SEM, 154–5, 158
Munday, C., 384, 385
Murphy, D. A., 260–1
Murphy, P. E., 168
Murphy, R. J., 418–19

N400 component, 428
National Hispanic Psychological Association,
    389
National Institute of Mental Health (NIMH),
    289, 346, 354–5, 367
    Clinical Treatment and Services Research
        Workgroup, 6, 310
National Institutes of Health (NIH), 63–4,
    67, 387–8

National Psychological Associations for the
    Advancement of Ethnic Minority
    Interests, Council of, 388–9
National Research Council (NRC), 398–9
National Science Foundation, 410
Native-Americans
    including in samples, 385–6
    research guidelines, 389
    studies of, 387
negative predictive power (NPP), 271–2
Neighbors, H. W., 384, 385
Nettlebeck, T., 318
neuroimaging, 252–4
    functional, 425–6
neuroscience
    research opportunities, 425–9
    see also brain
NIH *see* National Institutes of Health
NIMH *see* National Institute of Mental
    Health
Nisbett, R., 285–6
Nitschke, J. B., 243
no treatment comparisons, 337
Nolen-Hoeksema, S., 242–3
nonequivalent control group designs, 94
nonexperimental studies
    and effectiveness, 319
    and SEM, 165–9
nonnormality
    data analysis, 139, 158–62
    detecting and correcting, 131–2
non-randomized pretest–posttest control
    group design, 18, 94–5
Norcross, J. C., 408, 409–10
normal quantile–quantile plots, 132
normality, detecting and correcting violations,
    131–3
Norton, I. M., 385–6
novelty, effect on test results, 21
NPP *see* negative predictive power
NRC *see* National Research Council
NUDIST (software), 189

Oakland, T., 409
obesity, treating, 102–3, 359
observation, as data collection method, 184
Obsessive Compulsive Disorder (OCD)
    and threat-relevant stimuli, 238
    treating, 313, 341, 342, 423, 426

O'Connor, M., 47
ODD *see* Oppositional Defiant Disorder
odds ratios, 197
Office of Management and Budget (OMB), 388
Olkin, I., 197, 202
Ollendick, T. H., 309, 318
Olson, R. A., 400
OMB *see* Office of Management and Budget
one-group pretest–posttest design, 15–17, 197
Ones, D. S., 24
Oppositional Defiant Disorder (ODD), 232–3, 260–1, 316, 394–5
orbicularis oculi muscle, 243–4
Ordinary Least Squares estimation, 116
outcomes research, 307–53
   early studies, 308
   outcome measures, 319–21, 327–8, 343–7
   treatment outcome studies and sampling, 310–13
   see also effectiveness; efficacy
outliers, identification of, 130–1
outpatients clinics, research into, 400
overactivity
   measuring, 216
   see also Attention Deficit Hyperactivity Disorder
Oxford University Press, 404

p-values, 24
P3, 250–1
Padesky, Christine, 333
PANAS *see* Positive and Negative Affect Schedule
panic disorder, treating, 333, 334, 339, 340
Panichelli-Mindel, S. M., 327–8
Panter, A. T., 169
parallelism, test of, 107
parametric variation designs, 340
Parcel, G., 374–5
parent–child interaction therapy (PCIT), 315, 316
parenting
   and mental health, 357, 362
   parents as reporters of child cases, 319–20
   studies of, 184, 260–1, 315, 316, 318, 319
Park, T. L., 403
Parloff, M. B., 339
partialled products, 126

path analysis, and SEM, 139, 140, 147–9
patients, as research subjects, 58
Patrick, C. J., 245, 249, 250
pattern analyses, 224
Patterson, G., 362
Patton, M. Q., 180
Paul, Gordon L., 307, 331
payment, for research participation, 58
PCIT *see* parent–child interaction therapy
pediatric psychology *see* children and adolescents; diagnostic assessment, children and adolescents; therapy, children and adolescents
Pediatric Psychology, Society of, 309
peer influences, on mental health, 355
peer nomination instruments, 222
peer reviews, 36–7, 41
Pekarik, G., 402
Pelham, W. E., 260–1
performance-based experimental designs, 218
performance-based measures, 223, 266
personality disorders
   diagnosing, 295–6
   and ESTs, 422
Personality Inventory for Children, 296
Peruzzi, N., 406
PET *see* Positron Emission Tomography
Petti, T., 321
Pettit, Jeremy W., summary of chapter, 9
pharmacotherapy studies, 338–9, 423
   see also prescription privileges
phenomenology, 178–9
Phillips, J. S., 314
phobias, studies of, 237–8, 245, 320
physical maturation, measuring, 282–3
physiological measures, 243–54
Piacentini, J. C., 277
Pidgeon, N. F., 189, 190
Pittsburgh Youth Study, 232
placebos
   ethics of using, 65
   using, 317–18, 338–9, 352
   see also comparison conditions
plagiarism, 61
Poirier, J., 164–5
Ponterotto, J. G., 379–80
population samples *see* sampling
Positive and Negative Affect Schedule (PANAS), 159, 293–4

positive predictive power (PPP), 271–2
Positron Emission Tomography (PET),
    252–3, 426
posttest designs, 93, 94–5
posttraumatic stress, studies of, 380
posttraumatic stress disorder (PTSD), 282–3
    diagnosing, 296
    explaining, 430
Potthof, R. F., 107
power analysis, 23–4
power transformations, 133, 161
PPP *see* positive predictive power
PPPL *see Psychology, Public Policy and the Law*
practice research, 310, 399–402
PracticeNet project, 402
PRE *see* proportional reduction in error
prediction
    definition, 77
    examples, 78, 79, 81, 85, 87
prescription privileges
    challenges, 423–4
    surveys of attitudes to, 401, 408–9
    training in, 398
pretest–posttest designs, 15–17, 18–19,
    93–4, 94–5
    analyzing, 107, 107–8, 110–12
prevention, 10, 354–73
    classifying approaches, 357–8
    communities' role, 362–3
    ethical issues, 363–5
    indicated prevention, 358
    and intervention, 357–63
    measurement issues, 365–6, 366–7
    research priorities, 366–8
    research prototype, 357
    research vignette, 374–5
    risk and protective factors, 355–7
    tactic selection, 361–2
    target selection, 359–61
Prevention and Treatment, 42
Price, R. H., 357–8, 363
principal components analysis, 118, 119–20
privilege, psychotherapist–patient, 410
probit transformations, 133
problem-solving communication therapy
    (PSCT), 318
Prochaska, J. O., 408, 409–10
product moment correlation, 197
Professional Psychology, 409

Professional Psychology: Research and Practice,
    34
professional roles, 4
profiles, and developmental psychopathology,
    224
Project DARE, 364
Project HiPlaces, 361
projectives, 294–7
promotion, wellness
    benefits, 367–8
    and illness prevention, 355
    program targets, 361
    research vignette, 374–5
    typology, 357–8
    see also prevention
proportional reduction in error (PRE), 122
provocation paradigms, 223
PSCT *see* problem-solving communication
    therapy
Psychoanalytic Study of the Child, 34
Psychological Assessment, 139–40, 149
Psychological Clinic, 3
Psychological Study of Ethnic Minority
    Issues, Society for the, 388–9
psychologists
    attitudes and beliefs of, 408–9
    employment and salaries, 410–11
    as survey subjects, 401, 402
Psychology, Public Policy and the Law (PPPL),
    410
psychopathology
    developmental *see* developmental
        psychopathology
    experimental *see* experimental
        psychopathology
psychopaths, studies of, 245
Psychopathy Checklist, 245
psychotherapy *see* therapy
PTSD *see* posttraumatic stress disorder
pubertal status, measuring, 282–3
publication procedures, 8, 31–50
    content, 32–6
    editorial lag times, 46–7
    editorial review process, 45–9
    ethical aspects, 59–61
    meta-analyses, 198
    MS preparation, 43–5
    outlet selection, 37–43
    paying for publication, 41–2

quality, 36–7
rejection rates, 40–1
Puddy, R. W., 321
Punch, M., 192
Pupil Evaluation Inventory, 222
Putnam, Michelle, summary of chapter, 8

Q statistic, 204–6
qualitative analysis, 187–9, 190, 227–8
qualitative research *see* research, qualitative
quasi-experimental design, 94–5
  correlational group comparison design,
    17–18
  and effectiveness, 319
  interrupted time series designs, 95
  nonequivalent control group designs, 94
  non-randomized pretest–posttest control
    group design, 18, 94–5
  one-group pretest–posttest design, 15–17
  posttest control group designs, 94–5
  variables, 15
questionnaires
  and depression studies, 243
  and instrumentation, 16
Quillian, R. E., 352–3

r, 197
RAA *see* resting anterior asymmetry
race
  and research, 378
  see also cultural diversity issues; ethnic
    minorities, research among
Radtke, R. A., 352–3
Rae, William A., summary of chapter, 8
Rajab, M. H., 287, 288, 290, 291
Ramirez, R., 394–5
Ramsey, E., 362
Rand, Kevin L., summary of chapter, 7
random assignment
  free, 93
  matched, 93
random effects model testing, 203–4
randomized block design, 93
  analyzing, 104–5, 106–7
randomized clinical trials (RCTs)
  benefits, 332
  description, 317–18
  disadvantages, 309, 345, 421–2
  and treatment manuals, 333

rank transformations, 133
Rapoff, M. A., 400, 402
Ray, R., 282–3
Rayfield, A., 402
Raykov, T., 152
RCMAS *see* Revised Children's Manifest
  Anxiety Scale
RCTs *see* randomized clinical trials
Receiving Operating Characteristics (ROC)
  model, 272
record review, 184–5
recording, ethics of, 65
recurrence, defining, 345
regression analysis
  hierarchical linear regression, 225–6, 429
  model selection, 25
  ordinary least squares regression, 120–34
  software, 121, 124, 131
  statistical regression, effect on test results,
    17, 18
  stepwise regression, 121
regression sum of squares (SSR), 101
Reid, S. A., 247
Reiss, A. L., 282–3
Reiss, D., 357–8, 363
relapse, defining, 345
relative risk ratios, 197
reliability, and interpretations, 263–7
reliability estimates, and coefficient alpha,
  151–4
remission, rate of spontaneous, 330
repeated measures ANOVA, 110–12, 319
replication
  definition, 77
  examples, 79, 81, 85, 88
reporters
  adult cases, 343
  child cases, 319–20
  children as self-reporters, 274, 276, 291,
    319–20
  lack of agreement among, 273–6
  numbers of, 222–3, 272–7
  self-report inventories, 288, 427–8
repression, studies of, 238, 251–2
reproduced covariance matrices, 142
research
  importance of, 3–4
  opportunities and priorities, 5–6, 366–8,
    420–32

research (*cont'd*)
  relationship with practice, 6
  research into, 402–4
research, qualitative, 8, 176–95
  data analysis, 187–9, 190
  data collection methods, 181–5
  and developmental psychopathology, 227–8
  ethical issues, 191–2
  limitations, 189–91
  methods, 178–80
  sampling, 180–1, 183
  using, 185–7
research articles
  citation impact, 38, 404
  content analyses, 402–4
  publishing, 33
  surveys into helpfulness, 408
research planning
  ethical issues, 53–8, 61–8
  informed consent, 56–8, 63, 67
  institutional approval, 55–6
research records, handling of, 62
research subjects
  children, 220
  ethical issues, 62–3
  informed consent, 56–8, 63, 67
  patients, 58
  single cases, 8, 73–91
  students, 20, 57–8
  see also control groups; sampling
residual matrices, 142
resting anterior asymmetry (RAA), 246
reversal design, 79–80
Revised Children's Manifest Anxiety Scale
    (RCMAS), 291
Riech, W., 276–7
Riley, G., 316
risk analysis, 53–4
risk ratios, 197
risks, to mental health, 355–7
  and communities, 362–3
  risk constellation candidates, identifying,
    359–61
  and time periods, 361–2
RMSEA *see* root mean square error of
    approximation
Roberts, Michael C.
  case analyses, 400
  client satisfaction study, 402

contents analysis study, 185
ethical dilemmas survey, 406
journal article content analysis, 403
outcomes categorization model, 321
pediatric psychology trend survey, 410
summary of chapters, 8, 10–11
training survey, 397
Robiner, W. N., 399
ROC model *see* Receiving Operating
    Characteristics model
Rodrigue, J. R., 400
Rogosa, D., 107
Rogosch, F. A., 359
Romero, G. J., 379
root mean square error of approximation
    (RMSEA)
  definition, 144
  examples, 144, 146, 147, 148
Rorschach Inkblot Test, 295–6, 425
Rosenthal, R., 54, 56, 198
Rosenzweig, Sol, 330
Ross, L., 285–6
Rossi, P. T., 27
Roy, S. N., 109, 111
Rozeboom, W. W., 151–2
Rudd, M. D., 287, 288, 290, 291
rumination, directed, and depression, 242–3
ruminative response style, 242
Ruscio, A. M., 305–6
Ruscio, J., 305–6
Rutter, M., 216–17
Ryan, K., 400

Saadon, M., 407
Saccuzzo, D. P., 284
Sadler, Melody S., summary of chapter, 8
Safer Choices program, 374–5
Sales, M., 66
sampling, 340–2
  analog samples, 311
  clinical samples, 311, 312
  correlational group comparison, 17–18
  developmental psychopathology, 220, 232
  ethnic minority research, 384–6
  experimental design, 93–4
  families and children, 94, 220, 232,
    310–13, 317–19
  and internal vs external validity, 26–7
  multiple sites, 340–1

non-randomized pretest–posttest control group design, 18
norm-referenced scores, 268–9
normal and normative samples, 268
one-group pretest–posttest design, 15–17, 197
pretest–posttest control group design, 18–19
qualitative research, 180–1, 183
quasi-experimental design, 94–5
randomized clinical trials (RCTs), 309, 317–18, 332, 333, 345
selection bias, effect on test results, 17, 18
selection bias interaction, effect on test results, 18, 20–1
Solomon four-group design, 19
treatment outcome studies, 310–13
SAS (software), 105, 124, 131
Satorra–Bentler scaled chi square test (SB test), 161
Saxe, L., 307–8
SB test *see* Satorra–Bentler scaled chi square test
Schachar, R. J., 272
Scharrón-Del-Río, M. R., 313
Scheffe's method, 104, 109
Schiff, W. B., 319
schizophrenia
    diagnosing, 295–6, 401
    explaining, 430
    studies of, 238
schizotypal personality disorder, diagnosing, 295–6
Schmidt, F. L., 206
Schmidt, K. L., 291, 296, 297, 298
Schroeder, C. S., 402
Schumann, E. M., 316
SCID *see* Structured Clinical Interview for the DSM
scientific evidence, courtroom admissibility, 410
Scientific Study of Social Issues, Society for the, 42
scientist–practitioners, role, 4
scores, diagnostic
    cutoffs, 269–72, 278, 286, 291
    norm-referenced, 267–9
    predictive utility estimates, 270–2
    raw, 267

standard score conversion, 267
and structured interviews, 286
T-score, 267
test theory assumptions, 151
SD *see* standard deviation
Sedlmeier, P., 23
Segal, Z., 338
selection, forward and backward, 164–5
selection bias, effect on test results, 17, 18
selection bias interaction, effect on test results, 18, 20–1
self-esteem programs, 364
Self-Rating Depression Scale, 305
self-report inventories, 288, 427–8
SEM *see* structural equation modeling
sensitivity rates, 270, 271
sensitization, 20
service system research, 310
SES *see* socioeconomic status
settings, effect on test results, 20
sexual abuse
    adult survivors, 401
    detecting, 296
    by psychotherapists, 407
sexual behavior
    changing, 374–5
    studies of, 379
sexual offenders, studies of, 245
sexuality
    studies of, 182
    treatment training, 398
SFCES model *see* symptoms, functioning, consumer perspectives, environmental contexts, and systems model
Shaw, B. F., 336
Shinn, M., 365–6
Shipley, B., 161
Shirk, S. R., 314
short-term supportive expressive dynamic theory, 335
Shrout, P. E., 152
Shuman, D. W., 410
Sifers, S. K., 313, 403
signal detection theory, 272
significance testing, 24
    multiple dependent, 25
Silverman, N., 307–8
Simons, Anne D., 335
    summary of chapter, 10

Singer, J. D., 225
Singer, L., 400
single-case design, 73–91, 197
    efficacy evaluation, 88–90
    ethical issues, 80, 86
    purpose, 76–7
    therapist behaviors, 74–6
    types, 77–88
Sinnett, E. R., 401
skin conductance, and emotion, 243
Skinner, B. F., 354, 364
sleep disorders, treating, 352–3
Smith, G. T., 150
Smith, M. L., 186–7
Smith, T. S., 405
Smith-Boydston, Julianne M., summary of
    chapter, 8
smoking behavior, changing, 360
Sobel, A. B., 195, 400, 402
Sobel test, 129
social adaptation, and mental health, 366
social-cognitive mechanisms, and behavior,
    214
Social Science Citation Index (SSCI), 38, 404
Society for the Psychological Study of Ethnic
    Minority Issues, 388–9
Society for the Scientific Study of Social
    Issues, 42
Society of Clinical Child and Adolescent
    Psychology, 309
Society of Clinical Psychology, 34, 308–9,
    408, 420–1
    Task Force, 26–7
Society of Indian Psychologists, 389
Society of Pediatric Psychology, 309
socioeconomic status (SES)
    and ethnic minority research, 380, 382–3
    and mental health, 185, 356, 357, 382–3
software
    developmental psychopathology, 224
    multilevel modeling procedures, 134
    multiple regression, 121, 124, 131
    power analysis, 23–4
    qualitative analysis, 187, 189
    SEM, 117, 161
    and sums of squares, 105
Solomon, A., 403
Solomon four-group design, 19
Somer, E., 407

Southam-Gerow, M., 327–8
Spearman–Brown prophecy formula, 120
specificity rates, 270–1
sphericity assumptions, 110–11
spinal cord injury, studies of sufferers, 182
spread-location plots, 132
SPSS (software), 105, 131
square root transformations, 133
SRD *see* stress-response dampening
SSCI *see* Social Science Citation Index
SSE *see* sum of squares due to error
SSE(A) *see* sum of squares due to error,
    augmented model
SSE(C) *see* sum of squares due to error,
    compact model
SSI recipients, studies of, 185
SSR *see* regression sum of squares
SST *see* sum of squares due to treatment
Stagheeza, B., 277
STAI *see* State–Trait Anxiety Inventory
standard deviation (SD), 98–9, 197
standard score conversion, 267
standardized mean difference, 197
standards, meta-analysis, 198, 199
Stanley, J. C., 27
Stanton, A. L., 405–6
startle probes, 244, 245, 250
startle reflex, as measure of emotion, 243–5,
    249–51
State-Trait Anxiety Inventory (STAI), 292
statistical analysis *see* data analysis; meta-
    analysis; regression analysis; software;
    structural equation modeling
statistical conclusion validity, 23–6
statistical power, 23–4, 340
    and meta-analysis, 207–8
statistical regression, effect on test results, 17,
    18
Steele, Ric G., summary of chapter, 10
Steiger, J. H., 144
step-family design, 219
stepwise regression, 121
Stern, L. D., 241, 242
Stone, W. L., 399
Stouthamer-Loeber, M., 232–3
Strauss, A. L., 179
stress-diathesis model, 355–6
stress-response dampening (SRD), 248–9,
    249–50

strike behavior, studies of, 184
Stritzke, W. G. K., 249, 250
Stroop paradigm *see* emotional Stroop paradigm
structural equation modeling (SEM), 8, 134, 138–75
  benefits, 357
  and coefficient alpha, 149–53
  exploratory methods, 162–5
  in the literature, 139–40
  model equivalency, 165–9
  and multivariate analyses of means, 154–8
  and nonnormal data, 158–62
  overview, 140–9
  software, 117, 161
Structured Clinical Interview for the DSM (SCID), 288–9
Strupp, Hans, 331
Stuart, G., 334
students, as research subjects, 20, 57–8
study artifacts, effect on meta-analysis, 206
style guides, 44
submission guidelines, 44
substance use, studies of, 232–3, 287
Sugawara, H. M., 143–4
suicidality, diagnosing, 288, 406
Sullivan, Jeremy R., summary of chapter, 8
sum of squares due to error (SSE), 100, 101
  augmented model (SSE(A)), 121–2
  compact model (SSE(C)), 121–2
sum of squares due to treatment (SST), 100, 100–1
sums of squares, calculating for main effects, 105
survival analysis, 226–7
survivor function, 226, 227
Swales, T., 399
sweating, and emotion, 243
Sweeney, M., 379–80
symptom scales, 289–94
symptoms, functioning, consumer perspectives, environmental contexts, and systems (SFCES) model, 321

T-score, 267
t-statistics, 122
Tabu, 165
TADS *see* Treatment of Adolescent Depression Study

taste, and brain areas, 246
Tata, P., 239
TAU conditions *see* treatment as usual conditions
tau equivalency, 151
taxometrics, 297–8, 305–6
Taylor, S., 192
TDCRP *see* Treatment of Depression Collaborative Research Program
teachers, as informants, 274–6
Teasdale, J., 338
temptation provocation paradigms, 223
test design *see* design; experimental design and studies; quasi-experimental design; single-case design; structural equation modeling
test groups, selection and assignment *see* control groups, use of; sampling
testing, effect on test results, 16, 18
testing interaction, effect on test results, 19–20
testlets, 162
therapy, 10, 329–51
  acceptability, 344, 401
  adherence, 334–5
  comparison conditions, 336–41
  competence, 335–6
  diffusion, effect on test results, 18
  ESTs, 308–9, 321, 345–6, 398, 408, 420–3
  history of, 329
  outcome measures, 343–7
  research vignette, 352–3
  therapy selection, 314
  treatment manuals, 314–15, 327–8, 333–4, 401, 408
  see also effectiveness; efficacy; interventions
therapy, children and adolescents, 10, 307–26
  comparison conditions, 317–19
  early studies, 308
  efficacy vs effectiveness, 310
  ESTs, 308–9, 321
  evaluating efficacy, 88–90
  fidelity, 314–17
  nonpharmalogical, studies of, 179
  outcome measures, 319–21, 327–8
  research vignette, 327–8
  therapy selection, 313–14
  treatment manuals, 314–15, 327–8

Thompson, E. E., 384, 385
Thompson, M. P., 311, 313, 318
Thompson, Marilyn S., 164–5
  summary of chapter, 8
time-series analysis, 26
  interrupted time series designs, 95
Tolan, P., 400
Tomarken, A. J., 246
Tompson, M. C., 311
Toth, S. L., 359
training, 4
  ethical issues, 67
  research into, 397–9
transient error, 153
transformations
  inverse, 133
  log, 133
  logit, 133
  power, 133, 161
  probit, 133
  rank, 133
  square root, 133
  standard score, 267–8
trauma *see* posttraumatic stress disorder
Treat, T., 334
treatment *see* therapy
treatment as usual (TAU) conditions, 337–8
treatment mean square (MST), 100
Treatment of Adolescent Depression Study
    (TADS), 346–7
Treatment of Depression Collaborative
    Research Program (TDCRP), 334–5,
    341
Tremblay, George C., summary of chapter,
    10
trend analysis, 111
trend forecasting, 409–10
Triandis, H. C., 378
triangulation, 186, 228
Tryon, G. S., 401
Tukey, J. W., 104
Tukey-Kramer method, 104
twins, studies of, 219
Tymchuk, A. J., 406
Type I errors, controlling, 25, 103–4, 107,
    109, 165, 283

Uchino, B. N., 167
Uhleman, M. C., 407

unconscious, influence on cognition, 241–2
University Directors of Clinical Psychology,
    Council of, 397
utopian societies, studies of, 354

Valdez, A., 183
validity, and research, 13–30
  and attrition, 317
  construct validity, 22–3
  convergent, 118, 119–20
  discriminant, 118, 119–20
  ecological, 366
  and efficacy–effectiveness studies, 346–7
  and ethnic minority research, 386
  external validity, 19–21, 26–7, 310, 311,
    346–7, 386
  internal validity, 14–19, 26–7, 310–11,
    317, 319, 346–7
  and interpretations, 263–7
  and quasi-experimental designs, 319
  and sampling, 310–11
  statistical conclusion validity, 23–6
Van Horn, Y. V., 366
variables
  classificatory, 95
  confound variables, 15
  continuous, 95
  and correlational data, 116
  dependent variables, 15, 154–5
  effect on meta-analysis, 207
  grouping, 154
  inclusion in design, advantages of, 95
  independent variables and test validity,
    14–28
  treatment variables, 22–3
variance
  analysis of *see* analysis of variance
  correcting heterogeneity, 132–3
  detecting heterogeneity, 132
Vasay, M. W., 266
verification
  definition, 77
  examples, 79, 81, 85, 87–8
Vernberg, Eric M., summary of chapter, 9
vulnerable populations, as research subjects,
    62–3

Wada test, 246
Waddington, D., 184

Wade, W., 334
waitlist comparisons *see* control groups, use of
Waller, N., 298
Waltz, J., 334
Warman, M., 327–8
Watkins, P. C., 241, 242
Watson, D., 290
Weems, C. F., 282–3
Wegener, D. T., 167
weighting
  beta weights, 124
  effect sizes, 202
  information sources, 276–7
Weil, M., 374–5
Weisz, J. R., 311, 312, 320
Wells, K. C., 316
West, S. G., 127, 128, 160, 161
Westgren, N., 182
Wexler, B. E., 238
Whishaw, I. Q., 235
Whisman, M., 336
White, H. R., 232–3
Wildes, Jennifer E., summary of chapter,
  10

Wilkins, M. A., 405
Willard-Holt, C., 178–9
Willett, J. B., 225
Williams, J., 338
Wilson, D. B., 197, 198, 204
Wimberley, T. K., 406
within-subjects designs, 96
  analyzing, 111
Witmer, Lightner, 3
Wohlgemuth, W. K., 352–3
Wolf, F. M., 197
Wolff, C. B., 402
Wood, J. M., 295–6
Wright, H. F., 180
writing guides, 43

Yaryura-Tobias, J. A., 313
Yeh, M., 320
Yu, L. M., 398
Yuan, K.-H., 161

Zhang, H., 394–5
Zirkle, D. S., 418–19
Zvolenzky, M. J., 386–7